SURVIVAL OF THE FATTEST 5

D0999304

An alternative review of the
'98-99 football season

Compiled and edited by

David Jenkins
Judi Holly
Dave Thomas

Red Card
Publishing

Survival of the Fattest 5
An alternative review of the '98-99 football season

Front cover illustration by
David Banks

First published in 1999 by
RED CARD PUBLISHING LIMITED
23 Hamilton Road
Brighton
BN1 5DL

British Library Cataloguing in Publication Data.
A catalogue record for this book is available from the British Library

ISBN 0 9526610 55

Printed and bound in Great Britain by
Fotodirect, Brighton

For Thomas

CONTENTS

CONTENTS

CONTENTS

THE ANNUAL 'RANT'

1999 - the year I finally took the plunge. Actually, it was more of a giant leap, into the all-new, interactive, pay-per-view, digitally enhanced football coverage world of Dr Evil's Sky broadcasting empire. And whatever else has been said about the acquisitive Antipodean, his company certainly knows how to cover, and wring the last drop out of, our beloved game.

Mind you, it took the arrival of a new face at Red Card Publishing to finally get us to stump up for the dish. This new boy has proven himself to be prodigiously gifted - don't they all say that? - but infuriatingly temperamental at the same time. One minute he's up, smiling and ready for anything, but in the next he's making one of his catalogue of the same demands. There's little doubt that his presence has disrupted the harmony built up in the boardroom over the last four years, and his antics have caused many a sleepless night for the directors - hence the requirement for the dish. And yet, when all's said and done, at eight months old, teething and with a streaming cold, you'd still rather have him in your side than our friends Nicolas and Stanley.

Yes, the managerial duo of this esteemed organ has off-sprung, and it is truly amazing how the arrival of this little one has made us think about the past and future in equal measure - especially when it comes to football. Will he be a better centre half than me? I bloody hope so! Can he be brainwashed to follow one of our clubs? Or will he automatically succumb to the seduction techniques employed by one of the European, nay, Global football brands? And carrying on in that vein, will there even be a local club for him to support, or will the football landscape have changed so much as to render the old supporting habits as simply "something that my old man used to do"?

I admit it, I succumbed to the media hype surrounding the Kings Road Cavaliers as they stormed their way to FA Cup success in 1970. This was in the days when pictures were in black and white, Peter Osgood's side-boards were as evocative, if not as marketed, as Beckham's highlights and bum-fluff, and when the old trophy wasn't being shat upon by butcher's sons and politicians. Forget to polish the family silver at your peril, boys. Fortunately for *my* dad, back then, Brighton's Goldstone Ground was probably more welcoming than Stamford Bridge, televised live games were an annual event and replica shirts were bought just for Sunday morning teams.

So over the coming years we've got a challenge on our hands; one we won't shirk from. We're certainly not stuck in the past; we know that broadcasting is changing, and football seems to be falling in line with that change. But what's wrong with wanting your son to grow up having a love for his hometown club? In my case, for the moment, the picture looks a lot rosier than it has done for years. And, most importantly, the people running the Albion's show seem, for the moment at least, to genuinely have the interests of the supporters at the top of their agenda. What the situation will be like for all of us in five, let alone ten years, only Murdoch/Edwards/New Labour/God (delete as appropriate) knows.

Keep the faith.

Dave Jenkins, July 1999

THANKS

As ever, our main thanks go both to new readers, and to those faithful types who have stuck with us since the first ever *Survival of the Fattest*, which chronicled the events of the '94-95 season. Blimey, doesn't *that* seem a long time ago... Mind you, looking at the cover of SOTF1, it seems that some characters seem fated (doomed?) to crop up again and again; Merson and Grobelaar are still making headlines, anyway. But whatever happened to that funny French bloke?

For this issue of *Survival of the Fattest*, lack of space has unfortunately meant that for the first time ever we can't credit individual fanzine editors and contributors in the usual 'roll of honour'. (That will teach people to write such long articles - paper's expensive, you know). We've given a credit to each account's individual writer/s, but where these are not the actual fanzine editors (as often is the case), I'm afraid that this has meant no personal mention for the main protagonists. I am painfully aware that this omission has denied many the chest-swelling moment when they can take Grannie into Smiths, pick up a 'real' book (not "that funny old comic thing that you do, dear") and say "look - that's me!" All I can say is that we're sorry, and that normal service will (hopefully) be resumed in SOTF6.

Of course we owe a debt of gratitude to all of those insane fanzine people, who risk health, wealth and happiness in the pursuit of their obsession. Without them this book (obviously) wouldn't exist.

Other people we'd like to thank for their continued support are Maggie O'Connor and David Banks.

Finally, there is one person without whom this edition of SOTF absolutely would **not** have happened. Stepping into the breach in our hour of need, Dave Thomas (who, if he'd known what he was taking on, would surely have politely declined) has done a magnificent job editing the articles, working under enormous time pressure whilst putting aside other normal pursuits like editing his own fanzine, QPR's *A Kick Up The R's*, and having a social life (no - just make that having a life).

Dave, thanks a million.

Judi Holly, July 1999

BACK ISSUES

Limited numbers of back issues of SOTF are available from the publishers. Please send a cheque/PO or credit card details to Red Card Publishing, 23 Hamilton Road, Brighton BN1 5DL. Price: £9.99 per book, includes P&P.

SOTF1 ('94-95 season): ISBN 09526610 04
SOTF2 ('95-96): ISBN 09526610 12
SOTF3 ('96-97): ISBN 09526610 20
SOTF4 ('97-98): ISBN 09526610 47

2'S COMPANY 500'S A CROWD

Scarborough

As the old saying goes, "The show's not over until the fat lady sings." And although, on 8 May 1999, this particular fat lady had taken her seat at the McCain Stadium, it looked as though the concert was going to be cancelled and the UK tour moving onto Carlisle. However, as we now know, the great Scarborough public invited Mrs Fat Lady to treat us all to a wonderful exhibition. And, at 4:53pm, she gave the most rousing performance of her life, as her shrill voice sounded out over North Yorkshire, shattering the hopes and ambitions of loyal Seadogs everywhere.

After the disappointment of the play-off mauling at the hands of Torquay, things weren't looking too bad. We'd lost key players in Gary 'Mouldy' Bennett (sold to Darlington for £20,000), Ian Snodin (lured away by the call of management at his native Donny Rovers), Jason Rockett (who retired due to a pair of very dodgy knees) and Michael McElhatton (who left on request of the PA announcer, who'd had problems all season with pronouncing his name). However, we were comforted by the fact that we were about to get a new chairman, who promised much but, in reality, delivered little. The man in question was Anton Johnson, an ex-butcher from Essex with a decidedly dodgy past involving scandals at Rotherham and Southend. Mysteriously, the past was overlooked somewhat as the FA gave him the all-clear and Boro fans looked to go one better than the previous season.

Johnson was in charge for the first game, at home to Southend. Things were looking bright on that sunny August afternoon as Boro got their Third Division campaign underway. Six new faces took to the pitch: Paddy Atkinson, Jason Lydiate, Alex Mirankov, Wayne Bullimore, Jamie Hoyland and Ian Milbourne. We went down 2-1 in the end, but that wasn't so bad, was it? Southend had just been relegated and we had to bide our time until Micky Wadsworth was given some cash to splash. We were in for a long wait.

We were bottom after three straight defeats, but Wadders had just made his first 'signing' in the form of bald-headed, lardy-arsed striker Andy Saville.

Could he be the quality finisher we'd lacked for so much of last season? Saville was present at the home game against Brighton but couldn't play because he'd signed too late. However, just as Anton Johnson got to the supermarket checkout with his goods, he searched in his pocket for his wallet but came out with nothing. Saville returned to Cardiff later in the week, with Johnson supposedly "still sorting out our debts".

The financial problems were beginning to be well-documented after the Saville saga, with a proverbial tug-of-war for the club between Johnson and Russell. Various front-page stories were run about the whole mess and things came to a head when an unofficial fans' forum was arranged at the beginning of November. Russell attended; Johnson didn't - with Russell revealing that Johnson had borrowed £40,000 from the PFA to pay the wages. As a result of this, we could not sign players and Boro fans had doubts about the future of the club. This was a much different scenario from the one Johnson promised when he arrived.

On December 10, the Russells regained control of the club through the courts and began to try to stabilise. The PFA loan needed to be paid off quickly, as results were continuing to slide and Micky Wadsworth needed to bring in some quality players. This didn't happen (unless you count Glynn 'I don't know which is bigger, my pay packet or my big fat arse' Hodges as quality), and after a 1-0 defeat at Brighton, Tricky Micky resigned and joined Second Division Colchester. What a shame that one of our best-ever managers was forced to put up with an endless stream of shit coming from the boardroom. Good luck, Micky.

McHale and Mountfield took temporary charge, but after some heavy defeats, ex-Atletico Madrid and West Brom manager (did we forget to mention Newport County?) Colin Addison was appointed as manager. He came in like a breath of fresh air and signed some quality players in Darren Roberts, Tony Parks and Graeme Atkinson, and gave Chris 'Worst fake tan in the world ever' Tate his first real chance at league football. Tate didn't disappoint.

By April, there were three teams left scrapping for survival. We filled the last place, with Carlisle and Hartlepool just above. A 1-1 draw away at Hull in front of 14,000 (even though Boothferry Park's capacity is only around 13,500) saw us move up to the dizzy heights of 23rd. Oh the ecstasy on that sunny April afternoon. That was followed up by a crushing 3-0 win over relegation rivals Carlisle - Tate scoring a hat-trick. That seemed to have put us well on the way to league survival. This had to be the high point of the season, didn't it? A team inspired by a brilliant new manager. Bring on next season, we thought. However, being Scarborough FC meant that something had to happen.

The team cracked up and lost five games on the trot. Addison, though, remained confident as we went into the last three games bottom and knowing that we had to pick up points, and rely on Carlisle dropping some. We won away at Halifax (where it took the chairman and players ten minutes in a huddle to decide whether or not to clap the Boro fans for their outstanding support throughout the season, part-timers excluded of course), and at home to Plymouth - to leave us one point above Carlisle, with one game left. If we beat the Posh

2'S COMPANY 500'S A CROWD

on the final day of the season, then our Division Three status would remain. However, anything other than three points and Carlisle winning would see us drop down into non-league obscurity.

With no Premiership or First Division action, for once Boro were at the centre of media attention. Even the 2C team had a camera crew following us around all day. They were only interested in seeing despair and tears. And they weren't to be disappointed.

With a McStad packed to the rafters (once again all the part-timers in this town had got off their backsides and decided to see how 'their' team were doing), we reached half-time with the score 1-1 but, more importantly, Carlisle were losing 1-0. The job was half-complete.

With the Shed in full voice, 'the great escape' seemed on the cards. Early in the second-half, word got around that Carlisle had equalised. But we were still safe - just.

Then came one of those 'if only' moments, as Darren Roberts was sent clean through on goal. Dazza tried a cheeky lob over the goalkeeper but it dipped agonisingly over the bar. However, Carlisle were still drawing. The match at the McCain ended 1-1 and, with news of the same scoreline at Brunton Park, a horde of euphoric fans spilled onto the pitch. The jubilation was immense and the champagne opened. The escape of all escapes was complete - two months previously, we could only have dreamt of scenes like these. Then that same dream turned into one of the worst possible nightmares anyone could ever imagine (yes, worse than that one about David Mellor covered in custard). News of Carlisle's goalkeeper scoring in the 98th minute was at first treated as a joke. Then Boro fans faced the harsh reality that this was actually true. The chants stopped and were followed by a deadly silence as fans tried in vain to hold back the tears.

As if it couldn't get any worse, rivals York had just got relegated and the Carlisle goalkeeper who scored, Jimmy Glass (as if you didn't know), had been signed past the transfer deadline after being given special dispensation by the FA. Boro protests fell on deaf ears - whether this is because we didn't have a case, or because the dithering idiots at the FA did not want to admit to their mistake, is open for discussion. I suppose the fact that the FA were giving Carlisle special help for Michael Knighton's greed in selling their first choice goalkeeper on transfer deadline day for a measly sum isn't up for discussion. Have the FA and Carlisle ever heard of a YTS goalkeeper? It seems we received sweet FA from the FA.

Someone said that football is a cruel, cruel game and there is no better example of this than on the final day of our 98/99 season. We don't mean to be defeatist but things aren't looking good for the next campaign. Most of our away games will cost a small fortune to get to, we face the prospect of going part-time the season after next if we are still in the Conference, we still have an £800,000 debt to pay off, and our chairman has about as much money as Jonathan Aitken after he has just been mugged.

Still, looking on the bright side... is there a bright side?

Jonathon Cooper

SURVIVAL OF THE FATTEST 3

4,000 HOLES

Blackburn Rovers

A Clint Eastwood character once said: "If you want a guarantee, buy a toaster." Somebody should have pointed this out to Jack Walker when, during 1998/99, he allowed two managers to spend nearly £24m... and his team still got relegated. Admittedly over a quarter of that was spent on misfit Kevin Davies but, even so, we only laid out £2m in transfer fees the season we won the Premier League!

Colin Hendry shocked the club by asking for a transfer at the beginning of the season and, eventually, went to Rangers for "family reasons." This, despite having signed an extension to his contract only a couple of weeks beforehand. His reasons for leaving convinced no-one. What it did do was leave us without adequate cover at the back and thrust Darren Peacock centre-stage. From being signed as an understudy, he was now the star and, rather unfairly, was seen by a large section of the fans as a direct replacement for their hero Hendry. It also brought back memories of Shearer similarly leaving us in the lurch at the beginning of a season.

4000 HOLES

A NORTHERN HORDE OF UNCOUTH GARB AND STRANGE OATHS

INSIDE MONICA LEWINSKY ON GOING DOWN!

OR STAYING UP!

£1

The campaign began with Roy Hodgson as manager. The warning signs had been there the previous season as the team slumped alarmingly at the end, only just scraping a European place by winning our last match. Hodgson had bought Davies (£7.5m), Sebastian Perez (£3m), Darren Peacock (free), Christian Dailly (£5m) and Nathan Blake (£4.5m). By common consent he was paying ridiculous fees for amazingly average players, and by the end of the season the club had become a 'comfort zone' for mediocre players on exorbitant wages. Could that be why we got relegated?

One victory in our first eight matches set the tone for the remainder of the season. Certainly our inability to win at home, particularly against the other struggling clubs, was eventually to cost us our Premiership place. Ironically we were not playing that badly, but refereeing decisions, long-term injuries to key players and simple bad luck conspired against us. This enabled Hodgson to bring in youngsters, and whilst many of them were a revelation - Dunn,

Broomes and Johnson in particular - they were no substitute for experienced professionals.

As the team struggled in the league, we had a brief sojourn into Europe, against Olympique Lyonnais. After going down to a late goal at home, we battled bravely with ten men before going out in a 2-2 draw in Lyon. This performance gave hope for the future as we won our next home match, 3-0, but then went eight games without a win. It was this sequence of results which was to cost Hodgson his job. By now we realised that he talked a good game, quick with the ready-made excuses whenever we failed to win: injuries, refereeing, bad luck. It was to become his post-match mantra. Whilst he may have been the media's darling, there were rumours - later to be proved fairly accurate - that certain senior players no longer had confidence either in his training or man-management methods and were openly conspiring to undermine him, the unofficial spokesman being captain Tim Sherwood. He wanted to renegotiate his contract, hinting he would ask for a transfer if not successful. Off the field you might question Sherwood's attitude, but on the field he never gave less than one hundred per cent and when he finally left for Tottenham, after protracted negotiations, even his detractors would have to admit he left a void in midfield which was never filled. Hodgson was also struggling to justify Davies' fee. Admittedly the player had a serious throat infection which left him weak, then had a series of minor injuries. But he never seemed fully fit or committed to the cause, and naturally enough his confidence suffered. Fans can forgive most things, but not lack of effort.

Hodgson obviously realised he was under pressure but seemed quite content to carry on managing the club his way, trusting it would all come good in the end. What he failed to see was how much the club meant to its owner, Jack Walker. An hour after the 2-0 home defeat by Southampton, a game incidentally which we had dominated, Walker met with him and suggested a career-change opportunity. Hodgson was genuinely shocked and supposedly left in tears, with a sizeable chunk of Uncle Jack's fortune to dry his eyes with. Enter, stage left, Tony Parkes - once again to be caretaker-manager.

Despite various names being mentioned, it quickly became clear that Brian Kidd was their first choice. Initially, Rovers were rebuffed in trying to speak to Kidd. But United finally relented and, on 2 January 1999, he sat on the bench for the home game against Charlton. Kidd wasn't meant to take charge until the Monday, but within 15 minutes of the game starting, he was an animated figure on the touchline, waving, pointing, shouting and generally trying to cajole the players into some sort of order. This was to become a common sight for Rovers fans.

The initial enthusiasm generated by a new manager seemed to work as the team won 1-0, with Davies scoring his first goal. The team proceeded to go seven league and cup games without defeat, and by early February had reached the dizzy heights of 15th, including a 3-1 win at high-flying Aston Villa.

In reality, though, we were merely papering over the cracks. For once we enjoyed a fair amount of luck, although our disciplinary record was a major source of concern. Not only were we accumulating yellow cards at an alarming rate but frequently finished games with only ten men. We were not a dirty team but too often fell victim to over-zealous refereeing. A yellow card for a petty infringement would be followed by a legitimate yellow card offence, leaving the official no option but to send off the player.

Yet, in the short-term, this apparent victimisation by officials seemed to work in our favour, with the team suddenly developing fighting qualities that were sadly lacking by the season's end. We probably won or drew as many games with ten men as we did with eleven. In fact it was suggested, only half seriously, that we begin all games a player short!

This run of only one defeat in 13 or so league games came to an abrupt halt with a 4-1 home defeat against Sheffield Wednesday, a team supposedly in relegation trouble but who comprehensibly outplayed us in every department, especially midfield. This latter problem had been with us since the departure of Sherwood. Kidd had inherited the injury crisis and even managed to add to it along the way. The result was a total lack of quality midfield players in the team. Kidd rang the changes but it made little difference. Opposition players frequently dominated the centre of the park, as our midfield was invariably helping out in defence, leaving our forwards starved of good service.

Davies continued his nightmare season, mainly on the bench, as Kidd obviously had little confidence in him. Sutton always looked our best player, despite not being fully fit, and eventually his season was ended by injury - and, with it, our attacking potency. Defensively, Henchoz and Filan were magnificent and Peacock seemed to be winning the fans over until two horrendous mistakes against Liverpool cost us the game. This unsettled him and he looked nervous for the remainder of the season.

Kidd had strengthened the side by signing Keith Gillespie, who seemed a good buy but merely flattered to deceive; Jason McAteer, as a midfield player, but who was played at full-back due to injuries; and Matt Jansen, a precocious talent who scored a wonder goal on his debut but was similarly laid low with injury. One for the future, perhaps. Then we had Ashley Ward, who never gave up despite limited abilities.

The season was coming to its climax and supporters were now openly talking about the possibility of relegation. Games against fellow strugglers Southampton, Charlton and an already doomed Nottingham Forest would be crucial -and, needless to say, we didn't win one of them. No surprises there. Despite winning 3-1 with 30 minutes to go away at Southampton, at the end of 90 minutes we were lucky to escape with a 3-3 draw. At Charlton it was scoreless, with both teams lacking the will to take chances, even though with six minutes remaining Rovers were denied the most blatant of penalties as their goalkeeper brought down Ward. The referee indicated that Ward had dived, yet failed to book him.

Then came the Nottingham Forest game. They were already relegated, yet with ten men proceeded to win 2-1 - and we missed a penalty. The game was a shambles, with few of the team escaping censure for an abject performance.

It was clueless, passionless and heartless... and they were the positive aspects! This provoked Kidd into publicly criticising his players for the first time: "It's like a bunch of individuals who don't hurt enough and a lot of them are rubber dinghy men. The ship's going down, they're saying, "I'll go for help" - rubber dinghy men. I think the inmates have been running this club for too long." Strong stuff indeed. He'd obviously had his doubts about the team for some time, but whilst there was a chance to avoid relegation he kept quiet in the interests of team morale.

To look at the season simplistically, we only needed to have won two more home games and we'd have been safe. But our failure to win against any of the other struggling teams - Everton, Southampton and Nottingham Forest - was the deciding factor. These teams always seemed more aware that relegation was a possibility and had more urgency in their game; and, perhaps more importantly, played as a team. The Rovers players, instead of making things happen, just drifted through games hoping it would be all right on the night. This complacency and a lack of leadership on the pitch ultimately cost us dear. I would excuse the youngsters from criticism, but when they needed guidance from the more experienced players, the latter were nowhere to be seen. They bottled out.

Then came the Man United home match that ended our seven year tenure in the Premiership. Ironic that relegation was finally confirmed against Kidd's old club. Oh how we laughed.

If only we could have shown the same commitment and fighting spirit that we did against United during the rest of the season. Under normal circumstances, a draw was a good result - but not this time. It was win or be relegated. Ward had a good chance with six minutes to go but snatched at the ball and his shot went wide.

The scenes at the end were very emotional. The crowd stayed behind and cheered the team on a lap of honour, almost as if the players had won something - and in some respects they had: the confidence of the supporters. A quick return to the Premiership was just possible if the team could maintain that level of performance. But there was also frustration at what might have been; if only we could have played like that all season, if only we could have won two more games, if only 'that' penalty had been awarded at Charlton, if only Sutton had played all season.

If only...
Ian Ferris

A KICK UP THE R'S

Queens Park Rangers

"Six-nil to the Superhoops!" sang the delirious Rangers fans, jumping on their seats in a paroxysm of joy as we put yet another past the demoralised Crystal Palace. People were hugging strangers and shaking their heads in utter disbelief. I then looked round to see the sardonic smile on the face of Cilla Black, who was dressed only in the 1973-74 Sparta Prague away shirt, and realised that, in the words of Tom Jones, "Yes, I was only dreaming." I woke up in a convoluted mixture of sweat and deflated excitement, knowing that we would never beat Crystal Palace 6-0, and that forever I would be gingerly haunted by that image of the Scouse temptress.

≡ A KICK ᵁᴾ_ᴛʜᴇ R's ≡

£2.00

Issue 121

June 1999

STAYING UP! - RELIEF AT THE FINAL WHISTLE...
QPR v Crystal Palace
9 May 1999

An alternative view of Queens Park Rangers Football Club

There is a theatre in West London, found among the myriad housing estates of White City. Once upon a time, this theatre played host to some of the most prodigious and mesmerising actors the land has ever produced. Week in, week out the faithful audience would come and marvel at the dazzling performances these actors put on, believing that one day not only England but the whole world would bow down to the sublime talent of this small outfit from W12.

Now the stage has collapsed and the dream lies in ruins. The actors have turned into unknowns, spluttering their lines and missing their cues in dreadful plays that would be comedies if they weren't so tragic. A knife could now cut the disillusionment, where once it could slice the jubilant atmosphere. And yet this collection of bitter souls drag themselves on to the sound of the slow, dull beat of their weak hearts, hoping to avoid the ultimate humiliation.

The season began, predictably, with a 1-0 defeat at the Stadium of Light, yet it was the prosaic games against Walsall in the Worthington Cup and Bristol City in the league that set the tone for the rest of the season. Ironically, the glimmer of hope came from captain Karl Ready in the City game, when he equalised with a long-range effort in the dying minutes. I say "ironically" because it was Ready who personified the inane and clueless activity that we Rangers fans witnessed so often on the pitch. Karl's name is certainly no characternym. Indeed, it is about as apt as Dennis Wise's.

After being effortlessly knocked out of the Worthington Cup by Charlton (I would call it the 'Worthnothing Cup' - but since the last time we graced the hallowed turf of Wembley was in 1986 in this competition, I shall refrain), Ray Harford's job was in as precarious a position as our Division One status. A 2-0 win against Stockport eased worries slightly, as the fans found something to cheer about, and Kevin Gallen found both his 'magic hat' and his goalscoring boots.

Then came Saturday 26 September. Then came Oxford United. My name is Patrick Nathanson and I'm an Oxford United-hater. There, I've said it. And they claim that recognition is the first step to recovery. However, I'm not so sure, for I nearly despise the U's as much as I despise Chelsea. It all started on that fateful day in 1986 when, having beaten the mighty Liverpool in the semi's, we were hot favourites to win our first cup since 1967 - only for Oxford to go and thrash us 3-0. Certainly, if the mass of Rangers fans at Wembley were a beautiful sea of blue and white, then Oxford were the annoying little kids who ruined it all and pissed in that sea, turning the colours on the trophy from blue and white to yellow.

It is funny how things come full circle. It was last season when, on a bollock-freezing Friday evening at the Manor Ground, Ray Harford made his managerial debut for us and things were looking up. We then proceeded to get outplayed in every department, and lost 3-1. Worse was to come a year later. For on that sepulchral Saturday in September, I witnessed the most gutless, shameful performance I had ever seen, as we crumbled 4-1 without any hint of pride or defiance. Even the normally placid Ray Harford was outraged and said it was "pathetic". In the face of mounting pressure, Harford did the honourable thing and quit. However, his resignation was not met with the same unmitigated jubilation that greeted the departure of Stewart Houston and Bruce Rioch. Indeed, though I knew he had to go, the desperate picture of a lonely and dejected Harford returning from the Oxford game in his car, which had been broken into by fans for the third time in a month, soaking wet as the rain poured in, evoked immense sympathy on my part. He had the ability, but he was in the right place at the wrong time.

No, for me the real villain was a certain Vinnie Jones. Admittedly, he had played his part in keeping us up the previous season but his lust for money got the better of him, as he refused to even train after he was passed over for the vacant manager's job. Like an adulterous lover, Jones had blown kisses towards the Rangers faithful a few months earlier, only to show, with his disgraceful behaviour, how much true loyalty and honour he really possessed. He knew the parlous financial state the club was in but the only thing he cared about was the money. He eventually left, with a sizeable amount in his pocket, to pursue an acting career. If in the future I happen to win a holiday to Hollywood and I bump into Mr Jones, I'll... er, well, I probably won't do anything...

After the latest Oxford debacle, Iain Dowie was put in charge of the team for the game at Wolves. An untypically courageous performance produced a 2-1 victory, our first away win for a whole year. However, Grimsby brought us back to the harsh reality of Planet Nationwide Division One, beating us at Loftus Road the following Saturday. It was time for the Third Coming.

Gerry Francis had been a hero as the captain of the great 1975-76 nearly team. It was under his midfield guidance that we missed out on the championship by one point, as we were denied by the lethal combination of fate and a mid-table Norwich with nothing to play for. Gerry then returned to take the role of manager in the early Nineties. It was in the '92-93 season that we finished fifth in the inaugural Premier League and claimed the prestige of being top London club. But this new-found success did not last, as the then chairman, Richard Thompson, set about the systematic destruction of our beloved club. Gerry left in an acrimonious haze, burning with anger at Thompson's insatiable avarice.

Now, our sinking ship was desperately calling out for someone with a love for the club. Thankfully, Francis listened to his heart rather than his head, and in October he took charge. Our future, along with our hopes and dreams, seemed to be in safe hands again. This sudden optimism paid off immediately, as we went on a short run without defeat. Football fans being football fans, this ephemeral success was even met with talk about the play-offs, when really it was about as likely as Watford getting into the Premier League. QPR being QPR, they did not fail to disappoint the pragmatic realists among us for, after that brief flourish, we found ourselves getting beaten by a countless number of mediocre, yet hard-working sides.

The peak of the season came in the Sunderland home game. We had recently thrown away a win against Ipswich in the last few minutes, and now contrived to do the same against the formidable Rokermen.

However, the greatest mystery of the '98-99 season is not why Niall Quinn was allowed to head in the equaliser, or even how we managed to excel in being so hopelessly inept so hopelessly often. Rather, it is whatever happened to the repulsive, horrendously luminescent 'alternative' shirt. (By the way, yes, I did buy one.) The only conceivable explanation I can think of is that either the whole lot of them were taken back to the JD Sports shop in Chernobyl, where they were bought, or Damien Hirst nicked them and is currently using them in his next entry for the Turner Prize, having suspended them in a glass frame. Or maybe it was just that they were *so* repulsive and horrendously luminescent.

The inevitable cup exit at the hands of Huddersfield was memorable only for the ethereal hailstorm at half-time. It was as though the gods were expressing their displeasure and decided that, as the fans could not be entertained, they might as well be wet. Talking about a lack of entertainment, I found it deeply ironic that before the QPR v Bury game, the players lethargically trotted out to Robbie Williams' *Let Me Entertain You*. Needless to say, the game ended 0-0.

The possible divine intervention during the Huddersfield game brings me to the all-important question: is there a footballing God? Personally, I believe in a football heaven, a luscious utopia where true, loyal fans are rewarded with a place alongside the imperious Bryon Butler of 1986 *Radio 2* fame (give me Butler over the increasingly self-obsessed and egotistical Des Lynam any day), as a naked Karren Brady beguiles us with the euphonic sound of her flute, while all Chelsea fans and glory-hunting Cockney Reds are kept in check by a tailed and horny Mark Lawrenson.

Thump. I am brought back to reality with the memory of a mind-numbingly tedious scoreless draw against Bristol City, as we struggle to hold on to the point. Another three games without a win and it seems that no matter which way we QPR fans go after a match, we all seem to be on the same road. The sign of this road is clear. It says 'Nationwide Division Two'.

Relief came in the unlikely form of none other than Oxford United, as the on-loan Rob Steiner stole three points on a wet Wednesday night, with a goal that seemed to be an amalgamation of both a certain Diego Armando Maradona's brace in the 1986 World Cup semi-final against England; it had the cheeky, cunning element (i.e. cheating) of Maradona's first goal, along with the skill, luck and persistence of his second. Then, after losing three more games on the trot, we came up against a bored Swindon and came away with a 4-0 victory. It looked like we had made it, as all we had to do now was get six more points. Six points in eight games on the back of a 4-0 win? Easy. No problem at all.

Everybody was looking forward to a nice end of season run, which would see us pull away from the blood-sucking hounds who fight for every single last scrap of a point in the squalid quagmire that is relegation. Oh dear.

Many years ago (I think it might have been 1983), the people of Hartlepool found a monkey that had been washed ashore after a French boat had been shipwrecked. The monkey had been the mascot of the French sailors, and so they had dressed him up in a French uniform. The people of Hartlepool, having never seen a Frenchman before but knowing that the French were meant to talk in a wild and strange tongue (and were hairy and smelly) tried the monkey, found him guilty of being a French sailor and hanged him. They were wrong. In 1999 the supporters of QPR believed that they would escape relegation with ease. We too were wrong. What can I say? It happens.

After the Swindon game, we embarked on a diabolical run, managing only one win, a win which was incredibly fortunate to say the least; for, despite being outplayed by West Brom, we stole it once again in the last few minutes. The worrying absence of cohesion, confidence and, above all, goals culminated in an embarrassingly gutless 2-0 defeat away to Port Vale in the penultimate game of the season in front of 4,000 vociferous travelling supporters. It seemed as though the team did not deserve us; and, for some fans, the hapless frustration of our inexorable spiral down to Division Two obscurity was too much to handle. After Vale's second goal, the scorer, Carl Griffiths, showed an astounding capacity for stupidity in provocatively gesturing and celebrating right in front of the already volatile Rangers supporters. It all kicked off as police helmets went flying in a sea of abuse and a one-man pitch invasion was staged. When the anger had rescinded, we were left with the remnants of a dire display and the prospect of relegation unless we beat Palace on the final day.

That Port Vale game was one of the season's many crushing disappointments. As for the rare high points, Tony Scully's volley in the final few minutes of the season stands out. For me, it was something of a cathartic experience because it reminded me of Scully's similar volley in the last minutes of the Oxford away game, which we had lost 4-1, those few minutes being the nadir of a shambolic season and, indeed, our lowest point for many years. Then, of course, there was that whole last game of the season...

"Six-nil to the Superhoops!" sang the delirious Rangers fans, jumping on their seats in a paroxysm of joy as we put yet another past the demoralised Palace. People were hugging strangers and shaking their heads in utter disbelief. We had done it. We had beaten Palace 6-0 and stayed up. And guess what? Cilla was nowhere to be seen.

Patrick Nathanson

A LARGE SCOTCH

Shrewsbury Town

Pre-season optimism soon started to wane at Gay Meadow after only one win in the first ten league games and our failing to score in six of them.

It had all started so well. A 2-1 victory against one of the favourites for promotion, Scunthorpe, was followed by our obligatory first round exit from the Worthington Cup, this time to Bristol City - even though we scored four times in the home leg. Little did we know those goals were the last we would see for five consecutive games.

Supporters were starting to worry they would forget how to celebrate a goal. Thankfully, when

> **ISSUE 22   ONLY 50p**
>
> *S. T. F. C.*
>
> ## A LARGE SCOTCH
>
> You didn't tell me Beardsley takes size 7½
>
> Inside this issue:
> Media News
> Fair Shares
> Tribute to Paul Evans
> Zine Scene
> Play Station Competition
> Tales from the Bucks Arse
> and much more!
>
> **The Original & Best
> Shrewsbury Town Fanzine**

Kevin Seabury scored against Peterborough, our memories didn't let us down and we went mental. Five games without a goal really makes you appreciate when you finally do score. Unfortunately, Town couldn't hold on and we ended up with our usual score-draw against the Posh.

By now we had the indignity of being bottom of the league. Where were Doncaster Rovers when you needed them? There would be no safety net this season. Things were looking desperate. In an inconsistent division, every team appeared capable of beating anyone else on their day.

The turning point came in the home game against Carlisle. Town were desperate for the clubs above them not to open up a points gap. Former Town favourite Ian Stevens had put the visitors ahead in the 89th minute. Then, in the 90th minute, we were awarded a penalty – it was missed! Our hearts sank. We accepted defeat and the crowd started to leave the ground. However, as the referee started to check his watch, Town had one last attack and, somehow, Steve Kerrigan managed to scramble the ball home: 1-1.

Our chairman, looking to give the players a boost, enlisted the help of Richard O'Neill, an expert in positive attitude and a trained hypnotist. This got the club a lot of publicity, if nothing else. There were rumours that players had been hypnotised. In the next game, at Rotherham, we half expected the team to come out with a glazed expression, their arms stretched out in front, mumbling to themselves "We will win".

We did win 1-0, as we usually do at Millmoor. Had Mr O'Neill had an effect?

When I returned home after the match, I sat down to read the local paper. There was an article about Richard O'Neill. It started off thus: "Imagine the scene. Shrewsbury Town have just left the pitch to the cheers of the Town away following, after beating high-flying Rotherham. They have moved off the bottom of the league, never to return again." The article had been written the day before the match - and it had all come true. Scary stuff.

Manager Jake King was quick to play down O'Neill's contribution, stating that hard work had earned us a victory and that none of the players had actually been hypnotised. Well, whatever the reason, Town enjoyed ten league games without defeat.

It was time for the FA Cup - and we found ourselves drawn away to Rushden & Diamonds. We could only envy their superb ground, the size of their squad and the amount of money they have to spend. Once again there was a first round exit for Town. (We don't like cup competitions much. We also went out of the first round of the Auto Windscreens, to Wycombe.)

The cup game was seen as a one-off. We were still having a good spell in the league - that was until we lost four games in a row. We were starting to look over our shoulders again.

Boxing Day saw us comprehensively beaten - 3-0 at Cardiff - so it became even more important that we beat bottom club Hull City in the following home game. On a dramatic afternoon, Town won 3-2. It was a game that saw the return to form of talented striker Lee Steele, and was the start of a run of only one defeat in ten games. Once again we were starting to look towards the top of the table and the Promised Land of the play-off zone.

During this fantastic run, Town managed to score three goals in four consecutive home matches, a club record. Lee Steele scored quite a few during this period, with confidence at an all-time high, including a couple of fantastic individual efforts.

Transfer deadline day was approaching fast. As usual we had no money with which to purchase players to help in our push for the play-offs. In fact we had to sell star midfield player Paul Evans to Brentford for £100,000 to help balance the books. Evans would have been available on a free transfer at the end of the season when his contract expired, so he was doing the club a huge favour by going early and possibly doing himself out of a lot of money. His last game for the club was in the 3-0 home win over Darlington, Evans scoring the first goal from the penalty-spot. He was substituted near the end and left the pitch fighting back the tears after an emotional ovation from the crowd.

With no money available for a replacement, we all wondered how we would fare without our midfield linchpin. Our worst fears were realised, as we lost our next game, 2-1 to lowly Carlisle, their first win under Nigel Pearson. Our next match was away to Brentford.

Town's players seemed to have something to prove against their former team-mate and put in an excellent performance to come away with a 0-0 draw.

Evans received some good-natured kicks from his former team-mates during the match but it was all smiles afterwards as he received a water bottle soaking from his old pals.

The next two home games were the highlight of the season. We actually won a local derby for the first time in years, 2-0 over Chester. This was our one and only local derby in a season of long distance away trips.

Next, it was top of the table Cambridge at the Meadow on a Friday night. Sky had refused to show the match live. Shrewsbury and, until relegation cost them their league status, Scarborough were the only teams never to have featured in a live Sky match. It was Sky's loss - the match was an absolute cracker.

Town always play better against the top sides and this was no exception. We were all over Cambridge and had chance after chance. The Cambridge goalkeeper was having an inspired match. During the second-half, they scored against the run of play, but Town didn't give up and continued to dominate the game, creating enough chances to win ten games. With five minutes to go, the away fans finally started to sing, as they thought they had the match won. This just made Town's highest crowd of the season sing even louder still.

However, time was running out and the reserve official had already held up the board for added-on time. The crowd were willing the team to score. We didn't deserve to lose and the Cambridge fans were starting to get on our nerves. Then Town were awarded a free-kick. All the team piled forward, as Kevin Jobling curled the ball into the area and Kevin Seabury managed to beat the Cambridge giants in the air to head the ball home. The place went absolutely mad - you would have thought we had just won the FA Cup!

Whilst we were still celebrating, Town had won the ball back from the kick-off and were attacking once more. The ball came across to Mickey Brown but his point-blank effort was saved by the goalkeeper. If that had gone in, I can only imagine the scenes. This had been the best match seen at Gay Meadow for many a year, but unfortunately it was a game that we really had to win to keep alive our slim play-off hopes. Two defeats followed in the next two games, including 1-0 to bottom-of-the-table Hartlepool.

The players seemed to lose enthusiasm, as it was certain we weren't going to go up. Goals were becoming harder to come by again and all of a sudden we were starting to look over our shoulders as the bottom sides started stringing some decent results together. In the space of a month, we had gone from a side looking to get into the play-offs to a side in some danger of going out of the league. The loss of Paul Evans was beginning to tell, with only one win in the eleven games after his departure.

The eleventh game of this depressing run of results was at Orient, where Town found themselves 4-0 down at half-time! In the second-half, Town changed tactics, moving from 5-3-2 to a 4-4-2 formation, then promptly let in two more goals in the first five minutes. We had come from 2-0 down last season at Orient to win 3-2, so when we did score our one consolation goal, the Town following starting singing for all their worth, "We're gonna win 7-6." This earned a standing ovation from the Orient crowd.

We were still not mathematically safe when we entertained Mansfield in our final home game, although it was unlikely that the teams below us would all win. All the same, it was still a relief to win 1-0. The 6-1 drubbing had been forgotten and the usual last home game sing-songs began.

Torquay away was our last game of the season. We had been looking forward to this for a long time. Of course, we had been dreaming at the start of the season that this would be our seaside promotion party; but what the hell - we could party anyway. We were just pleased to be playing a club by the sea at a decent time of the year. Usually it's December on a cold Tuesday night.

A healthy 500+ Town following descended on Plainmoor, with most staying for the weekend. Town played superbly and raced into a three-goal lead and had two others disallowed. Why couldn't we play like this every week?

Neville Southall in the Torquay goal received plenty of stick throughout the game. "You're just a fat, scruffy Welshman," echoed around the ground, much to the annoyance of big Nev, who complained to the referee. Perhaps he was objecting to being called Welsh?

No more goals were added in the second-half, although we kept ourselves amused with non-stop singing. Then it was on to the nightclubs to celebrate with two-goal hero Steve Kerrigan on his stag night. What a weekend! If only the Football League's computer could arrange the same fixture next year. I'm sure big Nev would look forward to it.

Kevin Bright

Source: The Tea Party

A LOAD OF BULL

Wolverhampton Wanderers

Bye Bye Psychobabble, Hello Walsall

Always the bridesmaid and never the bride is the popular perception of us Molineux folk. And as Wolves' quest for Premiership elevation was again an ultimate failure, you could be forgiven for thinking just that. This time we missed out on the play-offs by a single victory. But the vision of Wolves fans crying into their pints of Banks' was never further away as we accepted our lot and muddled through our tenth consecutive season at this level. Incidentally, we have even given a nickname to a home we have become so fond of: 'The Division from Hell'. Even so, there was much to cheer. Perhaps the biggest

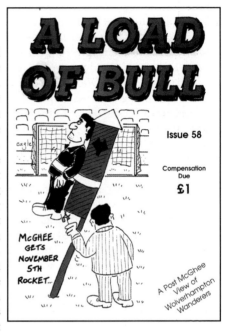

Issue 58

Compensation Due

£1

McGHEE GETS NOVEMBER 5TH ROCKET...

A Post McGhee View of Wolverhampton Wanderers

one was on Guy Fawkes' Night, when manager Mark McGhee got the rocket.

By then we were in freefall, with the best start for 30 years a distant memory. Inspired by the hard-running Steve Froggatt, Wolves romped home in their opening four league matches to storm to the top of the division by the end of August. The early promotion celebrations after a first-ever win at Oxford were probably a tad premature and our pleas for the season to end now fell on deaf ears. Shame really, as in our fifth clash we blew a two-goal lead against a Stockport team who seemed more compatible to the NFL than the Nationwide, and our first false dawn was over. Within days, Froggatt had run away to Coventry, Bully (showing some of his best form for ages) succumbed to an old knee injury, and when we were required to battle for our points, we displayed all the fighting spirit of a lemon. McGhee's stock started slipping when Sunderland arrived. It was great to sample a big match atmosphere, with the town buzzing and the pubs packed. It was the sort of day fans love - and the team responded, too. I thought the visitors weren't a patch on the previous season, as we carved out chance after chance. The game was all but ours after Robbie Keane had given us a second-half lead and it was well into the third minute of the three minutes' injury-time when they equalised. It was the game's last action... the drained, anguished, silent faces of Wolves fans leaving the

South Bank still haunt me now. We would have rather lost by four than go through that pain. At least the next match at Huddersfield could never be that bad... or so we thought.

With a soft underbelly now exposed, we couldn't even take with us the confidence of a decent performance, and were rubbish. We had all but accepted a 1-0 defeat as we approached injury-time, and guess what? Up pops Robbie with a Wolves equaliser. But the cheering had hardly died down, and there wasn't even time for the bloke behind me to mention "swings and roundabouts", as the hapless Steve Sedgley let Huddersfield in with the last kick of the game to send us reeling. Don't tell us how Bayern Munich fans feel.

As we stuttered into autumn, the season was taking a familiar shape. Bournemouth knocked us out of the Worthington Cup, the worst QPR team in history won easily at Molineux, and miserable defeats at Palace, Portsmouth and Ipswich spelt the end of McGhee. After nearly three years of promises, deceit and psychobabble, it was akin to an army at long last travelling on a full stomach as we journeyed with renewed hope to Bristol City. It was a brilliant day, made even better by going one down, as we went on to score six. The 3,000 travelling fans went mental and we had to rub our eyes in disbelief as the main predator was the cherubic David Connolly, an on-loan signing from Feyenoord, who had so far failed to hit the target, let alone score in more than a dozen outings. On this special day he managed four. It was kind of funny, though, that the main headliner was not our goal-scoring hero, but someone even chubbier - the Wolves mascot, Wolfie. As usual our hairy friend had been involved in a half-time *contretemps* with the opponent's mascot, but this time it was spotted by a smart lensman. Within days the image of him roughing up Bristol City's little pigs was being flashed around the world; the only thing that surprised Wolves fans was that his antics had not been picked up by the tabloids before. At least it gave us some well-deserved column inches in a season when non-Premiership football hardly got a look in.

All the hype of finding a new manager came to nothing as we continued in the more than capable hands of Colin Lee, McGhee's former right hand. His continuing presence confirmed the rumours that the two had long ago fallen out, and as Lee still had a contract to run to the end of the season it saved an ever-parsimonious board more cash. With former Seventies' goal king John Richards keeping a rather too close an eye on Sir Jack Hayward's purse strings, it was the dose of reality the fans had feared (or welcomed). He signalled limited spending in the transfer market and indicated the end of the gravy train of fat cat wages, mercilessly exploited by the likes of Geoff Thomas. The new-found spirit continued with another stunning win, this time against our rivals Birmingham City. Three goals in the last 15 minutes from youngsters Lee Naylor and Carl Robinson further justified the focus on homespun talent as we sent the blue noses snivelling back to New Street. This also put paid to an unwanted statistic which had emerged under McGhee and spoke volumes about our spirit, or more precisely lack of it. It went something like this... if the opposition scores first, that's it, Wolves lose. This malarkey had gone on for two and half years and no less than 40 league defeats. Then suddenly, under Lee, we come back from early reversals twice in a matter of weeks to win.

Lee, now entrusted to the end of the season, was joined by the ex-Bristol City manager John Ward. This new leadership team found faith in the fans and the players started performing like there was no tomorrow, which in a funny sort of way there wasn't, as most of their contracts were finished come May. Suddenly Keith Curle stopped moaning about his 'paltry' £400,000 a year salary and was back to what he does best. Dean Richards started to look like the sort of centre-half we always believed he was (i.e. he could do decent job for someone like Blackburn, Coventry or Southampton – ouch!), and the defence became one of the meanest in the division. It might not have been the prettiest Wolves team ever, but at least it had a fighting spirit and played for the full 95 minutes. Perhaps the one player to capture the mood more than any other was Aussie full-back Kevin Muscat. One swing of his right foot in the dying seconds against Ipswich put our season right on course, as he delivered to Wolves fans the perfect Christmas present - three valuable points. The *Top Cat* theme was adapted to fit our Steve Coogan doppelganger and, on the back of that 25-yard bombshell, a Black Country hero was born. We were lying 12th at the time, and from that point on hardly looked back.

There was real evidence to suggest that we could go all the way, albeit through the play-offs, as the team started gelling. Robbie Keane was delivering his wonderful potential with vital goals at Tranmere and an even sweeter brace to knock our nemesis, Bolton Wanderers, out of the FA Cup at the Reebok. It was an astonishing performance, as we played Robbie as a lone striker and, with a squad decimated through injury, had to field five YTS lads on the bench. Following much speculation, the Norwegian World Cup striker Havard Flo eventually arrived from Werder Bremen to take some of the load up front and his ability to strike the woodwork was uncanny as he searched for a first goal. It was well worth the wait when it did arrive - a brave headed equaliser against Arsenal in the cup. To cap it all, he was then denied a winner by... yes, a goalpost. At least we performed on this occasion, rather than the semi-final washout suffered at Villa Park the previous season. The arrival of Flo did spark more depressing reaction from managing director Richards, this time revealing the losses at Molineux (some £40,000 a week) and that this was the very *last* signing. Ironic really that the money which funded Flo's move was part of the £2m prised from Coventry for Froggatt. Funny how we could now do with a winger to supply his capable head with some decent crosses.

But we pushed on and it was amusing to see fans queuing for late season tickets to swell this loyal number to around the 17,000 mark. You really did wonder where all our money was going. But despite a setback at Sunderland - this time a last-minute Quinn goal beat us - our faith was repaid with fine victories on the road at QPR, Barnsley and Birmingham. The Barnsley one was particularly cherished as it was the sort of result that makes it worth going to 40-odd games a season. First and foremost it was against Barnsley, the team who literally mugged us for promotion two years ago. When the country sympathised with their plight and 6-0 hammerings amongst the big boys, I can assure you that Wolverhampton looked on with a smug smile. Initially things weren't too clever and to go 2-0 down was not the best way to take revenge. But even by our new-found standards of resilience, to come back and win 3-2 was simply staggering and, of course, the perfect riposte. At the final whistle the Wolves end went crazy with non-stop singing as we danced out of Oakwell, convinced a play-off place was ours.

Even though we maintained a steady rhythm and no small amount of effort, I'm afraid we didn't quite take account of Watford and a run that would take them past us and straight through to the Premiership. Fair play to them and there *are* many Wolves fans who will wish Graham Taylor the best. But to be honest, what chances have they and Bradford of anything but survival in the so-called promised land. Although there was certainly a touch of "it should have been us" on seeing Bradford celebrating promotion at Molineux, the reality was that we were not good enough. I doubt if we could take kindly to being whipping boys for nine months, get relegated and be patronised the way Charlton were. Not, of course, forgetting the long-term damage a drop like this can have. Wolves fans have long memories - normally to marvel at our great pioneering team of the Fifties. But these are scarred by our last humiliating sojourn to the top flight, when a hopelessly under-resourced squad were relegated by Easter and subsequent relegations all but put us out of business. There is no doubt about it, Wolves will come good again and if we make as much progress next season as we did in 98/99, we will have little to complain about. At least we have regained our sense of humour - as Bradford celebrated, it was the Wolves fans who caught the moment with a wonderful chant of "Walsall Here We Come".

Jim Heath

A LOVE SUPREME

Sunderland AFC

I really can't explain to you what it felt like. Michael Gray was to Sunderland what Lee Hughes would become for West Brom: raw local talent, nurtured into a quality product at the hometown club he adores. If Hughes bursting into the team and scoring 30-odd goals is every football child's dream, then Mickey missing *that* penalty after Wembley's finest final is the nightmare. The story of Sunderland's tragic denial was already irresistible, and if the media could tell it from the broad shoulders of a good-looking, talented footballer, then so much the better. Joe Public loves that. Mickey Gray became the emblem

of the club and, wherever Sunderland were mentioned, we saw his square jaw. Niall Quinn is quick to point out that rather than shying away from the pressure this brought, Mickey bleached his hair a brilliant white, encapsulating the team's attitude in quietly attacking the new campaign with a bitter resolution. Coming into the start of this season, we wore the play-off defeat like an 'I am 4' badge at a children's party.

There were surprisingly few additions to the squad over the summer. An unknown Danish goalkeeper by the name of Thomas Sorensen replaced the iconic, flamboyant - and occasionally shit - Lionel Perez (who unbelievably went to the Mags), and the gap created by Dickie Ord's departure to QPR was filled by the massive frame of Bury's Paul Butler. The two were hardly the big-name additions that Sunderland fans were desperate for, given the resources that were surely available in light of the previous season's attendances. Further signings Gerry Harrison (Burnley), Andy Marriott and Neil Wainwright (Wrexham) did little to appease the transfer junkies, who'd had all summer to wallow in play-off-losing, no-star-buying self-pity. Nevertheless, a £350,000 Kevin Phillips has taught us the lesson of planting acorns rather than buying oak trees, and over 40,000 gave Peter Reid the benefit of the doubt on August 8, for the visit of QPR to our little fortress.

Early season optimism allowed itself only the briefest of fleeting visits to the Stadium of Light, however, as Lee Clark was carried from the field in the late summer sunshine. A seemingly innocuous challenge by Keith Rowland left Sunderland's most influential player with a broken leg that was to see him sidelined for eight months. As we dragged ourselves towards a tedious 1-0 victory from the penalty-spot, many feared that without his creative guile in the centre of the park, Sunderland would become like the Angel of the North: plenty going on down the wings, but boring in the middle and looking rusty already.

The expected play-off hangover had presented itself only in the form of a slightly tepid start, but without the Alka-Seltzer that is Lee Clark, many feared that before too long we'd be moping around like a Geordie the day that Keegan quit the Mags (a wonderful, fantastic day, by the way). Within only a couple of weeks, however, we began to tonk people at a canter, without really playing all that well. In the last week of August, we faced Tranmere and Watford at home, and much-fancied (again) Ipswich away. We scored a total of eleven goals in those three matches, conceding only one. The tone had been set.

Generally we were solid enough, if a little boring at this stage. A monotonous grinding out of results was punctuated by the odd blinder - most notably, a late, late equaliser at Wolves, and a 7-0 thrashing of Oxford (who were unwittingly to become, incidentally, the latest team to fall victim to the curse of my birthday). At Chester in mid-September, however, things took a turn for the worse. Thoughts we had allowed ourselves of promotion were guiltily dismissed when Kevin Phillips limped off in the second round of the Worthless Cup. A minor niggle in his toe, we were told. A sodding minor niggle that was to keep him out for nearly four months, whilst the country's finest doctors contemplated their navels. "What's wrong with Kev?" - the eight-million pound question; "Buggered if I know" - the ubiquitous answer.

So Clarkie was crocked, SupaKev was knackered and, to add insult to injury, the Mags had binned Dourgleish and replaced him with football's golden boy, sexy Ruud Gullit. Marvellous. Just great. I spent three weeks walking around with a face like a smacked arse. John Mullin 'converted' (and I use the word like an estate agent... erroneously) into a central midfielder in a vain attempt to plug the gaping hole in midfield, and the Dichio/Bridges dream ticket stepped into the biggest (but actually quite small) boots on Wearside. Partly due to an old-fashioned combination of heart, honest hard work and ability in wide positions, but mainly due to three of the scariest men in English football (Peter Reid, Bobby Saxton and Kevin Ball) putting the fear of God up the lads, we held our own. And still we refused to lose.

Admittedly, watching Sunderland at times was like eroding granite with a leaky tap. We played our keep-ball game, tired teams out and tried to hit them in the last ten minutes - and, generally, we did it pretty effectively. When we weren't winning, we were drawing; and although the march towards the Premiership had become a crawl (actually we were lying on our fronts dragging ourselves towards the top flight by our eyelids), we kept on pulling out results when it mattered. In fact, there were one or two absolute crackers.

If Sunderland are rarely mentioned in the same sentence as Man United, then surely West Brom have never before been likened to Bayern Munich. But picture the scenes on a chilly Sunday afternoon when we turned a two-goal deficit into three points in the last 15 minutes of the game. Fair enough, it wasn't the European Champions' League Final, but it still gave you the rush, the football buzz; and if nothing else, it was worth seeing that little ginger bastard's irritating rag-doll celebration twice, only for him and his team to end up with sod all. Stick that on your transfer request, you spineless turncoat. Stepping away from the vitriol and bile for a moment, 3-0 away at Bolton was fairly satisfying too, if a little fortunate.

In the cup, the karma gods of football decided not only to draw Reidy against his old love, Everton, but to have the match decided on penalties to boot - an achievement in itself, considering that Sunderland were without nine of our first team. If ever there was a time to lay to rest the ghosts of last season, this was it. In the end, differences in the quality of the two teams were nullified by form. On the one hand, Sunderland, weakened though we were, were unbeaten all season and scoring for fun (ten in the previous three games). On the other, Everton were a joke at home, nowhere in the league, and couldn't hit a cow's arse with a banjo. We were always going to win the shoot-out - but to do it at the same time that the Mags lost on penalties to Blackburn was the little glacier cherry on top of the enormous and particularly delicious cake.

On November 21, we lost for the first time. The 3-2 home defeat to Barnsley was annoying when it came, not least because they scored the winner after Ashley Ward's sending off in the first-half. But these things happen to the best of teams, and the effect the loss had on us made it almost worthwhile. Our 4-0 trouncing of Sheffield United at Bramall Lane in the next match was, for me, the performance of the season. The match embodied our ability to play team football, and witnessing Mickey Bridges' two unbelievable goals gave us a feeling like copping off with the best looking lass in a nightclub.

Five wins on the bounce and a well-fought point at St Andrews looked like we might be set up for a very merry Christmas, but a Boxing Day defeat at Tranmere sounded the warning bells for a difficult January. Cup games against Blackburn and Leicester would at least give us some indication of how far we'd come since dropping out of the Premiership at Wimbledon two heart-breaking seasons ago. Not far enough was the sad truth. Whilst the fluid 4-4-2 system we play worked so well for us in the First Division, against Premiership opposition it was a different matter. In fairness, we were unlucky not to come away from Ewok Village with a point. But against Leicester, in particular, our lack of pace at the back was exposed.

Worrying, too, was the state of affairs down our left. One of the reasons we have been successful over the last two years is the partnership struck up between Mickey Gray and Allan Johnston - a formidable attacking force down our left wing in the Nationwide, a defensive liability in the Premiership. Nevertheless, we showed some character, especially in going ahead at Leicester. Press speculation over whether the bubble had burst was over the top, not least because we'd all but forgotten what to do when Sunderland lost a football match.

The results themselves we could take. "Them's the breaks," an Ipswich-supporting mate of mine always used to say (always, that is, until the last three seasons). What we were not prepared for, and what hurt more than being dumped out of two cups in three weeks, was the re-emergence of racism from a minuscule faction of the Sunderland end. If the outdated bigotry doled out to some of Leicester's players was sickening to the rest of the country, then believe me when I say that it can't possibly have shamed you as much as it did the thousands and thousands of Sunderland *fans* who turn up so regularly, so vociferously, without prejudice, up and down the country.

With Sunderland out of the cups, it was down to that old adage of concentrating on the leagues. I say 'leagues', plural, because whilst the first team were hogging the headlines in the Nationwide League, the reserve team - the killer Bs - were quietly dispatching Manchester United, in front of 25,000 at the Stadium of Light, and Liverpool, in front of 35,000, on their way to capturing the Pontin's League for the first time in the club's history. All of which bodes quite spectacularly well for the long-term health of the club in this Beckham, Giggs and Owen age, where the value of a strong youth set-up is banged on about *ad nauseam*. The black month of January had ended with a defeat for the first team on a bleak day at Watford. It was the third league match we had lost this season. It was also to be the last.

From thereon in, Sunderland were imperious, and January became April in the blinking of a red and white eye. Phillips and Clark were back, of course, and Phillips in particular was awesome, as his 25-goal haul in a much-shortened season testifies. At home, we were literally unbeatable, and whilst we never really lit the blue touch paper, we were all quite happy to sit back and watch it smoulder for three or four months. By the time we secured promotion, with a 5-2 win of some style at Bury, we were flying, securing the Championship four days later at Barnsley, where Roberto Carlos momentarily took over the body of Kevin Phillips to curl in a stunner.

We ended the season on a record 105 points by beating Birmingham 2-1, to notch up 19 wins in 23 home matches. In doing so, we achieved the unlikely distinction of beating every team in the league over the season, and were rewarded with full England call-ups for SupaKev and - oh irony of ironies - Michael Gray. There is no adequate cute proverb to summarise the turnaround of Sunderland's most infamous son of modern times; no tart quote that does him, or us, justice. I recommend quoting, "Oh, how the mighty have fallen" - and then turning it arse over tit.

But then, you're probably sick of hearing about the records broken and the renaissance of the north-east's least fashionable, but most credible team. And, at the end of it all, what have we proved? Yes, Peter Reid needs to strengthen the side over the summer, of that there's no doubt - we all know the standard of the top league. More revealing, though, is the realisation that Sunderland won the Nationwide Championship this season, not because of our Kevin Phillipses, Michael Grays and Lee Clarks, but because we were the only team in the whole league to play a squad system. Our first choice team was excellent, granted, but when key players were out, there was a string of quality understudies to carry on a sustained push. Just ask Steve Bruce, who played Ginger Rogers to Michael Bridges' Fred Astaire when the youngster led the experienced veteran a merry dance in November. Ask anybody at Grimsby who witnessed Andy Marriott's one performance - and clean sheet - of the season, deputising for a concussed Tommy Sorensen (a stunning 'keeper, by the way). Ask Wolves about Martin Smith.

These are just three examples of a wider trend at the club, exemplifying the high level of talent that couldn't get a game this season. We could afford to do it because we've had 40,000 plus at home since our new stadium was built, to add to our parachute money. We are the only team in this league with that level of resources. We are the lucky ones. And yet the realities of competing in the Premiership next year are frightening for us. Unless people stop talking about the widening gulf between the top two leagues and someone begins to subsidise lower-league teams with top-flight television money, the transition will soon become farcically impossible and free-market football will overheat as quickly as it has become so very trendy.

Peter Daykin

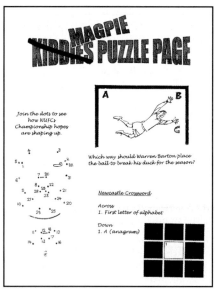

Source: *It's an easy one for Norman*

ANOTHER VIEW FROM THE TOWER

Blackpool

Until Blackpool finally achieve some long overdue success, May 1996 will be a month that Seasiders fans will continually refer to. That was the month that the club's owner and chairman started his vacation at Her Majesty's Pleasure, the team missed out on promotion in the most spectacular fashion, and the manager was duly rewarded with a P45. Since then the club's fortunes have dwindled in a way that even Nick Leeson would have trouble matching.

At the start of the '98-99 season there wasn't much for Seasiders fans to shout about. The pre-season friendlies revealed the club were still playing in the biggest

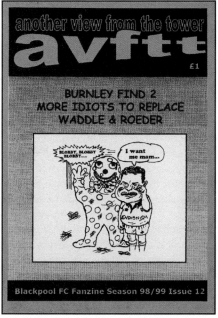

BURNLEY FIND 2 MORE IDIOTS TO REPLACE WADDLE & ROEDER

Blackpool FC Fanzine Season 98/99 Issue 12

toilet in the Football League, countless promises of a new stadium had failed to materialise, and you could see the away fans relishing the prospect of another rousing chorus of "Shit ground, no fans". (The latter not being entirely true: "shit ground, missing fans" being more appropriate.) Manager Nigel Worthington had been given a crisp new £10 note and told to go out and buy a new squad by the club's incumbent managing director, Vicky Oyston. ('Incompetent' would have been a better word, but you'll soon draw that conclusion anyway.) Worthington managed to lure Martin Aldridge, Steve Bushell and David Bardsley to the club, which led to us having to open a new wing in our injury room later in the season.

The season started with 3,000 Blackpool fans bathed in sunshine at Maine Road. So taken aback were we that football supporters could watch the great game in such palatial conditions, the 3-0 drubbing went largely unnoticed. There then followed an extraordinary string of results, which saw the side leap to third place in the league (tissues were handed out after most fans suffered a nosebleed) and manager Nigel Worthington handed the poisoned chalice (or the Manager of the Month award as it's foolishly known). In the meantime, the team had begun their annual attempt to get knocked out of the second round of the Worthington Cup. Taking a one-goal lead to Prenton Park after the first leg, we found the back of the net early on in the game to double our advantage. Fortunately the referee was on hand to make sure we didn't slip through the net and into the third round with the big boys, as he gifted the game to Tranmere with decisions that would make David Ellary seem competent. Who says that refereeing in this country is inconsistent? Far from it - it's consistently appalling.

Having had our confidence knocked, we expected a trip to the unbeaten division leaders, Stoke City, to be as worthwhile as a vote for the Conservatives - how wrong we were proved. The Potters were only halfway through telling us what they stuck in Delilah's mouth (and she laughed no more), when Aldridge and Ormerod demolished Little's men. Unfortunately all good things must come to an end – and, for Blackpool, the end came some seven months too early. Had our early season form continued we would have given Al Fayed's cheque book-busting team a run for their money. As it was, we'd run out of money and luck.

As the storm clouds started to gather over Bloomfield Road, a cold wind must have sent a chill down Vicky Oyston's spine. Blackpool fans had become increasingly despondent with our owner's attitude towards the club and, after a heated supporters meeting, it was decided the fans would do what the team had been unable to do for weeks - run unchallenged across the pitch. Chesterfield almost spoilt the demonstration by allowing Blackpool to take the lead in the game, but the referee's inability to see that the ball was still moving when the Spireites were taking a free-kick, led to a controversial equaliser and a pitch invasion usually reserved for happier times. After that incident, Vicky went in to full vindictive mode as she announced our best players were up for sale, she no longer loved the club, and Alan Ball and Gary Megson were a pair of little ginger pip-squeaks whom no-one liked. (Well, actually the last bit was made up, but a fair point well made we think!) Vicky announced it was her club, and if she couldn't enjoy it, then no-one would. The Oystons had control of the club and until a Seasider won £25 million on the Lottery, our only option was to march up to Vicky's palatial residence and protest about her regime. Unfortunately there were only a few smelly cows to greet us (I'll resist the temptation to draw an analogy), but we'd made our point, which would eventually prove fruitful. It was the first time for years that Blackpool received national TV, radio and press coverage; although again for all the wrong reasons.

Back on the pitch, Wigan inflicted another Springfield Park defeat on the Seasiders, this time in the first round of the FA Cup. The Tangerines had never won there and the whole of the Fylde coast volunteered to help bulldoze the jinxed ground at the end of the season. Stoke avenged their defeat at the Britannia Stadium by showing Blackpool the exit in the Windscreen Wipers Cup, and 1998 ended with Seasiders fans hoping for more than a pair of socks off Father Christmas - although asking for a new owner, stadium *and* team seemed a little optimistic.

By the time the tinsel had been taken down and January had dragged us all down to the depths of depression, Blackpool's fortunes were looking decidedly shaky. Despite the fact we'd completed the first 'double' of the season against the mighty Macclesfield Town, Blackpool's position in the league was as precarious as that of a policeman in the same toilet as George Michael. 'Going down' was the thought going through our minds. However, there's always someone worse off than yourself and, fortunately for us, when we visited the County Ground, Notts County were on the crest of a slump. Former Blackpool boss Sam Allardyce hadn't found life in the Second Division easy going and a defeat by the team who he had been sacked by three years earlier, must have been a bitter pill for him to swallow. (Still, this *is* football - tough luck, Sam, and thanks for the points).

In the meantime, our home form was more unpredictable than a Manchester United captain after a few drinks. The Bloomfield Road support was still particularly subdued, due to the uncertainty over the club's future, which led to the occasional unnecessary barracking of the management and players - and even the bloke who sells the half-time pies (although he deserved it!). The team were turning into a Jekyll and Hyde side, as one week they astounded us with their silky skills and attacking ability, whilst the next they looked like a gathering of the Dale Winton fan club - poncing about up-field and not very tight at the back. Gloomfield Road was living up to its name, as we threw away more matches than a reformed pyromaniac. At least our away form was giving us reason for cheer, and a fabulous win at Chesterfield helped us along the way to achieving the manager's target of 50 points.

What I've so far failed to say is that, during all our troubles, at least our Hillbilly neighbours in Burnley were giving us plenty of laughs (as usual). They'd employed Stan Ternent to get them in to the Third Division (after Chris Waddle had so very nearly taken them there the previous season) and the former Bury manager kept up their spectacular losing streak from the off. Unfortunately, there's always a fly in the ointment - and in this case it was Preston. For years, we'd enjoyed the Nob-enders shortcomings as much as we had those of the boys from Turd Moor, but something rather worrying was happening at Dungdale - they kept winning. When we faced them in April, they were within a whisker of achieving the impossible - automatic promotion. It has to be said: optimism is a key characteristic in any Blackpool fan, but even the most foolhardy couldn't have expected what happened that afternoon in Lancashire. The Tangerine army out-sang the Lilywhites from the start to the end, and the team's performance on the pitch reflected our support. A late Brett Ormerod winner sent the Blackpool fans in to a delirious state of ecstasy, whilst finishing off any hopes Preston had of an automatic promotion place - life doesn't get much better than that.

Having achieved our 50 points total, you might have thought that would have been the end of our season. But no, we *are* Blackpool, after all. And following defeat in our next two games, we had to wait until the penultimate game of the season, away at Wycombe, to earn the point which finally secured our Second Division status. Which meant the party could begin on the last day of the season. And what better way to end what had been a wretched season than with the re-opening of the Kop to Blackpool fans for the first time in nearly 20 years. This was the place that Seasiders had watched the likes of

Matthews and Mortenson, had enjoyed cup success, and had witnessed our steady decline in the late Seventies. The sun shone, the terrace was packed and the fans were soon rewarded for their support, as Brett Ormerod scored in the first minute. When Phil Clarkson scored just before the end of the game, the second pitch invasion of the season took place, this time in much happier circumstances. Blackpool had finally achieved a win at Bloomfield Road - something many of us thought we'd never see again.

They say that most good stories have a happy ending; Blackpool fans must wait another season for theirs. Next season should start on a better note than the one that's just gone. Vicky Oyston has now left the club and handed the reigns over to her son, Karl. So far the heir to the Oyston millions has done well, but with so many false dawns in the past, many Seasiders are reserving judgement. Manager Nigel Worthington has signed a new contract and we've seen the back of some of our most costly players (in more ways than one). The youngsters in the team are our best hope for the future – hopefully, you'll hear more from the likes of Brett Ormerod, Adam Nowland and Phil Thompson in the future.

Just to tie up the loose ends, it's with deep regret that we have to announce that Burnley weren't relegated (but there's always next year to look forward to), Preston spectacularly blew any chance of promotion in the play-offs, and Bolton manager Colin Todd is being sought by the police after he stole Steve Banks - Blackpool's best goalkeeper for years - for just £50,000 on transfer deadline day. Who says crime doesn't pay?

Blackpool fans are still talking about the 1996 season when we failed to go up. Just for the record, the club who denied us our place in the First Division that season? Bradford City... which just goes to show there's hope for us yet!

ANOTHER VINTAGE LIVERPOOL PERFORMANCE

Liverpool

We began the season with two managers - but ended it without a clue. It wasn't so much a roller-coaster as a helter-skelter of dull and increasingly desperate football. By April, Liverpool's play was in more danger of breaching the Trade Descriptions Act than winning three points.

Not that it was an uneventful season. Oh no. It's only the football that was shite. The Reds have to find other ways to hit the headlines these days, and '98-99 saw them come out with some corkers.

Having decided on the quickest route to mediocrity by appointing joint-managers over the

AVLP £1
Another Vintage Liverpool Performance
Or because we're confident for next season...1.45 euros

11 Trickier than a Heggem dribble   MARCH 1999

Mancs set for gay experiment

Manchester United have made football and television history by starting up a gay football TV channel.

★ Exclusive ★
By Willy Ryder

Well known for their innovation and ability to find a gap in the market and exploit it for all it's worth, the directors of the Salford-based club have decided to inaugurate a channel called Quanc TV. The channel, which will be broadcast between the hours of 3 and 6am, hopes to target football fans and players who have homosexual tendencies. The details of the pro-gramme are being kept secret by club officials but workers on the show have revealed that the contro- *Cont. pg Hooper*

Keane: sometimes a little too keen

Shock AVLP split! See back page

1 Paul Stewart

summer, the club showed no let-up on the road to nowhere as the campaign dragged on. We had Fowler trying to get someone to boot the ball up his backside, then trying to snort paint, Carragher enjoying livelier nights out than Dwight Yorke does nights in, McManaman playing with his mind on Spain, and Ince plainly out of his mind. It makes you wonder why Stan Collymore never really fitted in.

The first three months of the season were flushed down the bog like a morning-after dump. We all liked Roy but we knew he wasn't quite the man to steer the club to where we wanted it to go. He should have gone in the summer, but the board got all misty-eyed and appointed Gerard as a co-manager to ease him out after decades of unfaltering service. Not even Harry Enfield could have devised such a ridiculous scenario. Poor Roy deserved a more dignified send-off than the embarrassment his resignation eventually became. Gerard brought with him an astute brain, but anyone who says two minds are better than one doesn't support Liverpool.

Proof of this was seen in the side's defence. If it were a sitcom it would be top of the ratings. When neither of your managers can see that the team couldn't stop a tap, you wonder just how they can cash their wage cheques without hiding their faces. For a few months the pair kept up this far from convincing united front about how their revolutionary partnership would transform the club. How they expected anyone to buy it with Phil Babb still in the team is anyone's guess.

Belatedly, someone at the club realised that two blokes with one leg in an enormous pair of trousers didn't work, and Roy was granted parole. Out went one chair from the office, as Gerard was granted full control of all the drawers in the desk. The umpteenth false dawn of recent years had begun.

Gerard threatened changes. In came Song, Kippe and Ferri, and out went Harkness. Ruthless stuff, but nothing happened. Worryingly, the new guys hardly got a look-in and the plummet continued. The plane trips to Europe dried up. But we would have missed the boat there - even if Ferri was in the side - so bad was the fare. The new signings suggested more that Gerard was a frustrated tabloid newsman than a shrewd coach. Certainly his side played with about as much credibility as that section of the press.

You only have to glance through some of the results to see what a joke all the talk was of us being one of three clubs to join a European Super League. Points dropped against Charlton, Everton (again), Forest (yes, Forest!), Leicester and Derby would hardly impress the money-grabbing bureaucrats secretly plotting the downfall of the continent with this new competition. A couple of years ago we were questioning the commitment of one or two players. There's no need for that now. We know most of them can't cut the mustard. No longer are we an inconsistent side. We're now consistently crap.

You don't need to do much homework to know how to beat Liverpool these days. All you have to do is run at the defence and put them under a little bit of pressure. Even if that fails, a cross into the area usually does the trick. If you're not confident playing against defenders who can't tackle, can't head and get caught out of position in front of goalkeepers who flap, drop catches and charge off the line recklessly, you're probably Nottingham Forest; but even then you're still guaranteed a point.

Only twice - repeat, twice - in nine months did we see anything like the true Liverpool spirit. And both these performances happened to come against multi-Treble double, double Double, treble double-Double treble-winners Manchester bloody United. At Old Trafford in the fourth round of the cup, we matched and bettered the smarmy Manc sods pound for pound, ball for ball, man for man, but still came away with absolutely bugger all. The manner of their win, with two last-minute goals, was heart-shattering stuff. Who knows what a win would have done there? Certainly the lads did the Liverbird proud that day and were so close to a sweet, sweet victory. They showed they could do it on the day if the fancy took them. Pity they waited three months before doing it again.

Seldom has a season withered away with such embarrassment as it did from that late January Cup exit. A win could have turned the ship, but the loss sunk it. Until the Mancs returned to Anfield expecting their customary three points in May, for the rest of the season the team were about as impressive as Ron Atkinson's CV.

The Mancs arrived with the Treble well in their sights. Amazingly, 40,000 people turned up to witness the ritual caning. Yet, this time, things were different. The pressure of the battle for seventh place, for once, wasn't going to get to the lads. We fought back from 2-0 down, with Ince proving Fergie right and being a proper Big-time Charlie. His last-minute equaliser sent us into a frenzied delight in the deluded belief that we had broken their spirit and ruined their season. We took great delight in rubbing it in, too - even in the Main Stand. That would teach them to mess with us. We then parted ways. They went on and won the Treble... and we lost at Sheffield Wednesday.

Europe was its usual barrel of laughs this year. A couple of games against a crap side in front of three men and a dog, a bit of a tussle against a not-so-bad side in front of ten men, a dog and a few sheep, and then completely outclassed by a quality side. You can't just blame the players for this. The club could at least have tried charging just an arm, instead of both arm and leg for these games to generate a bit of atmosphere. Still, those of us who did pay to get in could sleep safe in the knowledge we had paid for Steve McManaman's car's next valet.

The Robbie Fowler incidents proved to Reds fans just how politically correct nonsense can destroy the entertainment factor in football. They also proved to Anfield regulars that there is no justice when it comes to Liverpool FC. In the year that we mourned at the tenth anniversary of the Hillsborough disaster, the punishment meted out to Robbie after the Le Saux and snorting incidents showed that there is an element out there trying to make Liverpool paranoid that things will never go their way.

To make Robbie more guilty than Le Saux (by suspending him for twice as many games) was a sick joke. If taunting (something which has gone on in professional football matches for years) is worse than being attacked by an opponent's elbow three times, then my name is Graham Kelly (which, thank God, it isn't).

The derby cocaine-snorting farce was almost as ridiculous as Gerard trying to pass it off as Robbie pretending to be a cow, which shattered his credibility completely. Evertonians would have been delighted that Robbie's perfect mimicking of snorting drugs took the spotlight away from their failure to beat our bunch of underachievers, but giving Robbie a four-match ban for this ranked almost as high in the 'season's worst decisions chart' as Kevin Keegan deciding Andy 'Barn Door' Cole was fit to play for England. In the era when football was a sport played by men and watched by real football fans (about 15 years ago and before), his celebration would have been laughed off and taken as it was intended - a joke. These days if a player so much as farts on the pitch, he's sent before the FA and given a twelve-month ban. The win in the derby, though, at least provided a glimmer of happiness for our dejected supporters. Everton have been truly awful in the Nineties but, as bad as they have got, they seemed to retain the upper hand in derbies. Before the April clash we were taunted for not winning a derby in nearly five years, but Robbie's double and

Berger's blast meant we had gone an impressive 18 since we last lost to that rabble. Figures are easy to twist.

Picking a player of the season was extremely difficult this term, but we were not without our good performers. Going into the season, Liverpool were given a decent chance of winning the title - and all because our side contained the biggest football star in the world in August. Following the World Cup, the name on everyone's lips was Michael Owen. He didn't take long to get into his stride and it was not his fault that Liverpool failed so miserably. At times he was our only hope. That's a hell of a burden for a man so young; but he carried it well.

Despite missing the last month of the season, he finished joint-top goalscorer in the Premiership - which is another feather in his plume-saturated cap. Buy of the summer turned out to be Vegard Heggem. Given Liverpool's ability to pick up Norwegians with less footballing talent than Julian Clary, the fans were a little sceptical at first. But his barnstorming runs down the right wing, having fear for no opponent, brought a smile to the hardiest of fans. Jamie Carragher, too, despite his appearances in the tabloids, had a fantastic season. Captain of England U-21s, the hunchback has been a rock in a field of pansies in the defence, making bone-crunching challenges and proving his versatility.

Gerard is now looking to rebuild a fallen empire but is having to do so with limited funds, whilst also looking to the future. Players like Traore, Kippe and Meijer may be good players but they are hardly the names you dream about when attempting to assemble a team to take on the world. Houllier has had his honeymoon period, even if it was spent in Bognor Regis rather than the Seychelles, and now it is time for him to prove his ability as a top class manager.

Still, the season wasn't all doom and gloom. How many other sides can say they have a flavour of crisps named after their star player?

Andy Hampson

BAMBER'S RIGHT FOOT

Torquay United

It has long been (and often) said by a few of those sad, deluded people who like to quote irritatingly inaccurate and spurious comments, that "a change is as good as a rest". As the season got underway, Torquay United were about to put that to the test, thanks to the not so much mass as key exodus at the end of the previous season.

Gone were the coaching duo of Kevin Hodges and Steve McCall to our hated rivals, and Division Three wannabes, Plymouth Argyle. Also leaving under a cloud was terrace darling Paul Gibbs, seemingly unable to reach an agreement with United

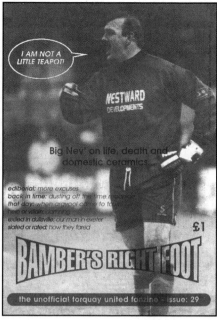

as regards a substantial and suitable increase in his weekly readies. His destination? Argyool. Then there was the case of the disappearing Player of the Year, in the shape of hardman defender Jon Gittens, who had played his way into the hearts of the Plainmoor faithful, but talked his way out of the club and off to our other less significant local rivals, Exeter City. This was a mess, and although we've been in more messes than Ron Atkinson's housekeeper, this was one we were going to have to wrestle with to resolve. The fans stood by and waited to see what the club would do. It was a fix that some thought we could not recover from and, in a sense, we haven't yet.

After the bitching, wrangling and mud-slinging had ceased over the contentious issue of Argyool grabbing Hodges and McCall, and the dust had settled on Plymouth's much-reported illegal approach for the pair's services, things finally started to happen. Not, though, before Torquay fans had shrugged their shoulders and conceded that, despite the acrimony, if Plymouth wanted Hodgie and McCall so badly, and they wanted to return to their former club, then what would have been the point in stopping them? And everyone knew in their bones that if this pair went to Argyle, then it was only a matter of time before Gibbs joined them.

So what were we going to do about it? First of all, former Torquay United legend Wes Saunders was appointed manager. This hero of the terraces in the early Nineties, who had led a triumphant United to promotion in a glorious Wembley win over play-off opponents Blackpool in 1991, would be the man to maintain the momentum the club had achieved under Hodges and McCall. Wes is a proud man, and certainly one of the modern day heroes of the Torquay United saga. With his never-say-die attitude, he had formed a formidable and memorable defensive partnership with Matt Elliott in his Plainmoor playing days. Now he was back with a new challenge ahead of him. Largely inexperienced and having been out of the game since retiring through injury, many people shook their heads and crossed their fingers firmly, as he set about making his mark. It was felt, and rightly so, that he didn't have the wherewithal, know-how or qualities that are required in management, especially when you're working at the arse-end of the Football League. The constraints and hurdles that a Third Division manager faces on a daily basis are a stern test for the most hardened man, and you need to have all your wits about you to fend off the jabs and uppercuts coming from all sides. Did Wes have what it took? To be fair to him, he was dropped pretty much in the deep end when he took over. It was late in the off-season, the pre-season was almost upon him and he had to get to work fast - there's no time to make a cup of tea and read the papers at this time of year.

The previous managerial incumbents had arranged a tour to Cornwall and this still had to be honoured. Nothing had been done, though, to sound out possible new faces to replace the departed players. One of the first tasks Wes had to deal with was the loss of Rodney Jack. The mercurial talent was heading out of Plainmoor, and no matter what positive noises Wes made about convincing the St Vincent pocket-rocket to stay, we all knew the board would never be able to resist the type of figures being quoted. Jack had done his job at Torquay - and we all respected him for that, and bade him a fond farewell as he set off to increase his lot with First Division Crewe Alexandra for a record fee of £650,000 in easy-payment terms. Not quite on HP, but a sort of direct debit arrangement.

With the season looming, there was a certain amount of uncertainty regarding who, if anyone, would be playing for Torquay. It was a far from ideal preparation, but that was hardly down to Wes. Many players he would have courted had already jumped into bed with another mistress.

These things always take time to resolve themselves, and steadily Wes started to get some faces in, but they were unknown and obscure ones - cast-offs some might call them, but players are notoriously hard to attract to this part of the world. Wes gave trials to a number of players, some good, some better, some worse. But we stumbled into the season with an assortment of wily old campaigners and youngsters. Wes talked a good game, but as the season progressed and United headed inexorably down the table, the wily fans began openly to question his motives and his ambitions, to say nothing of his ability to do the job. He had been out of the game for a long time, and although he had played for Newcastle earlier in his career, he had hardly set the footballing world alight. Did he have any contacts? Could he call on old friends for favours? Was his face well known in the footballing circles that mattered? The answer, unfortunately, seemed to be 'no' - and although those are not the only tools a manager needs to get on and get ahead in the game, they are pretty useful sidearms to have in your arsenal. His main allies are enthusiasm, determination and a fighting spirit, which are worthy attributes, but need to be complemented somewhat.

The season itself was very familiar to Torquay United fans, in that it was a huge anti-climax. It never really got going, and nothing happened that could even add a bit of spice to it all. A good draw in the Worthington Cup saw us take on Crystal Palace in a match televised by Sky. Does that constitute a highlight? The lads played very well against Palace, and Terry Venables popped back to do a bit of shopping a few weeks after they had knocked us out, taking young 'keeper Matthew Gregg for about £400,000. Many were very, very surprised at this, and it was one of the few times I would applaud the club, this time for almost ripping off Palace's arm when the offer was made. This put Kenny Veysey back between the sticks, and rightly so.

The FA Cup came and went, as it is wont to do in this part of Devon, although we did get past the first round this year. Worcester were put to the sword, before we were finally vanquished by the mighty Bournemouth. In terms of local derbies, we were spoilt for choice during the course of the season, and we didn't lose one of them – a proud record when you consider the pride at stake in these matches. We beat Exeter at home, drew with them away, and shared two draws with Plymouth.

The two breaks in the overcast skies of '98/99 were both Welsh. The arrival just before Christmas of goalkeeping legend and all-round good egg Neville Southall certainly raised a few eyebrows. The agreement was that he would locum between the sticks in place of the injured Kenny Veysey. It was really only supposed to be a temporary arrangement, but Neville agreed that he wouldn't just drop Torquay in the proverbial poo should a position become available which he wanted to pursue. He made it clear he was interested in going into management, but his playing performances impressed everyone from the word go.

Chris Waddle had spent a brief period at Plainmoor earlier in the season, but his performances were poor and ineffective. He was carried by the rest of the team, and Torquay never registered a win with him in the side. But Neville proved all those with reservations about his ability to be utterly wrong. He quickly achieved cult status, and proceeded to become a vital part of the Torquay side. The defenders seemed to have more confidence, with his barracking them from his goal-area, and his shot-stopping skills were regularly vital and world class. He was and is a colossus, who played an essential role in keeping Torquay in the Football League. His contribution to our season cannot be under-estimated. Of course, at the time of writing, the big man is in the frame for the vacant manager's position of the Welsh national side. Whilst it seems to be a conflict of interests because he would leave Torquay, we wish him all the best. He deserves our thanks - just as he deserved the Player of the Year award he won after only half a season.

The second reason for cheer was the arrival, on deadline day, from Barry Town of Wales B striker Effion Williams - or Effing Brilliant. He became, at £70,000, Torquay's record signing, and proved to be worth every penny. Many league clubs had been watching him and tracking him, and yet had failed to act. But the dallying of other clubs to take a risk on the youngster proved to be Torquay's ticket to grabbing his signature. He scored a hat-trick on his debut - which in itself is impressive - but you really had to have been there to see the quality of the finishing. Torquay fans knew that they were seeing something pretty special, and he was ours. He is certainly one to watch in the forthcoming season, and many people believe that his stay at Plainmoor may be a lot shorter than we would like. But he has pledged to stay, at least for the duration of the season.

The penultimate game of the season saw us travel to Hull. The day was significant in that it was Torquay United's birthday - 100 years old. The centenary celebrations have been low-key to say the least, and it will be interesting to see what the club will be doing to celebrate this proud and significant milestone in the club's history. A celebrity match was played in the close season, with an assorted bunch of minor 'stars' who had little or no connection to Torquay United, taking on the sun-tanned members of the current squad. In an eye-gouging atmosphere of tedium, and amid cringing displays of Christmas cracker humour, the honour of Torquay United was done no favours at all. The failure of certain big-name players to arrive at all ensured that the day was, as it always promised to be, a huge and disappointing anti-climax. The fact that, in their wisdom, the club scandalously decided to hike prices to £10 for a celebration match of this ilk, proves - if proof were needed - just how far out of touch the club is with the feelings of real fans. Most people stayed away, aware this would be little more than a futile exercise, hurriedly arranged as an afterthought, that would merely heap more insult on the put-upon supporters. With just a little imagination, it could have been a day for proud supporters to trek to Plainmoor in far greater numbers than did. With a lot more imagination, it could have been a great day of celebration for those who love this wonderful little club, and take its varying fortunes very much to heart.

Why *couldn't* the club have the sense to make this a special day? So much more could have been done, but in the pursuit of making yet more money out of the tightly-squeezed fans, the club once again showed the lack of invention, lack of understanding and disregard for the very hand that feeds. This would have been the perfect opportunity for the club to rebuild some of the bridges it has so willingly burnt in the past. But the small-time thinking that seems to pervade here just can't be wiped away, and now the chance is gone.

Hayden Jones

BEESOTTED

Brentford

He's Got White Hair, He's a Millionaire, Ronny, Ronny, Noades.

The season saw such a transformation at Brentford Football Club that, at times during the campaign, I had to rub my eyes and ask myself if this was really the same football club that I was following last year.

David Webb's tyrannical reign had left Brentford relegated to the basement and had seen asset-stripping on a quite obscene scale; so without the timely intervention of Ron Noades, our club's spiral towards oblivion would surely have gathered momentum. Instead of clinching the championship at Cambridge on the last day of the season, many Bees fans believed we would have been scrapping it out down there with Scarborough and Carlisle, fighting to stay in the Football League. Some even paint a gloomier picture than that.

Noades has certainly lived up to his Jeckyll and Hyde reputation since his arrival - although his spring-loaded gob and 'damn what you think' attitude have seen him at odds with the Brentford faithful, who have all but given up trying to work out how the Noadster ticks. But fans who would consider swapping Noades' eccentricities for another, more conventional chairman are very few and far between. Brentford's chairman/manager (who incidentally offers more than a passing resemblance to Monty Burns in *The Simpons*), may not be every football traditionalist's cup of tea, but it must be said that he has brought professionalism, direction and a genuine belief that Brentford Football Club really does have a healthy future. In league terms, we may only be back where we were a year ago - but, in terms of all-round health, our club has undergone a monumental and highly successful operation.

Some rival fans have likened Brentford's success this season to that of Fulham's under Al Fayed, arguing that with a rich man at the helm of a lower division club, success is almost guaranteed. But contrary to public belief, Ron Noades hasn't flashed the cash that much at all, to be honest. It may be more than most were fortunate enough to be able to shell out, but nothing too outrageous really. The balance sheet may show that £1.5m was spent in the transfer market, but you have to realise a few factors. More than half of that was spent on one player, Icelandic international defender Hermann Hreidarsson, a player who is a very close friend of Noades and who joined Brentford from Crystal Palace, a club owing our chairman a similar amount to the national debt of Russia. I'm not too sure if any money actually changed hands on that deal. As for the other new kids on the block, none of them cost more than £125,000. Surely that's not too much of an unfair advantage? With the exception of Leo Fortune-Waste (remarkably, Ron's only hiccup in the transfer market), the other rookies have all been shrewd, well-researched and timely purchases. Considering the amount of talent that was flogged off at knockdown prices by the rogue trader Webb, Ron has just been restocking the cupboards over the last three or four years. We've still sold more than we've bought. That's why we found ourselves in the lowest league in the land in the first place. Noades has simply gone some way to redressing the balance.

It wasn't all plain sailing last year, though. To be honest, Brentford looked pretty average at times and certainly weren't the obvious championship favourites the bookies had us down for. Away from home we were turned over constantly by teams who rose to the occasion of playing what they considered were the 'Big Time Charlies' from London, but who were, in reality, better equipped at that level than we were. Defeats against Scarborough and Hull City, who were both at the foot of the table when we played them, showed that when it came to rolling up our sleeves and battling for the right to win, we just weren't up for it enough. It was only down to our home form that we stayed there or thereabouts for so long. Once that bubble had burst at the turn of the new year, the alarm bells started to ring. Maybe the terrace songs predicting that ours would be a one-season whistle-stop tour of the Third were to be wrong after all?

We needn't have worried too much in the end. Two timely swoops just before the transfer deadline (traditionally a time when Brentford flog their best players) transformed the team from wannabes into deserved championship contenders. Paul Evans and Scott Partridge, from Shrewsbury and Torquay respectively, proved to be the missing parts of Noades' jigsaw and provided the adrenaline rush that started off the side's superb 16-match unbeaten run. A run that saw the side put in some awesome displays, notably against Southend away, and the home demolition of play-off semi-finalists Swansea. Brentford had become a class act and Cambridge found us too good for them, as we clinched the title in front of their own supporters. Still, they were promoted too, so there seemed to be no animosity. Or maybe it was the sight of thousands of Brentford fans wearing Noades-style white wigs that had them confused.

Without wishing to sound too much of a brown-noser, it must be said that Brentford has become a place of regeneration and hope under Noades, and despite the opinions of his many knockers throughout the game, and the continual threat of Noades moving back to Crystal Palace as a consequence of the drawn-out legal battle with Mark Goldberg, the new Bees chairman has shown what a shrewd football brain he has and how quickly he can adapt and breed success.

His real masterstroke was undoubtedly in securing a coaching line-up second to none outside the Premiership - namely, Ray Lewington, Brian Sparrow and Terry Bullivant; plus appointing a full-time scout, John Griffin. All four, along with the new club captain Paul Evans, have been instrumental in ensuring that the raw youngsters brought in by Noades have gelled together and developed in leaps and bounds. Noades readily admits that he has had a flukish year in the transfer market, everything the club has touched seems to have turned to gold, but the role of the coaching staff hasn't been overlooked either.

As I said at the start, I really can't believe what a turnaround our club has undertaken this season. In fact, anyone who remembers my contribution to *SOTF4* will think I've been abducted and brainwashed by the club. But it just goes to show what can be achieved when you've got a great little club, a great set of supporters and a man in charge who takes pride in success and is not on the fiddle.

Whether or not next season continues where the last finished off, obviously only time will tell. But whatever happens, I am confident Brentford will not struggle. I think the play-offs may just be beyond us as we enter the new Millennium, but as we leave the last century behind, I hope the countless years of under-achievement and under-investment are left behind with it.

David Lane

BERT TRAUTMAN'S HELMET

Manchester City

"Que sera, sera; whatever will be, will be..." I think it was fitting that, in the twilight of the Twentieth Century, the only team from Manchester should honour the national stadium with their presence. God knows, it had been a long time. In fact, for too long Manchester City had been absent friends and, as such, 1998/9 will be forever remembered as the season when they finally began their comeback, and on the greatest stage of all - Wembley Stadium. If a season can be encapsulated in one game – no, the last quarter of an hour of one game - then the Second Division Play-off Final between City and Gillingham was it.

Little of note had happened until the 81st minute, when the game exploded into life, with Carl Asaba giving the Gills an unexpected lead. Five minutes later, Robert Taylor made it two and, as Alan Brazil commented on Sky, "It'll be party time in Kent tonight!" Not so fast, Alan.

Back at Wembley, the word "Millwall" bounced around my brain as I rose from my Lilliputian seat, a picture of abject misery, and uttered to my girlfriend the words, "That's it, we're going." She wouldn't budge, which was just as well really as a) I may have been crushed in the rush to leave and b) I would have missed a modern day footballing miracle, as City staged the sort of comeback which had only ever been the sole preserve of other teams; in fact, every other team in the league, bar us. Even when Kevin Horlock hit his shot past Gillingham's goalkeeper in the dying seconds of normal time, I viewed it as nothing more than a consolation. "Why couldn't you have done that before?" I shouted to everyone and no-one. Too little too late, I thought, as tears of sorrow flowed down the faces of many of those around me.

But, roared on by the majority of the 40,000 Blues who had hung on, it happened. Some four minutes into injury-time, Paul Dickov steered the ball past Gillingham's 'keeper, to unleash the loudest cheer I have ever heard in my life. This was payback time, and from thereon in, there was only going to be one winner: Gillingham were finished. Extra-time came and went seemingly in a flash, whilst the penalty shoot-out found its own heroes - none of them Gillingham players - and unleashed a further flood of tears, only this time they were tears of joy.

While it was indeed strange to see Manchester City's players climbing the famous steps, never mind parading a cup around the equally famous turf, it was that moment when Dickov stuck the ball past his own best man that will stay in the hearts and minds of City fans for many a long year. Just as those who are old enough can remember where they were when Kennedy was shot, so too does every Blue know where he or she was when Dickov shot. For those watching at home, you have my sympathies, as even Sky's comprehensive coverage did not, and never could do justice to the unparalleled joy of actually being there for that split-second. And for those of you who were winding your way down Wembley Way, you too have my sympathies as, by rights, I should have been with you.

For those of us with fanzines to sell, leaving a game early is a necessary evil, unless of course you are at The New Den, where you're not even allowed to leave for a good half-hour after the final whistle has been blown, never mind early. Now, of course, The New Den and other such salubrious venues, such as Bootham Crescent and Springfield Park, or dangerously overcrowded grounds like Bloomfield Road and Moss Rose, have been banished to the back of our collective memory bank, not to mention the annals of history.

For Manchester City's supporters, much of the last season will be quietly forgotten as our famously underachieving, but beloved team attempts to gain a foothold on respectability in the next few years. And yet, ironically, and in keeping with the surrealism that hangs in the Maine Road air, whilst we all agree that relegation to what is the old Third Division was a bitter pill to swallow, ask any City fan if they'd have swapped the sheer drama and excitement of that Wembley afternoon, and I think you know what their answer will be.

Noel Bayley

BEYOND THE BOUNDARY

Oldham Athletic

I imagine many of this book's contributors, whose team failed to make any sort of impact on their division last season, would have been tempted to start their account with the line, "A season that promised so much..." I would have liked to do so myself, but as any Oldham Athletic fan will tell you, despite the arrival as manager of Latics favourite Andy Ritchie, the immediate prospects for us at the beginning of the '98-99 season were bleak to say the least. Having been told that our only hopes for the season lay at the feet of several untried youngsters, there were few who took exception to the pundits' predictions that we were heading for the Third Division. There was

one new signing, however: Steve Whitehall, the former Rochdale and Mansfield frontman, whose inclusion in the side throughout the season became increasingly mysterious. I have seen more than my fair share of donkeys in the many years I've followed Oldham, but Whitehall is by far the worst centre-forward I have ever had the misfortune to encounter.

If any Oldham fans had decided that, despite the obvious inadequacies of the side, we had as good a chance as anybody of going up, they were soon to be disillusioned, as on the first day of the season we lost 3-1 at home to newly promoted Notts County. We were not to know it at the time, but Athletic were about to embark on a catastrophic season at home, winning only eight, drawing four and losing eleven - an unequalled club record. Luckily, we seemed to have got over our previous season's failure away from Boundary Park - which, given the scrap for points at the end of the season, was to prove vital.

In October, with Athletic in the bottom four, manager Andy Ritchie managed to secure the services of former Bolton and Scotland striker John McGinlay and John Sheridan, once of Leeds and Sheffield Wednesday. Despite their combined age of 68, their experience, it was hoped, would rub off on the younger players. McGinlay's appearances were brief, however, due to injury but Sheridan soon proved that he could still play better than most players half his age. Whitehall, in the meantime, had obviously had a bonfire night rocket placed in a strategic position, as he managed to score twice in two games in November. It was not to last - and 17 games elapsed before he did it again.

A 3-1 win at Chesterfield on Boxing Day marked the halfway stage of the season, but the meagre total of 21 points looked like spelling disaster unless something was done to halt the slide. Meanwhile, there was the tasty prospect of a visit by Chelsea in the FA Cup Third Round to look forward to, after Latics had beaten Third Division Brentford on penalties in the second round. A 12,000 crowd squeezed into Boundary Park, and judging by the number of Latics shirts circa 1991, many of the people there hadn't visited the ground since we last played Chelsea in the Premier League. It seemed to be going fairly well (the Chelsea goal-glut hadn't materialised), until Dennis Wise knocked the ball into the net shortly before half-time. However, Babayaro appeared to have punched the ball, and as referee Paul Durkin went to consult his assistant, a well-aimed hot-dog struck him on the back of the neck. The incident filled quite a number of column inches the next day, as did the two goals from Gianluca Vialli, which finished off Oldham's cup hopes.

Such publicity comes thin on the ground at Oldham, but amazingly enough, six days later, Latics were in the news again - this time concerning an amazing outburst from chairman Ian Stott.

The day before the game at Notts County on January 9, the *Manchester Evening News* ran a story on their back page which claimed that Stott had had talks with both the Bury and Rochdale chairmen regarding a proposed merger of the three clubs. Furthermore, this new club would play at the proposed new stadium in Oldham and would be named Manchester North End. The announcement came in the same week Stott put his name forward for the vacant FA chairmanship. He was quick to claim that his comments had been taken out of context and that he had been the victim of an all-powerful and faceless press. This was a rather one-sided view of things as, for starters, it was Stott who had chosen to use that very same press to his own ends to announce his candidacy for the FA vacancy. Furthermore, even the briefest examination of his comments in the press on January 8 conveys a wholly different story from the one that subsequently emanated from Stott's corner.

He claimed that the merger talks amounted to little more than a four-minute discussion on a train some twelve months previously. However, this was not - truthful or otherwise - what he appeared to say when he revealed to the MEN that he had been giving "serious consideration" to the idea. If a four-minute chat on a train warrants the description of "serious consideration" in Stott's book, especially when we are talking about the future of three football clubs with hundreds of years worth of heritage, it makes you wonder just how much time was given to other important decisions concerning the club. Stott also went on to say that, "I have already discussed the possibility of merging the three clubs into one with my counterparts at both Rochdale and Bury, and like me, they can see the benefits of such a venture." This really must have been one hell of a four-minute chinwag don't you think? The pros and cons of a merger, the submergence of identities, concerns of hard-core fans, and the massive logistical problems - all touched on in some 240 seconds. That's fast talking in anyone's book. Not only that, we are supposed to believe that the trio also managed to find time to come up with the name 'Manchester North End' for the proposed venture. I think not.

Mr Stott, as he frequently likes to remind people, is a respected man, boasting years of experience of dealing in the corridors of power in English soccer and with the media. There can be little doubt, therefore, that he understood exactly what the main repercussion would be of him dropping the merger hints into his interview - publicity. It was no coincidence that Stott went on to announce his candidacy for the position of FA chairman the same day. And therein, of course, lay his motive in whipping up the whole tragi-comic affair. The interview was part of a personal re-launch, Stott was evidently keen to establish a new, higher profile within the game, casting himself as a visionary, a modernising figure, prepared to think the unthinkable. "I am nearer to the grassroots of soccer than the other contenders," he claimed. How ironic it was, then, that his comments would trigger an angry and universal backlash from supporters of the three clubs closest to his own locality within hours. Faced with condemnation from all sides and with chants of "We're not part of Manchester" ringing in his ears, he stepped aside from the Oldham chairman's post - and I am happy to report that not a squeak has been heard from him since.

One would have expected such unrest to have had a detrimental effect on the players but, surprisingly, the side went on to record their best run of results all season, winning four out of the next five games. The revival was short-lived, however, and only one win - at Manchester City - materialised in the next eleven fixtures. Athletic were now in real danger of a drop into the Third Division. Six games remained, four of which were at Boundary Park. But given Oldham's poor home form, there seemed to be little optimism around. The lowest home crowd of the season saw us beat Bristol Rovers 2-1, followed by a win at Wrexham four days later. It seemed as if we might need to win at Walsall, and also both our last games, to stay up. As it turned out, we lost 3-1 at Walsall, which guaranteed their place in Division One next season. But results elsewhere went our way. The penultimate game, against Stoke, resulted in a narrow 1-0 win. Finally, on the final Saturday, we needed Manchester City to beat York and, if we beat Reading, we'd still be in the Second Division. An early goal calmed the nerves, and after we'd gone 2-0 up, ears were glued to radios to see if City could help us out. They didn't let us down, sending York into the Third Division with a 4-0 win.

After putting up with some of the worst football for years, there was an enormous sense of relief that we'd managed to avoid the drop. The post-match view was that the club should heed the warnings of '98-99 or we would be in exactly the same position again.

From a personal point of view, I hope the youngsters manage to make a better impact than they did this season. There are at least three of them who have benefited from Sheridan's presence, and if they become anything like the gifted midfielder, we may have a side that at the very least stays in the top half of the league. Hopefully, this time next season I might not have to start my account with the words "A season that promised so much..."

Pete Mason

BLACK ARAB

Bristol Rovers

So that's it. Another season over and your scribe has the unenviable task of trying to make a boring season of mediocrity sound interesting. Well, sod that. I'm not even going to try. Even thinking about it is zz.zz.zz.zzz.zzzending me to zz.zz.z.z.zleep...

"What a magnificent through ball to Roberts... he's left Stam for dead, only Schmeichel in his way now... you are watching history in the making, as Roberts scores... with less than a minute of normal time left, it's all up for United now, who to be honest are lucky to be only 4-1 down... never mind the treble, Bristol Rovers are on the threshold of a historic quadruple, something never before achieved and unlikely ever to happen again... already Second Division champions with a record 123 points, this is their third visit to Wembley this season, having already lifted the Auto Windscreens Shield and the Worthington Cup... and are now only seconds away from adding the FA Cup to the list... and there it goes, the final whistle... Bristol Rovers have won the FA Cup...!"*

Wake up, you lazy bastard. Oi, wake up!

Oh shit, it was all a dream. So were there any highlights to talk about in this drab season? Well, we won 6-0 away at Reading, Jamie Cureton won the golden boot as the division's top scorer, we reached the fifth round of the FA Cup, we bought our own ground, and... Bristol City (1982) got relegated!

You know it's been crap when the highlight of your season is laughing at the antics of the red and white circus on the other side of the city, as they tumbled back into Division Two quicker than a bung finds its way into George Graham's back pocket. Star performer in all this was chairman Scott Davidson, whom we suspected of being a closet Gashead when he spent £1m on striker Tony Thorpe, who is unable to score unless wearing a Luton shirt. Davidson then moved into overdrive by forcing out manager John Ward, just months after gaining promotion, and replacing him with unknown Swede Benny Lennartson, who was immediately christened 'Benny Hill' by Gasheads (well, he made *us* laugh). Poor Benny, he has all the wit and charisma of David Mellor, and as much knowledge of English football as... David Mellor. When the task of ensuring relegation was complete, there was much rejoicing in Horfield as Rovers fans regaled Sky viewers during their home match with Manchester City with the song, "He's fat, he's round, he's taken City down, Benny Hill, Benny Hill..."

So that was the highlight of our season. Yet it had all started so promisingly. Even before a ball was kicked, Rovers fans were on cloud nine when we were given the news that the club had bought the Memorial Ground from its former owners, Bristol Rugby Club. For the first time in 50 years, Bristol Rovers OWNED their own ground. What a way to start a season! Okay, it's a bit of a dump at present, but even now, almost a year later, I still can't quite come to terms with it. I walk up to the ground thinking to myself, "This is OUR ground - we OWN this"; but it still doesn't quite sink in. When the only thing your football club has ever owned in your lifetime has been a minibus and a couple of portakabins, it really does take some getting used to.

But while all of us at *Black Arab* applaud the magnificent job the directors of our football club have done in getting us our own ground, we would say to them - please, don't ever let it slip from our grasp.

But back to the football. Our first home game, against Reading, gave us false hope. With new signing Michael Meaker playing against his old club, we went 1-0 down and Reading fans sang "Meaker, Meaker, what's the score?" to their ex-player. Moments later, it was 1-1. And when Meaker scored to put us 2-1 up, it was Rovers fans turn to sing "Meaker, Meaker what's the score?" - with repeat choruses at 3-1 and 4-1.

But supporters who got excited over this win were soon brought back to earth when, three days later, we made our annual first round exit from the Worthington Cup, this time courtesy of Leyton Orient. I really don't know why we bother to enter this competition. Surely it would be easier just to give the team drawn against us a bye into the next round, then I could put to much better use the money it costs to watch us lose - like the continuation of my quest to find the perfect pint of Blackthorn cider.

So that's one Wembley trip we're not going to make this year. What comes next? Oh yes, silly season. This is the period when Bristol Rovers feel it's unfair on the opposition to have to try to beat us when we have eleven players on the pitch. So to give the other team a chance, one of our players gets sent off and we play them with ten men - or, as happened on three occasions, nine. But even this didn't help Bournemouth, who played against just nine men in blue for over 25 minutes, yet still lost 1-0. A truly outstanding rearguard action by the Gas, helped by a totally clueless Bournemouth forward line.

We arrived late for one home match in November because the Gas Hit Squad were in action. I'd better explain. The Gas Hit Squad is a fanzine stunt. We find someone who calls him or herself a Rovers supporter but hasn't been for ages. We go to their house, kidnap them and take them to the football to remind them what they're missing. Good, eh? Anyway, we'd been busy kidnapping someone and arrived late. First thing we saw was this strange yellow object fall out of the sky. What is it? Is it a bird? Is it a plane? Is it a custard pie? No, it's just the new football they're going to use during the winter months. Well, our goalscoring hero Barry Hayles didn't like it. He refused to put it in the back of the net, and promptly buggered off to Fulham out of the way of it

That's it then. With our goalscorer gone, our season's over, thought most Rovers fans. Or is it? Step forward Jason Roberts. Over the next 15 games, Jason scored 15 goals, with just one league defeat. Jason formed a deadly partnership with Jamie Cureton, the like of which Rovers fans haven't seen for years, finishing the season with 52 goals between them. This (almost) unbeaten run included a few cup games, and we found we had sneaked into the fifth round of the FA Cup as if by accident. As usual, the Rovers fans did the club proud. If only we had a team to match the supporters. Having broken the ground attendance record in the previous round against Leyton Orient, with hundreds locked out, in a matter of hours we then snapped up the 4,000 tickets for the fifth round tie against Barnsley. But on a day when the team needed to rise to the occasion, the performance was in keeping with the rest of the season - patchy and disappointing. With our defence allowing Craig Hignett the freedom of Oakwell, it was no surprise when he scored three times to dump us out.

This cup defeat badly affected league form, and with five games left we were in some difficulty at the wrong end of the table, having only managed to win ten league games. How had we allowed ourselves to drift into this position when we had the deadliest strike-force in the division? One look at the 'players used' column gives you an idea. Thirty-four players used, 20 of them making their Rovers debut. Changes in tactics: four at the back; three at the back; players playing in defence one week, in midfield the next, then tried in attack the third week. No wonder players looked confused and unsure of their role in the team. Too many suspensions didn't help either (could have something to do with all those red cards earlier in the season). So it was to everyone's credit that, when it finally sunk in they were in serious danger of relegation, they finished off the season with a flourish - three wins, a draw and just one defeat, which saw us safely into mid-table. The campaign was rounded off nicely with a 4-3 win at relegated Macclesfield, after being 2-0 down, with Jamie Cureton scoring his third hat-trick of the season, to ensure he won the golden boot as the division's top scorer.

So we wave goodbye to what was for the most part a forgettable season, and look forward to a considerable improvement in '99-2000. Rovers fans deserve better than the fare they had to endure for the most part. And we will be renewing our rivalry with Bristol City (1982), despite the claim by an erroneously-named fanzine, *One Team in Bristol* (seems they get everything wrong), that the last-ever Bristol derby had been played in season '97-98. An opportunity next season for Rovers once again to be the top team in Bristol. Let's take it.

Ian Metheringham

BOB LORD'S SAUSAGE

Burnley

We finished fifteenth in probably the weakest Second Division since the league was reorganised, and ended the season unbeaten in eleven - yet for the majority of the campaign, the brown runny stuff was trickling down the inside leg of all but the most deluded and detached Clarets fans.

But I'll start at the beginning. Just as I missed the last goal of Waddle's disastrous previous campaign, I also missed our first goal of the 'rebirth' of Burnley Football Club. Once again I had to celebrate a goal in front of a urinal due to a combination of fanzine selling and an excess of beer. I wouldn't have minded but Andy Payton's second-

"The Meaty Burnley Fanzine With Only a Little Gristle"

bob lord's £1

sausage

Issue 7   Spend, Spend, Spend Edition   February '99

Stan Buys Mellon

Exclusive Interview With Clive Holt

minute strike against Bristol Rovers was the first goal of the English football season. The previous season, we were the last team to make the net ripple. A bad start for me, but not the team, as the 2-1 victory got us off to a flier.

Not only did the win prove to be a false dawn, it proved to be both a false noon and muthahumpin' dusk as well. The season's nadir (or so we all thought at the time) was reached in the very next home game against York City. One-nil down just before half-time, a veritable flurry of activity could be seen on the touchline as all three subs were forcibly ejected from the dugout and, to use a well-worn football phrase, warmed up like bastards. The Clarets side which emerged for the second-half had a strangely peculiar look about it. Lee Howey, Steve Blatherwick and Mark Winstanley, defenders purchased for a combined sum of £500,000, had been replaced by three complete rookies plucked from the youth team. Was it a tactical switch or were they injured? No, nothing like that. Stan 'Whip Cracker' Ternent had sacked them on the spot.

The press statement given by Ternent after the defeat that afternoon was easily the most incredible event witnessed at Turf Moor since chairman Frank Teasdale actually jumped out of his seat for a Burnley goal in 1985. It was revealed that the three players, along with Michael Williams, would never play for Burnley again. According to the gaffer, they weren't pulling in the same direction as himself. And damn right he was, too. East Lancashire went wild. Apocryphal tales emanated from all directions that fans drank the town dry that evening, such were the celebrations. Ternent had got it spot on. He had ditched the three so-called Premiership signings that Waddle had made and bundled in the worst Burnley defender in years - and that takes some beating, believe me.

In their place would come... er... hang on a minute... some youth team players. The sane reasoning was that although they lacked the experience, their commitment would make up for it. A couple of free signings were plucked from obscurity and the wheels were temporarily put back on the rickety old cart which was our season.

In the midst of all this was the protracted take-over saga, which seems *de rigueur* in non-Premiership land these days. With a backdrop of no money, a poor team and relegation threatening, the fans decided that enough was enough and a protest was instigated. The club merchandise boycott had been effective to the point that the shirt prices were reduced by the end of January - but the chairman still wasn't hinting at P45s. CISA took the initiative, organising a sit-in after the Notts County game in October. After an atmosphere-less 90 minutes it was heartening to hear the deafening holler of "Teasdale Out" reverberate around Turf Moor. It was incredible to see old men, kids and women sing with as much gusto as the thermos-flasked, beer-gutted, moustachioed season ticket stereotypes. The cause united us against the board - it couldn't fail, because we wouldn't let it. A 5,000-signature petition was handed in 15 minutes later, before retiring to the pub to soothe our larynxes.

And still nothing happened. Rumours abounded that the board was reeling and wary of future CISA action. Then, just as a red card protest threatened to emerge from the pipeline, Teasdale announced his intention to resign. Scratch card millionaire Barry Kilby was set to join the board and remove the chairman from his chair, so to speak. Not only that, he was underwriting a share issue to the tune of £4m. At last, we all thought, the perfect opportunity for us all to own a piece of the club that we cherish so dearly. "I'll buy ten shares," quipped one fan. "I'll buy twenty," piped another. "I'll buy none," said yours truly, as Kilby announced that they were £200 a shot. As the supporters gasped, the financial experts revealed that it was due to the huge debts run up by the outgoing chairman. The club was losing £80,000 a month and was £4m in debt.

Even as I write, there are a deluded few who refuse to blame Teasdale for the mess we were in. They all cite Frank's trump card of saving the club in 1985. Wrong, he took over in 1985 and frog-marched us to the brink of oblivion two years later. It was only the spirit of the players and the 17,000 fans who saved us on that glorious May afternoon twelve years ago. He took over a basement division club that was £800,000 in debt and left it 14 years later with debts that were five times larger and a team heading, once again, for the basement division. Well done Frank Teasdale. If he expected a golden handshake, he was sorely mistaken. A golden shower, on the other hand, was a distinct possibility.

With the new guy on board, the future looked brighter. Money would be forthcoming, but would it arrive in time to save us from relegation? After a dismal run of results, which saw us plummet down the league, Kilby dipped in his pocket and handed Stan Ternent over a million quid to keep us in Division Two.

I was on my deathbed with a severe bout of *crapfootballitis* (involving headaches, fever and reminiscences of Division One) when the news filtered through that we had re-signed Steve 'Stevie' Davis from Luton for a small fortune. The leap out of bed put Lazarus' rise from the dead in the 'Okay, but no Oscar' league. Within a week we had shelled out yet again, this time for a midfielder from Tranmere called Mickey Mellon. Oh, go on then, have a good laugh, you childish louts, but he was the creative midfielder we needed. In the club shop the counter staff were bracing themselves for an onslaught of female customers requesting 'Mellon' written across the front of their shirts, not the back. Form improved immediately, with back-to-back away wins at Bristol Rovers and Millwall. Things were looking up - but not for long.

Our home form had long been a reason for concern. In the absence of the never-to-be-forgotten Longside terrace, Turf Moor is no longer the forbidding cauldron it used to be, and just about all visiting teams have long since cottoned on to that fact. If the alarm bells were ringing after failing to beat Luton and Reading at home, the air-raid sirens were ringing by early March.

A conveniently-timed wedding by *Sausage* stalwart Grover fortunately spared us the embarrassment of the 5-0 pasting at home to Gillingham, so it's rather difficult to pass comment. All I remember of the day is fudging my trousers at the prospect of making the best man's speech, getting some Dutch courage from the bar, and being informed that my team had just let in five at home. It wouldn't have been so bad if the barman hadn't been a Blackburn fan. The real test of the team's mettle would be the next game - at home to Manchester City.

To say that being on the end of a 6-0 home defeat is embarrassing would be an understatement. But conceding eleven goals, without reply, in two home games is the second most humiliating experience that can ever happen to a football fan. Of course, the most humiliating experience is spending £100m and then getting relegated. That's not possible though... is it?

The long-awaited home victory finally came at the end of March, against Macclesfield Town. Tom Cowan and Paul Cook had both arrived for the previous game, against Preston and had looked impressive. At 2-1 down, Cowan produced the goal of the season, with a mesmeric overhead kick, which had Turf Moor in raptures. Coming from 3-2 down late in the second-half, Andy Payton ended his ten-game goal drought before Steve Davis thundered an injury-time header into the net to give us a sweet 4-3 victory. The drama didn't end there. Apparently, the Macc manager, Sammy 'Bad Teeth' McIlroy, was incensed at the Burnley crowd for their relentless booing of Efe Sodje, their bandanna-clad centre-half. During our earlier encounter at Moss Rose, this talentless lump of shite deliberately got Andy Cooke sent off and then, in the players bar afterwards, boasted to his team-mates that Cooke hadn't got anywhere near him, let alone hurt him. All this happened within earshot of Stan Ternent, who was justifiably outraged. In the aftermath of our victory at the Turf, McIlroy claimed that Ternent had called Macclesfield a pub team. What a shame they got relegated. I got a perverse sense of pleasure seeing the agony of defeat etched on the faces of the very same Pub Town fans who had sung "Can we play you every week?" at Moss Rose. The answer, quite clearly, is "No, not until you're good enough".

From that point onwards we played like a team possessed. The players gelled, fought for the cause and, for the first time all season, got the rub of the green. The team transformed itself from prime relegation candidates to the form team in the division. A memorable 4-1 thumping of Stoke on their own patch was followed a week later by arguably the finest performance of the season, as we sent home Mohamed Al Fulham with no points (as well as no British passport) - a victory which guaranteed us safety.

A fanzine review of the season would be incomplete without a comment about how *Bob Lord's Sausage* fared during the nine-month campaign. 'Eventful' would sum it up nicely. We produced the usual four issues a season, with the regular chairman-baiting and critical comment for which we are building a reputation. So well received was the *Sausage* that a number of fellow fanzine editors managed to make a couple of bob out of our work. Marcus Allin, editor of Bristol City's *Come In Number Seven, Your Time Is Up*, you know *exactly* what I'm talking about. And your team is second-rate as well.

The final analysis of '98-99 shows that it was yet another season of transition, though this time the change was where it really mattered: in the boardroom. We have a new chairman, who has recently created (and filled) a new post of general manager. The supporters clubs have a quarterly dialogue with the chairman. And - wait for it, folks - he actually listens to the fans and answers their questions. We have a new kit, which is made by a Burnley-based company and a feeling that our club is, at long last, in safe hands. Now it's up to Stan Ternent to give the 10,000 regulars the promotion-winning team they deserve.

Steve Winkley

BRIAN MOORE'S HEAD

Gillingham

It was one of the greatest seasons in Gillingham's history, but it ended in the cruellest of manners.

Picture the scene: The Second Division Play-off Final, the Wembley scoreboard reads **'GILLINGHAM 2 MAN-CHESTER CITY 0'**, and the clock stands at 89 minutes. The Gills are going to the First Division for the first time in their history, and ecstasy is written on every one of the 35,000 faces in our end, whilst the City end is a picture of sky blue misery. There are just 17 seconds of normal time left when Kevin Horlock pulls back a consolation. Seconds later, the fourth official holds up the injury-time board - it says **'5'**. Disbelief amongst the Gills support, and a period of frantic nail-biting and clock-watching ensue. In the fifth minute of injury-time, Paul Dickov levels the scores. The dream is over, we all know it.

That we ultimately lost on penalties didn't make it any easier to take, nor did the fact that we were denied a clear-cut penalty with less than ten minutes of extra-time left. It was afterwards that the recriminations began. Precisely where had referee Mark Halsey conjured those extra five minutes? He was the only person in the ground who considered it a just amount. There had been just one injury in the second-half, but Halsey attempted to justify his excessive additions by claiming that the various substitutions and excessive goal celebrating had been responsible. But everyone who was in the ground that day knew we were stitched up. Local radio commentators expressed their amazement, Radio Five commentators expressed their amazement, Sky commentators expressed their amazement, and even Man City fans admitted afterwards that there was simply no way there were five minutes of injury-time. Mr Halsey cheated us out of a place in the First Division, and he knows it. But to concentrate entirely on the end of season misfortune would be unfair to the players who gave their all throughout the campaign. They were heroes every one, and they deserved better than ultimate failure.

In many ways, the campaign could be summed up by the exploits of Bob Taylor. Signed for a record £500,000 (although this record was soon usurped by the £600,000 shelled out for Carl Asaba) at the start of the season, to replace the recently departed Ade Akinbiyi (flogged to Bristol City for £1.2 million), he initially found the weight of expectation a heavy burden to bear. He was unfit, out of touch and looked far from the half-million class. He was vilified by certain sections of the crowd, whilst his wife left the ground in tears, unable to endure the abuse directed at her other half. Yet, by the season's end, he was deservedly crowned Player of the Year, and it was recognised by all but the most blinkered that Super Bob was one of the finest players ever to pull on a Gills shirt.

The season's defining moments belonged to him. His last-minute winner against Al Fayed's mercenaries nearly took the roof off the Rainham End several months before its due demolition date. And when he scored all five in the 5-0 rout of Burnley at Turf Moor, Taylor simultaneously wrote his name into the record books, and Gillingham folklore.

But this was no one-man team. Everyone played a part, notably Andy Hessenthaler, who shrugged off the previous season's poor form to play like a man inspired, and Carl Asaba, who threatened to wage a one-man Goal of the Season contest. After a sluggish start to the campaign, caused largely by a less-than-potent strikeforce of an unfit Taylor and a past-it Steve Butler, the season was kick-started by the signing of Asaba. A previously goal-shy attack suddenly came to life, and goals were being scored from all areas - even midfield, which had failed to do its share for several years.

By the time a mammoth 17-match unbeaten run ended unluckily at Walsall (where the home side somehow defied a late onslaught), Gillingham had sneaked into the play-off positions, and could be considered a good outside bet for an automatic promotion slot. In the event, it didn't quite come off, as Fulham defied the collective weight of their wallets to speed away at the top, and big spending Walsall (well, they spent £35,000 anyway) held their nerve to clinch second spot - and should have won the admiration of everyone for the way they achieved so much on such a limited budget.

A club record-equalling fourth position saw us pitched into the play-offs against Preston, whose fans clearly reckoned they were going to dispatch us with the minimum of fuss. A goal up in the first-leg, they were singing the Wembley songs, but Super Bob's late equaliser ensured that we went into the home-leg as favourites. Andy Hessenthaler's goal after just 64 seconds set up a titanic struggle, played out before a passionate Priestfield audience. It was the farewell appearance of the ramshackle, but much loved Rainham End terrace - and what a way to go out, as the typically gutsy Gills team strained every sinew to clinch a deserved victory. The atmosphere was simply electric, and certainly by far the best I can recall in 27 years of supporting the club.

While it all went pretty much like clockwork on the field, the same, however, could not be said for what was going on behind the scenes. The relationship between chairman Paul Scally and manager Tony Pulis became increasingly strained, to the point where the two were not even talking. The main sticking point was money - or to be more precise - the fact that Scally was rather too keen to hang on to it, instead of giving it to the manager to spend on a new signing or two. But it also went deeper than that. It emerged that several players had found their wage packets light, the missing amounts being various bonuses they were due. Scally initially put this down to an "administrative error", but the manager retorted that this would have been more believable had it been the first time it had happened. This was a row that simmered throughout the season, and the Priestfield rumour mill span out of control as tales of the chairman's various alleged misdemeanours did the rounds. As is usually the case, it is often impossible to separate fact from fiction when hearing such stories, as we discovered when *Brian Moore's Head* published a spoof article claiming Scally had an unpaid milk bill totalling £4,000. The story was far too silly to be taken seriously by anyone... or so we thought. For within weeks it was being repeated *verbatim* as if an indisputable fact - which just goes to prove that people will believe exactly what they want to.

And so back to where we began - Wembley Stadium, venue of smelly toilets and over-priced lager. Looking back now, we all share a communal guilt. We had committed the cardinal sin of daring to believe we had actually done it. Captain Andy Hessenthaler admitted afterwards that he'd spent those moments visualising himself lifting the trophy. But then it was snatched away - which just goes to prove that it isn't over until the large female person sings, because until then there's always the chance that some cheating bastard of a ref will stitch you up.

Within days our mood was further shattered by the news that Tony Pulis - the best manager Gillingham FC has ever had - received a letter from the chairman before the play-off final informing him his contract was being terminated. In the Wembley aftermath, claim followed counter-claim. Scally denied Pulis had been sacked, Pulis denied having resigned, and the supporters were left dazed and confused, wondering how it could have been going so right one minute, and so wrong the next. As I write, Tony Pulis has just been appointed manager at Bristol City. But he will be fondly remembered for the team he built, one which took us closer to First Division football than any other in our history.

Simon Baker

BUILD A BONFIRE

Brighton & Hove Albion

1996 - finished 23rd in Division Two
1997 - finished 23rd in Division Three
1998 - finished 23rd in Division Three
1999 - mid-table obscurity amongst the Rochdales and Darlingtons of this world. Great!

Many Brighton fans felt relatively content by the end of the '98-99 season at finishing 17th in the table, thereby avoiding the usual relegation battle which has become synonymous with supporting the Seagulls in recent years. Others, including the Albion's fourth manager of this transitional season, Micky Adams, felt no cause for celebrating such a mediocre finale. Plans are being made for the Millennium season, but for once it isn't all doom and gloom around the club.

We kicked off our first full season with Dick Knight as chairman and the continuing push for the club to become solvent off the pitch. Former playing idol Brian Horton was manager and had made several new signings during the close season. Two of note were Paul Holsgrove and Gary Hart. Holsgrove had been signed on a free transfer, and played for half an hour in a pre-season friendly against Lewes, before being sold to Scottish side Hibs for a fee of £110,000, plus a cash bonus if they were promoted to the Scottish Premier League, which they duly were. Shrewd business, which gave the Albion a positive transfer dealings balance for the whole season, and goes to show how little was spent on quality signings. The majority of the new faces were free transfers, fresh-faced kids, or much-travelled old pros.

Gary Hart was one such fresh-faced youngster, plucked out of non-league football with Stanstead. We did splash out a fee for him, though - £1,000 and a new kit for his former team-mates. He struggled at first with the pace of playing football full-time, after giving up his job as a forklift driver, but adapted as time went on and has to be the find of the season. He finished as top scorer with 12 goals and has signed an extended contract. Many scouts from other clubs have had him watched, and he is now estimated to be worth at least £500,000 after his first season as a professional. Next season, with a stronger squad around him in support, he'll be one to watch. The next Alan Shearer? Possibly (and *Build A Bonfire* have got his first Albion shirt!).

The biggest, and only other amount paid for a player was for goalie Mark Walton, who cost £20,000. We started with a squad numbering 24, including seven new faces. Considering the team was basically the one that struggled for survival the previous season, why were we Brighton followers so positive at the start of the season?

The reason was the expected, imminent return from our exile in Gillingham. It was estimated the Albion would be playing back in Brighton, at the Withdean Stadium, by October 1998. Because of delays, this was later pushed back to March 1999, then to July of the same year. Hopefully, by the time you read this...

Brighton fans travelled 8,000 miles over the course of the season - and that was only to 'home' games. The club's time in Kent exasperated Albion supporters, players and board alike. Another year there would not only have left us on the brink of financial ruin, it would have pushed us over the edge into oblivion. The relief of everyone at the end of our final game was tangible, with the final whistle being blown on the most disastrous groundshare in English history. A final, curious fact to this matter - remembering that it was our previous, malignant regime of Archer and Bellotti who manipulated the fall of our great club: David Bellotti is now on the board at Gillingham, and their promotion push was partly financed from the extortionate rent paid to them by Brighton.

On the pitch, it was to be a record-breaking year for the Albion - both good and bad. The season started slowly, with defeats and draws galore throughout August. Things picked up towards the end of the month, though, with three wins in a row. September should be banned from the footballing calendar, with the Albion losing five games on the trot. This included a 1-0 defeat to the league's most welcoming team, fans, police and chairman: Leyton Orient.

The stark contrast of us hating playing at the Priestfield and preferring instead to go to away games was highlighted during October and November. Three games out of four were lost at 'home'. Compare this to our away results, and you see why we weren't going to get anywhere in the league. A club record of five away league wins in a row was THE highlight of the season, and showed just what we could have achieved with a home ground of our own. The team had the ability but not the belief to carry it through.

December actually saw us win a couple of matches in Gillingham. It also heralded a glimmer of a play-off place (briefly), with an excellent Christmas period of seven points out of nine, including wins over Brentford and Peterborough. The only negative during this time of seasonal joy and celebration was an injury to our wing wizard, Rod Thomas, in the 90th minute of the win against Peterborough. At the time, no-one realised the impact this was to have on the team - but it all turned sour as 1999 dawned.

This was to be the year for renewed optimism. We had a leader in Brian Horton, who was guiding us out of Division Three, we were going to return to Brighton in time to celebrate our promotion, plans for a permanent site to call our own were launched, and the whole year was designated 'Year For Youth' to promote football at grass level. We were even appearing on Sky Sports, against Chester, for our Fans United match. Then it all went wrong.

Chester proved to be Horton's final game in charge of the Albion. He was lured away to First Division Port Vale and left his job with us only half completed. In came Jeff Wood as caretaker-manager. Woody will always be a hero for his partnership with Steve Gritt two years ago, when saving Brighton from the Conference League. He started his leadership in full swing, with two wins and a draw. He was then offered the job full-time - and things went downhill fast. A new club record was again set, this time for the most consecutive losses, six in a row. In fact, the Seagulls only gained ONE point from a possible 30 through February, March and the beginning of April. Relegation was now more likely than promotion and we were looking over our shoulders again. Thankfully it didn't get to a stage of desperation and mid-table was beckoning.

With the sacking of Wood, in came our next caretaker-manager, Martin Hinshelwood. He only oversaw one match, but with his change in tactics, we actually won a game, after nearly three months. His reign was cut short with the appointment of our fourth manager of the season, Micky Adams. Now this *was* a manager backed by *Build A Bonfire*.

Micky's appointment also coincided with the production of the plans for Falmer. A new 25,000 capacity stadium was unveiled and detailed finance structures confirmed. The scheme is being backed by the local council and all of the main political parties in the area. A referendum by the local population produced a resounding 'yes' vote to the Albion having a new home. Planning applications and building will take about four years and the scheme will be called in by the Government. But it *will* happen, after 20 years of speculation.

Things were looking up again and this renewed optimism saw Micky win his first match in charge and guaranteed our mid-table berth. Adams then spent the remaining games assessing his squad and deciding which players had a future in his team set-up. Rod Thomas also returned to action for the first time in 1999, when he came on as sub for 20 minutes of our final match. Gary Hart received the Player of the Season accolade from all supporters groups, which the shy forward received sheepishly. The rough, uncut diamond was becoming a polished gem.

From the final squad of 27 players on the books, Adams retained only eleven. He is a man with strong ideas of what is required to get us out of Division Three and obviously felt that many of the playing staff just weren't up to the task. Some old favourites were dismissed, but we look forward to many new ones being introduced. Looking forward now seems to be the norm, rather than remonstrating about the past.

So the season petered out with a whimper - but, in the same fashion, it had kept us all enthralled. Eight away victories should have been good enough for automatic promotion. In fact, Brighton won more points on the road than at 'home'. The Seagulls lost a dozen times at the Priestfield, a statistic only matched by Macclesfield and Scarborough, the teams who finished bottom of Divisions Two and Three respectively. If more draws could have been ground out of the many losses, a play-off position would have been assured.

Positives for the year were the forming of the first-ever official supporters' football team, BHA United. They secured mid-table position, too, in their inaugural season. The Albion youth team also came through the year strongly, with some sound results. They even went on a fantastic cup run, only beaten by eventual finalists Coventry after some dubious refereeing. Some of these players have been recommended for advancement through the ranks and should have bright futures in front of them. With Adams guiding the club, we are all looking forward to a bright future.

Terry Brannigan

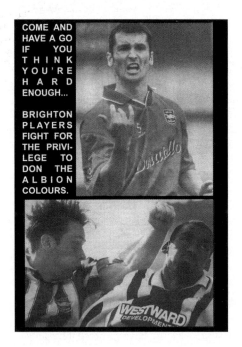

COME AND HAVE A GO IF YOU THINK YOU'RE HARD ENOUGH...

BRIGHTON PLAYERS FIGHT FOR THE PRIVILEGE TO DON THE ALBION COLOURS.

CHELSEA INDEPENDENT

Chelsea

For all of Chelsea's recent success, the Blues (nee Pensioners) cannot get out of the habit of the what-might-have-been season.

Having topped the table around Christmas and stayed in contention for the league until the penultimate game, we managed to throw it all away by drawing four of our last ten games.

Laying aside the disappointments of April and early May, we have rarely had a better season. We only lost three league games, conceded just 30 goals, collected our highest points total since romping the Second Division a few years back, and finished in our highest position since 1970. So gold stars all round then... except,

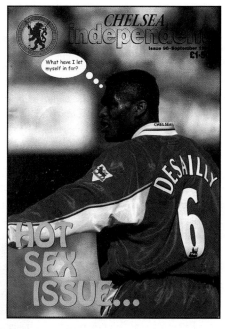

I suppose, when you consider that a bout of silly squabbling between the club and local council means that our ground is still half-built, and that a general breakdown in morals saw two of our staff charged with sexual misdemeanours (surely a Premiership record for a single season).

The season started with a touch of World Cup exhaustion. Having a record eleven players in nine international teams (let's face it, three Blues representatives would have set a new best) led to too many afternoons sitting behind closed curtains, trying to concentrate on the likes of Nigeria, Spain and Jamaica.

Having two World Cup winners in the side come August was an honour, even if it was one we had to share with the Gooners. And, yes, Chelsea fans did get sick of Frank droning on about it!

Consensus of opinion was that the arrival of Albert Ferrer and Desailly would turn our defence from comical to sound. A debate is still raging as to how many more points we would have garnered if Desailly had not been played 12 times in the middle. What we had forgotten is that Chelsea start the season a quarter of an hour after everyone else, so of course we lost the first game, at Highfield Road.

Chelsea stuttered at the beginning of the season. But we did get the chance to play the big friendly with Real Madrid in Monaco. The European

Super Cup turned out to be not so super, played on a Monaco car park, with a maximum capacity of 16,000 – and hardly any Chelsea fans could get tickets. In fact the atmosphere was so bad you could hear the players abusing each other on the TV coverage.

Still, when people say that Chelsea won nothing last season we can boast that we... er, won the Super Cup.

The midfield seemed to be our biggest headache at the start of the campaign. Dennis Wise only made guest appearances between suspensions. The highlight of his red cards had to be the two-footed clattering of a Villa defender in the Worthless Cup. Coventry fans might say "So what", but we were 4-1 up in injury-time when he did it.

Dan Petrescu could not get a game at the start of the year amid rumours that he was up for sale. Roberto Di Matteo struggled for form after a disappointing World Cup. And the combination of Babayaro and Le Saux down the left was almost absurd. Both left-backs by trade, they constantly fell over each other to be in the same space at the same time.

Jody Morris was the find of the season. Although he has been around for a few years now, he is really maturing after a few years developing his drinking arm. There is a feeling that Dennis' days might be numbered with such a classy home-grown talent waiting to replace him.

Off the field, a delay in the public enquiry into the development of the West Stand means that capacity remains limited to 34,000. While Man United add another 10,000 to their stadium, and the likes of Arsenal and Everton seek bigger premises, it seems absurd that a club the size of Chelsea should settle for 40,000. No wonder we pay the highest prices in the land. Given that Stamford Bridge sits on a site as big as Wembley, we could have hoped for a bigger ground.

The hotels that take up a substantial part of the site have not been breaking any booking records. Perhaps with the reputation of Bates Motel and the Chelsea Hotel, we should not have expected them to.

It was as early as November when things started to falter. Laudrup wanted away. He was struggling to settle and showed little of the incisive, attacking play his reputation promised. After scoring his only goal in a freezing Copenhagen, he left to join them. The spare, Bjarne Goldbaek, we picked up in return turned out to be the only player we signed all season - and one of the best midfielders we have signed for years. The goal he scored against Rottenham to preserve our decade-long unbeaten run at Three Point Lane was worth the price of half a season ticket in itself.

Then, in the next game after Brian had gone home, Casiraghi popped his knee in an alarming fashion. Given his age, he may never play again, although the club are convinced he will be back by Christmas. He was just starting to impress after having found the transition from Italy to England a bit tough. Zola and the boys paid tribute to him in our next league match; the part of the tribute he will not have appreciated is that we tonked three past Wimbledon with the strike-force we should have been using from the start.

So we were reduced to the strikers we thought of in the first place. When Flo took two months out injured, we were left grateful for the Finnish schoolboy Forssell (who did pass his English A' level, despite what people say) and that fact that the gaffer had kept his registration.

Scoring goals was a problem all season. Last year we seemed to crack five or six for fun. This season, Casiraghi struggled to come to terms with the Premiership and then got injured. Flo didn't get a look in until after Gigi's injury, and then picked up one of his own. The gaffer only scored in the cups and Zola, much though we love him, doesn't look like scoring 20 in a season.

The highlight of the year was the 0-5 win in the Worthless at Highbury. Detractors, and there were many, said it was an Arsenal B team. But the side put out was pretty much the second string we came to rely on when injuries further reduced the side, namely when Gus Poyet (again) and Ferrer (briefly) cut our squad to the bones.

Albert Ferrer has been one of the most underrated players in the Blues squad. Teams no longer attack down their left against us. He gets forward well and links with midfield effortlessly. But when the history of Chelsea is rewritten (at least twice a season at the moment), the absence of big Gustavo from our team for the middle of the last two campaigns will be cited as the single most important factor in Chelsea failing to claim a championship in the closing years of the century.

Ultimately the season slipped away after we lost to West Ham at home. While we were still in with an arithmetical chance, the faces of Chelsea fans down the Fulham Road that Saturday said it all. We lost five points and a striker to West Ham this season, and lost the championship by four points.

Others look back to being held, implausibly, by Leicester at home but we knew our chance had gone by then. Drawing 0-0 at the Riverside, four days before Arsenal won there by six, seemed to rub it in a bit.

Somehow we remained in touch until the penultimate game but a poor draw with Sheffield Wednesday after going out of Europe to Mallorca had kicked the final fight out of the team. We had all dreamt of securing the title at White Hart Lane – instead, our last chance blew up there, after Leboeuf had gifted a goal to Ginola.

Scratching around for other positives, the new kit, despite the odd white stripe out of place and the textured Bri-nylon, is at least the right shade of blue again; the *Chelsea Independent* continues despite financial problems that would make your hair stand on end; and we have been promised a few new Italians.

Give me some gossip about a left-sided midfielder and a chance of getting our old badge back, and we might just do something next season.

James Edwards

CITY 'TIL I CRY!

Manchester City

The Great Escape

"Don't look back in anger," warbled City's most famous fans, Oasis. "Are you 'avin a larf?" retorted almost every other City fan! As we faced the season ahead, plying our trade in the third division of English football for the first time in the roller-coaster history of our club, didn't we have just cause to be a mite pissed off? Unfortunately, 'looking back' was one of the few comforts left to City fans. And for season 1998/99, never was the warm coat of nostalgia needed more. However, once the shock had subsided, most City fans were surprisingly upbeat and positive

The THIRD WAY Manchester City fanzine!

about the situation. It was as if we had finally reached rock bottom and that the only way was up. Yeah, like City are *that* predictable. Following City these days is increasingly an act of blind faith, a defiant response to the Evil Empire of the rags. Most experts claimed that the crowd levels would be affected by relegation. They were right. They increased. This phenomenon had little to do with footballing matters, as being a City fan is more akin to membership of the Davidian Cult at Waco than one of those happy-clappy fans constantly portrayed on Sky. It is a statement of intent and cultural identity that most Home Counties rags could never comprehend. The priority for the club at the start of the season was to reduce the playing staff. Half a dozen different managers over the previous three years had seen the squad rise to 54 players, of which about half had been removed by the end of the season. The management had assured us that we were fitter, stronger, more motivated, had a better team spirit, and were more 'up for it' than the team which had previously humiliated us. Hmmm. We waited to be convinced.

First up was Blackpool at Maine Road. An incredible 32,134 attended - and most left skipping, as a 3-0 stroll prompted the typical over-optimism so inherent to Maine Road. This was going to be a doddle, we thought. This is City, we remembered. The popular view was that promotion would be assured sometime in February. Would it get any better than this? Well... er, probably not. Our next league match was away to Fulham, and around 4,000 City fans made the nightmare journey across London during Friday rush-hour to witness a performance we naively thought we had seen the last of. The wing-back formation and the lack of width even at this stage highlighted our inadequacies. And not for the first time this season, Joe Royle's judgement proved questionable. We were beaten 3-0, in front of the watching TV millions, and were once again embarrassed by a team we perceived to be inferior to us - although the end of season table showed that maybe, just maybe, Fulham weren't *that* inferior after all. One week into the season and two wildly differing performances. At least our inconsistency is... well, consistent. Things then settled into more of a routine. By Boxing Day, we were sitting pretty in 12th spot, about 14 points behind the leading teams. Gulp. But, the doom and gloom merchants were assured our 'run' was just around the corner. Didn't Alan Ball spout this nonsense? Didn't Frank Clark say something similar? The storm clouds were gathering over Maine Road, as Joe Royle and first team coach Willie Donachie then did what any self-respecting manager would do... they blamed the fans.

We were too "demanding", we were putting "pressure" on the players, we were being "negative".

City fans will put up with some right crap, but they will not tolerate someone trying to shift the blame. We had done our bit, turned up in our thousands, paid the wages of these ungrateful sods. Yet now we were being held responsible for the performances on the playing side. Within the week, the club had claimed that it had all been a bit of a misunderstanding, and that they were actually grateful for us turning up in our thousands every week. Which was nice.

But fortunately for the Blues, Big Joe was to be proved right in his assertions. A lucky 1-0 victory at Wrexham sparked off our season big-style. We then lost only two of our last 24 matches (at home to Oldham Athletic and Wycombe Wanderers, obviously) and roared into the play-offs, finishing third in the table. This season, though, was not just a turning point in the playing stakes for our beloved club, it was also the time when the media finally cottoned on to the fanaticism and loyalty of the hardy bunch of fans who follow Manchester City.

At a time when football is perceived as being only about money and Sky coverage, the media presented an alternative view of professional football at the grass roots level (well, that's what the Nationwide Second Division felt like!) and offered a contrary view to what was going on at one of our local rivals. You know the ones I mean, yes?

We were seen as carrying the banner for a more traditional support. We had a solid working-class image, with the ground set amongst rows of terraced houses; loud, raucous fans; people less interested in the souvenir shop and more concerned with partying in the pubs and bars; and we turned up in numbers every week. Our lowest crowd of the season was 24,291, higher than any other club's top attendance in the division, and our away attendances were inevitably the largest of the season. Of the 23 away grounds visited, 19 had their largest crowd for the visit of City. Two of the other four were for games on the last day of the season, and one was for a bank holiday match. Our allocations, whether small or large, were almost always sold out, as it appeared that the City fans had decreed that no matter what the failings of the football team, no-one could ever point a finger at them, in the time of their most desperate need. Unlike numerous other so-called 'fanatical' supports. Yes, I am talking about you Sunderland. And Newcastle United. And Leeds United. And Wolves. And Chelsea. And all the other hotbeds of soccer the media is so eager to tell us about. Where were they in their club's darkest hours?

For too long, the level of support at City was unappreciated, with unrealistic comparisons made with the other lot. Would any other club average getting on for 30,000 every week playing in the Third Division of English football? Somehow I doubt it. In a way, this 'cult' feeling about following City tended to attract more fans. It seemed we were the 'car crash' team of football... it was a horrible sight, but you just couldn't look away. As things have got worse around Maine Road, the fascination and urge to defend the club has increased. Who knows what the support would have been had we ended up in the Conference. The play-offs brought us a local derby against Wigan Athletic. For the first leg, at Springfield Park, City were allocated around 1,200 tickets in a capacity crowd of 6,600. It meant another early start queuing up for tickets and having to endure the club's inevitable lack of organisation. Every new regime taking over at Maine Road promises they will learn from the past mistakes. Well not about selling tickets you don't, you clots!

A 1-1 draw at their place set things up for the second-leg, and a capacity crowd set about winning the match for themselves. In all my long years of watching matches at Maine Road, I have never known such frenzy and noise envelop the stadium. A patchy 1-0 victory was greeted with joyous scenes rarely witnessed before in the club's history. At the final whistle, the outpouring of emotion and roar of the crowd brought tears to the eyes of even cynical, embittered seasoned campaigners - such as myself - as the crowd invaded the pitch to overwhelm the players. Even Joe Royle was taken aback at the scenes, as he wondered what it would be like when we actually did something. He didn't understand. But how could he? Managers come, managers go. But a fan goes on forever. But even that night was overshadowed by what was to follow. Wembley and Gillingham. Once again, the ticket arrangements were a huge cock-up, with the Football League, unbelievably, giving the Gills 34,000 tickets, when their average gate was under 7,000.

So there was widespread speculation about touts getting hold of tickets, about Millwall fans coming along for the day, rumours that City fans had been buying them up. By the time of the final, lower-priced tickets were going for £100 each. But not to fret, each Gillingham fan had been allowed eight tickets each to bring the missus, Uncle Ralph, Granny, the two kids, the wife's sister, and Scally the dog!

The authorities may have complimented us on our level of support, but they weren't going to play fair by us, that was for certain. The day itself is well-documented. Going 2-0 down with only three minutes left, we were dead and buried. A consolation goal in the final seconds (how cruel you are, Lord)... then the miracle - an equaliser in the fourth minute of injury-time and eventual success in the penalty shoot-out. Could it be any other way for a Manchester City fan? And I didn't even see it. As Gillingham's second goal hit the back of the net, I departed the stadium. The first time I have left a match early in over 15 years. By the time I had reached the bottom of the stairs, we had drawn level and watched as hundreds of City fans charged back into the stadium. But I knew I would have jinxed us had I gone back in. I was not meant to see it. So I headed out back to the car in Stanmore and walked into a pub full of City fans - at the precise second that Nicky Weaver made the final save and got us promoted. It was like a scene from the *X-Files* or *Close Encounters of the Third Kind*, as if it had been pre-ordained that this was the way I had to savour the joy. I don't regret not going back in to watch the extra-time, as I know that had I done so, things would not have turned out like they did. So a small sacrifice to pay.

And to think, I'm one of City's more rational, logical fans.

So the season had ended on a massive high. Or had it? Things are never that straightforward following City. A few days later, the Gillingham chairman called for the match to be replayed because the referee had been spotted in a hotel with City fans later that evening. Unbelievable or what? It could only happen to us, and it was almost a week before the authorities finally rejected the appeal. So finished the most traumatic season I've ever known following the Blues.

In spite of the routine inadequacies of those who have run the club over the past couple of decades, our support demands that we are still a 'big club'. And at long, long last, we now have a football team with a spirit that matches that of its supporters. Our day will come.

D'ya know what I mean?

Tom Ritchie

CLAP YOUR HANDS STAMP YOUR FEET!

Watford

Catching the Gravy Train

Your side has won promotion to the First Division. Do you:

a) Spend over £2m on two strikers, sack your decent manager, replace him with a clown, and sink back into the oblivion from whence you came;

b) Hover around mid-table, flirting occasionally with the play-offs, but finish the season with a job well done;

c) Spend virtually no money. Spend the vast majority of the season in the top six, fall away towards the business end of the season, before gatecrashing the play-offs and just keep on going all the way to the Premiership.

Clap Your Hands Stamp Your Feet!

No.51   February 1999   Back to £1

Well, a) is, hysterically, Bristol City; b) is what most, if not all, Watford fans would have settled for, but is actually Grimsby; and c) is what actually happened to Watford. I still can't believe it and probably won't do until the first *Match of the Day* of the season when Hansen, Brooking, Lineker and Lawrenson relegate us (and Bradford) there and then. But who cares?

The Premiership seemed a long way off on that first day of the season, at Portsmouth. Even the Pompey programme was against us, publishing a league table with no games played but cruelly putting the relegation line above Watford, WBA and Wolves. All the talk was of mid-table security. Even our Lord, Graham Taylor, wasn't sure what to expect and had no idea on what was his best team. We won with a hilarious own-goal and a Jason Lee bullet header, but it left us with more questions than answers. As indeed did the next game against Bradford, but we won that too. It all seemed to click against Bristol City. Richard Johnson blasted a couple of specials and three wins out of three - without looking anything like a side that should win three out of three.

We lost the next three, changed the tactics again, and won the next three. We hit another dodgy spell - and then came the game at Bolton. Our record in Lancashire is appalling and here we were faced with a side unbeaten so far and justifying their tag as one of the favourites. We were under the cosh from the off and fell behind. But just before half-time, Gifton Noel-Williams equalised and we held firm in the second-half, before a Micah Hyde cross, three minutes from time, was lashed home by Peter Kennedy. The thud as Kennedy made contact said 'GOAL'; you just *knew* it was in. We stole three points, and that changed the season. We even won our next game in Lancashire as well, as we embarked on a long unbeaten run, and kept our place in the top six; and, to top it all, playing some awesome football. At The Vic we seemed unstoppable.

The run had to end at some point. It was Grimsby who took the scalp and Watford hit another dodgy spell, where even goalscoring was becoming a problem. Spurs dumped us out the cup, although to be fair, Ginola clicked that afternoon and not many would have stopped him. At least we had the honour of scoring after 53 seconds and witnessing Richard Johnson getting his first-ever goal from inside the six-yard box. Johnno's previous 18 career goals consisting of 17 long-range missiles and one just inside the penalty-area.

Then came Sunderland, and even though the game wasn't all-ticket, it was a sell-out. We deservedly won. Tony Daley tore Sunderland apart in the first-half, setting up Nick Wright to score with a header. Sunderland equalised, but early in the second-half, Gifton controlled the ball and swivelled in one movement, striking the ball so cleanly it whistled in. Five minutes later he received a crunching tackle from Paul Butler and, although we didn't know it at the time, that was his season finished. Just as it looked like we were getting back on track, we were sent down the sidings.

The reality was that losing Gifton was a massive blow, and this showed in the results. A lone, deserved victory at QPR was all there was to show in the next two months, terminating with a dreadful performance at home to Bury. Everyone was resigned to another season of Division One football. Even at Fanzine Towers, we were saying that we should still celebrate this season, as the team had done everything we could ask for and more. Fortunately, one man refused to accept defeat and that man was Graham Taylor. There was a team meeting to discuss the problems; a sports psychologist was brought in. Would it do the trick? The answer, to start with, was 'no'. It needed one of those bizarre moments to kick-start the season. I felt another turning point coming on.

Tranmere, home, Easter Saturday. Thirty minutes to go, Watford one down. The season is not so much stopping as everyone mentally thinking, "summer holidays in a month's time." GT decides to make a substitution and the team appears in a 4-3-3 formation. Tommy Mooney, one of the substitutes, crosses and Peter Kennedy volleys first time into the corner of the net - 1-1, and the momentum is with Watford. Enter, stage right, John Aldridge. Richard Johnson tackles Kenny Irons, who falls as though hit by a thousand snipers. Aldridge leaps off the bench as though a thousand bees have nested there. The ref, having missed the incident, consults his linesman, who could not have seen the incident, and awards a second yellow card to Johnno. GT goes off to argue with the linesman. Aldridge invites some Watford supporters to punch him (if it weren't for a steward one would have been successful). Suddenly, the players are united, and the supporters get behind the team.

That wasn't the end of the incidents. Watford were awarded a penalty by the same linesman, who had effectively sent off Johnno. The arguments went on for ages. Peter Kennedy had his spot-kick saved, Michel Ngonge bundled home the rebound, David Kelly landed one of the greatest right hooks I've ever seen on Allan Smart, and utter pandemonium ensued in the penalty-area. How the very same linesman decided that Allan Smart should be the only one sent off, I'll never know. Only now can Watford thank John Aldridge and his team for their antics that afternoon. It got the season going again.

It was still a tall task to reach the play-offs but Birmingham and Bolton were beaten, to complete a memorable week, and suddenly the whole season changed: 4-3-3 was a success, but we had to keep on winning. And keep on we did. Crewe and Crystal Palace were dispatched, and the victory over Port Vale, to make it six wins out of six, put the Hornets back into a play-off place. Tommy Mooney was on fire, the defence resolute, the tide seemed to be with us. The winning run couldn't continue, but the draw with Barnsley relaxed everyone. One game and one win was the equation.

Vicarage Road was packed that Sunday afternoon for the visit of Grimsby, but a Peter Kennedy goal settled the nerves and clinched the points. Fifth place and the play-offs here we come.

We were not favourites to qualify. Indeed, as one paper put it: "Watford have no chance." Chris Kamara commented that we had over-achieved all season. 'Stuff them' seemed to be the attitude. Michel Ngonge scored early against Birmingham, and we should have had more. But we didn't and that left a very tense Thursday evening in the Midlands.

Birmingham threw everything at us; not surprising when you consider that their front two were both well over six-foot, but we hung on in there. And when David Holdsworth was sent off, it was there for the taking, but Birmingham looked the more likely. No-one scored, and it was penalties. Watford's penalty-taking is woeful. We've never really had someone who scores regularly, so most fans were probably fearing the most. We might as well have saved ourselves the bother. Each Watford player walked up calmly and, with the exception of Steve Palmer, scored with ease. Chris Holland stepped up nervously, the ground fell silent, and a chorus of "Watford" burst out from the away end. It seemed an age from foot striking ball to hand saving ball, but Alec Chamberlain guessed right and saved it. Delirium in the away end. Watford at Wembley. Players throwing their shirts to the crowd. Watford were at Wembley. Unbelievable!

By now superstitions must have taken hold of every Watford fan. Lucky pants, socks, shoes, T-shirts, friends, unwashed shirts, not wearing glasses - the list is endless. Even I was planning the week ahead thoroughly to make sure everything that needed to happen did. Come the big day and everything had gone according to plan.

The problem with a big day at Wembley is that you are desperate to take it all in, but it still passes you by. I could go on forever about what a day it was - but words really aren't enough. It is so difficult to convey the elation and ecstasy of the whole event from wake to sleep.

The game went so quickly - but then, I suppose, it always does when you win. Bolton had the better chances, but when Nick Wright's spectacular overhead kick hit the net, you sensed it might just be our day. We had chances to seal it, and one minute from time, Micah Hyde passed to Peter Kennedy, who squared it perfectly for Allan Smart. Smartie shot, and given that we were directly square on with the goal, I waited... and then the net swished. The greatest moment of my (and thousands others') life - although if you are female, 26-30, sporty, N/S and GSOH, you just might relegate it to second place in my case. At that moment, the beckoning finger of the Premiership was signalling to Watford. The final whistle blew and, amid the ecstasy, several people were pinching themselves just to believe it really had happened. The players collected the cup and their medals, and did their lap of honour; and the supporters went off to Watford to celebrate.

As I said at the start, I still can't believe it. That Bank Holiday Monday is still a blur and there was just too much going on. But one day it will sink in, and it will take a lot to wipe the grin off my face.

Sure, you dream that one day Watford will be in the Premiership, but never with just one stop at the Division One station. It's a bit like the Second Coming. When GT arrived in June 1977, it was a five-year plan to get to the old Second Division. It took two seasons. In June 1997, it was a five-year plan to get to the Premiership. Again, it's taken two seasons. *Deja vu*, anyone?

It's another success story for the 'small' clubs of this land. You sense that the other clubs of similar statue are willing Watford (and Bradford) to survive in the Premiership, but that the big clubs resent the two of us being there. We're the uninvited guests - and the quicker the riff-raff are cleared off, the better. Football would be very dull and samey if a fairy tale or two didn't appear in the Premiership every season. It gives the small clubs hope and belief.

At the start of the season, Watford will be amongst the elite, competing with the elite. You don't get there by luck. We have earned that right and now we will reap the rewards of the hard work and application shown throughout this successful season.

The final word should go to the supporters. Two-nil up and injury-time against Bolton: all season in the fanzine we've been going on about how unimportant singing about L***n T**n is. Never have the immortal words sounded so good. "Are you watching L***n T**n?"

Matthew Bentone

COCK-A-DOODLE-DOO

Tottenham Hotspur

Say what you like about the Worthington Cup, it is still larger and worth more than the empty space in the Arsenal trophy cabinet. While not quite an epic season for followers of the only English club apart from Manchester United to win a major trophy, it was more enjoyable than any of the campaigns previously recorded in this anthology.

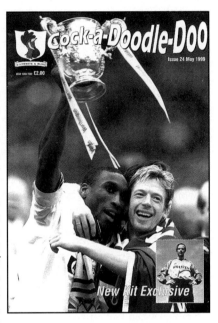

It all began so differently in August at Selhurst Park, where a fine summer's day found the Spurs support in boisterous mood, staging the usual flag-laden takeover of Selhurst. Then the team served up a pitiful display of soggy-spirited incompetence and lost 3-1, thoroughly deflating us. Tottenham were back.

Worse was to come as we were tonked 3-0 by Sheffield Wednesday in our opening home game. When the fixture lists came out, we'd drawn confidence from the fact that our opening games seemed to give us the chance to rack up the points before a tough series against the stronger sides. It wasn't happening, and the hapless Christian Gross was sacked. With no friends in the press, public criticism from the chairman, and a bunch of players who couldn't be bothered, it was hard not to feel sorry for him. But things couldn't go on as they were.

David Pleat was put in temporary charge, but the disturbing rumour began to circulate that a certain Mr George Graham was in the running to take over, prompting choruses of "You can stick yer George Graham up yer arse" at home games. This, combined with more lacklustre form, led to me and just one other of our bunch of regulars making the journey to Griffin Park for a Worthington Cup tie against Brentford. We won 3-2, but looked as if we'd found our level. An identical scoreline in the return put us through.

With Graham hotly tipped to take over at Spurs within days, one of those fascinating quirks of the fixture list saw his Leeds side face us at White Hart Lane. Barracked by the Leeds fans and pretending not to hear some of the chants directed at him from a by now deeply divided Spurs crowd, Stroller watched a thrilling 3-3 draw.

Graham was appointed days later, much to the glee of many opposing supporters, who waited to see how we could possibly live with it. There were three views. The first was that Graham was the Gooner Anti-Christ. The second was that he was a proven winner, something we needed. The third, and the one I held, was that the Gooner background didn't matter (I thought of it as revenge for Arsenal snatching my boyhood hero Pat Jennings) but the boring football Graham was famed for did. I could see the logic, but the dull tactics we now seemed doomed to watch offered only marginally more attractive a prospect than the rubbish we'd had to put up with for so long. Strangely, the Goons were livid, which made it more palatable.

The other thing that rankled was that Chairman Al had now appointed the only manager to be convicted of dodgy dealing. At the time of the bung scandal, Sugar had vociferously denounced the Arsenal board's hesitation in sacking Graham, using his saintly stance to justify the sacking of Terry Venables. Anyone can make a mistake or change their mind, but I resent paying £500 a season to watch the resulting wasted years.

But Graham was now firmly in charge. He made it clear he had no time for timewasters or grandstanders, and this not only led to the glorious silence of Chairman Al, but a steady upturn in fortune. Even George's most implacable opponents grudgingly acknowledged that things were improving; and, following an entertaining 2-0 defeat of Newcastle, something extraordinary happened. On the way to the pub after the game, I said to a mate, "That was great. I can't wait 'til next week." For a second, we fell silent to take in the enormity of the moment. For the first time in so long we wanted to come back after watching Spurs. We'd rediscovered the missing link - actually *enjoying* the game.

At a deserted Anfield on a November evening, we outclassed the worst Liverpool side I've ever seen to advance further in the Worthington. Just in front of where we stood, some of the loyal Scousers who did turn up provided the amusing sight of arguing with a gateman to let them out long before the final whistle.

There's nothing like having been down to make you take full advantage of others' misfortune when you're back on the up, as the wretched Pierre Van Hooijdonk found when, during a comfortable 2-0 disposal of Nottingham Forest, almost the entire Tottenham crowd informed him, "You're shit, and you've got no mates." An even greater joy, and surprise considering Graham's reputation, was the form of David Ginola. I will admit that, occasionally, he goes down a little too easily, but no genuine football fan can fail to appreciate his sheer class. It was a delight to see him week in, week out. In one interview, he said: "When you have the ability to beat someone with a football it becomes like a magnet. You want to do it again and again because it's fun." Like us, the players were rediscovering what football was really all about.

It kept getting better. In December, we became the only side in the world to prevent Manchester United winning a trophy, by beating an up-to-strength line-up 3-1 to reach the Worthington Cup semi-final. Even the suits in the West Stand stood and sang, and the particularly nasty hangover the next morning couldn't dull the sense of how great it was to be alive.

Beating Liverpool and drawing with Man United in our next two home league games proved our resurgence had substance and, following a five-goal spanking of Watford in the FA Cup, we embarked on a marathon against Wimbledon, playing them five times in a month, in a football version of *Groundhog Day*. By the time we put three past them in the FA Cup replay, we were sick of the sight of each other. Almost as sick, in fact, as Leeds fans were of George Graham. Inevitably, we got them in the FA Cup, away. With five cup-ties in Yorkshire that day, it made sense for the Highways Agency to close two lanes of the M1. We arrived, unfed and unwatered, outside Elland Road minutes before kick-off in the midst of an ugly atmosphere. A robust cup-tie saw us go ahead courtesy of a Tim Sherwood goal, before Ian Harte equalised with a superb strike. Outside was even worse than the way in, with two police horses caught in the middle of a massive punch-up, bits of wall flying through the air and police helicopters clattering overhead.

Finely poised in two cups, with Ginola, the majestic Sol Campbell, Carr, Walker and even Anderton in fine form, we entered the defining period of the season. First business was the Worthington semi. A win would take us to Wembley and, anticipating this, Tottenham swamped Selhurst and Norwood Junction. Unable to take a half-day, I arrived to meet the usual crew at about 6.30 to find astonishing scenes. Tottenham everywhere, pubs running out of beer, lots of singing and general upping of knees - I thought I'd missed the game and we'd already won. Thousands were there just to watch the game in the pubs or to taste the atmosphere.

It wasn't the best game of football ever. But who cares? Iverson's well-taken lob took us to Wembley, prompting emotional scenes and an old-fashioned pitch invasion to chair the players off at the whistle. We poured out of the ground eager to celebrate, but the police had closed every pub and the train station was running a reduced service. What should have been the conclusion of a night to remember instead petered out, as small groups of us hopped buses through the Godforsaken suburban wastelands of South London. I'd like to take this opportunity to thank the police and railways from the heart of my bottom.

The replay against Leeds was the best game of the season, with exciting football that was a pleasure to watch, and another excellent Ginola performance capped by a quite stunning goal. Then he bettered it against Barnsley in the next round, five days before the Worthington Final. Wembley may not be as fine a venue as some would have you believe but it still felt like coming home. The quality of the football was dreadful but the explosion of noise and emotion when Nielsen scored - so late we knew it was the winner - was something I'll remember for a long time.

Things had already been cranked up by Edinburgh's sending-off. Although foolish to raise his hand, Edinburgh was the victim of a blatant piece of cheating by Robbie Savage, who had been an advert for everything bad about football throughout. His reaction to Edinburgh's 'blow' came later than a Virgin train and was far, far worse than anything the oft-criticised Ginola had ever done. He deserved every bit of the vitriol unleashed on him by the Spurs support, but justice was done as we walked away with the cup and a place in Europe. With Wembley's witless selection of tunes preventing any real singing, we left to celebrate long into the night.

I remember returning to the Hilton, then leaving the curry house to clear my head, then getting lost. There was a message on my mobile from one of my mates saying, "We've won the cup. Where the fuck *are* you?" But I really don't remember how I got home.

League points were slipping through our fingers, but we had an Old Trafford semi-final against Newcastle to think of. Memories of our last, dreadful, FA Cup semi-final trip begun to resurface when the coach we'd booked didn't turn up, and we had to get 20 of us into cars and on the move at the last minute.

Tottenham's support, given three sides of the ground, was magnificent. A turning point came when, after a particularly fierce bit of touchline gesticulation by George, everyone of us sang "Georgie Graham's blue 'n' white army" (rather than "Man in the raincoat's...") for the first time. My previously hardline anti-George mate was reduced to pointing out that Graham's choice of brown shoes with a blue suit was a bit of a fashion crime.

Of course, it wasn't to end well for us. Campbell's uncharacteristic error was judged far more harshly than Dabizdas' identical offence, giving Newcastle the lead before a well-taken Shearer goal wrapped things up. Shamefully, many Spurs fans left early after that, refusing to clap off a team who had performed much better than the bunch who capitulated to Everton in our last semi. If we'd had a halfway decent striker, we would have won the game in the first-half, but we missed our chances. Newcastle weren't much of a team and, as fate would have it, the point was proved when a halfway decent striker who we sold to Man United and got fuck all for (thanks Al) destroyed them in the final. We would have given United more of a game, as we proved in the final Premiership game of the season when, unfortunately, we couldn't quite help our old mates at Highbury to get the title - even after they inflicted a gut-wrenching 3-1 defeat on us at White Hart Lane.

We finished the home campaign on a Monday evening - it doesn't seem quite right - by laying the Chelsea jinx to rest and finishing off their title hopes in the process. Another sublime goal from double Footballer of the Year Ginola helped ensure Chelsea would be the great pretenders they always have been for yet another year.

Maybe Graham will attempt to sneak in a vanload of centre-halves under cover of the close season, but we look unlikely to lose anyone due to a Chairman Al tantrum and, if we offload some of the inadequates who talk a better game than they play (you know who you are, Les), and make two or three intelligent signings, we should be looking at top six, a European run and maybe a trophy or two. With the joy of football rediscovered, by George, I think he's got it.

Martin Cloake

COMMUNITY SERVICE

AFC Bournemouth

"And don't think you'll be going *this* season," she said.

In fairness she had a point, of sorts. After all, only a week prior to the big kick-off she had delivered, with the sort of impeccable timing which would have once made Ted MacDougall proud, a first born. My personal contribution to the whole conception process - several pints of lager (easy on the lemonade top) and a bunch of battered roses picked up at Charing Cross by way of a romantic gesture - were, if memory serves me well, the prelude to considerably less than 90 minutes of duvet match action. Given my involvement, I really ought to have been planning trips

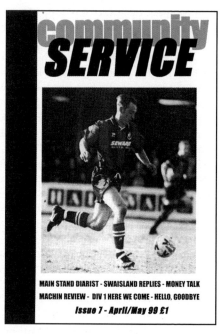

MAIN STAND DIARIST - SWAISLAND REPLIES - MONEY TALK
MACHIN REVIEW - DIV 1 HERE WE COME - HELLO, GOODBYE
Issue 7 - April/May 99 £1

to Mothercare and thrusting myself forward to join up with the Saturday morning coffee brigade. Tempting as cappuccino was, I reasoned that I'd done more than my fair share of thrusting a mere nine months earlier, and chose the much more demanding schedule of attending all 46 league games for the first time.

Onwards then to pre-season and expectations were, as with every other born optimist, remarkably high. Indeed, I'd predicted a top-six finish for Boscombe. Of course, I'd worked through the permutations of highs and lows that the play-offs might bring. On the one hand I'd decided I'd only want to get there if we were sure of getting through. On the other, I'd argued that losing the final at Wembley would ensure sufficient funds were raised to pay off the remaining debt, without incurring the additional expenditure required to survive in Division One. Without the benefit of a third hand it was difficult at the outset to predict how I'd cope with the emotions that losing out on sixth spot on the last day of the season - despite occupancy for the previous six months - would bring.

Prior to battle commencing, Mel Machin had delved into the transfer market to snap up the ageing pro (Mark Stein), the maverick Johnny Foreigner (Mohammed Berthe), and the discarded juveniles of the Premiership (Richard Hughes and Jason Tindall). Chairman TrevSpeak had, during a particularly expensive call to the premium-rate line, which "updated me on all the latest news from Dean Court, although we may pan it out, and we'll be starting the interview any minute now, if we can just string it out a few more minutes" enthused about Berthe having the hardest shot he'd ever seen, before raving (literally) about Tindall's ability to "ping passes over 20, 30, even 40 yards!" When you are easily excitable, such comment is bound to easily excite.

Such unbridled enthusiasm carried us through our opening few matches. First day visitors to Dean Court, Lincoln City, were dispatched with little ceremony. I had been uncertain of our chances when City turned up in the green and white hoops of Celtic, with heads dyed a collective blond, and several players sporting multi-coloured footwear. Teams who adopt such an approach in my local Sunday League tend to be either far too good for the rest of us, and therefore able to shrug off the pisstakes, or adopt such strategies to divert the opposition from their all-round lack of ability. Lincoln proved to be the latter, despite a more bruising second-half performance, which prevented Stein *et al* from building on a comfortable half-time lead.

Towards the end of the first month, we had remained unbeaten, culminating with a well-earned point at Fayedham. Post-match lagers (heavy on the lemonade top - I'd learnt my lesson) with the locals suggested our humble division had found another ManUre in the making. The wealthy ones put-down was that we weren't even in their league. Our retort that they'd be relegation fodder by the time they visited Dean Court went down less well than my five-pint imagination imagined it would do. Our escape was aided by the Fayedhams being temporarily distracted by a Michael Jackson lookalike, talking animatedly about the glory days of Johnny Haynes. As if.

The onset of Autumn brought the giddy excitement of cup football and a tie with the Wanderers of Wolverhampton in the League Cup. The board announced a voucher release for the forthcoming bank holiday fixture with our arch-rivals Blackpool. Well, arch-rivalry had apparently been detected by the local constabulary, who decreed that this violent disorder clash must be moved to the Tuesday night. The voucher issue was just in case the cup-tie became all-ticket, which it didn't. But it could have been, had anyone been brainwashed into believing it was Wolves circa 1956, with Billy Wright, and those sisters he used to knock around with, coming to town. Still, having dispatched McGhee's All Golds with a fine rearguard action in the second-leg, we were more than willing to play up their pedigree.

The following round brought an exit at the hands of Barnsley, and the commencement of a dismal run of form that saw us fail to win in seven outings. This included defeat at nine-man Bristol Rovers, solace from which came in a football cliché and a little applied logic. As it's always been harder to beat ten men, if a team loses two players they must become twice as hard to beat. So no wonder we lost. Given this particularly grim spell of form, there were those of us urging Machin to play with eight to test our theory further. He declined, and having decided Berthe wasn't up to the task, hard shot or not, brought in an unlikely couple of replacements. Roger Boli had pedigree: he had topped the goalscoring charts the previous year for Walsall and made the PFA divisional line-up. Daniel Rodrigues Fernandez was an unknown Portuguese U-18 starlet, snapped up on a three-month loan with first refusal rights secured (or so we were led to believe).

Remarkably, the return from injury of Steve Fletcher who, but for the limited number of clubs in his portfolio, can best be described as a journeyman footballer, saw a club record eight straight victories counteract the previous seven without a win. Meanwhile, Boli had picked up a calf strain and a Eurostar ticket, and wasn't seen at Dean Court for weeks. The starlet who had, by now, shortened his name to Danny, plus one of his two surnames, had yet to start a game. Machin was apparently convinced, though, and it was announced that he had signed a two-year deal. At the outset of the loan we'd been told the fee had been agreed at £100,000. Chairman TrevSpeak boasted how, on the advice of the Football League, the club had reneged on payment of the fee, but that due to the loan contract and retention of the player's registration, there was bugger all the Portuguese could do. Whilst TrevSpeak was throwing in a few Portuguese chairman impressions for good measure, the club were reminded by FIFA that we didn't have international clearance, that it was very rude to stick your tongue out at other's misfortune, and Danny would, in fact, remain the property of his former club. Until they sold him for £175,000 to Southampton a week later, that is. Nothing underhand there, then.

Despite all this, thanks largely to stoic defending and the goals of a very much in-form Mark Stein, Boscombe were well ensconced in the top six. Transfer deadline day and Easter were now looking like the crucial periods. The (partial) firesale of the outstanding left full-back in the division, Jamie Vincent, raised many an eyebrow. Vincent had been stretching away at the top of the goal-assist charts and a ready-made replacement, at such a crucial stage of the season, did not appear to be waiting in the wings. Instead we saw the arrival of William Huck, the third rejected Gunner to arrive in the year. Having sworn blind that the French experiment was at an end, following the Berthe and Boli debacles (and that's without boring you with the tale of Kadar Seydi), TrevSpeak was far more confident during initial negotiations with Huck. Remarking that no doubt William would like to retain his Dutch passport, so that one day he might make the Holland team, TrevSpeak was knocked sideways as the youngster remarked how pointless that would be, given he was French.

Nevertheless it appeared Machin was going to gamble on Gallic flair to ensure we rode into the play-off zone on the back of a string of thunderous attacking displays. Defeat at Northampton and the GillyLongBallers over Easter suggested otherwise, and Cautious Mel, having announced we would need no more than 76 points, replaced the flairs with drainpipes and sought to grind out eight goalless draws in the eight remaining fixtures. When we'd lost to Wigan in late February, Machin confidently predicted that we'd not be looking over our shoulders at them come the end of the season. And how right he was, as Wigan cleared the last hurdle to the play-offs, whilst we stumbled to a final goalless draw at home to a Wrexham side who had a greater desire for Boscombe to win than it appeared Boscombe did.

When you've been through receivership and you know that your club is still in need of debt clearance to ensure its long-term survival, seventh place might well seem an achievement in itself. My left hand reminded me that, perhaps, it was better after all not to get through to the play-offs and be faced with the sort of heartbreak faced by the GillyLongBallers at Wembley, while my right punched a wall in bitter disappointment.

At the season's end, I'd even missed out on hitting my 46-game target by a margin of six, largely as a result of compromising the likes of Oldham away with a trip around Tescos, pushchair in tow. Never before had football been so reminiscent of a young man's awakening teenage hobby. Whilst really looking forward to it all starting and enjoying it immensely at the time, afterwards there was a certain guilt and (in my case, due to the season's tearful last rites) damp tissues to dispose of. And, just like the teenager promises his mum he won't get caught doing it again, so I have promised to stay home next season. In order to get through the summer recess with relationship intact, I have even agreed to host a coffee morning and talk, at length and in a pleasant way, about the relative merits of breast over bottle and retractable car seats.

Now, *where's* that fixture list...

Jerry Tosswell

DERANGED FERRET

Lincoln City

Lincoln's fate in the '98-99 season was, like the previous two, not decided until the final game. That we'd kept the season going, if not exactly kicking, until the last act was something of a miracle. But our ultimate destiny was the one that had been predicted virtually from day one - relegation.

One win in the first eleven league games, including an incredible collapse from 3-1 up at home to Preston with 12 minutes left, only to lose 4-3, saw us floundering on the pitch. Off it as well, we were having problems. Shortly after the season started, chairman John Reames put the club up for sale. He had no serious response. A public meeting was called and, on the day, the local media reported the chairman as saying the club was close to being put into administration. A packed Centre Spot at Sincil Bank heard Reames say that would never happen whilst he was in charge, and admitting he had shot himself in the foot by making the announcement.

DERANGED FERRET

1998-99 SEASON

ISSUE 5. [No.43] PRICE: £1

A LINCOLN CITY FANZINE

STAYING UP OR GOING DOWN...

ALWAYS LOOK ON THE BRIGHT SIDE OF LIFE.

Lincoln City were, he said, losing around £1,000 a week, despite being the second lowest wage payers in the division. (One summer signing, however, was rumoured to be on £90,000 a year. Hardly surprising then that he was farmed out on loan and eventually sold for £65,000. At least he had come on a free!) Even by increasing admission prices from £10 to £13, a break-even attendance of around 5,500 was needed. But we only managed that six times in the league all season. Of course, as seems the norm at these crisis meetings, an impromptu whip-round was held and raised a couple of hundred pounds. Lincoln fans have not in recent years been noted for their generosity in giving money to the club, and with the chairman pledging not to let the club die whilst he was in charge, perhaps the seriousness of the situation wasn't fully appreciated. One positive to come out of the meeting was a promise that if the supporters could raise £25,000, we would be allowed a representative on the board. So, after several further public meetings, Impetus was born.

On the pitch, an exciting 3-2 win at Notts County brought our first away success, and only our second win of the season. Was it to be the start of a revival? No, as we lost four of the next five, seeing us go bottom of the table. The stormy 2-1 defeat at Walsall spelt the end of manager Shane Westley and his assistant Wally Downes. But instead of an experienced manager, the replacement was none other than chairman John Reames himself, following in the footsteps of Michael Knighton and Ron Noades as a chairman/manager. The popular Phil Stant was to carry on in the coaching role he had held under Westley, but team selection was down to Reames.

At least he got off to a positive start, with a 1-0 win in a tricky FA Cup tie at Cheltenham, and then oversaw a 4-1 thrashing of Stevenage in round two. The after-match press conference for the latter game produced the amazing comment from Stevenage manager Paul Fairclough that Lincoln had been very lucky and, "...apart from the four goals, Stevenage had been the better team." Even his own local media were apparently struggling to keep a straight face as he spoke. In the league, home form improved, as did the style of play. Out of the window went the long-ball method preferred by most previous City managers, but away from home we were abysmal. We even had the farcical situation of Bruce Grobelaar signing for the Imps... farcical, because he stayed two games at who knows what cost; and for the second, at Wycombe (he let in four), the club apparently weren't sure if he would turn up, and had to arrange for John Vaughan to travel down with the team to make sure we had a recognised goalkeeper.

Our two cup wins earned us the reward of a home tie with Sunderland but a freak early goal saw an unimpressive Wearside team go through. Impetus, after being on the receiving end of some stick from the chairman for promising much but delivering nothing, handed over its first cheque, for £12,000. Only about 100 City fans had bothered to join. Apathy rules... or perhaps the fact that watching football, with all the costs like food, programmes, souvenirs, etc, on wages that most people earn in Lincolnshire means that finding an extra £50 to join a movement like Impetus just wasn't an option. On the same day, the club announced the extended loan signings of Tottenham pair Neale Fenn and Peter Gain until the end of the season. On paper, this seemed an exciting move. In reality, Gain was used as a sub a couple of times, yet we signed him for £15,000; whilst Fenn, despite Reames describing him as the most skilful player at the club, fared less well and was probably on the pitch for no more than 20 minutes over the rest of the season. "Learning about Lincoln City discipline" was the reason trotted out for not using him. The rumour amongst fans was that he had turned up late for a game, and generally had an attitude problem, so Reames wouldn't pick him.

One defeat in seven league games in late December/January and early February saw us climb out of the bottom four and even start to dream of Wembley in the Auto Windscreen, until we lost on a goalden goal at home to Wrexham. Even worse, was the fact it was an own-goal that did us. Still, we bounced back with only our second away win of the season, at Blackpool, and in the process scored our first goal at Bloomfield Road since the 1913/14 season. It didn't herald an upturn in our fortunes away from Sincil Bank, as we lost the next five away games: 5-0 at Preston, 1-0 at Fulham, 4-0 at Gillingham, 2-0 at Stoke (who had lost their previous six home games) and 4-0 at Manchester City.

Since Reames had taken over, we hadn't lost at home in the league, and only this was keeping us in with a chance of survival. Unfortunately, fortress Sincil Bank was breached at the wrong time as York won a crucial six-pointer on a Sunday in March (their first win in eleven). Strangely, when they had beaten us at Bootham Crescent earlier in the season it was their first win in twelve. If you're on a bad run, look forward to playing Lincoln City. The York defeat was followed by visitors Notts County beating us on Easter Monday.

With twelve games to go, Reames had said five wins would ensure we stayed up. With six to play, we still needed five wins. One came at Luton, where we won for the first time since 1900, but two more defeats meant three wins out of our final three games were the only hope we had of staying up. Even then it needed others to mess up. Win one came at Colchester where, as we were walking back to the car, some of their fans came up to us and said we were the best team that had been there this season. Not many other supporters would have said that of the '98-99 Imps. A grim Tuesday night battle with Wrexham saw a last-minute winner. Which brings us to where we started... the final game.

Lincoln had to win, Northampton and Oldham had to lose. To add spice, we were playing Wycombe. If they won, they were safe - as long as either Northampton. Oldham and York lost. Two early Oldham goals killed us off; Wycombe's late winner saved them.

The season ended with us still up for sale and no buyer in sight. We've still no proper manager, as Reames has announced his intention to carry on in the role next season. Impetus has been absorbed into a new membership scheme. And possibly the cruellest blow of all was the fact that Scunthorpe got promoted via the play-offs. Still, optimism reigns supreme, we've had a taste of the higher division and maybe, come May 2000, we'll be celebrating promotion again.

Gary Parle

DRIBBLE!

Ipswich Town

Oh no, not the play-offs

I am writing this article before the Division One play-off final. I was hoping to write it after a Wembley win, but for the third year running, we ended up losing in the play-off semi-finals.

The season started with plenty of hope. The previous season's team was kept almost intact and the division looked weaker than the season before. Ipswich fans knew this was our last chance of keeping young stars like Richard Wright and Kieron Dyer. The club lost one Dutchman, to Fulham, and acquired one more Dutchman from the continent.

We started the season in our

December 98   ISSUE 53

50p

DRiBBLE!

The Ipswich Fanzine

MID SEASON SALE

usual slow way - not that anyone was bothered, after the previous two years. We started to put some results together, and then came a Saturday night game at home to Sunderland. Those who turned up, or watched on Sky, soon saw that Sunderland were the team to beat. The defeat seemed to be the boost the Town needed and we soon found ourselves in the top six. The only blip along the way was a League Cup defeat by Luton. But just as we found ourselves in position to push Sunderland at the top, we sold three players. The first, Danny Sonner, was expected, as he had broken manager George Burley's strict disciplinary code. The fee from Sheffield Wednesday may have been small but was OK for a player we had got free from a German Fourth Division side. The shock was that he left us as a squad player and ended up as a first team regular at Wednesday. The next departure, Alex Mathie, was not a popular one with the fans. Alex was a great favourite all over the town and had placed himself up with the favourites of the '62,'78 and '81 teams after his hat-trick the previous season against the scum up the road. For those who could look more rationally at it, it seemed a good fee from Dundee United for an injury-prone player, who needed first team football. The next transfer caused the most uproar, as Mauricio Taricco was sold to Spurs.

The fee seemed too small for a player who had been the star of the team over the last two seasons. What made it worse was that as well as the fans loving Taricco, he also loved them; and it was obvious he did not want to go. Other ill feeling was caused by the fact that the chief scout at Spurs, Charlie Woods, had only just left the Town after almost 30 years on the coaching staff. This transfer even led to attacks on chairman David Sheepshanks in the local paper, almost unheard of before. In the end, Taricco was not missed as much as we thought he would be, mainly by the superb form of the remainder of the defence. Tony Mowbray found a season clear of injury, and Mark Venus had an outstanding campaign. Jamie Clapham ended his first full season at the club as the Player of the Year, and there was the arrival of two outstanding (and at bargain price) continentals, Manuel Thetis and Fabian Wilnis. The player most missed was Alex Mathie, as injuries to both Scowcroft and Johnson forced Burley to hit the loan trail again. Samassi Abou and Marlon Harewood were the replacements. Both tried hard, but in the end we only had a couple of goals to remember them by - and Marlon will want to forget his open-goal miss that made the top three misses in the Sky end of season poll.

After Christmas, we started our usual run of good form, and after a narrow and dubious defeat at Everton in the FA Cup, we could concentrate on chasing Sunderland. We had to rush both Scowcroft and Johnson back but were still not scoring like in the previous two seasons. This did not matter so much, as new first team coach Stewart Houston had really got the defence organised - and the team would end the season with a club record of clean sheets. By the time we had our return game at the Stadium of Light, it was obvious that Sunderland were already up but the performance we delivered in the north-east showed we could match them on our day. The trouble was our home form: silly defeats to the likes of Grimsby and Barnsley, and the last-minute defeat to Bolton, would cost us dear. These slip-ups coincided with the departure of Houston to Spurs. This again caused trouble as it seemed Spurs had not been above board with their approaches to him. Houston was quickly replaced by John Gorman. This saw the town return to a more attacking style and led to our best display of the season, a big away win at Swindon. It set up a two-horse race between ourselves and Bradford City. Bradford were the shock team of the division, alongside Watford. It was obvious they were serious as, to boost their hopes, they spent yet more millions to bring in Oxford's Dean Windass, as well as Lee Sharpe on loan. Meanwhile, we lost the influential Dyer to a broken leg against Watford. This forced the board's hand and Jim Magilton was brought in from Sheffield Wednesday. He was much needed, and scored a cracking winner against Stockport. Both Ipswich and Bradford kept dropping stupid points but we were still in the driving seat until the, unbelievable, home defeat by Crewe. This led to the last game of the season, and us relying on Wolves beating City. We accounted for Sheffield United after a shaky start, but Wolves let it slip; and it was Bradford who deserved their promotion. This leads me back to where I started, the bloody play-offs. We played Bolton - and lost. The second-leg was outstanding, and at least we have now won a play-off game - our first in eight. But it was our home form where we lost it during the season, even though we were not helped by a dodgy ref in the game at Bolton, where we should have had a penalty. So where do we go now?

As I say, I'm writing this before the Play-off Final, whilst we still have all our players. Dyer is now on the list, with Leeds the favourites. If we get the seven million we are asking for, that should be enough to get the bank manager smiling - and let George spend a bit. Richard Wright would be a bigger loss, and he has just been named in the full England squad. Playing in the First Division won't harm his chances. If anything he is better off playing for us than sitting on some Premier club's bench. David Johnson has always made it clear he wants to play at the top, but he may have shot himself in the foot by choosing to play for Jamaica. Holland and Scowcroft may also be tempted to leave, but I think we can keep most of the squad together; and we have some more Suffolk-born youngsters waiting in the wings, Richard Logan and Titus Bramble the pick of the bunch. The league itself will be stronger next year, with two rich clubs - Fulham and Blackburn - joining from opposite directions. Charlton and Man City will be a threat, along with Wolves, Birmingham and the new moneybags club, Huddersfield. But at least we should make the play-offs. Off the pitch, we also saw the death of Alf Ramsey. The thing I found strange was all the attention his death brought - whereas I, as an Ipswich fan, didn't feel too much. I think it was the way he ignored Bobby Robson. Ramsey was a private man and, unlike Robson, didn't do much in the local community. It may also because I am too young to remember the '62 Championship team. All the same, it was appropriate that Ipswich Town announced his death, and there is talk of a statue of him being built at the ground, alongside one of Robson. Actually, I think they should build one at the new Wembley. Chairman David Sheepshanks may not have delivered Premiership football to the town, but he has got the club on an even keel financially and the club is now a real part of the community. And now... only 367 days to the next play-off final.

Alasdair Ross

Sonner set to lose "Ipswich Reserve" tag as sponsored motor is delivered

Source: War of the Monster Trucks

EVERYWHERE WE GO

Nottingham Forest

"It couldn't get any worse than this" - a simple sentence, first heard echoing around the streets of Nottingham in early August 1998. It is a phrase which conjures up feelings of despair, and a sign that a situation has generally reached its lowest ebb. Sadly, these seven words would be repeated with frightening regularity during the following months. Welcome to our *annus horribilis* (again!).

The writing was on the wall before a ball was even kicked, as we became the first club to actually weaken its squad following promotion to the Premiership. First up were the reigning Double winners and their line-up of World Cup stars. Forest meanwhile handed a debut to Glynn Hodges, and our previous season's 57-goal strike-force were highly conspicuous by their absence. The following day saw the news that inspirational captain Colin Cooper would, like Kevin Campbell, be plying his trade away from the City Ground. Meanwhile, Pierre Van Stroppydonk decided that the best way to earn his keep would be to remain in Holland and sulk. Apparently Forest wouldn't provide the right kind of conditioner for his hair, or something. The first home game would, therefore, happily coincide with the first protest against the board.

A steady slide down the table saw us begin October with a 'must win' game against Charlton. Of course, we didn't - and so began our permanent residence in the bottom three of the Premiership. That prolific hernia-carrying marksman Neil Shipperley was brought in to bolster the non-existent strike-force, and a visit to Anfield saw the first serious drubbing of the year. It would not be the last. As the cold, icy, autumnal winds blew across the North Sea, Pierre began to shiver in Breda and so decided a return to the tropical climes of the East Midlands was in order. He needn't have bothered. The orchestra had changed but we were still playing the same tune. Sometimes we played well, sometimes we were unlucky, sometimes we were awful, but the distinct lack of victories remained consistent.

A miserable Christmas saw the return of the 'post-match car park protest' ritual, and things appeared to come to a head with an early cup exit to struggling Portsmouth. "It couldn't get any worse than this" was uttered once again, and the calls for the manager and the board to go were long and loud. Manager Dave

everywhere we go

An Independent Nottingham Forest Fanzine

Issue #4   February 1999

WRAY, SCHOLAR, SOAR...

WHERE'S THE MONEY GONE
SACK THE BOARD

TIME TO GO!

We want OUR Forest back

£1   SACK THE BOARD SPECIAL

Bassett went; sadly the board remained and, in their wisdom, appointed a manager who at this time of crisis was topping up his already golden tan in the Caribbean. Welcome aboard, Big Ron - wish you were here.

Sitting in Coventry, having opposing fans (quite justifiably) enquiring exactly what it was like to be outclassed, led many to believe once again that it "couldn't get any worse than this". Big Ron finally put in an appearance and it was only a matter of seconds before he had the Forest crowd cringing once more, as he marched straight past the Forest bench and promptly sat himself down in the Arsenal dug-out. Maybe he was jet-lagged. In just two weeks, though, he delivered the first Forest success since August, with a win at Everton. Was this the beginning of the miracle, the fightback and the surge up the table? Er... no.

In early February, with confidence rising, Manchester United came to town and delivered one of the darkest days in Forest's history. At 4-1 down, the majority of the crowd had accepted defeat and were making their way back over Trent Bridge. The news that greeted them as they returned to their respective cars, pubs and homes was devastating. We had ended up losing 8-1 at home. Irrespective of the opposition, this was low. We would find ourselves sitting uncomfortably in the record books and be the laughing stock of the football world. Could it get any worse than this?

Following this humbling experience, the final march towards relegation was now a formality and most people's eyes were on which game would actually see us put out of our misery. Performances were uninspired, as teams came and went, taking an easy three points and hardly having to break sweat in the process. It was a tactic Pierre Van Hooijdonk was attempting to use but without the same degree of success. The board tried to hasten our departure from the top flight by selling Steve Stone and Scott Gemmill, and an Easter rising saw the dissenters once again return to the car park to politely voice their constructive criticism to the powers that be. Thankfully, results meant that our inaugural visit to Gay Pride Park could not result in the final nail being driven into the coffin. It did, however, provide one last chance for some semblance of Forest pride to be restored. Pierre Van Hooijdonk managed to win back some favour from the fans by putting a Derby defender in hospital early on with creative use of his elbow. However, a late strike from the sheep left their fans bleating and left us once again considering if it were possible to feel any worse.

Relegation was finally confirmed at Villa Park at the end of April, and was greeted in the now traditional Forest style, with an all-singing, all-dancing carnival atmosphere, celebrating the fact that the year of crap we'd been through was now almost at an end. The party continued right through to the end of the season, and our ability to win meaningless games meant that we actually finished the year as the Premiership's form team. Big Ron clearly enjoyed his Forest experience so much that he decided to quit football; and the boardroom wrangling continued, threatening to drag on long into the summer.

In the past, older supporters have always referred to the early Seventies as being the darkest days for Forest. Now they are beginning to change their tune, and the end of the Twentieth Century is quickly becoming a time to forget. As for the new Millennium... well it couldn't get any worse, could it?

Ed Shirbon

EXILED

AFC Bournemouth

I have to admit, it hardly seems like twelve months since I sat down to pen the season's review for *SOTF4*, but here we are with *SOTF5*.

So, you've no doubt been asking, "What's been going on down in sunny Bournemouth?" I thought you'd never ask. In response, I'd have to say it has not been a dull year at all for one reason or another; ranging from progress in the cups, excitement (and tedium) in the league, and progress towards the new stadium.

In the run-up to the season, most of us thought the club had committed a dreadful mistake in signing Mark Stein on a permanent move from Chelsea. You may

EXILED

THE OFFICIAL MAGAZINE OF THE
AFC BOURNEMOUTH EXILES CLUB

SCOTLAND v NORTHERN IRELAND
OUR INTERNATIONAL STARS!!

NON-MEMBERS £2   SPRING EDITION 1999

recall he joined us for a loan spell towards the end of the previous season, which had been less than successful, so to have him back did not appeal. But give him credit, he scored against Lincoln City, as did Ian Cox, in a comfortable opening day win. Making his debut in this game was Mohammed Berthe, a tall Frenchman whose stay at the club was thankfully brief - more on him later. With the opening three games all ending in victory, we found ourselves sitting in second place following a home draw against a well-organised Blackpool side. Unfortunately we never quite reached the giddy heights of second for the rest of the campaign.

Having played Fulham ten days earlier, we then had to tackle the two most difficult away games of the year - Stoke City and Manchester City in three days. Thanks, Football League. A creditable draw against Fulham, defeat at Stoke (why do these new grounds have to be so far out of town?) and at Maine Road was the outcome. League action was replaced with a Worthy Cup encounter against Wolves over two legs. Having been held to a draw at Dean Court, we managed to edge out Wolves at Molineux in a gripping game in which goalkeeper Ovendale was outstanding and little Mark "Like, you know..." Stein popped up to snatch the winner. The victory was put down (in part) to the club publicising the team selection on the official website beforehand. Checks were made to see whether Wolves had 'hit' the site to see that we were fielding a weakened side, and once confirmation had been received that they had visited the site, the real team was then posted. Nice one – and a change for us to out-fox (out-Wolf?) our opponents. Victory against Oldham four days later was the last for seven games as we slipped down to 11th in the table. That period wasn't without incident. Since Pulis left and joined Gillingham, taking a few ex-Bournemouth players with him, and seemingly turning the entire Gills side into a bunch of hired thugs intent on kicking their way to three points at every opportunity, there has not been a great deal of love lost between the two clubs. I don't know why, as I have never had any problems in Gillingham, or seen any down here. But on the pitch there's always a bit of needle - and this game was no exception as it ebbed and flowed to a 3-3 draw (we had to equalise in the dying seconds to secure the point). The next league match saw us up against our nearest and dearest from Berkshire - Reading. In the past we've trudged up to stand out in the open at Elm Park, but no more. What a fantastic new stadium they've got these days. Pity they finished it and opened it without any proper access road. Whoever planned this one must have been drunk at the time; or maybe this is a characteristic of Berkshire planning. Who knows? Whatever, it took nearly 90 minutes to get from south of the M4 to within spitting distance of the ground. The service inside is equally slow. Haven't they got to pay for the stadium?

Again, another great game of football, as 2,508 travelling fans out-sung the home faithful, and Bournemouth fought their way back from 3-1 down to another 3-3 draw. Yep - another last-gasp equaliser, this time from a Mark Stein penalty. The locals were not happy at all as we shouted and sung the praises of the lads - a thoroughly deserved point, methinks. This game was also graced by Mohammed Berthe, who was playing wide right - not wide right enough, which unfortunately meant that he was actually inside the stadium and on the pitch. On his day, he could be quite good and, on another, absolute crap. Today, he was the latter. In one sweeping move, the ball was fed out to him. He moved forward, his gangly legs taking him on. Getting to the bye-line was fine, but the delicate cross to the far post? Well, to say that the cross almost landed in Oxfordshire is an understatement. The final straw for all of us came two weeks later in the FA Cup, against Basingstoke. The non-leaguers of the Ryman Premier couldn't believe their luck having such a player against them. He couldn't keep hold of, or control the ball and was substituted before half-time. Funnily enough he's not played for us again, and was shipped off to (and just as quickly out of) Hearts before transfer deadline day.

Into December, and an away win against Torquay saw the mighty Cherries embark on a record run of eight straight wins, which took us firmly back in to the play-off places and into the third round of the cup against the Baggies. Much was made of this game, as the country's two leading scorers were pitted against each other (Mark Stein and Lee Hughes). For a First Division side, West Brom weren't up to much, and defender Eddie Howe finished off a well-worked corner routine to score the game's only goal.

The first league match of 1999 took us off to Lincoln City on a damp and cold Saturday morning. Lincoln bottom and Bournemouth fifth – an away win, surely? No, of course not. On the ground where we notched up our heaviest-ever defeat (0-9) way back in the Eighties, we managed to lose 2-1. One thing that did surprise me was the Sincil Bank pitch markings. I hadn't realised that the Football League allowed pitches to be systematically scarred. Needless to say, we slipped to defeat. The only consolation of the day? Their bacon butties - fantastic - and being able to accuse the opposition of being a bunch of 'Newarks' (work it out for yourself). A fine home win against Notts County seven days later (Cox and Stein the scorers) led us nicely into the fourth round of the FA Cup. For the second time this year we traipsed up to Barnsley (having already rolled over and gifted them a Worthy Cup win back in October). This time we did slightly better - we scored. But still ended up with two more being put past Mark Ovendale.

Next up at Dean Court were Preston North End. At the time, Preston were going great and looked as if they were playing some terrific football (given the limited amount of highlights on Sky/Meridian). So we were expecting a tough encounter. I have to admit I was surprised when they only started to play once we were three goals to the good. The result took us back up to fifth - and serious questions were being asked about automatic promotion.

For me, one of the best games I saw during the season was the home match against Stoke City in February. Not because we played them off the park, for a four-goal win, but the way in which we played. The passing movement was just superb, as was the amount of work coming from the players. All this from a team depleted because of injury. Roger Boli started his first game in absolutely ages in place of Mark Stein, who had picked up a virus infection during the week. He, in customary fashion, got himself injured within the first quarter of an hour, and on came Jamie Hayter, one of the up and coming youngsters at Dean Court. He worked his socks off - and scored a good goal to go with it as well. The Stoke keeper obviously thought that someone so young would never get past him, but cool, calm and collected, Hayter neatly side-footed the ball past his man for it to nestle in the bottom far corner of the net.

Seven days later, we entertained Manchester City to a 0-0 draw at Dean Court. The game was livened up enormously when Pollock (renamed Pillock) got himself sent off for yet another disgusting challenge on John Bailey, and Horlock for alleged "aggressive walking". The way the ref reacted, I thought Horlock might have said something in passing - but aggressive walking it was, and who am I to argue with a newark of a referee. (Ah, *now* you've worked it out.)

One thing about the fixture list is that there are games you can pick out and say with some measure of confidence "We'll beat them"; or "Oh well, we've not beaten them in years". So when it's time for us to play Bristol Rovers, you can usually guarantee three points to the home team. The Bristol clubs must hate Bournemouth, as they never seem to do that well against us. So it's a big welcome back to Division Two for Bristol

City. As for Rovers - we won, this year by a solitary Eddie Howe goal. Then disaster struck, bloody Reading came and spoiled our unbeaten home record, winning 1-0. They, of course, went home quite happy, having gained revenge for us nicking a point at their place.

One of the highlights of the season came during the home match against Colchester United in March. OK, we won 2-1, but to see ex-player (and incredibly fat) Warren Aspinall crumple in a heap, having received a hefty blow to the bollocks, from an attempted punt forward by Christer Warren was absolutely hilarious. Not to mention the miracle that Warren found such a small target.

In putting this together, I have been umming and arring over what to say about the televised game against Gillingham. Having been unable to get away from work in time, I managed to persuade a pub in Portsmouth (where I live) to do the decent thing and show the game. We went one up from a nice Steve Robinson glancing header, one of 16 goals he scored. But what I saw from Gillingham when they'd had enough of playing 'pretty football' was disgusting. Never in all my days of watching professional football have I seen a worse display of pure thuggery from a team of professional footballers. Anyone who watched the match would have winced at the leg-breaking tackles that Gillingham were getting away with. Unfortunately, we couldn't match their physical style and eventually lost 1-2. In complete contrast, Walsall came to Dean Court three days later, played football how it should be played and deserved to win through a marvellous Wrack goal. Thoroughly deserved.

The last five games of the season were highly frustrating as we dropped points left, right and centre - this from a team in the top six for most of the season. We just could not score to save our lives, let alone win. We chalked up a success at York City - but no-one else seemed up for it.

Players who had signed new and extended contracts appeared to become complacent, confidence disappeared and Wigan caught up an incredible number of points from seven games in 15 days to nick the last play-off place from under our very noses. After that game I sent off a number of e-mails to their various websites to congratulate them on their achievement. Thanks for the replies, guys - appreciated (why did you sack your manager?).

In summary: gutted we lost out in the end - very disappointing - but not as disappointing as losing a play-off final at Wembley on penalties. In the final analysis, we have finished the last five seasons under Mel Machin with more points and in a higher league position than the previous year. If that's not progress, then I don't know what is. So for next season, it has to be "Up those Cherries" - and with backing from Bournemouth Borough Council, which (it has to be said) is long overdue, there is every reason to be optimistic that work on the stadium development project will start early in the New Year - and not before time. But that's another story - probably for *SOTF6*.

Andy Burton

Scunthorpe United

As a certain national team coach discovered this season, talking about your personal beliefs can be dangerous, but here goes anyway. I believe that there's a higher power 'up there', among whose duties is arranging for football matches to have the most dramatically satisfying outcome. In ten years as a Scunthorpe United fan, this belief has been tested many times, but it's held firm.

At the start of the season, the omens looked good. It was the club's 100th year of existence, and surely that would count for something with the Scriptwriter in the Sky. What's more, *Fe* had finally gone from a vague idea to a fully-fledged fanzine. On the playing side, the team that

Brian Laws' long lost brother found

See inside for more details

Fe

56
26

Issue three   Price 50p

had narrowly missed out on a play-off place the year before had been strengthened by the addition of John Gayle, who could help us kick our way out if all else failed.

Such was the pre-season optimism that a 2-1 defeat in the first match was hailed as proof that we were bucking our recent trend of a brilliant start, then downhill for the rest of the season. After winning the second match (at which *Fe* was launched to general indifference) we were eighth in the opening league table. Later that week, I left the country. I felt slightly guilty for deserting the Iron, but it seemed that my absence did them good. I returned to find them in second place after three straight wins. A fortnight later, for the first time in my Iron-supporting life, I tasted the heady joy of going top.

Ten years of supporting Scunthorpe have taught me to enjoy these pleasures, since they never last. I fully expected them to come unstuck, and they did so in style, with a 4-0 defeat. A succession of draws and defeats convinced me that we'd had our chance and lost it, and we'd have to settle for a play-off place. But no, we got another chance to go top in October - and we took it, despite doing our best impression of a charitable foundation (4-0 up with 20 minutes to go; final score 4-3).

The first round of the FA Cup sent us to Woking, and the second issue of *Fe* went on sale before a fairly comfortable 1-0 win. Could it be that selling fanzines brought the Iron luck? A victory in the next game, with *Fe* still on sale, lent weight to this theory, but the quality of the opposition (Woking and Hull) tended to cast a bit of doubt. The second round pitted us against the lamb dogs of

Bedlington (just look at their club emblem), who had already humiliated Colchester. We won through comfortably, no thanks to Darryn Stamp, whose open-goal miss will probably give Iron fans nightmares for years to come.

Our league form, meanwhile, was starting to look decidedly dodgy. We hadn't won away in months, and a home defeat against leaders Cardiff set us up for a pretty rough Christmas. But obviously turkey agrees with the Scunny players, because after Christmas we did nothing but win in the league all through January. Or maybe the signing of Andy Dawson and the replacement of Tim Clarke with Tom Evans had more to do with it.

In the third round of the cup, meanwhile, faith in the Scriptwriter in the Sky was shaken once again. We were playing Wrexham, who had undeservedly knocked us out two years ago. If everyone had read the script, this was our chance for revenge. Allowing Wrexham to score three goals was probably not part of the plan, but the dramatic fightback that saw us level the scores with minutes to go was surely the perfect way to catch the Scriptwriter's attention. Last minute, a Scunny player brought down in the area - penalty and a famous victory for the Iron? Sadly, the referee hadn't read the script. He waved play on, and while the Scunny players struggled to believe it, Wrexham went down the other end and scored.

OK, Mr Scriptwriter. You get one more chance. Give us promotion in dramatic circumstances, and I'll believe in you. Revitalised - who cares how? - and without the distraction of the cup, we climbed back up the league, reaching second spot in mid-January. Then February happened.

Don't ask me what it is with February and Scunthorpe United. If we're going to have a month when we lose every match and sack our manager, you can put money on it being February. A 0-0 draw against Cambridge, immediately above us, was all that brightened the proceedings; plus of course, the knowledge that we'd got the month finished with Lawsy still in a job. Even selling the third issue of *Fe* failed to prevent defeat at home to Rochdale.

With the mid-season slump behind us, we tried to put right some of the damage. By Easter, we had climbed back to fourth, the top play-off spot, but couldn't seem to regain an automatic promotion place. Remembering what my absence had done for the Iron at the beginning of the season, I decided to spend Easter in Germany. It didn't have such a dramatic effect this time. Scunny remained just within reach of third place, and I returned just in time for our last throw of the dice. If we could beat Cardiff, we could snatch their promotion place. We chose this moment to hit a goal drought, and could only manage a goalless draw.

We went into the last match knowing we couldn't finish any higher than fourth, or any lower than fifth. The fans were all concentrating on a burning issue that would be settled that day: would Lincoln City be relegated? They were, which lent some enjoyment to an otherwise dismal day. We lost 1-0, and dark predictions abounded as to how badly we would fare in the play-offs.

Despite this and a 5:30am start, hundreds of fans made the journey down to Swansea for the first leg. Balloons, jesters hats, and even the odd inflatable sheep were also at the Vetch Field, but the Iron's performance was disappointing. Swansea scored from a free-kick, while we were still disputing it, and although we piled on the pressure, we couldn't seem to equalise. In fact, Tim Clarke, back in goal for no readily obvious reason, had to pull off several saves to keep the score at 1-0.

So, at least we knew what we had to do in the second-leg. Something we hadn't managed in four games: score. But if we, as fans, could help at all by turning up in numbers and making as much noise as possible, we were determined to do so. I had forgotten my ultimatum to the Scriptwriter, and turned up half-expecting a defeat. But, within a minute of the kick-off, Andy Dawson levelled the tie and restored my faith.

After this promising start, nothing happened for 90 minutes. Well, both sides had some shots on goal, and my fingernails became bloody stubs, but nothing that affected the promotion challenge. Our newest hope, Gareth Sheldon, came on as substitute towards the final whistle, and my kid sister predicted he'd score a hat-trick. But he failed to do so before the 90 minutes were up, and the tie went into extra-time.

Within a minute of the restart, Sheldon gave us an aggregate lead. When the hugging and cheering had died down, we all began to wish that Sheldon had scored two minutes earlier, or that the goalden goal applied in the play-offs. There was nothing we could do but offer up prayers to whoever was listening that the Iron could hold out. Then, Swansea scored. For a moment, we collectively refused to believe the ball had crossed the line. Then, slowly, the implications sank in. I'll come clean and confess: it was only the fact that I was already wrung dry that stopped me bursting into tears. Swansea had got an away goal. Once again, the Scriptwriter had kicked us in the teeth.

But I had underestimated the Scriptwriter's sense of drama, Scunny's resilience and Gareth Sheldon. Again, within a couple of minutes of the restart, he restored our lead. This time, in spite of having John Eyre sent off for a second booking, we managed to hang on. The dying seconds, knowing that at any moment we could seal our trip to Wembley - or have it cruelly snatched from us, set a new standard in tension, against which everything else will now be judged. But the final whistle delivered us. We swarmed the pitch, already dreaming of a day out beneath the Twin Towers.

Not wanting to take any more risks, the Scriptwriter made sure everyone knew what was expected for the final. The sun blazed down and the Scunny fans, despite being outnumbered by the Orient contingent by about two to one, created a fantastic atmosphere. When the match was only seven minutes old, Alex Calvo-Garcia, my choice of player of the season, got on the end of a cross from Sheldon and put us into the lead. Now all we had to do was hang on for another 83 minutes!

And that was just about what we did. We had a few chances to extend our lead and win in style, and we had a few scares, especially second-half. But we held out, and for the first time in our history, we had won at Wembley to earn promotion.

As the fans began their long journey home, the heavens opened with a spectacular thunderstorm. Most people thought it was just ordinary weather, but I knew better. It was a final theatrical flourish from the Scriptwriter in the Sky, letting me know that he'd done Scunthorpe United proud at last.

Nick Kiddle

FLASHING BLADE

Sheffield United

If I were to tell you that a football club could, in less than two years, lose four managers, two assistant-managers, a chairman, three chief executives, the club physio, the club kit man, the company secretary and the commercial manager, and that directors would be threatening to sue each other, you'd think I was either having you on or writing a script for a new football-based soap series.

But honestly, it's true. Has a football club ever experienced such a turnover of high-profile non-playing staff in such a short space of time?

And just to add a bit of spice to it all, towards the end of the '98-99 season, Sheffield United plc chairman Carlo Colombotti issued a writ against fellow director and largest shareholder Mike McDonald and two other directors for "conduct detrimental to the football club".

WAS IT GOODBYE OR MERELY AU REVOIR? No.66 May 1999
Amid threats, writs and accusations, don't rule out a return to the helm for Mike McDonald

Let's try and ease you through it, although I can't be sure I've got everything in exact chronological order. In the summer of 1997, Howard Kendall decided he would like to go and manage Everton again (daft bugger) and took his assistant Viv Busby with him. At this point, nobody was particularly concerned as, despite his leading United to the play-off final at Wembley, fans were a bit fed-up with Kendall's 'conservative' (i.e. boring) style of play; and when Nigel Spackman, who had impressed everybody with his care of the club immediately after Kendall's departure, was appointed full-time, things appeared to be looking up.

We had signed returning hero Brian Deane and Paul McGrath, who, despite being 38, made everybody marvel at what a player he must have been ten years earlier. A 12-game unbeaten start to the '97-98 season ensued as Spackman's side played the best football we had seen since John Harris' team of the early Seventies.

However, there were undercurrents of unrest, most of them emanating from the perceived meddling in team affairs of chief executive Charles Green. A host of letters to the local sports paper even accused Green of picking the team. United then sold Carl Tiler and Mitch Ward to Everton, when neither of them wanted to leave, and tried to offload Gareth Taylor to a number of clubs, with the player himself not having a clue what was going on. Supporters suspected the work of Mr Green. Things came to a head during and after a post-Christmas match at home to Charlton. Blades fans chanted Taylor's name throughout the game, while in a live after-match interview on Sky, Spackman was clearly and visibly frustrated and angry at the prospect of having his team pulled from under him.

In mid-January 1998 came the bombshell, as United sold Deane and Jan Aage Fjortoft on the same day. At an away match at Loftus Road, a few weeks later, Blades fans sang, "Charles Green, he sells the team, Charles Green, he sells the team!"

The natives were getting restless; they weren't the only ones. In early March, Spackman resigned, feeling unable to do his job in the face of the interference from above. The next game was at home to Ipswich, where a pre-match demonstration in the Bramall Lane car park ended with the resignation of chairman Mike McDonald, who stated that if the fans didn't want him, he wouldn't stay.

The team's promotion drive faltered and eventually stalled in the first round of the play-offs, while over the summer, club chairman Kevin McCabe and the still influential McDonald battled to win control of the boardroom. One result of their scrap was the firing of Charles Green (albeit with a pay-off of over a hundred grand) and the appointment of Ian Townsend, another plc director, in his place. Townsend had already been rumoured to be a key player in the leaving "by mutual consent" (believe that if you will) of long-time commercial manager Andy Daykin. Stories abounded that Daykin was given 20 minutes to clear his desk (very mutual), while mischievous (or possibly not) accounts alleged that the reason for Daykin's rapid exit was that he had something on a senior person at the club involving 'extra curricular activities' with a female employee.

Meanwhile, newly-appointed manager Steve Bruce was told he had £5m to spend. He didn't part with a bob until after Christmas, when he forked out the grand sum of £15,000 on an unknown 31-year-old Norwegian centre-half. He had to be thankful for that, as only two months into his tenure, he learned that there wasn't any money available after all.

At the same time, McDonald was negotiating the sale of his shareholding to a Welsh-Italian London-based lawyer, whose escorts in an apparent 'living it up' lifestyle included songstresses Sinitta and Shirley Bassey. Honestly, none of this is made up.

Now, if you're still with me, the new chief executive Ian Townsend decided to stand down to concentrate on his own business, but was still to maintain his place on the board. We're now in November 1998, and the Welsh-Italian London-based lawyer, Carlo Colombotti, had agreed a deal with McDonald. Colombotti's sidekick, an actual Sheffield United supporter called Phillip Wood, was appointed to replace Townsend. Club chairman Kevin

McCabe reported that the board was now in harmony.

At the Sheffield United plc AGM in December '98, it was announced by Colombotti that the sale of McDonald's shares to him was done and dusted. Early in the New Year, it was discovered that this was not quite so, as a further announcement was made to the effect that a sum of a million pounds still due to McDonald would now be put into the club instead - leaving Big Mike remaining as the major shareholder. The recipe for more trouble was beginning to bubble nicely.

Just before the transfer deadline in March, Steve Bruce got good news - he wouldn't have to sell anybody. Two weeks later his two best players, David Holdsworth and Graham Stuart, were on their way for a combined fee of around £2.5m. But no matter, he would get three-quarters (according to one director) or two-thirds (according to another) of the money to spend. He was allowed £275,000. Ian Townsend (remember him?) now quits completely, complaining that decisions have been taken which he was not party to and which he did not agree with.

The boardroom rumblings went on. Mike McDonald was beginning to make noises about being unhappy with the way Colombotti was running the club. It culminated in April, with Colombotti accusing McDonald and a couple of other directors of holding a board meeting without his knowledge. So what? They had a quorum. The next thing we know is that Colombotti wants to sue them. Harmony indeed. The threat is later withdrawn.

When a board meeting is finally held with everybody present, the outcome is that chief executive Phillip Wood, in the job for less than six months, is sacked, most likely at McDonald's insistence.

The season ends with Steve Bruce somehow managing to keep his team in reaching distance of the play-offs, even though they ultimately fail to make it, and promise for the future in the shape of several good young players, not least 19-year-olds Curtis Woodhouse and Lee Morris (if we don't sell them first). However, almost immediately after the season is over Bruce resigns, citing interference from above, making his position "untenable". A favourite story of local reporter Tony Pritchett is that when he mentioned to Bruce that he had been speaking to the chairman, Bruce would ask, "Which one?" You can understand his confusion, as effectively we had three: chairman of the plc (Colombotti), chairman of the football club (McCabe), and the largest shareholder (McDonald), who still effectively wields the power.

But wait, we're not finished yet. David Capper, a decade-long veteran of the post of company secretary, and who is also a director, resigns as well, he too talking of "interference". Capper's resignation causes as many, if not more, shockwaves as Steve Bruce's, as for years he has been the steady, seen-it-all-before rock who has stood firm throughout many a troubled time at boardroom level.

Where do we go from here? A board meeting on June 7 apparently decided that McDonald and Colombotti would become joint-chairman of the plc and that a new, independent chairman would be appointed "at the earliest opportunity", although I doubt whether anything can be taken at face value.

Matthew Bell

FLY ME TO THE MOON

Middlesbrough

The Season of Consolidation

Middlesbrough had returned to the Premiership at the first attempt, and this time we were determined to stay there, at all costs. This meant turning our backs on the promising youth policy of the promotion season and building on experience for this, the season of consolidation. Gary Pallister was brought back from Man United to replace retired club skipper and inspiration Nigel Pearson, with more than a few raised eyebrows at the fee of over £2m.

He joined the golden oldies, over-30s club of

FLY ME TO THE MOON

THE OFFICIAL 'UNOFFICIAL' VOICE OF THE BORO   PRICE £1... A STEAL !

issue 215   v   Everton | Carling Premiership 19th September 1998

MERSON LOSS HITS BORO HARD!

Who's gonna drive me home from the pub *now* ?!?

BACK ON THE BOOZE - WE JUST CAN'T LOSE!!!

Townsend, Mustoe, Gascoigne, Vickers, Fleming and Branca, and soon to be joined by a second prodigal son in 'super' Colin Cooper. Middlesbrough became the Saga holiday camp of the Premier League. Flair would be sacrificed for a strong back five and a workmanlike midfield. There would be none of that fantasy football of Juninho, Emerson and Ravanelli, because this time it was survival at all costs. Build from the back to beat the drop and no more trips to Wembley... please.

Hamilton Ricard was a player reborn and his 15 goals proved absolutely invaluable to a team which had lost their first choice strike partnership in pre-season. Alun Armstrong's second major injury of the summer months would see him sidelined until April, while for Marco Branca it would be a tragically fruitless season-long fight against retirement. The main attacking outlet would be newly-signed flying wing-back Dean Gordon, whose starring performances really should have seen him ahead of Michael Gray in the England pecking order. But perhaps Gordon suffered from being in the media shadow of Paul Gascoigne and the perennial question of should he or shouldn't he be welcomed back into the England fold. But more about Gazza later. Much more.

Middlesbrough's season started cautiously. A team ravaged by suspensions and injuries were happy to settle for a 0-0 draw at home to Leeds in an altogether quieter affair than our last meeting two seasons ago when Middlesbrough's dream ended in the pain and tears of relegation. There followed a defeat at Villa and a draw at home to Derby - and then our old 'friend' Colonel Controversy reared his ugly head again, as fans' idol Merson spat out his dummy and Middlesbrough were embroiled in yet another media storm. Boro's hero and salvation, Paul Merson, opened his heart in the tabloids about his battles against temptation and the evils of boozy, betting Boro, the Sodom and Gomorra of English football.

Middlesbrough were stung into two away victories, Gazza opening his account with a glorious free-kick at Leicester and Ricard devastating the shaky Spurs back line with a brace at White Hart Lane. *Fly Me's* emphatic message to Merson was, "Back on the booze - we just can't lose." Only later would the real facts emerge as the England man admitted that his "devils" had followed him to Villa. His real battles, of course, were within himself, not Boro.

There followed a couple of months of solid performances. Ricard was joined up front by the Dane, Mikkel Beck, and they seemed to be hitting the heights together. Beck's best was reserved for a couple in the season's most emphatic victory, a 4-0 drubbing of the goddam awful Sheffield Wednesday. We were clambering up the league pretty much unnoticed in this, as yet, most low-key of Premiership campaigns.

But things were far from low-key off the pitch at Boro. Paul Gascoigne commandeered the team bus from the new training ground at Hurworth, pulled into a bus stop and said, "Any passengers for Darlington?" The early pantomime season spread to the south coast, when referee Paul Alcock proved he was still in mental torpor over his Di Canio moment. He red-carded two Boro midfielders at the Dell, and then allowed Ostenstat to barge both the ball and goalkeeper Beresford into the net. Cometh the hour, cometh the man - and former coach driver Paul Gascoigne lifted himself to his greatest performance of the season, and with not a little help from his Italian friend Gianluca Festa, Boro fought back to a brilliant battling draw. It was a great second match after his breakdown and fortnight in the Priory clinic, and promised much for the rejuvenated Gazza. Unfortunately it would not prove so simple, but then again nothing ever is with Gazza.

Only a last-minute equaliser from Anelka prevented an historic victory at Highbury, where the recently-signed front man Brian Deane, another not short in the birthdays, had put us ahead. But a couple of weeks later the history books had to be reopened, as a Gazza-less Middlesbrough marched to an incredible 3-2 win at Old Trafford. At one point, the Old Trafford scoreboard read 3-0 to Middlesbrough. It was the most sensational away performance anyone could ever remember. There we were at Old Trafford singing "We're going to win the league" (a little prematurely as it turned out), followed by "Bernie, Bernie show us your bum". Or words to that effect, as former local goal-hero-turned-commentator Bernie Slaven was summoned to make good his threat, or promise, if Boro should do the unthinkable and win. The next week he stopped traffic in central Middlesbrough, disrobing in Binns' window before a massive crowd, larger than had recently greeted Father Christmas.

We are strange folk up here on Teesside, but then again we went one step further than either Arsenal or Bayern Munich. Champions of Europe, therefore - now that *is* worthy of celebration.

Bernie's arse seemed to give our season the bum's rush, as it all seemed to go a little Stephen Pears-shaped from then on. The normal post-Christmas slump came early and saw us plummet from the title fringes to the fringes of relegation. Our proud undefeated home record fell on the very last game of the year, in a Boxing Day defeat by Liverpool. From then on all we could manage at home were goalless draws. Worse still, on our travels, defeats came thick and fast. Criticism began to mount on Bryan Robson but he stuck stubbornly to his back-five plan. People began to point the finger at his overly long-in-the-tooth squad but he refrained from bringing in youth or new signings. Eventually it paid off, as the death drive was aborted, but not before an utterly humiliating night on Merseyside, where Everton, who had previously only managed a mighty three home goals all season, clocked up five against us. Just to add even more insult to injury, it was Nicky Barmby who opened the Toffees' account.

Anyway, I'm getting a bit ahead of myself here, because February was blighted by the biggest PR own-goal Middlesbrough have scored for many a day - well, since they announced the signing of Keith Gillespie in the middle of a pre-season tournament, only for the deal to fall belly up the next day. This time, with the world's media encamped at the training ground, manager Bryan Robson called a press conference to announce he was a non-starter for the England job... oh, and by the way, we've nearly re-signed Juninho. Cue mass celebration, triumphant headlines in the local press, spontaneous outpourings of joy, street parties - which lasted all of an hour until the news filtered through from Madrid that the deal was off, done for and dead in the water.

Robson had joked in the 'Juninho' press conference that he still had a few more traumas to go through in club management. Well, he certainly didn't speak too soon.

Just when things were looking very, very dodgy, the slump was ended with 3-0 home win over the pitifully bad Southampton, a match that I will always remember for the worst-ever shot seen in the Premiership. Sparky Hughes, once the king of the volley, turned on a sixpence to slice a shot so woefully, it actually finished up arcing out of play behind him. Who needs Flo anyway, Mr Vialli? Middlesbrough now went off on a bit of a run, with victories at Nottingham Forest and Coventry, and creditable draws with Blackburn and championship-seeking Chelsea. Oh how we would have loved to have beaten Chelsea, after all the pain, torture and misery they have inflicted on us. But at least we more or less ended their title challenge in a performance epitomised by Hamilton Ricard's human battering-ram against Desailly.

Unfortunately it was almost the last bright spot of the season as, apart from a draw at the Cup Final-obsessed Newcastle, our form foundered on a few of the sharper Premiership hazards. After the Chelsea game, expectations were high for the arrival of champions Arsenal, but our European ambitions were shredded in a whirlwind performance that saw us sink to our record home defeat, a 6-1 mauling from Anelka, Viera and the devastating Kanu. Incidentally, we had tried to buy Kanu two years' previous, but now our feet were very firmly back on the ground, courtesy of the giant Nigerian. We recovered to threaten a first-ever double over Man United, before falling to an 'offside' strike from Sheringham, and then finished up getting hammered away again to the... er, Hammers.

But the main thing is we are back to face another Premiership campaign. We finished in ninth place, our highest for 20 years and were the top-placed north-east club. Best of all, we avoided the Inter-Toto Cup. Imagine the embarrassment of playing in a competition named after a dodgy soft-rock band?

Robert Nichols

MERSON " OH YE ! I LARV IT UP EE YA I DO, SIGNED A BLEEDIN 5 YEAR CONTRACT AINT I, WANNA BE THE MANAGER EVENTUALLY, KNOW WHAT I MEAN, ANY HOW I'M OFF NOW, THANKS FOR ALL THE BANGERS & MASH (CASH) , TA-RA "

PINOCCHIO MERSON IS OFF TO VILLA WHERE ALL THE PLAYERS SET SUCH A GOOD EXAMPLE, JUST ASK ULRIKA JOHNSON

C ANDY BLAND

FOLLOW THE YELLOW BRICK ROAD

Mansfield Town

Well, whaddyaknow? You go and spend ages writing a *résumé* of the season and, as soon as you finish it, your manager goes and resigns. Didn't think it was that bad myself.

If you'd have told me after the dismal 3-0 loss against early-season title-favourites Brentford in August that, come the end of the season, Mansfield Town would finish eighth in the Division Three table, four points shy of a play-off place, then I would have probably bitten your hand off.

But if, after relieving you of your hand, you then went on to inform me that, during the course of the same season, Mansfield Town would top the table, possess one of the division's leading scorers, give Huddersfield Town a run for their money in the Worthington Cup, beat Manchester City at Maine Road, and spend all but six weeks in the play-off places, not to mention residing in the top three for a good part of it, then I might feel rather inclined to ask - what went wrong?

Mansfield Town Football Club - The Stags, Barry Fry's pre-season tip for relegation to the Nationwide Conference, surprised most observers throughout, not least their own fans. Having lost the club's leading scorer and fans' favourite, Steve Whitehall, to Oldham during the summer break, we could all have been excused for thinking that the season would be one of toil and trouble at the wrong end of the country's bottom professional division.

With Whitehall heading for the exit door for an undisclosed fee, coming the other way were ex-England under-21 defender Stuart Ryder on a free from Walsall and Tony Lormor... hells bells, have we gone mad? An ex-Spireite? (Spireite, pronounced - spy-r-i-yet; definition - a person who it has been proved beyond reasonable doubt to reside/have resided in a place known for having a bent religious structure.)

With echoes of a transfer embargo, the players' wages going unpaid, on/off ground redevelopment plans, and protests against the club's owner still ringing in our ears from the previous season, the Stags began at Griffin Park

Follow The Yellow Brick Road

Number 2
Issue 38

Season 98/99

Johnny Miller Interview

Whitehall Replies

Show Me The Money

Grounds For Concern!

Two Hearts Beat As One

plus... Loads More about The Super Stags

£1

An Alternative View of Mansfield Town F.C.

determined, it seemed, to prove the obese one right. But, from that day on, things took a decided turn for the better - on the field at least.

Huddersfield were pushed all the way in the Worthington Cup, both at the McAlpine Stadium and the return leg at Field Mill, and Plymouth were swept aside, 2-0, in our first home league game. Throughout the course of late summer and autumn, things were going strangely well. In addition to residing in the higher echelons of the division, Mansfield were gaining a reputation for playing the beautiful game the way it should be played.

The beginning of November saw a pivotal moment that was going to have a bearing on our eventual outcome in the division. It was Tuesday 10 November, to be precise, and Mansfield came away from the Victoria Ground, Hartlepool armed with three points as reward for a 2-1 win. Little did we know then that this match would prove to be the last time Mansfield would win away from home in the league. We came mightily close once or twice - especially at then league leaders Halifax on the last Friday in November, when the referee decided, firstly, to add six minutes of injury-time and, secondly, in the fourth-minute of that injury-time, to award a very dubious penalty. It resulted in an equaliser for the home side after ten-man Mansfield had held a two-goal lead going into the second-half.

Looking back, it was probably our failure to secure three points in any of the remaining 12 away league games that was to prove the undoing of all the hard work. Perversely, the *very* last time Mansfield won away in the '98-99 season was at Maine Road in early December, when we beat Man City 2-1 in the Auto Windscreens Shield. Football, eh?

Two weeks in early December really told the story of our whole campaign better than I ever could. We were famously dumped out of the FA Cup at home to Southport on the Saturday, beat Man City on the Tuesday, and went top of the table for the first time in aeons when beating Shrewsbury on Friday night. Then, the following Saturday, we crashed 4-2 at Ninian Park in a top-of-the-table clash against Cardiff, after outplaying the home side for the majority of the game.

Off the field, things weren't going half as well. The long-promised ground redevelopment entered its fifth year of promises and its fifth year of disappointments. The local Mansfield MP, Alan Meale, a constant companion and supporter of chairman and chief executive Keith Haslam, was 'exposed' in the *Sunday Times*. Meale, a frequent commentator and defender of Mr Haslam's tactics prior to then, has been strangely subdued to the point of silence since.

We turned for the home straight with probably Mansfield's best performance of the season, when turning over eventual-Champions Brentford 3-1 at The Mill. It was probably the point when we peaked; and also the point when, in many observers' eyes, Mansfield should have strengthened the team to consolidate their position. The problem is that to be able to strengthen the team, you have to be able to acquire new players; and to acquire new players, you have to rely on the fact that you aren't working with an embargo on incoming transfers. A transfer embargo is imposed when a club borrows money from the PFA, and is lifted when the money is repaid.

This wasn't the case at Mansfield Town, with the transfer embargo only lifted twice during the entire season - once in December, when Stuart Naylor was brought in to allow our regular goalkeeper to have an urgent groin operation, and secondly, 48 hours before transfer deadline day. Stuart Naylor's wages were also paid by the Support Our Stags (SOS) organisation. Unfortunately, he got injured on his debut, so our regular goalkeeper had to postpone his operation and resume playing

The following two weeks not only proved to be the main turning point - as from here onwards Mansfield only picked up 27 more points (a similar record to relegated Scarborough) - but also showed the financial gulf that exists between the country's professional football teams and players.

Firstly, Tony Ford broke the outfield players' appearance record when playing his 825th match. In this money-soaked era of football, Tony's achievement stands out the proverbial mile. Tony was the centre of much local and national media attention in the weeks running up to him equalling, and eventually surpassing, Terry Paine's 22-year-old landmark - and rightly so. By the age of 39, most top footballers have finished playing, having retired due to insufficient motivation. Often, they've earnt so much from football that there is no need for them to continue to play the game that so many of us would give our right arm to have just 45 minutes at. At 39, most top footballers are veterans in the media circle. Tony has never been paid more than £1,000 per week, and most of the current Premiership footballers who earn more in seven days than Tony earns in a year are not worthy to pack his kit-bag.

Secondly, our regular goalkeeper, Ian Bowling, had been playing through the pain barrier for three months. He had a groin injury that required surgery, but played on and was probably on the verge of causing himself serious damage. It wasn't that he was ordered to, and probably not because he wanted to, but because he had no choice: the transfer embargo meant we had only one goalkeeper - him.

At the same time as these occurrences, Peter Schmeichel needed a Christmas holiday because he was "tired" - don't make me laugh. Dean Sturridge pulled out of a match because he wasn't "mentally prepared" - what a disgrace. Paulo Di Canio stayed in Italy because he was "stressed". These people are being paid weekly wages that would be enough for clubs like Mansfield Town to consider themselves wealthy. Professional football is in a crazy state.

Ford's love of the game, and Bowling's loyalty and bravery, stand them head and shoulders above any *prima donna* Premiership footballer. This game will never make them millionaires but they have something more than wealth. They have pride. And they have commitment.

We then invited Sky to film us play a home game against fellow promotion contenders and local rivals Rotherham. They'd been pestering us for years, but we couldn't fit them in due to other contractual obligations (BBC, ITV, MTFCTV, etc). We then duly did the falling-apart trick we always reserve for Sky viewers. We dominated the first 45 minutes and had two goals disallowed, then went and conceded three in the second-half. Both managers in this game were wired to heart monitors to test the stress levels of football managers. Before the game we heard about pulse rates and the like, and how anything above 80 *whatevers* was bordering on dangerous. I don't think Steve Parkin's was below 130 at any stage of the game - definitely heart attack material.

This defeat was the second game in a run of four losses in five matches, a run which also saw us concede 13 goals. Mansfield were never the tightest team in defence: the style of football always dictating that there would be gaps at the back. But the goals were going in at an alarming rate. It may also have had something to do with the fact that our loan goalkeeper was in for four of those five games.

Mansfield carried on misfiring for the next month, scraping points here and there. But the confidence, conviction and fear-free free-flowing football of pre-Christmas had vanished. Another defining moment of the season was away at league leaders Cambridge in mid-March: we were mauled 7-2. Mansfield didn't play as badly as the score suggested. In fact, after the game, a lot of Cambridge fans e-mailed the Mansfield Town website, congratulating us on being the best team to visit the Abbey Stadium so far that season, a sentiment echoed by the Cardiff fans back in December.

But Steve Parkin had seen enough. Armed with his new-found freedom in the transfer market, albeit only 48 hours before the transfer deadline, he signed three players on loan - two defenders and a striker. He then proceeded to drop the entire back-three and made a total of five changes for the next game, away at Peterborough. The subsequent 1-0 defeat at London Road saw Mansfield drop out of the top seven for the first time since mid-October. The loss wasn't the worst thing about this result - it was the significant change in playing style that concerned the Mansfield faithful.

From this day on, we should have strolled into the play-offs, with six of our remaining nine games being at Field Mill, and only Brentford having a better home record. But the introduction of the new back-three had a more far-reaching effect than just plugging the leaks in defence. Mansfield's tactics were founded on a strong belief in playing football properly, with all players contributing. A lot of our attacks were initiated by the defence coming out with the ball, playing it through midfield and up to the forwards. But our new back-line seemed only interested in hoofing the ball as far down the field as possible. The midfielders and forwards were not used to playing this way - and the results showed.

After the 2-0 home victory in early April over Brighton, who were probably one of the worst teams to visit Field Mill all season, Mansfield failed to score in five of the next six games. True, they weren't conceding, but with the team's balance affected, we weren't scoring either.

Disappointing home results followed that afternoon against Southend, and on the Tuesday night, against Halifax. Both performances were poor but the Halifax one was particularly upsetting for a number of reasons, not least the 1-0 scoreline. Mansfield were booed off the pitch. It was the first time all season that the fans had turned against the team and the manager, but it was a purely understandable reaction. The fans knew what the team were capable of; and not only were they not producing it at a key point of the season, they didn't actually look like they wanted to.

Personally speaking, I have never been so frustrated watching a football match in my entire life, and was still kicking the cat a full five hours after the final whistle. They played as if they didn't *want* to get promoted.

As author of the Mansfield Town section of the regular slot on regional Teletext, 'Fanscene', I put forward some forthright opinions about the game:

"Could things get any worse after Saturday? Well, try Tuesday for starters. Are the players on a stay-down bonus? We are told that 16 out of the 21 players are out of contract in May and no new offers have been made. We can't afford the wages of a loan player, whose wages we aren't even paying, so we send him back, and we've started to play like Lincoln! Don't even get me started on the ground."

By all accounts my piece didn't go down well with Steve Parkin so I called him to put across my side of the story. After getting through all the initial expletives, threats of libel and getting the players to sort me out, I managed to have my say. Thirty minutes or so later, he'd grudgingly accepted that I was entitled to my view but was only willing to let the matter be forgotten if I wrote a letter apologising to him and the players. No way. He did get a letter in which I re-stated my case together with an accompanying video showing the goals we'd scored this season to remind him of what the team were capable of.

Mansfield were stumbling towards the finishing line, and their hopes were finally extinguished when fellow play-off contenders Swansea beat the then leaders Cambridge to put the play-offs finally out of our reach. We all knew it was going to happen, but we didn't want to believe it *could* happen - not after being in pole-position for most of the season. Mansfield had blown it. From being in a position in mid-season where nothing but promotion would have been acceptable, they had slipped so alarmingly as to stumble out of even the play-offs. At the end everyone just wanted to forget about it - it had been heartbreaking.

This all seemed to pale into insignificance when, in June, Steve Parkin resigned, citing the recently re-imposed transfer embargo as making his position "untenable". Parkin then said that, because of a back injury, he would be out of the game for about five to six weeks. Exactly two weeks later, he was appointed manager of Rochdale. Most Mansfield fans with Internet access had known even before Parkin had resigned that he was on his way to Rochdale. The rumours were too strong to ignore and they eventually became true.

At the time of writing, Mansfield have appointed Billy Dearden as manager, have nine senior players, are under a transfer embargo, and have two ends of their ground closed due to safety reasons. Things as they say, can only get better.

Mark Watson

GOODBYE HORSE

Charlton Athletic

End of the Roller-coaster

They came to bury Charlton, not to praise them.

As Barnsley found out before us, and as Watford and Bradford will find out this season, the Premiership is a new place, different from the cosy old world when it was simply known as Division One (of four). Today, the country's top professional league is a members only club, with no room for the likes of us.

One of the regular features of *Goodbye Horse*, in its inaugural year, was the Fantasy Cliché League. This featured regular highlights as the big boys of Fleet Street (well, more often than not, Wapping) fought on a level playing field with the nation's local press to write off Charlton's chances and disparage the efforts of the new boys. It really was quite amazing. Charlton never seemed to put on a good performance in the Premier League, but an awful lot of the Big Boys had off-days against us!

And bad days they certainly had. Of the top four in the Premiership, Arsenal only managed to score one goal - a penalty - against us and, in truth, should have lost at least one, if not both of our encounters; Manchester United had to rely on a Ferguson-added-time winner at The Valley; Chelsea relied on another late winner at The Hotel and suicidal Addick defending at The Valley; while Leeds escaped an away defeat by the margin of a missed penalty.

And it wasn't only the 'big four' who had scares against us. Villa were under the cosh for the whole game at The Valley but still escaped with a 1-0 win thanks to an own-goal. They didn't escape at Villa Park in a tremendous penultimate match of the season, when an 88th minute netbuster from soon-to-be England international Danny Mills kept The Addicks' hopes alive into the final week of the season.

Meanwhile - joy of joys - after all of the dodgy decisions and thrashings at the hands of the mighty Liverpool in our last spell in the top flight, the Anfield machine managed to rescue only one point from two games against everybody's whipping boys - and that was courtesy of more bizarre refereeing from Mr Balance himself, Paul Alcock.

It all started out so brightly when, after the ten men at Newcastle came away with a goalless draw, Charlton produced fireworks to match those greeting them onto the pitch as they walloped Southampton 5-0 in the bright August sunshine, to go top of the Premiership and leave the rest of the country spluttering in their cornflakes. Sure, there were only two games gone. So what? We were certainly going to enjoy the moment.

Despite leading the country's goalscoring charts alongside Manchester United and Chelsea in the early weeks, and a very satisfying 4-2 win as part of a double over the West Ham childsnatchers, we never quite reached similar heights again. Indeed, a lack of goals and an inclination to miss gilt-edged chances, particularly penalties, proved to be our undoing.

A terrible run of a big fat zero points in just under two months didn't overly help the cause as we slid from a comfortable mid-table position (11th after Keith Jones snuffed out Gazza in a 1-1 draw against Middlesbrough) to an entrenched relegation-zone 19th in the table after a humiliating revenge stuffing at Southampton. (By the way, have any other team's supporters *really* only got one song to sing?)

There were, believe it or not, two positive aspects to take from this dismal run. One was that, with the exception of a couple of dismal performances in the wintry north, we were never truly outclassed by anyone and we were genuinely unlucky in a number of games. The other was, courtesy of an abysmal team in Nottingham Forest, the fact that we never sunk to the bottom of the league and always stayed in touch, somehow, with the teams above us.

Our apparent saviour first appeared as a substitute in the last game of the barren run, at Southampton, and immediately showed the sort of ball control skills that we just weren't used to at The Valley. By the time Charlton played host to Newcastle in a televised match eight days later, Martin Pringle had settled in after his loan move from Benfica and was ready to help us out of our goalscoring crisis.

This he did in some style, dispatching a goal against the Geordies, with style and smoothness and, most importantly, a calmness that had been somewhat lacking from the Addicks' attack since the enforced lay-off of Super Clive Mendonca earlier in the season. That goal helped the Addicks to a precious point, but could have been three without more poor refereeing.

Two more goals, against Wimbledon and Derby in the next four games, underlined the importance of Pringle's addition to the side. And then the inevitable happened. Desperate to ensure that we kept hold of the services of our new-found saviour, and with a keen eye for a bargain, Alan Curbishley splashed out £800,000 to make our new signing permanent earlier (and more cheaply) than originally agreed with Souness. And guess what happened? That's right, missed sitters replaced the goals and the Super Swede failed to score again before the end of the season.

Although a winning streak in February, without conceding a goal in four games, raised the spirits once more, a record of only two wins and four draws in our final dozen games was not the form required to avoid the despair felt on the final day, and the sighs of relief heard from behind the crocodile tears of pundits up and down the country.

There is no doubt that, looking back at the season, our lack of goalscoring prowess, with the injury-stricken Clive Mendonca top scoring with only eight goals, was a major factor in our failure to prove the critics wrong. But it is equally clear that we were not as hopeless as many forecasts claimed and we certainly didn't require a league to ourselves as that doyen of football writers, Danny Baker, hopefully predicted. (Well done on getting to Wembley in that competition for the little clubs, Danny.)

Unlike Barnsley the season before, or indeed Forest last season, we were not on the end of any humiliating scorelines. No team beat us by more than three goals, and only Spurs managed that margin of victory at The Valley, despite our disappointing home record. And we certainly handed out a few football lessons of our own, including a rather delightful double against West Ham (oh, sorry, have I mentioned that already?).

However, despite assertions at the start of the season about learning from the rough experiences suffered by Barnsley, we were victims in the end of our own naivety and inexperience. Failing to kill off teams when the opportunity presented itself cost us dear, as did a misguided persistence with Neil Redfearn when his performances clearly didn't merit inclusion. Had we signed Graham Stuart that little bit earlier, perhaps things might have been different.

Despite Charlton's widely-lauded youth policy, it is also the view of many fans that Alan Curbishley's reticence to blood clearly talented products such as Scott Parker and Paul Konchesky had a negative effect on performances. Certainly they never looked out of their depth in their brief appearances but the reluctance to throw them into such a high-pressure situation was perhaps understandable.

Injuries also played a major role, with the two first choice goalkeepers both suffering from lengthy periods out during the season, and Matty Holmes never recovering from the assault by Wolves' Aussie assassin Kevin Muscat the previous year. The enigma that is Paul Mortimer failed to display his undoubted talents on the big stage one last time due to constant injuries. We have now bid a fond farewell to a modern legend at The Valley.

John Barnes came and went, with only one storming performance, in the second half of the double (oh yes, that again!) against poachers supreme West Ham. Perhaps his class, incisive passing and footballing brain were underused. They were certainly misused appearing on one of the league's worst pitches at Coventry, but not against Leeds or Middlesborough, where he may have made a difference.

Excuses or not, at the end of the season we failed to attain the number of points required to consolidate our dramatically-won Premiership place. Every fan would have done something different, but no-one is to blame. The board did not make more money available because they did not want to repeat the mistakes made by previous newly promoted teams and sink into the oblivion currently inhabited by Crystal Palace. Alan Curbishley did an excellent job in the circumstances, borne out by two Manager of the Month awards and the affection of supporters who waited back over half an hour for him to reappear after the final game of the season.

The job now is not to look back but to fight back. The process was started early with the inspired capture of Republic of Ireland goalkeeper Dean Kiely from Bury and perhaps, just perhaps, a bright future beckons.

By the way, as I write this, it has been announced that Charlton are considering taking West Ham United to court for the kidnapping of teenage prodigy Jermaine Defoe. Too bloody right! By the way, did I mention that we did the double over the Hammers last season?

Andy Lopata

Source: Sky Blue Army

GRORTY DICK

West Bromwich Albion

"Tell me why - Fab don't like Mondays?"

Chant at Loftus Road, five days after the Crewe debacle...

It wasn't exactly an auspicious season for The Baggies. Perhaps the weight of expectation on the part of supporters, and heaped on the shoulders of both management and staff, proved in the end to be too burdensome. Perhaps, with a tad more ambition, if we had retained Super Bob (who went on to do such sterling work at Bolton, getting well into double figures for them) as the perfect foil for Lee Hughes. Perhaps, if certain of our finest had shown more commitment to the cause. Perhaps...

The season proper for us opened on a baking hot early August day at Oakwell - and what a game. A bit like a beach party in reverse, so to speak. It was rare to spot the Albionite not clad in T-shirt and shorts as the many coaches spewed forth their loads onto the away car park and down the short walk to the away turnstiles. A creditable result. Strikes from Richard Sneekes (plus ponytail) and James Quinn put us 2-1 to the good - until Old Inevitable itself, the dreaded *Semper Te Fallant* factor, reared its ugly head. Bang - 2-2. Still, we mused, not bad for starters.

The following week we were in league action again (more of the League Cup in a later paragraph). This time Sheffield United, the Blades, Sean Bean's lot, provided the opposition. More cause for optimism as The Brummie rang to the sound of 'boings' a phenomenal FOUR times; remember, United were in the play-off zone the previous campaign. Fifth in the League, early doors maybe, but we were cooking on gas.

Then came the downer - Brentford. A scant four days after walloping the lads from Yorkshire, we journeyed to Griffin Park. It should have been a doddle: thanks to the home leg, we were 2-1 in front thanks to strikes from Lee Hughes and our own 'Mr Injured', Mickey Evans. However, some of our finest seemed to take it into their heads that, although we were performing on a muckheap, the result was cut and dried. They failed to notice the small detail that Brentford, managed by none other than erstwhile Palace supremo Ron Noades, were totally, totally committed. Predictably, we paid the price - a 3-0 drubbing. I felt sorry for young striker Brian Quailey, who was the subject of much vituperative comment from our away following. Had two fleeting opportunities gone the lad's way, he would have been the hero of the hour. As things transpired, an eventual loan move to Exeter City proved to be the kindest thing to do, given The Brummie's unpleasant ability to seek out a scapegoat with the unerring ability of a Cruise missile.

And so the season plodded on. One step forward, two steps back. The first was due to the phenomenal form of Lee Hughes, the fairy-tale hero of last season's Crewe game. Even in his first season of league footie, he'd managed to get into double figures; this time around, he was knifing into opposition defences with a vengeance -and no-one seemed to have the answer. Tallies of two and three goals per game proved to be the norm. The nationals and TV started to take notice. On one memorable occasion, I was plodding wearily home from work, only to encounter Lee standing outside the Balti a few doors away from where I live. When questioned, it transpired Sky had arranged to capture the lad doing what he did best - when not scoring goals for the Baggies, that is. Our defence, quite frankly, was proving to be a mess - totally negating the sterling work performed by Hughes at the opposite end of the park. On a totally embarrassing Bank Holiday Monday, we were trounced 5-1 at Blundell Park by Alan Buckley's lot. To add insult to injury, shortly after, we suffered a 3-2 last-minute defeat by play-off finalists Bolton - after being two goals to the good, thanks to Kevin Kilbane and Sean Flynn. Where was the defence, for God's sake? Some things never change.

Late September, October and early November saw us yo-yo around the upper reaches of the table, but never quite attaining the glittering prize of a top-six position. Again, defeats in important fixtures (Blues and Sunderland at home, spring to mind) exposed our defensive inabilities, somewhat embarrassingly, in front of the whole nation. One interesting (and hypothermia-inducing) interlude was the away fixture at Swindon, which took place in the teeth of a torrential downpour and what appeared to be a force nine gale. Guess where we away supporters were situated? That's right, in an enclosure totally bereft of any cover whatsoever. I can honestly say, in nigh on 40 years of watching the Baggies, I've never experienced conditions like it. Believe it or not, several Albionites were treated for exposure.

Come November's end, came the usual bi-annual bloodletting versus The Tatters, who had play-off ambitions of their own - shame we beat you 2-0, wasn't it chaps? And yet, despite all this, the Lee Hughes goal machine steamrollered on: three hat-tricks and the nation's leading goalscorer - not bad for a Smethwick lad.

Space 1999. Lots of it, mostly in our penalty box. By now, our 'goals against' tally was racking up faster than an old-fashioned pinball machine. The difference between tenth spot and the relegation zone was proving to be the exploits of Lee Hughes. Additionally (unsurprising to most Baggies, for whom a cup-run is a distant memory) we were unceremoniously dumped from the FA Cup by a lively AFC Bournemouth. If only their ticketing arrangements were as good as their side. When the tie was announced, Baggies were told terrace places were to be in short supply - this, at a ground where the average gate is lucky to get into double figures, I ask you. No-one had thought to make the game all-ticket. Consequently, Albion supporters travelling on the day of the tie were seemingly involved in a race against time - to get in the queue outside the ground before the main rush of travellers arrived. Then Bournemouth (or the police - believe whatever you will) changed their minds, and all away supporters gained admission. Not that it did us any good, mind - a 1-0 defeat ensured our cup-run came crashing to a halt even before it had gained momentum.

Paradoxically, after that defeat, a run of favourable results ensured a steady climb up the table. The signing of goalkeeper Phil Whitehead had helped steady the ship, between the sticks, somewhat. Whitehead seemed to have far more command of his area than Alan Miller and was far more confident on crosses. In short, a good, sound First Division goalkeeper. The highlight of this period was a 2-0 win at Watford - a 'double', in fact, over the eventual play-off winners. Although this was swiftly followed by defeats at the hands of Bolton (yes, referee, Lee Hughes' strike was over the line and should have been the equaliser), a lucky last-gasp home draw versus Bristol City, and a narrow reverse at the hands of promoted Bradford City, we were still in there pitchin' by virtue of the fact all our fellow play-off hopefuls seemed to have suffered similarly damaging results. By early March, home wins versus Stockport and our old friends Oxford had put us in that coveted sixth spot. Holidays were booked with the play-offs in mind - and the talk was of an Albion v Tatters fixture. We winced at the prospect. Then it all turned pear-shaped.

The rot commenced versus Blues at St Andrews. The collapse of the men in blue and white was totally comprehensive from the moment the first goal went in - and yet it could have been so different. For the first 20 minutes we appeared to have the upper hand, possibly due to promotion-nerves on the part of the Bluenoses. With that defeat, any thoughts of being play-off contenders went totally out of the window. The plain truth was, we simply weren't good enough, despite the best efforts of Lee Hughes (whose goalbusting exploits had distinctly turned stale during early 1999, it must be said). Then came the visit of Ipswich to The Shrine. The 0-1 scoreline hid the stark truth: namely, the trashing our finest received at the hands of the country bumpkins with upwardly-mobile ambitions. And so to The Stadium of Light. Sunderland were sweeping all before them in their clean-up of Nationwide Division One. We travelled not in expectation, but rather in the hope the inevitable stonking wouldn't prove too painful. Prior to the match, gallows humour abounded in the vicinity of the away-end bar.

"My garden shed... is bigger than this/My garden shed is bigger than this/It's got a door and a window/My garden shed is bigger than this..."

And, inevitably, the goals rolled in - three of 'em to be exact. By that time, we were past caring - and undulatedly joined in the Mexican Waves carousing around the ground, courtesy of that red-and-white striped tame Nuremberg Rally, commonly known as The Mackems. Great day out, shame about the result. And then there was Crewe...

In retrospect, all the ingredients for an overturn were there. Crewe were jealously guarding their hard-won First Division status much as a she-cat will protect her litter against a predatory Rottweiler. We were vapour-trailing downwards into 'also-ran' status. The mood was ugly. Already, the first dissenting voices had been heard *apropos* the future employment of manager Denis Smith, plus the general fitness of the board to run the club. Selling outside The Hawthorns prior to the game, two rumours reared their heads:

a) Fabian DeFreitas (our alleged striker) had, unbelievably, thought that an Easter Monday fixture meant a 7.45pm kick-off and consequently didn't turn up at all - not only that but;

b) Defender Andy McDermott, late because of reasons beyond his control, caught the full onslaught of the Smith fury, the principal cause of which was (a). Without the chance of an explanation, he was summarily sent forth homeward - and all witnessed by a (for once) lost-for-words Martin Lewis, one of our sellers.

This sort of thing isn't exactly conducive towards harmony within the ranks. Admittedly, within minutes of the kick-off, we should have had a penalty - the match officials thought otherwise. Then Crewe, with the determination that's born of desperation, began to turn the screw. Our pusillanimous performers had no answer -and the goals rained in. Inevitably, the mood began to turn ugly. Chants like "You're not fit to wear the shirt", "Sack the board", plus the inevitable "Smith Out" abounded. One supporter dashed onto the pitch and hurled his shirt, disgustedly, in front of the directors box. Another, in a meaningful gesture, kissed the badge adorning his, in front of our manager. Final result - 1-5. Not surprisingly, there was an after-match demonstration. What was surprising to us was the subsequent *Daily Mirror* report. For the benefit of those journalistic chaps and chapesses, let's get one thing straight: the glass doors in Halfords Lane were NOT smashed, as reported by that erudite journal. Not only were we present at the time, we passed that way some three hours later - and the doors were still in pristine condition. Still, can't let the truth get in the way of a good story, can we?

One ray of sunshine did emerge from our Easter Monday 'Crewcification' (but not resurrection). The following Saturday, at Loftus Road, I heard our away following bellow one of the funniest spontaneous one-liners I have ever heard. I used it for the title of this piece...

Talking of one-liners, we now proceed (reluctantly) to Wolverhampton Scrapyard. Again, the ingredients of this encounter blended nicely. A defeat would mean the prospect of our manager looking at his P45. The Tatters needed a win to boost their chances of a play-off place. Pre-match, the pot was bubbling nicely - our friends from Wulferampton were under the impression we were lambs to the slaughter, given their recent run of form. But it was our lads who took the lead thanks to Mickey Evans, newly raised from the dead for this occasion. Oh dear, they do not like it up em; from my vantage point behind the touchline (I had a photographer's pass), I captured pictures of numerous dissatisfied Tatters - I think the expression 'bulldog chewin' a wasp' says it all!). Eventually, Wulves did equalise - but then came one of the funniest moments of my spectating career. Wulves gained a rather dubious penalty. Up stepped one Keith Curle, the own-goal 'hero' of the previous season's fixture, and principal cause of my dodgy back (for details, see *SOTF4*). The tension was unbearable, as Curle laid the ball on the spot, made his run... only to see his kick score what would have been a lovely conversion had he been playing rugby league.

Mother Gravity reclaimed what was rightfully hers, amidst much derisory hooting from the lower section of the John Ireland Stand. And then - I don't know which genius thought up the chant - but within minutes it reverberated throughout The Scrapyard, and seemingly throughout the whole of Wolverhampton. The tune is *Go West*, the rest I leave to your imaginations:

"Keith Curle is an Albion fan, Keith Curle is an Albion fan..."

The black-and-gold clad braindeads had absolutely no answer to this superb jibe. Reduced to silence, they fumed the remainder of the match. So did their favourites. That draw was to prove the effective difference between a top-six place and also-ran status.

It's now the end of the season and our club is in turmoil. Will Lee Hughes go? Personally, I think the lure of Mammon will prove to be too much, despite his Black Country roots and his avowed love of the Baggies. There's also unrest in the boardroom. It does the club no good at all to be seemingly involved in internecine warfare. Why is it the recent (and not so recent) history of our favourite football club seems to be permeated by schisms and rumours of schisms? Surely, we all want the same thing - a place in the sun for West Bromwich Albion. The gap between the Nationwide and the Premiership is rapidly becoming a chasm; few clubs have managed to bridge that gap and go on to survive in the Realm of Murdoch. If Albion truly want to evolve as a football club, the foundations have to be set in place *now*.

Two or so seasons hence will be too late, I fear. Albion, like many others, will descend into a *cul-de-sac* from which they will never escape. Sorry to sound so gloomy, folks, but, as I pen this piece, the lyrics of Talking Heads reverberate through my brain, constantly:

"We're on the road to nowhere..."
Glynis Wright

HANGING ON THE TELEPHONE

Huddersfield Town

Things Can Only Get Worse would have been the title of a successful hit record if a Huddersfield Town supporter had been responsible for the lyrics. Having seen so many false dawns over the last 25 years and more, there is a natural, if unhealthy cynicism ingrained deep within the psyche of every Town fan. Without it life would simply be too much fun.

Little surprise to the travelling faithful, then, that following The Great Escape of '97-98, the season got underway with a miserable defeat, in which new Belgian 'keeper Nico Vaesen was sent off after only nine minutes.

The pattern for the season perhaps? But no! Beyond our comprehension and wildest expectation, the boys in blue and white embarked on an unbeaten run that saw them top the First Division for six weeks in September/October.

Peter Jackson is a god.

Terry Yorath, despite being Welsh, knows how to coach a football team.

Surely now the only way was down? But no! "Multi-millionaire suitor courts Town take-over" the local paper screamed. "Millions to invest in push for Premiership" it continued. Let the good times roll.

Oh how we drooled;

Oh how we dreamed.

Oh how the hell did we let in seven goals at Oakwell during our annual ritual embarrassment? As the nation watched on TV, pointing and sniggering, the alarm bells were ringing loud and clear that strengthening was required.

Yet the loss of Barry Horne in midfield was never redressed (crunched in a scything tackle from a Sadford opponent - although, unlike our neighbours in a similar situation, we didn't immediately reach for our lawyers). The consequence was that we were consistently overrun and had to depend upon a defence so poor, even OJ Simpson would not have been happy with it; and who, without the brilliance of 'keeper Nico Vaesen, would have crumbled even more embarrassingly on many more occasions.

Town continued to stutter along and by Christmas were just outside the play-off positions, and slowly but surely Great Expectations were giving way to A Bleak Mid-Winter.

A brief cup run took us as far as a fifth-round replay at Derby in which, as appeared to be the case throughout the season's cup competition, a Premiership referee helped a Premiership side get the upper hand, and that was that.

By now the cracks were beginning to turn into chasms and a record of only three wins in the second half of the season was suggestive of what we suspected was a growing sense of disharmony within the ranks.

Every cloud has a silver lining, however, and our usual points haul at Valley Parade was even more rewarding than any of us could have hoped for.

What a game this was.

Crap defending to hand them the lead; Three goals in 12 minutes to take command of the match and silence the gobby shites in the other three stands; Captain (and crap Welsh defender) Steve Jenkins dismissed before half-time for making no contact with Peter Beagrie in an attempted slide tackle, but rather (presumably) for frowning menacingly at him thereafter; One-time Town target Dean Windows scoring a second for the scum, which is followed by a back-of-the-net assault on goalkeeper Vaesen by Gordon "I never want to see this type of challenge in football ever again" Watson; The referee awarding a controversial penalty eight minutes from time, which Windows blasts hard and low but which Nico palms over the top (cue pandemonium in away end).

Fantastic.

That aside - and it was no more than that - little could detract from the fact that Town were little more than a mediocre mid-table outfit (as testified by the final position of tenth). An abysmal record of never having kept a clean sheet in 23 away league matches speaks for itself.

That the take-over wasn't completed until late February was a cause of great consternation to many, as most felt that with investment at the time when we were top of the table, things could have been quite different. Most fans, however, felt that progress had been made over the previous season (which was spent largely in the bottom three), but rumours of Jackson's imminent demise were circulating from the time of the take-over, and no (kiss of death) vote of confidence seemed capable of displacing them.

As the season ground to a halt with a 0-0 draw against Crewe, most Town fans went home content in the knowledge that Jackson and Yorath would be able to bolster the squad in the summer with the promised millions, and wondered what on earth they were going to do for the next 14 Saturdays.

That Jackson in particular didn't get the opportunity, being sacked the following morning, was greeted by gob-smacked disbelief, as a hero was seen to have been felled in his prime.

But if it is possible to consider your club and not let your heart rule your head, then it must be conceded that the new board's assessment that Peter

Jackson, fine job that he had done, was ultimately not capable of delivering on the promises the new ownership regime were making was probably correct.

That latterly most of his team talks began with "You'd better play better today 'cos my job's at stake" might illustrate that even he knew the game was up.

To me it was most interesting that supporters who had bemoaned the board for lacking the ambition to propel the club back to the heights of English football were now savaging it for showing no loyalty. Perhaps the two are mutually exclusive?

Having unceremoniously ditched Jackson, we held our collective breath as the big-name, high-profile appointment we had all been waiting for was made... er, Steve Bruce.

"Is *this* the man to lead us to the promised land of the Premiership?" cried the Jackson faithful (some of whom by now were threatening to march on the ground for his reinstatement). What has *he* ever done that Jackson hasn't? Where's *his* pedigree? How will *he* attract high-calibre players to the club, etc, etc?

I'll take my time to judge him by results, not reputation. But as the signings begin to roll in (Donis, Irons, Sellars, Lucketti - with more promised) and pre-season ticket sales breaking all records, it would seem that, finally, Town fans might have to believe that things will only get better.

Watch this space.

Mick Green

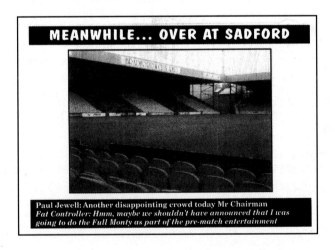

MEANWHILE... OVER AT SADFORD

Paul Jewell: Another disappointing crowd today Mr Chairman
Fat Controller: Hmm, maybe we shouldn't have announced that I was going to do the Full Monty as part of the pre-match entertainment

HEROES & VILLAINS

Aston Villa

The prologue:

Dwight Yorke spent most of the close season moving, inexorably, towards Old Trafford and the lair of the Demon King.

Alex Ferguson admitted that he had been approaching Yorke for twelve months, showing that Manchester United care as much for the FA's rule on poaching players as they do for any other rule. Faced with this admission of an obvious breach of their regulations, the FA did... nothing. Well, it was Manchester United involved so we should all bend over backwards to help them for the good of English football. But we only hate them because we're jealous, aren't we? And so on to the roller-coaster that was '98-99.

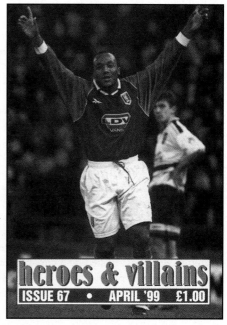

heroes & villains
ISSUE 67 • APRIL '99 £1.00

Act One:

The season got underway with a 0-0 draw at Everton. Mark Bosnich had a typically quiet game, saving a penalty and then being reported to the FA for making gestures to Everton supporters. Yorke played, but didn't look interested.

Five days later, Villa accepted a £12.6m bid for Yorke. It wasn't a particularly happy parting. Yorke said he'd always wanted to play for United, John Gregory made his infamous quote about wanting to shoot the player - and supporters reacted with the usual mixture of anger, bitterness and resignation.

With wonderful timing, the Aston Villa AGM was held that evening and for two hours supporters railed against the board, and Doug Ellis in particular, for lack of ambition. One shareholder read out a list, stretching back over 50 years, of players whom the club had been unable to keep. As a cathartic exercise, it was marvellous; but ultimately futile.

And the football continued. Middlesbrough were the first visitors to Villa Park, and we won that one. In fact, we kept winning. All the pre-season controversy was quickly forgotten, as Villa went on a record-breaking run of 12 matches unbeaten.

An injury to Bosnich meant that more by accident than design, we were fielding an all-English team and being held up as a shining example to the United Nations squads of Chelsea, Arsenal *et al*. John Gregory was lauded for his honesty and straight-talking, even the perennial black cloud that is Stan Collymore seemed to be enjoying his football.

Of course, it couldn't last. Liverpool came to Villa Park and in the midst of a marvellous game, Stan was sent off for attempting to murder Steve Harkness. Villa lost 4-2 and, more significantly, Collymore was never the same again.

The results continued to be promising, though. Yorke returned with the rest of his entourage, and was lucky to get away with a 1-1 draw. He also got booked for arguing with the ref, which was obviously something else he'd learnt at Old Trafford. On a personal note, to the journalist who made up totally false quotes attributed to me in the week leading up to this match (you know who you are)... I hope somebody causes you as much inconvenience one day.

A week later came the match that could have been so significant. Two down at home to Arsenal at half-time, the second-half was delayed following a horrific accident when a parachutist crashed into the Trinity Road stand. A storming comeback, helped by a blatantly offside goal from Dion Dublin, and a 3-2 victory, could only really be celebrated when news came through that we hadn't witnessed a fatality, thank God. With our rivals starting to stumble we were beginning to think we might, after all, go the distance. The size of the squad was a worry, but surely with the chance for glory so close, the money would be available for more new recruits.

Christmas came and the curtain fell with Villa, amazingly, top of the league.

Act two:

The portents were there for the rest of the season at Ewood Park, where Blackburn got a 2-1 victory1 following Michael Oakes' dismissal for accidently carrying the ball out of the penalty-area. Except that it was proved later that he didn't.

January arrived and with it the latest chapter of that long-running tragedy 'Aston Villa in the FA Cup'. A home tie with Hull City saw top of the league versus bottom for the first time since nobody knew when and a 3-0 victory that was uninspiring, to say the least. Then the first real turning point of the season.

We'd been linked with Juninho for some time and the story flared up again. He wanted to join, his club were happy to sell - even Pele was reported as saying we were the right club for his countryman. Finally, the Brazilian was photographed leaving Villa Park and we awaited the press conference. It never happened. The whole sorry saga fizzled out, with Villa claiming he wanted too much money.

Not only had we failed to sign a world class player, who could have transformed a season which was starting to go wrong, the club also reinforced what supporters have long since suspected. The people in charge have no vision, live in a past where a million pounds is still a major transfer fee and are content with jogging along, never willing to make the gamble which could turn the Villa from a large provincial club into a major international one. As was reported at the time, big clubs sign players first, then work out how to afford them later. Villa ask the price, count their loose change and walk away.

While the Juninho farce was limping to its inevitable conclusion, the second downturn came. Fulham at home in the FA Cup Fourth Round, and the most embarrassing defeat I can remember - 2-0, and it could have been more. And didn't that little Canadian goblin, Mr Karren Brady, enjoy it. Rumours flew all weekend about the non-appearance at the match of Stan; and when he finally surfaced, he was off to a clinic, suffering from stress. The stress of knowing what to spend £20,000 a week on, according to the more cynical.

The perfect end to a perfect month came at Newcastle, with defeat and Ugo Ehiogu becoming the latest player 'accidentally' crippled by Alan Shearer. This was the start of a nightmarish league run of one point in eight games, highlighted by heavy home defeats, courtesy of Blackburn and Coventry.

The soap opera continued, with Paul Merson falling off the wagon with a vengeance, Stan making daily headlines, and Gregory proclaiming how he couldn't understand players nowadays.

We eventually pulled out of it and actually won three matches in a row. The highlight was a 1-0 win at Anfield on the tenth anniversary weekend of Hillsborough, which was the second reminder of the season that football really isn't all that important.

Mark Bosnich suffered a mysterious injury, which meant that he coincidentally missed the defeat at Old Trafford, which was where he'd been linked with a move all season. Villa ended '98-99 with two more frustrating defeats. We managed the difficult task of losing at home to Charlton in spectacular fashion. Despite equalising three times and them having their 'keeper sent off and an outfield player having to go in goal, Villa were still able to concede an injury-time fourth - which summed up the season. Losing at Highbury on the final day meant that a team who were top of the league in January finished sixth and even managed to miss out on the dubious delights of the Inter-Toto Cup.

The usual suspects were lined up. Collymore, naturally, led the list of over-paid, under-achieving players. John Gregory took the credit for the good start, so must shoulder some of the blame for the appalling finish. His preference for English players sometimes bordered on the obsessional and meant that Villa paid out some strange transfer fees: £4m for Steve Watson and £5.5m for Steve Stone, for example. His regular outbursts became embarrassing at times and his man-management left something to be desired. Still, the general consensus was that he'll come back better for the experience.

But suspect number one... step forward once more Herbert Douglas Ellis. There was a time during the season when I really thought the Villa could win the league. Just a couple more players and we'd be there. No chance. Altogether, we spent something like £8m net. I know that supporters of most clubs will be wondering what we've got to complain about, but that sort of money when you're chasing a place in the Champions League really is peanuts. Yet again, Villa showed that they always fail to take the final step.

The epilogue:

Bosnich left for Manchester United on a free. He got married the following day, after being released from police custody hours earlier following an incident involving his stag night, a strip club and a photographer. Perhaps it's an Australian custom. His replacement is well-known disaster area David James. The suspicion that James arrived because he was cheap is difficult to shake off. We were interested in Oliver Dacourt. A price was quoted - we made our excuses and left. At the time of writing, Villa are waiting for Coventry to drop the asking price for George Boateng, with several other clubs ready to take advantage of Villa's dithering. Ugo is making ominous noises about wanting reassurance regarding the club's ambition. And his Villa future is far from certain, with several clubs wanting to sign him. *The Evening Mail* regularly prints letters from supporters bemoaning the lack of ambition and vision (those words do keep cropping up). All is worryingly ominous, yet strangely familiar.

Dave Woodhall

Source: *Clap Your Hands Stamp Your Feet!*

HEY BIG SPENDER

Derby County

There can be no doubt that the event which had most effect on the Rams this season was the calamitous fall from grace of Blackburn Rovers. When, during the early days of the campaign, they required extra central defenders for their short but ill-fated European jaunt, they offered big money for Christian Dailly, and we are talking BIG money. Barrowloads of the stuff. Derby snapped up an offer that even the player said was beyond his worth.

Roy Hodgson - or 'Woy' as he's known - stated that he saw Dailly as an ideal replacement for Colin Hendry: ideal presumably in the same way that Mike Tyson would be for Tinky Winky. Don't

FREE LAGER see page 27

HEY BIG $PENDER
an independent derby county football club supporters' magazine
ISSUE NO.32 • DECEMBER 1997 • ONE POUND

get me wrong. I think Christian was a great player at Derby, but not in the same mould as Hendry.

Before fans had time to speculate on who the big money replacement would be, Jim Smith rushed out and bought the utterly dependable Spencer Prior from Leicester for well under a million.

Solid, reliable and runner up in the supporters' Player of the Year vote suggests that Hodgson would have done himself a huge favour by sending his scouts to watch Leicester reserves instead of our first team.

The Dailly transfer, along with other expensive signings that our Woy was unable to knit into a cohesive unit, saw one of the bookies' favourites for the England job only a few months earlier depart from Ewood Park to be superseded by Brian Kidd.

Alex Ferguson wanted the best possible replacement for his trusty lieutenant and, sadly for us, found him working alongside Jim Smith.

Steve McLaren (for it was he) had proved an enormous influence on Derby County Football Club during his time here, and although Jim Smith acted quickly to bring in Ray Harford - a highly-rated coach of the old school - it seemed inevitable that at some stage the innovations which McLaren introduced to keep us up with the big boys would be sorely missed.

Lee Carsley was the last Derby-Blackburn crossover of the season to depart, and although the Birmingham-born Eire international had his critics, he did a vital job for Derby this time around, just in front of the defence. It was surely no coincidence that his departure corresponded with the once-impregnable Rams defence suddenly shipping goals with the same ferocity as the Titanic leaked water after its meeting with the iceberg.

Maybe things would not have been so bad had Seth Johnson agreed to sign at the first time of asking.

Another club whose destiny was closely linked with our own was Arsenal. The mighty Gunners conspired to remove us from both knock-out competitions, embarrassingly by bringing a virtual reserve side to Pride Park and ending our interest in the Worthington Cup, while we held a full Arsenal team right until stoppage-time in the FA Cup before home pressure told and Kanu got the all-important, but cruel, winning goal.

As the season progressed, Rams turned from a side who did not score or concede many to a side who just did not score. All the regular strikers had leaner times this year - although how much of that was down to the absence of Francisco Baiano, through injury, is hard to tell.

Best of the bunch was the previously much-derided Deon Burton, who suddenly sprang into goal-scoring action after being shipped off to Barnsley on loan. Having been to Barnsley, I can well imagine what a culture shock it must have been to someone playing in the World Cup only months earlier.

Improved though Burton's contribution was, Derby never looked totally convincing in front of goal, and if the defence had not been so frugal in the opening months, it could well have been Derby who took the drop.

The first months were professionally fought, though with an early season visit to Villa Park seeing the team with a chance of going top for the first time in 25 years. One goal, sadly, settled it and we never reached such stratospheric heights again.

Let us not be too pessimistic, though. Derby were never in trouble at any stage of the term and had European qualification as a very real target for much of the time - until UEFA moved the goalposts, dictating that the spot we thought would be the reward for finishing fifth was handed to Newcastle, for no other reason than to be bloody-minded, because our governing body insisted that the Worthington Cup winners retain a European place.

After the decision had been made, you could see some of the spirit drain from the players. They knew that fifth was possible, but at that stage were aware that fourth-placed Leeds were unreachable, being 16 points ahead.

High spots for most people would have to be defeating Liverpool at Anfield - a feat not managed previously in a generation - and completing the double over them for what seemed like the first time since Methuselah had a ticket for the boys' pen at the Baseball Ground.

Doing the double over Leicester was also nice, although it was a sign of our goalscoring problems that the 2-0 victory at Pride Park proved to be our largest winning margin of the league campaign.

Despite their own record-breaking season, Nottingham Forest held us to a draw at their place, and we could manage no more than a one-goal victory at Pride Park, courtesy of a late Carbonari strike. If many Rams fans were sniggering at their demise, I was certainly not one of them. Give me a 17-mile journey over a trip up the A1 to the north-east any day!

Incidentally, Carbonari managed the double twice, scoring home and away against both Forest and Chelsea.

Best league display was probably Middlesbrough at home during the Christmas period, with a late, great winner from Jonathan Hunt, who we seemed to spend the majority of the year trying to offload to anyone and their uncle.

The FA Cup managed to draw us away to every far-flung corner of the Empire that it felt we were unlikely to visit in normal circumstances, although it did allow me to tick off several pages of my I Spy 'Little Chef' book - even if overdosing on all-day 'Olympic' breakfasts is harmful to the cholesterol level.

Thinking about it, the whole season seems to have been measured in toilet stops and big breakfasts, with roadworks on the A1 being particularly troublesome. How joyous to see Sunderland added to our journeys in that direction for the next term.

The lowest points were probably the final three home games, against Forest, Southampton and Coventry. We managed to score an aggregate total of one goal against three teams who were all there for the taking, that UEFA ruling again depriving Rams of the impetus to finish on a high.

As far as personnel were concerned, early departures for Gary Rowett, Chris Powell and Christian Dailly were disappointing. It is sad to think that we will see none of them in league action with visiting teams at Pride Park next time around (transfers notwithstanding) but, as mentioned earlier, we may have missed them as individuals but the defence seemed stronger for the changes.

Similarly, Igor Stimac's absence did not cause the lowering of standards that he suggested was the case.

Incoming players seemed in the main solid, if unspectacular. Youngsters like Harper, Christie and, most notably, Adam Murray (the most exciting home-grown talent for some time) suggest that Jim Smith's pronouncements about building a young team with a few top quality foreigners to add the sparkle are taking shape.

In closing, I guess that we can say that this season was not as exciting, or possibly entertaining, as previous ones, but it was progress of a very real kind.

In a Premiership where tea ladies seem to change hands for seven-figure sums, just being there fighting your corner without mega-bucks budgets is success. When you also improve positions and/or points, it all bodes well for the future.

Phil Matthews

HEY JUDE

Brentford

Brentford in the Third Division was not the most appealing of prospects, and certainly took a bit of getting used to. After Ron Noades bought out the hated Dave Webb's majority shareholding for the princely sum of £850,000, frustrated Bees fans faced up to the stark reality of at least a year in the basement division. But what a season it turned out to be.

Chairman Noades immediately installed himself as team manager and appointed, what he called, some of the best coaches in the country - Ray Lewington and Brian Sparrow (from Palace), and Terry Bullivant, the former Brentford player.

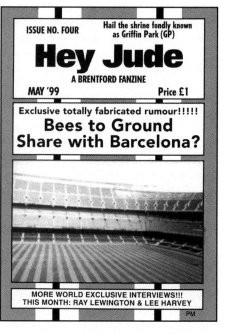

ISSUE NO. FOUR — Hail the shrine fondly known as Griffin Park (GP)

Hey Jude

A BRENTFORD FANZINE

MAY '99   Price £1

Exclusive totally fabricated rumour!!!!!

Bees to Ground Share with Barcelona?

MORE WORLD EXCLUSIVE INTERVIEWS!!!
THIS MONTH: RAY LEWINGTON & LEE HARVEY

PM

Lewington is the man many Palace fans attribute to their various successful periods, and he was officially head coach. Crucially, John Griffin also joined the club as chief scout (via Palace). His contribution was to prove immense.

Noades arrived at Griffin Park with the reputation of being an outspoken, colourful character (to say the least). But he was welcomed with open arms by Brentford fans, who were just relieved to see the back of Webb. He, no doubt, was sunning himself and counting the fortune he had 'earned' out of our club. Noades, or Uncle Ron as he was to become known, made all the right noises on his much-publicised takeover, although some Bees fans remained fairly sceptical towards him. After the traumas of previous seasons, fans needed to be won over by Uncle Ron. This was achieved - but not without a few hiccups along the way. Noades criticised his popular and highly respected predecessor, Micky Adams, for the pre-season friendly schedule, which had intended to visit southern Ireland (a trip many of us would have gone on) and, apparently, a dodgy pitch at Bashley. Although I thought these sorts of comments were both petty and unnecessary, they were something we would grow accustomed to.

The season kicked off with mercurial striker Robert Taylor moving on to Gillingham for £500,000, to join all his ex-Brentford buddies and spearhead their play-off push. Noades tried desperately to persuade Taylor to stay, offering him a huge contract. But the striker's mind was made up and off he trudged to ramshackle Priestfield, Kent's answer to Underhill. I could understand Rob wanting to leave but it was nonetheless more than irritating to see Gillingford (as we call them) enjoying such a good season, with the backbone of their side having made their names at Griffin Park. Popular Carl Hutchings was sold to Bristol City for just £135,000. This left the team requiring almost total rebuilding, a fact not unnoticed by clubs in the division, eager to put one over on what we were, for the first time, to become known as - "Moneybags Brentford".

The team's surgery began. In came Quinn, Boxall and Folan from Palace, Martin Rowlands from Farnborough, Darren Powell from Hampton (remember that name) and Lloyd Owusu from Slough Town. All six proved to be shrewd acquisitions - and all six were bought for a song. Darren Freeman also arrived on a free - from Fu**am - but did a good job early in the season. Ron later signed Hermann Hreidarsson (of Iceland and... er, Palace) for half a million pounds (yes, Brentford paid £500,000 for one player!) and the classy Gavin Mahon from Hereford for £90,000 - a steal. Although Bees fans had to check their programmes to learn who was who, the results were impressive and the football exciting. West Brom were disposed of in some style (3-0) in the Worthington Cup and Tottenham were dead lucky to overcome the Bees over two legs in the third round on a 6-4 aggregate.

Brentford won ten out of the first eleven home league games. The only slight problem was the away form. Brentford's biggest opponent was the complacent attitude shown on their travels. Poor results and performances at places like Torquay, Scarborough, Shrewsbury and Rochdale (who all treated our visit as their cup finals, it seemed) were deemed unacceptable by the fans and Noades himself. Only the still excellent home form was keeping the team in promotion contention. Sandwiched in between all these games were a couple more controversial outbursts from Uncle Ron. He criticised attendances, more than once he threatened to quit the club, and blasted the fans for apparently barracking the young side he had assembled. With Noades, what you see and hear is what you get. I suppose we can't have it both ways. On the one hand, you want to know what's going on at the club and you want frank comment. On the other, sometimes you don't like what you hear. On one occasion Ron described a section of Bees fans as idiots and morons. He also complimented W***, despite knowing how despised he was at Griffin Park. Sometimes I got the impression that Ron was trying to wind up the fans. At one stage, I even wondered whether Ron perhaps preferred the sound of boos (which he was used to) to cheers (which he obviously wasn't). A reluctant hero? Yes. Jekyll and Hyde? No. Victor Meldrew and Captain Sensible? Maybe.

Throughout the season, Bees fans were accused of being arrogant by some of our, albeit mainly northern, counterparts. If the truth be told, perhaps Bees fans enjoyed being a bigger fish in a smaller pond. If the enthusiasm was occasionally over the top, it was only to be expected. Okay, we may have considered ourselves 'too big' for the division W*** had dragged us into (via the gutter), but you'd have to be a Brentford fan to appreciate fully the positive turnaround in the club's fortunes since Noades' arrival. For me, one statement summed up the club's new, professional and more ambitious attitude. At a sell-out fans forum at the club, held on transfer deadline day, Noades was asked if he had received offers for any of his highly-promising young players. The answer was sweet music to the ear of any Bees fan: "No. Clubs realise we're going for promotion, they'd be wasting their time." That refreshing stance was unique for us. If I just mention the names of Andy Sinton and Nicky Forster, Bees fans will know what I mean...

There was no contest for the *Hey Jude* Idiot of the Season award. So-called referee Kevin Lynch, a name not unfamiliar with the pages of this book, won this dubious 'accolade' for his performance at Leyton Orient. With the Bees 1-0 up, Orient turned the game on its head with two goals, aided by a couple of highly debatable decisions. With gusto, over 2,000 away fans sang in unison, "2-1 to the referee" - and were amazed to see Lynch theatrically bow in front of them. Not the most sensible of reactions by Lynch (who nearly was) and this provoked trouble in the stands. I've followed Brentford for a long time - this was the first time I'd ever seen Bees fans ripping up seats. Though not an excuse, it was the fault of the referee and his equally inept linesman and lineswoman. Lynch later received a ticking-off from the FA following complaints by Brentford officials and fans alike.

Boxing Day saw Griffin Park resemble Beirut as Cardiff City 'fans' descended on West London for a promotion six-pointer. The away end at GP (affectionately known as The Wendy House) only has room for 2,400 visitors. When Cardiff do well, their away support miraculously increases ten-fold, it seems. Brentford gave them an extra 900 seats in the main stand but still an estimated 1,000 Taffs were locked out for a match that, incredibly, wasn't all-ticket. Chelsea yuppies like Banks and Mellor can prattle on as much as they like about hooliganism being a thing of the past. The residents of TW18 and regulars at GP can tell a different story - dozens of cars (and even some houses) around the ground were trashed at will. Next season, if Cardiff are languishing in mid-table or lower, I expect they will bring their usual 250 or so to the shrine of football. Fickle? No, surely not.

With Brentford hovering around the top three places, Noades once again conducted some interesting transfer business. Out went the promising and popular striker Kevin Rapley, crowd favourite Warren Aspinall, 'keeper Kevin Dearden, followed by club captain and Brentford legend, Jamie Bates, a veteran of over 500 appearances. It's fair to say Noades was taking a chance by releasing those players, but in time he was to be proved correct. Two players arrived at £100,000 apiece - Paul Evans from Shrewsbury and Scott Partridge from Torquay (which pissed off Helen Chamberlain big time, bless her!). Evans was immediately installed as captain and added a new dimension to the team from his midfield berth, whilst Partridge gave the free-scoring cult figure Owusu the strike-partner he required.

Bingo! The new additions were the missing ingredients - neither Evans or Partridge appeared in a losing Brentford side, as they embarked on a 16-match unbeaten run.

If the (alleged) attendance figures at GP didn't properly reflect the feel-good factor returning to the fans, the fever a good run brings was there for all to see for the Southend away game in April. Over 200 pissed up Bees fans took an astonishing four hours travelling up the Thames from Westminster to Southend on the BeesBoat! An easy 4-1 win ensured the pre-match party atmosphere was retained for the entire evening.

Further celebrations followed the Exeter game (when promotion was confirmed), the 4-1 demolition of Swansea and, last but far from least, the final-day 1-0 win at Cambridge, which clinched the title and sparked jubilant scenes around Brentford that evening. Success can bring its problems, especially if you're not as accustomed to it as you'd like - the hangovers tend to feel worse than normal, don't they?

Step one of the rebuilding process has been completed but there are some concerns about the club's immediate future. Uncle Ron has stated that there's no future in Griffin Park and is adamant that Brentford need a new stadium. What worries the fans is that he's prepared for the club to groundshare on an 'interim basis' until our new ground is ready - QPR were approached, but thankfully rejected the suggestion. That idea might be reluctantly bearable if our new home was at least under construction but, as I write, planning permission has not even been granted. Wary of the problems at Wimbledon and Brighton, Bees fans are obviously concerned we could end up homeless if GP is sold, we lodge elsewhere and a new ground isn't guaranteed.

Our other worry is that Noades could yet return to Palace as his protracted dispute with Goldberg rumbles on. I have a view on what happened at Selhurst but, let's face it, what's it got to do with us? (No disrespect intended to Palace fans, by the way). However, if Ron were to return to Selhurst, he would leave himself open to much criticism at our end. He wouldn't be the "football man" he calls himself. He would prove himself to be motivated by money and nothing else.

Whatever people say about Uncle Ron, it's a case of so far, so good at Griffin Park. He's done the club proud (at the time of writing!) and certainly proved himself in footballing terms. Some may scoff and say it's down to Lewington *et al* - but Ron employed all these guys (and put real money into the club), so the credit is his as I see it. Not only has he brought success to the club, he's acquired some fantastic young players (at least two future full internationals) and provided some genuinely thrilling football for the fans. Uncle Ron proved a hell of a lot of people wrong, me included if I'm honest. What's this? *Hey Jude* praising the management? Send for the men in white coats.

The only other blips in an otherwise excellent Brentford season were QPR somehow staying up, Fulham going up, and Watford going for nine months vacation in the Premiership. So our only local derby is against Millwall. Better than Barnet, though.

Roll on next season. Let's hope Brentford's renaissance continues. I'm confident of at least a play-off spot.

Come on, Brentford.

P Johnston

HIT THE BAR!

Carlisle United

The Great Escape

Everybody in the world now knows how our season ended. A jammy 94th minute goal hammered in by our on-loan 'keeper Jimmy Glass keeping us in the league for, at least, another season.

How did it come to this? Why should a club who 25 years ago sat proudly on top of the old First Division be fighting for its existence in the last ten seconds of the '98-99 season? I'm afraid the story is a familiar one - of lack of investment, lack of money and lack of vision throughout the intervening years. All of that changed, we thought, in 1992

when Michael Knighton took over. Knighton was big on change, big on investment, big on publicity, big on vision - but sadly for the club, it appears, not too big on money. To be fair to the man, he always said that he would get us to the top, whilst not paying big transfer fees and by ensuring the club did not become insolvent. Nevertheless, swept along by his enthusiasm and astute financial management, the club turned loss into profit, failure into success; and a Championship, a promotion and a Wembley win later, we couldn't believe our luck.

Then it all went wrong - badly wrong. Our director of coaching, Mick Wadsworth, left for greener pastures (Norwich, Scarborough and Colchester) and the team and its tactics suffered. His successor, Mervyn Day, and Knighton never saw eye to eye, and Day was soon relieved of his duties. After the extraordinary came the bizarre. Knighton appointed himself manager (assisted by the youth team trainer and 'football in the community' officer), changed the tactics again, and although relegated, still believed he could turn the situation around himself. In the close season, he signed a new defence, letting some under-performing, but good and popular players leave for nothing - or next to it.

The season began badly and the new team never formed or performed. A 1-0 win over Brighton was hardly a convincing start; and the writing was on the wall just two weeks later when we lost at home to Rochdale. A week later and we were on the bottom of the division. A 3-0 thrashing of Southend lifted us up to mid-table and talk of the play-offs, but two weeks later we were down in the bottom four again. With no midfield, we had to knock the long ball over the top to our forwards. It was not pretty stuff and soon the ageing - sorry, experienced - forwards gave up chasing lost causes. Once the goals had dried up, nothing could start them coming again. We didn't score a single goal in November, and only managed four in the whole of December. Knighton eventually admitted defeat and appointed the ex-Middlesbrough and Sheffield Wednesday star Nigel Pearson as manager. Pearson's arrival tightened the defence, increased the commitment and brought some much-needed tactical savvy to the side. After an initial purple patch in which we did the double over both Brighton and Southend, we discovered we had a side that even Alex Ferguson couldn't have helped; and, consequently, the results failed to improve.

We had a diversion at Christmas, when the club shop began to sell Carlisle shirts with a number '7' and the name 'Beardsley' across the back. Peter Beardsley was exactly the sort of midfield player we so badly needed and he very nearly rejoined the club who launched his career. But it all ended in tears, with Knighton, who wanted to sign him, and Beardsley, who wanted to join, somehow failing adequately to communicate the relevant facts to each other.

As the transfer deadline approached, the fans were now calling for Knighton to get out his chequebook. Following three 1-0 defeats in March, we expected the side to be strengthened. But instead, on transfer deadline day, we sold our best midfield player, Paul Boertien, to Derby; our only goalkeeper, Tony Caig, and our improving midfielder, Andy Couzens, to Blackpool; and one of our experienced strikers, Steve Finney, to Orient. In replacement, we got two young reserve strikers, a reserve midfielder and Derby's third team goalkeeper on loan. Guess what happened to our results?

Half the problem had been that no-one had thrashed us. Thirteen of our 19 defeats had been by a single goal. It gave us all hope that it would still work out. When Paul Boertien scored at Swansea in February, on his reappearance from injury, we thought our problems were solved. This goal should be commemorated. In some ways it was the goal of the season. It was, in fact, the only goal scored in open play by a midfielder. After only six games last season and seven games this time around, Paul joined the list of young Carlisle players snatched by bigger clubs before they could ever really show us their best. Steve Harkness, Paul Murray, Matt Jansen and Rory Delap are others who immediately spring to mind.

It was a season of few highlights. Billy Barr's amazing 20-yard volleyed own-goal at Brentford, seconds after we had taken the lead, would have been typical of the type of fluke that would have put us down, had he not tried it again two weeks later at Swansea. The ease with which we won at Brighton, including a splendid free-kick from Scott Paterson and an individual goal from Scott Dobie, stands out in the memory. Light relief was provided in the Mickey Mouse Cup where we beat Scunthorpe on penalties, only to lie down and let arch-enemies Wigan walk all over us at Brunton Park in the quarter-finals.

In August we had a team who had forgotten how to win. Now we had a team who had never seen a win. With things getting sticky, we managed our best win at home to Torquay in front of a good crowd on Easter Saturday (3-0), only to record our worst defeat two days later at Scarborough (0-3). It suddenly began to look very bleak. We looked at the remaining fixtures for each of the bottom clubs, totalled up the prospective points, and realised that we needed Scarborough, Southend and Hartlepool to keep losing.

If this wasn't bad enough, we started to get reports from Scotland that Clydebank wanted to merge with us and play from Brunton Park in the Scottish First Division. Can you imagine it? Scotland v England every week - trips to Inverness for London branch fans. Not a big vote winner. If Knighton wanted to win friends, then he needed to distance himself as far as possible from the rumours. Instead, he said that he shared some similar views on football with Clydebank's chairman and the fans would have to decide on this interesting idea. Most of the fans did, and the letters piled in to the local paper - almost all of them condemning the prospect. Still, the rumour fails to lie down and die, and scarcely a day passes without my e-mail being added to by a plaintive plea from another Bankies fan to help them save their club. We'll do what we can.

When Southend accelerated away, and then Hartlepool - aided by Beardsley - picked up some points, it was left to a dogfight between ourselves and Scarborough. Obviously there was only ever going to be one winner - until, that was, Scarborough ended Halifax's play-off hopes and we began to worry again.

So it all came down to the last game. Our first problem was to present the award to the Player of the Season. Most of the candidates had ruled themselves out by leaving. McGregor, Caig, Boertien, Finney and Scott had all left or failed to have been signed after promising loan periods. The award went to Stuart Whitehead - certainly a player to watch for the future - for just staying there and not giving up, really.

An amazing record under Knighton of play-offs, championship, relegation, promotion, and relegation in successive seasons was now going to have oblivion added to it. Or so it seemed, until 7,599 fans waved Glass up for the last corner of the match, Dobie headed it goalwards only for it to be pushed out by the 'keeper to the feet of the onrushing Glass, who smashed it into the back of the net.

I have never witnessed or experienced such blatant raw emotion - getting to the First Division, beating Everton at Goodison, winning the Third Division Championship, winning at Wembley - all paled into insignificance when compared to this.

With tears in our eyes, our voices hoarse from shouting, the tannoy played the theme music to *The Great Escape* and we basked in the vision of an ageing motorbike leaping over a wire fence, being ridden by Jimmy Glass and disappearing into the sunset...

Malcolm Fawcett

HOOF!

Plymouth Argyle

It's difficult to write much of worth about the first 36 weeks of last season. I would like to be able to say what a pleasure it was to follow my team, but until May there was only a *soupcon* of interest. I would like to have commented on how glorious it was to travel the country watching The 'Gyle in a distant utopia; but, no matter how you try, Rotherham and Leyton do not exactly match the awayday exotica of a trip to, say, Anfield, nor even a Maine Road.

Pre-season began as ordinary as pre-seasons can be. A couple of high-profile Home friendlies (against Birmingham and Sunderland) were followed by more traditional away fare visiting

Hoof! ISSUE SEVEN JAN 99 - now 50p

WRITTEN BY ARGYLE FANS FOR ARGYLE FANS

Bad Karma Day in Exeter!

URI GELLER'S PLAN FOR A CITY WIN BACKFIRES

BELIEVE, TRUST, EXETER WILL WIN!

1-0 TO THE ARGYLE... 1-0 TO THE ARGYLE

the local non-league grounds. Personally, I was only able to get to the Yeovil fixture. Off the field, the club was in a transitional period. Relegation stemming from that last-day defeat at scummy Burnley (I have hope - what goes around comes around!) had cost popular manager Mick Jones his job. His replacement was former Argyle hero Kevin Hodges, who finally returned Home after a successful spell at Torquay. Along with Hodgy came another former 'Gyle, Steve McCall. This seemed like a good move - McCall could bring his UEFA Cup winning experience alongside a man who truly loved the club. Could this be the dawning of a new era?

On paper, at least, we had secured the names of some decent players. Lee Power had joined us on a free transfer from Hibernian, who had signed two Argyle summer targets, Mixu Paatelainen and Stuart Lovell (who said The Greens settled for third best?) We had also secured the services of ex-'Gyle Sean McCarthy. Team McCarthy up with Hodges and McCall, plus our backroom team of Geoff Crudgington, Kevin Summerfield and Tommy Tynan, and we now had a true Argyle 'Team of the Eighties'. Typical West Country - ten years too late! Also making the short journey from Torquay with Hodgie was Paul Gibbs - boyfriend of Sky's Helen Chamberlain.

Hoof!

Notice how all of these players were obtained on a free - chairman Dan McCauley obviously not backing his faith in the manager enough to give him money to spend.

The season began with the slight glimmer of expectation that all first days bring. They usually last for 90 minutes. However, to be fair, our opening day excursion against Rochdale was a scorcher. The new 'Retro Argyle' outplayed The Dale in all departments and a 2-1 Argyle win flattered the Lancastrians (stick to cricket, lads).

The boys in green were brought down to earth with a bang at Mansfield. Field Mill may only have two sides these days, but there was only one side on the field, as The Stags' strike-force - Lee Peacock in particular - took us apart, scoring two goals without reply.

We fared a little better in the newly-named Worthington Cup against old dockyard rivals Pompey. A 3-6 aggregate scoreline was not as bad as it may appear: the performance at Fratton Park was reasonably enjoyable for the considerable Argyle contingent present.

A good run towards the end of August saw us maintain the high position that the bookies had predicted, whilst September brought Argyle an indifferent seven points from 15.

Our first local derby saw Argyle travel to Plainmoor, where as normal we took three sides of the ground without much resistance from the stewards. Opposing colours were being openly worn side by side and the nearest thing to crowd trouble in Torqueer that Saturday would have been found down on the promenade, where thousands of old grannies were fighting to feed the birds in an end-of-holiday-season melée.

In such a tranquil atmosphere, it was surprising that the match was threatening to boil over at times - Paul Gibbs not being made welcome at his former club - and, in the end, Argyle were lucky to take a point back to Plymouth.

Before the injury sustained after the Torquay game, Argyle fans were beginning to doubt all the hype that Gibbs had brought with him. His defending was a little suspect and many - myself included - doubted his commitment to the club.

November hinted at what Argyle's season would ultimately become - we secured a great 3-0 win against Ron 'Ego' Noades' high-flying Brentford, yet lost at lowly Hartlepool, where fans' feelings against the static and cumbersome Lee Power threatened to boil over, after the hapless striker (the term being used loosely) made hand gestures at the loyal travelling support. Ultimately, Power was only to make one more appearance for Argyle before being hounded out in his straitjacket to the unfortunate Halifax institution. Fan power lives on.

The trivia buffs among you will know that it is possible to win the FA Cup in six games. Argyle took three to even reach round two. It took a dramatic penalty shoot-out at Aggborough to knock out plucky Kiddy Harriers after they drew at Home Park in the original match. The replay, scheduled ten days later, was abandoned at half-time, due to a severe case of traffic congestion wafting over from nearby Birmingham. No it wasn't fog, honest!

In the second round it took another replay to get past Second Division Wycombe, a team who gave us a real hammering on our last visit (I refuse to mention the score). Heroics at Adams Park from what was basically a rookie team earned us the right to a Home replay, which we duly won 3-2, and a trip to Dreamland in round three.

Before we could worry about Derby in the next round, we had a derby of a different kind to look forward. It's always fun to play the crap up the road (whose name I conveniently forget), if only to see the looks on their sorry faces when we beat them. Of course, today was no different, as the Scum lost to a superbly taken goal from Howard Forinton, our on-loan star from Birmingham City.

Unfortunately, this euphoria didn't continue into the New Year, as we lost 3-0 at Home to Derby County in the third round of the FA Cup. *Match of the Day* didn't seem to care, as the game wasn't deemed fit for broadcast. Perhaps Des, Gary and co realise that Argyle away is no longer the threat of yesteryear. Anyway, who cares about the FA Cup now it's been bought by an insurance firm?

By now, Argyle had a considerably younger looking team than had started the season against Rochdale. The three players who stood out were full-backs Jon Ashton and Jon Beswetherick - the latter replacing the injury-prone Gibbs - and midfielder Darren Bastow.

Despite a fresh injection of young blood into the side, and although we only lost two of our next eleven games, most Argyle fans were dismissive of our promotion chances. We had managed a respectable draw away at St Blames' Park, Excreta (Howard Forinton yet again) and, to the neutral, Argyle's future would have looked 'wear your Ray-Ban's' bright. However, two defeats followed (against lowly Hull and Chester of all teams) and seemed to suggest that us ever-knowledgeable 'Gyles were correct. But two smashing results followed to put possible egg on the doubters' faces, including a 5-0 thumping of Scunthorpe (and looked where they ended up).

By now, Super Howard Forinton had gone, but we found another loanee terrace hero in Steve Guinan from FOREST (Fighting Off Relegation Every Saturday Tea-time). Guinan scored seven goals in eight games for Argyle and was our second-highest goalscorer of the season.

In the midst of all this, yet another ex-'Gyle terrace hero had returned to the club. It was unfortunate that Nicky Marker's second coming coincided with a four-game run in which not one goal was scored by an Argyle player, including a 0-0 Home draw with Torqueer. Welcome Home, Nicky!

Four defeats in April condemned us to another season in Division Three, but I have never known a week as entertaining or exciting in all my time as a football supporter as the final week of the season, which put Argyle in the headlines.

It all began with a trip in the *Hoof!*-mobile from Southampton to Scarborough, hijacking Steve from *Rub of the Greens* on the way. Our intention was to threaten to strip him naked if Argyle won, but a pathetic 3-0 defeat saved his (and probably our) blushes.

We decided on a drink in the Boro Social Club before our long trip back south. What we intended on was a quiet drink - what we got was a full-scale knees-up with what must be the friendliest club in football. Everyone was there celebrating - fans, players and chairman all together. We ended up swapping scarves and promising to return on Saturday after we visited Carlisle.

Unless you were holidaying on Mars, you will know that Scarborough and Carlisle were scrapping it out for league survival. Again, we drove up north, this time to Brunton Park. Our hostage had decided not to join us this time - he made his own way up.

Despite the fact that Carlisle were fighting for survival, you would have thought this was a routine end-of-season mid-table amble. Carlisle lacked the will to win, and we couldn't help wonder what would happen to us if we were to send them down. Most Argyle fans were talking about leaving early when Lee Phillips got his first senior goal to put us in front.

The Scarborough boys who we met earlier on the week were now on the phone to us as injury-time commenced. It was real nail-biting stuff - Carlisle were going down and had the seats ripped up ready to take it out on some poor unfortunate away fans. I was now in full Motty mode to my Scarborough pal on my mobile. The tension was mounting - surely this was the last corner? I was on a roll: "Their goalie's coming forward... the ball comes in from the left... it's inswinging... our 'keeper's come for it... he misses with the punch... it goes straight to their 'keeper... GOAL!" I didn't want to be excited for Scarborough's sake, because they treated us like royalty, but this was without doubt the most exciting match I had witnessed away from Home. To be fair, the Carlisle fans were as nice as Cumberland Pie. Both sets of fans invaded the pitch together at the final whistle, we pluralled their chants of "There's only one greedy bastard" at their reviled chairman, Michael Knighton, to include our own megalomaniac, Dan McCauley.

It was a shame that one team had to go down and I hope with all of my heart that Scarborough can come back up next year, though it will be hard. But as we failed to win at Carlisle, and Exeter won, the plot took a new sinister twist. Not even the hilarity of Gillingham being finally humbled by Man City in such amusing circumstances, or Burnley losing by a cricket score every week, could lift us from the embarrassment of finishing below the Scum.

So it was certainly not the best season in Argyle's history. It was the first time that we'd ever finished in the bottom half of the bottom flight. Under McCauley's dictatorship it is probably, like the group who sang it, only a D:Ream that *Things Can Only Get Better*, if you'll excuse the pun. It has been TWO YEARS since we last bought a player. I can no longer keep the faith. This is what it has come to. This year, maybe we will know how it feels to be Carlisle. Only with our luck, we won't have Jimmy Glass in goal.

Blake Hall

IN THE LOFT

Queens Park Rangers

Being a QPR supporter these last few years has not been the most comfortable of rides. Since relegation from the Premiership in 1996, we're currently on our fourth manager in an attempt to get back to the Promised Land, but the only division we've been most likely to join is Division Two. For a team who spent the first half of the 1990s living comfortably with the best in the top half of the Premiership/Division One, to say the last few years have been rather less than enjoyable would be a massive understatement.

The surrealism of Sunday 9 May, though, will live long in the memory of all QPR fans.

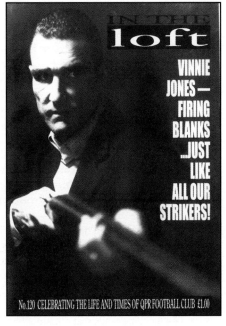

No.120 CELEBRATING THE LIFE AND TIMES OF QPR FOOTBALL CLUB £1.00

Needing a win against Crystal Palace to guarantee safety from Division One, we'd have all settled for a scrappy 1-0 victory - "scrappy" being the most common word to describe QPR's performances this past season - but to win 6-0 was quite unexpected, almost shocking for a team which had struggled to score goals throughout, and whose top scorer remained Mike Sheron, who left the club in January with the modest total of nine goals.

All fans have witnessed their team run up a cricket score at least once in their lives, but the whole manner of the victory over Palace made it much more than just a convincing win. The general feeling amongst a lot of fans was that if QPR could avoid relegation, next season under Gerry Francis would see a turnaround in fortunes. As each goal found the back of the net, it seemed to carry the message of "wait 'til next season". It would be premature to suggest the win will see a rebirth of QPR as a potent force, but as a season's worth of frustration was expelled that Sunday afternoon, a major barrier had been overcome. How I wish every match could be like this. A full house, a roaring atmosphere and a tremendous win. Relegation would have been disastrous but, under Gerry Francis, I believe we can look forward to next season with a great deal more enthusiasm than how we had started this one under Ray Harford.

The required win against Palace would not have been necessary had QPR not lost their five previous matches, which made the trouncing of Palace so much more remarkable. A week earlier at Port Vale, 4,000 QPR fans made the journey to Vale Park, hoping for the win that would see us safe, but left brimming with frustration and anger - there appeared to be no escape route. It seemed this once respectable little club from London W12 had finally paid the price for years of mis-management.

When QPR were relegated to Division One in 1996, Chris Wright - our supposed knight in shining armour - was soon expected to get us back on the right tracks, having taken over from Richard Thompson as chairman. If Thompson was ridiculed for not spending any money, then in Chris Wright we had the total opposite. For the first two years, Wright gave his managers an almost endless supply of money in a bid to return to the top division, failing to check regularly our true financial situation, in the blinkered belief that a return to the prosperity of the Premiership was only another signed cheque away.

Like a kid alone in a candy store, he'd eaten all the sickly sweets and was now paying the price for it. The feeling of satisfaction didn't materialise - QPR remained in the wrong half of the division, as huge debts crept up from almost nowhere - from financial security to almost bankruptcy in just two years. By September 1998, QPR hit rock bottom. As debts of £5m+ were announced, Gerry Francis was called upon to pull off the great escape act, combined with the task of helping to reduce the debts. A slight inroad was made when Francis purchased a million shares - total price: £110,000. Had he purchased a similar amount in January 1997, it would have set him back close to £1.2m.

The fact that QPR still remain a First Division club owes much to Gerry Francis. It would be too much to expect him to enjoy the same kind of moderate success he had in his first spell as manager, but as anyone who was at that final fixture of the season against Crystal Palace can vouch, the heart of QPR is still beating loud and strong - all it needs now is some greater exercise.

Howard Prosser

IT'S AN EASY ONE FOR NORMAN

Sunderland

In *SOTF4*, I confidently predicted in the aftermath of THAT shattering play-off defeat that Sunderland would win automatic promotion the following season. However, I didn't predict just how dominant Sunderland would be.

A total of 105 points (18 clear of second-placed Bradford), 93 league goals, and just three league defeats. Oh, and the small matter of defeating every Division One side at least once. In a season of superlatives, it is difficult to know where to begin.

Put simply, Sunderland were far too good for the rest of Division One, something I suspected might be the case, even

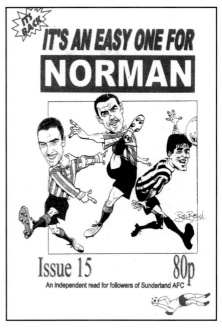

IT'S BACK

IT'S AN EASY ONE FOR

NORMAN

Issue 15   80p

An independent read for followers of Sunderland AFC

when walking down the steps out of Wembley after the Charlton epic. Despite this feeling, there was nothing inevitable about Sunderland's march to the Championship. The history of the play-offs is littered with examples of losing play-off finalists sliding into mid-table mediocrity the following season. The main reason Sunderland bucked this trend is the superb, close-knit atmosphere fostered by Peter Reid and assistant-manager Bobby Saxton at the club, and epitomised by Niall Quinn just minutes after the Wembley final, when the Charlton players were still cavorting on the pitch. In front of the Sky cameras, he said the players could either feel sorry for themselves or be up and ready from the start in August. And so it proved.

With key players such as Kevin Phillips and Lee Clark pledging their futures to the club, and in general, a solid infrastructure in place thanks to the new stadium and a united boardroom, everything was in place for a successful season. The fans played their part, too, with an average attendance just under 39,000, the third highest in England, after Man United and Liverpool.

There were obviously many highlights - early away victories against promotion rivals Bolton and Ipswich gave sign of intent; victory at West Bromwich Albion, after going 2-0 down with 30 minutes left on the clock, demonstrated the mettle and never-say-die attitude of the team, which would brush so many others aside on their way to the Championship.

Perhaps the best home performances were the 3-0 victory over Bolton (particularly sweet given Bolton manager Colin Todd's confident prediction just weeks earlier that his club could catch and overtake Sunderland at the top) and the 3-0 Easter Saturday hammering of West Bromwich Albion, a dazzling display which was a joy to watch.

The final home game, against Birmingham City in front of another capacity crowd, was obviously a special occasion: another victory and the Championship trophy held aloft by captain Kevin Ball for the second time in three years. Any comparisons with the team and circumstances of 1996 should end there, though. A casual look around the packed Stadium of Light will have convinced anyone with memories of Roker Park that the club is in a far healthier and stronger position to compete with the Premiership big boys than was the case last time. The squad itself is also far stronger, epitomised by England call-ups for Kevin Phillips and Michael Gray, and a regular Scottish international in Alan Johnson. Throw in Peter Schmeichel's Danish understudy, Thomas Svenson - an exceptional goalkeeper - and you can understand why Sunderland fans are more confident this time round.

Whilst pundits constantly decry the huge and 'unbridgeable' gap between the Premiership and Division One (conveniently ignoring the likes of Leicester, Derby and Middlesbrough, who have shown that it can be done), Sunderland now have the resources to consolidate themselves in the top flight, something they have conspicuously failed to do ever since they were relegated for the first time in 1958.

With the club already submitting a planning application to take the capacity of the stadium in two stages up to 53,000, it is clear that the board - at long last - are starting to share the ambition of the fans.

It's no exaggeration to say these are the best times for the club since the 'Bank of England' days of the 1950s - a time when Sunderland were one of the biggest spenders in the game and strived to compete with the best.

However, before I get too carried away, it is important that everyone concerned with the club keeps their feet on the ground. Survival must be ensured next season, and with one or two quality signings this will be achieved.

So here's to *Premier Passions 2* - only this time with a happy ending.
Mark Jennings

IT'S THE HOPE I CAN'T STAND

Sunderland

As I sit down to write our annual review of Sunderland's season, the fixtures for '99-2000 have just been published, and Sunderland's first game will be at Chelsea. The following week we host Arsenal. I'm sorry? Surely that should be Millwall and Watf... er, Luton. It goes on. On Boxing Day we visit Everton and, two days later, play host to Manchester United. The week before Easter we go to Old Trafford, and there's a game against Liverpool somewhere in there too. Our last game of the season is at White Hart Lane. And, of course, battle will be resumed with the old enemy - Newcastle. All famous names, and all to whet the appetite of your average English football fan. And we, Sunderland (yes, Sunderland), will be going there. Granted there's Wimbledon, Watford, Bradford, Southampton and Coventry to remind us what life is like in the Nationwide, but for the most part this is where most (if not all) Sunderland fans would say they deserve to be. It's only when the fixtures come out that the magnitude of last season's efforts become obvious.

But this time last year, it was so different. The Premiership seemed like an unachievable dream. Stunned by the penalty shoot-out defeat at Wembley, things could have taken a disastrous turn. Kevin Ball, the lion-hearted captain of the side, revealed on the end of season video that the team had stopped off for a quick pint after the play-off final. That quick pint turned into a full-scale drinking festival, replete with Henry V style speech by Niall Quinn, which inspired this season's stomp through the First Division. Top by October 24, the team was never displaced. The main question in supporters' minds for most of the campaign was when, rather than if we were going to win the league.

Ipswich and Bradford were irritatingly dogged in keeping our lead at the top of the First Division to single figures. Fans kept trannies glued to their ears, listening out for the scores of the two teams, leaving with long faces when they both won. Indeed, our lead was kept below ten points until we actually clinched promotion on April 13 at Bury. The team thrashed a soon-to-be-relegated side

5-2, with Sunderland's best player for years, Kevin Phillips, scoring four goals - the first time he had ever achieved a hat-trick in a league match. After clinching promotion, the sides below us started losing for fun (apologies to Ron Atkinson) and the final table showed us with 105 points, 18 points ahead of second-placed Bradford. All kinds of records were broken (although not the one in which Peter Reid says, "I'll only buy if he's better than what we've got at the club already!").

With a record points haul, Sunderland beat every other team in the division at least once (we did the double over eight teams) and achieved plenty more feats which better anoraks than I can still remember. I won't bore you with a blow-by-blow account of the season, but highlights included: the 4-0 away thumping of Sheffield United, in which some say Michael Bridges played his best-ever game; victories over Bolton Wanderers, 3-0 away and 3-1 at home ("Can you catch us, Colin Todd?"); the away win at Bradford, in which Quinny not only scored the winner, but went in goal for the last 15 minutes after our 'keeper, Thomas Sorensen, had to go off injured. The promotion-clinching game at Bury was magic, as was the Championship-clinching game at Barnsley. Best goal of the season? Well there was Kevin Phillips' half-volley from the outside of his boot at QPR. This in his first game after four months out injured. Niall Quinn's goal against Birmingham came at the end of an exquisite move, involving Phillips and Summerbee. But our first goal at Ipswich in August involved a superb cross-field ball from Nicky Summerbee (my player of the season), which was picked up by Allan Johnston; Mickey Gray overlapped and crossed a ball for John Mullin to bundle in. That would be my goal of the season.

So it was a wonderful nine months, rounded off with a festival put on by the club for the Championship presentation at the final home game against Birmingham. It was fun, fun, fun 'til daddy took his T-bird away. But it all seemed a bit glitzy for the down-to-earth, good folk of Sunderland. All the fireworks and geeing up by the man with the mike didn't suit the club. It's the kind of trick those up the road go for, but not us. We don't need to be told when to sing and when to start a Mexican wave. If we feel like it (which is usually when the team is playing well), we'll do it. It gives a tiny pointer as to what we can expect off the pitch next season. I once accused Newcastle of being all style and no substance. In that last game, I saw a danger of my club going down that same rocky road. Are we getting just a little too cocky for our own good? Do we believe our own press releases too much? I hope not. Don't get me wrong, the club has definitely been turned around in the last four years and particularly since the move to the Stadium of Light two years ago. The club is becoming, once again, a centre of the community, but there is a danger of the administration taking away from the fans what is rightfully theirs; of the people who run the club cashing in on the fans' fanaticism. But that's for another place.

So we're now back where we belong. Last year was fantastic and we'll never forget it. But as we get well into the close season (and I'm sorry to spoon on a dollop of caution here), many Sunderland fans are getting a real sense of deja-vu. We've all been here before. The summer of 1996, to be precise (and of 1990, for that matter). To be fair, Reid took up a team of journeymen and no-hopers against everyone's expectations in 1996. This time we were everyone's favourites to go up (by a long mile) and the team is unrecognisable from that of 1996. But similarities do exist. The fact that no-one of substance has been added to the squad is a big worry. Even Kevin Phillips (on his wedding day, no less) was quoted as saying that he was surprised that the manager had not brought in anyone new. He did add the caveat that he was sure that he would before the season starts. I know a few supporters who aren't as confident as our top striker.

But this is Sunderland. It's the fans' job to be pessimistic. I mean, when have we ever been successful in the last 50 years? Sunderland haven't finished in the top half of the top division since 1956, for God's sake. To give Reid credit, this year's team won the First Division Championship with far more style and panache than his team of 1996. Then we clinched the title without kicking a ball and celebrated it with a boring scoreless draw at home to a dogged Stoke. Then the writing was on the wall, but now some are saying it's possible that the current squad could hold its own in the Premiership. Even the bookies agree. They reckon we'll finish about tenth. Well, they're not often wrong, so that's all right then... what am I worried about? I've had enough of clutching at straws. In the middle of last season, when we were doing so well, some readers were asking if we were going to change the name of the fanzine, because the hope had been realised. Well, I beg to differ, the hope has just been increased ten-fold. Never has the title of our organ been more appropriate. It really *is* the hope I can't stand.

Nic Wiseman

JACKANORY

Swansea City

The jail door was ajar and a ray of light entered our cell. An escape route from the dungeon presented itself. But instead of springing to our feet and grasping this lifeline to the Second Division, we stumbled, tripped and fell in an exhausted heap at Glanford Park. So, for us Jacks, it's another season in the Third, a division devoid of decent football, where the standard seems to be getting worse with every passing summer. The only consistent thing about the teams who play at this level is their inconsistency.

Who's to blame for consigning us to another year in hell? Well, the board (surprise, surprise) must take a lot of responsibility. Chairman Steve Hamer and sidekick Neil McClure invested nothing in the team last season. When the club hit an injury crisis during the early months of 1999, the board, as well as manager John Hollins, refused to bring in any loan signings, insisting that the squad was good enough to get promotion. Sadly, they weren't - much to the annoyance of the passionately loyal thousands, who keep turning up at The Vetch in blind optimism. This vociferous support from the stands and terraces at Swansea lifted the players and you could see them respond, but it shouldn't be up to the fans to motivate and encourage the team every week. They should play for the white shirt with pride and passion, even if no-one's there.

The season itself had few highlights - although we were treated, at last, to a decent run in the FA Cup. This put Swansea City back into the media spotlight, with the tabloids preferring to focus on an eight-foot white swan called Cyril instead of the merits of players who had overcome higher opposition in the form of Millwall, Stoke and West Ham (and who also deserved a replay against Derby County). The club's mascot arrived on the scene in dramatic style on the first day of the season, by abseiling down one of the floodlights. This was amusing - but not as hilarious as the opening day news from Hartlepool, where the game was held up because a Cardiff fan had knocked himself out cold on a goalpost while celebrating a goal.

A Swansea City Fanzine

Jackanory

Issue Ten - Oct/Nov 1998 - 50p

Police Raid Cyril's Bedroom Ahead Of Cardiff Game

INSIDE

Queen Mum in Garibaldi Shocker, The Ex-Files with Dave Stewart, Exclusive Interview with Cyril the Swan, Swansea Till I Die plus lots more rubbish !

Cyril had arrived. A commercial manager's dream. Dolls, cushions, sandwich boxes, even a *Nice One, Cyril* CD appeared on the shelves of the club shop, alongside the unsold maroon and white fudge. Not content with prancing around the pitch and taking penalties in his big fluffy boots (which were to be replaced by Adidas Predators before the end of the season, as the half-time shoot-outs became more like Euro '96 than *It's A Knockout*), Cyril decided to get in on the action during the 90 minutes.

Norwich coach Bryan Hamilton was the first one to get 'Cyril-ed', when the Welsh fowl collided with the Ulsterman during a Worthington Cup tie. Next to get the wrath of the big bird was a linesman, whose running of the line and flag-waving was mimicked by Cyril in hilarious fashion. What was to follow proved the last straw for the Welsh FA. Not happy with a place on the touchline, he decided to invade the pitch and celebrate one of our goals against Millwall. For fans who do that, it's a life ban; but for a fan dressed up in a costume, it's instant celebrity status.

He started to behave from then on and really hit the big time when we defeated West Ham at the Vetch. Hollins and Cyril adorned every national newspaper the following day. Cyril-mania had swept Britain. Think Swansea, think Cyril. It's sad - but that's what any punter in the street would say. The novelty has worn off since then but he still has his moments. His party piece is to lie on the floor and wave one leg in the air while the North Bank cries, "Cyril, do a Beckham. Cyril, do a Beckham..." He's yet to run his beak along the touchline, though, in response to our chants of "Cyril, do a Fowler, Cyril, do a Fowler".

The mascot's identity was kept a closely guarded secret by the club. Amongst the fans, rumour was rife on who could be donning the white costume. Was it ex-chairman Doug Sharpe? Was it former boss Alan Cork? It *was*, on one occasion, our striker Julian Alsop, who missed a game through injury. He dressed up as Cyril, entered the North Bank and began signing autographs! Maybe this will start a new craze and we'll see Alan Shearer running up and down the stands in St James' Park dressed as a giant Newcastle Brown Ale bottle.

Cyril wasn't the only thing to emerge from the club during the FA Cup run - a complete lack of respect for the loyal supporter was shown by the board in 'Ticketgate'. The farce which surrounded the distribution of home tickets for the Irons' replay was sad. 'Watch Gillingham in the Autoglass and guarantee yourself a cup ticket' was the club's slogan. It later turned out to be 'Queue at the back of the North Bank for a programme which contains a voucher, miss the entire first-half and then get to the front of queue, only to be told "There ain't any programmes left, mate".'

Swans fans fought amongst themselves for the last matchday mag, whilst others kept hands in pockets as they protected their stash of five or six programmes, collected via the 'know the programme seller' method or the 'let's move from one part of the ground to the other, where the queues are shorter' route. Those who did get vouchers weren't as lucky as first appeared, as cock-ups in ground capacity, forgeries and some dubious distribution meant the police (some on horses) were called to the club shop to restore order as rain-soaked supporters rioted when they reached the 'sold out' sign on the front door.

As this proves, success brings its own problems, especially when the club is run by those with no forward planning or common sense. Whether we taste success in the form of another cup run or a promotion next season is very much dependent on the chequebook coming out, and Swansea holding on to stars like Stuart Roberts, Richie Appleby and Jason Smith. We have the team to play at a higher level, but not the squad. Fringe players just weren't up to it but, having said that, we were still good enough to take four points off the Bluebirds. As we said in last season's round-up, some things never change.

Geraint Jones

Manics New Single

"If we tolerate this,

Aug 22 Leyton Orient (Home) 1-1
Aug 31 Scunthorpe United (Home) 1-2

then the Conference will be next."

JANUARY 3, '88

Portsmouth

In 1996 we left it to the last day of the season to secure survival. In 1998 we did the same. In 1999 we left it until five days after the season had ended.

Not our First Division status, you understand. No, this time around we had enjoyed the luxury of avoiding relegation a full week before the finish - although that had more to do with others' failings than our own abilities.

This spring, though, relegation was the least of our worries. The very survival of our club was the heaviest cloud hanging over our heads.

Most of the campaign was spent wondering not who would be in the team for the next game

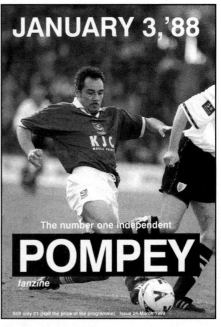

(although we ended up with so few squad members, we couldn't even take our minds off our troubles with selection quandaries) but, rather, whether we would still be in existence by the next game.

Serious financial problems dogging the club began to come to light after only a few weeks, by which time it had already become apparent '98-99 was to be a season of struggle and not one dominated by the mid-table security we'd have settled for. Martin Gregory was still at the helm but he was steering an increasingly uncertain course. (What's a Pompey review without a couple of ship references? No, *ship*, I said).

As the winter closed in, so did the people owed serious amounts of money by PFC - builders and the taxman amongst them. Gregory gave a new meaning to the phrase 'low profile' by not only refusing to communicate with fans through the local paper but trying (unsuccessfully) to stop the paper reporting on games.

It was no surprise when the administrators were brought in. But until the High Court approved their taking-over of the running of the club, it had been touch and go whether winding-up orders would be survived. Not even a big Fratton Park cup-tie against Leeds could divert people's attention from the troubles. And anyone who did forget them for a while was soon brought back to reality with a 5-1 defeat.

Thanks to the efficiency and business acumen of the administrators Tom Burton and John Ariel, overheads were chopped, unnecessary expenses were ruthlessly cut, and talks were opened and progressed with a number of interested parties.

All the groups who had come and gone during the previous few years threw their hats into the ring - the northern businessmen, the Florida tycoons; all the usual suspects. But on Thursday 13 May, wealthy Serb Milan Mandaric, with a consortium involving our ex-director David Deacon and the former Arsenal player Bob McNab, agreed a deal to buy Portsmouth for £4.6m. A week earlier the group's very existence had barely been known about. Suddenly they had become front-runners and done the business. Supporter scepticism about the way they had kept quiet about their bid was overcome when they declared their hand after shaking hands on the deal. Early mutterings were positive ones - Alan Ball would be given a chance as manager, he would have money to spend and ticket prices would be frozen. As I write, the necessary dots and crosses have still to be applied, but even allowing for the fact that if something can go wrong, it normally will at Fratton Park, nothing else is expected to get in the way of our brave new world.

Interestingly, fans seem to be staying realistic. No-one's roaring about us running away with the Championship; inevitably a few are talking of play-offs - but, hey, there's probably even some Port Vale fans thinking about those. Well, if Watford can win them...

All the post-season excitement meant the on-field activity of '98-99 was soon forgotten, which although no great shame, as it hadn't been the most memorable year, meant a few highs and lows were consigned to history's bin a little sooner than they might otherwise have been.

It took us until the last day of August to secure our first league win - but that was at home to QPR, so it didn't really count. September gave us all false hope. We won three games in a week, including a hard-grafting Worthington Cup win over Wimbledon and a 5-2 romp at home to Swindon, in which our goalkeeper gave the opposition a much-needed helping hand by fainting during one of their attacks. We didn't have much luck with goalkeepers in Swindon games, strangely, as in February the same one, Aaron Flahavan, was stretchered off during the first-half, only for his replacement, centre-half Russell Perrett, to let in two softies in a few minutes, before unexpectedly keeping a second-half clean sheet to help us draw.

But if September had raised our hopes, October and November did a fine job of dashing them to pieces. By the time December began, we had to win at home to Crewe to restore fan confidence and ward off the threat of a slump right to the bottom.

The poor run's highlight was a sit-in - well a standing-up sit-in, actually - after the final whistle at Crystal Palace, during which we chanted Alan Ball's name non-stop. You wouldn't have thought we'd lost 4-1. The reason for the overwhelming show of support was to get at the two Terrys - Venables and Fenwick - who at this time were in charge at Selhurst, having taken our club to the brink during their ill-fated spells at Fratton. Before the November reunion, Fenwick had had a go at the Pompey fans for expecting too much and had claimed we would soon turn on Ballie if results went badly. Wrong again, Tel. Sadly the dastardly duo had left Palace by the time the Eagles came to Fratton, so what could have been a spicy afternoon turned into a dull one.

Selhurst was not the only great show of Pompey fan camaraderie last season. In mid-December we hosted Grimsby at Fratton Park, and with the Sky team present we turned it into anti-Martin Gregory day. There were banners, chants and pitch invasions. We all felt better at the end of it - and happier still when he resigned as chairman six days later, to take another step towards his eventual departure from our affairs altogether.

January saw strength in adversity - an upturn in our form at a time when the club's survival chances were looking bleak. We won at Forest in the cup to secure the Leeds tie, which was great fun for the two minutes that we were 1-0 up but a trifle embarrassing after that. We went two months without a league defeat and the previous season's relegation battle seemed a long time ago.

But you know us, we never like to make things easy for ourselves. We always knew the start of March was going to be tough, with trips to Sunderland and Birmingham in the space of five days. No points there then. Although we recovered with four points from two homes, thanks largely to Andy Awford's first goal at Fratton Park in eleven years with the club (and probably his last for another eleven years), we then plunged ourselves into the basement battle (as the tabloids like to call it) by taking just two points from our next six games.

We suffered at this point from a puzzling inability to win home games on any day of the week other than Saturday. We only lost one Saturday home game - that was against Watford on the opening day, when a spectacular own-goal helped the Hornets off on their top-six assault - but lost three Tuesday night home games, one on a Bank Holiday Monday and two on Sundays.

Our ill-timed dip in form left us, with three games left, desperately needing to win at home to Stockport. One thing about Pompey is that when we really have to win, we do - witness those 1996 and 1998 great escapes - and it was no different on this occasion. And, fittingly, it was one of our heroes of the season, if not heroes of all time, Stevie Claridge, who calmed us down with a great early goal.

Claridge went on to win the Player of the Season title. Few argued, even if, at times, he had struggled to impose himself on matches. He could have been out injured the whole season and still got a few votes. My own player of the season, and many others' too, was Jeff Peron, a French midfielder bought from Walsall, who often shone out from matches in which no-one else did. He has superb close control, vision and passing ability - and there ain't much of that in today's First Division, is there?

Other troupers who won a few plaudits were skipper Adrian Whitbread - one of those who makes up what he lacks in ability by sheer determination and shouting a lot; veteran stopper Alan Knight - who's lost little of his agility despite his edging nearer all the time to the pension queue; loan goalkeeper Andy Petterson - whose three-month spell from Charlton did enough to convince all fans we ought to buy him (and we still might, as I write); and our old goalscoring hero, Guy Whittingham - who's done so little for every club he's played for, and so much for us (seven goals in nine on-loan games were vital this spring), that he really ought to build himself a house in Southsea and sign a life contract.

And the season's reflections can't end without a word or two for Alan Ball. He had his critics during a difficult season - some of his selections and substitutions were interesting to say the least - but how many managers would have stuck by a club that gave him no money to spend, sold some of his top players against his wishes and gave him no long-term job security? He loves the city and loves the fans - and of course the city and the fans love him back. Now he will have to prove he can produce a successful team with a bit of cash behind him - but, succeed or fail on that score, he'll forever be remembered as the man who guided us through one of the most nightmarish periods of our existence. Raise your flat caps in his honour.

Steve Bone

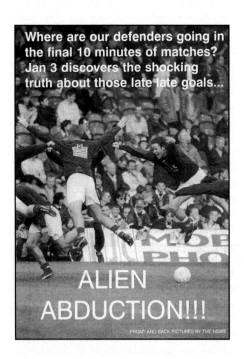

JUNCTION 11

Reading

We win!

Without a shadow of a doubt, the most welcome visitor to our brand spanking new £37m 25,000-seater Madejski Stadium this season was the Official Receiver. That may seem a strange statement, but he was called in to help sort out the finances of our tenants, the unwanted egg-chasing cuckoos of Richmond Rah-Rah Football Club. He came through in the best way possible and helped to close them down.

Thus a season which promised much for Royals fans, but which ultimately brought only disappointment, was at least followed by a significant victory.

Reading fans have been accused of arrogance in the past, notably by Stoke City fans after they've watched their team get beaten by us yet again (six more points last season). It's fair to say that this reputation was well-deserved at the start of the season. We all expected to be promoted at the first time of asking, after our disastrous flirting with the failed taxi-driver-turned-manager-turned-unemployed Terry Bullivant and the ignominy of last place in a poor First Division. Apart from confidence about our results on the pitch, we had also said a fond farewell to Elm Park and were looking forward to moving into a new stadium.

The August opening day at Madejski Stadium was a splendid event. Big crowd, party atmosphere, bank holiday weather, Stuart Hall, marching band (unfortunately), balloons, skydivers, parade of former heroes - and, most importantly, a one-sided 3-0 win. It all made for an unforgettable day. And we even had an excellent reminder of the incompetence of football administrators, after they blithely announced an attendance figure several thousand lower than the number of advance tickets sold, without even considering that this might appear odd. (It turned out that some of the turnstile counters weren't working properly.) The club also decided to borrow our fanzine name, so that the Royals now have the shortest address in the country - Junction 11, M4.

One home victory didn't lead to the great revival we all expected, though, and our season quickly became one to be remembered only for mediocrity, with few further notable events. Thus it was that the fans' attention started turning to other issues. Exactly why did we only buy Scottish players? And why was it that the ones we got were the few Scots with no apparent fire in their bellies? Where was our chairman, and in particular, where was his money? Why were there no Reading Football Club signs outside our stadium? Why were there never enough buses back to the town centre for the home fans?

But there was one question uppermost on every fan's lips - why was our pitch brown, rather than the traditional and more usual green?

We (by we, I mean every single fan, and apparently not one single club employee) knew the answer to the last question, of course. Someone high up in the Reading Football Club plc power structure had decided that we would take in some impoverished homeless tenants and help them set up a sporting organisation in the Reading area. You might think that that was a pretty stupid decision in itself, but it was even worse than that. Our pitch suppliers had warned the club against over-use in the first year - but we knew better, didn't we?

And so it was that a bunch of overweight, upper class, outcast egg-chasing hooray henries arrived from Richmond (somewhere in London apparently), bringing their silent three-figure crowds with them. The local media fawned over them. Why is it that the English press always suck up to those involved in public schoolboy sports, even though fewer people care about them than the average Ryman League team? Hockey, polo, egg-chasing, show-jumping, rowing - add them all together, and they've still got less paying spectators than Manchester City. Richmond themselves set about the goal of spreading their message by poisoning the minds of our children.

Remember that egg-chasing only exists as a 'sport' because some toffee-nosed public schoolboy cheated during a game of football by picking up the ball and running with it. Apparently the rah-rah philosophy of cheating on the pitch caught on with some of our other visitors, with Bournemouth in particular benefiting from a ludicrous penalty decision after a penalty-area dive by that perennial cheat, Mark Stein.

Another ugly interlude occurred after a comfortable home win over Preston North End. In a display of pique entirely suitable for our tenants (but not for proper sportsmen), one of the Preston players kicked in the door of the referee's dressing room. I don't know if the culprit was identified, but everybody knew that at least it couldn't have been Kurt Nogan, as he hadn't been able to hit a barn door all day!

The lush green surface of that opening August day quickly came to resemble the rubbish tip that had previously occupied the site, with all the billiard-table properties of the Somme landscape in 1916. Now, if Reading were long-ball hoof-merchants like Gillingham, this might have been a positive advantage. However, our manager, Tommy Burns, believes in the beautiful game and an uneven pitch was something that we definitely did not want.

It was interesting to watch the comments of club officials change during the season. At first, their reaction to bringing in tenants was only positive.

They would talk about increased income, extra media attention directed towards the town, more use of a tremendous facility, and so on. But by February, Tommy Burns was rightly criticising the pitch after every game, and our creative midfield genius Darren Caskey said that he would rather play in the car park, as at least the surface there was level. (Ironically, the car park would have been a more suitable location for the rah-rah tenants to play, as their pitiful crowds would have looked less out of place there.)

In April, we lost at home to Fulham despite being the better team. Our Liberian superstar Mass Sarr missed an easy chance to put us ahead when the ball bobbled on some scrum-damaged turf (or at least something vaguely resembling turf), and after the match Kevin Keegan had a go at the pitch. Given that his (then) team had just won, he had no axe to grind; but, as befits the England manager, he took a wider view and spoke up for football.

By this time, even Reading officials were trying to work out how to get rid of the egg-chasers without losing face, but fortunately we didn't have to leave it up to them. This brings us back to the start of this article, and to our good friends appointed by the Official Receiver to run Richmond's affairs. They knew that no-one cared whether a rah-rah club lived or died (the attendance for what proved to be Richmond's last-ever home game was 2,613, if you want an idea of just how much their fans rallied around the club). The imposed administrators therefore helped to bring about the end of Richmond (and of London Scottish, whoever they were) with a take-over by some more nonentities called London Irish.

The take-over of Richmond - officially a three-way merger, but only a moron would fall for that one - directly affects several groups of people. For Richmond's 2,000 fans, and London Scottish's 1,000, it represented survival. For London Irish's 3,000 fans, it meant very little. Of course, for all the morons running this country's media the events surrounding these tiny 'sporting' organisations is very important, but the only true winners are Reading Football Club's 11,000 faithful (not to mention the few thousand extra we will attract by playing attractive football on grass). The 1998/99 season should have been our new beginning, but at least we have learnt an important lesson.

All of this leaves Madejski Stadium as a football-only zone for the new Millennium. Our chairman, John Madejski (bit of a coincidence him having the same name as the stadium, isn't it?), has returned from a period of self-imposed tax-exile and business opportunity in Malaysia, and everything in our garden is rosy. Reading fans are preparing for the 1999/2000 season in the full knowledge that this season we are going up in style as Champions.

Arrogant? Us? Never!
Steve James & Ray Curry

KING OF THE KIPPAX

Manchester City

On the final day of the '97-98 season Manchester City were relegated to the real Third Division for the first time in their history. Three years after playing Liverpool, Arsenal and Chelsea, we faced the prospect of playing Colchester, Lincoln and Wycombe.

King of the Kippax

ISSUE 71 Oct '98 | 10th Anniversary Special

A Manchester City Fanzine For the Fans, By the Fans

I've got just the thing to get us UP this season

VIAGRA

£1

The main reason for our rapid decline had been a lack of goals. We picked up a few victories of course, but were let down by an almost continuous stream of narrow defeats when our strikers looked as if they'd never seen a football before.

The new season didn't look to offer any improvement as Gio Kinkladze, our most skilful player, and Uwe Rosler, our most consistent goalscorer of recent times, were both allowed to leave. If that wasn't bad enough, we also started the season without a recognised wide player, unless you count the increasing girth of Jamie Pollock.

We started brightly, beating Blackpool 3-0 in front of over 32,000 in our first game, and a few days later won 2-0 at Meadow Lane in the League Cup. The joy didn't last long, as Fulham panned us 3-0 in front of the Sky cameras in our second league fixture. That game also meant the end of the season, through injury, of our Georgian central-defender Kakhaber Tskhadadze, who had scored in the two wins.

We bounced back to beat Notts County 7-1 in the second-leg of the League Cup, but in the league were beginning a disappointing spell that would last until Christmas. We still won a few, but the draws and defeats were often caused by a lack of firepower. We would dominate games but just couldn't find the killer touch. We also produced a few performances more reminiscent of a non-league team than of a side playing in the Premiership just three seasons earlier. Supporters of Wycombe and Lincoln may have seen two particularly abysmal performances, and will know I'm not exaggerating.

Everything seemed wrong. We had no width, no pace and no left-back. Joe Royle had pointed out these three weaknesses when he arrived at the club, but eight months later they were still there. Goater and Dickov were picking up the odd goal, but both were missing chances galore.

The autumn also saw the sale of Lee Bradbury. City had paid £3m for him in the summer of '97 and sold him for half that 14 months later. The loss on the deal was bad enough, but Bradbury was actually playing quite well when we decided to sell him.

Off the pitch, we were having adventures of another kind. The restricted ticket allocation at most away matches meant tickets for these games were sold to regular season ticket holders on a first come, first served basis - a 'regular' season ticket holder being one who had held a ticket for at least five seasons.

Macclesfield was the first real test of the system, but the allocation of around 1,600 tickets meant anyone willing to queue up at Maine Road a couple of hours before the ticket office opened managed to get in. Northampton, with the smallest allocation for visiting fans, was another problem game, but again the early birds got their tickets. This ritual of queuing continued all season, and whilst Maine Road may be wonderful at 7.00am on a Saturday morning, I can think of better places to be.

Later in the season our ticket office showed their legendary lack of competence by making a complete balls-up of distributing tickets for the play-off game at Wigan. They screwed up again for the final, when some season ticket holders ended up queuing for over 12 hours in order to get a seat at Wembley.

We also had the chance to visit a few recently-built grounds. In previous seasons we'd seen new grounds at Sunderland, Middlesbrough, Huddersfield and Stoke. Now we had the opportunity to visit the relatively small Bescot Stadium, the tiny Sixfields Stadium, the dickhead-filled asylum known as The New Den (where old habits die hard) and the much-too-large-for-Reading Madejksi Stadium. The second round of the League Cup took us to another new ground, Pride Park in Derby.

These new grounds are not particularly interesting, as they tend to be pretty much the same. Some of the smaller ones may have the occasional unique characteristic but, in general, the new crop of purpose-built grounds have no character of their own. I suppose the unusual roof design at Huddersfield may be worth a mention, but as the design is responsible for lots of people getting wet, we'll give it a miss. The other problem with many of the new grounds is the crap parking facilities. Clubs want fans to use the car parks, so the surrounding streets don't get clogged, but they seem to forget that most fans don't want to spend an hour in a car park after each match.

After that little moan, we'll return to the action on the pitch, starting with a minor miracle. In October, Joe Royle signed a bargain. This may not mean much to some, but to City fans it is almost unique. When City are interested in a player, they make an enquiry and, as if by magic, the player's price rises. If we remain keen, the selling club invents a few bids from other unnamed 'interested parties' and the price rises again. Finally, the City directors panic and end up paying twice the original offer. This is often four times what the player is really worth.

Joe broke with tradition when he bought Andy Morrison, a central defender from Huddersfield Town. Unfortunately his physique was the first thing to catch the eye, and many thought he'd been bought from Huddersfield's rugby league team, who share the McAlpine Stadium with the football club. These fears were quickly dispelled and we stopped leaking goals almost as soon as Andy arrived. In Morrison's first 12 league games, City conceded only three goals. At the other end, Morrison scored four himself, the most stunning being at Oldham when his 20-yard thunderbolt sealed a 3-0 victory.

Our season finally came to life with a 1-0 win at Wrexham on Boxing Day. Some say it was lucky, and the home side certainly made our goalkeeper Nicky Weaver earn his wages, but we also created a lot of chances. The margin of victory would have been higher had one of our star strikers not lifted the ball onto the bar from only two yards out.

That game marked the start of a 12-game unbeaten run in the league, and it also marked our first sight of Terry Cooke, who was on loan at Wrexham. Cooke was a winger from Stretford Lepers and was trying to get match-fit following a long injury. He looked too skilful for us, but Royle signed him on loan when his spell at Wrexham was over, and he scored seven goals during our march up the league. Three of those were direct from free-kicks, and we finally had some options from dead-ball situations.

The unbeaten run included seven wins and five draws, the final game being a 6-0 victory at Burnley, where Shaun Goater bagged a hat-trick. The thirteenth game proved unlucky, as Oldham won 2-1 at Maine Road. We shot ourselves in the foot during that match, missing a host of chances, including a penalty when only 1-0 down.

In the past we would have fallen apart, but we rallied and won our next four games to set us up with a real six-pointer at Preston on Easter Monday. At the time it looked as if Preston would go up with Fulham, and we believed our only chance of snatching second place would require a win at Deepdale. The 1-1 draw didn't help either side, but we reacted better than Preston, and won the next three without conceding a goal, and moved into third place. With second place still a remote possibility, we produced a dire performance at home against Wycombe and lost 2-1. The following week we threw away a two-goal lead at Bristol Rovers, a few hours after Walsall had clinched the second promotion place.

We started the final day in fourth place, level on points with Preston. We beat York 4-0, whilst they lost at Fulham - so we finished in third place and had to face Wigan in the play-offs.

In the last game to be played at Springfield Park, we were 1-0 down after 20 seconds thanks to an amazing fuck-up involving Weaver and Wiekens. However, we equalised late on to leave the tie finely balanced.

A crowd of over 31,000 saw Shaun Goater score the only goal of the second-leg to send us through to a Wembley final against Gillingham. (It could have been a bit different had the referee spotted a foul by Wiekens in the first few minutes - but let's not worry about that.)

The ticket allocation for the final was a farce, with Gillingham receiving about 34,000 tickets compared with our 37,000 (or 39,000 depending on which paper you read). This was a strange split as our average gate was over 28,250 and Gillingham's less than 6,750. Somehow they managed to get rid of their allocation, and the crowd was a record for the Nationwide League Second Division Final. It also beat the crowd for the First Division final the following day.

The match itself wasn't a classic, but in a game like that it's the result that counts. We should have had a penalty for handball in the first minute, and also hit the post at 0-0, but Gillingham scored two late goals and looked to be heading for promotion. With a few seconds left, Horlock pulled it back to 2-1, but I hadn't seen the fourth official indicate five minutes of added time, so I was deep in panic mode. With about four and a half minutes of added time played, Paul Dickov blasted the ball into the roof of the net and over half of Wembley erupted. Things like that just don't happen to us.

Extra-time didn't help either side, so we were left with the nightmare of penalties. We'd only been awarded three all season, and although Horlock had scored his, Goater and Taylor hadn't. Not only that, but Weaver had never saved a penalty - and the rumours from the training ground were that he'd not saved many during the intense penalty practice sessions before the final.

We put those problems behind us as Horlock scored and Weaver saved. Then Dickov hit the post, and they missed. Terry Cooke scored, so did they, but then we played our joker. Richard Edghill was rumoured to be our eleventh penalty-taker and many fans thought even that was too high up the order, but he stepped up and blasted home the fourth penalty. Nicky Weaver saved the next kick and we were promoted.

Weaver set off on a run around Wembley and would probably still be dancing on the pitch now had it not been required for the next day's game. The fans just went wild, and for half an hour we completely forgot that all we'd done was escape from the real Third Division.

The season had been characterised by opposing fans taking the piss out of our lowly status. They were so keen to laugh that 20 teams enjoyed their highest gate of the season when we were the visitors. Our home gates were also reasonably impressive, and the 23 highest attendances in the division were for our 23 games.

We also managed a decent turnout at Selhurst Park for the FA Cup tie against Wimbledon, when our travelling supporters not only out-sung the home fans, but also outnumbered them. According to the official attendance figures, there were 6,312 City fans in a gate of only 11,226.

Our adventure is over. We've been to some new grounds, visited some new pubs and sold fanzines on some new street corners. We've also met a great bunch of people who follow their teams through thick and thin (generally thin) and aren't blinded by all the hype from the Premiership.

One of my ambitions is to see City on all the grounds in the league, and a few were crossed off the list last season. I just hope I get to do the rest in cup-ties.

Ged Isaacs

LAND OF SHEEP AND GLORY

Carlisle United

It's Saturday 8 May, 4.54pm. Carlisle United - you know, that team who no-one is bothered about - are one minute from relegation to the Football Conference. All around Brunton Park, faces are red - some with tears, others through hatred towards our chairman. At 1-1, against Plymouth, we get a corner with barely ten seconds left. In one last act of desperation, the bench urge our on-loan 'keeper to go up. He might as well, if only to cause confusion. The ball is put in, a blue head sends it goalbound, the 'keeper parries it out, and... well I think you all know the rest. With one swing of his boot, Jimmy Glass

L.O.S.A.G.

AN INDEPENDENT FANS VOICE OF CARLISLE UNITED F.C.

COME ON YOU BLUES!

ISSUE 7 - AUG 98   £1.00

became a legend... well, around these parts anyway. All of a sudden the pitch was covered by a wave of ecstasy as the man in the red top was swamped. Even the ref got rugby-tackled. The game restarted for *one second*, then the whistle went. Grown men cried, hugged and kissed, our Jim was carried aloft, and the Plymouth fans just laughed. We were safe and every other team cursed when they realised they would have to still make the long trek next season.

So how did all this commotion come about, you might be asking? Well, to be quite honest, we were the worst team in the division - and until my dying day, I'll still maintain that some sort of divine force was watching over us on that final game. There had to be - I mean, can you imagine approaching *Roy of the Rovers* with that script? They'd laugh at you and say it was too ridiculous.

Let's now rewind to August 8, the first day of the season. United scrape a 1-0 win over Brighton in an unconvincing display. Well, it is only the first game, we tell ourselves, we've got to give the new players time to gel. Except they didn't really. Three defeats on the bounce proved that. And this was to be the story of the season. The odd win here and there, a lot of draws (thank God) and a lot of defeats. Just when you thought things were on the upturn, we'd shoot ourselves in the foot. A little salvation came from our loan players. First up was Rob Scott from Fulham. He scored a couple and looked what we were missing up front. A deal was done but apparently Rob's agent was pricing him out of the move. It fell through, he sacked his agent and went to Rotherham

instead. Next up was the rock 'n' roll star Paul McGregor, from No[...]
Forest. He came, got injured a lot, then showed his skill with som[...]
finishing, before ending up at Preston in March because we were [...]
over his contract. The long-haired lead singer wanted to com[...]
dithered and missed out.

By this time there was a realisation we wouldn'[...]
this season. Christmas came and went, and even Sant[...]
coach to replace Knighton and the Yes Men failed to stop th[...]
New Year see a turn for the better? Well, no, to be blunt. Even tw[...]
in a fortnight, at Brighton and Southend, were merely papering over th[...]
Yet still we talked of how we could make the play-offs. The fans' problen[...]
that we were too optimistic to see the terror slowly unfolding before our eye[...]

Transfer deadline day came - and suddenly there were more comings
and goings than Waterloo Station in rush hour. We sold Paul Boertian to
Derby, Andy Couzens to Blackpool and, bizarrely, Tony Caig (our only fit
goalkeeper) to Blackpool. Oh and some bloke called Steve Finney to Orient.
Apparently he was our striker, but judging by his scoring record and the size of
his belly, it seemed like he was *on* strike. In came Rotherham's David Bass and
Richard Tracey, Barnsley's Paul Bagshaw, and Derby's third 'keeper Richard
Knight. The team who played at Cardiff two days later contained five 19-year-
olds and the rest, bar two, were under 24. Not exactly the experience needed
for the relegation battle we were getting sucked into.

Yet, despite the team's troubles, the fans refused to blame the players or
coach Nigel Pearson. In the eyes of many, only one man was to blame, a
certain 'tashed chairman. A failure to buy in players (we only deal in frees,
loans and Derby juniors) and the sale of our better players was quite obviously
not working.

The last seven games were going to be the most important in our
history. First up were fellow rivals Scarborough on Easter Monday. A 3-
0 defeat saw their fans singing "Bye-bye to the Football League" at us. You
may have won the battle, but ultimately we won the war. A 1-1 draw
against Peterborough and a 0-0 with Hull, both at home, were points; but
we needed more. Rotherham then tanked us 3-1 at their spot, before a 3-
3 draw with Darlington at home. This match saw the arrival of unknown
goalkeeper Jimmy Glass. Special dispensation was granted for us to sign
him, as Derby had had to recall Richard Knight.

We travelled to Hartlepool, all 1,200 tickets soon going. Within ten
minutes came the news that Scarborough were 2-0 up at Halifax. Nothing was
going right. Our game ended 0-0, with the score reflecting the nerves of the
two teams. Scarborough had won 2-1. They were two points behind us, with
a game in hand. Wednesday saw Scarborough beat Plymouth, our last
opponents, 3-0, to move a point above us, each with one game left. Going into
the last weekend of the season in 92nd place is a funny feeling. Everyone who
had stayed away all season returned. The game kicked off - and, within seven
minutes, Peterborough were one up at Scarborough, according to hundreds of

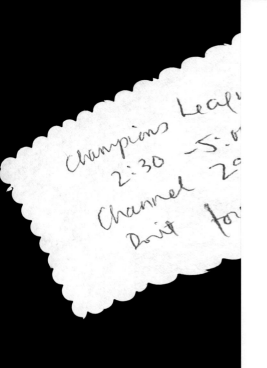

radios. Our game had a nervy feel to it and the first-half was cagey. Half-time - and the news was Scarborough had equalised. Plymouth then took the lead after four minutes of the second-half and all eyes turned on the directors' box. Then, on the hour, the first glimmer of hope: centre-back Dave Brightwell hit a 25-yard low drive into the far corner of the net. The great escape was on. But chances weren't being taken, and when Scott Dobie put wide with injury-time already started, our worst fears were about to hit us full on. Then the moment, which will be talked about in our town forever more. I won't describe it again, but forget your Wembleys; this goal meant everything to the people of Carlisle. Our league existence was preserved by an on-loan Swindon 'keeper, who used to train up front with Ian Wright when he had a bad wrist injury whilst at Crystal Palace. It really is a funny old game.

The final verdict:

Team: Just not good enough, it's plain and simple. We won the fewest games and scored the second-lowest number of goals. Defence is spot-on, but a midfield and a six-foot plus target man are needed if we are to climb once more.

Players: Stu Whitehead is class and will surely move onto higher things. Damon Searle has a never-say-die spirit, which is vital. Scott Dobie and Peter Clark have the potential. And the rest? Well choose any word between 'average' and 'very poor'.

Coach: When Knighton was in charge, along with Sooty and Sweep (aka John Halpin and David Wilkes), it just wasn't happening. Nigel Pearson came in and tried, but inexperience combined with the view that his hands were tied, meant he couldn't improve the situation. Top bloke, though. We've just replaced Pearson with Keith Mincher, so we'll have to wait and see this coming season.

Chairman: During April and May, the most hated man in Cumbria. Says he will sell to the right offer, but can't see it happening at the moment. Policy of selling anyone with an ounce of class must be slowed down. Needs to do some very quick bridge-building to simmer ill-feeling towards him.

Overall: Our club can never be allowed to be in such a precarious position again. It's going to take some guts to do, but we'd like to see the good ship Carlisle United sailing in calmer waters this coming season. If we had a school report it would surely read: "A disappointing season, needs to work much harder, and stop messing about during class." Better start doing your homework, boys, because we expect better this season.

Daniel MacLennan

LEYTON ORIENTEAR

Leyton Orient

A campaign that started with supporters and chairman exchanging insults ended on a scorching afternoon at Wembley, where the mighty O's fell agonisingly short of a rare and long overdue promotion success.

What an unbelievable season it turned out to be. There were times that Orient, resplendent in their Croatia-style shirts, looked the real deal when talking about promotion candidates. Players such as Matt Lockwood, Simon Clark and Belgian import Wim Walschaerts became the backbone of the side, whilst the arrival of former French international Amara Simba added real style to an otherwise ordinary attack.

the alternative **leyton orient** supporters fanzine

I CAN GET THAT TURQUOISE SHELL-SUIT NOW

"GRIFFITHS WHERES THE MONEY GONE?"
Price: £1.00 Date: Apr/May 99 Issue: 118

However, after a nightmare first six weeks of inconsistency that brought some horrific home defeats, notably 1-5 v Forest in the fizzy pop cup (sorry - that's the fizzy beer cup) and 0-3 against Scarborough (which also brought forth an angry exchange between Barry Hearn and some irate supporters in the main stand), promotion was looking light years away.

Consistency, as any fan will tell you, is the magic ingredient required for success. Despite those early disasters, through the months of October and November we had it in spades. High-flying Scunthorpe and Halifax were overcome in appalling conditions, whilst our away form - for so long Orient's achilles' heel - held up remarkably well. The FA Cup brought forth a confrontation with arch-rivals Brighton and Kent Albion, which was played against the backdrop of a white hot atmosphere. After falling behind early on, the O's put four past the Seagulls and themselves into round two, with blond bombshell Tony Richards helping himself to a superb hat-trick. The fact that Tony ran along the length of the stand housing the Brighton support with his hand to his ear was the ultimate insult, and it was no surprise when a section of the visiting hordes tried to climb into the home end via the burger bar for a little 'hand to hand'. Ironically, the poor sods would never have got through the queue for starters and we had a real laugh at their expense. By the time November was over, both Brentford (in more than controversial circumstances) and Plymouth had been dispatched and things were looking good. But you have to remember that this is Orient we're talking about, and failure to register a win in the league for the next two months resulted in a tumble down the table. An appearance in the fourth round of the FA Cup for the first time in seven years almost made up for the slump. But a harsh 0-3 reverse at Bristol Rovers ended our interest in that route into Europe. It was to be the defining part of the season.

The following week, Taylor signed Scott Barrett, a goalkeeper from Cambridge, and dropped the out-of-form Chris McKenzie after a string of giveaway goals. From then on, the soft goals that had cost us dearly were stemmed and five victories on the spin were recorded, with the help of a rejuvenated Carl Griffiths, who had enjoyed a series of run-ins with the manager all season. Darlington, Cambridge and Brighton (yet again) were brushed aside and February's Manager of the Month, Tommy Taylor, claimed a nice bottle of Scotch, which must have reminded himself of the days he ran a pub in Leyton. Only this time the booze wasn't watered down...

So all was set fair for the run-in. Or so we thought. Griffiths was sold to Port Vale for £100,000 and not replaced, whilst suspensions began to take their toll as the O's clocked up over 80 yellow cards during the campaign. Two bad home defeats, to lowly Hull and Southend, set the pattern for the final few regular-season games as Orient staggered into play-off territory, whilst the dream of automatic promotion evaporated with a mixture of bad and brilliant performances (the 6-1 demolition of Shrewsbury was as good as anything witnessed at Orient in years).

So this was the deal. Rotherham over two legs, then on to Wembley to play the winners of Scunthorpe v Swansea: Simple enough really. So we took on the men from South Yorkshire, mindful of the fact that they had tonked us twice already in previous encounters. After a drab goalless first-leg in Leyton, it was all to play for at Millmoor three days later. Even before a ball was kicked, there was controversy as Orient supporters were turfed out of seats they had paid for, so that Rotherham could squeeze in a few more of their fans. Some Orient fans refused to move and were left unprotected, whilst the police and stewards did nothing. I thought this kind of thing was made illegal under the Taylor report – and ten years after presiding over the biggest sporting disaster in history, South Yorkshire police still can't get it right. The match got underway and, sure enough, a classic enfolded. Although the game was excruciatingly tight, the O's battled every step of the way. With the last kick of full-time, Scott Barrett pulled off a stunning save from a free-kick to take us into 30 more nerve-shredding minutes, and then on to the dreaded penalties. Could we take any more of this? Would Orient's legendary lack of bottle come to the fore yet again? The answer was an emphatic NO, as all our spot-kicks hit home, whilst that man Barrett saved two Rotherham efforts. Cue delirium and scenes of utter joy among the 2,500 travelling support. It was simply the best day of my 20 years as an Orient fan, with Wembley looming large before us. Could it really be true?

Well, it was no dream - and 20,000 Orient supporters, including those who don't normally visit Brisbane Road on a regular basis, turned out for our big day. Alas, there was no happy ending. Our first-half performance was nothing short of dire and Taylor's tactics played a big part in Orient's downfall. Despite changing things around at half time and dominating, Orient just couldn't pull back the goal that finally denied us Second Division football next season. It was the day that the sale of Griffiths came home to roost, as we needed somebody of his quality to open up a tight Scunthorpe defence. After all the effort of the previous nine months, to walk away with nothing was a real sickener and numbness began to creep as we made our way homeward.

When all is said and done, the 98/99 season put us back on the map and saw some pride restored to the club (this despite a tie-up with Bravo TV, a cable television station with a liking for porn). The team almost pulled off an unlikely looking promotion and, for the most part, played some excellent football. Our ground is being redeveloped at last, although Barry Hearn and the local authority are still stalling over a long-term lease that will give the club real stability. The future, on the field, looks good, with the youth set-up the best for years and some exciting players being recruited for next season. Although knowing Orient as I do, it could still go horribly pear-shaped. Roll on next season.

Jamie Stripe

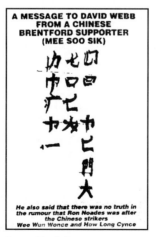

Source: *Hey Jude*

MAN UTD ARE ON THE TELE AGAIN

Norwich City

Norwich City began the season with a new managerial team in the shape of Bruce Rioch and Bryan Hamilton. Over a year after being sacked, former manager Mike Walker still hasn't got a job. Why doesn't someone give him a chance?

Many fans had written off Iwan Roberts at the end of the 97-98 season after the gap-toothed striker (who cost nearly a million pounds from Wolves) had netted a measly seven goals. However, after shedding a stone and a half in weight during the summer, the new lean, mean Roberts' transformation was reminiscent of Arnold Schwarzenegger's cyborg in *The Terminator*. A unanimous winner of the club's Player of the Season award after netting 23 goals in league and cup (and this after failing to make the starting line-up in the first six games), big Iwan is now the most popular player at the club - and he's worked bloody hard for it. It would have been nice if Keith O'Neill had taken a leaf out of Iwan's book whilst he was at Carrow Road. However, the greasy-haired Irishman's attitude stank and few City fans were sad to see him move to Middlesbrough for a modest fee. O'Neill has got tremendous ability but he's an enigma and is always injured. I'm sure he thought that actually being fit for a game was all he had to do. A God he definitely isn't.

The turning point of the season for me was the 2-2 draw at Wolves in December, when City threw away a two-goal lead in the last ten minutes. There's little doubt the players' concentration was badly affected by a scandalous challenge on Craig Bellamy by Kevin Muscat. Amazingly the referee didn't even award us a free-kick. More importantly, our Welsh international wonder-kid was stretchered off and sidelined for over two months, which meant bye-bye to the Premiership for another season. At the time of his injury, 'Bellers' had scored 13 goals in Division One. (He scored just four more after his return). Kevin Muscat, meanwhile, just carried on playing as if nothing had happened. You ruined our season, you bastard.

Bruce Rioch's first season as Norwich boss started really well. After a 2-1 home victory against Bristol City in December, the Canaries were comfortably perched in the top six in Division One. However, it was to be two months before we won again, at Bury. Indeed, in 1999 we only won three times and, incredibly, if it wasn't for a last-minute wonder goal by Paul Hughes (the only decent thing the on-loan Chelsea reserve did for us) against Swindon, the Canaries would have failed to register a single home victory in the New Year. Despite our pathetic second half of the season, we still managed to finish ninth, our highest position since leaving the top flight in 1995.

It's expected that there will be a big clear-out during the summer and it's not before time. In fact, at the time of going to press, Neil Adams has returned to his old club Oldham. Sadly, as yet Rioch hasn't been able to dispose of Peter Grant. Amazingly, this poor excuse for a midfielder has been capped by Scotland. A decrepit tortoise has got more pace!

As far as club chairmen go, Robert Chase was the ultimate anti-hero. Even though he regularly sold all our best players, he still left the club £7m in debt. Bob Cooper is now chairman. I met the former Sainsbury's director in January and he seemed a decent bloke. However, when I kept trying to convince him that Rioch needed to strengthen his squad if we were to have any realistic chance of making the play-offs because we were beginning to fall away at this point, Cooper kept insisting that we didn't need any new players - which was absolutely bollocks (we somehow managed to lose 3-2 at Crewe after being 2-0 up with eight minutes to go, for example). Even though he had a lot of good points and took a double subscription out to the fanzine, Cooper's unrealistic views on team strengthening had 'Robert Chase' written all over them.

Cooper and his colleagues did eventually release some funds for Bruce Rioch to acquire some players (four actually) but not until transfer deadline day, when it was mathematically impossible for us to reach the play-offs. Phil Mulryne (a bargain buy from Manchester United for £500,000) scored a cracking goal on his full debut against Grimsby (a Beckham-style free-kick) and looks set to be a highly influential player for us in 99/00. Great things are also expected from Frenchman Cedric Anselin and Paul Dalglish, son of Kenny.

Casting my mind back over the season, I can recall very few highs, several lows and a lot of 'if onlys'. The outstanding highlight of yet another tepid campaign that seldom set the pulse racing was City's fine away win at the old enemy - Ipswich. It was by far our best away performance of the season at a time when we were threatening the top of the league. Sadly, as some of you may be aware, the Canaries have a tradition of sliding down the league after the second week in December. City put up a solid defensive performance (yes, there was one last season) and scored a great goal through Bellamy on the counter-attack. In reality it could have been more, with plenty of good chances squandered (no surprise there then). It was a well-earned victory that put the memories of Feb 98 (when we were thrashed 5-0) to rest.

The trip: there was apprehension as the train pulled into the scum stronghold of Stowmarket. I'm not going to pretend to be one of those fans who relishes the ugly side of football in local derbies, so unwelcome memories of some of the violence at this fixture in recent years flashed through my mind as we entered Suffolk. However, there is nothing I want more from a season than a glorious campaign and beating those bastards twice. This match was perfect, the atmosphere intense (despite their fans being a little quiet) and - despite sensational local newspaper reports - very little trouble, except some smashed toilets (which for some reason merited a mention in one of the national broadsheets, highlighting the sort of vile behaviour still occurring in football).

For once the rival teams slugging it out on the pitch made the news, rather than the rival fans outside Ipswich station. Which made for, in my opinion, the most enjoyable City game seen since we were in Europe. I pray for a similar outcome next season.

Being a Norwich fan these days is a bit boring. Stuck in Division One with hardly any money, while our fiercest rivals (Scumwich) have been grabbing all the media attention because of their three consecutive play-off failures.

What we really need is a scandal. It's four years since Norwich City were embarrassed on the front page of the *Daily Star* when it was revealed that Robert Chase was charging the Carrow Road ball-boys £2 for the privilege of picking up the ball after Mike Sheron's wayward shots. These days our rare mentions in the press are usually preceded by a predictable headline such as "Delia's Recipe For Success". Yawn! Oh for some controversy. I actually feel jealous of Swansea City who were fined £1,000 last season when the club mascot celebrated a goal with the players. This was an injustice of the highest degree - like the time I was reprimanded at school for writing the lyrics to the Goodies' *The Funky Gibbon* on a desk. Why? Because the desk belonged to a girl with the surname Gibbon! Talk about coincidences, how the hell was I to know? I'd love to see our club mascot Captain Canary have a scrap with the opposition equivalent like the Wolves one did last season. However, goody-goody Norwich have only gone and given him a girlfriend. (Actually, the person inside Captain Canary is allegedly also of the female gender. Could there be a lesbian scandal developing here?!) Sadly 'scandal' is not a term associated with Norwich City these days.

Favourite moments of '98-99:
1. Beating Ipswich at Portman Road.
2. Seeing Echo and the Bunnymen play live at the UEA.
3. Tim Blyth (more about him in a moment).
4. Bellers' hat-trick against QPR.
5. Seeing the Ipswich fans crying after they had missed out on a Premiership place, even though they'd just beaten Sheffield United 4-1.

In a season of few highlights, the funniest moment occurred in the midst of despair at the end of a 4-3 home defeat by Port Vale. City's appalling defensive showing was too much for the burly figure of Barclay Ender Tim Blyth who, after peeling off his Norwich top in disgust, ran onto the pitch and was chased by a trio of stewards as he made his way towards the dug-out to chuck his shirt at Bruce Rioch. You've got to hand it to him - the bloke had balls (and a rather flabby stomach). Tim Blyth is now a Carrow Road legend.

I'm quite confident about next season. If the likes of Eadie, Bellamy, Roberts and Mulryne can steer clear of injury, I think we'll do well.

Duke Macmaster & Dave Greenwood

MATTHEW HARDING'S BLUE AND WHITE ARMY

Chelsea

Blue is the colour, libel is the game

So, a gripping season comes to an end and sees the Chels finishing with their highest league placing for 29 years, the best away record in the Premiership and a place in the Champions League. Not bad - unless you read the national press who, amongst other things, solemnly refer to the Blues as "trophy-less". Trophy-less? Yes, it would have been nice to end up with a tin-pot or two but what people tend to forget is that no-one ever supported Chelsea because they win trophies. Twenty-seven years without silverware is testament to that. No, blessed with

Matthew Harding's

Blue And White Army

Issue 2 - £1.00   April 1999

"HARDING BELIEVED THAT CHELSEA WAS DOING FAR MORE FOR BATES THAN BATES HAD EVER DONE FOR CHELSEA"

C.£.C. C.£.C. ... C.£.C. C.£.C.
C.£.C. C.£.C. ... C.£.C. C.£.C.
C.£.C. C.£.C ... £.C. C.£.C.
C.£.C. C.£.C ... £.C. C.£.C.
C.£.C. C.£.C ... £.C. C.£.C
C.£.C. C.£. ... £.C. C.£.C
C.£.C. C.£.C ... £.C. C.£.C
C.£.C. C.£.C. ... .£.C. C.£.C.
C.£.C. C.£.C. ... .£.C. C.£.C.
C.£.C. C.£.C ... £.C. C.£.C.
C.£.C. C.£ ... £.C. C.£.C.
C.£.C. C. ... £.C. C.£.C.
C.£.C. C. ... .C. C.£.C.
C.£.C. C. ... C. C.£.C.
C.£.C. C.£.C. C.£.C. C.£.C. C.£.C. C.£.C.
C.£.C.   (T RUBYTHON, BUSINESS AGE, FEB 99, NO86, P58)   C.£.C.
C.£.C. C.£.C. C.£.C. C.£.C. C.£.C. C.£.C.

eternal patience, Blues fans visit the Bridge to watch scintillating, attacking, passing football, which has always been a hallmark of our team, even with Vinnie Jones in the starting XI. So, yes, whilst we're slightly disappointed with how events turned out this season, you won't find too many Blues fans complaining. This is by far and away the best side at the Bridge in most fans' living memory, and with players of the calibre of Zola, Desailly and... er, Mark Nicholls strutting their stuff on the Bridge turf, it shouldn't be too long before more pots find their way to the Bridge trophy cabinet.

By way of contrast, events off the field couldn't be more different, and have been a mixture of the downright depressing to those of pure farce. All can be laid at the feet of our not-so-popular chairman, Ken Bates, the man who looks extraordinarily like an ugly version of Captain Bird's Eye. No amount of words could adequately describe this curious mixture of Goebbels, Robert Maxwell and Napoleon, but I'll leave you with one - Tit.

Captain Bird's Eye, known simply as 'the Captain', has kept a close eye on the Chelsea fanzines all season, and letters from London's most expensive law firm, the celebrated Peter Carter Ruck & Partners, regularly find their way into the editors' postbags. As a result, most fanzines, including ours, have given Bates a lot less grief than he might otherwise have deserved. However, there was one notable exception during the season when the Captain made a mind-boggling gaffe that has given us pages of hilarious content, libel free. You see, it's official, Bates suffers from premature ejaculation. Allegedly.

It all started off rather innocuously with a passing comment Bates made in his regular programme column. Bates usually reserves his programme notes as his personal 'hate-site', which gives his victims no right of reply. Indeed, his very last end-of-season column said of one fanzine editor, Alan Collis of *Red Card*, "you are pathetic, grow up, get a job and get a life." Anyway, in his programme column for the February midweek game against Blackburn Rovers, Bates started bragging about his sexual exploits. Describing the previous Valentine's weekend he'd had with his fragrant dolly bird, Suzannah Dwyer, the Captain proudly told us, "...emulating Di Matteo's 1997 FA Cup Final goal, I scored early before going to work." Given that Di Matteo scored in only 43 seconds, that's a cut and dried case of premature ejaculation. Either that or Bates' buttocks operate like a well-oiled piston that would not only put a Ferrari to shame but would also be able to warp time. Given that Bates is 67 years old, I'd plump for the former.

You can just imagine it. Bates gets down to business and 30 rapid strokes later lets out a muffled grunt (or should be roar?) from behind his white beard - 43 seconds exactly. What a grotesque thought. The Independent Supporters Association, the compassionate lot that they are, subsequently had a whip-round and sent the Captain a self-help book by Dr Ruth entitled *Lasting the Distance*. Given that no lawyers letters landed, we can only assume that, for once, we've got the Captain by the balls (no pun intended).

Other off-the-field events have been a mite more depressing. Most conspicuous of these has been the never-ending saga of our unfinished stadium. Bates is to construction what Hitler was to diplomatic relations. By way of example, in the time it took 'Boro to build the Riverside from the ground up, the Captain built us... a car park. In particular has been the problem with the West Stand. Yet again, the past season has seen 6,000 Blues fans get pissed on from above, while the away fans are kept nice and toasty in the East Stand (the most expensive stand at the Bridge). The problem has been one of planning permission, which for reasons unbeknownst to anyone but the Captain was applied for after the rest of the ground had been built. The propaganda regularly wheeled out from the Bridge tells us that the local residents, who live in one of the most exclusive residential addresses in the whole of Britain, are opposed to the size and capacity of the stand. Not so. After the Second World War, we had over 100,000 pack the Bridge for a visit by Dynamo Kiev. By 1970, we still had over 50,000 traipsing to the Bridge, so the question of ground capacity objections is a red herring.

No, the problem is that Bates wants to incorporate a 900-capacity nightclub into the West Stand. As far as the local residents are concerned, the prospect of nearly a thousand people stumbling out pissed onto the streets at 2.00am and regurgitating their Bridge kebabs onto their doorsteps is not particularly appealing, and therein lies the problem. Rumour has it that a compromise has now been struck, which will also limit our capacity to 41,500 at a time when clubs like Newcastle and Man United are all increasing theirs to well over 50,000.

This leads us nicely on to the Captain's other Stamford Bridge developments, namely the hotel and restaurants. The hotel's 1998 launch was marked with flowing champagne, canapes and vol-au-vents but was missing one vital ingredient: paying guests. Indeed, paying guests have been rarer than a well-timed Paul Scholes tackle, and there is a fanzine sweepstake to see who can be the first to find one. Admittedly, the hotel launch was not helped by the sacking of the hotel manager for 'misappropriating funds' - that's 'putting your hand in the till and taking your gay lover on romantic Venice weekend breaks' to you and me. The restaurants haven't fared much better, with an *Observer* review absolutely hammering Fishnets. The reviewer was trying to be kind but could not help including the words "shockingly pretentious", or noting that the final bill was, quote, "insultingly preposterous". Strong stuff. But that's not all. Rumour has it that there is so much unsold food, it has started to appear at the South Bank soup kitchen. Apparently even the tramps avoid it.

It is therefore no surprise that the debacle that is Chelsea Village has seen its share price plunge from a high of £1.50 to its current altitude-defying height of 65p. That's still 65p too much, given that no-one knows who owns the club (Bates merely "represents" the majority shareholders). Indeed, City insiders secretly argue that, at best, Chelsea Village is a 'penny share' – and, at worst, have given it 'junk bond' status.

At least on the pitch the players did not sink to the gross incompetence of Captain Bird's Eye. Throughout the season they were superb. A special word has to be said for our defence, which is not something the Blues have been noted for down the years. Desailly *et al* were nothing short of outstanding and, having conceded only 30 goals, beat the record for the best Chelsea defence ever. In fact, the only defence better than us last season was the Arse, who themselves have the best defensive record in Europe.

This has all been part of Vialli's pragmatic approach to management, which has seen us adapt a more 'Juve-style' pressing game, rather than the free-style 'sexy football' that Gullit had us playing. No disrespect to Gullit, who I admire greatly, but three defeats as opposed to last season's 13 tells its own story. The improvement in our defence has been down to the addition of two players: Marcel Desailly and Albert Ferrer. Much has been written about Desailly but very little about Ferrer, or 'Chappie' as he is known to the players. Chappie is many fans' player of the season and his accomplished style, along with his technical flair, has won him many admirers at the Bridge. What is even more incredible is to think that the Barcelona and Spain right-back only cost us £2m, when inexperienced, homegrown players like Danny Mills are fetching double that amount. No wonder we buy abroad - and long may it continue if we keep buying players of Chappie's quality.

That we didn't win the league has been put down by some observers to the loss of Casiraghi and Laudrup early in the season. However, to be fair, Casiraghi looked like a pup, with his sell-by-date long behind him, and Laudrup was an inconsistent luxury. No, the league was lost with the injury to Gustavo Poyet at Southampton on Boxing Day. Coming at the same time as a two-month injury lay-off to Tore Andre Flo, our attack was decimated. It was at that point Vialli should have bought a new striker, which would have also given us fresh impetus for the end of season run-in. However, he didn't and the rest is now history.

And what are the prospects for next season? Mixed, I'm afraid. Contrary to the hype, we're skint, and Vialli's published aim in a recent club magazine article is to hang on to what he has got. That doesn't bode well because it is obvious to all Blues fans what is needed - a striker. Not an ageing pup, not an inexperienced kid and not 'one for the future'. We need a striker and we need him now

Jez Walters

Source: *Spitting Feathers*

MONKEY BUSINESS

Hartlepool United

Peter Beardsley in a Hartlepool shirt, Pools live on Sky, the division's leading goalscorer leaving in unusual circumstances, and the usual end of season nerve-jangling finish. Yes, yet another roller-coaster season for Hartlepool United fans, with the now customary start, which flatters to deceive, a period of apparent comfort, followed by a headlong dash towards the Conference. This season's traditional flirting with the drop went much closer to the wire for the well-being of the nerves and fingernails of the Pools faithful.

The close season began with the ongoing contract dispute between owners IOR and manager Mick Tait, who was not convinced that he had their full backing. He had earlier objected to what he felt was undue interference with his duties from a board who wanted to impose a Norwegian coach on him. Tait's discomfort intensified with a dispute over goalkeeper Martin Hollund, who Tait didn't want on his retained list, but IOR were said to have insisted. The Norwegian stopper was given a one-year contract. IOR's subsequent explanation that they had not interfered, but had signed Hollund because they wanted to make sure the club had goalkeeping cover was somewhat less than convincing. Certainly, Tait never seemed to have access to promised transfer funds sufficiently large to both sign players and fund their wages.

The season started with a distinct rarity - we won a trophy. Not that the Tweedmouth Feast Shield, fought over two days at Berwick Rangers' speedway stadium cunningly disguised as a football ground, made many headlines outside of Berwick or Hartlepool, but we hoped it augured well for the season to come. Early away wins at Barnet and Cambridge, coupled with a very creditable performance against Bolton in the League Cup added to the usual early doors expectations.

September brought an early highlight, with Pools' first-ever appearance on Sky, in what should have been an excellent party night for the fans regardless of the result. That it was not to be was due in no small part to the actions of

Monkey Business — No 45 — Apr 99 — Still £1 Or 1.50 Euros!

The Independent Voice of Hartlepool United Fans

HERE WE GO AGAIN !

host club Halifax Town and those so-called guardians of the peace, the West Yorkshire Police. From the day the fixture was announced, it was obvious that there was going to be a large contingent travelling to Yorkshire. The club even laid on subsidised bus travel to help swell the support, and this generous offer was fully subscribed. In spite of the numbers travelling, assurances were given that the game was not all-ticket, and there would be plenty of room.

I remembered Halifax's shambolic Shay from years gone by, when turf was laid on boards to make up the corners of the pitch cut off by the speedway track. Visiting fans were shoe-horned into a corner of the ground with such shallow terracing and poor diagonal view of the pitch that any more than 100 visiting fans would make it impossible to see the game. Still, no need to worry, the game was being played at the now re-named New Shay, and it had all been re-built... hadn't it? Certainly, a magnificent new terrace had been built behind one goal on the site of the former shale heap. We arrived to learn that in spite of appearing almost finished, it had been refused a safety certificate, and we were once more being forced into that dark corner terrace with no view and even fewer facilities.

We arrived early to soak up the pre-match 'Sky' atmosphere (sad, I know!) and realised that things were not right. A safety steward was asking if we knew when the official coaches would arrive as they only had 69 tickets left and there were more than that number already queuing. The official coaches arrived close to the kick-off, but fortunately the club had ensured that the vast majority already had tickets. However, the queuing fans were not pleased to be told that there were no tickets left for a match which they had been told was not all-ticket. Eventually they were allowed to buy tickets for the small stand beside the terrace, and another small area of terracing on the other side of the stand. Everyone got in - but, once there, were cramped into totally unsafe areas. The 700 fans now packed onto the shallow terrace had the luxury of four Portaloos - with no separate facilities for female fans.

On the pitch, the occasion was obviously too much for the team, and we conceded two goals in quick succession midway through the first half. As the game went on, the crowd became increasingly restless at being penned in, and many climbed over a crush barrier and stood between it and the advertising hoardings. At half-time, one fan ran onto the pitch, and gestured towards the huge empty terrace in complaint at the overcrowded conditions. He was pursued by a steward, and eventually rightly detained.

This, however, seemed to be the turning point of the evening. The stewards summoned police help, who decided to push fans back from behind the advertising hoardings to behind the crush barriers. They did this in an inflammatory manner. How they expected fans stumbling backwards with a baton in their face to climb a three-foot high fence and enter an already dangerously over-crowded area is unclear. Those already behind the barriers resisted and fans at the back pushed forward. This was the signal for the police to extend their batons and start hitting anyone within reach over the head and to the body - seemingly at random.

Within seconds, a number of supporters suffered gaping head wounds; some fell to the floor, but were still hit. An eight-year-old boy caught up in the incident received similar treatment until he was helped by other members of the crowd. I was always under the impression that police presence at games was to stop trouble, not cause it; but I am obviously mistaken. I was also under the impression that police officers were under a legal obligation to identify themselves (i.e. give you their number) when asked - again I'm obviously mistaken, unless that is, every member of the West Yorkshire police force is called "Fuck off".

The subsequent FA Whitewash - sorry, Enquiry - amazingly decided that the facilities had been fine, and that no-one had been at fault. The internal police disciplinary procedure is still "on-going" - they are obviously working on the principle that the longer they take to do it, the more visiting supporters are likely to drop their complaints. Back on the field, Pools played a lot better in the second-half, and a great solo goal by Chris Beech pulled one back, although we were always chasing the game.

Beech was Pools' most influential player by far and was also leading goalscorer in the division by the end of October, with nine goals. However, he played no further part in the season. He had been in contract dispute with the club all season, playing on a week-to-week contract. His salary demands were in excess of what the club could justify under their limited pay structure, although negotiations were said to be closing the gap. Beech then acquired an agent, a certain David Speedie, who arranged a deal with Sheffield United for the midfielder. Although obviously a good move for Beech, the downside for the club was that rather than a cash transfer deal, it involved the return of Jon Cullen, sold to the Blades months earlier, and for whom we had not yet received the final transfer payment. He had not played a competitive game all season, and would require a salary of at least twice the amount that the club had been unable to pay Beech in the first place. Not surprisingly, the club felt unable to accept the deal; and, as a result, Speedie advised his client to walk out on the club.

Beech ended up in limbo, out of favour at the Vic and unable to play for another club. He later went on loan to Huddersfield for a month, but they had no cash to buy him either. Eventually after a take-over had gone through, the Yorkshire club decided to buy him, and in spite of their previous valuation in the region of £250,000... offered £20,000. This was obviously part of the traditional pre-tribunal posturing and, true to form, the tribunal awarded us £65,000 plus appearance add-ons.

The absence of Beech, with his extremely valuable goals from midfield, only served to emphasise the obvious lack of goalscoring forwards. Senior striker Paul Baker had suffered the agony of three broken legs within the space of 18 months and was destined to play a part only in the tail-end of the season. This left the onus squarely on the shoulders of the diminutive Craig Midgley and converted midfielder Steve Howard. The former simply didn't score enough goals, although would probably offer lack of supply as his main defence. The latter was still learning his trade as a target man, and was soon bearing the brunt of criticism from sections of the support for failing to score. He battled on through the bad times and, as the season wore on, won back the fans with superb displays - sadly without the necessary support to convert the chances created into goals. He eventually moved on to Northampton for a significant fee.

Help arrived over Christmas, with the signing of Peter Beardsley on his release from Fulham. He scored a blinding 20-yard volley on his debut and the scene seemed to be set for cameo performances to bring a fairy-tale end to his career. It didn't work out like that, as he ran hot and cold, and found difficulty with our playing surface, which had been ruined by an ill-fated groundshare with our rugby-playing neighbours. He also found difficulty finding players on the same wavelength, and a lot of his prompting went unexploited.

Indifferent performances and a steady slide down the table inevitably cost Tait his job. The owners' less-than-overwhelming support meant that Tait played out every permutation of his wafer-thin resources without finding the Midas touch solution he sought. For a month, they didn't even appoint a successor, and all-time hero Brian Honour stood in, achieving a couple of vital victories. Ex-Man United and Sunderland goalkeeper Chris Turner arrived from Wolves, and brought the new face that many fans had demanded. He certainly stepped the club up a gear in many ways - and the funds which had been so elusive to Tait, suddenly were made available. In came experience in the form of Notts County man-mountain Gary Strodder, last year's Golden Boot winner Gary Jones, also from Notts County, and Chris Freestone from Northampton (who had previously signed the much-improved Howard) .

All three were to contribute in a major way to our survival, and Beardsley found kindred spirits in the form of Freestone and Jones. The former England maestro scored the winner against Leyton Orient with a cool finish under pressure, and destroyed Scarborough almost single-handedly, setting up a Freestone strike and a penalty for the ex-Middlesbrough and Northampton striker to convert, with quickly-taken free-kicks. Strodder only played 13 games, but to such an effect that a couple more and he would have been voted Player of the Year.

Following a club like Hartlepool is very much an acquired taste, and one alien to the glory-hunting fans that you see around many of our towns and cities proudly wearing the replica shirt of whichever club they have decided to attach themselves to, in their search for a little reflected glory. As with many lower league fans, the banter on the terrace with your own and visiting fans often helps to keep you sane. The other vital element is the away trip. Being located where we are, most of these are a bit of an expedition - but even the shorter ones can be memorable for a variety of reasons. This season yielded several notable ones. Halifax, for the reasons outlined above, will stick in many people's memories (and throats). London area trips are usually best done by train, Kings Cross being a mere two and a bit hours from Darlington (the place does have its uses!). But the FA Cup trip to Fulham was only finalised a week or so previously, due to their replay. Being mid-December, all of the cheap train tickets had gone to Christmas shoppers, so mini-buses galore were arranged. We twice came from behind against Keegan's eventual giant-killers, but two late goals finished us off.

The New Year saw an horrendous sequence of away games that would stretch the stamina of even the most committed of fans. Exeter, Peterborough, Plymouth, Torquay, Shrewsbury, and Swansea were regurgitated by the league's fixture computer in the space of eight weeks, the latter on a Tuesday night to rub salt into wounds. I chose to miss the Exeter game, a good decision with hindsight - 1-0 going into injury-time, we allowed the Grecians to score in the 92nd and 96th minute to steal victory. Peterborough and Plymouth were excellent battling draws under new manager Chris Turner. The Torquay game was a 12.00 kick-off to allow for England v Poland at 3.00, so we drove down on Friday and took in Exeter v Darlington that evening - or half of it... all we could stomach. With a good following of Poolies (Torquay is always a popular weekend away trip), we lay down and let them walk all over us, giving debutante Effion Williams a hat-trick. At least the long journey home was made in daylight.

Turner's arrival saw form pick up, but four successive draws allowed Hull, Scarborough and Carlisle either to overtake us or close the gap. A nail-biting end to the season ensued, and the critical result was probably a 1-0 away win at Shrewsbury, where Paul Baker vitally slotted home the rebound from a penalty save in the 87th minute. A 3-0 home win over Scarborough, inspired by Beardsley and finished by Freestone, in front of a crowd of 5,098, calmed the nerves. Various combinations of results meant that a 0-0 draw at home to Carlisle in the following home game was sufficient to guarantee safety and a leisurely last-day trip to Southend. This was memorable for a variety of reasons, including spending the night on the floor of a fire station recreation room (don't ask!) and an excellent turnout to follow the 1,000 or so who had been at Mansfield a fortnight earlier.

The last three home games saw average attendances in excess of 4,000, which, coupled with the excellent away followings throughout the season shows that there *is* support for the club in the town. As safety was secured with the wins against Scarborough and Orient, and a draw against Carlisle, you would have thought we had actually won something, and not simply survived. The club will hope to build on the euphoria for the coming season, and I'm sure the fans will go into it fuelled by their usual blind faith and optimism. The squad we finished with certainly looks to have the makings of our strongest for a long time. Much will depend on how Turner spends his budget over the summer to add to those retained. Beardsley will not be there - he did his bit, but younger legs will be needed, along with a creative brain. Following Hartlepool United is certainly never dull, and is often controversial - and I haven't even mentioned Jimmy Glass... not that he should have been allowed to play for Carlisle in the first place.

Paul Mullen

MOULIN ROUGE

Rotherham United

August 8 dawned bright and warm (the first day of the football season always does, doesn't it?), and several hours later the masses had gathered down at the Millmoor Academy, resplendent in their new 'One2One' team shirts, hoping that this was going to be THE season. I had spent the summer editing my first edition of *Moulin Rouge*, founding editor Matt Norcliffe having decided to call it a day after 22 issues (he deserves some kind of medal). With his help and the contributions of the usual suspects, the process was not as painful as I had imagined; and thus I found myself outside Millmoor, the first issue in my hot, sweaty little hand (oo-er missus!), looking forward to

THE ROTHERHAM UNITED FANZINE

ISSUE 23   *AUG/SEPT 98*   £1

our opening day clash versus Dull City. Having just missed out on the play-offs the year before, optimism was high and, despite going a goal down in six minutes, a 3-1 win added fuel to our optimism. It's unfortunate, therefore, that I belong to a strange cult of people whose only common trait is that of following the worst and unluckiest sports teams that they can find. In fact we are so unlucky that if we fell in a barrel of bosoms we'd come out sucking our collective thumbs. The win against Hull should have been a starter for 90 points and automatic promotion, but all that remains now, ten months later, is that gut-wrenching feeling of failure yet again... Thirty-one years of hurt (sounds familiar), and a campaign that promised so much, but which ultimately turned into a smack in the face with David Beckham's damp jock-strap (very unpleasant I'm led to believe). The play-off semi-final second-leg ended horribly, and as Leyton Orient's left-back danced a jig of delight in front of us after he had struck the winning penalty of the shoot-out at Rotherham, I turned away and felt like crying. After three years of torture and suffering, surely we had deserved a break or two? But no, just like most lower league football fans, we're stuck with reality; we have no other choice. But there's always next year, isn't there?

Looking back, most of the past season is a blur, partly due to constant sleep depravation caused by my son, who was born just as Marcel Desailly was getting his red card during the World Cup Final, and partly due to the roller-coaster ride our beloved Millers took us on from September to May (I feel a song coming on). The four-win opening burst which shot us to the top of the league, oddly enough culminated in the August Manager of the Month award going to Ron Nodules, Brentford's owner/manager/lap dancer/all-round good egg and media darling. This despite Brentford having lost one of their league games. (We, strangely enough, were unbeaten, though we prefer not to mention our defeat over two legs in the Bad Beer Cup to the Direshites...) These four wins had us believing in our own publicity but, whatever, we looked forward to cementing our position at the top during the early days of September.

However, the type of shite 'service' any Roth fan worth his/her salt would recognise as commonplace, was resumed with the shock of two awful defeats against Sarfend (3-0) at Roots Hall and our first home defeat, 2-0 to Plywoodmouth - the only redeeming feature of these putrid experiences being the discovery of a cellophane-wrapped Pukka Pie at Sarfend. It was gratifying to see that the missionary work had percolated so far south. After the debacle of Plymouth, inquests were held, youngsters were added to the squad and a week later we were stuffing the arse off Nodule's lads at Griffin Park, 3-0. Now, having already beaten Cambridge and Cardiff during our initial four-win spurt, this win at Brentford meant that we had beaten all of the eventual automatically promoted teams before mid-September, and herein lies the rub. Cuffing the better teams and then making an arse of ourselves against the so-called lower lights ultimately cost us automatic promotion. This was further borne out a couple of weeks later by a defensively inept 4-2 defeat at Barnet, closely followed by a sad 1-0 reverse at home to the then bottom of the league lads from Shrewsbury - this, to anyone with a modicum of realism and honesty at Rotherham, began to cast huge doubts over our promotion credentials.

October carried on this zig-zag trend, none more so than Scunny away, where, when 4-0 down with 15 minutes to go, our lads suddenly realised that fingers ought to be extracted. Roared on by what was left from an initial following of 1,500 Roth fans (not many, I can tell you) and helped by three injudicious substitutions by Brian Laws, they started to run around like men possessed, scoring three goals in 15 minutes and ending up nearly drawing a game that they had never sniffed. The last match in October saw us go top for the last time that season (oh, the heady heights...). Struggling 2-0 down at half-time to Barry 'Fat' Fryer's Posh, I had a *contretemps* with a Millers fan who refused to buy a mag unless it contained, "...summat about Ronnie Moore gerrin' t'sack." Four magnificent second-half goals without reply and three points later, the guy changed his mind and bought the fanzine on his way out - fickle folk, us from Rotherham. The subsequent 4-0 drubbing we gave Scarborough seven days later turned out to be Leo Fortune-West's last game for Roth, as his loan spell from Lincoln had expired and, after much messing about, he was finally tempted back to London and Brentford Nylons FC by Ron Nodules (yes, that man again!). The lack of willingness on our board's part to stump up the cash for him did not help the situation. Claim and counter-claim bounced back and forth from the club about Leo's desire to move back to London, although I still maintain that we did not try hard enough. At this vital stage in the season, it seemed to me that Leo had provided a spark that had been lacking a month before. And our failure to sign him first time around, I believe, went some way towards fatally harming our hopes of automatic promotion.

Following his departure the wheels began to come off what remained of our championship wagon. Leo had scored four goals out of 14 in the five matches he played, compared to the whole team managing only seven in the next five games (four of those were against non-league Emley in two FA Cup matches). The term 'couldn't hit a cow's arse with a banjo' started to be bandied about down Millmoor way, and despite the signing of Rob Scott from Full Ham a week after Leo's departure, we still couldn't pick ourselves up. By the end of November, we had slipped down to fourth on the back of three draws. Two of these were goalless and the third should have been a defeat, as we proved yet again that our propensity for scoring late goals, introduced last year, was still intact. Torquay outplayed us at Millmoor the Tuesday after Leo's last match, but conceded two fortunate goals in injury-time to throw away two of the three points that had looked destined for Plainmoor all night. This game was finally to see the demise of Leo's so-called 'replacement' from the reserves, Gisbjert Bos (giraffe-like, Dutch cheese and all-round shite footballer), who gave what is commonly agreed by Millers fans as the worst, most uncommitted performance ever given by someone wearing the Millers colours... and he only had 45 minutes in which to do it. This was his first appearance of the season, and it was to be his last. Ronnie replaced him at half-time with Trevor Berry, who is half his size. Weeks later, Gisbjert's contract was cancelled.

December dawned dark and dreary, the only bright spot being our wins in the FA Cup, which took us into round three. The rest was a disaster. We were knocked out by Wigan in round one of the Auto Plated Doo Dah Shield competition (we won it in 1996 and haven't won a tie since), one of their goals being scored by Paul Warne, who was to join us in January to great effect; and we failed to win a league match before Christmas. Our 'push' for promotion was taking on disaster proportions as we copped three real drubbings: Brighton 4-1 and Cambridge 3-2, both away; and, worst of all, Chester beat us 4-2 at home. Ronnie looked humiliated after this match and certainly appeared as though he wanted to rip off someone's head. We were down to tenth and looking for inspiration. Christmas had been spoilt (again), and something had to give.

Salvation came initially in the form of experienced midfielder Steve Thompson, who had been mysteriously missing from first team action since early September. The best passer of a ball in the division, his return coincided with a year-end 3-1 win against Halifax Town. Apart from a dreadful, gutless team display at Dull City (or "Pull Titty" as one *Moulinrouger* has it) in early January, he was instrumental in an upturn in form, which saw three excellent wins in January taking us to fifth. The 3-0 win at Mansfield (or the Shags as they are affectionately known) came in front of the Sky cameras, and given that twelve months previously we had thumped Brunley at Turf Moor in front of the same TV audience, we are still considering an application for the permanent residence of satellite TV at all Roth's away games. By the way, the Dull City match saw the re-appearance of my mate from the Posh game, still bibbling on about Ronnie getting the sack. This time I nearly lost control - I mean, wouldn't you? The team was playing crap and I was having to put up with his endless stream of bollocks at the same time. What he doesn't seem to understand is that in these current 'Snouts in the trough, Premiership, pull the ladder up Jack, I'm OK' times, no other manager could hope to do any better under the same financial restraints. Ronnie is the best chance we have at the moment. He's Roth through and through - and if anyone can, Ronnie can... I hope!

Unfortunately Ronnie seems unable to cure the ever-present, rampant inconsistency of the team, and this trait reared its ugly head again in February as we slid to ninth on the back of two draws and two defeats. The last defeat came at home against Brentford Nylons, who took their revenge and cuffed us 4-2. This was the turning point. Leo Fortune-West came on as sub for Brentford and gave Vance Warner a real kicking. This must have jogged a memory or two because six days later Leo had returned to Millmoor in a deal worth £35,000. He was to form a partnership with Paul Warne, who was signed from Wigan in January to cover Lee Glover's long-term absence through injury. Glover did his hamstring in the FA Cup Third Round defeat against Brissel Rovers and did not play again. Warne turned out to be an excellent signing, who never gave less than 100%, chasing lost causes in the style of our old hero Dave Gwyther from the Seventies. Further injuries were biting, and at the beginning of March we had a whole defence and forward line out for the rest of the season. Ronnie was forced to bring in three fresh defenders (two on loan, Phil Whelen and Will Varty), and with these guys having only met the Friday before, the team ran out magnificent 4-0 winners away at Scarborough the day after. This set us up for a steady rise through March and April, culminating in a play-off spot. Eight back-to-back matches were played in April, and apart from two dismal showings in the south- west, at Exeter and Torquay, we maintained a steady stream of points sufficient to clinch fifth place. This part of the world proves a constant puzzle for the Millers: 1-0 at Plymouth, 2-0 at Torquay, 3-0 at Exeter; any further up the coast and we could find ourselves on the end of a 6-0 drubbing from Yeovil Town. I think the overnight stay deadens the senses - or could it be too much room service?

Glossing over the play-offs would be ideal but after finishing fifth and joint-top scorers in the division, with 79, we spent 210 minutes huffing and puffing against Orient, before going out on penalties after two goalless draws. The God of Shite Footie teams had once again dumped on us from a great height... nuff said, it's too painful to delve any deeper. The 9,500 crowd at Millmoor for the second-leg showed that people will come and watch if there is something on offer. Three and a half thousand extra

Roth fans took the trouble to turn out. But where do they come from? Plastic fans? I think not (we aren't in the right division). Nosey-parker Washday fans? Maybe (looking for tips for their next failed Premiershit campaign). Or long lost Millers fans? Let's hope so. We need home support and too often this past season, the barracking has been unacceptable. Hardly surprising when put in the historical context of the 96-97 season (the worst in our history). Wounds take time to heal and even with Dr Moore in charge, sporadic crap performances are like salt to those wounds, and the patient does not take long to start squealing. But it has to stop. We need to get square behind the lads next year - it's the only way forward.

So what of next season? We are short of a quality midfielder, and two quality full-/wing-backs. The board have already told Ronnie that there is no cash to spend, so Bosman signings it is. But with the excessive signing-on fees and wage demands that come with these players, we could be hard pushed to improve on last season's position. It was an achievement in itself getting to the play-offs, considering the injuries we had and the lack of form we showed on many occasions, and it says a lot about the fitness and spirit of the team - but too often we lacked quality. Boothy, our septuagenarian chairman, must dig deep so we can climb out of this bloody league, because every year we miss out, the job gets that much harder the following season. We are not helped by a somewhat intransigent board, who contribute not much at all, the financial burden falling on Boothy and his scrap business. They remind me a little of how the Kremlin used to operate. Secreted away in the bowels of the main stand, they appear every so often, to give the proletariat a wave... sometimes a full hand is used, if we're lucky. The club is patchily run, with Phil Henson, our ex-manager now occupying the post of chief executive. Not a guy well-endowed with PR skills, he does not give the club an approachable face and his management of such things as whether or not to make the Orient second leg all-ticket, and his *fait accompli* handling of increasing standing season tickets by 30% to bring them in line with those who sit, leaves much to be desired. We still have no discernible policy of going forward (e.g. the stadium), apart from an attitude of, "Well, we'll get there eventually..."; which makes the progress Ronnie has made on the pitch so much more surprising. This progress must be continued next season - and that means automatic promotion. With prudent investment in the playing staff and a shrewder more street-wise attitude on the pitch, I believe we could... nay, *must* do it.

Steve Exley

MY EYES HAVE SEEN THE GLORY

Tottenham Hotspur

Of all the clubs in all the world, he had to become manager of ours. Of all the things that could have happened at Tottenham this season, George Graham's arrival was probably the least expected. This had followed the most likely thing to happen - the dismissal of Christian Gross. Unfortunately for him, the knowledgeable Swiss manager was never likely to become the big cheese at Spurs. He kept Tottenham up the previous season and then they let him down after a couple of months of this.

After three games, it looked like the run-in at the end would be crucial for Tottenham. Liverpool away, then home games against Chelsea and Arsenal, before we visited one ground from which we regularly return empty-handed, Old Trafford. As it turned out, those games, which only produced one point for the club, came after just enough points had been accumulated to see Spurs safe. But I am jumping ahead of the game.

The Tottenham defence had been leaking goals and was as 'holey' as the cheese for which Gross' home country is famous. But after a brief period when Pleat took the reins, the shock appointment of GG saw the back-line tighten like Alan Sugar's purse strings. But there again, Graham was not a man to be trifled with and the money was spent to make short-term gains. At one point it was between German or Cameroon internationals as to who would be the first arrival. Spurs fans weren't sure if it would be Freund or Foe. As it turned out the German came and found a medal in his kitbag before he had even unpacked properly. The other worrying rumour was that Spurs were set to get Munitis. No, not a nasty tropical disease, but a Spanish striker with Racing Santander (which is not a colloquialism for a dose of the runs). For other members of the squad, it was a time of long knives and prospective short careers at the club. Those who incurred the wrath of George were soon banished to the nether-world of the Combination League, rarely to be seen again. Moussa Saib sought to play for Algeria when he had been suffering from a back injury

- and he played out the season as captain of his country and midfielder in our reserves. From a stiff back to a stiffs midfielder.

Some found that GG's style suited them nicely and had a renaissance. The vilified Vega became a sound centre-half, Edinburgh got stuck in at left-back and Walker produced some good form that saw him back in the England squad. Tim Sherwood left Blackburn to come to join the revolution at the Lane and he steadied the ship as well as scoring a few goals. While not the most obvious of players, his contributions were valuable to the club's progression in the FA Cup and gathering league points. He was unlucky enough to have to sit and watch the victorious Worthington Cup side, while his challenge in the FA Cup faltered at the semi-final stage. The match against Newcastle was poor and the ref and linesman both managed to avert their eyes when Dabizas palmed the ball away in the box, but were sufficiently alert to see Sol Campbell knock the ball away with his hand at the other end. The Toon never looked like scoring until the penalty, but by then Spurs were out of it and would probably have lost in the final anyway. But coming away from Old Trafford, the feeling wasn't one of resentment, because there was already a trophy in the cupboard and a place in Europe too - which, if anything, was even more important in attracting top players to the club. At times, Tottenham seemed to be playing like they had done before Graham took control, so the UEFA Cup campaign may be as short as those that many English teams have had recently. I hope there will be a few of the famous European nights under lights at White Hart Lane before the competition is flooded with the Champions League rejects.

The Spurs fans had a terrible time trying to decide whether George Graham's tenure at the club would be a good thing or a bad thing. Had he come as a Gooner in Spurs clothing to finish off the club we loved, or would he be our knight in shining blue and white armour to carry Tottenham forward into a successful Millennium? The debate raged, with heated views on both sides. The cannon on his patio became a crucial talking point and it was thought that, unless it went, he could be buried under it if the side didn't do well. His love affair with the Highbury outfit is only natural, as his most successful times as a player and manager were there, but he assured fans that he was Tottenham now and would do all he could to put the club back on the right track. He was making all the right noises, but still had to convince the Spurs faithful. After the Wembley win there were a few bars of song praising him, but it was the touch-line argument he had with Gullit at the FA Cup semi-final that won over the majority of the fans. A five-minute long version of "Georgie Graham's blue and white army..." followed, leaving the Toon Army wondering what was going on. While some still have their doubts, many feel he is the only manager who could have taken on the task of reviving Tottenham at that time. But we all know that he will always have red and white in his heart.

On the pitch, Tottenham's best spell of football throughout the whole season came between the marathon saga of five matches against Wimbledon (some fans never made it through... they will always be remembered; which is more than you can say for some of the football) and the FA Cup semi-final.

The Wimbledon games will only be recalled with fondness by those who have seen Tottenham capitulate to the Dons so readily in the past. Les Ferdinand went through a spell of suffering head injuries, which we hoped might have knocked some (goal-scoring) sense into him. The Leeds FA Cup replay at Tottenham was probably the best the side played all season, as Ginola did everything that Tottenham fans were hoping he would do since joining from Newcastle and that he would reproduce on a regular basis. His run across the pitch, beating players with pace and style, ended as much of the season's play did - without a goal, Martyn's slightest finger-tip on the ball diverting it against the post and out. Ginola was not to be denied, though, and hit a bouncing volley from 20 yards that went in for the second goal. Even Darren Anderton weighed in with a cracker of a goal, which Spurs fans could cope with seeing him do more often.

Daveed was saving his best, though, and it was for Barnsley, who had knocked Spurs out of the FA Cup the previous season. The original date had seen a covering of snow on the pitch, and although it was rumoured that certain footballers had been invited in to sniff it all up, the game had to be postponed. The re-arranged match took place on a Wednesday night in front of a fired-up Yorkshire audience. Last time, Stephen Clemence had been dismissed for diving, and on this occasion, the red card saw Adie Moses depart - opening up the red sea of shirts defending their goal and allowing Ginola to dance between the challenges to stick the only goal of the game past the 'keeper. Oh, if Ryan Giggs hadn't done something similar to the Arsenal back-four - but then again... It was enough to secure the Double for Tottenham's Frenchman - the PFA and the Football Writers' Player of the Year trophies. He was rumoured to be one of the first victims of Gross and Graham, but has knuckled down to produce more effort and, hopefully, more result from his mastery of the ball.

For the high point of the season, the final minute of the Worthington Cup Final takes some beating. Mainly because the preceding 89 minutes had been so dull. It was nerve-racking stuff, with Justin Edinburgh getting a red card for re-arranging Robbie Savage's hair. It's so unfair when you try to help someone like that. Anyway, as the time ticked away and the vigour of the tackles on the said Welshman increased, the Leicester manager saw fit to replace him with extra-time looming. His walk to the bench with a great big greenie hanging from his nose is an enduring image (isn't it, Ron?) and the fact that Tottenham scored almost immediately made things a tad more enjoyable. In a season of crucial last-minute goals, this was one of the first - and gave Tottenham a trophy and a European passport for the first time in eight years. The relief at winning what most people consider a Mickey Mouse competition was huge, as three games into the season such a feat looked as remote as the chances of a goalkeeper scoring a last-minute goal to keep a club in the league.

It saw the last vestige of any decent form as the club played out the rest of the season. Some thought that it was because of Ramon Vega's injury in the final, some because of Edinburgh's suspension, but most because of Houston, that we had the problem. The introduction of Stewart Houston as Graham's number two caused some concern amongst Tottenham fans. Chris Hughton was seen as the last Spurs link in the backroom staff and he seemed to be getting edged out. Jokes about Adidas' design for the new Spurs kit involving red and white shirts were not going down well.

One of the strangest things of this season was the exposé by Joe Kinnear that referee Dermot Gallagher had asked David Ginola for his shirt after the FA Cup tie at Selhurst Park. The ref had wanted it for a charity raffle, but Smokin' Joe (from his ears, no doubt) wanted the official banned from taking charge of the replay as, because of his actions at the end of the first match, he was an unsuitable choice. Well, he reffed the replay, and despite all Kinnear's tricks, he didn't get his way - on or off the pitch, with Tottenham going through 3-0 to the next round.

The season didn't end with meaningless games, though, as three of our last opponents were going for the title. Arsenal won at the Lane and Chelsea got a draw to prolong the sequence since we beat them to ten years. It all hung on our last match against Manchester United as to whether our neighbours would take the title or not. It started so well (for some), with Les Ferdinand losing his fear of being in front of goal and lobbing the despairing Schmeichel, who comically got tangled in the net as he failed to keep the ball out. Then, things started swinging the other way. It didn't take long for the home side to start piling on the pressure and Walker's earlier botched clearance attempt, which saw the ball bounce back off Yorke, onto the post and into Ian's arms, was redeemed by a series of saves that kept United out almost until the break. Then Beckham struck, followed by Cole's neat lob minutes after the break, and it was really all over. For us and for Arsenal. As the team who stopped Manchester United winning the lot this season by knocking them out of the Worthington Cup, we couldn't do it again to stop them winning the Premiership. But, hey, you can't win them all. Well, not if you are Tottenham Hotspur anyway.

Wyart Lane

NEW FRONTIERS

York City

Despite losing to Sunderland in round one of the Worthington Cup, York's season got off to an unusually bright start. Ten-man City held Fulham to a 3-3 draw at Craven Cottage and we were challenging for a play-off place in October. As well as two stunning goals at Fulham, Steve Agnew's all-round play suggested that he would be a vital cog in the side, playing the sort of role that another wily old veteran, Barry Lyons, had played when we last won promotion into the top two divisions, 25 years ago.

Then the rot set in. It wasn't until mid-December that we won again, and a bright Christmas suggested renewed play-off aspirations. These games saw debutant Andy Dawson strike the winner against Manchester City with his first touch, Oldham were comprehensively outplayed (and beaten) on their own ground, and a win at Wycombe followed.

Issue 41
£1
Apr-99

Little Out

no change?

new frontiers

But, no-one could remember when we last kept a clean sheet, as a New Year crash gathered momentum. Alan Little paid the penalty. After almost six years as manager, he was sacked in March. It's probably true to say that he had become stale and needed a fresh challenge. He appeared unable to motivate the players any longer. Watching, it was hard to see what the players did in training - set-piece play had become non-existent.

Around the same time, Steve Agnew had a falling out with the club. On the field, it was precipitated by his reaction to City supporters when subbed, but I wonder whether there were deeper undertones. Anyway, he was banished to the reserves, where he can serve out the remaining two years of his contract if no-one else wants him. If rumours are to be believed, he's the top earner at the club on over £1,500 a week.

Neil Thompson was appointed caretaker-manager. Performances improved slightly. Certainly the players seemed more motivated. As caretaker, he made four signings. Craig Skinner's signature prompted wild celebrations on Wrexham's websites - they couldn't believe they'd got as much as £30,000 for him. We paid a similar fee for Halifax's Marc Williams. He scored a few goals but looks distinctly Third Division class (read what I said about Richard Cresswell last year and you'll know that's not an insult). Matt Hocking, a Hull reserve defender, looked useful. However, those three purchases indicated the way we were heading.

Successive wins in late April made us favourites to stay up. Entering the final week, we could only go down if both Wycombe and Oldham won their two remaining games, and we lost at Maine Road. Guess what? Wycombe and Oldham won midweek. Oldham took an early lead on the last day of the season; we soon went a goal down and crumbled in the second-half, to lose 4-0. Our woe was complete when, in the 83rd minute, Wycombe scored a winner at Lincoln to stay up and send us down.

Two days later, Neil Thompson was confirmed as manager. With five experienced players (all high earners) transfer-listed and others freed, there should, hopefully, be a little room for newcomers this summer. But with five juniors signing professional contracts, probably not too much room.

The perceived wisdom is that Thompson is a good choice as manager. I've yet to be convinced. He took over in mid-March and took us to our lowest league position of the season on the final day (21st and relegation). Whilst it could be argued he took over a bad, demoralised side, Lawrie Sanchez, admittedly with a few more weeks, motivated Wycombe to safety from a far worse position than City.

Thompson's transfer policy to date is also open to question. Skinner hasn't proved anything, whilst the other three (Hocking, Williams and Chris Fairclough) fitted into the side well, without setting the world alight.

His transfer-listing of Andy McMillan didn't go down well with the majority of fans, and certainly not with the player; whilst he dismissed Mark Tinkler, probably our classiest operator, as not having the right attributes for a Division Three side. I can see some logic in both decisions, others don't. After over ten years, McMillan, who is approaching the club record for appearances is certainly nearer the end of his career than the start, and is facing increased pressure from three youngsters for the right-back shirt. Tinkler's disciplinary record leaves something to be desired. I believe both are out of contract next summer and that may have more to do with the transfer-listing than anything else.

One bright spot was a new openness displayed by our chairman, Douglas Craig. Our first-ever fans' forum was held in November and attended by about 200 supporters. A second one was held in March, when Craig opened proceedings by announcing that Alan Little had been sacked as manager after six years in charge. Craig also attended a fans' forum held by the London & South-East Branch of the Supporters Club. His frankness earned him a lot of respect and many fans gained a far better understanding of why the club is run the way it is. When wages are twice as much as gate receipts, it doesn't leave much money to go splashing around on big-money signings.

Many were amazed when we got £750,000 from Reading for Graeme Murty last summer, and you'd have been locked up for suggesting we'd get £950,000 for Richard Cresswell during the season. Cresswell wasn't guaranteed a place in the team at the start of the proceedings, but he'd grown physically over the summer and soon displaced the very disappointing Neil Woods as our main striker. Goals flowed, his hard work was a feature of his every performance, the goals his reward. No-one thought he'd make the England Under-21 side, but he did, earning his first cap before his transfer to Sheffield Wednesday. Before joining the squad, Peter Taylor took Jon Greening aside and said he was to room with a newcomer from York called Cresswell. "Talk to him and make him feel welcome," Taylor instructed. He didn't realise that they are best friends having shared a room together for three years in York. By the end of the season he'd been joined in the Under-21 side by three more players who had started their careers at York (Jon Greening, Darren Williams and Curtis Woodhouse).

On the bright side, once again our youth team did well, reaching the last-16 of the FA Youth Cup, before losing 5-0 to the eventual winners, West Ham, after a replay. Joe Cole ran the show, and 5-0 was no disgrace, as West Ham went on to beat Arsenal (4-0), Everton (3-0) and Coventry (6-0) to win the trophy. The highlight of their cup campaign probably came at the hotel meal before our victory at Stoke, when the youngsters scoffed the pasta and chicken meal that had been laid on for Manchester United reserve side who were on their way to a game at Villa Park. Hotel staff seeing the York side walk in wearing their red blazers thought they were United. As the York side was leaving, in walked the United side. It's not recorded what they thought of their beans on toast. The youth side rounded off their season by winning a 20-team, eleven-a-side tournament in Holland, where they beat the finest from Holland, Belgium, Yugoslavia and others.

The juniors coming through represent our best bet for a successful season. Lee Bullock and Christian Fox down the right, and James Turley and Michael Dibie up front could go places. Already established in our first team is 19-year-old Martin Garrett, and he could be our first million-pound player. Wednesday, Leeds and Blackburn are said to head the queue for his services.

With experience on the transfer list, it remains who will join the club this summer. City would like to make loanee Chris Fairclough a permanent signing. His influence was felt when he joined us, but at 35, he doesn't represent the future. Last summer's gamble on experience didn't do too well. Neil Woods had his contract paid up recently after only a handful of games and no goals, Agnew's on the list and even Thompson himself was out injured for much of the season.

But with relegation and five youngsters joining the professional staff, there isn't much room for manoeuvre on the transfer front. A goalkeeper, centre-back, striker and midfielder top the shopping list.

Until we know who is coming, it's hard to get enthusiastic about the new season. Even more so when you realise that the last two occasions on which we've been relegated to Division Three, it's taken us eight years to gain promotion.

As previously mentioned, with players' wages more than double gate receipts, prudence is the order of the day. Last season's side contains no-one who is guaranteed to set Division Three alight. Whatever else happens, though, you won't hear York City mentioned next to financial crisis clubs, Scarborough, Portsmouth, Hull and Crystal Palace.

Chris Forth

NO MORE PIE IN THE SKY

Notts County

Should I stay or should I go? (the choice is yours mix...)

Prologue: The end of season celebrations refused to subside as Heather continued to party hard until the last rays of sun receded from view. The Music *did* Sound Better With You, as she sang along to the holiday hiatus anthem. As the tempo of summer began to cool, she chilled out and reached new highs with the Verve at their homecoming zenith. But she'd pushed her body to the extreme and it was time for nature to have its payback. As the comedown approached, Heather started to feel the chill; she shivered

A NOTTS Co. FANZINE
ISSUE # 31
(April 98 - Aug. 98)
(*"50 Cups of coffee & you know it's on"*)
£1

"Dad, can I have the new Forest kit for my Birthday ?"

"No Son, I'm not going to be ripped off spending £45 on a football top, you can have a Notts Co. one like the rest of us."

ALSO INSIDE :- Pre-Season Match Reports, Where Are They Now ?, Reviews of the 1997/98 season, France 1998, The Ultimate Football Challenge, Zebra's, Zebra's and more Zebra's !!! + all the usual crap.

at the thought of a long, bleak and enduring winter. The memories of sunshine fun soon faded, replaced by the dark shadows of the night. She needed to rest. To sleep. Oh how she needed to sleep...

Side 1 - Blown a Wish

Intro: If You Tolerate This Your Children Will Be Next - Manic Street Preachers

There's ninety-odd clubs in the four divisions. That's four titles to be won, one FA Cup, one Worthy Cup, The Ratshit Windows (or whatever they call it these days) Cup for the no-hopers, European qualification and various promotion and play-off places to go for at the start of the season. Everyone thinks during the pre-season that it'll be their season, even if deep, deep down you know that your bunch of has-beens and wannabes have as much chance as My Bloody Valentine releasing a new album before the Millennium. But, for just a few weeks, we can all dream; and the sad thing about it is, we do - we all do... well, most of us anyway.

The reality is that very few of our teams *are* successful. After Man United have taken their share of the pickings, it's left for the rest of the others to scrap around for off-cuts. For some, there's always the threat and thrill of a relegation battle; and, for those supporters, survival is their success. For others, there's season upon season of mid-table mediocrity. I bet even some QPR fans were secretly pleased that there was a relegation battle for change. Teams like Rochdale always seem to finish 14th, or thereabouts, every season - a pretty boring existence, you must admit.

So what of our troupe, Notts County? It's guaranteed that we'll be either pushing for promotion or wrestling with relegation - no mid-table mediocrity for us. Still buzzin' on the euphoria of last season's record-breaking championship ride, expectations were high. An influx of eight new players gave supporters the idea that Sam Allardyce knew exactly what he was doing, and that success was unavoidable - just a matter of turning out each week and hanging around the top spot with promotion favourites Fulham, Stoke and Man City. Promotion, via the play-offs, was only 40-odd games away...

Track 1: Don't Believe The Hype - Public Enemy

The summer had been spent being encapsulated by the Verve's Haige Hall homecoming, emotionally emptied by England's Bitter Sweet Symphony, breakdancing to the latest sonic delights from The Beastie Boys, and dreaming of Notts and F****t in the same division come the Millennium. Thoughts were racing skyward as Notts ran out on a cold and blustery Boundary Park. Ninety minutes later and this promotion daydream looked to be realistic. A 3-0 annihilation of the Latics had seen the players continue from where they'd left off last term. But just as you've let you defences slip, football has that knack of kicking you in the balls, bringing you back down to earth.

The Worthington Cup saw an early exit, as promotion favourites Manchester City gave us a right Royle hammering - 2-0 at the Lane, followed by a 7-1 nadir that kept Sky viewers wondering if they were watching live football or a goals roundup from the weekend. But Notts fans are renowned for their sense of humour, and we took immense pleasure from a group of City stewards who'd placed a bet on City winning 7-0. With their winnings already spent, the first of many on-loan waste-of-space strikers did his stand-and-deliver impression with a consolation goal in the 85th minute. Stewards 0 Ladbrokes 1.

The league offered a home defeat at the hands of Bournemouth; the return of our old friend, the late goal, giving Northampton a point; and a pride-restoring point against City (our third game against them in six outings). With a 1-0 win away to the Macc lads, this concluded an up and down August. MTV could have done worse then use this month's exploits for the video of those horrendous Vengaboys.

Track 2: You Get What You Give - New Radicals

Inconsistency was the name of game throughout September; both Wigan and Blackpool winning 1-0. Andy Gorman came out of retirement and made his one and only Notts appearance, then disappeared from wherever he'd come. Keegan's Fulham were sent home pointless thanks to a superb performance from Darren Ward and a goal from one of a number of quality signings from Bradford, Shaun Murray. But another live Sky game for Allardyce's men could only mean one thing - defeat. Although we did manage to lead for part of the tie, we all knew we'd fuck it up come 90 minutes. But, like the previous month, Notts finished with another win, this time Millwall the casualties.

September also saw the door shut on Chris Billy's career as a Magpie. Signed in the summer, Billy will be remember for not being remembered, if you catch my drift. He's probably one of the biggest wastes of space (and I've seen a few during my footie watching days) ever to grace the turf of Meadow Lane. I thought I was crap, but there's hope for everybody, if the likes of Chris Billy can make a living from the game.

Track 3: You Don't Care About Us - Placebo

October was pretty poor to be honest. We scraped a last-gasp draw at Wycombe and wondered why we hadn't stayed in the picturesque settings of The White Horse and its back-to-nature entertainment! Local rivals Lincoln once again twisted the knife of hate. Stand-in goalkeeper Brain Parkin gifted them the first two and it wasn't until we were 3-0 down that we begin a fight-back. But it was too late in the day and the Imps rejoiced with their 3-2 prize. After an improved performance at Turf Moor, where once again we chucked away three points in the last minute, all was set for a cold, wet and miserable jog up the road to The Spireshites. My love of football and music are normally able to live quite happily side-by-side. But tonight I made a bad call, a very bad call. One of the best bands around, Placebo, were playing Rock-City, *Pure Morning, Teenage Angst, Nancy Boy,* etc... mouth-watering stuff. But I have the crazy notion that I have some bizarre allegiance to this club and have a duty, whenever humanly possibly, and often when inhumanly possible, to attend every game home and away. Some seasons I've actually managed to attend all of them (sad, but true). But if I miss one, I'm made to feel guilty. So, along with my dad, a Carlisle fan, who decided to treat (?) me for my 31st birthday, we jogged up the road to Saltershite. We met up with *Tora! Tora! Tora!* contributor and top bloke Chris Snell before the game for a few beers, and it's a good job I did sink a few, as the long-ball excuse for footie saw our bunch of non-performers reduced to a 3-0 deficit after an hour. I wanted to go then, but managed to endure another 15 minutes before concluding that never again would I choose footie over music.

Track 4: The Great Depression - The Jam

November saw little sight of fireworks. The first round of the FA Cup took us south down the M1 in search of a Sunday morning pint in lifeless Hendon. We eventually found one open in Golders Green and managed to neck two quick jars before being relieved of twelve quid for a 90-minute endurance test. Just because the game was played on a Sunday didn't mean that we had to play like a Sunday league side (although that's being disrespectful to Sunday league players). Back in league land, we lost - as is expected - to Seventies throwbacks Colchester United, and away against Wrexham. With Christmas just around the corner, we'd slipped down to just above the relegation zone - not exactly what we'd hoped for back in August.

Track 5: Bring The Pain - Method Man

December saw FA Cup hopes gather momentum. We eventually disposed of Hendon and then Wigan (after a penalty shoot-out) to give us the prize of Sheffield United in the third round. As for our league form, defeats against

Preston and Gillingham were beginning to become embarrassing. The Auto Windscreens tie against Hull, which we lost, did offer some ray of light in the night sky. A youngster named Jermaine Pennant made his debut at the tender age of 15. His 20-minute spell captivated the 1,109 fans with a display of more skill, passion, fight and pride than the rest of the squad had managed since the opening day. With the kitten out of the bag, it wasn't long before the Premiership fatcats came sniffing around. Pennant eventually joined Arsenal for an undisclosed fee, leaving both Notts and the fans to wonder what could have been. But you can't help wonder whether the player would have been better learning his trade with the club who had nurtured and brought him into the football world, instead of being dazzled by the bright lights of London. Boxing Day actually saw us win, 3-1 against Northampton - a result and display that had home fans wondering just how much booze they'd consumed the day before.

- End Of Side 1 -
Side 2: To Here Knows When
Track 6: What Is It Like - Everlast

The New Year party continued as 2,400 hung-over Magpies travelled north. Bramall Lane has always been a happy hunting ground for Notts during the Nineties, and today was to be no exception. A deserved draw kept both the fans and money-hungry Pavis smiling. A return to league action was once again marred with defeats, lowly Oldham and high-flying Bournemouth the bearers of pain. The state of our pitch had been a major problem. Constantly waterlogged, it wasn't until fourth round day that our third round replay eventually got the go-ahead. The delay gave the 7,500 fans the game of the season. The first-half saw honours even at 1-1, but Notts had been by far the better of the two sides. The second saw a contender for goal of the season, as Shaun Murray's strike gave the 'Pies the lead. And with Gary Jones' second on 83 minutes, you'd be forgiven for thinking that a fourth round place was ours. Our players must have thought it every bit as much as the visiting fans, as they began an exodus, intent on beating the traffic and getting home. But regular readers of our exploits will know that we're long-time sufferers of the late-goal syndrome, and once again it was to raise its ugly head. Eighty-five minutes - and it was 3-2; 89 - and it was honours even. Blades fans frantically backtracked to their seats for another 30 minutes of cup action. Even when United took the lead, we still had chances to win the tie. But we'd been given our opportunity - and were left to ponder what might have been, down at Highbury.

Track 7: Papa's Got A Brand New Pigbag - Pigbag

Following three successive league defeats, we reached the make or break fork of the trail. Our lack of goals was a prime factor in a relegation scenario. Jonna had lost his pair of golden boots, Duane Darby and Faz were AWOL with long-term injuries, whilst a whole array of ineffective loan signings had failed to find the net. Quality was not just a necessity but a priority. Allardyce was finally given the funds for new ammunition. Peter Beadle, Gerry Creaney and Kevin Rapley were quickly signed and almost immediately the effects were Viagra-like. Rapley scored on his debut and gave us an almighty lift. The small band of fans who travelled to Luton midweek returned with the fire rekindled.

Track 8: The Magnificent Seven - The Clash

The next six games saw only one defeat - an unlucky 2-1 at Maine Road. By now Mark Stallard had joined the new inter-ballistic strike-force and our rise back up the league even had some fans joking about a possible play-off spot come May.

Track 9: Survival - Bob Marley

April provided revenge over local rivals and further points bagged, in what was still a closely fought dogfight at the foot of the table. A slight hiccup midway through saw Colchester take their by now obligatory three points from us; while our 1-0 over fellow strugglers Wycombe made Notts all but mathematically safe.

Track 10: Always Look On The Bright Side Of Life - Monty Python

The season drew to a close with a couple of draws to confirm our safety and Division Two footie come the Millennium. But even though life has been far from rosy this season, for many Notts fans it had offered one almighty highlight and source of constant entertainment. Across the water in the Temple Of Sin, the Spawns of Satan had languished at the bottom of the almighty Premiership for months. However bad we'd played, however poor *we* were, one glance over the Trent and a wry grin would fill our faces. boardroom bickering, The PVH debacle, player exodus and TV pundit Big Ron's transfer floundering all added to a most memorable season for F****t fans. Thanks lads - thanks a lot.

End Of Side 2

EPILOGUE: The ear-splitting pulse of techno and drum'n'bass had become a parody of itself. No longer was it raging against the machine; it had become but a mere cog in the engine. A fresh approach, a new inspiration was what Heather needed. As the sinister sonic soundscapes subsided, she began to hear the strum of acoustics and a chilled-out, uplifting rhythm, with attitude to boot. A hip-hop fusion with blues was just the tonic needed as a perfect pick-up. Full of new hope, she sat back and listened as 'Whitey Ford sang the blues'. With the Millennium now only months away, it was time to find herself, to become what *she* wanted, not what society dictated, and not what her friends and family expected. It was time to become Heather...

Ivan 'Bart' Bainbridge

NO-ONE LIKES US

Millwall

The dominating event of our season was a trip to the Twin Towers. We didn't care that it was the Auto Windscreens Shield, it was Wembulee and it was over fifty years since we'd been there. It was a helluva party and the disappointing final result hardly mattered. Flags and facepaint was the order of the day, and even arriving well ahead of kick-off, we had to struggle through thousands of old friends having a party. We struggled because our son was in his pushchair, and I was delighted to be able to take him with me at only ten months old (and thinking all the time he'd maybe have to wait another fifty years). I don't mind if he turns out a wrong 'un in some ways - but if he suddenly

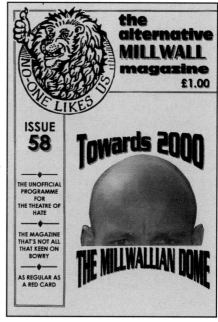

the alternative MILLWALL magazine £1.00

ISSUE 58

Towards 2000

THE UNOFFICIAL PROGRAMME FOR THE THEATRE OF HATE

THE MAGAZINE THAT'S NOT ALL THAT KEEN ON BOWRY

AS REGULAR AS A RED CARD

THE MILLWALLIAN DOME

decides he wants to go to Palace, he'll have to buy his own tickets.

At least the last-minute goal gave us the chance to get to the tube station, while the rest of our crowd were still sitting in a state of shock. I'd seen grown men in tears at the kick-off. Our editor, the Albatross, was celebrating his 50th birthday that day and couldn't have wished for a better present. We left vowing to return soon for a better result. It couldn't be Millwall, of course, without the papers putting the boot in - dear God, they even suggested we were somehow linked with the Stephen Lawrence tragedy. Before Wembley they had stories about how the visit of our lot would save the job of demolishing the old stadium, but they were disappointed. Out of 50,000 of us, five managed to get arrested and even when comments were made about noise during the minute's silence for Hillsborough, it turned out that a poor Millwallite had suffered a heart attack and his family were trying to get help. There are worse ways to go, I suppose.

At the end of the season, we could tot up the pluses and minuses. The pluses took the form of the young players who had come into the side and gained valuable experience. As had our old hero and new manager, Keith (Rhino) Stevens. Rhino hadn't had to change clubs to see different management styles. He'd seen plenty come and go here - Graham, Rioch, McCarthy, Docherty, Bonds and Nicholl. Nor did he have to visit clubs with different fortunes - he'd seen the boom and bust years here, and a change of ground. He knew a good player when he saw one because he'd played alongside Sheringham, Ruddock, Babb, Cooper and Keller. He'd seen some bloody awful signings, such as Wilkinson, Allen (two of that family, in fact), the Russians, Uwe, Malkin, Dair, and many other villains. Rhino didn't sign any players this season but unloaded some rubbish and brought in the kids, who didn't disappoint. He's what many fans want - an honest, common sense manager. Rhino wasn't scared of the fans and understood their utter devotion to the Lions. I got extremely annoyed during the Wembley party when I felt the chairman was a bit jealous of what Rhino had achieved and tried to undermine him in various ways. He'd better be careful...

Unfortunately, the 'bad boys' tables in the crappy football mags made us look dirty, but at least three sendings-off were down to young players retaliating to violent challenges and wind-ups. At least one was bullied off his game at Wembley. Those things really piss off supporters. I suppose every club sees one of those in a season but we had more than our fair share because of inexperience. Next season we'll see how much our kids have matured. Overall it was a real 'win one, lose one' season. I know every other writer here will talk about inconsistency but I defy any of them to match a record of two - yes, a mere two - consecutive league wins; while it was the same picture with defeats, so at least we bounced back. We never had a period of continued success and the only real slump came, understandably, post-Wembley.

As to old rivalries, we're sadistic buggers as everyone knows, so we enjoyed seeing Palace suffer what we had suffered, and delighted in Noades' destruction of the club. The hamsters conceding eleven goals in two games raised a smile; and whilst QPR crawled to safety, at least Charlton claimed their rightful position. And we could enjoy the sight of Lord Edward of Sheringham showing those infidels that God had indeed been reborn here at Millwall. Speaking of Manchester, we were smeared after a visit to the slums and drug dens of Moss Side, but even the FA understood it was a bit hard for us to smash up our own coaches when we were locked in the ground helping the police test out their new truncheons on our heads.

We're not savages, friends, we have the same problem as nearly every other club. We must meet huge overheads but keep our best players and retain our fans. Our headache is that the chairman says he has to sell a million pounds worth of talent every year but we ran the well dry a couple of seasons ago and relegation was the consequence. We don't want to lose another Teddy but we may be made an offer we can't refuse for a star such as Monkey Harris. That offer would be a blessing if we can make vital signings; every other club seems to have one or two goalies a season, while we've had four, with the latest only with us temporarily. We've no passer in midfield and no true wingers, but just a couple of lucky signings and we'd be a real force. At Wembley, it was asked where all these fans had come from, but I was more concerned about why they'd forsaken us; it was down to all those sales over the years. This season could be a great one for us if we can keep our best players and even improve the squad. We seem to be getting over recent upheavals and perhaps the club is now more professionally run. Maybe another visit to Wembley is close, maybe this season, maybe next. And maybe next season, Rodney, we'll be millionaires.

George Craig

ON THE TERRACES

West Ham United

If you ask anyone who is not a fairly fervent follower of the Hammers whether or not they think the club had a good season, the answer would have to be a very resounding "yes". Not just a good season, but a bloody fantastic season.

In case you didn't know, West Ham finished in fifth place in the Premier League and - for the second season in a row - above far richer, more illustrious clubs such as Liverpool, Spurs and Newcastle. For the third season in a row, we also finished well clear of perennial relegation strugglers like Southampton, Coventry, Sheffield Wednesday and Everton.

On top of that, West Ham's youth team were so head and

shoulders above every other young side in the country that they won their divisional Premier Youth League before the end of February (without having lost a game) and cantered towards a triumphant League and FA Youth Cup double, playing along the way some of the finest and most exhilarating football, I have seen in my thirtysomething years of watching the game. The record books were rewritten as they laid on an absolute feast for a 28,000+ crowd on a balmy Friday evening in May at Upton Park. Sky viewers were privileged to see Joe Cole and his team-mates put six goals past Coventry to take the FA Youth Cup by an unprecedented (even by Manchester United standards) aggregate of 9-0. Their season culminated a few days later when they beat Sheffield Wednesday in the Premier Youth League Final.

Joe Cole is a name you are sure to hear a lot more about. Although still a teenager and yet to play a full 90 minutes for the first team, he has several lucrative sponsorship deals under his belt, recently copyrighted several obvious media headlines ('Goal King Cole, 'Joe Goal' - that type of thing) to ensure his merchandising rights; and, perhaps more importantly, was called into Kevin Keegan's (doomed) England European Championship qualifier preparations over the summer. In this day and age of extreme hyperbole (thank you Andy Gray and Jonathan Pearce), when mediocre talents such as Tim Sherwood set foot on the international stage, it would be very easy for the cynic, and those yet to see him, to wonder if young Cole is not just another in the endless search for the new England saviour, a flash in the pan waiting to happen, a kid whose meteoric rise is merely the prelude to a Gascoignian demise into alcoholic oblivion. Of course, none of us can predict what the future holds for Joe Cole, but rest assured, this lad can do things with the ball that you and I can only fantasise about in our wettest dreams; what's more, you're sure to see him pulling off his flicks and tricks during the course of a game, and when he does, you're likely to be as open-mouthed as all of us have been. I have my fingers crossed that fame, fortune and sponsors do not spoil him. He has world class potential and it would be a crying shame for fans of the beautiful game, and a tragedy for him, if it were not realised.

However, do not let it be thought that our youth team is a one-man band. Joe missed the first two months of the season with a foot injury; and anyway, there is no way a team can dominate in the style and fashion that West Ham's youngsters did, without a good squad and equally as good management and coaching. The latter came courtesy of Tony Carr, under whose astute guidance West Ham's once proud Ford-like production line of talent has been returned to its former glory days of the early/mid-Sixties. Where once it was Moore, Hurst, Peters, Brooking, Lampard, Redknapp, etc, it is now the likes of centre-back Izzy Iriekpen, strikers Michael Carrick and Gary Alexander, goalkeeper Stephen Bywater, and right-back Adam Newton (to say nothing of Joe Cole, Rio Ferdinand and Frank Lampard junior). I hope that all will feature in manager Harry Redknapp's thinking during this season. All are good enough and more deserving of a chance than any number of multi-million pound so-called superstars, has-beens and never-will-be's taking football for all they and their agents can get.

You might be forgiven for thinking that, despite all the positivity in the preceding paragraphs, there remains a nagging thought at the back of my head that all is still not rosy in the West Ham garden. As far as some of us are concerned, it isn't. Not only is there this unshakeable feeling that the whole lot could come tumbling down at any minute, but also that that minute could come at any time.

Having suffered so many years of underachievement, the club seem to have assumed that Harry's uncanny ability not only to keep us in the Premiership, but rarely outside the top ten, is sufficient to get us bowing down before them in the kind of show of loyalty that led to their hatching of the odious Bond Scheme (anyone remember the FA Cup semi-final of '90-91?). I don't think they can quite comprehend that there is still a fairly large and vociferous element within the ranks of Hammers fans, who still regard their every move and utterance with the sort of suspicion that, were it not so true, might be viewed as verging on the paranoid.

Whilst Harry is more than happy to lap up the media column inches with his often Lewis Carroll-like post-match conferences, West Ham chairman Terence Brown plays the deaf, dumb and blind man with all the skills of Roger Daltrey's Tommy character in the eponymous film. Whilst most Premiership club chairmen are a bit too eager to lay before us their thoughts on the game (and in loudmouth Ken Bates' case, just about everything else, including the legal system and how he can reconcile himself to stick up for, and be willing to re-employ Graham Rix), Terence Brown maintains a profile that's - appropriately, some might say - lower than a snake's belly. During the past year or so, he has overseen the complete restructuring of the club, dividing it up into separate companies and, like Martin Edwards at Manchester United, has removed the words 'Football Club' from the club crest.

Under him, we have seen the price of our season tickets go up by some 400 or 500 per cent in the past four years, mostly under the guise that players are demanding such huge wages that we have to help foot the bill; but did anyone ask us if we wanted to pay Ian Wright £25,000 a week? No, of course not. Perhaps the main and most justifiable complaint that can be laid at the feet of Terence Brown is that he has failed to invest a single penny of his own money into the club. From a shareholding that cost him about £2.5m five years ago, he has seen that 'investment' inflate to some £30m (and rising by the day). And yet, whilst imposing swingeing increases on fans, he doesn't want to use any of that immense profit for the good of the club. If the club are to continue to prosper, and not fall down like a house of cards within the next few years, Mr Brown has some very hard thinking to do. There is no way that the forward momentum of the past couple of seasons can possibly be maintained, unless the capacity of Upton Park is upped to 35,000, or the club sell the ground and move elsewhere. I think they will pick the latter, and in defence of that decision, is there really any point in spending £20m on redevelopments, when selling Upton Park could probably raise about £12m, and with the sooner-rather-than-later sale of one or more of our most precious assets (i.e. Rio Ferdinand, Frank Lampard, Joe Cole), they could have £40m+ at their disposal to relocate to a 40,000 super-stadium in either the Essex heartland or Docklands. A bold and brave move such as that COULD be the making of West Ham, and herald a time when our bubbles don't simply fade and die.

It is also quite possible that Harry resigns in the wake of the (not for the first time) enforced sale of one of his players, others then hand in transfer requests quicker than David Unsworth at Aston Villa, Terence Brown cashes in on his profit, and West Ham end up back where they were when he first poked his nose in - struggling against relegation and a legion of discontented fans. This time, however, I fear that there will be no way back.

The ball is in your half of the pitch, Mr Brown...
Marc Williams

ONE MORE POINT

Crystal Palace

In years to come, people who glance through the league tables will see Palace in mid-table and assume that, for once, the club had a mediocre season, with no relegation or promotion battle - the first since 1992, in fact. What the league table won't tell them, however, is that this was the most turbulent season in Palace's 96-year history and, as I write this in June 1999, the very future of the club is still in doubt.

It had all been so different a year ago. After discussions, which had begun shortly after the Ice Age, new chairman Mark Goldberg finally got his man and Terry Venables was reinstalled at the club he'd originally cut his managerial teeth on 20 years previously. I was optimistic. But older fans remembered how he'd shafted us in 1980, and were dubious of Tel's motives for coming back. And just a few months later they would able to say to us youngsters, "I told you so." Goldberg's background was in the IT recruitment industry; and from what we were told, his company, MSB International, was worth £100m. He breezed into Selhurst, lauding the so-called five-year plan which would see Palace as a player in Europe by 2003. A few questions had to be asked, though. If he really was worth in excess of £100m, why had it taken Goldberg so long to raise £22m to buy Crystal Palace? Furthermore, why had he accepted a deal from previous chairman Ron Noades that didn't include the purchase of Selhurst Park itself? However, his business record seemed great, so we merrily went along with the hype.

Throughout the Venables reign, things never really got going. In a complete reverse of the previous season, our home form was magnificent, whilst our away form was distinctly non-league standard. After a mixed bag in the opening six matches, we then won every home game until late November, whilst losing every away game until mid-December. Anyone doing their pools coupons knew not to bother putting an X next to Palace. During this time, El Tel embarked on a remarkable transformation of the squad, with a string of 'interesting' deals. The few players who'd proved they were Premiership-quality, like Edworthy and Shipperley, were sold for well below their value and replaced by inferior players for the same money. It soon became a case of Palace becoming a refuge for former players from Tel's previous two teams: Portsmouth and Australia.

Rumours abounded as to Venables' motives for this transfer policy; including whispers about the financial gains Tel was personally making through these deals. Needless to say, when the home form started to dip before the away form started to pick up, the fans started getting disillusioned. For every great display, like thrashing Norwich 5-1 or Wolves 3-2 (I know it doesn't sound much, but believe me, it *was* a thrashing!), there was a 4-0 defeat to Barnsley or Huddersfield lurking around the corner. Opposition fans would gleefully sing "Terry, Terry what's the score?"; and, increasingly, Palace fans would join in, furious that this overpaid team were folding once again.

In fact, having Venables as manager ensured we kept in the media despite our very ordinary form on the pitch. Not a week went by without Ceefax or the radio informing us that one organisation or another was checking the books for financial irregularities, including the FA and the Inland Revenue. At one stage I was half-expecting the Mafia to get involved, it was that bad.

There were a few plus points to all this. The inspired signing of Fan Zhiyi and Sun Jihai, the Chinese equivalent of Shearer and Owen, had seen us getting audiences of 100 million (twice the population of England) in China for games such as Sheffield United's visit in September. From our position in the middle of Division One, we could justifiably claim to be the best supported club in the world. With a head count of well over a billion, the Chinese market was simply awesome, and we waited for the orders to come in from Asia to make Palace a very rich club indeed. The marketing team were even on the ball to the extent of arranging a PR stunt, with Tony Blair being given a Palace shirt in front of the cameras whilst he was out in China. Half a year on and I can tell you that sheer incompetence and laziness has meant this opportunity has slipped by, possibly forever, due to a £20,000 Internet fee not being paid to the Chinese government. The significance here is that in China there's only one Internet Service Provider, namely the government. If you piss them off, then you've had it. In other words, for the sake of one week of Lombardo's wages, we've missed out on the chance to make literally millions.

With Palace falling behind in the promotion race, the media had a field day at the turn of the year, predicting which star would be next to leave. The obvious one was Italian ace Lombardo, who was linked with Chelsea amongst others. However, the real interest centred around the young jewel in the Palace crown, Matt 'Magic' Jansen. He'd been signed for a million in February '98 but was attracting bids of five or six times that figure. At one stage, Capital Radio announced both Spurs and Arsenal were prepared to pay over £7m for him. Insiders told me Goldberg had turned down Villa's £6m at around the time of Yorke's departure. Goldberg calmed the fans by saying Magic wasn't going anywhere. However, it was at this time that Palace's dire financial problems were starting to emerge, and it wasn't long before Jansen was on his way to Blackburn... for £4m. It was a terrible loss to Palace, and on a personal level it was particularly annoying, as I'd only just put his poster up in my lounge.

Also in January we lost the services of the stylish Paul Warhurst, Marcus Bent (two more whose posters were on my lounge door) and Lombardo, who made the amazing leap from Nationwide League obscurity to the very top of Serie A with Lazio. No longer would it be trendy to be bald in SE25.

The start of 1999 marked the end for Venables. A battling 2-1 defeat at Newcastle in a great FA Cup tie was followed by a crass 0-3 reverse at Bolton in front of the Sky cameras. It was at this stage that I started questioning why I'd decided for the first time to make a concerted effort to do every Palace league game for a season. I'd always been one or two short previously, and had decided this season would be a good one to do every game, seeing as we'd no doubt win the title. How wrong can you be?

With Venables gone, the five-year plan was in tatters... or was it? Goldberg again tried to show the fans all was rosy and insisted everything was still on course, promptly reinstalling Steve Coppell as first team boss, having moved him 'upstairs' less than a year previously. This was the fourth time Coppell had some form of control over first team affairs and some questioned whether it was wise to have him back yet again. The first few weeks of the Coppell reign were mediocre to say the least. Three home draws and three away defeats meant that, against all expectation, we were looking increasingly likely to find ourselves in a relegation battle. The three home draws had at least preserved our fabulous unbeaten run at home, which had stretched past the five-month mark, even though we'd had to rely on a freak 30-yard, 91st minute own-goal against Birmingham to snatch a draw in early February.

At the end of January, Goldberg scored a major PR victory when he attended a fans forum in Croydon and seemingly laid all the cards on the table. He raised his hands and basically admitted he'd been naive and had made mistakes. By dispensing with the lavish expenses of Venables and the ridiculous entourage he'd brought with him, he'd set the wheels in motion to right the wrongs. It was a smart move because it bought him time. However, barely a month later and it transpired we simply didn't have the money to pay the players' wages. Palace were in a mess. The next few weeks brought further news of just how much shit we were in. For the Barnsley game the players played without having been paid.

This game on the last day of February, to my mind, was pivotal. With the game being shown on Sky, a previously unknown fan came to the fore. Through the excellent e-mail Palace bulletin service provided by a guy called Ray Bateup, 'Al from Bromley' made his mark and decided Goldberg had to go. In the final analysis, about 2,000 people waved the red 'Goldberg Out' posters which Al had made and distributed before the game. I was concerned about lending my support to this on the basis there didn't appear to be anyone else to step into Goldberg's place. Whilst it was very much a peaceful protest, the message was clear: 'Goldberg Out - you're not fit to run a bath' proclaimed one bedsheet-cum-banner. The other thing about the game was that we won for the first time since Boxing Day and, not only that, kept our first clean sheet since September. A 1-0 win against Barnsley is hardly earth-shattering, but what followed was the most satisfying period of the season by far.

Crystal Palace went into administration, with Goldberg saying this was a new beginning for the club. The man sure has some front! I'm sure a nuclear bomb could hit Selhurst and he'd still announce that it was just the break Palace needed. Despite the fact the players didn't have a clue where their next pay cheque was coming from, they embarked on the longest unbeaten run enjoyed in nearly three years. Away draws at Sheffield United and Bury preceded a fabulous 3-2 win against promotion-chasing Ipswich. This game saw two of our youngsters stake their claim to being Palace's No.1 assets.

Hayden Mullins and Clinton Morrison got the goals that night to all but end the lingering fears of relegation and, not only that, it showed the Selhurst faithful there was life after Lombardo, Jansen, Shipperley and co. Mullins is very much out of the Gareth Southgate school, in that he can play proficiently in midfield but is top class in defence. Morrison, on the other hand, is the first out-and-out poacher at the club since the Crimean War. In the last decade we've seen the outrageous talents of Ian Wright, Dougie Freedman, Chris Armstrong, Mark Bright and Matt Jansen, but none of these were six-yard box players. Morrison has been compared to Wright and, in terms of speed and agility, there's a definite similarity. However, Wright (aka Judas in certain quarters of Croydon) could score from all angles, whereas if Morrison were to score a penalty, it would be the furthest out from goal he'd ever scored from. Both are names you should keep an eye out for. They can make it to the top, but whether it's with Palace remains to be seen.

A draw at Pompey stretched this most unlikely of unbeaten runs in a game which represented the first-ever fixture to be played by two teams in administration (good little note for you trivia buffs out there). The following week saw a remarkable 3-1 win v Grimsby in that, having gone behind, Palace scored after 44, 45 and 46 minutes. Comically, a lot of fans went to the bar just before half-time cursing the incompetence of the team, only to hear two roars from the crowd (two more for Morrison) before they'd even been served. Then, just as they were finishing their pint right at the start of the second-half, Mullins had made it 3-1. Ironically it was the second game on the trot for this sort of thing, as we'd scored against Ipswich after 45 and 46 minutes as well.

Later that week saw the transfer deadline and, in a bid to reduce the crippling wage bill, five first team players went on loan. With a depleted side fielded for the following game against Bradford, we feared the worst - only to see our team of kids put in a great display for a 1-0 win. Amazingly we scored after 45 minutes yet again, thereby ensuring everyone was back to their seat when the second-half started. Needless to say we didn't score after 46 minutes this time. The worse it got off the pitch, the better it was on it. On this basis, I even suggested paying the players pocket money and playing with coats for goalposts. The Easter trip to Norwich came amid the news the players would go on strike for the following game v Sunderland. As I entered Carrow Road, there was even talk it would be Palace's last ever game. It was confusing to say the least. What happened that day will live with me forever. With the youngest team Palace had ever put out, the team played for their lives and won 1-0. The support that day was off the scale. The win was greeted with fans crying for joy, such was the sheer emotion. The players came and hugged the fans like we'd won promotion. Anyone who'd ever doubted Coppell had the ability to turn things around gladly accepted they'd been wrong. In the most restricted conditions, he'd transformed a team of kids into one capable of playing anyone in the division. The Sunderland game was played after all, and thanks to inspired keeping from Miller, we held the runaway champs 1-1, to make it nine games unbeaten.

April 8 marked the ninth anniversary of the greatest football match ever played, namely Palace's 4-3 defeat of Liverpool in the 1990 FA Cup Semi-Final. It also saw Mark, Simon and myself, worried for the future existence (let alone prosperity) of the club we love, meet in a pub by St Paul's Cathedral to set the wheels in motion to try to bring down Mark Goldberg. He, on the other hand, tried to counter fan discontentment by organising his own forum.

I sat there, along with a thousand others, cringing - it looked like his well-polished routine would win over those fans still on the fence. Then, he scored the own-goal of the season. PR man Terry Byfield attempted to enlist star players Morrison and Mullins onto the stage for an impromptu Q&A session, to the vocal disgust of the fans. "Don't get used," we screamed. Morrison looked upset, while Mullins was clearly embarrassed. They'd been used by Goldberg but the fans were having none of it. It went downhill for the chairman from there onwards, as embarassing and awkward questions were fired at them from the crowd. Not even Goldberg's ringers in the crowd, apparently brought in to ask 'nice' questions to make him look good, could help.

Evidence had been coming my way which undermined Goldberg's trump card of being a true Palace fan. This had stopped many fans from turning on him over the year, but there were many pieces in this jigsaw, and when put together there was a totally different picture developing from the one which had originally been presented to us. The last *One More Point* of the season carried the biggest story of ANY Palace fanzine in presenting this evidence. By now, the momentum was relentless. A poll in the *Croydon Advertiser* had 91% of fans demanding the chairman leave. Everything was geared to the May Day home game v Huddersfield and, thanks to dubious delegating, I was nominated to dress up as the Grim Reaper and lead the march to present the petition. The week leading up to it saw us gain good media exposure. The *Evening Standard* printed the story that two players had signed the petition, whilst the *Mirror* claimed that the club had launched a probe into the identity of these players and said that I had resisted all attempts to get me to spill the beans. I had to laugh. The club never contacted me once and I'm not even sure they were aware of players signing. A brief spell on ITV's *Sports Show* on the Thursday was fun, although I nearly passed out in the Grim Reaper costume under the heat of the studio lights.

May 1 finally arrived and expectations of 500 people joining in the march were soon put to one side as about 2,000 turned up, with another 600 or so lining the route. Two thousand people in colours, led by the Grim Reaper made for a spectacular sight as the procession made its way to the ground. On police advice, Goldberg was not allowed to go out and receive the petition. Instead, the police had arranged for three of us to go into the club building and present it to him.

As I walked in, Goldberg was in front of me surrounded by four heavies, including well-known hardman Dave Courtney, who'd previously served nearly 20 years for attacking five Chinese waiters with a meat cleaver. On my side I had a plastic scythe, which came with the Grim Reaper costume I'd hired. Needless to say, the old sphincter was twitching somewhat. As I handed over the petition sheets the room fell silent. "Damn, what happens now?" I thought. With all eyes on the 'Reaper', I made some sort of speech to Goldberg about how he MUST save the club and do whatever it takes. Annoyingly, although the hood of the costume covered most of my face, Goldberg was so bloody short he could look up at me (I'm pretty tall you see) and see my face. Bollocks - I didn't want him to be able to identify me to his nutter bodyguards. He then made a speech of his own, but despite the seriousness of it all, I have to admit I couldn't help but wonder why he wasn't laughing. I mean, if some punter came up to me in a hired costume and a plastic scythe I'd be wetting myself. It was certainly a surreal moment.

I went back out in the sunshine, where 1,500 people were still gathered to hear what had happened. I made an announcement along the lines of "Let's stick together and save the club we love". Everyone cheered, and to my horror a chant of "Sit down if you hate Goldberg" went up. NOOOOOOO! I had to get round the other side of the ground to sell the fanzine and suddenly instead of filing through the crowd, my way was blocked by hundreds of people sitting down. I eventually tiptoed through and sold the mag. The final part of the protest was the distribution and release of 15,000 black balloons as a mark of respect to the 46 members of the Palace staff who'd been sacked without pay on April 1. These were ordinary people on ordinary wages and they'd been dismissed in the harshest of manners. As I write, comedian and TV presenter Kevin Day has organised a comedy night in Croydon, from which all the proceeds will go to the sacked staff.

On the final Sunday, I woke up in Nottingham at 8.00am needing to be at QPR at 1.30pm to complete this most turbulent of seasons. I was hungover and the thought of spending two more hours in bed recovering with the mystery blonde next to me was too much to resist. Well, I'm only human. I eventually rolled into Loftus Road half an hour late and virtually fell into my seat. I'd done it. I'd actually done every Palace game for a whole season for the first time in my life. And how did Palace reward my loyalty for this enormous achievement? By losing 6-0.

Now I know exactly what you're thinking - which players signed? To this day Goldberg still doesn't know, because under strict instruction, I took the relevant sheet of names out and it's currently sitting beside my PC here in my bedroom. Don't tell him, though - I understand he's still scouring the list!

Cris Lehmann

ONE-NIL DOWN, TWO-ONE UP

Arsenal

ISSUE 65 SPRING 1999 £1.50

ONE-NIL DOWN
TWO-ONE UP   THE ARSENAL FANZINE
FAREWELL

After eleven years and 65 issues, *One-Nil Down* is no more. The spotty youths who began the magazine back in 1987 are now high-powered middle-class achievers, with little time for the unwholesome plebs who go to football matches. Life has moved on, and I for one am glad that I no longer have to stand on a freezing street corner mingling with people who are far below me in terms of wealth, position and intellect.

Of course, the above is complete bollocks. Being an Arsenal fan now means mingling awkwardly with the elite. I've seen Melvyn Bragg, Jeremy Paxman, Nick Hornby and (loud fanfare of trumpets) Perry Groves walking up Avenell Road before games recently. So despite the upturn in my fortunes due to *One-Nil Down* (and Tony Willis in particular), I'm still way down the social scale. Football has changed, especially in London N5, and I'm not sure that I totally approve.

Back in 1988, for example, we would think very carefully before selling the magazine when playing the likes of Spurs and West Ham. A tattooed fist in the Hampsteads (teeth, dear reader) was hardly the best appetiser for a game of soccer, and the thought of having a wedge of 50 fanzines forcibly inserted into an intimate orifice was not an appealing prospect.

What a difference eleven years make. Nowadays when Spurs come to Highbury the worst that happens is a tad of high-spirited banter. "I say, Julian, that new away kit of yours is a trifle loud, don't you think?" Julian (Eton and Caius College), a lifelong Spurs fan for three years, is never lost for a reply. "Perhaps, but I cannot imagine Mr Stephen Bould advertising L'Oreal with the same élan as our own Monsieur Ginola." Gosh, they're so cruel! Even West Ham seem to be followed by goofy train spotters from Gants Hill these days. "You don't know if any of the local newsagents stock *Steam Monthly* do you, old chap?" Where have all the ICF gone? What has the world come to?

Well, the football world has come to Big Money in our neck of the woods, and the game seems to be run for the benefit of the players and Sky. If Manchester United want exemption from the FA Cup, then I want exemption for Arsenal from the Premiership for a season. This would enable us to concentrate on Europe and the Worthington Cup - which we now have to blag, simply because Spurs won it last season.

Such an arrangement would also allow the perennially-knackered Emmanuel Petit to have a break from his exertions. This is the man, you will recall, who lifted the World Cup with France, won £17,000 on a fruit machine in Monaco, and then spent the entire season whinging about how onerous the fixture schedule was. Never mind that he was out of action for about two months suspended - for Manu the pressure of work was just too much.

And you can see his point. You may think you've got it hard when you get up at 6am, catch a crowded bus or a train and then spend eight to nine hours with people you could cheerfully strangle - all for a tenner a week. Imagine how much harder it would be if you had to work eight hours a week, 40 weeks a year (maximum) and only took home £750,000 per annum for your troubles. And, if that wasn't enough, you had all that worry about your ponytail. It's enough to make you weep. And they say footballers are tough.

Anyway, after our Double triumph of the previous season, hopes were high for a storming nine months, especially in Europe. No chance. The opening game in Lens (which is the most boring town anywhere on earth) looked good for a while, with Overmars scoring a good goal (but missing some sitters). So what happens? The Arsenal defence thoughtfully lets in a goal right at the death and we come away with only one point.

Thus the scene was set for a scrappy and unsuccessful campaign, despite Arsene Wenger's much-vaunted 'intelligence'. I attended the match at Wembley against Dynamo Kiev (or Dinamo Kyiv as some train spotters in the posh papers called them) and the lack of true European class was obvious. Kiev, on the other hand, were breathtaking. They were lightning fast in attack, superbly organised in the middle and resolute at the back. Arsenal looked very ordinary indeed, and when Bergkamp scored with a diving header (yes, you read that correctly) we looked to have struck lucky.

However, justice was done when Kiev equalised right at the death, but I don't blame the bloke behind me for wanting to "sort out some Russians" after such a bitter blow. Ah, sod it. We were never going to win the Champions' League anyway, although the identity of the eventual victors still causes me nausea whenever I think about them.

We fared little better in the Worthington Cup. I knew Wenger wasn't really serious about this competition when I received a second class letter on the morning of the game against Chelsea asking me to play. I couldn't make it (luckily for the Blues) and it was no big shock when Vialli's men ran in five against an Arsenal team comprised largely of boys from the local primary school. Although some argued that the competition was unimportant, the point is that Arsenal treated their fans with contempt by charging full admission prices for a game they blatantly didn't give a toss about. Still, as I said earlier, it's all about the players and Sky these days - so bollocks to us lot.

We knew Wenger had his work cut out in the league, especially after the magnificent conclusion to the '97-98 campaign. And to be fair to the Frenchman, he made a far better fist of defending the championship than George Graham ever managed. And, yes, we knew George was dodgy. But to go to Spurs as their manager took the proverbial biscuit as far as most Gooners were concerned. We can only hope Mr Sugar has a lock on the petty cash tin at White Hart Lane (to help prevent accounting inaccuracies, you understand).

And one of the Premier highlights of the year for me was attending the screening of the Spurs game towards the end of the season. For the benefit of those who still support ordinary football clubs, this means that for a tenner (maybe what you pay for a *real* game) you get to watch live action on a big screen set up in the middle of the pitch. What happens on these occasions is that suddenly all the old faces come back (because the season ticket holders have travelled away) and the atmosphere is better than that at a 'live' game. When Petit opened the scoring, it was just like being back in the early 1980s, with complete strangers hugging each other and generally going mental. When Kanu notched the third, it was even better. The look on George Graham's face spoke volumes. Football used to be like that all the time.

Anyway, it was a grim irony that we were ultimately denied the championship by David O'Leary's Leeds, who beat us 1-0 at Elland Road right at the death. And it was a double disappointment that Nigel Winterburn, my Arsenal player of the year by a mile, was carried off with a badly broken nose during the game. Winterburn is one of those players who quietly gets on with his job (as opposed to Dennis Bergkamp, who is often just quiet) and does more work in 90 minutes than some of our 'superstars' do all season (goodbye and good riddance, Nicolas). Still, no real complaints, apart from the plunging and appalling form of Ray Parlour, who Kevin Keegan rewarded with a place in the England squad for his troubles. Oh, Kev, you're going to regret moving from Fulham.

The less said about the FA Cup the better. Dennis missed the penalty and Ryan Giggs scored The Goal of the Millennium, as we all know very well. Perhaps the outcome would have been different if David Seaman hadn't decided to do his Kermit the Frog impression at such a vital moment, but we'll never know. It was just one of those bloody nights.

And that's about that. I've enjoyed my time in the fanzine world immensely but I think that at clubs like Arsenal, 'alternative' publications have had their day. When we started there was a distinct mass of people who would get together for football matches, and you could legitimately call this mass 'the Arsenal fans'. These days we attract coach-loads of Scandinavian and Japanese tourists, affluent day-trippers from the suburbs, and Islington yuppies who, whatever else they could be called, are not Arsenal fans. The only sales we got from them was when we pretended *One-Nil Down* was the official programme, which is what they all want.

Never mind - as I've said, things move on and we've certainly moved into a new era of football now. Harping on about the past has no useful purpose and, in a way, this is what most of the Premiership fanzines are now doing. The game is now geared to the needs of the players and shareholders. And although we were once the true shareholders of football, we're now just a paying audience. The people at the top just don't care about us anymore, so enough's enough. Come on you Reds.

Mike Collins

ONE-ONE

Wycombe Wanderers

If the Wycombe Wanderers board have come in for a bit of stick in recent years for their slightly corporate attitude, then some explanation for the low esteem that some Wycombe fans hold them in arrived at the start of the '98-99 season. The optimism that generally comes with a new set of fixtures was immediately doused with reality when the Wycombe board once again showed their unstoppable commitment to increasing ticket prices at Adams Park. For a club desperately needing to attract back old fans who have found more enjoyable things to do, this wasn't a step in the right direction. Still, things on the pitch are what count, and there

shouldn't be too many problems there, right? Er... wrong.

Three points from 12 games and the pant-wettingly funny 'What's the difference between Wycombe and a fork?' jokes seemed to be coming from everywhere. It wasn't that the other teams were good, aside from Preston, who looked a bit tasty when they nonchalantly outplayed Wycombe to an embarrassing degree at Adams Park - rather, that Wycombe were crap. The meeting with hated rivals Colchester United ended in a 1-2 defeat after a last-minute penalty and things couldn't get any worse than losing to our old Conference enemies.

With the majority of Wycombe's support being of a sickeningly benevolent disposition, the manager and the players came in for very little criticism during this bleaker than bleak time. Even at Gillingham (a 3-0 defeat, which could have been at least twice as heavy), the players received a warm ovation as they left the pitch. In fact it took a tormenting home defeat to York City and a 4-1 home destruction in the Autumn Windowledge Beaker at the hands of Third Division Brentford before there was eventually some disquiet on the terraces. However, it only took one more predictable defeat at Luton, where even the characters in *Willow* would complain about the legroom in the away end, for the money-crazy Wycombe board to decide enough was enough.

Manager Neil Smillie is an affable old chap, but there's no room for sentiment when you're propping up the table and have a defence who look like they've been studying Laurel and Hardy films a bit too hard, and the fire-power up front of a broken spud-gun. Smillie was sacked and everyone really agreed with the decision, despite his excellent work bringing through youth team players. He'd often been quoted in the local press saying that the players preferred to play wing-backs, so the team played wing-backs, even though he personally preferred 4-4-2. Perhaps he really was too nice, or maybe he just wasn't any good. Whatever the reason, he was soon down the job centre and everyone put their mind towards who would take his place.

It's fair to say that the position of Wycombe manager was turned down more times than Janet Street-Porter on a night on the pull. Name after name was thrown into the hat, with such luminaries as Mickey Adams, John Ward, John Rudge and Bryan Flynn among a cast of thousands telling the board they had something better to do, although local rumour has it that Flynn wanted the job but couldn't reach the postbox to send back his application. Club physio and brutish one-time centre-back Terry Evans took the caretaker job for the Millwall game the week after (but I didn't see him doing much tidying up - ho ho!). Wycombe lost that as well; and the week after we lost again, at Chesterfield. The Wycombe job was the least attractive thing around (except for maybe Noel Edmonds wearing nothing but a G-string) and Wanderers fans couldn't think of anyone who hadn't already turned down the job.

Suddenly, just before the crucial home game with Fulham, ex-Wimbledon defender Lawrie Sanchez was appointed as manager, a decision that was warmly welcomed from all sides. If there could be an opposite of Smillie's wishy-washy tactics (such as never making a substitution until the last three minutes of a game), then Sanchez was it. Yet not even he could turn water into wine - and, despite a plucky 1-1 draw with Fulham, results continued to be piss poor.

The return match with Colchester led to an increase in the suicide rate in the High Wycombe area, such was the sodding jamminess of the Essex side. A tense atmosphere was not helped by Colchester United fans invading the pitch a couple of times and a few of them getting thrown out before an ending that sent even the most serene of Wycombe fans into a fit of rage. Basically this vomit-inducing match entered its seventh minute of injury-time, with Wycombe leading 2-1, when a late penalty was given after an idiotic challenge by Wycombe 'keeper Martin Taylor. They scored. That's all you need to know. God, how we hate Colchester United.

The following week, a defeat at home to second from bottom Northampton Town took Wanderers to a new low. The winning goal came as the result of yet another 'Dog and Duck' style defensive error by captain Jason Cousins, who tended to play brilliantly all game and then pull something disastrous out the bag late on. Unfortunately for us, Cousins did the same a week later at Reading's character-free Madejski Stadium, gifting the Royals their first goal. Reading's ground was all very shiny and big but why the hell do they need it? The stadium was less than half-full and that was helped by a large away following from Buckinghamshire. Can't they groundshare with Wokingham Town or something? Surely that would make more sense? A first-half penalty miss by Dave Carroll added insult to injury, and Reading went 2-0 up in the second-half - undeservedly, as we had the better of the chances. Wycombe's latest loan signing, Sean Devine (remember him?), from Barnet came on as substitute and scored the second best goal of the season from 25 yards out. It finished 2-1 - and we left Reading to enjoy their stadium. They get three seats each, you know.

Performances had improved immensely since Sanchez's arrival, yet stupid errors were costing us dearly and looked like sending us down. Bottom of the league once again after the Reading game, Wycombe staying up looked about as likely as The Vengaboys being inducted into the Rock & Roll Hall of Fame. Unexpectedly, however, the seemingly stagnant corpse of Wycombe Wanderers kicked into life. Bristol Rovers were beaten when the impossible was finally achieved - Wycombe won away. For the 200 or so of us there, it was well worth waiting for. But this wasn't just a one-off. After steamrollering Oldham 3-0 at home, the Blues went to Macclesfield and won 3-1. Even the disappointment of a 2-0 home defeat at the hands of Gillingham couldn't stop the momentum of a barely unrecognisable side, not in terms of personnel but in terms of effort, commitment and ability. We went to Wrexham and won again, and drew away at Stoke, with new hero Sean Devine scoring a late equaliser. But if these results seemed incredible to Wycombe fans, who had witnessed an amazing transformation of the team by Lawrie Sanchez, then it was nothing compared with what was to come.

Saturday 24 April 1999 will live in the memory of all Wycombe fans, particularly those who travelled up to Maine Road to witness the Blues complete the double over Manchester City. Seated in the corner in a temporary stand that was reminiscent of that Pink Floyd concert at Earls Court, the travelling contingent of 1,000 roared the side on to a famous 2-1 victory, with youngster Andy Baird (remember that name) and - wait for it - Sean Devine scoring our goals. A truly heroic performance, where, as a *One-One* contributor put it, the only thing that caved in all day was the back window of the supporters coach.

This excitement was quelled by a 2-2 draw with Blackpool (Devine scored again by the way), Wycombe twice giving away the lead. However, on a wet Tuesday night, we pulled off another good win, this time against a very tired Wigan side. This result left us one place above the relegation zone and safety was at last in our own hands. The Blues now had to go to Lincoln on the last day of the season. Technically we could have stayed up with a draw if Northampton and Oldham were to lose - although, realistically, the Blues had to go and win.

The importance of the this game was made even clearer when manager Lawrie Sanchez had the idea to run free coach travel to the game at Sincil Bank. The directors duly stumped up the £15,000 to do it and perhaps shut up a few of their critics, at least for an afternoon. Quite how many coaches they expected to pay for I'm unsure, but on the day 30 left Adams Park at 9:30am as the Blue Army went on the road. Considering we've taken around 200 to places like Gillingham, 2,800 to Lincoln was a bit of a surprise.

Not surprisingly, the atmosphere in the away end was electric. Unfortunately, the game itself was not. As it stood at half-time, with the score at 0-0 and fellow strugglers Northampton and Oldham both winning, Wycombe would be relegated. The travelling fans felt worse than a man on a 22-hour flight sat next to Jim Rosenthal. The second-half was equally scrappy - and, after 80 minutes, things were as desperate as Tom O'Connor's jokes on *Crosswits*. Then it came. Paul Emblen headed home with seven minutes remaining and everyone around me went ballistic. The final whistle went amid scenes of utter jubilation as the Chairboys' Barmy Army sang and danced on the terrace, while some ugly looking Lincoln fans tried to start some ugly scenes, before they realised they were all 14. The celebrations went into the early morning and players and fans alike partied into the night.

So there you have it, a season that promised so little and didn't deliver much either. Lawrie Sanchez changed a crap, unmotivated side into a team who, while still not the most technically brilliant in the world, had enough fight in them to beat off relegation when all seemed doomed. Sean Devine must also get a mention, but I won't say too much in case any of those big clubs with money are reading this and come and poach him off us.

The days at City and Lincoln will go down the history of the club, and we can look forward to next season with some optimism. Some old cliché-ridden hack would probably label this "A season of two halves", or perhaps "A tale of two managers", but I can't be bothered. I'm just glad we're up and it's over, and we can look forward to stuffing Oxford and Colchester next season.
Ross Marvin & Chris Wildey

ONE STEP BEYOND

Walsall

Joe Royle, Brian Little, Tommy Burns, Tony Pulis... your guys took one hell of a beating! OK, I may be overdoing it, but you get the picture. Set up by all and sundry (including this author) for a long and ultimately fruitless battle against the drop, Walsall FC confounded everyone, probably even themselves, and wound-up the season second only to Fulham's mega-bucks.

What made the achievement more remarkable was the backdrop against which we kicked off at a sun-drenched Priestfield Stadium. We'd avoided relegation by four points the previous year; a season that if it had been maybe four games longer

ONE STEP BEYOND...

Two Down...

One to Go!!

Issue 4   50p

Laughing in the face of the big boys.

The Independent Walsall Fanzine.

would have almost certainly seen us go down. Our crazy-haired, portly-but-popular Danish manager Jan Sorensen inevitably became the scapegoat, despite the fact that he never received the support from the board that his successor enjoyed. Many fans were unhappy at Sorensen's dismissal, and it is has to be said we were hardly placated by the appointment of the little-known Ray Graydon. Ominously, we travelled to Kent for one of the toughest starts we could have wished for, away at Gillingham. We won 1-0.

"Going up", we joked that night in beer gardens around the borough. But deep down we felt that it was a freak result. We'd caught Gillingham cold but we'd soon get our comeuppance. However, our friend Mr Comeuppance had, like many Walsall folk since the late Eighties, pissed off to support the Villa (they were his team for '99) or even Wolves (he was seen sporting the old gold and black when Wolves flirted with the play-offs). Rather than slip into the relegation mainstream as we expected, we carried on picking up points.

Ten points came from the first four games, as we headed to Maine Road in good heart. We froze, however, and despite a second-half rally crashed to our first defeat. We lost the next one as well (the only time we would lose consecutive matches all season), but we soon picked up the trail again, nicking away wins at Chesterfield and Luton, and defeating promotion rivals Preston and Blackpool. It wasn't all plain sailing, though. We handed Reading their first away win in nearly twelve months, and at Wrexham blew one of numerous chances we had to go top. Things started to look bleak towards the end of October, when we were thrashed 4-1 at Craven Cottage. We then had a haunting start to our Halloween fixture at Bristol Rovers, going 2-0 down after five minutes to a team who'd turned their home ground into the proverbial fortress. We showed our mettle, however, to come back and win 4-3 in the last minute. It has to be said that many Saddlers fans at this stage were still highly sceptical and waiting for the bubble to burst. But after this performance we began to believe that the play-offs at least were a realistic target. This confidence was repaid as we cruised through to Christmas, picking up four wins and a draw from five games, culminating in a clash with Stoke, who at the time were top. The equation was simple: beat Stoke, and provided Fulham don't take maximum points at Preston, we'd be top for Christmas. We kept our part of the bargain but, alas, Fulham stole three late points at Deepdale. A slight wobble of a mere two points from three games was put right early in the new year, when we completed the double over Gillingham, handing them their first defeat in 20-odd games. A capacity crowd then saw us share the points with a resurgent Man City, a satisfactory result in itself but one which saw us drop into the play-off quagmire.

Fulham had started winning games with their eyes closed and their legs tied together, and were not going to be caught. It was therefore increasingly apparent that there was only one automatic promotion place available, and it appeared to be between Preston and ourselves. Our performances had started to dip, but we still carried on picking up points. Results were now being ground out, and we did not *look* a good side. But August and September are the times to look good. From Christmas to the season's end it matters to *be* a good side. Under the consummate professionalism of Ray Graydon, our merry band of youth and experience simply would not lie down. Rambo Rammell's goals had started to dry up, but he was still leading the line like the starship trooper he was. Jimmy Walker was at his best 'twixt the sticks. Ian Roper continued his amazing progress from likely cast-off to first choice centre-half, leaving the vastly experienced and thoroughbred Adrian Viveash and Richard Green fighting it out for the right to play alongside him. Darren Wrack was beginning to make Alan Buckley look a bit of a fool by handing him a free transfer, as he went on his way to plundering 14 goals from right-midfield.

Perhaps equally as important as these contributions, however, was the unusual phenomenon of the board supporting the manager at key moments. The previous season had seen a striker from Rotherham reserves sign for us on transfer deadline day, a move which was transparently an attempt by the board to be seen to be doing something. But this time, whenever Sir Ray needed players, they were made available. OK, we didn't (and probably never will under the current regime) spend a fortune on transfer fees, but we consistently recruited quality players throughout, whether on loan, short-term or medium-term contracts. In particular the club used the loan system fantastically well, and because of this we were able to field a virtually full-strength side time after time, with only the left-midfield role occasionally providing trouble.

Our decent squad also helped lend a hand to our 'double' attempt, as for the second successive year we reached the Area Final of the Auto Windscreens Shield. For reasons unbeknown, we could just not take advantage of penalties and failed to convert five consecutive spot-kicks. Bizarrely, however, the route to the Area Final saw us excel in three penalty shoot-outs out of four ties. Alas, Millwall deservedly thwarted our promotion-cup glory double. And although it didn't feel like it at the time, we had bigger fish to fry.

A two-week break at the end of March did us the world of good. Preston had started to bottle it big time, and we were able to take second place again during Easter. In fact, Preston had slipped so badly that a subsequent defeat at Deepdale proved only to be a setback and not a disaster. Manchester City had become the biggest threat to an automatic place, but they couldn't handle the pressure when it mattered at home to Wycombe, whilst we ground out a 1-0 win at Lincoln. The remaining two points we needed were sewn up with a 3-1 victory over Oldham, and we secured automatic promotion with two games to spare.

Discipline and organisation, along with effort and teamwork, played a major part in this success, but the architect of it all was undoubtedly manager Ray Graydon. His signing raised a few eyebrows but it turned out to be a stroke of genius by the acting chairman. Graydon has already been raised to the super-hero standard, and if he maintains our position in Division One, he'll be cast as a demi-god. Needless to say there were plenty of folk gorged on humble pie.

Any promotion is a good one, but this one was particularly special. Not simply because we were favourites for the drop, but also because it was one in the eye for an unimaginative national media. The press paid us scant notice, instead preferring to focus on the Fulhams, Man Citys *et al.* We smirked at Sky's expense after our promotion rendered meaningless a match broadcast live involving Man City. And while we're on the subject of City, to all you City fans who contributed to our Walsall FC Internet discussion site, we apologise for having the audacity to finish above you. We really ought to know our place.

Eleven years ago we climbed into the second-tier and slipped straight back down again, a fall from which we have only now recovered. There's no doubt Division One is going to provide a very tough test and we'll be most people's favourites for the drop again. But with Ray Graydon at the helm, adequately backed by the board, there's every chance we'll at least make a fight of it.

Pete Holland

ONE TEAM IN BRISTOL

Bristol City

As August approached, everyone was still on a high from the marvellous promotion season we had just enjoyed. At last City were back where we belonged, Division One. The land of better grounds, bigger crowds, a larger piece of the Sky cake - and, of course, only one step away from the promised land of the Premiership.

Our preparation seemed to be going just about perfectly. Our season ticket sales created a record and we had addressed our main area of concern, the replacement of goal-scorer Shaun Goater, one of the reasons why we handed Watford the Championship back in May. Just to be safe, we bought not just one, but three strikers in the summer, splashing out a previously

unheard of amount of money, and not getting much change from £3m. Ade Akinbiyi, Tony Thorpe and Soren Anderson joined to make the squad look a little top-heavy. The loss of Shaun 'Thou shalt not pass' Taylor during the previous season (the other reason we failed to win the Championship) unfortunately had not been resolved to the same degree, something which would be embarrassingly highlighted again and again as the season progressed.

Manager John Ward revealed his summer was spent watching videos of all our new opponents in action, learning how to combat our step up to a higher level. However, not many games were available on Betamax. The pattern of the season was there for us all to see in our first couple of games. We were pretty awesome up front, but pretty awful at the back. As early as our first away trip at QPR, two more patterns were set. One, that City fans would fill most away ends, and in some fixtures spill over into the home ends, with incredible loyal support backing the team in their thousands until the bitter end. Second, we would concede late goals to deny us a well-deserved victory.

By the end of September our optimistic prediction that we could attain mid-table consolidation in our first season back in a higher league was dwindling. Realism had set in that the gulf between the divisions was much greater than we had thought. Our theory that we could outscore our opponents, and therefore hide the problems in defence, wasn't working. John Ward's attempt to shore up the defence, which had conceded 23 goals in 12 games, was bringing in, on loan, Dutch defender Clemens Zwijnenberg, whose only claim to fame was his surname was once used as the Countdown Conundrum. Still there was always Dyche and Watts to fall back on.

The month of October saw a turning point. From going in a reverse direction, we put our foot down... and went backward even faster. After an earlier defeat at Ipswich, manager Ward astonished the fans with the comment that he had run out of ideas and needed the help of a coach. His suggestion was Ray Harford. Many fans choked on something hard and jagged; Harford's career not exactly filled with success.

The board appointed their own man. One of the most admired, respected and knowledgeable coaches outside the Premiership; someone whom any Scandinavian club would sell their Abba record collection to have coach their side. He helped Sweden to the World Cup Semi-Final in USA 94, and wrote the words to the successful Eurovision Song, *Waterloo*. Benny Lennartsson was the highly recommended man to help John Ward turn our season around... Benny who?

John Ward walked out. Many thought he could at least have tried the partnership for a month or so, but his pride was hurt and John felt he would lose the position of being in overall charge. This debate split the fans down the middle for the remainder of the season. Whilst all this was going on, Bristol Rovers fans were using their only brain cell to come up with various Benny Hill jokes. The last laugh was on them when it was pointed out that whilst we may have Benny Hill, *their* manager was the small bald guy he used to slap on the head repeatedly. Serious stuff, this rivalry.

So, with Benny promoted to boss, our season really was at the Crossroads motel. We waited with bated breath to see how he could transform our poor results, which had seen us win just three games all season and left us teetering on the brink of relegation. His first two games in charge were Bradford City 5 Bristol City 0, and Bristol City 1 Wolves 6. Gulp! The latter made the headlines on *News at Ten* - nothing to do with the football, but the half-time scrap between the mascots. Wolves' Wolfie attacked our Three Little Pigs, and all hell let loose. After many punches were exchanged, sanity was restored. That was until our other mascot - a cat - downed Wolfie in the tunnel. Now *that's* what you pay your entrance money to see.

A regular criticism of Benny was that he had an uncanny knack of playing players out of position, something kindred with people who have close dealings with national sides, no doubt. In fact results did start to improve after that inauspicious start to management in England. Indeed, we won two games in a month. Maybe it will take him time to get the players to adjust to his way of playing we thought, and we can look forward to the biggest coup in English football.

A whole host of players with completely unpronounceable names were brought into the club, the majority of them leaving after unsuccessful trials. After our Boxing Day win against local rivals Swindon, and a battling display against Everton in the FA Cup, only spoiled by a couple of goals in the last five minutes, we seemed to be a team full of confidence and belief. That lasted about as long as the New Year hangovers.

The significant game was at The Hawthorns against West Bromwich Albion on February 20. All City fans would unanimously agree that this game probably ended our hopes of staving off relegation. After a catalogue of poor refereeing decisions all season, something certainly not unique to Bristol City, we were really picked on for this game. Probably two of our best players were also to finish their season that day. Firstly, Mickey Bell, our deadball specialist and usually the team's second top scorer (not bad for a left-back), broke his leg, and Ivan Testimatanu twisted his knee, *a la* Gascoigne, condemning both to the treatment table until May. At half-time, thanks to a bizarre decision to allow 4,000 City fans to sit alongside the home fans, with just some nylon netting acting as the first line of defence, the inevitable happened and ugly fighting broke out and continued for at least 20 minutes - that was, until the infamous West Midlands Police could make it from the local nick.

This incident - another reported on *News at Ten* - held up the start of the second-half, but amazingly City played probably their best 45 minutes football all season, scoring twice to lead 2-1. The fourth official raised the board to show that an extra five minutes were to be played. The clock behind us read 5.00pm already. However, at 5.09pm, Lee Hughes equalised. It was reported in the paper that on the way back to the restart, our players asked the ref how much longer. He informed them two minutes. We kicked off and he blew the whistle - and with it our hopes. Bastard.

Despite not winning a game in 12 outings, we still had hope when Easter came around. Especially as we had to play a couple of relegation rivals. The last time we won had been on a bank holiday, back at Christmas; and sure enough Easter Saturday and Easter Monday saw us repeat that holiday feeling, winning back-to-back games. This was followed a week later with another victory. All of a sudden the great escape was on.

That was until one of those refs appeared again, this time at home to another Midlands side, Birmingham. We had a handball decision turned down; a goal disallowed because a Birmingham defender collided with his own goalkeeper; and, just to rub salt in our wounds, seconds later a dive that Greg Louganis would have been proud of was declared a penalty. To cap it all, at the end of the game Trevor Francis apparently attacked one of our stewards who couldn't control the anger of the City fans (oh, how I cheered when Birmingham missed that penalty in the play-offs).

When the dust settled, it was clear we would be playing Second Division football again next season, a fact mathematically confirmed the following week at Bramall Lane. But those bad refereeing decisions were not the real reason behind our demise. That was down to the poor pre-season preparation, the departure of John Ward, the arrival of a man who knew nothing about the English game, the board's failure to appoint a manager to replace John Ward and stick to the original plan, and the failure to replace Shaun Taylor.

However, next season we will be back with a bang; already we have sold more season tickets than the same time last year. Optimism is already starting to build. As they say, what comes down must go up!

Rob Humphries

OVER LAND AND SEA

West Ham United

If the shit is going to hit the fan, you can bet as much as you like that it will be everyone else's shit - and a West Ham fan who gets hit. And so it goes on. And if there is going to be something totally unfair and outrageous, once again, the Happy Hammers will turn out to be the nation's fall guys.

Over Land and Sea

Issue 200

**West Ham United v Middlesborough
Sunday May 16th 1999**

And if you're starting to believe I'm paranoid, forget it. I know I am. But regardless of that, looking at things in a logical kind of way, can anyone anywhere tell me the justification in not allowing us to gain an automatic place in this season's UEFA Cup after finishing fifth last season?

Fifth place has seen entry for various clubs for no less than the last ten years plus. In fact, the season before, West Ham finished in eighth place, just one point behind Villa, who managed to get a UEFA spot for finishing seventh.

Yes, I'm whinging. But surely I'm entitled to after this. It's neither fair nor funny. And because the goalposts were once again moved, we have the pleasure of the Inter-Toto Cup to contend. And if anyone thinks that it's funny and not worth a wank, try telling that to Juventus, who find themselves scratching through the same competition. Quite frankly, it stinks. The governing bodies just couldn't give a flying toss about your average run-of-the-mill clubs - and it quite blatantly and highly irritatingly shows.

The turning of the European Cup into the Champions League - or, as it is now, the Not-quite-the-Champions-but-the-runners-up-as-well-oh-yes-and-even-the-third-place-team-gets-in-now-Cup. What a load of bollocks. Talk about defacing the game. I know it is a widely-used cliché, but nonetheless the facts remain - the richest clubs keep getting richer... and fuck all the others.

Getting off my soapbox, I suppose I ought to drift back through the time tunnel to last season. I say 'last season', but considering we're playing the Inter-Toto Cup matches in July, that's not strictly true, is it? It's more a couple of weeks ago.

As usual, if you were looking for a complete contrast in fortunes from one club, we're the boys to trust. For example, we can give you the fifth place if you want it but, for that, you'll have to go out of both cups at the first hurdle. And both times to Second or Third Division teams. Nothing new there. It's a trait of the club that we get dumped on by the likes of Northampton Town (League Cup) and Swansea City (FA Cup), so they were just playing along with the rules. Of course it wasn't that they were any better than us. Or that they had more guts, more fight and a bigger desire. No, no, no. Who would even dare suggest such a thing? They both just beat us because... well, you can make up your own minds.

And of course the mandatory reverse double by an end of season relegated side came along as well. This time our one-time lodgers Charlton threw the spanner into the already creaking works. But saying that, it wasn't as if we didn't let them get away with it. At one stage we were 2-0 up at half-time, 2-2 with two minutes to go, then lost 4-2. We don't do things by halves.

But even that was surpassed by the home game with Wimbledon, where we went in at half-time sitting on a stunning first-half performance that saw us 3-0 up. Full-time saw us run back in 4-3. To them. At Upton Park. And that was some thing of a trait for the whole season. Yes, we finished fifth, but not many West Ham fans will tell you that we played all that well.

Sure, in patches we were the dog's. But, like everyone else apart from the big three, we didn't have many patches such as those. In fact, I reckon most people would be surprised to learn that a team who conceded four goals on no less than seven occasions could ever finish above halfway in the table, let alone near the top. Yet that's exactly what happened.

But I don't want to go on and on about results, except to say that it was magnificent, almost to the point of orgasm, to stuff the Totts twice. And for that matter to do Vialli's millionaires on their own turf. Personalities are much more interesting. And they don't come more interesting than some of those you'll find at Upton Park.

Long-time enemy, and still somewhat unpopular at Upton Park, Ian Wright came, scored, and if it wasn't for a four-month injury lay-off, may well have conquered. The boy did OK, even though most of us wouldn't have pissed on him if he was on fire just a few months previous. Whether he will continue this year, who knows? It will depend on who stays fit.

We also made what most people thought was a somewhat bizarre signing when we took Paolo Di Canio off the nutty doctor's bench and stuck a pair of white boots to his feet. But, and I say this without so much as a smirk, that signing was one of the best Harry has ever made - so far. The guy is quite brilliant. But I did say 'so far'. I'm not blind to the fact that he has got something of a reputation and, yes, I appreciate he will go off the rails again sooner or later. But until that happens, I will continue to watch and appreciate his magnificent array of skills. And laugh like a drain when he tears into the referee, the opposition, or even his own team-mates. And he does all three continuously.

And if there is one thing I wouldn't want to be, it's Di Canio's face as he always seems to be slapping himself in it. Last year also saw the return of Julian Dicks, albeit briefly. But it was one hell of an achievement to see him playing again, especially when you consider the fact that the world's leading surgeons all said he wouldn't.

And although he has had to face the inevitable now and retired, his nine appearances last season were worth the entrance money alone. I just feel sorry for those who only caught their first glimpses of him last season. They missed one hell of a player. The sad fact was that he couldn't compete in his left wing-back slot, and Harry wasn't prepared to move him into the back three, which I would have liked to have seen. But there you go. I'm sure he will get ably rewarded with his testimonial and there is the likelihood that they will be queuing around the block long after kick-off to get into that one.

Of course the season couldn't go by without the standard farce amongst the personnel. And that came about this time when Chilean Javier Margas went AWOL. This occurred after a particularly shit performance at Leeds, where we were stuffed 4-0. Margas could take the blame for all of them.

He was slaughtered in the papers, on televison and on the terraces (see, it still comes naturally to say that; it's never been the same with seats). He disappeared and, as far as I know, hasn't been seen since. Well, that's a little white lie. Everyone knows where he is, but they're ignoring him. Apparently he wants to come back and try again, but Harry would rather set his pubic hair alight than have him back at the club.

As far as departures go, the most significant wasn't John Hartson, although that has to go down in history as one of the most ridiculous of all time. Now tell me Joe Kinnear left Wimbledon to take over one of the top boys. Who'll touch him after spending £7m - or whatever it was - on Big Bad John? That was probably the reason Joe had his heart attack. No, to me, the one big departure was that of managing director Peter Storrie, who didn't have his contract renewed at the end of the season. Storrie was the club's fall guy. He was the one who answered all the questions, took all the flying shit, and still dragged the club kicking and screaming into a new era.

It's some feat to turn around feelings the way he did in his ten-year spell with the club. For the first five or even six years, most people at West Ham would have wanted him to burn in hell - some even wrote him letters telling him that - but he turned things around with hard work and a dedication to the club that others would be advised to follow. And he was always accessible. Always there on the end of a phone for a chat, on or off the record. And if anyone had a problem, he would try his best to sort it.

Peter Storrie opened up West Ham again from the dark distant days of the Cearns cartel, when no-one except those in the inner sanctum knew anything about anything. I suppose that's one of the reasons they outed him. A return to those days appears to be drawing nearer. And that will be one hell of a big mistake.

Oh yes, and the final issue of the season saw me reach my 200th issue. And I would like to thank everyone who has played a part in it over the last decade. I did think of packing it in when I reached this target, but the way football is going, I reckon there's more need than ever to keep going. Someone has to stand up for the rights of the fans now more than ever.

Gary Firmager

PEEPING TOM

Coventry City

It has been noted that Emperor Napoleon didn't care whether his generals were any good at their job, he only wanted to know whether they were lucky or not. Now, Napoleon was quite a bright chap. He did well for himself. In fact, as emperors go, he was the second most successful of all time, being marginally outshone by Ming the Merciless of Mongo. We could all learn a lesson from Napoleon. But if Gordon Strachan had signed up for the French army under Napoleon, it is safe to assume he would still be the lowliest private, or a reserve drummer boy, or even the lad who holds the sheet music for the drummer boy - because Gordon

Strachan is not a lucky general. In fact, Coventry City have had so much bad luck this season, you rather wonder whether his drive to work each morning leads him straight past a home for retired black cats and under a factory that manufactures ladders.

They do say that you make your own luck in football. If that really is the case, then Strachan ought to nip down to his nearest DIY superstore and invest in a huge self-assembly luck kit, because we were certainly out of it last season. The catalogue of poor refereeing decisions, injudicious arithmetic when calculating extra-time, and cruel hands of fate bestowed upon Coventry City Football Club in '98-99 would fill a couple of editions of the *Fortean Times*.

Our injury list reads like an episode of *Casualty*, with extras walking on, getting struck down with some terrible injury and then being written out of the script. In fact, we have had so many career-threatening injuries this season that *Peeping Tom* seriously considered starting an obituary page. Belgian World Cup comet ('star' sounds a bit too grand for a Belgian) Philippe Clement fractured his cheek in pre-season, and Belgian 'Wonder Kid' Lauren Delorge lasted half an hour before shattering his leg. But this was an eternity compared with the nought minutes played by Croatian World Cup hero Robert Jarni before he disappeared to Madrid. Add to that, Wallemme's quick return to France and you have to say that the pre-season signings didn't settle in too easily.

Gordon has said that he is used to this sort of thing now, and although he doesn't like it, he has to put up with it. Poor refereeing decisions may decide where the championship ends up and who gets into the European Champions, Runners-up and Odds and Sods League. More importantly, it often ultimately influences who goes down. We are owed so much luck now that next season we should be able to field a team from our injury list and still win every game by a comfortable margin. Sadly, luck doesn't work quite like it is advertised.

Wee Gordon appears never to have heard the saying 'Too many chiefs and not enough indians', as his policy on signing new players seemed to be based solely on whether they are currently a team captain or not. Jean Guy Wallemme was the Lens (then French League Champions) captain when we swooped for him. He joined a Sky Blue side with two captains, namely Judas Dublin who was leading CCFC, while Gary McAllister (Scotland captain) was in for repairs, alongside former Brummie captain, Liam Daish. These top dogs were soon to be joined by Crystal Palace captain Marc Edworthy and Bosnian captain Mo Konjic. It's not a policy that many other clubs are rushing to copy.

During the season, Gary retired from international football, Wallemme got homesick and Dublin disappeared without trace. This did have some positive returns, as our defence became stronger, with Richard Shaw outstanding at its heart. Around him, Paul Williams, David Burrows and, especially, Roland Nilsson all performed beyond expectations. Sadly Nilsson has now returned to Sweden but the arrival of Mo Konjic, the return to fitness of Daish and Hall, the versatility of Telfer and Edworthy, and the decision by Breen not to go to Blackburn (I wonder why?) has left us a few options. The departure of our talismanic bald striker allowed Darren Huckerby and Noel Whelan to forge quite a partnership. The arrival of John Aloisi reinforced this attack, with the result that we recorded our first league win at Villa Park, with a four-goal hammering of our local rivals being the one real highlight of the season.

As we drifted around the bottom of the table, never far from the relegation zone, at times rock bottom, the consensus of opinion was that we were too good to go down and that we would soon be shooting up the table. The reality was that we only got out of trouble with one week to spare. We were saved our usual last-day dysentery thanks to a dismal goalless draw with Derby County. The Sky Blues were guaranteed a 32nd year of top flight football due to some fine goalkeeping by Magnus Hedman and some farcical finishing by Derby's strikers Abbott and Costello. With two candidates for miss of the season, they should have been tested for performance-inhibiting drugs. Mind you, given their accuracy, I don't suppose anyone could be found who was willing to hold the pot. And that about summed up the whole season. No shortage of graft and effort, but as Thomas Edison once said: "Genius is one per cent inspiration and 99 per cent perspiration." Sadly we lacked that crucial one per cent.

Mind you, deja-vu rhymes with Sky Blue for good reason, as I've got a strange feeling I may have already said. If this season was less than memorable, it's probably because we've been here so many times before.

The first game arrives and supporters harbour lofty ambitions and dreams of greatness for the coming months. Eventually all these possibilities become impossibilities and we spend the final ten matches praying that we can do enough to try again next year, when perhaps we'll have a bit more luck. This season ended with an unusual situation on the final Sunday, when so many players had been carried off that we actually ran out of stretchers. There was a beautiful moment when everyone noticed at the same time that Whelan was going to have to stay on the pitch, despite the ref's wishes, because both our stretchers were already in use. With the summer break the players have two months to overcome our huge list of injuries, and then next year we'll have some more of the same no doubt.

Not that I am complaining. I believe that people support Coventry City for the same reason they like eating in American fast food chains. It's not because the food is so fantastic that it is unparalleled elsewhere. No, people eat there because it is comfortable, easy to get to and you know exactly what you are going to get when you arrive. No long queues, fancy menus or strange foreign named dishes to get your tongue round. Just plain fare at a fixed price - and fast food is just the same.

Paul Wheeler

RAGE ON

Oxford United

What's the best thing about the summer? Lack of football of course!

Although sometimes there's all these national teams playing each other, and two or three times a decade, something called the World Cup. Never understood it myself. I support my local league team - and would support a national team containing any number of players from my team. The nearest we manage at the moment is Matt Elliott.

Over the close season... not a lot happened. Rumours of takeovers were rife but not a cherry picked. No millionaire saviour's bids coming to fruition.

Oh, we did buy Dean Windass (ego as big as his ears) and Andy Thomson (not so much of a feather as a down weight) - both with impressive careers in the Third Division and in the Scottish League. Would they hold their own (or each others) in the heady heights of Nationwide Division One?

Sorry, didn't clarify why no footie for three months was a good thing. Well it boosts the optimism, doesn't it? And a draw at big spenders Bristol City and a win at Luton away in the Worthington Cup helped to ice that mood. It went a bit sticky after that, leading to the first *Rage On* of the season (in a controversial new home kit of pastel yellow cover) to scream 'The honeymoon is over, darling' to last season's messiah, manager Malcolm Shotton. Surely the fickle fans had not turned on their former hero already? Only time would tell...

A couple of months into the season, gloom and doom were growing, both on the field and at boardroom level, interspersed with glimmers of hope. Rumours had been circulating suggesting the existence of a consortium who were about to buy United. They were due to be announced at the AGM. There seemed, however, to be a lot of secrecy surrounding this so-called Grenoble consortium - as no-one knew all the individuals involved. Fans were worried at the probable involvement of Martyn Deaner, who allegedly asset-stripped Newbury Town. Memories of the Maxwell era could not be forgotten so soon, and fans were sceptical about the takeover involving another of the Maxwell ilk. The secrecy surrounding the potential buyer of the club planted yet more seeds of distrust in the board and, more importantly, Keith Cox. Disillusionment with the board had already grown, as there still seemed to be no answers with regards to completing the half-built rusting stadium at Minchery Farm, or any means with which to clear the £13.5m debt, which was steadily increasing by several grand each week.

The scene on the field had also been inconsistent, with some dismal games being followed by some surprisingly better ones. But if relegation was to be avoided, the club desperately needed to invest in a striker who could actually score goals in every match. Players also needed to avoid defensive mix-ups like the Whelan-Whitehead one at Barnsley, which gave away three vital points. Oxford couldn't complain of being completely without luck, as the Pompey game showed. The U's, to the astonishment of both sets of fans, walked away with three precious points thanks to a couple of dodgy refereeing decisions and the intervention of Mother Luck.

One of the biggest blows to United was the 4-1 crushing defeat at Swindon. Prior to the match there was a glimmer of hope - surely it was the U's turn to come home with an away win from the local derby. Unfortunately the players did not seem to have the same faith in themselves and gave up possession of the ball much too easily. It was inevitable that the U's were doomed to defeat with a strike-force who couldn't score, a defence who couldn't defend and a weak midfield who couldn't do either.

A hope-giving draw against Ipswich was then followed by an almighty 7-0 pounding by Sunderland at the Stadium of Light. United would rather not have entered the record books for their largest-ever defeat and, in a brief resolution to make amends, picked up three points in each of the following two games, against QPR and Ipswich. Normality soon resumed, with two further defeats, plus an unexpected away 1-1 draw at Bolton.

Also at this time the club, being concerned about its influence on the younger community, started a 'Cut it out Campaign' in order to try to stop some of the more obscene chanting that generated from London Roaders. *Rage On* supported this campaign - although felt that the chant's targeted ("Agggghhhh you're shit" and " It's nice to know you're here [now fuck off]") were probably two of the least offensive ones.

One of the results of the campaign, particularly noticeable at the Tranmere game, was that it limited the repertoire of the London Road. What *Rage On* felt was really needed was a chant unique to Oxford, the irksome rendition of "Oxford till I die" being borrowed from other teams. Unfortunately Gary Glitter's 'involvement' with the younger generation meant it was no longer suitable for the club to continue playing *I'm the Leader of the Gang* as United took to the field.

The third *Rage On* of the season featured as its cover star one of the most inept players ever to pull on the Oxford goalkeeper's shirt. He only made one appearance for United, at home to Birmingham, but in those 90 minutes had the singular distinction of conceding another record-breaking seven goals, although admittedly only four of them could be attributed directly to Mike Salmon's incompetence.

Unfortunately the on-field debacles were overshadowed by the shenanigans in the boardroom. In fact so much was going on that our usual one-page editorial had to be edited down to fit onto two sides, and we didn't even mention the football. It mostly centred on the withdrawal of John Gunn from the Grenoble consortium, who were apparently negotiating the purchase of the club from owner Robin Herd. This followed an article in the local paper outlining Gunn's previous financial problems, which MD Keith Cox blamed for Gunn's departure, although Gunn himself criticised Cox for providing him with misleading financial information. Gunn was the main backer behind Grenoble, and his departure threw the whole package into serious doubt. All this came on the back of having to sell goalkeeper Phil Whitehead (to Denis Smith's West Brom of all teams, which really hurt) and the club's only left-back, Simon Marsh, to Birmingham, in order just to play the players' wages. (The non-playing staff, including manager Malcolm Shotton, went unpaid for over two months.)

The rumours and speculation concerning the club's imminent demise led to the formation in November of FOUL - Fighting for Oxford United's Life (crises are always good breeding grounds for acronyms) - an independent supporters group. FOUL immediately increased its effectiveness, if not its universal appeal, by refusing to mount an anti-Cox campaign. It claimed that its sole aim was the survival of the football club and that as there was no-one around to replace Cox, his going would be counter-productive. Whatever the merits of this argument, there was no doubt FOUL was immediately successful in its initial objectives of raising awareness of the club's plight and mobilising supporters via a packed public meeting at the Town Hall.

An interesting diversion at this time was the appearance of another Oxford United fanzine, *Shott Away*. It lasted for two issues, both of which made for quite painful reading, before fading into the oblivion where it belonged. Whilst this in itself is meaningless in the greater scheme of things it was of significance to ourselves and fellow fanzine editors at *Yellow Fever* in that it showed that our club is really only capable of supporting two fanzines, unless perhaps something extraordinary comes along.

When our March issue came out we had, for the first time in ages, just the slightest glimmer of hope. Keith Cox had finally done the decent thing and resigned as managing director. Having allegedly paid himself £67 an hour to patronise supporters, whilst taking the club deeper into debt, he was decent enough to take our advice from the previous issue. Yes, the words ship, sinking, jumping and rat sprung to mind, but so did good and riddance.

Almost immediately, London hotelier Firoz Kassam appeared out of the blue and asked whether he could buy the club. He realised that the land surrounding Minchery Farm was ripe for development, and stated his intention to build a multiplex cinema, a hotel and other leisure facilities adjacent to the stadium. His arrival and subsequent purchase of Robin Herd's majority shareholding met with an inevitable mixture of cynicism and hope. He was greeted as a hero at Oxford Town Hall when, during another packed FOUL meeting, he made an unscheduled appearance. Others suspected his intentions, worried that without any football background he may simply use the club to help him achieve other business ambitions. We stuck his picture on our front cover with the headline 'If Anyone Can Kassam Can'. With a big question mark, of course.

There was some football to watch, too, including *that* FA Cup tie against Chelsea. Three minutes into injury-time, 1-0 to Oxford. Then Kevin Francis tackles Vialli in our box, taking the ball cleanly. Vialli throws himself in the air, collapses in a heap and referee Mike Reed awards a penalty. Le Boeuf strokes it home, and the Blue Poo escape by the skin of their teeth. We bayed for Mike Reed's blood, the Chelsea supporters breathed a sigh of relief and the back pages the next morning echoed everyone else's outrage. 'No Justice' proclaimed the *Daily Mail*, and for once *The Sun* got it right with 'Oxford Cheated'. We lost the replay, of course, but then that was just for a laugh. Everyone knows who the real winners were.

Our league performances around this time ranged from the joyous (2-0 against a Swindon side who patently didn't care) to the commendable (a hard-earned point at Wolves) to those that had relegation written all over them. The 1-0 defeat in a hailstorm at QPR was a case in point, a game in which Dean Windass (destined for a move to Bradford City) simply couldn't be arsed. Cheers Deano.

By the time the final *Rage On* of the season appeared, relegation was inevitable and we celebrated by producing one of the best editions we could be bothered to cobble together. It was considered by most supporters an achievement that we still had a team to follow, so demotion to the Second wasn't greeted with as much despair as might otherwise have been the case. However, despite Kassam's involvement, the club's future is still precarious and there's no guarantee that we will get to play a Division Two game next season.

It all hinges on United being able to complete the stadium at Minchery Farm in time for the start of season 2000/01. According to Kassam, this itself is reliant upon the club being granted planning permission to incorporate the multiplex cinema into the adjacent leisure facilities, for which permission already exists. This is to make the site valuable enough to sell to cover the costs of completing the ground. The major obstacle to all this is that Kassam said right from the start that if this planning application gets called in by the government, a process which could add a year or more to the procedure, then he doesn't have enough money to sustain the club for that period and will walk away, leaving the club once more in the lurch.

This would hardly be a major loss to Kassam himself – he bought the controlling interest in United for just one pound (taking on the £13.5 million of debts) and his only investment so far into the club is a commitment to pay the running costs during the close season. He's told Shotton that he must cut the playing squad to just 20 professionals and that there is no money to buy new players.

The good news is that, when Kassam introduced the concept of a Creditors Voluntary Arrangement (CVA), in order to strike a deal with the club's creditors, the board at long last resigned. Throughout the past few seasons the board members have proven singularly inept at just about everything except licking the arse of Keith Cox, and their resignation was due to the fact that the CVA, if accepted by 75% of the club's creditors (by value), meant it quite likely that Cox would get nothing of the supposed £250,000 he had loaned the club. As Taylor Woodrow, the stadium contractors, favour the CVA idea, and their debt is almost the required percentage of the total, it is quite feasible that the CVA will go ahead.

So now it's all up to the Government Office of the South-East (GOSE). By the time this book appears they will have made their decision whether or not to call in the planning application. Kassam will have walked or he will still be there. If he walks, then it's unlikely that United will be able to provide the financial guarantees required to compete in the league next season. The Millennium issue of *Rage On* might yet be written in support of a Rymans League club.

Martin Brodetsky

United Stars on the Bog:
No. 4: Keith Cox

Source: Yellow Fever

RAISING THE COFFIN

Preston North End

The '98-99 season didn't feel like Preston's most successful for 20 years. With David Moyes in his first full season in charge, and one of the smallest squads in the division, the fans expected nothing. What they got was a championship chase that lasted for all but the final few weeks, an unforgettable cup run, and Deepdale's biggest attendances since the early Seventies.

Ultimately, the play-off defeat by Gillingham is all we will remember. But it could have been so different. Here are the ten minutes that made our season what it was and, in the end, what it wasn't.

10 August 1998 - 12:00: Lee Ashcroft is transferred to Grimsby Town

Selling your leading goalscorer on the opening weekend of the season isn't great PR, but in the case of Lee Ashcroft it simply had to be done. Whilst Ashy's ability was unquestionable, his temperament was. Preston through and through he may be, but when a player is able to choose where he wants to play, you know you've got a problem on your hands. He was like a spoilt kid in the school playground, begging manager Moyes to play him at centre-forward so he could net a few more goals and a earn a bit more personal glory.

So, with Lee gone, the question was: "Where will the goals come from?" Despite the worry, we spent most of the season as leading scorers, and ended up with 78 - the same number we scored when we won the Division Three Championship in '96.

Meanwhile, Ashcroft spent much of the season on the bench - be it the physio's or the subs' -and you can count his goals on the fingers of one hand. It's ironic isn't it?

15 August 1998 - 16:12: Michael Appleton is sent off at Luton

In August 1997, Michael Appleton became Preston's record signing - and because of the £500,000 fee, and the fact that he had seen so little first team football in his first season with us, Appleton was an automatic choice for a shirt. He simply had to be given a chance.

At Luton - our second league game of the season - he undid all his good fortune when he lunged at an opponent and was red carded. Appleton's suspension kicked in with the Lincoln away game. He'd worn the number seven shirt in the five games that preceded it, but would only start another nine games during the eight months that followed.

Despite being the club's biggest buy, Appo has never enjoyed a settled run in the first team. He is a tenacious player, who has yet to prove himself, but who undoubtedly has vision and imagination worthy of a higher level. Who knows how the team would have performed with Appleton in every week, and who knows how Appleton would have performed. All we do know is that Paul McKenna deputised for Appleton during his suspension, and hung in there until December, a period in which the Whites established themselves as genuine automatic promotion contenders.

12 October 1998 - 21:30: Preston win 1-0 at Manchester City

When you look back at the start Man City made to the current campaign, it's hard to believe they ended up being promoted. When North End arrived at Maine Road - a match switched to a Monday night due to City's international absentees - the Blues were struggling to string two wins together, in a division they were expected to win, and win easily.

City started well, but North End started better. Roared on by more than 3,000 travelling Whites, North End made City work as hard as anyone had all season. In the second period we got even more into the game and, with 20 minutes to go, sub Jon Macken was brought down in the box. Penalty. Gary Parkinson strode up to the ball and swept it with pace into the roof of the net - 1-0 to Preston, and with the nation listening to full match commentary on Five Live, we held firm to secure a famous win.

In terms of confidence, the result was invaluable. In terms of points, it was another three for us - and another blank for what were now serious promotion rivals. The momentum of this victory won us eight points from the next 12, and was another major step towards establishing Preston as genuine automatic promotion candidates.

26 December 1998 - 16:50: Preston win 1-0 at Stoke

Our Boxing Day victory over Stoke was significant in many ways. On this blustery afternoon we made it clear to the rest of the division that we were not going to lie down without a fight.

Back in August we had faced Stoke with more than a degree of trepidation. They were a big club with a big-name manager, a big new ground and a genuine belief that they could make an immediate return to Division One. Despite the fact they beat us that day, we had managed to cling on to their coat-tails ever since, and arrived at the Britannia Stadium with the division's best away record and a strong sense of self-belief .

With two minutes on the clock, David Eyres swung a looping ball over for Michael Jackson to head home but the referee mysteriously ruled it out. Four minutes later we conjured up a carbon copy - and this time it stood. A textbook example of holding a lead meant another three points for the Whites, and the start of a spectacular slide for Stoke. By March they had lost all form and looked destined for mid-table. With Man City and Stoke out of the way, PNE were second only to Fulham. Could we hold on?

4 January 1999 - 20:21: Kurt Nogan puts PNE 2-0 up against Arsenal

All Preston fans remember where they where when the draw for last season's FA Cup Third Round was made.

Having neatly dispatched a well-organised Walsall side in the second round, all North Enders were hoping for a rare crack at one of the big boys on our own patch - and they don't come any bigger than the reigning Double winners. When the night of the big game came, the buzz around the ground was bigger than it had been for years. And so was the crowd - 21,099 inside a Second Division ground for a match nobody gave us a hope of winning. And who could have predicted what was to follow?

North End were on top from the word go. We worked hard to win the ball and when we did, passed it fluently and created a string of half-chances. Arsenal weren't in the game. With 20 minutes on the clock, a swift move down the left led to the ball being fed into Eyres, who laid it back for Nogan to fire home. Two minutes later the same player darted to the back post to head home a PNE corner. Preston 2 Arsenal 0.

It stayed that way until the stroke of half-time, when Arsenal scraped one back. Immediately after the break, Nogan came within a whisker of killing off the game when Manninger's clearance rebounded off our centre-forward, only to hit the side netting. A Petit free-kick brought Arsenal level, and with ten minutes to go, the goal that should never have been put them ahead, Ryan Kidd left floored by a deliberate elbow. Overmars' late strike flattered the Champions. "Preston played like Brazil," said Arsene Wenger.

6 February 1999 - 16:00: Steve Basham makes his PNE Debut

Bringing in a new face - preferably a star name - towards the end of the season is a common tactic. It lifts the rest of the squad. At North End, John McGrath did it with Frank Worthington in 1987; Gary Peters with David Beckham in 1994; and this season David Moyes tried it with Stuart Pearce.

Steve Basham was more than that, though, he was an all-round quality striker... precisely what we needed. He never suggested he was interested in a permanent move, but made it perfectly clear he was going to do the business whilst here. Basham came off the bench to help the Whites to a 2-2 draw at home to Bristol Rovers - a match that looked lost before his arrival. His impact was such that he was rewarded with a start alongside Kurt Nogan from then on, and five goals in three games was a fine way to repay the gesture.

Basham was Premiership quality. He'd seen plenty of first team action at Southampton and in Division Two, he was a class above the rest. A superb first touch, an even better second, and an unstoppable finish - including a spectacular 25-yarder against Northampton. Basham netted two that day, and further strikes against Manchester City and Macclesfield (two again) made it ten in eleven starts alongside Nogan. For the Blackpool home game, Nogan was dropped. It turned out the partnership had played its last game. Alongside Macken, Basham failed to score in four games.

As loan signings go, we got a remarkable return from this man, even if Kurt did dry up a bit without Macken in the side. It's just a shame Steve chose not to sign on for the play-offs. Fortunately, he chose to make the move permanent in mid-June. Roll on next season.

23 February 1999 - 21:30: Ryan Kidd and Lee Cartwright are injured

Blaming injuries for your team's failings is always an easy option. It's right up there with referees, isn't it? In fairness, our injury list was reasonable enough to be described as average last season. What has crippled us is that they all came at the same time - and with the notoriously lean squad, we immediately looked threadbare. Right-back Gary Parkinson was the first to go in late January. We even managed without left-winger David Eyres for periods from February onwards. The real blow came in the home encounter with Lincoln. We won the match 5-0, but it was a result that cost us dearly.

Ryan Kidd and Lee Cartwright had been involved in all but a handful of matches as the team soared to second place (and even first on three occasions). Kidd's commitment and Cartwright's pace were major factors in our success, and it is no coincidence that these were our two longest-serving players. These two were playing for the badge. Having formed a formidable partnership with Michael Jackson in central defence, Ryan Kidd missed the next 13 games through injury, during which time we clocked just four wins. Cartwright, too, played only one of the next 14 games as we slid away from second spot.

Add to these shorter-term problems with Ludden, Nogan and Basham, and you can see how our small squad suffered. Who knows where we'd be now if Kidd and Cartwright had been in the side.

6 March 1999 - 16:50 :Last-minute Equaliser conceded at Gillingham

Few fancied our chances of a result at Gillingham. With the home side enjoying their best spell of the season - a spell that had made them look outside possibilities for the automatic promotion place we held - there couldn't have been a tougher test for our boys.

In our last 14 meetings with Gillingham, either side has only scored more than a single goal on three occasions. Put simply, these are generally 'tight' affairs. On a brisk spring afternoon, the Whites made a gutsy start, matching their opponents physically. On ten minutes came the breakthrough, when Mark Rankine's long-ranger was deflected in off Sean Gregan. We spent the rest of the afternoon defending resolutely, as our opponents had done to us on so many occasions.

At 16:50, and with all the other results in, Robert Taylor headed an equaliser with seconds on the clock, to loosen North End's grip on second place.

24 April 1999 - 16:50: Last-Minute equaliser conceded at Millwall

Having established ourselves as favourites to join Fulham in Division One next season, our automatic promotion chances took several knocks as we won just one of our last nine games. Dropped points at Colchester and Macclesfield, and in the home game with Blackpool, were almost fatal, but a 1-0 win in the six-pointer with Walsall put us back in with a shout.

We went to the New Den believing that we were back in with a real chance. If our rivals slipped up today and we won, we would be within touching distance of Walsall in second. The first-half was evenly balanced, with either side dominating in spells, but neither able to score. Immediately after the restart, Julian Darby fired home a superb 25-yarder and, shortly after, Michael Jackson scored with a trademark header from a corner to seal the points.

Except it didn't. On 84 minutes. Millwall - with nothing but pride to play for - pulled one back. As the match moved into injury-time, it was disaster for this particular promotion push, as Jackson failed to clear properly and Millwall took full advantage to equalise.

16 May 1999 - 16:36: Robert Taylor curls the Ball past David Lucas

As David Moyes had said beforehand, the play-offs were the start of a new season of three games. If we won all three we would be in Division One. Two might do it, but we certainly needed to win the home leg.

With more than 18,500 in the ground, it was another superb atmosphere. This time it was more important, though. This was what all our work had been for. The return from injury of several of our key players - Nogan, Cartwright, Jackson, Gregan and Eyres - meant the slate was wiped clean following the previous week's defeat at Fulham. This was pretty much the side that had got North End into such a strong position to start with, Gary Parkinson being the only absentee.

As the fans made their way into the ground, much of the debate centred around the famously negative tactics of our opponents. Gillingham were well known for being a team of well-built six-footers, who were more than capable of holding out defensively. There was never likely to be much in this game.

The players came out to rapturous applause, but started badly. In truth, the first-half of this match was poor, with both sides too tense and tight to take even the slightest risk. To make matters worse, Sean Gregan played the entire game on a yellow card having been booked just 20 seconds into the game. There was relief for both teams as they made their way to the dressing rooms all-square. Moyesie's team talk had obviously stressed that, this being the home leg, it was our best chance of putting some daylight between ourselves and the Gills.

The second period saw a much more positive North End, who deservedly took the lead on the hour when David Eyres looped a header over the stranded Vince Bartram. The atmosphere immediately changed as the Whites poured forward to a backdrop of 'Wembley... Wembley...' from the terraces. The visiting fans were silent. Two-nil would have been a great scoreline - and we looked well in with a chance of getting another goal, when Michael Appleton stumbled over the ball in the centre of the park.

Bizarrely, the ref chose to award a free-kick from which Gillingham's Robert Taylor was allowed to pass through three defenders before curving his shot around Lucas. The goal was fatal for North End, and although later described as a goalkeeping error, there were others at fault in defence. The goal meant we had to score at least once at Priestfield. The pressure was suddenly on us when such a short time ago they had looked desperate. The only goal of the second leg came in the opening minute, and it went Gillingham's way. The rest, as they say, is history.

Steve Brennan

RED ALL OVER THE LAND

Liverpool

Nothing Was Delivered II

(See *SOTF4* for part I - to prove that nothing changes...)

In the close season, following our failure to make any real impact in '97-98, although we finished third, I expected the Liverpool board to sort things out. In the Sixties, under Bill Shankly, Liverpool set out to achieve what was a modern miracle; and from the ruins of what were the Fifties a new Liverpool rose, with the Liverbird doing a phoenix and ascending from the ashes. Inside 30-odd years Liverpool became the greatest football club that this country had ever seen. Forget the Arsenal of the Thirties, the

Wolverhampton Wanderers of the Fifties or the Manchester United of whatever decade they think they dominated, Liverpool were supreme. No one side had ever dominated like they did. From the mid-Seventies until 1990, the English League was in danger of becoming just like its Scottish counterpart and being totally monopolised by one club.

Then came the Nineties - 'The nightmare Nineties' as it is now being called. The hunger for more glory was kicked into touch and the star-studded names flocking to Anfield to wear the shirt with a Liverbird upon its chest became a bunch of overpaid, egotistical nonentities. By the end of the '97-98 season, the fans had just about had enough. Since Kenny Dalglish left, we had been put through the grinder. Graeme Souness arrived and not only brought Phil Boersma with him but also a lorry load of players who shouldn't have been allowed on Merseyside, let alone inside Anfield. But arrive they did; like refugees from the footballing backwaters, they descended on Anfield and we were forced to give them not only a home, but also a game.

Those of us who follow Liverpool know the story: Souness went and the club appointed that nice Mr Evans - Uncle Roy - to run the show, steady the ship and take us back to where we once belonged. Roy, bless him, tried. He tried very hard. Roy certainly steered the ship back into calm waters. Unfortunately the crew, who had mutinied under Souness, saw Roy as a soft touch and they all ended up sunning themselves on the luxury liner, whilst forgetting that they were supposed to be in search of the land of gold and silver

- or trophies as we used to call them. The problem was that Roy loved them so much, he kept giving them pay rises for failing to deliver, when he should have been wafting the cat o'nine tails around their arses.

But back to last summer, and the board of directors who sensed that all was not well and decided that it was time to take Liverpool back to where they once were. Unfortunately, the deliverance was not back to the glory days but back to the pre-Shankly dark times. What they did was to make the proud name of Liverpool Football Club a laughing stock. Here's what happened.

The football world was wafting with the fragrance of the World Cup. To some it had been a bit of a disappointment, but the men in the suits who count pennies not trophies, and prefer cash to class, had been rather pleased. Football had sold itself a bit further and the only areas left untapped as far as marketing the game was concerned were in outer space, where no doubt you'd probably find a few Man United fans anyway. Arsenal had won the Double with a French manager in command and a fair sprinkling of French talent to boot. As football today is as much about fashion and trends as it is about the game down on the pitch, being French became fashionable - heaven help us, I say. So, having witnessed that France had done rather nicely in their World Cup and Arsenal had done pretty well thank you very much in the English game with a French boss, it was time for the once leaders to become dedicated followers of fashion. We had to have a Frenchman.

Step forward one Monsieur Gerard Houllier. I bet that out of the 40-odd thousand who attend matches at Anfield, only a handful would have known who Gerard Houllier was. And OK, I bet the percentage of Arsenal fans who had ever heard of Arsene Wenger, was about the same or maybe even less. But it didn't matter because Monsieur Houllier wasn't just French - and a member of the backroom staff who had helped win the World Cup - he had also lived in Liverpool during the Sixties. He probably could list a few Beatles albums and the odd Cilla Black seven-inch vinyl amongst his record collection as well. But his track record in football was good... or was it? I mean he was in charge of the French team who failed to qualify for USA 94, so does that mean he is worthy of a job with the most successful of all English clubs? By the same token, Graham Taylor had made a pig's ear (and a laugh-a-minute, swear-a-minute film) of the England job in '94, so why not him? It can't be pulling power, can it? Houllier's track record in French club football - hardly the greatest league in Europe, even if two of their clubs have stuffed us in recent times - was not exactly sensational. I think he won a title sometime back in the Eighties but it didn't register at the time, and I've forgotten who it was with anyway. But based on having Gallic blood being enough to make you flavour of the month, Gerard 'I've stood on the Kop' Houllier was brought in. However, not to *replace* Roy, but to help him. In the distance there were two distinct sounds - one the sound of Kopites sighing and the other the sound of football laughing. Oh dear, we now had not one, but two managers. Some said: "Two heads are better than one"; while others chipped in with, "Too many cooks..." We being loyal fans defended the issue because it was Liverpool and our club. Roy was a lovely man and we didn't want to see him hurt, so maybe bringing in the Frenchman was a good idea. Deep down we knew it was destined to end not only in failure but also total humiliation for Roy Evans and, more importantly, Liverpool Football Club. And so it proved.

The season started reasonably well - two away wins on the bounce and a home draw with the Double boys of Arsene and Arsenal. Fans pointed to the difference that Gerard had obviously made, by commenting on our warm-up procedure. And, after four matches, Liverpool were top of the pile. The good old days were back. Oh no they weren't... From here onwards it was to go pear-shaped. In fact it was to go all shapes apart from the right one. Hindsight is a wonderful tool to have in the cupboard, and when we use it now, things fall into perspective. We won at Southampton, who struggled against relegation all season. We won at Newcastle, who never really threatened and, apart from getting to Wembley, their season was a shambles as well. We drew 0-0 with Arsenal at Anfield - the Champions were still finding their feet. We beat Coventry 2-0 at Anfield - but Coventry were destined to fight against the drop for most of the campaign. So, in hindsight, the start was good, but in reality any side hoping to challenge would have probably done the same. Then came West Ham.

It was a funny day. Most of the gang were looking forward to the away leg in the UEFA Cup against Kosice - a new country for most of us and the guarantee of cheap beer. West Ham had just been stuffed at home by Wimbledon and wouldn't worry us, the league leaders. One man had made a lot of difference to the team, and although he was a foreigner, he was German not French. Karlheinz Riedle was a star in the eyes of many. He had looked fit in the games mentioned and was the best supporting act the star of the show - Michael Owen - could have. Michael was still running about with his 'L' plates on despite his meteoric rise to fame, and KHR was the master he could learn from. How we loved the German genius. The talk amongst Reds was about the impact of KHR on Michael. Give this guy the job of partnering Owen and things would blossom - and we also had Robbie almost fit again to join the strike-force. Happy days, we thought, were here again.

Outside Upton Park the rumour mill produced a tale that was soon proven to be fact: KHR had been left out of the side. Dropped or rested, who cared, he was only sub. "It must be Roy Evans," moaned the fans in unison. Gerard was exonerated. Only later did we find out it had been his idea and not that of the much-maligned Royston. Given they had nobody to mark, West Ham defenders were free to join their attacking pals and cause havoc. It happened. Michael Owen ploughed a lonely furrow but made no impression. Only incessant calling for KHR and the Hammers second goal finally woke up the Liverpool bench, "Bloody hell, 2-0, we'd better do something about it!" However, his introduction was too little too late. Although he scored, the brains had screwed up big time and we were never again to threaten the coveted top spot.

The rot set in and spread faster than a rash that had been encouraged by constant scratching. It was our first false dawn and the mood of the masses was not a happy one. We drew 3-3 with Charlton at Anfield and should have lost.

Then we went to Old Trafford to play the enemy and got stuffed 2-0, thanks again to some inept tactical work and some absolute rubbish on the field. The Mancs didn't play well; in fact at times they looked ordinary. But we were so poor it didn't matter. One of summer signings was Vegard Heggem and he actually looked like a full-back who could play a bit. But someone - we think it was the one with a French accent - decided he was tired and rested him from this game. Not a big game, the one against the Mancs, good game to do a bit of experimenting in... and back came Jason McAteer.

As defeat followed defeat and the likes of Derby County could win at Anfield, someone would surely have to pay for all this. The gallows were constructed, the noose put in place and the fall guy was Roy Evans.

It was hard not to feel sorry for Roy but he had not done himself any favours. In truth he should have gone after the '96-97 season with his head held high, but now it had all gone sour. The board had set up a farcical situation with their rank stupidity in going for the so-called 'partnership' - and now the club and fans were paying the price. There have been many great double acts - Morecambe and Wise, Laurel and Hardy, Cannon and Ba... no, forget them - but our pair were Useless and Clueless, and I didn't know who was who. But Gerard got the nod over Roy, and Roy got shown the door.

Many fans heaved a sigh of relief that Roy had taken his leave of us and thought that with the French tactical genius in command, aided and abetted by ex-Red legend Phil Thompson, things would return to normal; and the glory that was, would once again be. We were spared David Moores doing the "exist only to win things" speech, but whilst some looked for an immediate return to glory, others weren't so sure. We now had a manager who had not managed at club level for 15 years and had never managed in England. But of course he was French - and therefore must be good. We had a second-in-command who had been out of the game since getting the boot by Souness from the job of managing Liverpool reserves.

It wouldn't be Liverpool with another false dawn though, would it? After a dismal run of defeats and performances that left much to be desired, there was another. We suddenly won some matches. The might of Sheffield Wednesday were put in their place, then we stuffed Middlesbrough away and Newcastle home, and in those last two games there can be no denying that the team played extremely well. Port Vale were duffed up in the FA Cup and as we left Vale Park we heard that our fourth round tie would be against Manchester United. But we then went to Arsenal and drew 0-0, before crushing Southampton 7-1 at Anfield, and we thought that at long last the sun might be breaking through. But we then lost in the FA Cup (more of that later) and it meant that we were left with just a decent league place to go for.

To cut a long story short - Houllier failed. When our supporters went into delirious delight when we managed to draw at home with Manchester United, their actions summed up our season perfectly. By the end of the most forgettable campaign in the modern history of Liverpool, we were feeling reasonably happy to finish above halfway.

Travelling abroad to watch your team is something to savour. When you travel abroad to watch Liverpool you get to understand just how big the club is - or maybe now that should read *was*. Our first sortie to foreign parts took us to Slovakia to play Kosice. It was football fans' heaven. Nothing to do with the opposition because playing against Kosice in front of 3,000 odd fans is nothing special. Playing against the likes of Barcelona, AC or Inter, Juve, Real Madrid - now *that's* special. But travelling to Kosice was different and brilliant. A stop-off in Prague, strong lager at about 30p a pint - that's special. Drinking in the bars of sleepy Kosice and finding the beer even cheaper - that's special. And beating a team like Kosice wasn't difficult either. Then we found we had to play Valencia. At this point Roy and Gerard were still doing the 'double act' and for some strange reason they decided to give little Michael Owen a rest for the home-leg - and, no, we don't know why either. But a rest he was given, and we were lucky to survive and get away with a goalless draw. So it was off to Valencia and another memorable trip. That is, the drinking was memorable. On this occasion the football wasn't too bad either: late goals, red cards and gritty determination to win out. Scenes of great jubilation at the airport and a happy band of fans travelled home to find out that we were going back to Spain, this time to Celta Vigo. By now, Gerard was in control (if that's the right word) of the good ship Liverpool. In Vigo we went one up, but then in the second-half, Liverpool dug deep into the locker of embarrassment and we gave away goals that would have shamed a poor pub side. We were out, the home leg went to Vigo as well, and we just wondered what the hell was going on.

So to the FA Cup and having won at a canter 3-0 at Port Vale, the next step on the march was Old Trafford. Now this isn't the ideal place to visit in January when your season looks like hinging on one match. But for 88 minutes it looked like glory at 1-0 up. Three minutes later the final whistle blew - 2-1 down. Now *that's* heartbreak. It was all over: the match; the cup run; the season.

We hoped that Gerard could do something. We hoped and prayed that he'd get players in to sort out the mess. From the day he joined, we hoped he'd sort out the defence. When he took over full command, we hoped he'd make a difference. But no.

When Bill Shankly took office he performed a modern-day miracle. He built not only a team but also a club. From obscurity to glory, through Shanks, Bob, Joe and Kenny, the glory went on and on. But now those in control of Anfield, those who represent the board, the management and the players have performed another modern-day miracle. They have taken Liverpool back to obscurity. In the past, even during the darker times there has been a chink of light. Under Souness it was the emergence of the likes of McManaman and Fowler. Under Evans we were given hope in the shape of the boy wonder, Michael Owen. But last season there wasn't even a crumb of comfort, no straw to clutch and no chink of light. It was the worst for 40 years, no matter what they say. Once again we went in hope, but once again 'Nothing was delivered'.

John Pearman

RED ARMY

Manchester United

Some things in life are best left unexplained. Like, why do you travel thousands of miles over the course of nine months, spending thousands of pounds in the process, all in the name of watching a group of millionaire prima donnas kicking a bag of wind around a patch of grass? Even the most ardent of football supporters would struggle answering this question posed by a sceptical relative or friend - but this season has seen all of our time and effort made worthwhile in the greatest of fashions, with some exhilarating football and fairytale finishes that even Roald Dahl would have struggled to produce. Every pound spent and every mile travelled has been made worthwhile, as the

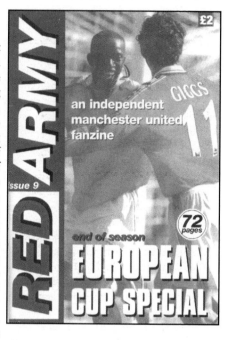

final two weeks of this history-making season saw all our loyalties rewarded in the finest possible style.

On Sunday 9 August 1998, the whole of England was against United - nothing new there. The ABUism had reached its ultimate climax as Beckham had "cost England the World Cup", we had just forked out £10m on a 'donkey' of a defender and as a disastrous pre-season warm-up in the Charity Shield against the deserved Double winners, Arsenal, ended in a 3-0 reversal, the whole of the nation was rejoicing as the mighty monster Manchester United had fallen from its pretty perch in such dramatic fashion. Or so you all thought.

He signed for Man United 'cos...

United's league campaign opened at home to Leicester with a disappointing 2-2 draw in which we were lucky to take a point. One aspect of the game that stood out for me, though, was the newly-crowned 'hero' Teddy Sheringham coming off the bench to a crescendo of boos from an element of United's fickle support. You should never boo your own, and the imbeciles who joined in these disgraceful events should be too ashamed to step foot inside Old Trafford ever again. A conversation with a Red was had at the next home game and he proudly admitted that he was on his feet booing every time the "Tottenham reject" touched the ball. OK, Teddy's attitude and commitment at times looked, at the very least, half-hearted and a lot of the criticism he received was deserved. This isn't any sort of apology because those who doubted have nothing to apologise for. Admittedly,

I had personally questioned our number ten's commitment to the red shirt but you would never stoop so low as to boo your own.

United Against Murdoch

Whilst in the light of this season's obvious glories, we mustn't forget one major victory on behalf of the supporters, which has saved the face of the beautiful game - for the time being at least. David proved victorious against Goliath, City scraped past Gillingham, and the Manchester United supporters defeated the powerful Australian money-making megalomaniac, Rupert Murdoch. As news broke of the proposed takeover back in September, the general opinion was that Murdoch would take control of the club, football would be totally defaced and the working class game would be taken over by geriatric fat cats, only there to line their pockets. Despite the pessimistic attitude, there was still the thought that we had to fight for the slightest chance of victory and, after seven agonising months of campaigning and turning as many people against the decision as possible, Murdoch was defeated. IMUSA (Independent Manchester United Supporters Association) and SUAM (Shareholders United Against Murdoch) had done us all proud.

The End Of An Era

On Thursday 12 November 1998, Peter Schmeichel shocked football by announcing that he was to quit Manchester United at the end of the season. It was a decision that I had been dreading for a few years as the big man has been one of the greatest servants ever to appear in a United shirt. Between then and the end of the season, people just took him for granted. A catalogue of errors over a two-month period had the doubters rather amusingly and somewhat prematurely starting questioning the Dane's ability between the sticks and some even believed it was "about time he retired". Tossers one and all. Unsurprisingly, it is probably the same mindless individuals who booed Teddy, called Stam a "donkey" and thought that Cole is a waste of space. The final bow in a United shirt brought to an end the career of one of United's most influential footballers and no doubt greatest goalkeeper. Although a lot of people will disagree, Peter Schmeichel became probably more important to Manchester United than a certain French genius. Blasphemous maybe, but deep down there is an element of truth.

2-1 To The Champions

In one season's action, you are lucky if you get two or three games that you know will stand out for the rest of your lives. But in this season alone we had over half a dozen memorable games. Because of the limit posed on this article it will be impossible to cover them all, so instead we'll concentrate on just three games, each ending in the same result.

Liverpool - FA Cup Fourth Round

No victory is sweeter than that against your closest and most deadly rivals. We hate Liverpool with a vengeance and they hate us - always have done and always will do. So put yourselves in our position. The last couple of minutes of an FA Cup tie, on your patch and the Scum are beating you. Ten thousand of the bastards are singing their hearts out, as they believe victory is only moments away. You are sitting, literally, three or four seats away, and it hurts. Then the sound to your left is overshadowed by the immense roar, as you equalise in the last minute. The Hub

Cap Collectors are crying. Yes. Then plans are made for the replay - and before you can talk about possible allocations, you've scored a winner. Sheer ecstasy as your rivals drown in a sea of their own tears. They are dumb, not even able to reply to your irresistible taunts. Nothing could better this, could it?

Arsenal - FA Cup

For a team who couldn't give a toss about this competition and a cup which had apparently "lost its magic", United were doing pretty well and this match once again pushed the boundaries of sheer orgasmic ecstasy. This game had it all. Following a game that had a perfectly legal goal disallowed for a decision which still confuses every United fan, this one was always going to be tense. The match wasn't a sell-out and the hard-core supporters were here in abundance as the daytrippers and plastic supporters made their excuses and watched this spectacle on Murdoch TV. Those who were there witnessed something spectacular. A beautiful opener from Beckham. A deflected equaliser from Bergkamp. Anelka goal. Arsenal fans on pitch. Disallowed. Arsenal arrested. Keano getting sent off for a second bookable. Ten men. Shit. Last minute. Arsenal penalty. Double shit. Schmeichel save. Yeeeeessssssss. Extra-time with ten men. Giggs runs. And runs. Past another. And another. Surely not. Yeeeeessssssss. Shirt off. Fans on the pitch. Full-time. Invasion. Better than Liverpool?

Bayern Munich - European Cup Final

After knocking out the cream of European football, the only team that Manchester United had failed to defeat were Bayern Munich. Two group games. Two draws. We were favourites and in the last few years, the underdogs have won. Dortmund, Madrid, Ajax and even Juventus have lifted the trophy in previous years as second-favourites, and before the game my attitude was rather the opposite to the majority of United fans. We'd mess this one up. Six minutes gone. It wasn't a free-kick. Goal - 0-1. The Germans are pretty handy at defending 1-0 leads. Ten minutes remaining. Still 0-1. Five minutes to go. Told you. Ninety minutes. See, what did I say? Five minutes later. Manchester United - Champions of Europe. Tears streaming down my face. Not ashamed. It just didn't sink in. We'd prepared ourselves for over an hour that Bayern Munich would be victorious, and within two minutes at the death we'd switched the game around in possibly the greatest finale to such an important game the world has ever seen. The only thing to spoil the trip, though - other than the huge element of tossers supporting United - City won. Two goals in the last three or four minutes. "Anything United can do, City can do just as well," said the papers. Yeah, right. I really wish I was a City fan this season...

Player Of The Season?

And so how do you chose a single Player of the Season in a year which has seen your team produce some of the most scintillating and entertaining football you are ever likely to witness, and in a campaign which produces three finely-crafted lumps of silver. The answer is you can't. Each player has been magnificent - but five players stand out slightly above the rest.

David Beckham. According to all but the loyal Red contingent, this would be the year that would see Beckham fall to pieces. As the New Radicals would appropriately put it, "You've got the dreamer's disease" - a disease that spread faster than the plague. His character has been built immensely and he has provided us with his most consistent season in his beloved shirt. The World Cup experience has made him stronger and his 'no shit' attitude has seen him give his all to the cause this season. His passing at times has been unbelievable, *a la* Milan, and has provided us with numerous stunning goals. In Barcelona - along with Gary Neville - Beckham appeared to be the only player on the park truly giving it his all, with the sort of grit and determination that he has reflected throughout the team during this near 60-game season.

Jaap Stam. To say the very least, it has been one hell of an impressive season from the big Dutchman. Built like something more recognisable to Arnie Schwarzenegger in *Terminator 2*, Jaap has certainly been the missing brick in the defensive wall, and with him in the team we look awesome. Add to this his will to win, his appreciation for the shirt on his back and the sacrifices made to join us in the first place, he is rapidly establishing himself as a true Red Legend.

Dwight Yorke. A dream debut season for our much loved number 19. Just like Ole, he plays the game in the correct fashion and has earned massive respect not just from United fans but from other quarters as well. Many remained pessimistic when Fergie splashed out over 12 million big ones for a striker unproven at European level, but playing for Manchester United has given him the platform to perform... and perform he most certainly has. Valuable goals against minnows from places such as Milan, Barcelona, Munich and Juventus have seen him reach the ultimate pinnacle in goalscoring feats. Not to mention a memorable equaliser against the Scouse in the FA Cup. Pure class.

Peter Schmeichel. Another exceptional season from the world's greatest, who has sadly played his final year in the green jersey of Manchester United. A shaky spell early on in the year has no doubt been erased after a number of superb performances, most notably on that wonderful night in Barcelona. Ended his career in a typical Roy of the Rovers style finish by captaining his club on his final appearance and lifting the European Cup, and thus adding to two previous medals this season, resulting in an historic treble.

Roy Keane. Back with a vengeance. Although he was absent in the Nou Camp and missed the majority of the Cup Final, Keano's influence on this season has underlined the importance of just how much his presence was missed last term. His attitude after the victory over Juventus, in which he received a booking that would rule him out of the biggest day of his career, he showed his true character by admitting, "The club is bigger than any one player." His disciplinary record has also been superb. Is Keano going soft? Are Manchester City a successful club?

And Not Forgetting Those Less Fortunate

So our good friends from down the road, "we lost the league on merseyside..." the scousers will probably tell us that they have won the European Cup four times, and that "it isn't winning the treble that counts but retaining it".

Congratulations, Sir Alex.

David Bergin

RED PASSION

Wrexham

At 4.26pm on Saturday 8 August 1998, ageing (but legendary) Wrexham midfielder Peter Ward played a delicious one-two with ageing (but legendary) centre-forward Ian Rush, making his Wrexham debut. The touch from Rush was subtle and superb; the finish from Ward was deft and delightful. The sun was shining, a massive crowd of 6,671 had come to see Rush's first game in Wrexham colours, and the 3-0 victory over potential pace-setters Reading was convincing. We could go up on this form. Surely?

That was August.

By May 1999, Ward was sounding off in the local paper after being released by the club and 'goalscoring legend' Rush was still to break his Wrexham duck in front of goal. The sunshine of August 1998 was but a quaint, beautiful memory. Who said football was a funny game?

The truth, sadly and unfortunately, was that Wrexham's '98-99 adventure peaked in August - at 4.26pm on the first Saturday of the season. We were third in Division Two after the fundamentally brilliant Reading display; on May 8, after our last league game against Bournemouth, we'd settled for a final placing of 17th. That's football. That's life.

There were other statistics that told a poignant story: we scored only 43 league goals all season - only relegated Northampton, Lincoln and Macclesfield had similar or worse records; we had the third-worst average attendance figure in our division (3,948) - only Wycombe and Macclesfield suffered lower gates; we had the worst home attack in the division - 21 goals in 23 games; and if it hadn't been for our out-of-this-world run of five away wins (January to March - Colchester, Macclesfield, Luton, Stoke, Northampton) we would definitely have gone down.

Beyond the figures, though, this was a fascinating and intriguing season, with myriad themes and sub-plots.

First, there was Rush: the icon, the legend, the idol, the hero - the man who, in the end, could not net a single goal for Wrexham. It is very easy to make fun of Rushie's void in front of goal. For the whole season, fans were just dying for him to score. Everyone was itching to be at the game in which he eventually did score - so they could legitimately say "I was there" for the rest of their lives.

But it never happened and, to be honest, it didn't look like it was ever going to happen. OK, he hit the crossbar and the post, he brought a couple of brilliant saves out of opposition goalkeepers... and he did hit the target for the reserves. But here we have to remember that Rush had experienced barren spells at Leeds, Newcastle and Sheffield United. So why should his time at Wrexham, his first Welsh league club, be any different? When he signed for the Reds in sun-drenched August, he made the serious mistake of saying, "I'll be surprised if I don't score lots of goals at this level." Fatal words, indeed.

The man with the moustache did have his moments, though. Some of his touches were heavenly and several good Wrexham's goals bore the hallmark 'Made by Rush'. He also worked very hard - whether up front or in a withdrawn midfield role - and always had his head up, talking, encouraging and hoping to inspire those around him. Anyone and everyone who played and worked with him attached the phrase 'model professional' to him. As player-coach, it is clear that he was a brilliant influence on young players, and as an employee of Wrexham FC (he asked for no special terms regarding remuneration) he was a hard working and dignified ambassador in and around North Wales. However, the fact remains that Flynn was in need of a striker and Rush failed to deliver. Wrexham's 'goals for' column did not make pleasant reading and the feeling among some fans is that the Rush money could have been invested more profitably in a proven lower-league goalscorer (if any, actually, would have come to North Wales - they invariably seem to turn us down anyway).

So, all those Rush photos, Rush T-shirts, and Rush posters sold at the height of Rushmania c.August 1998 soon looked a bit dated. A dream 'marketing opportunity' he may have been, but Rushie's future now lies away from the Racecourse (the dilapidated but gradually improving football stadium). I'm afraid that all those 'Goal Rush' headlines went unused after all. But thanks anyway, Ian.

Rush might have been the season's big story - or the season's damp squib - but there were other things happening as well. Or not happening. In the league, Wrexham were poor and suffered their worst season since graduating into Division Two in 1993. To be honest, there was just unadulterated mediocrity. OK there were breathtaking highpoints - *that* Reading game (easier-than-easy 3-0 stroll), Stoke away (brilliant 3-1 win) and Man City away (incredibly valiant 0-0 draw). Funny in fact how our best performances came against a trio of rich and fancied clubs.

For the most part, though, it was average, if not worse than average. Our home form in particular was dreadful (9 wins in 23 games) and when fans were feeling in a particularly intellectual mood they constantly debated one big question - why so? Theories abounded. Predictable and unvarying tactics? Perhaps. Unsupportive and fairly negative and abusive fans? Perhaps. Ghostly 'this ground is being rebuilt' atmosphere? Definitely. But take your pick really. Whatever the reason, the fare served up wasn't pretty.

And apart from a crazy sequence of five consecutive awayday triumphs in the New Year - Colchester (3-1), Macclesfield (2-0), Luton (2-1), Stoke (3-1), Northampton (2-0) - the mediocrity was also a constant away from home. It may be difficult to pinpoint exactly why Flynn's boys started winning on their travels. A kick up the backside? An overdue injection of class in two loan signings, Whitley and Griffiths? Or just a run of good luck? The scary reality is that without those lovely 15 points we would be looking up the route to Cheltenham this coming season. It was a truly bizarre and spellbinding flush of success on the road - and desperately required. We finished 17th in the Second Division and, as all genuine footie fans know, the end of season table does not lie. Yes, we were poor.

There was the odd glimpse of light relief, though - and it was usually in a cup competition. We played in four knockout tournaments (well, five, if you count the outrageously-named 'Isle of Man International Tournament' - a leisurely pre-season experience) and in each we came tantalisingly close to doing something. In the League Cup, we recovered a two-goal, first-leg deficit against Halifax - only to go out on penalties; in the FA Cup, we fought hard and doggedly - and were just edged out by upwardly-mobile Huddersfield; in the Auto Windscreens Shield we reached the Northern Final - and narrowly missed out on a first-time visit to Wembley; and in the world's least glamorous competition, the Welsh Premier Cup, we were eclipsed in the final by the mighty Barry Town - and are a cool £60,000 poorer as a result. Somehow all these harrowing cup exits said something quite profound - like, we just weren't good enough.

And it was in one specific cup encounter - Wigan at home in the second-leg of the AWS Northern Final - that our one perennial problem was gratuitously exposed: our goalkeeper. The unassuming Mark Cartwright, heir to the late and lamented Andy Marriott, became the ultimate dodgy 'keeper. In the Wigan game, he made one outrageous misjudgement - which effectively ended our Wembley dreams - and he was crucified for it. For various reasons, Cartwright is an extremely likeable chap, but Wrexham fans are not the most charitable where their own 'stars' are concerned; and Cartwright's career at the Racecourse was effectively killed by some of the most unpleasant terrace abuse you could ever have the misfortune to live - or play - through. "What's it like to catch a ball..."; "There's only one Andy Marriott..." - the list does not end there. Mark's mishaps led to a swift re-christening: 'Carthorse', 'Can't catch', 'Can't punch', 'Can't kick', and finally 'Coco'. No prizes for guessing the implication here. Cartwright's league career may not survive this mauling. Late-season stability was restored by Man City loan man Tommy Wright and young gun David Walsh, but it was all far too late. Cartwright needed a breather well before he was eventually dropped - a serious management blooper.

It was no surprise that, in the end, a loan signing helped save our season. No surprise - because Flynn's mastery of the non-permanent transfer market was a consistent feature (and has been a consistent feature of his whole management career). The late-season capture of Newcastle reserves skipper Stuart Elliott may have been the most over-hyped loan signing of all time, but with Terry Cooke and Jeff Whitley (both Man City) and Carl Griffiths (Leyton Orient), the Wrexham boss struck gold. Cooke was quality on the right-wing - and we got sick of hearing how, when he left North Wales, he helped turn Man City's season from the very average to the very good. Whitley was a willing workhorse - and steadied the ship superbly in the first three months of 1999. But it was Welshman Griffiths who took the real plaudits: a local lad, a guy who supported Wrexham as a kid, and a natural goalscorer, who bagged four goals in five vital post-Christmas games. So why couldn't we sign him permanently? Discuss.

The loan captures *had* to be good because nobody wanted to come to Wrexham permanently. Andy Rammell, John Hodge, Gavin Ward, plus a plethora of anonymous continentals, seemed interested - but didn't sign. OK, they all loved the "Premiership-quality training ground" but they didn't seem to appreciate the rest. This was, and will continue to be, a big problem.

So Flynn, Reeves, Jones, Rush and Pejic (the best backroom five-a-side team in Western Europe?) had to make do with an old-look squad. Most fans in fact would argue that the management team at Wrexham have been particularly charitable in the way that they have retained, and continued to trust, thirtysomethings like Kevin Russell, Tony Humes, Peter Ward and - of course - Rush. Journeyman Russell in particular came in for Cartwright-style abuse this season. Good brain, but lack of movement - that was the diagnosis offered on the terraces (well, the politest one anyway).

That said, though, a blend is needed. Given Wrexham's excellent youth policy (which has seen Bryan Hughes, Neil Wainwright and Dave Brammer all progress to First Division clubs recently), it is probably sensible to retain a few wise-ish heads to gee up and encourage the current crop of youngsters, most notably wingman Gibson, right-back McGregor, centre-forward Roberts and goalkeeper Walsh.

The sale of Hughes (Birmingham), Wainwright (Sunderland) and Brammer (Port Vale) would actually have been vaguely palatable if the money that accrued (c.£1.6m), or even a modest proportion of it, had been spent on new players. The reality though is that this money has been paid into two bank accounts, one marked 'New Stand' and the other 'Good Housekeeping'.

Unfortunately, Wrexham have had to cough up a considerable amount of dosh for the new Mold Road construction - The Pryce Griffiths Stand. Fans might moan about this, but the fact is that the dilapidated, derelict old stand was a disgrace and the club risked becoming a laughing stock if they had stalled even further on turning a three-sided embarrassment into a four-sided palace - so that's fair enough. However, the chairman's constant emphasis on thriftiness - and the need for a 'Good Housekeeping' account - is a source of both pride and annoyance. Of course, the club must remain solvent and financially stable, but - for heaven's sake - we must have the most expensive housekeeper in Western Europe. Surely just a small proportion of the Hughes/Wainwright/Brammer pot could have been used to good effect in the transfer market?

So, Flynn might be going stale - the phrase "He's taken the side as far as he can" keeps cropping up - but we can't really complain. Next season, for the first time in ages, we will have a real, genuine, authentic four-sided stadium. And I've got a funny feeling that ground improvements could have just the same positive effect on us as they've also recently had on teams like Huddersfield, Sunderland and Middlesbrough. New Millennium, New Promotion Push - that's what I say.

Peter Davies

RUB OF THE GREENS

Plymouth Argyle

What Have I Done To Deserve This?

This season was the worst-ever for Plymouth Argyle Football Club. That is the bare bones - I will try to put some 'meat' on the story. The previous 'worst-ever' season was '94-95, when we finished fourth in Division Four (yes, let's call it what it is), but we finished that year on a high by being promoted via the play-offs. Although I am not a fan of this system, I felt our promotion was justified, having finished in what would have been a promotion position in pre-play-off days.

This year was to offer no such let out, although with a week of the season to go, we still had a (very slim) mathematical chance of making seventh place. Defeats to the two bottom sides - including the surreal last day at Carlisle - finally did us in. To be clutching at such straws to get out of a division that is clearly very low on quality, though, is sad indeed, as there was not one really decent side around. We failed because of our inability to beat - or even score against - the teams at the bottom, such as Hull (0-0, 0-1), Hartlepool (0-0, 0-2), Scarborough (0-0, 0-3) and Southend (0-3, 0-1).

Champions Brentford beat us well at Griffin Park, but we wiped the floor with them at Home Park. Cambridge were a disappointingly dirty side - so much for Roy MacFarland's claim that they were a 'footballing' team. Cardiff weren't bad, but even their fans would probably agree that they were lucky to beat us at Ninian Park. The best individual performance I witnessed was Peterborough thrashing us at Home Park. We were lucky to get nil on the day. It was indicative of the league, though, that we had completely outplayed them earlier in the season at their place.

Argyle's lack of success can be placed fairly and squarely in the hands of one man - chairman Dan McCauley. This is the man who took over at Home Park in the early Nineties, and has held power at a time of endless failure. When he arrived he was hailed as some sort of knight in shining armour, as the club had financial problems even then. At the time we were in the (old) Second

Division playing the likes of Newcastle, Leeds, Blackburn, Leicester, Sunderland and Middlesbrough.

Sadly, the relegation in his first season was indicative of his stewardship. He has hired and fired a series of high and low profile managers since then, throwing money at Peter Shilton and Neil Warnock, but refusing it to Mick Jones and the current boss, Kevin Hodges. (I would suggest that Kevin Hodges leaves his mobile phone at home when he goes on holiday this year.)

Hodges arrived from Torquay's unsuccessful play-off bid last summer, with Argyle on the crest of a slump, having been relegated. The Torquay chairman accused McCauley of poaching, but Hodges - and his assistant Steve McCall - had not signed contracts at Plainmoor. Unfortunately, by the time they arrived, most of the out of contract players had left, including Corazzin (Northampton), Logan (Scunthorpe), Billy (Notts County), Saunders and Williams (the East Kent home for retired Pilgrims).

The incoming signings were of an obvious lower quality - Sean 'Sumo' McCarthy (Oldham), Chris Hargreaves (Hereford), Lee Power (Hibs), Richard Flash (Watford) and Paul Gibbs (Torquay). Just to prove our chairman's ambition, only McCarthy was given a contract to last beyond 1999, and none of the players commanded a transfer fee. In fact, we haven't paid a transfer fee for a player since Jon Sheffield in the summer of 1997.

The success of the incoming transfers was somewhat limited. McCarthy, Hargreaves and Flash spent over half of the season injured. Power looked good against various Cornish sides in the pre-season games, but in the real thing he couldn't hit a cow's arse with a banjo and was soon on his way to Halifax. Gibbs was the worst signing of the lot. How he made it into the divisional select team, I and all the Argyle faithful will never know. He was injured for half the season, suspended for five other games, and a liability for the rest. I can think of at least one other left-back better than him in Division Four, and that's Jon Beswetherick, his understudy at Home Park.

In fact it was only the products of Argyle's excellent youth team - under the guidance of Kevin Summerfield - that made it worthwhile watching the Greens. Jon Ashton, Jon Beswetherick, Lee Phillips, Paul Wotton, Darren Bastow, Kevin Wills, Liam Ford, Steve Adams, Jamie Gill and Brendan McGovern all made appearances at first team level and all acquitted themselves well - certainly better than the majority of the loan signings, most of whom shouldn't have bothered. The exceptions were Steve Guinan (Forest), who scored a few goals at the end of the season; Howard Forinton (Birmingham), who scored the goals that earned a win and a draw against Excreta; and Guy Branston (Leicester), who was an excellent defender. The other five - Crittenden (Chelsea), Sale (Colchester), Marker (Sheffield United), Edmondson (Huddersfield) and Taylor (Swindon) - might as well have not bothered. In reality you have to question the chairman, who is in the top 500 richest men in the country, on why he thinks we should rely on free transfers, loanees and youth players to gain promotion.

The only good news on the transfer front was the arrival of former 'Gyle, Dwight Marshall. Even he had to play on non-contract terms before earning a contract... to the end of the season. How typical of McCauley. Dwight finished up as top scorer with 12 - nine more than our new striker McCarthy. Just to show how well our season went, Guinan was second on seven!

Dwight also starred in one or two surreal moments. He scored the opening goal at Chester and was milking the applause of the away contingent, when one of the Argyle fans ran on the pitch to join in the celebration. The fan slipped, crashed into Dwight and caused him a nasty injury, requiring ten minutes of treatment.

The second surreal experience was at Carlisle on the last day of the season - and I don't mean their 'keeper scoring the winner six minutes into injury-time. We had lost at Scarborough on the Wednesday, which meant that Carlisle had to win and hope that Scarborough didn't, to retain their league status. OK, you'd expect a tannoy announcer to 'gee up' the home supporters when giving the teams before kick-off and after the half-time break, but the Carlisle guy was *joining in with the chanting*. Not only that, but when the Scarborough game finished, he announced the result and told the Carlisle players they had four minutes to score the winner. I'm not sure this is allowed, is it?

The season did offer a few highs: winning away to Brighton (albeit at Gillingham) for the first time since 1951 (my in-laws are from Hove); slaughtering Scunthorpe 5-0; the win over Shrewsbury, which allowed my daughter to break her 18-month non-winning sequence; and she also enjoyed presenting one of the Player of the Year awards. We also had some great days out - including a few games of football against opposition fans. At Carlisle, that meant a 4.00am start from Devon. My favourite day out was at Scarborough, where everyone at the club treated us well, even before they beat us. Oh, and the youth team were a joy to watch.

Unfortunately the lows outweighed the highs: Paul Gibbs; dire performances at Mansfield, Shrewsbury and Scarborough; and those at home to Hull, Scarborough, Southend and Brighton. Finishing thirteenth in such a poor division is bad enough; finishing below Excreta is even more difficult to take. With McCauley at the helm, things will only get worse. Fans of Brighton, Bournemouth and Doncaster will know how we feel in believing that Plymouth Argyle are a definite possibility for the Conference in the Millennium.

Cheltenham and Withdean here we come. Roll on 2000.

Steve Nicholson

SATIS?

Everton

Apart from the usual battle against relegation at the end of the season, '98-99 will be remembered by all Evertonians for one reason: the eventual resignation of chairman Peter Johnson. From supremo to loser, it all happened over a period of just seven days.

SATIS?

Volume 1, Issue 10 For Thinking Evertonians   May 1999

Appearing in a Cup Final near You!

Please note: apparel may differ from this photo

November 23 (Monday Evening, Newcastle United, home).

On my usual pre-match perch selling fanzines. A light drizzle starts to fall. Ken, a subscriber from the Midlands, stops for a chat about Bakayoko. Why am I so critical of the man? Because I think he's crap, says I, and I think we've bought a dud. You never know, says Ken, look at Ricard - crap last season and now a star. Good this season, says I, but it'll only be a temporary thing and, in a few years time, he'll be remembered as a failure. Same with Bakayoko - except I don't think he'll have even limited success in the Premier League. It is just too fast for him, and he can't adjust to it. Never mind, we agree, we still have big Dunc.

Not two minutes later, Wigan George rushes past en route from the Winslow to the Spellow, a pint in every pub on Goodison Road before the match. What did I think about Ferguson, then? What about him? But George is on the run, and already out of earshot.

Angie arrives with Elyn in tow, on their way to the lower Gwladys. "Some fella in MacDonalds says Ferguson's on his way to Leeds, dad." "Rubbish," says I, the lifelong Evertonian. "No way will they ever sell Ferguson. Trust me, he's going nowhere."

Meanwhile, in the Winslow Hotel, Goodison Road, Duncan Ferguson's father is sipping the nippy sweeties, saying that his son is on his way to another club, "Leeds or Newcastle, one of those up there." "Another Scotch, Mr Ferguson? Tell us more! You ARE joking, aren't you?"

The word is starting to spread.

Ferguson is injured and taking no part in the match . In the dressing-room, Walter Smith prepares his team for the game ahead. In the boardroom,

Peter Johnson, Everton chairman, meets Freddie Shepherd of Newcastle United, and Duncan Ferguson. The deal is being done. Ferguson is astonished and hurt that the club is letting him go. In the previous League Cup tie, he had refused to take a penalty in the shoot-out against Sunderland, and was criticised by fans as a result. Did Johnson tell him that the fans didn't want him any more, and neither did the manager?

Later, in the stadium, the match. Everton, through a Michael Ball penalty, take the three points. For once, none of the kids need a lift, so it's a quick getaway and home. I rewind the tape of Sky's coverage and watch the post-match interview with Walter Smith live. Andy Gray and Richard Keys are in the studio. "Any truth in the rumours about Duncan Ferguson going to Sunderland?" asks Richard. (That's a new one, I thought - Sunderland now!) "Absolutely no truth in the rumour," says Walter. "Duncan will be in my squad at Charlton on Saturday."

Hah! Told ya!

Walter deals with the media. Elsewhere, other matters are in hand. The room overlooks Goodison Road, and the blinds are not properly closed. Fans look on as Freddie Shepherd and Duncan Ferguson are in deep conversation. A handshake. The rumours are now spreading like wildfire - Duncan is going. The big man emerged from the club offices and quickly dives into his Bentley, ticking over outside. His wife is driving, and dad is in the back seat. They speed away into the night. Not a word to the fans. No change there, then.

November 24

I stop off at the newsagents on my way to the office. The *Daily Post* carries a front-page banner headline 'EVERTON TO SELL HERO FERGUSON'. I stare in total disbelief. It is a done deal. Seven million and another million after 30 appearances. What the hell's going on? The paper speculates that Walter Smith knew nothing of the negotiations. I saw him on TV, and I'm certain it's true.

Not an easy day at work. Red noses pop up all over the place. "Where's ya totem pole now, kiddo?" "Well," says I, the lifelong Evertonian, "you guys might even be able to contemplate the outside chance of a remote possibility of winning a derby match now, whaddya think?"

"Looks like Johnson did it all behind Walter's back," they squeal. "Looks like you lost another manager, then!" I am inclined to agree. If Smith knew, then his position is untenable after what he said last night. If he didn't know (as I suspect), then he will walk, simple as that. And that would make four managers gone since Johnson took over four years ago. Jeez.

There is a queue at the shop for the *Liverpool Echo*, the local evening paper. 'SMITH READY TO QUIT' screams the front-page headline. Good grief.

November 28 (The Valley, Charlton away).

In the pubs, the Bluenoses have only one topic of conversation - Johnson has to go. It has gone beyond all hope of reconciliation, and the man is a complete washout and is ruining our club. We know that Walter Smith is considering his future, and some of the more senior players might also be looking to ship out unless the club is returned to more sensible management. The Independent Blues are organising a demonstration at The Valley, showing the letters INDEPENDENT BLUES SAY JOHNSON OUT across the Blue support behind the goal. It is agreed that a meeting be called to organise support for the cause. The Everton Fans Forum is born.

November 29
Early evening. Telephone call from Gary of the GFE (Goodison for Ever) Committee. A public meeting is set for tomorrow evening at the Blue House pub next to Goodison Park, and all of the fans' organisations will be there - am I up for it? You bet! Apart from *Satis?*, the other two fanzines have been invited, plus the Goodison for Ever campaign, the Independent Everton Supporters Club, and Boardwatch, who keep an eye on things in the Everton boardroom.

The pressure is mounting on Peter Johnson. All of the media will be present. And there is a strong rumour that Walter Smith has issued an ultimatum that either Johnson goes, or he does.

November 30
Mid-afternoon. A phone call at work from a colleague in London. "Allo, skarse git. Let me be one of the first to congratulate you and your anarchist buddies up there!" How it was that a Crystal Palace fan found out before anyone in our large office block on Merseyside is beyond me, but there you go. A few calls confirm the news that Peter Johnson has resigned as chairman of the club, and is to sell his majority shareholdings in Everton. Was it the fans or the manager? I think probably a combination of the two. One thing is for sure - the supporters groups and the fanzines have proved they *can* make a difference.

It is still crucial to have the meeting, which goes ahead as planned. To the Blue House. Chaos. Granada TV, Sky News, and two radio crews - all looking for quotes. Gary points me at a radio man. "This is Phil Pellow of *Satis?* fanzine, he'll talk to you. See ya later, I've got to do Sky."

I am ferried out of the pub and over the road to the deserted Goodison Park car park, and a radio vehicle. It is freezing. A guy from Boardwatch, another from GFE, and me. We stand for 20 minutes listening to the phone-in programme at the studio before we are eventually patched in.

I am asked an inane question about club finances. I ignore it and pitch in about communication. The club must learn that the fans *are* important and must be kept informed about the current situation, whatever it might be. I cite Peter Johnson's barbed remarks at a couple of the Independent Blues in the hotel on pre-season tour: "Three wins and the other fans won't want to know you. You'll be history." This kind of arrogant dismissal cannot be allowed to continue.

Bill Kenwright is a media man. As the new vice-chairman, he must appoint a media man to the board, to talk to and listen to the fans. There can be no more of the long silences punctuated by patronising statements from the boardroom - it will not wash.

We pad back to the Blue House. TV and radio crews are still here, guys are still giving interviews. Fans everywhere, waiting for something to happen. We decide to get on with it. The meeting is brought to order. One by one, any Evertonian who wants to can say his/her piece, and there follows a couple of hours of lively debate, covering the board, the finances, the players and the manager, and other things Evertonian. Despite the chairman having no experience of meetings, everyone has their chance and things are done with good manners and respect all round.

As to Johnson, we are all still suspicious. He may have resigned as chairman, but he still owns 68% of the Blues. Until he has sold out, we are unable to rest easy. Who comes in? Will they be any better? A plan of action is proposed. Leaflets at the Chelsea match next Saturday, and a boycott of club merchandise, to attempt to deflate the value of Johnson's shares and make it easier for someone to buy them.

There are two drunks. One wants to talk all night, most of it meaningless drivel. He is allowed a little time, and then the meeting shuts him up. The other staggers to the front and sings, "AND IT'S EV-ER-TON, EVER-TON-HON EFF CEE!" he roars. He is allowed to finish the verse, and is then ushered back to his place. He sheepishly realises that he would have been wiser to wait until the end.

Next morning, on *Sky News*, they show about four seconds. Of the drunk singing. But the Everton Fans' Quorum is born. And we will never go away. We are watching.

Post Script

Later that week, Everton secretary Michael Dunford, on the instruction of vice-chairman Bill Kenwright and chairman Sir Philip Carter, invites the fans' leaders into Goodison, for the first of many future meetings. The atmosphere is cordial. Dunford asks for patience, but understands that the Fans' Quorum is a positive thing for the club. *Progress.*

There is no doubt that Walter Smith's stand against Johnson was instrumental in forcing the resignation of the ex-chairman. But let there be no doubt that pressure from the fanzines, the Independent Supporters Club, Boardwatch and Goodison for Ever, all had a profound effect on the outcome.

We will continue to fight for the rights and views of the fans, in a football world which today owes much of its allegiance to media and business interests. The shareholders own the shares in Everton, but the club belongs to us, our children and their children. The new owners, whoever they are, will do well to recognise this inalienable fact. And listen to us.

Phil Pellow

SEASIDE SAGA

Brighton & Hove Albion

Did you enjoy *your* birthday? I spent mine wandering around the streets of Hove tying green balloons to trees and lampposts. Not for the first time in my life, I wonder if I'm quite all there.

You're probably assuming I was drunk, and it was a sad attempt to liven my evening up, but no. I was stone cold sober. So go on, guess why I'm tramping the streets with bin bags full of inflated balloons. To give you a clue... the balloons have 'YES YES' written on them, and the previous fortnight had been spent going from door to door, getting my fingers caught in gates, my hand stuck in letterboxes, and running for my life as ferocious dogs leapt for my throat. Gosh it's fun being a Brighton supporter.

A Brighton & Hove Albion Fanzine

YES
YES
May 6th

48 Pages Inside

ISSUE 28 MARCH 1999 - £1

You're quite right, it's our annual campaign. I have a horrible feeling we're never going to make it through a season without having one. It's traditional, becoming addictive, and now a sort of a superstitious thing. We're always going to have a ritual 'Lucky Campaign'. Bring out the T-shirts, the balloons, car stickers, the video starring supporters, the multi-coloured leaflets, the never-ending meetings, and the Internet web page devoted to The Campaign.

It's the 'YES YES' campaign (bear with me, I'll get to the football later) and Brighton & Hove Council in their wisdom, decided to hold a referendum on May 6. They asked the good people of the two towns to vote on whether or not the Albion should come back to the area, and also whether we thought the Council should back the Albion's bid for a new permanent stadium at Falmer.

Actually, I'm writing this backwards, aren't I? It's the end of the season and I'm rambling on about events in May. I really ought to start at the beginning...

The season began with its usual optimism. We all buy our season tickets, and await the first game at Withdean (announced as the Mansfield game - 17 October). Nothing against Gillingham and the Priestfield Stadium - thanks for having us - but it's a long way from Brighton. One season wasn't too bad, but we couldn't wait to come back home, Withdean being our temporary lodging place for a little while.

As it turned out, we didn't make it back to Brighton. By mid-March it came as no surprise when the club announced we wouldn't, after all, be playing at Withdean this season. A marvellous array of compensation options are offered to season ticket holders, with a large number choosing to leave their money in the club. Sadly, I'm more greedy than most, choosing the free programme subscription for the '99-2000 season. Did someone just call me sad? Hey, I could have gone for free cup tickets.

Apart from the campaigning stuff, the season was fairly unexciting. It started OK, got better, and we started getting all sorts of nose bleeds as we rose through the division. The improvement started in September at Cambridge, where we won 3-2. It carried on at a rain-soaked Barnet, with a player called (hang on while I check the spelling)... Emeka Ifejiagwa.

It goes without saying he's foreign, which seemed to lead to some sort of problem with his work permit, so we didn't have him for long. But at Barnet, he was magic. He scored the only goal of the game, and even though we were all soaked to the skin, it was one of the best bits of the season. January brought with it the sad departure of Brian Horton. It came as something of a surprise. We assumed he would stick with us for the duration. However, the offer from Port Vale proved too tempting. We were all sad to see him go. But at least we can remember him as a great player and a good manager. He brought in some good players for us - Gary Hart and Rod Thomas, for instance - and he left us in a better state than when he joined us.

Everyone had their own idea of who should replace him, Micky Adams and Jeff Wood (the on-hand assistant) being the favourites. And Jeff was given the job until the end of the season.

Back at the start of the season, I thought the fanzine ought to try to plough some of the immense amount of money we make (?) back into the club by way of sponsoring a player. Well, let's be honest, I could only afford half a player, and opted for the cheapest half - the away kit. I made a unanimous decision, going for my favourite player, 17-year-old Ben Andrews. What a wonderful choice that was, I thought to myself, as he was injured during training in mid-August and was never seen again...

Part of the sponsors' package was some free tickets for a home game of your choice, and having your photo taken with 'your player'. So with the shrewd, knowledgeable judgement I'm famed for, I decided the Darlington game (March 13) was the best bet.

We lost 4-0. We'd lost the previous five games, too. Jeff Wood was clearly not the manager we'd hoped for. It was possibly the lowest point of the season. The team performance was absolutely diabolical, the spirit at an all-time low - the sort of game you wouldn't want to take a child along to as their introduction to 'Albion football'. So I took along my son's best friend - the Man United fan, William. His first Brighton game. The game started, William and Jonathan (my son) tucked into their bag of snacks. (I took along a lot of child-friendly comfort food, to pass the time, if things got boring.) I felt a tug on my sleeve, and glanced round at William. His hands were clasped to his face and there was blood everywhere. Surely this must be the ultimate nightmare when you take someone else's beloved offspring out for the day.

"Who hit you?" "No-one. My tooth just fell out."

Phew! That's all right then. Panic over, I search in my bag under my seat and grab my antiseptic wet one and wipe his face and hands. However this wasn't the end of the story, as he'd spat out the tooth (still attached to a Chewit) and couldn't find it. He's a shrewd young man, and was already anticipating a visit from the tooth fairy that night. So, there I was, my face in everyone's lap, grovelling under the seats searching for the missing tooth. You know how cramped it is, with your bags, coats, boxes of unsold fanzines, etc already wedging us in tightly. I was facing a losing battle, and soon gave up.

A traumatic, miserable afternoon, but one must pick oneself up, and after the game we dragged the boys into the sponsors lounge. The boys enjoyed their photo session and complimentary glass of coke, but the highlight of the day (they informed me) was watching the TV as the Premier League results come through. We did take William along for a second game. Actually he asked to come, amazingly. The funny thing was, another of his teeth fell out. What are the chances of that happening? I doubt his mum will let me take him again; she must have visions of her child wearing dentures by the time he's 12.

We continued to lose under Jeff Wood and, by the beginning of April, it was clear we had another fight for league survival on our hands. We were in 17th place and moving down the league every week. The fans were calling for Jeff Wood to go. It was becoming clear we couldn't afford to keep him until the end of the season.

The 3-1 defeat at home to Cambridge on April 6 was the final straw, and Jeff was sacked. A few days later Micky Adams was placed in charge. We won a couple of games, which meant we could relax and breathe again. We could enjoy the football and concentrate the main effort on The Campaign.

The referendum had been announced back in February, and our YES YES campaign kicked off shortly after. What fun, eh? Special mention must go to Ian Morley and Tim Carder. They were wonderful, and put in loads of work. (That should keep me in their good books!) The main bulk of the work came in the few weeks leading up to the vote on May 6. Our supporters turned out in force, and they leafleted over 100,000 households twice. Hard work indeed, but the results made it worthwhile.

Of those people bothering to vote, 84% wanted the Albion back, with 68% thinking Falmer is a good place to build our new home.

I really think we'll do well next season. With Micky Adams in charge, playing back in Brighton, with real hope of a new stadium, I can't see us anywhere but somewhere at the top of the table. I hope all the other teams in our league will enjoy their visit to Brighton, and I look forward to meeting up with all my friends. Of all the games, I really do hope we manage to beat Leyton Orient this season.

I would like to thank everyone who helped with the fanzine this season, all the writers, and especially Ben and Phil, Jonathan and Dave.

Jackie Mooney

SHAYMEN DOWN SOUTH

Halifax Town

"Shaymen are back... Shaymen are back..." The beginning of the season saw the phoenix-like return to the professional ranks of one of the Football League's perennial strugglers. However, apart from the tendency of those in charge to press the self-destruct button when things began to go too well, the new Halifax Town bore little resemblance to the old Halifax Town who slipped almost unnoticed out of the Third Division at the end of the '92-93 season. The Shaymen have returned from the Conference a much leaner and fitter outfit and they now play at a redeveloped stadium in front of respectable

crowds who actually expect them to win games. So how was Town's first season back in the Football League? Well, let's have a look.

The pre-season preparation started well. Manager George Mulhall and assistant manager Kieran O'Regan kept most of the Conference-winning squad together and the prospect of 'doing a Macclesfield' seemed to be very much on the cards. Friendly games, including a respectable draw against Burnley (3-3) and a 1-0 win against Huddersfield Town, further fuelled most Town fans' optimism. By late July we were all really looking forward to the big kick-off at Peterborough. Then, with the start of the season only a few days away, our recently reinstated chairman brought his brother-in-law, Peter Butler, to the club to be the new player-coach. This really upset the status quo and resulted in George Mulhall resigning (although he subsequently went on to become Town's director of football) and Kieran O'Regan taking over as manager. It was always planned that O'Regan would take over from Mulhall at some point in the season. No-one expected that it would be before a ball had been kicked in anger.

The day of the big kick-off arrived and by 2.55pm most of the 800 or so Town fans in the away end at London Road were desperately trying to keep their pre-season optimism going. Not only had the club lost one of their most successful managers ever, they also had three first team players unavailable. We should have known better than to doubt the ability of our beloved team, as they outwitted the Posh and fully deserved their 2-0 victory, courtesy of goals from Dave Hanson and 'Super Geoff' Horsfield. At 4.45pm, I really wished I could have seen the look on the face of the local radio bloke, who before the game was thanking the fixture list computer for giving Peterborough such an easy opening fixture.

Town's good form at London Road proved not to be a flash in the pan and, a couple of weeks later, a Friday evening fixture at the Shay against Shrewsbury gave the Shaymen the opportunity to go top of the table. Goals from Geoff Horsfield and Kevin Hulme proved too much for the Shrews, and by the end of the game the now familiar chant of "We are top of the league..." was ringing out from the Skircoat.

September started with a live game on Sky against Hartlepool United. The game itself was very entertaining, although it will probably be remembered more for the Hartlepool United fans fighting amongst themselves at half-time than the 2-1 score-line. The rest of September was a pretty mixed bag. Those friendly folk from the Welsh valleys came to the Shay and scored two late goals to break our unbeaten home record that stretched back to March 1997. Four days later, Division One runners-up Bradford City made the long journey south and were made to work hard for their 2-1 second-round, first-leg Worthington Cup victory. A week after that they were made to work even harder for their 3-1 second-leg win.

Early October saw the transfer of Geoff Horsfield to Fulham for the princely sum of £300,000. Most Town fans didn't have a problem with Horsfield leaving the Shay. He was clearly destined for better things and deserved to show off his talents on a bigger stage. What many fans did have a problem with was the size of the fee, and this was put into perspective a week or so later when Fulham signed the arguably less-talented Barry Hayles from Bristol Rovers for £2m. The first games without Horsfield went pretty well. A 4-0 score-line at Scunthorpe was swiftly followed by a 1-0 win at Cheltenham Town, which added the highly prestigious Conference Championship Shield to the now bulging trophy cabinet. However, by the end of the month the post-Geoff cracks were beginning to show. The club was still handily placed near the top of the league but the exciting flowing football from the Conference was now but a distant memory.

November started with a hike up to the Scottish Borders. Yorkshire-based Town fans had the opportunity to make their way up north on the scenic Settle-Carlisle railway line, whereas we southern-based supporters had to rely on Virgin Trains. To be fair to Virgin the journey was pretty trouble free (honest!), with the only hiccup been one our own making. Our bargain-ticket holder was still at home when the train to Carlisle was due to depart Euston. Fortunately, the nice people at Virgin accepted his oh so true story about broken pipes and allowed us to use the ticket on the next train. The actual game will be remembered most for the second-half performance between the sticks of Town midfielder Kevin Hulme. A scandalous first-half lunge on 'keeper Tim Carter (who was making his Town league debut) forced him to retire to hospital at half-time. Hulme put in a competent, if not textbook, performance to keep Carlisle out and his efforts were further rewarded after 89 minutes when Paul Stoneman fired home a Jamie Paterson cross to steal all the points. Three days later, against Chester City, Hulme turned from hero to villain when he was sent off for his part in a 21-man brawl, which incidentally included a contribution from the Chester bench. Fortunately for Town they were able to cope with Hulme's dismissal and scored three goals to Chester's two. The resulting three points meant that Town went back to the top of the league.

The following weekend was FA Cup weekend. After two seasons of not making it through the qualifying stages, it felt good to be involved in the first round proper again. The ball-feelers from the Football Association paired the mighty Shaymen away to fallen giants Manchester City. Sky obviously thought that an upset could be on the cards, as they chose the match as their Friday evening feature. On the night, however, Town weren't good enough and City ran out comfortable winners, 3-0. A number of people blame the defeat on the chairman's decision to ban Kevin Hulme from the proceedings for his part in the Chester incident. With hindsight, I don't think he would have made enough of a difference; and, looking on the positive side, the chairman's prompt action almost certainly saved the club from a hefty fine from the Football League.

A win and a draw in their next two games saw Town maintain top spot until the start of December. Performances throughout the month were not up to standard, and two draws and two defeats saw Town drift down into the play-off places.

The New Year started with a trip to Gay Meadow. Player-manager Kieran O'Regan restored himself to the starting XI after recovering from injury and his presence made a significant difference. In fact it was the player-manager who earned Town a share of the spoils with a thunderbolt of an equaliser after 85 minutes. For the final five minutes Town were back to their passionate Conference best and the Shrewsbury defence had to be at their best to keep hold of a point. If, for the rest of the month, Town had played like they did at the end of the Shrewsbury game, they would have been back up with the front-runners by early February. Unfortunately we only saw flashes of passion and the cause wasn't helped by the extended run of Tim Carter in goal. Carter was desperately out of form and the defence clearly had no confidence in him. It was rumoured that Martin was fit by mid-January, which leaves some possible question marks over the manager's decision to keep on playing Carter.

February was more of the same, although we thankfully saw the return of Lee Martin to the goalkeeping position. Martin's presence gave the defence a more solid look, but only one win from four league matches meant that Town slipped out of the play-off places. The Shaymen also bowed out of the Broken Windscreen Trophy at the quarter-final stage, when Rochdull won their 'home' tie 2-1 on the goalden goal rule. The game was switched to the

Shay after numerous attempts to stage the match at the ever-waterlogged cow field, commonly known as Spotland, were thwarted.

March proved to be a month of mixed fortunes. It started with an embarrassing defeat at Torquay, when a technically full-strength Town side were lucky to escape only conceding four goals against an overweight ex-international goalkeeper and a bunch of part-time teenagers. If Torquay was embarrassing, then the match at Swansea towards the end of the month was a real tonic. The Shaymen coped with the hostile atmosphere at the Vetch Field very well and fully deserved their three points, courtesy of goals from Jamie Murphy and local hero Jamie Paterson, who was playing his first game since a second hernia operation. The hostile atmosphere at the Vetch Field has to be seen to be believed. I have never seen such a well-fortressed away end, although I think it is there more for the visiting fans' own protection than anything else.

April provided us with a few surprises. Early in the evening of April 6, it was leaked to a local radio station that Kieran O'Regan and Andy May had been sacked. Later that evening a director who was part of the unanimous board decision denied this. However, the following day the sackings were confirmed. O'Regan was a very popular person at the Shay and his sacking sent shock waves reverberating throughout Calderdale and beyond. The quality of football played under O'Regan's stewardship had deteriorated somewhat throughout the season, and the club were beginning to feel the strain of running with a very small squad due to the failure to sign anyone on or around transfer deadline day. But as Town were still within a shout of the play-offs, most fans were extremely disappointed with the timing of the decision. Football's a funny old game - until you're dumped on.

With no permanent replacement in sight, the board turned to Dave Worthington to see out the season. Apart from asking George Mulhall to come back into the limelight, this was probably the only internal appointment the fans would have accepted. Worthington's tenure started with a 4-0 drubbing at Cambridge. After the game, thoughts of the play-offs were all but extinguished. But a good run, consisting of three wins and a draw, saw Town back in the play-off places. By the time relegation-haunted Scarborough came to the Shay for Town's last home game of the season, their destiny was almost in their own hands. A win against Scarborough and a win at Exeter would almost certainly have seen the Shaymen in the play-offs. Unfortunately two defeats gave Swansea the coveted seventh place, leaving Town five points off the pace in tenth position.

Now that the dust has settled, I think we can look back at last season and describe it as 'almost but not quite'. At the beginning we had a team who could match any in the division. However, boardroom unrest, management changes, the sale of 'Super Geoff' and a general inability to strengthen the squad, all played a part in ensuring that the mid-table mediocrity many fans would have secretly been happy with at the beginning of the season became reality as the proceedings came to a close.

Simon Denton

SHAYVEN HAVEN

Halifax Town

We're back... after five years of non-league oblivion, Town had managed to get themselves promoted to take their rightful place at the bottom of the Third Division... or were they?

The season started with everyone still high on the euphoria of promotion. But a bombshell was waiting. George Mulhall, who was to be the oldest manager in the Football League, moved aside and midfield leprechaun Kieran O'Regan stepped into his god-sized shoes, while George moved upstairs. Sir George had taken Town from near relegation from the Conference to the Football League in one year, and was rightly hailed as a living god.

NOW ON TELETEXT EVERY THURSDAY p178

SHAYVEN HAVEN

The Crazy World of Tim Carter

The Official Unofficial Fanzine of Halifax Town

In this exciting episode : Freddie the Fox, Mystic Megson, Hulmey makes a tackle (once again), and much, much more.....

This fanzine does not represent the official views of Halifax town AFC. This is not a match day programme. **Issue 4 Only £1!!!**

Whatever you want, we've got it...

This wasn't the only pre-season turmoil. Hometown boy Peter Butler had signed over the summer from West Brom and was rumoured to be refusing to play because of confusion over his promised coaching role.

This confusion continued all season, with the rumour mill working overtime (good for fanzine writers), but little response from the club, and particularly the chairman, Jim Brown. Jim is not a particularly popular figure at the Shay - being at the helm when Town went down and then moving on, only to reappear when Town were on the up.

All this aside, the prospect of revisiting old friends like Rochdale, Cardiff and Scunny filled the Town faithful with joy. Let's not joke about this: non-league football is hell - and you're never on the pools coupon. It has a few advantages, though, not least a tolerant attitude to alcohol and many interesting grounds next to cattle markets. After years of having to qualify for the first round of the FA Cup, we could be knocked out straight away without having to try to scrape a result at Nowhere United.

When Town got to the serious business of playing football, things went rather well. The first game ended with three points for us at Peterborough, who seem to have some of the politest hooligans going.

Posh hooli: "Fancy a rumble, lads?"

SH: "Er, no thanks."

Posh hooli: "OK, sorry to bother you."

This was followed by a win in the League Cup at Wrexham. All was going well. This good form carried on for a while, until the unthinkable happened: Super Geoffrey Horsfield, who had scored a hatful of goals in the promotion season, was surrounded by transfer rumours, and finally signed for Fulham for £300,000. To the neutral this might seem like a fair price for a striker who had yet to prove his worth in league football, but to the Shay masses it was worse than robbery (Torquay had sold a teenage 'keeper for £400,000 the previous week). Geoff was a hero for Town, and still is, and would be a hard act to replace. Most Fulham fans probably wouldn't have heard of Geoff when they signed him but ended the season chanting "Horsfield for England". Geoff finished the season Town's second highest scorer - and he left in October. If anything tells a tale, that does.

The money from the sale of Geoff, and televised games against Man City and Hartlepool, stuffed the coffers as they have never been stuffed before; so much so that Jim Brown declared we were one of the richest clubs in the lower leagues. The money came as a boost, and it was wisely spent tarting up the bar in the boardroom...

Town laboured with various striking partnerships over the rest of the season, none of them sparked: Lee Power, Justin Jackson, Marc Williams, and *SH*'s number one fan, Dave Hanson, all ploughed an honest furrow but without ever coming up with the goods. Someone joked if you took two stones off Lee Power and put it on Justin Jackson, you might end up with two decent players. Willo also put Town on the map when he became only the second Town player ever to represent his country at any level, when he set Wrexham alight for Wales B.

Town also struggled at the other end of the pitch. Lee Martin is a good goalkeeper but had problems with injuries all season, giving Tim Carter a shot between the sticks. I'd heard Tim was a good 'keeper in his day... that day was 15 October 1989. Before then, and since, he's been shit. It would be harsh to pin Town's failings on one player but Tim managed to throw the ball into the back of the net, and games with it. Town's undisputed goalkeeping hero of the season was midfield hardman Kevin Hulme, twice taking over in the pegs and keeping clean sheets both times.

Town hit the headlines mid-season (well, in the *Halifax Evening Courier* they did) when the game against Chester descended into a 21-man brawl in the middle of the pitch, when Kevin Hulme was attacked by a man in a kagoule and was promptly sent off, chasing Chester's Chris Priest down the tunnel. (Question: if Chester are so skint, why did they have 15 substitutes that day?)

The steam train began to slow down in the meantime, as we lost our 18-month unbeaten home record, to Cardiff. Town struggled to maintain consistent form all season with frustrating results. It might just be me, but we always seemed to be battling back from 2-0 down.

The other villain of the year was Town's mascot, Freddie the Fox. It's not personal (despite what he thinks) but I've never seen the point. I'm sure you're scratching your head thinking of a connection between Halifax and a fox - and to be quite honest there isn't one. Apparently, a couple of years ago, it was rumoured a fox was living in the Shay, but that's tenuous to say the least. On top of all this, though, he managed to lose a penalty shoot-out to a seagull at Scarborough. Since then we've found the perfect replacement. The Tod Shaymen (Tod or Todmorden is a sleepy backwater between Halifax and Burnley, which is populated by Burnley fans from Yorkshire and a few honest Town fans) discovered Pork Pie Man. What better example of true Yorkshire grit than a man made from pork pies representing the Shaymen.

Town season ended in confusion and acrimony. Kieran O'Regan, who had steered an uncertain course all season and had managed to bundle Town into the play-off places, was duly sacked. The timing was bizarre. Seven games from the end of the season, in the play-offs, and you sack your manager. I'm not saying it was the wrong decision - just the wrong time. Kieran was great servant to Town as a player and as an assistant to George Mulhall in the Conference promotion season. On his own, things didn't quite work out, even with the help of tactical genius Andy May.

Dave Worthington (brother of the legendary Frank) stepped into Kieran's boots. Dave didn't have a lot of management experience, despite taking Shelf United down, but bravely took Town to Cambridge and promptly got stuffed 4-0. Anyone who fancied travelling down to Mansfield must have been mad... so off I trotted and witnessed a battling performance to send us back into the play-offs, and those Twin Towers were looming. There are now only ten sides who have never been to Wembley. I hope and pray we won't be the last, but you have to accept that it's inevitable.

The run-in was highs and lows. A win over Brighton (are all their fans left-wing radicals with beards?), who wanted a pitch invasion to protest the sacking of Keiran, which was met by the usual apathy of Town fans. Next, the *SH* awayday to Chester ended in a 2-2 draw, and things were starting to look shaky again, before being followed by a win over Scunny. The unthinkable happened next - a home defeat by Scarborough (the team who were finally relegated managed the Double over us) finally put the mockers on thoughts of Wembley, as we had to win at Exeter and other results go our way. In the end it wasn't to be. We lost at St James' Park and that was it. We finally finished tenth and had to settle for another season in the absurd Third. (It couldn't even be brightened by welcoming Burnley to the bottom flight, as they evaded relegation yet again.)

Was it a bad season, though? Before it kicked off, most Town fans would have settled for tenth place. But over the course of the season, we know that we threw it away. Jim Brown and others said that we should be happy, and anyway look where we were only twelve months ago. The last good thing you did should measure success. The last great thing Town did was top the Third Division but failed to capitalise. Poor home form, silly results, and a negative stance from management (too cautious) and the board (the men in black - bank account defenders) meant that it wasn't to be.

Matt Blackburn

SHRIMP SEASON

Southend United

Deja-vu 2: "Nellie the Elephant packed his trunk and said hello to The Cricketers!"

White Elephant - 1) a rare albino variety of the Indian elephant, regarded as sacred in parts of South Asia; 2) a possession that is unwanted by its owner; 3) a rare or valuable possession, the upkeep of which is very expensive. OK, that's the *New Collins Concise Dictionary* version of a Southend United manager, it seems. More so in the last couple of seasons. Poor old Chipmunk - Alvin Martin - had lost his nuts as well as his sense of direction. When we meant 'up', he meant 'down'. He told us we would be in the play-offs by Christmas, but we knew better; it was all OUR fault anyway.

Yes, it almost happened again. That dreaded word 'relegation' hovered over OUR beloved Roots Hall for a third successive season just like Death with his scythe waiting for the inevitable to happen, but as in all good horror movies there is a saviour who rescues the day. But a little (excuse the pun) more of that later.

After a second successive relegation at the end of the '97-98 season, Southend United supporters' belief in Chipmunk seemed to have been rewarded, as this season saw us start with four straight victories.

It began with a trip to the highly-rated Scarborough, who had a certain Anton Johnson sitting in the wings. (You didn't listen did you, Scarborough? There is no such thing as a butcher on a white charger.) We were off to a good start in the league and it included knocking Gillingham out of the Worthington Cup over two legs. More new faces were brought in. (No excuses, Chipmunk, they were your men this time.)

So we thought... maybe Chipmunk has got it right. They were not convincing victories, but they were victories. This was followed by boring draws and games where we dominated but ended in defeat. Those feelings of deja-vu again!

When we went to Coventry in the Worthington Cup in the middle of September, we were in eighth place in the table, with everything looking rosy, and OUR bets we had on us winning promotion looked safe. OUR display at Coventry was pure class, as we took the game to OUR Premiership opponents. But what, in the end, would prove to be Chipmunk's downfall was OUR inability to score goals. At the risk of repeating OURselves (something that Chipmunk was also good at), there were many classic examples of us dominating a team from start to finish but ending up on the losing side. This was simply due to the fact that we could not put the ball into the onion bag.

We could not carry on where we had left off in the Worthington Cup tie at Coventry and were dumped out of the competition 4-0 at Roots Hall, 5-0 on aggregate. So much for cup success. So please don't mention Doncaster...

Many draws and losses followed. By this time we'd had enough, and the first signs of OUR frustration came in the home game against Mansfield. We were a goal up but proceeded to lose 2-1. And, as the second goal went in, the "Martin out" chants went up again. Things really came to a head against Conference side Doncaster Rovers in the FA Cup. The game was on the back of two defeats against Exeter and Brentford, when we felt it could not get worse. It did. It was after the Exeter game when Martin said: "If we are not in a play-off position by Christmas, then I will review my position." We could have played all afternoon and still not scored against Doncaster. Still, Martin hung on to his position, despite OUR protests.

By this time, Uncle Vic Jobson had accepted an offer he couldn't refuse and John 'Passion Man' Main took over as chairman with Martin Dawn plc in overall control. It seems that OUR new owners had given Chipmunk their full backing. But, as with most playground romances, it was to end in tears (literally). They gave him money to buy players, something that had been unheard of in the last two seasons of Uncle Vic's reign. Chipmunk also brought in a few loan signings to plug the ever-increasing gaps in OUR defence and bolster OUR ammo for the shots on OUR opponent's goal. Even with this injection of new players, results did not improve. As they say, it's all about management style. Chipmunk's style was to play pretty football. He thought he was still with the Hamsters and not in Division Three. A defeat by Barnet, in what was Roots Hall's 1000th league match, didn't help Chipmunk's now precarious position. Subsequent defeats against Torquay, Shrewsbury, Carlisle, Halifax, Cambridge and Darlington saw us perilously close to OUR third relegation in a row. Those feelings of deja-vu again!

So it was... *Et Tu Bruté...* beware the Ides of March, Chipmunk. Nevertheless, a sixth home defeat of the season, to a Hull side who had previously been rock bottom of the league and heading for the Conference, was the final straw. It saw many of us demonstrating after the game. So it came of no surprise that Chipmunk's resignation was announced by a tearful John Main to a not so tearful group of supporters. It seems that Chipmunk was a man of his word. But three months too late.

The next game was against Rochdale, with Micky Gooding in charge. It was the same old story. A lacklustre display and another defeat. Poor old Mick lasted only one game and it seems OUR next manager had been watching it anyway. By then OUR saviour was on his way down the A1. It was The Yorkie Man himself, Alan Little, OUR former player (and brother of the not-so-famous Brian.)

Little's first game in charge was a tough game away to promotion-chasing Orient. His signing prompted over a thousand of us to travel to Brisbane Road. The atmosphere amongst OUR supporters and the players was in complete contrast to the previous weeks and months. It seemed that the new messiah had arrived in the East (London), as Orient were stuffed 3-0. Or had he? Everybody was brought back down to earth, as the next three home matches were defeats. This would continue to be the theme until the end of the season. Home defeats, but superb performances on the road seeing us eventually escape the dreaded drop into non-league obscurity.

So the final curtain came down on another disappointing Roots Hall season. With Alan Little in charge and a new-found confidence amongst OUR players, it's those feelings of deja-vu again.

So, as per usual, as far as we are concerned, the future looks bright. With two of OUR players being picked for the Republic of Ireland, and with the reserve team back in place next season, things can only get better. Let's hope so.

Ian Kemp

Source: Moulin Rouge

SHRIMPERLERO

Southend United

Two Hundred Streets Under The Sky

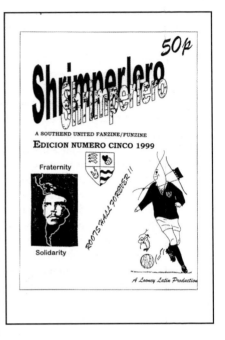

Crumpled crisp packets lie empty. Beer glasses, encrusted with rings of froth, await collection. Ashtrays are close to over-spilling with stubbed out ciggies. Twenty minutes to kick-off. Just around the corner, down the road, there are battleship grey stands and four floodlight pylons. We are in a football paradise. It is called Roots Hall, home of Southend United. In the Golden Lion pub, Hartlepool and Southend fans mix happily in a relaxed atmosphere. There is no tension. Both clubs had avoided falling through the Conference trapdoor. It is the last game of the season.

Roots Hall, built by and for supporters and the community in 1955, will not be the Shrimper's home for much longer. The ground is being sold, a sacrifice on the altar of market forces and the unacceptable face of capitalism that represents professional football in these credit card, 24-hour society, pre-Millennium days. This spiritual home of Southend United FC stands in the parish of Prittlewell, a little suburb with grids of neat and not-so-neat terraced houses and bungalows, interspersed with the odd sub-post office, newsagents and corner shop not yet put out of business by the multi-national supermarkets encroaching the environs of Southend. From whatever direction you approach the ground, you can see the proud spires of the twelfth-century Church of St Mary share the skyline with the tall floodlight pylons that peep above the rooftops. The floodlights stand out like beacons, beckoning the faithful to the Saturday ritual. The faithful? Around three to four thousand on average. Boxing Days excepted of course. The area around the ground is a little untidy. An obsolete hotel, an obligatory charity shop, some boarded up shop fronts, graffiti-free! There is a legendary chip shop and two traditional pubs. On match days there is a resigned atmosphere. There have been better times. Perhaps you can hear echoes of glorious moments. A snow-covered Roots Hall in January 1978, where only desperate defending by Emlyn Hughes and the brilliant goalkeeping of Ray Clemence prevented Southend knocking

Liverpool out of the FA Cup. The classic Rumbelows Cup tie with Spurs, when we ran out 3-2 winners on the night, but lost on the away-goal rule.

Andy Warhol once said that everyone should enjoy 15 minutes of fame. In football terms, Southend's moment probably came on 4 May 1991 at Gigg Lane, Bury, when Blues striker Ian Benjamin slammed home the goal that sent Southend into the old Division Two for the first time in their modest history. The yo-yo existence of life between the old Divisions Three and Four had been exorcised. Under manager Dave Webb, we had at last seemed to have stability and confidence. Heady, halcyon days when, for a few hours on 1 January 1992, we led the Division Two table after tonking Newcastle 4-0 at Roots Hall. Was it really ten years ago that Dave Crown and Gary Bennett were banging in goals from every angle? The bone-crunching tackles of Peter Butler and Dave Martin that made Ince and Keane look like blushing choirboys at a Black Mass? The silky skills of Andy Ansah and Steve Tilson? Brett Angell hovering in the air like a giant bird of prey before powering home an unstoppable header? Dave Webb departed under acrimonious circumstances and we had to put up with a negative and sterile system of play under Colin Murphy. Murphy's reign was only relieved by the arrival of a dusky colossus called Stanley Collymore. The North Bank heaved in delirium as Stan scythed his way through opposition defences with awesome power and skill.

Collymore's goals could not save Murphy's job, and Blues chairman Vic Jobson rescued Barry Fry from the Stan Flashman-induced nightmare at Barnet. Fry gave Southend a short but sweet period of attacking and exciting football. Collymore had been sold to Forest for over £2m, with add-on clauses. Fry brought in Jon Hunt, Dereyk Payne and the Black Maradona, Ricky Otto, a winger from Orient, with a veritable magic box of football tricks and pace. Otto - a wizard and a true star. Then big dollars at Brum lured Fry and his backroom staff to St Andrews. The squad he left behind were in great shape as ex-Shrimper Peter Taylor took over. Things began to go wrong. Perhaps it was the hangover of Fry's defection. Quality players were being sold and not replaced. Taylor lasted 18 months, and towards the end of season 94/95, Blues were staring relegation in the face. Steve Thompson came in to steady a rocking boat and a sudden surge of goals (and form) from Gary Jones saved the day. Unable to accept terms from Vic Jobson, Thompson decided to jump ship and join ex-manager Colin Murphy at Notts County. The popular Ronnie Whelan stepped up as player-manager. Behind the scenes the financial state of the club was bad. The money from the Collymore deal had enabled the club to purchase its own training complex and adjacent night club, but getting top quality players to come to Roots Hall was getting more and more difficult. However, Whelan's influence helped Mike Marsh and Paul Byrne join what was still a reasonable squad.

The Bosman ruling and subsequent restricted transfer market hit hard and Southend, like many teams with limited resources, found the going tough. We were in trouble, and the end of season 96-97 saw us relegated from Division

One as bottom club. Whelan left, claiming he was still owed money from his outstanding contract. Alvin Martin, ex-West Ham stalwart and Leyton Orient coach, was appointed new manager. Morale was low, as was skill and motivation. The reserve side had been sacrificed in a cost-cutting exercise. There was no money for new players, and some existing players were still on long contracts, with Division One wages. Alvin Martin had to rely on free transfers and short-term loan signings. We knew by February 1998 that relegation to Division Three was inevitable, and the under-achieving players obliged by finishing bottom of their division for the second year in succession. During the close season, chairman Vic Jobson agreed to sell his majority shareholding to Martin Dawn plc, a local firm of property developers. New chairman John Main assured fans that the club was in safe hands, although in the long-term the club must sell Roots Hall to help fund a new stadium and commercial facilities situated, hopefully, near the club's training complex.

This season started in fine style. We had managed to buy defender Rob Newman from Norwich, and attacking midfielder Alex Burns arrived on a Bosman from Dutch club, Heracles. Four wins on the trot and a great display at Highfield Road against Coventry in the Worthington Cup had the fans happy for a change. Had the tide finally turned? Apparently not, as bad habits began to resurface and gnaw away like an old nagging toothache. On an October evening, in a miserable display against Mansfield at Roots Hall, the chants of "We want Martin out!" cascaded around the ground. Funds had been made available by the new board, and Martin invested £90,000 in Manchester City's Barry Conlon, a striker, and defender Dave Morley for £10,000. It did not get any better, and perhaps the 0-1 defeat by Donny Rovers in the FA Cup First Round was the beginning of the end for Alvin Martin. Donny were bottom of the Conference at the time and played Southend off the park. Another striker, Neil Campbell, who could not get into a struggling Scarborough side, was bought for £10,000. Results continued to be patchy, and Alvin kept the players locked in the dressing-room for inquests over defeats on a regular basis. We were in free-fall.

Then came the Ides of March. We were told by Martin Dawn plc that the club were nearly £4m in debt. Creditors included the Inland Revenue and Customs & Excise. The club had just lost a legal battle with ex-manager Colin Murphy over unpaid commission on the Collymore transfer deal. The club could not (or would not) pay up the insurance on the injury that wrecked former player Mike Lapper's career. Roots Hall had to be sold and the club pay a rent of £400,000 per annum over the next four years. Planning applications would now have to be prepared for submission to the Council for a new stadium. The club has no security of tenure, so technically we are homeless as well as insolvent.

After a pathetic 1-0 home defeat by fellow strugglers Hull City, the final nail in Alvin Martin's coffin was hammered home. Alvin resigned within an hour of the final whistle. Assistant player/coach, Mick Gooding, took over for the following Tuesday's game at Rochdale. Another 1-0 defeat and the club were at their lowest ebb for well over a decade. Returning home from Spotland and walking home along the silent, deserted streets of Prittlewell at 3.00am, we realised that the door to the Conference was creaking open wider and wider. Within days John Main appointed ex-York City boss Alan Little as manager. Perversely, our away form, so abysmal over the last two years, improved beyond recognition. Home form was still non-existent, but with the inspiration of Lee Hodges, on loan from West Ham, we won three and drew one of our remaining four away fixtures. Hodges became our very own Ariel Ortega and with 'keeper Mel Capleton doing a reasonable impersonation of Pat Jennings, we clawed our way to safety.

So as we walk down to the familiar turnstiles and take our place in the usual seat, we can enjoy the final game of the season against Hartlepool. During the summer, we will walk along the pier with our 'kiss me quick' gas masks, candy-floss glued to our cheeks and toffee-apples stuck to our teeth, safe in the knowledge that our league status is intact, our reserve team reinstated, and that hopefully a Lib-Labour Council will look favourably on plans for a new stadium. Hope springs eternal in Shrimpland.

'Argentine' Pete Hanscomb

Source: Spitting Feathers

SKY BLUE ARMY

Coventry City

If enthusiasm was dynamite, then this season hardly generated enough to blow the gruff nuts off my backside. After last season's eleventh place and quarter-final of the cup, we had great expectations for this year. But as usual with Coventry City, where there's expectation there's disappointment.

There were highs, like shitting on the Villa and dumping Leicester out of the cup, but there were far more lows and a fair sprinkling of mediocrity. We started OK with our second opening-day win on the trot over Chelsea and we finished OK with a fine display against Leeds. But unfortunately we had to endure too much dross in the middle. Could a season in which we beat (sorry, thrashed) the Villa be so bad, or was I just too pissed to remember all the good bits?

S.B.A.

Sky Blue Army Fanzine.

It's huge I tell ya... huge man !

Gordon Strachan having just seen Dion's pay packet.

ISSUE 55

Sky Blues v Arsenal Saturday 31st October 1998.

£1

Well here's the A-Z of a Coventry fan's season.

Annihilations, Atrocities and Johnny Aloisi: Like lambs to the slaughter came Macclesfield in the FA Cup Third Round. To be fair, they weren't as bad as the 7-0 score-line suggested (bullshit - of course they were; they were crap), but these are the sort of games that us Coventry fans have learnt never to take for granted. Remember Sutton, Northampton, etc? So it's always nice when we can go into smug mode for a change. As the seventh hit the back of the net, we were all feeling pretty pleased with ourselves... well, nearly all. 'Brave Sir Tomo' was actually pretty pissed off. He had Froggatt to score the first (which he did) and us to win 6-0. Ain't life a bitch?

On the receiving end, we only conceded more than two goals twice all season - both against Newcastle, 1-5 and 4-1. Of course we were far better than the score-lines suggested - but we never recovered from taking the lead in both games!

At one stage we had the top-scorer in the Premiership, in Johnny Aloisi. Admittedly they were all for Portsmouth - although he did score on his debut, coming on to equalise against Spurs. He finished the season with 22 (five for us), not exactly living up to expectations, although I won't hear a bad word said about him since he scored two of the goals that helped us beat (sorry, stuff) the Villa. That alone was worth the £650,000 we paid for him.

Bye Bye Blackburn and Brave Sir Tomo: It was a long time coming - November 7 to be precise - but we secured our first away victory at Blackburn... and typically it was the first game I missed. We had a disappointing draw with them at our place, but the four points we took off them was enough to make sure it was Blackburn, not us, who took the dreaded drop.

Now your probably asking yourself, "Who the fuck is 'Brave Sir Tomo'?" Well, last year we had a minor run-in with some Tottenham boys. Tomo was conspicuous by his absence, walking so close to the wall that he left skid-marks. So this year we unveiled a plaque for him on the said wall, down the side of the Spurs ground. It read something like: "Here forever lies a piece of Brave Sir Tomo's arm - lost in action 15th April 1997." Most of the Spurs fans wondered what we were doing, but it was still there at the end of the game and had a steady flow of admirers.

Come-backs, Clean Sheets and Cheeky little Cockney Chappies: In general terms, once we went behind, we stayed behind. Only against Charlton did we actually manage to come back from a goal down to win, and that was only because we had one of our players sent off.

We kept seven clean sheets all season - our worse record since '83-84 - which may give some indication where our problems lay; although, individually, our defenders all had a reasonable season.

Our record against London sides read P12 W3 D4 L5. Beating Chelsea in the first game of the season was the most memorable, especially seeing that they didn't lose another game until about February. Then again, we hardly won one.

Mine's a Double: Thank you Sheffield Wednesday, since you were the only team we did the double over this season, Dublin scoring with his unfeasible large knob at Highfield Road, and Macca and Whelan scoring in Yorkshire. As for doubles against us, thank you Arsenal, Man United and Newcastle.

Everton: Having comprehensively outclassed Everton in a 3-0 beating at Highfield Road, we went to Goodison with high expectations and a huge following in the fifth round of the cup. This was the low of the season, as we simply did not perform, and lost 2-1. Since our league position suggested we were no better than Everton, we had no right to expect to beat them. But we did. There was, therefore, a huge cloud of despair coming back down the M6. Just to rub our noses in it, they also beat us 2-0 in the league a few weeks later, which well and truly kept us in the mire.

FA Cup escapades: It doesn't matter how bad we are doing in the league, we always have high hopes (often unfounded) in the cup. Having disposed of Macclesfield 7-0, then came the other high point of the season, when we beat (no, trounced) the sad bastards from up the M69, 3-0. Although the ground's a dump - with one stand the size of a planet, the rest straight out of a subuteo box - the atmosphere at Filbert Street is always intense. Having fucked up our own ticket arrangements, we ended up in the Jupiter stand. It was hard up our own ticket arrangements, we ended up in the Jupiter stand. It was hard work not standing up and shouting "Stick that up your country bumpkin arses, you simple Leicester folk" as Whelan, Froggatt and Telfer took it in turns to stick the ball in the back of the net. The game itself was a classic cup-tie, with us down to ten men after George Boateng had been sent off, them missing a penalty, and then us hitting them on the break as they laid siege to our goal. Cracking stuff.

After this euphoria, the Everton game was a huge disappointment.

Georgie Boy: Although hugely talented and a snip at £250,000, George Boateng's season was somewhat disappointing. He managed to go missing in too many games - although I will not hear a bad word said about him, since he scored two of the goals that helped beat (sorry, crush) Villa 4-1.

Mad Hatters and Hedman: The other major low of the year was our Worthington Cup exit at Luton. Dublin had decided he didn't wish to play because of his pending move to the Scum, so the rest of them decided to come out in sympathy. We were a disaster and the chants of "You're not fit to wear the shirt" were well warranted. The biggest joke was that we still had to pay Judas, since Strachan's attempts to stop his wages were overturned by the PFA.

One plus of the season was the form of Magnus Hedman. The Swede is class - and now has only 3,401 games to go to beat Oggy's appearance record.

Iffy Hair Cuts: There can be few worse haircuts than Richard Shaw's cow pat surprise. Fortunately the fact that his mop looks like an explosion in a cushion factory hasn't effected his game. He was brilliant and, hence, voted our 'player of the season'.

Jinger Jocks and Judas: You might think that after such a poor season, the daggers would be out for Strachan. But not so. I just wish a few more of the players could show the same passion on the pitch as Strach does on the touchline. The way Dublin orchestrated his leaving hardly adhered him to the Coventry fans - needless to say we gave him a huge amount of grief when we played at Villa Park, which was made all the sweeter with us beating (no, demolishing) them 4-1.

His departure was messy and with him scoring goals at will and Villa sitting at the top of the league, it looked like all our nightmares had come true. So, there was only one thing for it - I transferred Dublin into my *Sun* dream team. Result - he hardly scores another goal and Villa go down quicker than Monica Lewinski in a cigar factory. Since I have this knack of giving the kiss of death to any player I have in my team, next year I'm going to have a team full of Villa and Leicester half-wits.

Mighty Mo Konjic: Although he only played a couple of games, this guy could be massive. Well, actually he already is. At 8' 6" and 24 stone, he will hopefully scare a few strikers shitless next season.

Limp-wristed Linesmen: We were denied getting anything off the Villa at Highfield Road by a limp-wristed linesman. Merson was so far offside, it was obscene. The linesman said he was "sorry" - but, as Strachan put it, "Sorry, doesn't keep you in a job."

Macca's Miracle: Although the jury is still out on Gary McAllister, his form after coming back from injury was drastically improved and instead of groans of frustration he actually got a standing ovation at Sheffield Wednesday.

Our 'other' Macca is Gary McSheffrey. By coming on at Villa, at 16 he became the youngest-ever player to play for the Sky Blues (shame he didn't actually touch the ball) and he actually made the bench for a couple of England U-21 games. Not bad for a kid.

Mr Nice Guy Roland Nilsson: Although his career with Coventry was pretty short, Roland Nilsson will probably go down as one of the best full-backs we've ever had. He is class. Sadly he decided to call it a day and has retired to play out his days in Sweden.

Open Goals: A goalless draw at Derby secured our Premiership safety. This was somewhat a luxury as far as Coventry fans are concerned, since we still had a whole game to go. It was secured thanks to an horrendous goal-line miss in the dying seconds by 'You've only got Wan Chop'.

Piss ups and parties: As far as piss-ups are concerned, the cups have been kind to us in recent years, with seaside trips to Blackpool, Scarborough, Plymouth, Hull (Hornsea), Gillingham (Herne Bay). So before the Worthington Cup draw was even made, we had decided that we wanted a jolly boys' outing to Southend.

And Southend it was. Needless to say it didn't disappoint, although some of the pubs were straight out of the *Twilight Zone*. One on the front was full of some very strange characters indeed. I think just about every alky and loony in Southend used it for their local. One guy, who was slumped unconscious in the corner yet still hanging on to his pint for dear life, unwittingly became the entertainment for the next half-hour. His bald head was just perfect for target practice, with extra points if you could bounce nuts off his head and into his pint. Unfortunately, this game was brought to an abrupt end when he sat up with a jolt, took a swig of his beer, and then threw up all over himself . It was time to leave. For once, the team didn't manage to ruin the day out and we won 4-0. Just to give you some idea how pissed we were, we spent half of the following Saturday arguing what colour kit we had played in.

Quiet days out: As well as the quiet day at Southend, we also went on the razzle in St Albans for another all-dayer before the Luton game. With a coachload of us wearing halloween masks, goodness knows what the locals made of us. The day was ruined by the news that Dublin was going and the subsequent arguments on who should replace him. The day was ruined even further with a totally inept performance on the pitch.

Red Cards and wanky Referees: Although Mr Strachan had his fair share of run-ins with the normal bunch of 'shit for brains' referees, we actually had to thank them for our two sendings-off this season. Firstly Georgie Boateng at Leicester, which inspired us to beat them 3-0, and then John Aloisi, whose sending off against Charlton totally transformed the game in our favour. A goal down and playing crap, we suddenly looked like world-beaters once he had got his marching orders. This was a vital win, since Charlton were above us in the league at the time. Maybe we should play all our games with ten men.

Staying Up: The biggest revelation of the season came from a book called *Staying Up*, a behind-the-scenes diary of a season with Coventry City. The revelation? That Dublin has a pork sausage the size of an elephant's trunk! You have to take your hat (or helmet) off when you consider the extra weight he's been carrying. Apparently, he does well not to keep standing on the thing.

Unlucky Thirteen and Thirty-Nine steps: To emphasise the point of a crap season, the 13 away defeats was our worst-ever in the Premiership, as was the 39 goals we scored, the lowest since 1991.

Under-21's: There was some success at the club. The U-21s, with McSheffrey firing the bullets, got to the FA Youth Cup Final. The first time since we won it in 1987. Admittedly we got hammered by the Hammers in the final, but it was still a worthy achievement.

Villa Park Hoodoo: What fucking Villa Park Hoodoo?

Naughty Noel Whelan: Having missed a fair bit of last season by having an altercation with a shop window, he was at it again. This time managing to get two barrels of shit kicked out of him for getting involved with a West Brom player's sister at a party in Derby, or was it a Derby player's brother at a party in West Brom? I get confused. He's not exactly Mr Sensible - but having said that, he's still class and finished our top scorer with 13 goals.

X marks the spot: In all we had ten drawn games, of which four were 0-0. Six were against the same teams, drawing home and away against Leicester, Derby and Spurs.

Yokel Derbies (Sorry, I'm getting a bit desperate): We played played nine, won three, lost two and drew four. Beating Forest 4-0 was pleasing and the 3-0 victory at Leicester was awesome, but the one that mattered came on Saturday 27 February 1999, when we beat (sorry, annihilated) the Villa 4-1 to secure our first-ever league win at Villa Park.

ZZZZZZZ's: So has this season really sent us all to sleep? Well to be honest, yes. The sad thing is that we've had our best average attendance since 1978/79.

But then again we did beat (sorry, shit on) the Villa.
David Rose

SON OF A REF

Scunthorpe United

Now My Heart Is Full

It's Saturday 29 May 1999, 3.07pm, and Spanish midfielder Alex Calvo-Garcia has just scored the most significant goal in 15 years for Scunthorpe United. I am drunk and upside down across the lap of someone I don't know, two rows in front of the seat from which I had leapt when Garcia's beautiful Basque forehead connected so perfectly with the ball.

Considering 1992's Wembley defeat on penalties, United finished the season with promotion by the best route possible - a play-off final victory in the (ahem) national showpiece stadium. It really didn't matter that

our opponents were Leyton Orient - it could have been Brazil, or Manchester United, or Arsenal, or France. We would have beaten anyone. We were there en masse as a town to exorcise ghosts and move inexorably forward through to the next chapter of our history book. Calvo-Garcia ensured there would be a gold-embossed leaf or two dedicated to him.

At about 4.50 on the same afternoon, I turned round and hugged the hardest men in Scunthorpe. We stood in each other's arms and wept like babies, huddled together in brilliant release from 15 years of frustrating underachievement. When the referee blew that shrill final whistle, it might as well have been an angel's trumpet, its sound was that sweet. It fanfared in a new era and played the last post for an old one. I sat back down for a few brief seconds, still in tears, and a whole bunch of dark years flashed before my eyes in an intense burst. In tandem came vivid glimpses of a bright future. This was undeniably the defining moment of the year.

Scunthorpe United had been stuck in the basement division of the Football League for my entire adult life. I was only just a shaver, and a scantly necessary one at that, the last time they tasted success, and finding out what all the fuss was about as far as women were concerned was still three years away for me. I had yet to leave comprehensive school, yet to taste my first pint on its way down and its way up, and had yet to decide what I wanted to do with the rest of my life. I really didn't know until this last year.

It was one of those incredibly long and winding years. One of those that carries a tense and almost tangible - there's no other word to describe it - "magic" in the air. One of those years when you really get down to business. It was make or break time, time to move on, or stay still forever - and hell, didn't we move on? Didn't we just have a time? The *best* time?

I began last year's SOTF contribution with an appropriate quote from Nick Hornby's *Fever Pitch*, and so I make no excuses for including one this time round. As the summer of 1998 began, I nervously started to implement plans for my future, and for the following nine months my confidence was buoyed along by the success of the team I spend so much time thinking about. There were two significant victories come the end of the season: "It was if I jumped on to the shoulders of the team, and they carried me into the light that shone down on all of us." In truth, I always had the sneaking suspicion that this year would be the year that both myself and Scunthorpe United would show what we were truly made of.

It started well, everyone operating on a clearheaded level, with me trying to stop the personal rot by tentatively, but optimistically, enrolling as a mature student on a local college film course, and United manager Brian Laws quietly, assuredly, understating his belief that we would get promoted. See, for years United managers seemed content to aim for mid-table status, with the play-offs - should we find ourselves in them come judgement day - a happy bonus. Laws, however, believed that we would be in them as the absolute minimum peak of our achievements. What a refreshingly positive attitude - but what was more refreshing was that, as the early weeks of the season peeled away, it was clear for all to see that he had actually built a team who were, indeed, capable of achieving promotion through either of the two routes. Whether we gathered enough points to go up automatically, or through the only real national lottery, would surely come down to pure luck over a few results.

By the final Saturday in September, United sat two points clear at the top of the table, and my stepfather's sixtieth birthday party that same night was a real blast. I breezed through it, cap at a jaunty angle and smile burning brightly, putting away my trademark Lloyd Cole frown and self-consciousness, opting instead (as if you have a choice when you're top of the table!) for a Robbie Williams grin and an air of confidence. A very rich local businessman was engaged in friendly conversation, and pressed as to how he could cope with the dishonour of spending so much money on very expensive cigars (I think I called them "turds", actually) when he hadn't invested money in the club he claimed to support. He was left hiding away in a corner, shamefaced and apologetic.

College work began to really pile up, and for a few months I was an underpaid slave to my computer, knocking out a script for a short autobiographical documentary I had to make as part of my college course. It was bloody hard work, and my lungs took a severe hammering from the cigarettes, but somehow I did it. There was a bit about the moon landing in 1969, the year I was born, and a bit about the traditional mini-crisis at turning

30 and some about moving forward into further education. I called it *Small Steps & Giant Leaps* because I had a feeling it was to be a year of both.

Though the documentary had nothing to do with football, I'd wanted to imbue it with the sense of optimism and determination on weekly display down at Glanford Park; an optimism and determination that was rubbing off on me so strongly. I wanted people who saw the piece when finished (and doubtlessly myself also) to realise that I too could be a winner, an achiever, a person who could say what he was intending to do, however ambitious; and unlikely as it might sound, then be a deliverer. Work, work, work... win, win, win... Although film-making was a process of which I remained unsure with regards to my own ability and progress for a long, long while, I guess I figured that if I began and then completed my project with the earnest Brian Laws' ethic of working hard to get things dead right every step of the way, then there was a strong likelihood I would be successful in my endeavours.

I'd think a lot about Brian Laws as I worked on my project. I'd think about how dedicated he was to his job, about how seriously he thought through the minute details, about how much care and attention he put into it all. He was my role-model, if you want to put it that way, for the duration of my course. Silly? I dunno. When you've a reputation as an underachiever, and you then turn a corner on your own stagnation, then it's just like that, sometimes, isn't it? You need to believe in something else as well as yourself. Maybe so that, if you fail, you don't have to feel totally culpable. Or if you succeed, you don't have to cope alone with the equally scary prospect of success.

Well, whatever. Good results came and went (as did some bad ones), but United and me... well, we were consistent in that our overall determination and commitment never dampened. Spirits flagged occasionally, but only in a very small way, because we had toiled and toiled and built ourselves up; and belief had finally begun to rush in. Brian Laws occasionally blew his top at the poor standard of refereeing (and, by God, it was sometimes very poor indeed) on display during seemingly every other game United played, and I skipped the occasional lecture to lazily drink cheap coffee in the refectory. There are no real parallels between the two activities, other than the fact that this was about as dark and negative as it got all year. Mostly, things just ticked over week by week in that determined and positive way. United played like they knew they could finally get out of the dungeon, and I began to think that I maybe did know what I was doing, film-making-wise.

By Easter I had all my filming and a portion of editing complete, and United looked to be strong contenders for fourth spot in Division Three, possibly pushing up into third place if they could edge themselves into a strong, late burst. It wasn't to be: Whitney Houston summed it all up, away at Halifax on the Tuesday night that sealed our place as play-off participants. We stood on a cold terrace and she put her arms round us and sang "It's not right, but it's okay..." as the team trudged off, beaten 1-0. Only two or three better results over the past few months and we would have gone up automatically. But not to panic - for the first time in many long and miserable years we still had the opportunity to achieve something.

The play-off semi-finals saw us face Swansea, right around the time that I had to hand in the final edit of my documentary. It was a nervous period all round, and worry beads would have been put to use, had I any, following the 1-0 defeat away to the Welsh club. Swansea certainly offered nothing United couldn't handle, but we had failed so many times at this stage of the play-offs that it wasn't easy to deny the negative aspects of our history as they crept into our minds.

Three days later, on the greatest night at Glanford Park, self-doubt was blown completely out of the water. We cancelled out the one-goal deficit as early as the second minute, with a blistering edge-of-the box strike from the recently-signed full-back Andy Dawson - a player so young and already so assured that he looks like being one of Scunthorpe's all-time greats. This was the perfect start, but what was to follow was the highest drama indeed. An 18-year-old local boy called Gareth Sheldon, who had made only a handful of appearances before this night, was put on as a late substitute and scored within a couple of minutes of the start of extra-time. United fans couldn't believe their eyes, and Sheldon must have thought this was the best moment of his career. Not so... Swansea equalised after a defensive melee, and it looked as though we were on the decline, while the Swans were going to win through in their second wind. Not so... The incredible Dawson tirelessly burst up the wing, just as we'd seen him do many times before, and the ebullient Sheldon, as we *hadn't* had the chance to see him do many times before, turned in a low cross with all the measured precision of your Owen or your Shearer. What an incredible goal, somehow perfectly summing up the youthful drive and never-say-die attitude of this season's United side. This, surely, was the greatest moment of Sheldon's fledgling career? Not so...

Somewhere in the midst of all this, United's powerhouse midfielder/striker John Eyre contrived to get himself sent off, and therefore suspended should we win out and reach Wembley. On the night of the semi-final victory this seemed little more than a minor irritation, but when we did finally win out, and as the hysteria died down over the following week, it became clear that it was much more. Eyre had signed for us four years previously after a successful loan period (about a million goals in one game) but had failed to fit into any of the previous manager's gameplans with the ease or respect that his excess of real talent deserved. Brian Laws put this right by giving him a sort of free-reign, with special detail to be paid to attacking teams down the right. Eyre repaid his manager's faith by turning in one of the best individual seasons I've ever seen from a Scunthorpe player. So many of our goals this season came from Eyre runs, crosses, dinks and drives, that Wembley without him began to seem daunting.

On the day, Laws pleasingly picked the obvious replacement to deputise, and in the seventh minute the greatest moment of Sheldon's career finally arrived. He performed trickery of which the entire Magicians Union would be envious from one so young, stopping just short of chopping the Orient defender in half in the box. He crossed, and Alex Calvo-Garcia made 12,500 Scunthorpe people jump for joy.

Isn't that where we came in? Yes. We've gone full circle, and in little under two thousand simple words I've tried to explain the season for you. I've given it a bloody good go, but I know that really I've failed. There are actually no words yet created which are adequate enough to describe the depth and breadth of the brilliance of it. Even the poor results (0-5 away to Plymouth, or a 'B minus' for a tossed-off essay about *The Crying Game*) seem great. So, as you can see, perspectives have not, and probably will not, be regained for a very long time. If you drop me a line in about 40 years time, I might just be able to string a few decent, rational sentences together about it all. There was so much in the feeling of rushing forward to embrace the future, crystallised perfectly in my head during that brief moment I sat down after the final whistle at Wembley and saw it all flash before my eyes, that I'm exhausted - I reckon I've earned the right to be perpetually giddy about last season. I'm going to have a very giddy and very sociably silly drunk summer.

I just hope that Brian Laws is a good a man-manager as we think he is, and is able to clear the players' heads of any Wembley hangover in time for the start of the next campaign. Without the sharp intelligence of John Eyre (buggered off to Hull City, where he will be a very, very big fish in a modest pond) and the goalscoring of Jamie Forrester (25 or so goals, some derogatory comments about the town, and then a wave goodbye as he too buggered off, to FC Utrecht, where he will be a very small fish in a modest pond), we are looking forward to the unknown with a mixture of fear and excitement. Whatever happens next season - even if we sign Ronaldo and somehow end up as Champions of Division Two - I still don't think anything will quite eclipse this season's sense of our liberation from the dungeon division. Although it pains me to say it, when the bods at Wembley played M People's *Movin' On Up*, they got it dead right on every level.

This had been the greatest and most significant year of my life so far - my endeavours at college rewarded with a grade of which I am incredibly proud, and the documentary seeming as though it might open a few doors career-wise. Finally - a winner, an achiever, and a deliverer. This was the year that Scunthorpe United and I, walking hand-in-hand all the way with the diligent and resolute Brian Laws as our guide, finally took Small Steps and made Giant Leaps.

Now for the future, where the real hard work is!
Steve Graham

SPEKE FROM THE HARBOUR

Everton

Only eight minutes into the season and new signing John Collins, fresh from scoring a penalty against Brazil in France 98, was unable to replicate the feat against Aston Villa. It was going to be another long season.

With four new signings, in the shape of Olivier Dacourt, Marco Materazzi, and Scots duo Alec Cleland and John Collins, there was an air of cautious optimism at Goodison. An improvement on fourth from bottom was expected with a few of the more hopeful dreaming of mid-table. As it happened, we managed to finish fourteenth, but that did not tell the full story of a season which was to prove every bit as

SMITH FINALLY LANDS NEW PARTNER FOR DUNCAN!

The Alternative Everton fanzine

ISSUE No. 25

depressing and stomach-churning as the previous one.

Scoring goals was to be the first obstacle for an Everton side which, Smith had obviously decided, was going to concentrate on defending. The adoption of the negative 5-3-2 formation, especially at home, was winning him few friends. However, we thought that if that was what it took to steady the ship, then we would have to be patient. He was not helped by his limited choice of strikers: John 'Tries hard, but isn't very good' Spencer, Danny 'Headless Chicken' Cadamarteri, Michael 'Barn Door' Branch, Mikael 'I don't like him and I'm not playing him' Madar and Duncan 'Scoring's not my strong point' Ferguson. The Goodison faithful were therefore 'treated' to three home league goals during the first four and a half months of the season (ten games). This was a statistic made all the more embarrassing by the fact that Manchester United had managed to score four at Goodison in just 90 minutes. Smith had attempted to alleviate this problem with the recruitment of the Ivory Coast international, Ibrahima Bakayoko, for £4.5m from Montpellier in France. His first league goal was to come two months into his Goodison career.

Dixie Dean had nothing to worry about.

The date that all Evertonians will remember from the season was 23 November 1998. Two major events were to unfold after the now infamous Newcastle United game screened live on Sky that fateful Monday evening. A rumour started to circulate before the game that terrace idol Duncan Ferguson had been sold to Newcastle. This was dismissed as idle gossip by most - and even by Walter Smith himself live on Sky. It was only later on that evening, when it was found out that Duncan's dad had been in the Winslow pub, opposite the ground before the game, confirming the fact, that the unbelievable news began to sink in. Duncan was reportedly in tears himself, being given no option by Peter Johnson, who had told him of the club's perilous financial plight and the fact that he was the club's most saleable asset.

The Blue threequarters (© Olivier Dacourt) of Merseyside was dumbfounded. It emerged that Walter Smith himself had not known about the sale. Duncan had been sold from under his nose and now the speculation switched to whether he would quit himself after being treated so shabbily by Johnson. Peter Johnson was obviously intent on being remembered as the Liverpudlian who ruined Everton. In four seasons, he'd managed to do more damage than even old big nose himself, Ian Rush, had in 15 years!

Duncan Ferguson was an icon. A figurehead to lead Evertonians forward. A young man with his best years ahead of him, and there was never any doubt about how much he loved Everton. He was the player opposing teams were frightened of. Awesome jumping and heading ability, a strong desire to win, and deceptively good on the ground for a big man. He may never have been the 25-goals-a-season striker that we were crying out for but, during his last 18 months at Everton, he had started to show a greater consistency and had developed his all-round game. But the thing that stuck in the throat the most was Johnson's involvement. If Walter Smith had come out and said Duncan was being sold but he was using the money to strengthen other areas of the team, there would still have been plenty of dissent. However, if he could demonstrate that in the long-term that it was in the best interests of the club, you would have had to have accepted it.

November 30 was an all-round happier day for Evertonians, when Peter Johnson announced he was stepping down as chairman and was prepared to divest himself of his 68 per cent shareholding in Everton Football Club. Ex-chairman Philip Carter and impresario Bill Kenwright were to step in as chairman and vice-chairman, with the latter rumoured to be intent on raising the necessary cash to buy out Johnson.

The local media was flooded with questions about Johnson's mismanagement.

How was the club able to buy Dacourt, Collins, Unsworth, Bakayoko, Materazzi and, most suspiciously, Steve Simonsen from Tranmere Rovers, if we had no money? Now that Duncan had been sold, we were told that all the proceeds were to be put towards the overdraft. Why bother spending £4.5m on Bakayoko (a player Arsene Wenger rejected only twelve months previously) when we couldn't afford it, and even more mysteriously, goalkeeper Steve Simonsen, for a record £3.5m, when we already had two decent 'keepers? Why make mention of a ground move to a new space-age, out-of-town stadium when we had the equivalent of a Third World country's national debt? The fact of the matter was that Johnson was out of his depth. He could not fully comprehend the difference between being chairman of a little First Division outfit with 5,000 gates, who were happy to steer clear of Division Two every year, and being chairman of Everton, average gates of 36,000, nine times League Champions, five times FA Cup winners, and fourth most successful English club of all time. The only thing that worries me is that as I write this, some seven months later, Johnson is *still* the majority shareholder at Everton.

However, the season wasn't all doom and gloom. There were a couple of reasons for Evertonians to get excited. A decent cup run was curtailed only at the quarter-final stage by eventual runners-up Newcastle and the emergence of a bright young talent in the shape of teenage striker Francis Jeffers. Things could have been considerably different if it hadn't have been for the actions of the Trabsonspor chairman in February.

When the dull 0-0 draws started turning into defeats, our perilous fifteenth position in the league saw us getting sucked towards the relegation zone at exactly the wrong time. An absolutely dire 1-0 home defeat against a seemingly doomed Forest side started the alarm bells ringing, and seven days later Derby dumped us into seventeenth place. Although we did have the surreal experience of seeing five Everton goals in one game, against Boro ten days later, we knew it was going to be a brief respite, with four of our next six matches being against Leeds, Arsenal, Liverpool and Manchester United. Sure enough we managed a meagre four points out of a possible 18 and we were back in the mire.

However, two masterful swoops by Walter Smith before the transfer deadline were to transform our season and prove to be the difference between playing at Highbury next season or just playing Bury. Scott Gemmill had been out of favour at Forest since the arrival of Big Ron and was set to quit the club on the Bosman in the summer. Smith nipped in and picked him up for a bargain £250,000. But it was to be the loan signing of Kevin Campbell from Trabsonspor which to prove most decisive. Having been labelled a "discoloured cannibal" by his chairman, he vowed not to play for the Turkish side again. With Bakayoko still firing blanks and Francis Jeffers understandably still settling in to the first team, the priority was to find somebody to score goals. Not everybody thought Campbell was the man to do it. Having been offloaded by Arsenal and only really having had one good season for Forest (and that being in the First Division), the Gwladys Street faithful had their reservations. However, with no money to spend, Smith snapped up Campbell on loan until the end of the season.

The chance to pull clear came at home to Sheffield Wednesday, a team who had lost their previous five games. Having taking a first-half lead through Francis Jeffers, two howling errors by £4.5m David Unsworth gifted Wednesday the three points and saw us drop into the relegation zone with only six games to play.

A vital home win against Coventry with a Campbell brace was slightly overshadowed by the man in black once again. Rob Harris seemed to know as much about football as his namesake Rolf, as a truly inept performance culminated in his dismissal of Marco Materazzi. Decision after decision perplexed the Goodison crowd - with nobody able to guess 'what is was yet'.

So it looked like we'd finally blown the European Fair Play League place in next season's UEFA Cup!

And whilst on the subject of referees, it was a season which was to provide dozens of utterly bewildering decisions by officials against Everton. Here for your delectation are the top ten, in no particular order:

1. Duncan Ferguson's disallowed header against Spurs.
2. Uriah Rennie's entire sorry performance in the Huddersfield away game, especially his failure to spot either of the two blatant handballs in the box.
3. Dacourt's booking by Jeff Winter for taking a free-kick too quickly, away to Sheffield Wed.
4. Beckham, Neville and Schmeichel convincing Peter Jones to book Bakayoko when he had previously waved play on. If I hadn't seen it with my own eyes, I wouldn't have believed it.
5. Mike Riley's decision to send off Materazzi for being pushed over v Ipswich.
6. Neale Barry fails to give the most blatant penalty at home to Wimbledon, when Michael Hughes' clumsy lunge takes out Michael Branch.
7. Blackburn's Andy Johnson not sent off for two blatantly bookable offences in the space of 20 minutes.
8. Uriah Rennie's decision to send off Don Hutchison in the Arsenal home game, for jumping.
9. David Elleray, chairman of the Liverpool supporters club (referees branch) - Anfield.
10. 'Rolf' Harris' dismissal of Materazzi for his 'foul' on submarine Huckerby against Coventry.

Four more goals from Super Kevin Campbell in his next two starts, along with a superb volley from Gemmill against Newcastle, brought relief to many Evertonians. However, it wasn't until the second to last week of the season that all fears of relegation were finally banished. A truly outstanding display saw Campbell grab a hat-trick in the 6-0 mauling of West Ham.

As for my man of the season, well there were few candidates. Jeffers looks like he has a bright future ahead of him, whilst Myhre and Watson were both models of consistency, barring a few uncharacteristic mistakes. However, the player who epitomised the skill and determination associated with the great Everton sides of the past was Don Hutchison. Whilst he may not be blessed with great pace, he more than makes up for it with the other fine qualities he possesses. Skill, vision, passing, the ability to hold and release the ball at the right time, tackling, consistency, anticipation, bravery and leadership. In fact on the few occasions he wasn't in the team, or had an off-day, it was no coincidence that Everton had an off-day too.

Here's hoping that the takeover is concluded by the time you read this and the cancerous tumour that is Peter Johnson is consigned to the Everton FC history books.

Mark Staniford

SPITTING FEATHERS

Sheffield Wednesday

When it was announced that I was going to cover the SWIFTA awards ceremony on behalf of Richard and Judy, I thought I might as well tell the readers of *SOTF* all about it as well. What? You've never heard of them? SWIFTAs - The Sheffield Wednesday Independent Film and Television Awards. All the regulars were there: Hugh and Liz, Tom and Nicole, Brad, Cameron, Mel and Arnie... yes, the Old Crown on Penistone Road must have been empty that night.

The Sheffield Wednesday players were out in force at the City Hall. Goalkeepers Pressman and Srnicek waved to the crowd, who threw bouquets at them... sadly

ANOTHER SEASON ENDS BUT WE'VE GOT ONE THING TO CELEBRATE...

turn to back page

An Independent View of Sheffield Wednesday

most of these ended up on the floor. Des Walker, meticulous in his designer suit arrived and, after a brief wave to the onlookers, stepped in for his award and got out of there as soon as possible. Once again, Wim Jonk failed to notice that the fans were cheering him... in fact he looked somewhat lost when he realised there were no options available and Peter Atherton was not to his right. The Wednesday captain was in fact doing a man-marking job on tonight's master of ceremonies, Steve McManaman. There was crowd favourite Emerson, who spent so long signing autographs outside the City Hall that the ceremony was over before he got to go in. Juan Cobian and Dejan Stefanovic were both there... tearful as they took the plaudits from the crowd. Bargain buy Danny Sonner arrived wearing a cheap suit but still looked reasonably good in it. Andy Hinchcliffe hobbled in on his crutches. And Player of the Year, Beni Carbone, spent so long getting ready that he missed the ceremony altogether. Andy Booth will no doubt turn up tomorrow... bless him.

Inside, there wasn't much doubt about who was going to take the **Best Actor** award and no-one was surprised when Leonardo Di Canio stepped up to receive it (although he had to sign a waiver saying that he would return the award in time for next year's ceremony). His performance in *The Italian Gob*, in which he tells his adoring fans how much he loves them will never be forgotten, although it will no doubt be repeated (at West Ham in the near future... and it's not sour grapes, because Celtic fans told us exactly the same and we didn't believe them either!). Surprisingly, Di Canio also took the **Best Actress** award for his performance as Greta Garbo ("I want to be alone") after he disappeared to Italy and refused to talk to anyone for months on end. Di Canio took the opportunity to thank a certain Paul Alcock ("...without whom all this would have been impossible."), who was also there to pick up the award for **Best Animation**, his short film *Man in Black* was likened to Disney's *The Wonderful Thing About Tigger* excerpt from *Winnie the Pooh*. **Least Animation** went to Wim Jonk.

Best Supporting Actor went to Des Walker for the sixth year running, Des has been supporting the rest of the Wednesday defence for some years now - and it was fitting that in the season that Wednesday, for once, had a somewhat capable defence, Desi was also presented with a **Special Award for his Service to the Industry** (despite being rumoured that he wants to get out of Hillsborough).

Best Supporting Actress went to Kevin Pressman for an enigmatic performance in *Whatever Happened to Baby Kev?* The film revolves round the mysterious disappearance of a quite capable goalkeeper who is replaced by a far more erratic one (Pavel Srnicek because of a clash of personalities with the club's manager, Danny De Wilson). *Whatever Happened to Baby Kev?* is still playing in Sheffield, but Kev might be appearing at a club near you in the next few weeks.

Best Foreign Film was easily won by Emerson Thome for his enthusiastic characterisation in *Life is Beautiful (in Sheffield)...* which should be required viewing for all footballers who fear living in the North. Surprisingly, we *have* got electricity up here now, so you can set up your Playstation just the same as you can in London.

Best Drama went to the media for their continuing performance of *Vanity Fair (Play Awards)* in which they dragged out the fact that Wednesday just weren't willing to tackle anyone because of an obsession with qualifying for Europe through the Fair Play Awards. Which we didn't... being sabotaged by that well-known Leicester fan Mike Reed in an overzealous card-and-gore fest at The Valley on the last day of the season. The media seemed totally unaware that even if we did qualify, there was still the little matter of being lucky enough to beat odds of 5/1 in the deciding lottery. With relegation always a possibility up to the last few weeks, did they really believe Wednesday didn't want to compete for the sake of a one in five chance of Europe? The only reason we didn't compete was because we had a midfield who would struggle to dominate the cast from *Cocoon* in a kickabout.

The lesser awards such as **Best Costume**, which once again went to Tango, that most underdressed of Wednesdayites, who showed off his latest outfit to the crowds outside the City Hall - although one little boy had the temerity to say, "He isn't wearing any clothes!": and another said, "Yes he is, but surely he could have ironed them!"). Other nominees such as

Wednesday's new shirt didn't really stand much chance. Pyjamas never do well in this category.

Best Soundtrack went to the Wednesday Kop Band, who have further increased their profile by appearing on Channel 4's *Cutting Edge...* look what that did for Graham Taylor's career. The documentary told of a rift between the members of the band. Yes, even a couple of drummers and assorted brass who follow Wednesday (and England) around can be torn apart by "musical differences". Just like The Smiths.

Best Production went to the Wednesday Youth Academy, who at last seem to be producing something that Wednesday have consistently failed to do for a long time now - good young players. Watch out for McKeever, Quinn, Haslam, and a certain young lad called Alex Higgins... apparently he's a bit of a maverick.

Best Lighting went to the subs bench, which actually looked like we had five footballers who were capable of making a difference to the game sat on it... amazingly, it was all done with mirrors.

Best Make-Up went to Dave Richards for constantly making up stories about money being available when Danny Wilson needs it.

Best Director was awarded to nobody as the concept is a paradox in itself. However, Wednesday director Joe Ashton was nominated for his performance in *Anna and the King of Siam Sauna* - although it should be stressed that this film should not be confused with Kevin Costner's latest *Massage in a Brothel...* for obvious reasons.

When it came to **Best Film**, there were one or two who had their backers. *Titanic* - the story of a fight to save a sinking ship was a strong contender from Sheffield's other production company. *Mission Impossible* - Barnsley's attempts to return to the big time. *Notting Ham* - the tale of an ordinary bloke who gets involved with all the big stars and still gets relegated at the end. All had their supporters - but it was the tale of the club who just seem happy enough to stay in the big league that took the honours this time. Yes, **Best Film** went to Hillsborough Productions for *As Good As It Gets*.

Of course when it comes to **Best Supporting Fans** well... need you ask?
Graham Lighfoot

TALES FROM SENEGAL FIELDS

Millwall

The end of the '97-98 season saw the mighty Lions scrabbling about in an undignified manner for Second Division survival. The arrival of Billy Bonds, albeit accompanied by the usual bullshit about having watched the Lions as a boy, was almost universally greeted with disdain and scepticism by the majority of supporters. Would he be able to give Millwall the same sort of commitment that he gave to the hampsters? The answer, as it turned out, was 'maybe'; but commitment proved not to be enough. Theo Paphitis, the Millwall chairman, unceremoniously dismissed Bonds back from whence he came, adding

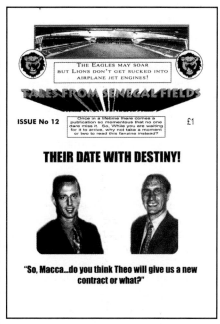

THE EAGLES MAY SOAR BUT LIONS DON'T GET SUCKED INTO AIRPLANE JET ENGINES!

ISSUE No 12   Once in a lifetime there comes a publication so momentous that no one dare miss it. So, While you are waiting for it to arrive, why not take a moment or two to read this fanzine instead?   £1

THEIR DATE WITH DESTINY!

"So, Macca...do you think Theo will give us a new contract or what?"

curiously that Bonds was, "A very good manager... but not at this level." In his place, he installed Keith 'Rhino' Stevens and Alan 'Macca' McLeary, both players who had enjoyed a long and, at times, over-indulgent relationship with Millwall fans, Stevens in particular attracting the sort of quasi-hero worship normally reserved for the likes of Harry 'Arry Boy' Cripps, Barry Kitchener and Teddy Sheringham.

The fans' reaction was mixed. No-one doubted the qualities that the pair would bring to the team: commitment, fire, passion and determination... the qualities so admired and respected at the Den, both new and old. But the big question was, "Are they experienced enough?" In an uncharacteristic display of benevolence, many Millwall fans questioned whether it was right to elevate Rhino to a position where he was susceptible to humiliation should he fail.

Things got off to a good(ish) start, with Paul Shaw scoring the only goal away at Wigan, sending Wycombe packing in the first home league match of the season, before going to Bournemouth to get well and truly stuffed. And that was to be the story of the season really: indifferent displays when the form book and Division Three table suggested otherwise; diabolical displays when the players forgot the gospel according to Rhino; and scintillating displays when least expected. Away at Stoke City, for instance, the Lions played the home side off the park for 90 per cent of the match, only to fall to a sucker punch and the only goal of the game. Against a poor Macclesfield Town, the Lions struggled to achieve a 0-0 draw.

As far as the fans were concerned, the big match of the season was to be against Manchester City – and, in terms of significance, so it proved to be. For some strange reason, someone in power decided that it would be a good idea to stage the game on a Tuesday evening at the New Den, with Fulham the only other side playing in London. It didn't take an idiot to work out that there would be trouble. Thus the New Den was besieged by Chelsea and West Ham fans, most of whom declined to enter the ground, but decided to bide their time in the local hostelries. Despite all the media hype about Manchester City's enormous following, only 1,800 bothered to make the trip to South Bermondsey... a disappointing turnout following the mountain of rhetoric. Millwall decided to have one of their better days and basically tore them apart. The much-vaunted Shaun Goater found the class and experience of ex-Spur Stuart Nethercott too hard to break down, and Manchester's attack was reduced to a shambles of long hopeful punts upfield. At the other end, the young pretenders, Tim Cahill, Neil 'Bomber' Harris and Lucas Neill, were having a field day. Bomber latched onto a lovely through ball, beat the offside trap and gleefully smashed the ball home. The goal was greeted by about 12 youngsters jumping onto the cinder track to celebrate - a gesture which Joe Royle would later describe as "an intimidating pitch invasion". City did manage to score in the second-half to snatch a point, but were poor value for the money they supposedly had. Royle, one of English football's elder statesmen and, according to the media, all-round good guy, then shifted his rhetoric gear stick into overdrive, claiming that his team were intimidated throughout the match; and, more famously, claiming that the players were scared to go for a winner because they felt they might not get out of South London alive. In actual fact, what happened inside the ground was basically nothing of note, apart from an incident that was greeted by a very drunk Arsenal fan (don't ask!) weaving onto the pitch to have a go at the referee from a distance of some 50 yards. Still, Royle was in full flow, as were the group of some 2,500 assorted thugs hanging around in the streets, all of whom were demanding that they be allowed to get at the visiting supporters from "oop north". The Police, bless 'em, were having none of it (no sense of humour), and a pitch battle began, which quickly turned into a running street battle as the authorities realised that not only were they inadequately prepared, but were seriously unable to deal with the ferocity of the violence. It took around two hours before relative peace was restored, by which time Royle had produced enough soundbites to keep David Mellor happy for the rest of the season.

Not a man to waste the opportunity of grabbing the wrong end of the stick whenever the opportunity arose, Mellor launched into an anti-Millwall campaign at the earliest opportunity. Armed with none of the facts and a ceaseless desire for credibility, Mellor took no prisoners, even allegedly calling for Millwall chairman Theo Paphitis to have it out with him on air. Strangely, when Paphitis phoned in, Mellor wouldn't take the call.

Just a couple of matches later, Fulham visited the Den, and a couple of idiots ran onto the pitch and attempted to attack Rufus Brevett. Neither were Millwall supporters, one claiming to be a West Ham fan, the other a Spurs aficionado. Thankfully, Kevin Keegan calmed the situation by saying, "They're passionate here... if you take the passion out of football there's nothing left." It was noticeable that after these two matches, the standard of refereeing changed at the Den. Suddenly Millwall players were picking up red and yellow cards as though they were going out of fashion. At first the fans didn't realise what was going on, but by the time we got to the caravan park in Kent (that's Priestfield, home of Gillingham, to you) it was clear that the referees had issued the word - "Get Millwall!" Thus we saw Carl Asaba, much-vaunted by the pikey hordes who follow the Gills but frustrated throughout his match against the Lions, headbutt Gerard Lavin. It was one of those feint things, where contact is minimal. However, Lavin (sensibly we felt) was not going to make a meal of it and stayed on his feet... only to be sent off by the referee. Ironically, Asaba headbutted someone else a few weeks later and was sent off - but appealed and got off. No justice.

Millwall have emerged as officially the dirtiest team in the division and probably the league. By this time, the Lions had managed to make their annual exit from the FA Cup, being destroyed by John Hollins' Swansea at the Vetch Field, but had begun to make progress in the Auto Windscreens Shield. They had dismissed Cardiff at the Den, slaughtered Brighton, thanks largely to a comical display from their 'keeper, and become the first team to beat Bournemouth at Dean Court, albeit on penalties. In the next round they faced the Gills at the Den, but first it was off to Maine Road. Ever since the first game, the Man City fans had been promising Millwall fans a "good old-fashioned Manchester welcome", via the Internet and on the City websites. Once at Maine Road, there were some 3,500 Millwall fans in the visitors section, separated from City's finest by three rows of seats, some plastic netting and a few nervous looking stewards. Indeed, City fans proceeded to 'give it the biggun', but were noticeably reticent about actually following up their bravado with anything more solid. Therefore it was left to the riot police to kick it off with the Lions fans. Sadly the words "indiscriminate" and "brutal" spring elf-like to mind when describing their conduct on the day. City fans bravely joined in by hurling seats, triggering off a major terrace battle the like of which had not been seen since the bad old days of the Seventies. Despite all the same tired old bollocks from Mellor on Radio Five, City fans aren't unused to this type of thing, and there were reports of similar incidents against Stoke and Burnley. Following this, the Manchester Constabulary are under investigation... Joe Royle should also be there (but isn't) for having written in his programme notes that, "We have some scores to settle with Millwall" - now what did he mean by that?

Back in the Auto Windscreens Shield, Gillingham were dismissed via a goalden goal and we headed for Walsall nurturing a slender 1-0 lead. Millwall fans had begun to give up on reaching the play-offs, thanks to some mediocre displays and terrible results - defeats at Chesterfield, Notts County and Lincoln, for instance. Therefore the Twin Towers of Wembley began to look more likely in the Shield. The Lions had appeared in a cup final there in 1945, but statisticians refuse to acknowledge the fact, as it has been classified a "war-time cup final". So a Wembley appearance had become something of a holy grail for Millwall. Up at Walsall, although only 1,900 tickets were officially available, around 2,500 turned up from London. A party atmosphere began as soon as the fans entered the ground some 25 minutes before kick-off. There was a feeling Millwall couldn't lose. So dominant were they, in fact, that the only surprising thing was they only managed one goal. Walsall equalised, but it was very much a consolation goal, as the Millwall celebrations began in earnest.

Both on and off the field, the league programme took second place as Wembley fever gripped the club. The players were, perhaps understandably, worried about getting injured and form suffered. Everyone was obsessed with getting a ticket for Wembley. When the big day finally came, 48,000 Millwall fans swamped Wembley in what had little to do with football and everything to do with celebrating the fact that they had got there. Seven thousand Wigan fans bravely sang their songs, but for most of the time were drowned out. The fairy tale was nearly complete... and then the ball came across, was blatantly handled as the Wigan player controlled it... 55,000 saw it, one man - the referee - didn't... and by the time we had finished protesting, the ball was in the back of the net. Despite losing, Millwall fans celebrated. Defeat was a minor irritation. The Lions had reached Wembley,

Millwall had taken over for the day and there was no trouble whatsoever. Good result.

The best team to visit the Den were Preston, who played some terrific football and deservedly took a two-goal lead. However, as stated at the beginning of this piece, the one thing that Keith Stevens has instilled into the players is a sense of pride and commitment. The Lions came back, scoring through Australian Tim Cahill and the youngster Paul Ifill. In the end, Millwall finished tenth in the table, a position that other teams' fans might describe as mid-table mediocrity. However, for us this represents real progress from the previous season and proved that, after years of sub-standard disappointment, not only is there light at the end of the tunnel, but real hope that if consistency and perhaps a few half-decent players can be added to the repertoire, then promotion is more than a possibility next season.

Mike George

TALES OF A CHAIRBOY

Wycombe Wanderers

Chairboys? What's that all about then? It's a question commonly asked of Wanderers fans. The answer is that when the Wanderers were founded, way back in 1884, the town of High Wycombe was renowned for its furniture-making industry. A few of the workers decided to set up a footie team and Wycombe Wanderers were formed.

We have experienced a fair few peaks and troughs in our six years as a Football League club. The messiah, Martin O'Neill, almost led us to the promised land of Division One. Alan Smith (spit) nearly sent us back from whence we came. John Gregory saved us that season, only to flatter to

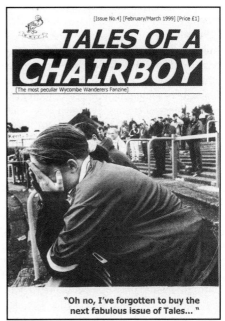

[Issue No.4] [February/March 1999] [Price £1]

TALES OF A CHAIRBOY

[The most peculiar Wycombe Wanderers Fanzine]

"Oh no, I've forgotten to buy the next fabulous issue of Tales... "

deceive the next. This didn't deter Aston Villa, however, who pinched back their former coach. Youth team coach Neil Smillie was appointed caretaker-boss and guided us to safety. Fittingly, his reward was to be given the job on a full-time basis. Being the cynical wretches that we are, this was probably more to do with him being the cheapest option for the powers that be. This theory was given more credence when the board announced in the summer that Neil Smillie wasn't going to receive any money to strengthen the team. It wasn't too long before it became apparent that it was going to be a long, hard season. It was at a pre-season friendly, a 2-0 defeat at Kingstonian on a balmy July evening, that the seeds of doubt were sown.

The first issue of *Tales...* went on sale on August 7 at home to Luton, our first game of the season. Luton captain Steve Davis (no, not that one) thundered home a 30-yard free-kick and that was it. Swindon were disposed of over two legs in the Worthington Cup. However, our league form went from bad to worse. Three defeats left us with the same points total as Norway's entry in the Eurovision Song Contest. We finally earned our first point of the season with an injury-time equaliser at home to Bristol Rovers. September saw our second point earned, with a draw at Burnley. Middlesbrough cruised through to the third round of the Worthington Cup with a 3-1 aggregate win. Four more league defeats left us marooned at the foot of Division Two. October started with an injury-time equaliser from a woeful Notts County, meaning our third point of the season was less than gratefully received. Two weeks later, Issue 2 of *Tales...* hit the streets, the same day as a bottom of the table clash with Macclesfield Town, which we won 3-0 to earn our first three points of the campaign. Another 3-0 victory followed this time, with Wrexham the victims. November saw progress in the FA Cup, with a 1-0 win over Chesterfield. The biggest result through was a historic and memorable 1-0 triumph over Manchester City. A Michael Simpson penalty earned the Chairboys three valuable points and gave the Wanderers faithful the opportunity to give the Gallaghers some much-deserved abuse.

December saw Plymouth Argyle gifted all three goals to win 3-2 in an FA Cup replay. The following Saturday, we faced Lincoln City in a proverbial six-pointer at Adams Park. Issue 3 of *Tales...* was unleashed on the unsuspecting public, hoping that we had become a lucky charm after the Macclesfield victory. Well, who needs lucky pants? The Wanderers produced an excellent performance to see off the Imps 4-1, Jermaine McSporran scoring the goal of the season past Bruce Grobelaar. Christmas was a happy one with a draw at high-flying Walsall and a win at home to Chesterfield. January saw the Wanderers with a golden opportunity to climb out of the bottom four with a home game with York City. We never turned up and deservedly lost 2-1. Smillie admitted in the local paper that the players hadn't been up for it - an admission that understandably didn't go down to well with the Wanderers faithful. A shambles of a performance followed at Luton Town. A 3-1 defeat was the last straw and Neil Smillie was sacked. Lawrie Sanchez was appointed the new manager of Wycombe Wanderers on February 5. Not 24 hours later the Wanderers faced Fulham at Adams Park. To make it a day to remember, Issue 4 of *Tales...* also went on sale. The result with Keegan's millionaires was a creditable 1-1 draw. A 2-0 win at home to Burnley two weeks later was our first victory in almost two months. Relegation rivals and 'hoofers' Northampton visited Adams Park, and a quite remarkably inept performance handed the Cobblers three points on a plate. The short trip for the local derby with Reading followed. On a cabbage patch of a pitch the Wanderers shot themselves in the foot. This was especially ironic, as you wonder how on earth they would manage to hit such a small part of the human anatomy when, for the majority of the match, the Wanderers shooting was akin to that of a blind centipede trying to hit a cow's arse with a banjo. It all ended in a 2-1 defeat, loan signing Sean Devine scoring our consolation. So Division Three it is then, at least that's what we told the Wycombe public as Issue 5 of *Tales...* went to press. The following day we travelled to Bristol Rovers still without an away win all season. It was bound to happen, wasn't it? Eight minutes in, 'Captain Marvel', Jason Cousins, headed home a corner to put us in front and himself out for the season with an ankle injury. The Pirates weren't up for the fight and, with eight minutes remaining, Sean Devine scored to send the Wanderers fans into heaven. Oldham Athletic produced possibly the worst performance we witnessed at Adams Park, as the Wanderers comfortably won 3-0. We had given ourselves hope and now faced an away game at Macclesfield in a proverbial six-pointer. On a gloriously sunny day the Wanderers were soon a goal behind. We then gained control and two goals just before half-time put us in the driving seat. A goal early in the second-half secured a crucial 3-1 win. Issue 5 of *Tales...* hit the streets on Easter Bank Holiday Monday when the Blues faced Gillingham. We were soon brought back down to earth as Gillingham showed their 'class' with their usual blitzkrieg tactics. The Wanderers had to bounce back and they did so with a gritty performance at Wrexham. Two late goals secured a 2-0 victory. Four days later we visited Stoke City and, after controlling the first half-hour, snatched a point in the last minute to draw 2-2.

Things looked ominous as our next game was away at an in-form Manchester City. A thousand Wanderers fans travelled up to Maine Road hoping for perhaps a much-needed point. A quarter of an hour in and Andy Baird fired home after a glorious flick from Sean Devine. On the half-hour, Andy Baird returned the favour for Sean Devine to run on and hit an unstoppable 20-yard shot past the bewildered Nicky Weaver in the City goal. Two-nil up at Man City? Most Wanderers fans were pinching themselves. Shaun Goater pulled one back for City right on half-time and the Wanderers fans were in for a nail-biting time. Whilst City pressed for an equaliser, it was never a siege; and although City came agonisingly close on three occasions, the Wanderers held on for a famous victory and became the only team to do the double over them. Defeat followed at Notts County, losing 1-0 to a disputable penalty. Next up was a home encounter with Blackpool. Not a minute had gone before Sean Devine had headed us into the lead. However, the nerves began to show and, a quarter of an hour later, Blackpool levelled. Wanderers went straight back up the other end and Dave Carroll headed home to put us back in front. On the hour, Blackpool made it 2-2 - and that's how it stayed.

Wanderers then faced, at Adams Park, a Wigan Athletic side who were playing their sixth game in eleven days. It didn't seem to affect them, as they took the lead seven minutes before the break. However Sean Devine levelled right on half-time. The Wanderers then went in front four minutes into the second-half when Paul Emblen deflected home a shot from Michael Simpson. The Wanderers held on to win 2-1.

Saturday 8 May. Lincoln away - and 2,800 Wanderers fans travelled to cheer their team on to safety. The atmosphere soon built up as kick-off approached. It was an untidy game with few chances. Andy Baird should have headed the Blues in front after ten minutes but headed over. Just before half-time, referee Gurnham Singh missed a blatant handball in the Lincoln box. On the hour and Imps defender Stuart Bimson cleared an effort off the line, against his own crossbar - and away. It was beginning to look as if it wasn't going to be our day when, with just seven minutes remaining, Sean Devine crossed from the left and Paul Emblen headed over Lincoln 'keeper John Vaughan. The ball glided under the crossbar and nestled in the bottom corner of the net. Cue delirium among the mass ranked Wanderers fans at the opposite end. The seven minutes remaining seemed like seven hours, but the final whistle blew to signal mass celebration and singing and drinking which went on long into the night.

Dale Hurman

TALK OF THE TYNE

Newcastle United

Belgrade - Once More Into The Breach, Dear Friends

Partizan Belgrade 1 Newcastle United 0

Without wanting to tempt fate, I felt there was never a better chance for the Toon to pick up silverware in Europe than this season's Cup-Winners' Cup: 49 clubs from 48 countries (England boasting two teams due to Chelsea qualifying as the holders) and the English clubs apart, only Paris St Germain had ever won a European competition before. So, with only five rounds (including the final), we were looking at a wonderful opportunity to actually win something. Take away PSG, Lazio

and Chelsea, and there was no-one to fear. All we had to do was squeeze past Partizan and opportunity was knocking.

The problem with getting to Belgrade was plain and simple... it was on the verge of being a war zone! The Serbs were having a bit of a tiff with Kosovo and Albania, 'ethnic cleansing' and the like, and NATO were on standby waiting to flatten military targets - primarily those in Belgrade. All chartered flights into Belgrade were cancelled for obvious reasons, and the whole package became a massive disaster. NUFC wouldn't touch the deal with a barge-pole and had no intention of running an official trip, so we were left to fend for ourselves and make our own way there.

We scoured the map of Eastern Europe and came up with two possibilities: a flight to either Budapest (Hungary) or Vienna (Austria), then complete the journey by train. It looked simple enough on paper but putting the whole thing into practice was a lot of hard work. Budapest was the more practical, as it was only 256 miles from our destination (Vienna being 411) and it was possible to get a flight on the Tuesday direct from Newcastle. The problem was getting back to Budapest for midday on the Friday for our flight back. The Republic of Yugoslav Embassy offered little encouragement, saying they would not advise any tourists to travel by train between Hungary and Yugoslavia: "We have reports of muggings every day. Tourists are an easy target and gangs of thugs take their money and their hand luggage. It happens

---

all of the time. Anyway, there are problems on the border and I cannot see you getting back to Budapest in time." So that was that idea out the window. Next up, a company from Manchester came up with a strong possibility, with a package flying from Manchester to Hamburg; Hamburg to Munich; and a small business flight from Munich to Belgrade. Cracked it. Still very few of our friends believed we would make it, so to give us an extra incentive we contacted the local newspapers and asked if anyone would like to sponsor the huge flag we hump around the continent for Newcastle's European games. Two quid and we would write the sponsors' name on the flag - all money going to charity (multiple sclerosis in this case). The idea was a great success and we raised £300. The train to Manchester (and back) knocked us £41, £35 for a visa, £10 insurance, and £350 for the flights, and before we knew it, the two of us had coughed up £431 each and we hadn't even left the country.

We ended up sleeping on the floor of Manchester airport with a group of Heart of Midlothian supporters, who were bound for Majorca to watch their team in the same competition as ourselves. Lucky buggers. By 6.00am the airport was full of Man United fans who were heading vaguely in our direction - Munich - only we were taking the scenic route via Hamburg, basically to avoid them like the plague. The first indication that things weren't exactly going hunky dory was bad news that greeted us in Munich. Not only was our flight delayed because of minor engine problems with the modern day equivalent of a Messerschmitt Bf 109 that was going to take us to Serbia, but Belgrade had been hit by an earthquake that recorded 5.8 on the Richter scale. Once we became airborne, a Polish businessman gave us kind advice on how to stay alive in Serbia: "Never, ever, argue with a Serb. They carry guns, and the way things are going over there they don't take too kindly to English people." Point taken. The hotel we booked was ideally situated in the centre of the city, but there was a minor catch. We paid for a five-star hotel, but the local police and the hotel management decided we should go to the adjoining building, which was about four stars less and doubled as a brothel and a drugs den. Refund? As we were to find out later, there is no such thing as a refund in Serbia. The rooms were like something out of a 1960s TV programme. We had a bright orange six-foot standing lamp, which Mark kept referring to as "Zippy's head stuck on a stick", and the wallpaper was like a psychedelic Jimi Hendrix poster. Apparently water was in short supply. The toilet wouldn't flush (there was a large 'flush brush' provided) and you were expected to use the shower, not the bath, so all plugs were confiscated. As for toilet paper... well, that was a story in itself. One rather large Toon fan asked the cleaning lady for a toilet roll and was handed three squares. I kid you not. She gestured "Do you want more?" and he replied: "Here's me arse, pet, what do you think?" By this time we were probably 15-strong and the police decided on a 24-hour armed guard, yet at no time did I believe this was for our own protection. The Partizan fans, known as 'The Gravediggers', could be a problem, but the police were ten times worse. They didn't need provocation to lash out with batons; it was just the done thing. If they wanted you to go in one direction, they would simply knock you until you happened to point that way. We had an arrangement to meet up with a photographer from the *Evening Chronicle*, for a picture to confirm we had made it to Partizan's JNA Stadion. The rendezvous went according to plan and we even bluffed our way into the ground to watch the team train. The quote of the whole trip came from a young female reporter covering the story for a local newspaper: "Excuse me. Were you Newcastle fans frightened to come to Belgrade?" "No. Why should we?" I replied. "I live here, and I am terrified!" Poor girl.

Next we met a Serbian by the name of Miomir Jugin, who became our guide for two days. A chance meeting, yet this man went out of his way to make sure we came to no ill. I cannot thank him enough for what he did for us. He took five of us to a pub on the outskirts of town, although I have to admit I had reservations at first. He insisted on phoning the pub first to say he would be arriving with a group of English fans, which at first I took to mean they would be waiting armed up to the eyeballs. The female reporter had warned us that the English hooligans who rampaged through the French town of St Etienne in the 1998 World Cup had been given full coverage in her country, and Newcastle fans were thought of in a similar light. Let's say I was cautious at best - terrified at worst. We got to the pub and only came across three old men sat in a corner. Something wasn't right. It was ten o'clock at night and the streets were buzzing, so why was this place almost empty? I couldn't settle. Five minutes passed, the beers were handed around, and still no sign of life. I asked the way to the toilets and was directed up a small set of stairs that lead to, what seemed like, the attic. I got to the top and flicked the light switch and there must have been 70 or 80 teenagers sat huddled together drinking beer. It frightened the life out of me. It reminded me of the film *Schindler's List* when the Nazis searched for the Jews in a block of flats. There was not a sign of them, yet when the floorboards were pulled up scores of them trundled out.

We had a great evening, got back to the hotel in the early hours and fought our way past the drug barons, prostitutes and pimps to get into the lobby. Next morning our 'leader', Steve Burns (landlord of the Black Bull next to SJP), had his room door burst open by the Serbian SS. "Can we talk to you Mr Burns? You only have a party of around 15 in this hotel and so far one has been hit by a car (a Lada of all things), one is in hospital with a broken ankle, two have been attacked by a gang with baseball bats, one is suffering a broken nose, and one lad was so drunk he has been to hospital to have his stomach pumped! Where is it all going to end, Mr Burns? You have been here less than 24 hours."

We visited the home of Red Star, the most impressive of all the seven Premiership clubs from the capital, and once again bluffed our way inside. A Red Star fan had just arrived back from Metz in France for a European tie, and we nabbed him as he got off the coach and he got us inside the stadium.

Belgrade is a strange, unattractive city that has little to commend it. Hardly surprising, considering it has been flattened and rebuilt 36 times since its founding in the third century. The most attractive parts are the areas that man hasn't touched for centuries, i.e. the river Danube and the old Kalemegdan fortress that stands where the Danube meets the river Sava. It is the most complex and culturally diverse city I have ever visited. The walls are covered in graffiti, either showing the red star of communism or the swastika of fascism, and what was once the country of Yugoslavia is now six independent states. Nobody seems to know what the hell they want from their country.

As we walked to the ground for the match, there was trouble three hours before kick-off, thankfully none of it involving Newcastle fans. Groups of lads fighting with each other and gangs wanting to fight with anyone. Newcastle shirts with 'real' Adidas logos were much sought after. Everyone seemed as though they were prepared to offer anything for a swap, which was hardly surprising because we later found out they could be sold for £60... the equivalent of a month's wages. Inside the ground the intimidation started, and not just from the Partizan supporters. The police were in their element, striking anyone who did anything other than stand motionless. One Toon fan fell down the steps as he walked into the ground and was immediately kicked in the face by the Plod. I tried to tie the flag on the perimeter fence and was struck on the arm because the Plod said it was "too high". Why didn't he just say so? The so-called 'segregation' insisted on by UEFA for European games must have been relaxed for Serbia. The only obstruction detaching us from the Partizan supporters was a line of coppers who were even more threatening than the fans behind them. When the players walked out of the tunnel they could be excused for thinking it was Guy Fawkes night, as fireworks lit up the stadium in spectacular fashion. The team had midfield hard-man David Batty back in their ranks for his first game of the season after a six-match ban and surgery on his achilles. But how ironic it was that he was the culprit who hauled down Vladimir Ivic in the 53rd minute to send the Serbs into the next round. United fought all of the way and no-one could doubt their commitment. They even had three players booked in a ten-minute spell. But in the end they were left to rue poor a pass from Ketsbaia after he carved a hole in the Partizan defence and had the goal at his mercy. He waited until he could see the whites of the goalkeeper's eyes and teed himself up perfectly, only to have second thoughts when Shearer, standing unmarked, waved frantically for service. He opted to pass rather and shoot and Vuk Rasovic appeared from nowhere to hook the ball away. Not only was the Partizan defender the hero in this instance, but it was he who scored the two hotly-disputed penalties that gave his side ultimate victory.

The referee brought an end to the game and the players ran to the safety of the dressing-room. Only Warren Barton, who didn't take any part in the game, ran to the fans to applaud their support, and he even threw his training shirt over the eight-foot high fence. We were showered with coins, batteries and cigarette lighters, and the end brought about a pre-planned riot at the opposite end of the ground to ourselves, as two gangs slugged it out toe-to-toe. Hundreds of seats were ripped up and thrown onto the pitch, and the whole scene became increasingly ugly. A riot squad water cannon was brought to our section of the ground, but thankfully it wasn't put into action. But let us not forget the actions of the police that went way above the call of duty. These loveable chaps went out of their way to make us feel secure and safe from the rabid mob that congregated by the exit. We were escorted out of the ground and taken the full journey back to the hotel, kept in line by police who weren't too shy to swing their batons. They made conversation by taunting us with: "Partizan 1 Alan Shearer 0." "Partizan 1 Newcastle 0." "Tony Blair is a fuck!" Steve Burns was struck on the arm with a baton and insulted by a copper who scoffed at Newcastle's defeat. Steve put the fear of God into him: "Don't treat me like an animal! You're a big boy with a piece of wood in your hand. Let's see how big you are without your stick and your mates. Me and you... outside!" The Serb, as you would expect, bottled it. Back at the hotel the police insisted we stayed in the town square, but three of us met up with our Serbian friends and made an exit down a side street. Miomir and his stunning girlfriend, Natasha, ushered us to their waiting cars, their pride and joy, two identical 1969 Escort Mk 1, and we set off in search of beer and adventure. Back to the hotel at 4.00am and at 10.00am we were woken with the news that all British subjects had to evacuate Belgrade as soon as possible because NATO were on red alert. A flight to Munich, another one direct to Manchester airport, a train journey home providing us with just enough time to unpack, get a bath, then head off to Highbury for the Arsenal match.

FA Cup Final - Newcastle 0 Manchester United 2 (Sheringham, Scholes)

We hadn't won in seven matches, and come to think of it, I don't think we even came close to it, but we approached Wembley with the usual blind faith we are famous for. I was as gullible as the next man, even though Newcastle have an abysmal FA Cup record of only once in 23 years having beaten a club higher placed than themselves (Blackburn, 1995). The thousands of Geordies who packed Trafalgar Square on Friday evening was a true testimony to football fanaticism. Without doubt the most passionate supporters in this country. There was not a Manc (or Cockney) to be seen anywhere. We'd all read the reports the Reds were up for a confrontation, and Trafalgar Square was pencilled in as the meeting point, but there was not one single arrest. The chants of "Man U, where are you?" could be heard down the Strand a mile away. Could I give credit to the way the police handled the evening. Looking at the photographs of the Bigg Market after the cup final, there was undoubtedly a larger gathering at Trafalgar Square this particular Friday evening, yet the police were superb. They were in the area, and strong in numbers, but never at any stage moved in to fuel the fire. Nelson's four lions struggled under the strain of scores of Toon fans hanging off every crevice, and the fountains were like the Wet & Wild swimming baths. But the police accepted the fact this was a celebration, not a war. Perhaps the plod in the Bigg Market should look hard at their own strategy. The trouble in the Bigg Market, just like twice previous (end of season 1996 and cup final last year), only kicked off when the riot police moved in.

Saturday, if anything, saw Toon fans in a more positive mood than the previous year. Charvet, Glass and Ferguson hadn't completed a game between them in two months but everyone seemed to believe it would all come together on the day. The Duke of York and Railway Tavern at Kings Cross, as always the traditional places to rally the troops for a London game, did a roaring trade. Everyone was up for it... the Mancs had other things on their mind and the cup was destined for Tyneside. Winding our way down to Baker Street, we surfaced from the underground to join the sea of black and white outside The Globe. Once again, not a Manc in sight. They surfaced at Wembley Way, but even then they seemed to be outnumbered five to one. Anyone wearing a coat (and this was a blistering hot day) obviously had something to hide. Either that or there was a stand inside Wembley selling Man United shirts! Unlike the friendly banter the year before, when Gooners and Mags embraced and shook hands, this was strictly "You go your way, we'll go our way". Taunts from both sides, the most notable from the Mags being: "Live 'round the corner; you only live 'round the corner." From there it was into the piss-ridden paddling pool that is our national stadium. Noble and magnanimous from Wembley Way, one step inside is like walking into a raw sewer.

Harper, Griffin, Charvet, Dabizas, Domi, Lee, Hamann, Speed, Solano, Ketsbaia, Shearer.

The 30,000 bonnie lads and lasses - all with smiling faces gannin' along the Wembley Road - coughed up four weeks' wages: £43 for the new replica shirt, £40 for the ticket, God knows how much for transport and digs for the night, plus the ultimatum that season tickets (£386 at least) must be paid forthwith. As for the dream, well... that lasted ten minutes. Newcastle had been saving themselves for two months, hardly taxing their muscles and treating each game as a training exercise as they waited for 'The Big One'. Wrapped in cotton wool, plodding through games with the minimum of effort, avoiding physical contact wherever possible. Their opponents, however, played every game during those two months with 101 per cent commitment, as they stretched their elastic nerves to shredding point. Teddy Sheringham scored after ten minutes and there was never going to be a way back. It's not the losing which offends. Christ almighty, these fans have had a bellyful of defeats in their lifetime and you have to be a bloody pensioner to remember the last time a Newcastle captain lifted a domestic cup. It's the pathetic way the players throw in the towel.

Manchester United players were willing to risk a place in Wednesday's European Champions League - the ultimate prize in club soccer - to fight for a cause that many thought was the last thing they needed four days before Ferguson's holy grail. Gullit says he wants players who don't make a mistake. Well, isn't it about time we had a manager who doesn't make mistakes. Because he is starting to pass the buck, when we all know this team is no better now than when he first took over almost a full season ago. Charvet will be blamed for every sin in the book. Gullit says he's not a centre-back, and we all know he's not a centre-back. The player would probably be the first to go along with that assessment... so the ultimate question is "Why play him there?" Spider Heed distanced himself from this defeat. And that, in my opinion, was the ultimate sin because he has sat back and watched his side disintegrate over the last two months without putting a Doc Marten up their proverbial arses! Two-nil was a let-off. I thank God they had Europe on their minds because they scored and took the foot off the gas when they could so easily have topped the 4-0 Charity Shield victory.

Like it or not, Man United and Arsenal are our yardstick. They have what champions are made of, and I ask you, how many players from our team at Wembley would get a place at Highbury or Old Trafford? I wrote in the match report for last season's cup final that a Gooner approached me on the tube after our 2-0 defeat. He pushed a match programme in my direction and said: "You have a squad of 40-odd players, and take away Shearer and I wouldn't know one of them!" Have any of those 40-odd players made a name for themselves since? When Keegan left we were two players short of a Championship-winning team. Now that's <u>nine</u>. Take away Shearer and Hamann and we are struggling. OK, the manager talks about building a team around Howey and Ferguson, but perhaps he should look at the stats. Neither has averaged 20 games a season in the last six years. That's less than half the matches. It's not for me to doubt their ability, but it's a hard fact that they won't be available for more than half the season. A year ago we castigated Dalglish for negative tactics, but what on earth was Gullit thinking of when he replaced Hamann? Throwing on Ferguson was indeed positive, but at the expense of Hamann? The only high ball Ferguson was fed came in the 89th minute. Yes, we've heard Gullit is planning a summer clear-out. Perhaps he thinks he looked the part in his Armani suit as he strolled out at Wembley in the city he feel s more comfortable in than Newcastle. The sexy manager with the sexy ideas. Let's put this 'sexy' quotation into plain Geordie... Ruud, you fucked up big time!

Kev Fletcher

THE 69'ER

Swindon Town

This could have been a humorous piece, but I have a feeling it's downbeat and rather tedious. But then again, this is apt, as 'downbeat' and 'tedious' resemble the season just gone by.

For the first time in several years, I genuinely considered my options last year. Did I really want to be bored watching a team so ground down after three and a half years of McMahon? To go to away games when I knew that, if we were lucky, we were probably going to get beaten; and if we were, humiliated as well? To go to home games, when the whole atmosphere was so negative and the source of that pervaded up through the dressing-room? Rikki Hunt, chairman of Swindon and the man who said that he would never sack Steve McMahon, probably wants people like me not to bother. He even suggested we 'morons' should go and watch Oxford. And no sooner had I paid for my season ticket than we started losing. Not so bad? Bad enough if you'd had to sit through the end of the previous season and seen it all coming.

Issue 29
September 1998

80P

The 69er

THE SWINDON TOWN FANZINE

It's Football, Jim, but not as we know it.

When Swindon supporters look back, the season may well be remembered for one thing - the pitch invasion. Why? Because pitch invasions really aren't all that common these days; they are illegal for a start. It was because the pitch invasion was largely unorchestrated, yet was portrayed otherwise; because the pitch invasion probably wasn't the real reason why Steve McMahon finally resigned, but was said to be so by the club; and because it was probably the best thing that happened and the most fun I had in '98-99. Apart from Steve McMahon resigning, that is.

Our whole season really hinged on three games at the beginning of September. Two crunch games happened to be local derby fixtures at home, on the back of five league games without a win. If we were to lose both, McMahon would have to go... we thought. So, our dilemma was obvious. These are local derbies, games you want to win. But derby games are, in reality, not the lifeblood of a club, nor its reason for existence, and for a Division One side with little more than Division One survival on its mind, there just had to be more to it than beating Oxford. But for many others, this was it. Far more important than the good of the club, was spending whole seasons singing songs about another club, who were really no threat to anyone. Anyway, we won both games and disappointingly, McMahon announced joyously that he was staying. The local paper, the *Evening Advertiser*, which had up until then been pretty steadfast, yet not overt in its support for him, boomed his decision triumphantly in their next edition.

As it turned out, his reprieve was short-lived. Influenced into staying by "The support he had received during the Oxford game", a 5-2 defeat at Portsmouth quickly followed. He just hadn't wanted to acknowledge that some supporters that night would have cheered anyone. He may also have based this self-gratification on Rikki Hunt's figure of "99.9 per cent" of Swindon supporters being completely behind him. As a representative of the supporters through the fanzine, I was asked to do something; but, as it turned out, I didn't have much of a hand in things.

It seemed to everyone concerned a purely spontaneous gesture. Not the result of a poor start to the season, but the result of several seasons' worth of dismal football; of 'here we go again'. Well, we definitely didn't want to go there this time around. And there might have been several reactions from the club. They might have echoed the concern felt by the fans at the direction in which the club was headed. They might have castigated those involved and taken security measures to make sure it couldn't happen again, but nevertheless praised the spirit in which the invasion was conducted. After all, the police made no moves to clear the pitch and spent their time chatting to supporters they knew and many they didn't. Instead, with steam still rising from under his collar following McMahon's resignation just days afterwards, Rikki Hunt announced that the 500 people who had taken part in the on-pitch protest would be banned from the County Ground for life, if it took him "until the end of the season to find them". As an exception, he was prepared to let off people who wrote to him apologising and admitting they were wrong.

The whole situation was almost too ridiculous to describe and the arrogance of the club's attitude positively astounding. Everyone who had not actually participated in the protest knew at least one other person who had, and probably many more. These were not people the police would probably speak to in a lifetime of football policing, other than to give directions. Most supporters were livid - even those who were against pitch invasions in principle - at the sheer arrogance of a club banning a set of supporters, the majority of whom would regularly be seen at away games. OK, this was an illegal act, technically speaking, but the good-spirited nature of the protest had been there for everybody to see. One "assault on a steward" was quite clearly only a bit of push, a shove resulting from that steward shoving the supporter first. Much of the time spent by supporters on the pitch (nearly two hours in all) was spent wandering around singing, talking and sharing views. And there was a game of mass football, the likes of which will never probably be seen again on the

County Ground. Now if that constitutes damage to the pitch, then the pitch is obviously not as robust as it should be.

I don't know anyone, or know of anyone who knows anyone who wrote to Rikki Hunt to apologise, although he claimed to have received many letters in support. Over the next few days, which then ran into a few weeks, even the *Evening Advertiser* moved over to the side of the supporters, at least in the context of trying to get the 'life' ban overthrown. It was a long, slow process, with Hunt first insisting that he would not back down and saying, almost with hatred in his voice, that these were not the sort of people he wanted at the club. When he did change his mind, coincidentally or not, it came shortly after the *Advertiser* printed another spread of letters under the banner headline 'Has Rikki lost the plot'. Quite clearly he had.

He did a U-turn for one main public reason and a whole range of private ones. The public reason was that he realised, through talking to people, the genuine concern of the supporters who invaded the pitch, and now thought that they shouldn't be punished. How we laughed. In fact he had to back down because he completely underestimated the tidal wave of feeling. One of the rumoured private reasons was that there had been no signs round the perimeter of the pitch advising the illegality of pitch invasions, and that he might have had trouble enforcing the ban. He probably also realised that he had cornered himself with the logic behind the ban and had to find a quick route out.

After the first 69er of the season, when the editors called for a management change and did a lot of well-reasoned slagging, I had a letter accusing me of "not wanting the side to win" and of being not just ridiculously anti-McMahon, but anti-STFC, the very club I purported to follow. The same person who wrote those lines wrote again a few months later to apologise and offer his support. I got some pleasure out of that letter, but not because I was glad to be right.

Jimmy Quinn came in as manager and, for a time, things looked brighter. It was as if a huge weight had been lifted from everyone's shoulders, fans and players alike. Staying up was still a struggle; but we did it.

For a club like Swindon, with no new money forthcoming, little is going to change this season. Maybe we were spoiled by that ten-year period of championship, play-offs, relegations and demotion - and, now, mid-table security is not enough. But looking on the bright side, at least up until now, Quinn hasn't recruited anyone who looks like he's 50 and who can almost be remembered from the days of the bubble-gum card. That was one of McMahon's trademarks - and another we are not sorry to see the back of.

Anna Merriman

THE BLUE EAGLE

Colchester United

So here we are at the end of yet another long season, and it doesn't seem a year since we were stumbling drunkenly around the streets of Wembley trying to comprehend the fact that, at last, I had seen a Colchester United side promoted out of the basement division. It was always going to be a struggle not to go straight back down through the trapdoor, not just because the big names and big wallets we were lined up against, but for the fact that, although most of the other teams fell outside this category, none really looked like dead-certain relegation-fodder. Our mission was simple: not to finish in the bottom four, 20th-place would be fine, but anything else that came

The Colchester United Fanzine Written by Supporters for Supporters

Colchester's defensive tactics are taken to extremes in a bid to earn a point!

along, preferably involving a meeting with Bill Borrows, a dark alleyway and a Watusi ritual disembowelling spear, would be most welcome.

Certainly the friendlies went rather well, although the opposition was not of the highest quality. A good unbeaten run always does wonders for the morale, so personally the season began with reasonable hopes. And with Chesterfield providing the opening day opposition at Layer Road, the chances of getting off to a good start were better than they might have been. The manner in which it was achieved was far from relaxing - the only goal of the game an injury-time winner by the Tree (aka Mark Sale, nicknamed the 'Tree' not only because of his great height, but for the fact that he moved around the pitch with the ease of a diseased Dutch Elm), which had the Sale doubters eating a few words in the pub afterwards. Sadly, though, as the months wore on, you realised there was more chance of finding a Dodo egg on the Barside (being closely guarded by two frantically copulating Giant Pandas) than seeing the Tree hit the back of the net again at Layer Road.

Still, as usual, I digress. Sandwiched in between the annual low profile fizzy-keg-shite cup exit - this season at the hands of Bournemouth - was arguably the best win of the season, a 4-2 tonking of Wrexham on their own patch. It was simply superb. No other words can possibly describe it - although manager Steve Wignall didn't quite share our sense of humour, light-hearted chants of "What the fuck is going on" were met with a 'Wiggy slams doubters' headline in the local

Evening Gutsache the following Monday. Ho hum. Still, these heroics put us right up with the top boys after the first two games. (Sad, I know; but, hey, how often are Colchester in the top two of the Second Division? We have to enjoy these things whenever they happen!) Some of those big spenders were visitors to Layer Road in the opening month of the campaign. Both Fulham and Stoke somehow escaped from Layer Road with 1-0 wins, the former thanks to the cheating antics of stumpy half-pint tosspot Paul Peschisolido, the latter thanks to a blinding strike by Graham Kavanagh, the only real effort the visitors had on goal in the entire second-half.

The trip to York is certainly worth more than a passing mention (isn't any away win?), but it was notable for more than just the 2-1, last-minute victory. Picture the scene: a pub in York, not long before kick-off, and renowned David Essex look-a-like and renowned Tree basher Julian (we'll keep his surname a mystery, but he knows who he is!) is chatting away to a man and a women whom he mistakenly believes to be followers of the Minstermen. "You are about to see," begins Julian, blissfully unaware he is about to heap more ridicule upon himself with two words that his retro-coiffure could manage in a year, "the worst player you have ever seen on a football pitch." The couple are evidently intrigued by Jule's musings, and politely enquire as to the identity of the aforementioned player. "His name is Mark Sale," he proclaims triumphantly, awaiting a reaction. "Mark Sale, eh?" replies the man, "Well, I'm his dad." The sound of Julian's jaw hitting the floor at the speed of light is masked only by the lady of the piece chipping in with: "And I'm his sister." We didn't laugh too much, of course, especially when the story made the news in a light-hearted column of the local paper the next week, and certainly would never dream of photocopying the cutting several dozen times and posting it up around the walls of the local pub.

So, back to the adventures of Stevie Wignall's blue and white army, by now comfortably nestled in a mid-table slot. It was rather less comfortable ten games later, with just one win in this period, yet again sealed in the last minute at home to old Conference sparring partners Wycombe. But just to add extra satisfaction to the occasion, it was a dodgy penalty won by - yes, you guessed it, Mark Sale. A forgettable trio of results started to raise concerns as the north-west trio of Oldham, Burnley (total away wins until playing at Layer Road - nil) and Preston found the U's easy pickings, with no danger of troubling their goals-against column. Sale and Neil Gregory were forming the most laughed-at strike-force in the division as the leaves started to fall from the trees. Autumn is the perfect time to visit Maine Road, as it's always nice to have something soft to lie on if you're going to get the shite beaten out of you. I dread to think what might have happened had we won, or even drawn, as the City fans displayed why Manchester is everyone's favourite place, seeming not to care whether they picked on men, women or even kids in the streets after the game.

Not us, though, we were hiding out in a Moss Side boozer, protected by our bodyguards, the rather more friendly lads of the Man City Internet team (actually they were top lads, and saved our necks on more than one occasion that weekend). Strangely, though, the question on everyone's mind was not, "How the hell are we going to get out of here alive?"; but rather, "Who the bloody hell are Bedlington Terriers?" Yes, it was the fateful day we heard the draw for the first round of the FA Cup. I thought it was a wind-up at first, not knowing that Bedlington a) existed; b) had an association football team; or even c) had a rather strange looking dog named after them. Three weeks later and the fateful day arrived. Now, it is always a great day when you beat a team from a higher division in the FA Cup - the most prestigious footballing competition in the world, Man United take note! If you not only beat them, but tonk them 4-1 (having been 4-0 up), then you get a mention on the back pages of the Sunday papers. And if the team you've beaten are actually three divisions (or is it four?) higher than you, then congratulations, you win this year's giant-killers' award. Now, whilst it's always nice to be thought of as a giant (well, you have to be, to be the victims of giant-killing, don't you?), it was just a tad depressing when Bedlington Terriers joined Sutton, Gravesend & Northfleet, and the several others in recent years to knock the U's out of the FA Cup. It's the other footie fans at work who are the worse, as you struggle to convince them that, despite all you've said over the past ten years, you're not really that much of a supporter and the defeat doesn't really bother you in the slightest... but God help you if you mention it again!

But, of course, in true U's style, we beat Notts County 3-1 the following week at the County Ground, just to remind us all (along with regular readers of *SOTF*) that inconsistency is the most consistent thing about Colchester United.

And so the bleak midwinter set in. As we shivered on the terraces up and down the country, it just seemed to get worse and worse. An early chance to make amends for our awful cup form reared its head in the form of the Auto Windscreens Shield, not so ridiculed in these parts after the Wembley run of a couple of seasons back. But even that managed to turn into a nightmare as Gillingham laughed all the way back to Kent with a 5-1 win. Meanwhile, we were banging on the door of the pub by 4:20pm. But if this alone has caused you a nervous breakdown, remember I said worse *and* worse. In the eight games after the win at Meadow Lane, we managed a pitiful five points. The trapdoor was creaking open below us, and when I put the light out at night, I suffered horrible images of the collective populations of Hartlepool, Chester, Mansfield and Plymouth grinning maniacally as they beckoned to us, and we were powerless to resist the relentless slide downwards. We all thought it couldn't get worse when Bristol Rovers (total away wins up to playing at Layer Road - nil) tonked us 3-0, with a bit of help from Embo, followed by another away defeat, 3-1, at Chesterfield, notable only for the first appearance of, and first goal for, new-found wonder-kid Lomanu Tresor Lua Lua. Remember that name: he'll be tormenting a defence near you sometime in the future. It was all capped with a piss-poor 3-1 defeat on a grotty Friday night at Layer Road, the slayers being the mighty Wrexham (total away wins up to playing at Layer Road - nil). Something had to give, fans were crying out for change, but we were all still a tad shocked when Wiggy fell on his sword the following week and walked out of Layer Road for the last time.

You see, the trouble with Wiggy resigning was not so much losing his managerial talents, but the very real risk that ultra-evil assistant-manager Steve

Whitton and his deadly army of burger-hurling ninja contacts was a hot tip to take over. Worst fears were half-confirmed the following day when the burgermeister was appointed joint caretaker-manager with youth team boss Micky Cook, an all-round good egg, holder of the record number of appearances in a U's shirt and generally loved by all. Saturday arrived and we set off for Stoke with some trepidation, easing the nerves by flooding the 'other' section of the *Evening Gazette's* "Who should be the new manager" poll with false votes for terrace legend and fightstarter, twisted-fightstarter, John Raymond Basil Tweed (we felt it best to give his full name at all times, so as to avoid any confusion with little-known termite farmer John Aardvark Tweed of Antwerp). At first we started off with feeble efforts to cover our tracks. Names were pulled out of stories, and telephone numbers were taken from the classified pages of the self-same *Gazette*. (At this point, I would like to offer my sincerest apologies to anyone in the Rabbits and Guinea Pigs section who received strange phone calls that weekend). Boring of this, names and numbers were supplied by passing coaches and lorries, and as the number of pub stops increased, it just all got rather silly - although I thought my Shaggy impression was pretty good, even if I do say so myself.

The actual game (we were on our way to Stoke in case you have forgotten amid yet another ramble) turned out to be a stormer, the Burgerman/Cook partnership got off to a blinding start, the lads showed all of the tremendous spirit we knew they had but had rarely been on show in recent months: 1-0 up after nine minutes, 3-1 down at half-time, then a superb second-half fightback capped with a late equaliser to make it 3-3. They never gave up and it was a joy to watch (except when we were getting thrashed in the first-half). Dismay returned on Monday evening, though - the *Gazette* had somehow managed to discount all of our votes for the Tweedster. We must have made getting on for 40-odd, yet somehow only about half a dozen appeared in the 'other' section in the poll, with no mention of JRBT in sight. However, justice was done and full credit was given in Friday's edition, as the same column that had left Julian rather embarrassed in those heady, late summer months made Mr T red-faced as well, much to our silent mirth.

The week passed, and with a day or so to go to another tricky awayday, this time to Bristol Rovers, Mick Wadsworth was proclaimed the new messiah of Layer Road. The trouble was, as he received the vestments of power, half of the U's fans hadn't heard of him, and the other half had noticed with some concern that his previous job had seen him skilfully pilot Scarborough to the lofty position of only being the second worst club in the entire Football League. He did have his good points, though, having taken the very same Boro to the play-offs the previous season on a budget that even our own chairman Gordon Parker would consider mean, and he actually had quite a good pedigree when you looked below the surface, including a stint as England U-21 manager under the patron saint of farmers, Bobby Robson. Still, the McWhitton/Cook partnership remained at the helm for the Brizzle trip (if you visit Bristol next season, go to the Highbury Vaults - a superb pub you'll do well to top elsewhere in the Second Division). Another battling performance, another last-minute equaliser, another point. We were happier than we were two weeks previously, in the aftermath of the Wrexham bloodbaaaaaaath.

The Wadsworth regime got off to a great start, helped no end by the appearance of something we were beginning to wonder if we would ever see again around these parts - a couple of quality signings. York and Wigan were duly dispatched with 2-1 scorelines, backed up with battling points on our travels to Gillingham and Wycombe, after trailing with ten men; but frustrated with 1-1 draws at home to Reading and Oldham, whom we both led and should have beaten. The Wycombe match was sweet and sour - another injury-time winner, another penalty, another great away trip (especially seeing all their red little faces as they stamped their feet at the final whistle), but it was tempered by the loss of Aaron Skelton, a revelation since his return from injury. He suffered a broken leg after an innocuous collision with Keith Scott. No blame attached, but he was sorely missed for the rest of the campaign...

...which was a bit of a mixed bag really. Macclesfield ended the mini-unbeaten run, with a 2-0 win at the Moss Rose swamp, The Sky cameras came to Layer Road for a narrow defeat at the hands of Man City, which featured a brief but brilliant 15-minute cameo from Fumuca, the only Brazilian ever to play in a U's shirt, ending only when he was knocked out and signed for Barnsley in a daze. Bournemouth snatched a 2-1 win at Dean Court, only to suffer at Layer Road later on in the season, the last in a run of four straight home wins over good sides (Preston and Walsall, two other notable scalps in the quartet), and it was this brief return of Fortress Layer Road that effectively kept us in the Second Division for another year. The away form was patchy at best and horrific at worst, straight defeats at the hands of Burnley and Millwall's youth team (particularly distressing), but we recovered to gain a crucial point in a 3-3 draw at Northampton that wiped the smug grin off the face of former U's manager, now hated Brummie tosser, Ian Atkins. Hope he also wishes he'd never spouted "We'll stay up and you'll go down" bollocks in the *Gazette*, as his team of untalented hoofers slipped through the trap door to Cheltenham.

May hovered into view with only a mathematical miracle in the goals-scored department of our rivals posing any threat to the U's survival mission. So it was typically good spirited of the U's to give Lincoln all three points from our final home game of the season; after all, we were nearly safe now, and they needed them far more than we did. So it was left to a wild weekend in Blackpool to put the season to bed. They took the three points with a late goal, but it was a gutsy show from a U's side containing four youth team debutantes, and besides, it didn't matter - we were already safe, albeit by the skin of our teeth. We went on the Big One; we drank far too much beer; and generally released all the pent-up tension that had built up over nine long, nerve-jangling months. But then again, when the result turns out the right way, you really don't mind that much, do you?

Jason Skinner

THE CIDER'ED

Bristol City

The mid-afternoon sun slants across an early season cricket match. A random couple toss a Frisbee to each other. John and Vicky stroll hand in hand past the lake, ducks just existing, slowly. Emma, sunglasses pushed into her hair, sleeps next to Will, pouring white wine. It is the day after Bristol City have been relegated.

It is the calm after the hurricane, the tension has been released after such a cruel prelude and I can live again. Why do I subject myself to this? I wanted to leave but stopped, condemned to my team, and disillusioned by it. Vague notions of faith and loyalty. Why analyse them? I can't escape.

I am free though, now the season is over. I am free from the despondency of the Carling Atyeo Stand and the City Away Travel Service. Saturday afternoons painless, Tuesday evenings dry, free from tears. The daily 302 Teletext ritual ended, and the newspapers read from the front. Free, but only until the first week in August.

This harsh, harsh game is unerringly compulsive. For eight long, dreadful months I hoped, child-like, that the inevitable would prove a mirage. As we sank, uselessly, to our peril, I found a hundred ways through that thick black line, separating 22nd from heaven. The team could find none of those hundred ways. Relegation shimmered in the distance for half a year and then pounced. Over so quickly but after such hideous, unbelievable anticipation.

How can such promise deliver so little? A summer spent basking in the glory of promotion, constructing dreams of greater success, became an autumn searching for a turning point, a winter despairing of our luck, a spring praying for a miracle, a May Bank Holiday recovering - the barrel of the gun we had looked down for so long finally firing on a warm afternoon in Sheffield.

And what an afternoon that was. Benny Lennartsson, often vilified by the fans yet stoical, dignified, pacing the touchline, falling to his knees, maniacally waving his arms, distraught at the death. Shaun Taylor, the ultimate captain, a maestro at the heart of the back four but his season pitilessly ended by injury just weeks after he had returned from a year out to galvanise his team; inspire three victories; give us hope. Adam Locke, offered a first team reprieve by the Danish coach after Christmas, tirelessly committed, but left to the torture of failure at the whistle, tears dripping miserably onto his yellow and green shirt. Ade Akinbiyi, mercurial but beaten, a 23rd goal of the season against the Blades, but each one futile in the final analysis. Jim Brennan, Aaron Brown and Louis Carey, the kids, the future, but thrust into a campaign of abject ruin. And Brian Tinnion - did anybody hurt more than him as our ignominious decline was completed at Bramall Lane?

Never can a season have offered up so much drama, such palpable fear, such basic apprehension, such entertainment, yet have left the audience disgusted by it all, unable to realise the truth.

The departure of John Ward in October, incomprehensible. Replaced by an unknown, ushered into position with the battlecry "Judge me on my results" still ringing. Well, thank you Benny, you struggled, you kicked every ball, you screamed, you flapped that white baseball cap, but you didn't have a chance. The damage was long done.

The team was defenceless: Dyche and Watts, so uncommanding, the source of uncountable opposition goals; Clemens Zwijnenberg, arrived on loan from Aalborg and utterly inept, a frustrated throw of the dice by Wardy, admitting after a 3-1 defeat at Ipswich that he didn't know what to do next; Bell and Murray, moving forward incessantly, instinctively, exposed when called upon to track back. The centre of midfield no better: Hutchings, a liability; and Hewlett, forever the kid with unrealised potential; Doherty, too often injured, like Edwards.

And up front: £1m for Tony Thorpe but a starter just half a dozen times and ending on loan at Luton; Andersen, a Danish international convinced of his own ability, unready to pass, too often the exquisite soloist when the orchestra demanded silence; and Akinbiyi, a record signing at £1.2m but bemused by it all, a glorious talent who suffered by those around him.

So, as All Saints Day came, Benny Lennartsson arrived to guide a squad perplexed. Where was Ward gone? They took a month to understand. A 5-0 defeat in Benny's first match, at Bradford. Then the complete, most desperate loss of a terrible season. Beaten 6-1 at home by Wolves. Only the warring mascots could divert our attention from that golden-shirted carnage. And the game was up by then anyway. Humiliated at Ashton Gate, jeered by the opposition, laughed at by Rovers. The most irrational 90 minutes of football many will ever witness. Eleven players entirely confounded; new tactics, new confusion. They looked vainly to the bench for guidance. Professional footballers unable to understand Benny's 'diamond' formation. From the kamikaze football of Ward to the incoherent, suicidal style of Lennartsson. It couldn't get worse. The problem was, it hardly got any better.

Sure, Benny made changes: international defenders Ivan Tistimitanu and Vilmos Sebok signed for the club; Cramb, Hutchings, Welch, Dyche, Watts, Hewlett, Murray and Goodridge were all consigned to the reserves, some to the transfer list. The Danish coach tinkered with the team: Shail was brought in to partner Carey at the back; Torpey played up front; striker Soren Andersen played on the left-wing; left-back Brennan played at right-back; first Steve Phillips, then Bo Andersen took over in goal; and Locke was used in the centre of midfield. He altered the formation as well: for weeks we veered, uncertain, confused, between 4-3-3, and 4-4-2, and 4-3-1-2, and 3-5-2. But it didn't matter: whatever combination of players, whatever formation, whatever tactics, something went wrong.

Palace won 2-1 with a last-minute goal; at the Hawthorns, Bell broke a leg, Tistimitanu damaged ligaments, and the team conceded after seven minutes of injury-time, three points metamorphosing instantly into one; in the return fixture with Wolves, Steve Phillips allowed a back-pass to roll slowly into the net; Sunderland were given a 90th-minute penalty with the score at 0-0 and Kevin Phillips made amends for his miss from the spot in the 1-1 draw at the Stadium of Light; from 2-0 down against Bradford, City equalised before gifting the Bantams a third; in the match with Ipswich, Akinbiyi fired wide from half a yard with the 'keeper stranded, subjecting the Ashton Gate faithful to defeat by a single goal yet again; and Birmingham came to Bristol and stole the points after referee Mike Dean put in what many present described as the most inept performance from an official seen at the ground (and this from fans not noted for hyperbole).

How easy all this is, though: to blame bad luck, poor refereeing, an unending injury crisis, and missed chances. How easy, and how clichéd. It is the preserve of every relegated team; the prerogative that says there must be an extraneous reason for failure.

The reality is that there can be no accurate analysis, and the points above are more excuse than reason. There is no consensus of opinion among fans. Debate rages on as memories of '98-99 blur: some remain indignant that John Ward should not have been allowed to leave; others support Benny's tenure fully, considering that his task was impossible and the damage done by the time of his arrival. How can there be a conclusion? Even with hindsight the answer is elusive. All that I am certain of is that it seems strange that the board planned a dual-aspect managerial team but instantly settled on a one-man show when JW departed. The more cynical suggest a boardroom conspiracy. Constructive dismissal has been mooted. But that is unfair to directors who have done so much for our club. An error does not necessarily constitute a premeditated decision. But this is to open another debate, one that has been fought without resolution many times before and can only reopen wounds that are best left untouched.

It is less strongly disputed that a key element in the decline was a division in the changing room; a collapse of team spirit. Rumours persist that a drinking culture prevailed: the likes of Thorpe, Murray and Cramb leaving a trail of empties in Bristol's darkest watering holes. One-time captain Mark Shail is reputed to have been heavy-handed in analysis of his team-mates, alienating some. There are indications that a split emerged between the substantial foreign legion and the British players; Canadians, Hungarians, Moldovans and Danes mingling uneasily with Geordies, Cockneys and the Bristolian talent. Colin Cramb has stated publicly that many players had no respect for their manager, and disagreed with his methods (a point mitigated by Cramb's public statement of his desire to join Bristol Rovers, and reported lack of fitness). Others responded well to Benny's extra training sessions and emphasis on technique: Brennan, Locke, Akinbiyi, Torpey, Carey, and Doherty have all improved since the Dane's arrival. Much is conjecture, but one tends to ask: so much smoke without fire?

These points are inconclusive, and neglect the most important matter of all: the football itself. Ultimately, a team is relegated because it does not play well enough. Above all else that is true of City. Defensively the side was naive: concepts such as marking and closing down seemed alien until Christmas. There was not enough inventiveness going forward, and it was said all season that we needed a creative midfielder. Indeed, it is instructive that when David Howells arrived on loan on transfer deadline day the team secured three consecutive victories - but a season cannot be saved in a month. When Lennartsson arrived he reined in the freedom given to expressive wingers. An expansive game that left the team vulnerable at the back gave way to a tighter system that conceded, but also yielded, fewer goals. The most effective front pairing was never found. BL was right to say that Akinbiyi and Andersen did not complement each other well enough, yet Soren's replacement, Steve Torpey, hit only three goals despite being a near permanent fixture from the New Year. And a genuine leader was missing: it was not until Shaun Taylor, at 36, returned from a year-long injury crisis, over the Easter weekend, that the team had a dominating presence to look to for guidance.

It is hardly surprising that such extensive problems in the dug-out, in the dressing-room and on the pitch resulted in relegation. So, where now?

Indications are the majority of the squad will stay: vital is that a cash injection from the board means Ade Akinbiyi, rated at £3m, does not have to be sold to cover the cost of relegation. There is an abundance of youth talent ready to make its mark: to join the established Bristolian triumvirate of Brown, Doherty and Carey come Alex Meacham, Joe Burnell, Kev Langan, Andrew Jordan, Lorenzo Pinamonte, and Matt Hill, all of whom have now appeared, and impressed, for the first team. Lastly, there remains a senior group who have experience of the last Second Division promotion campaign: Taylor, Tinnion, Torpey, Bell and, possibly, Locke will complement the more rugged talent of the kids.

So, we are optimistic. Many predict immediate promotion back to the First Division. The infrastructure of the club seems capable of supporting football at a higher grade, and there appears to be a growing determination to atone for last season. But we are also wearied by this season, and less idealistic. We entered the First Division confident, certain of ourselves, and we failed hopelessly, unprepared for the experience. At the start of August those vague notions of faith and loyalty will re-emerge, and I'll try to believe again. The Second Division season will approach and the mid-afternoon sun will slant across Ashton Gate, instead of that early season cricket match. City will be back.

Ed Hayes

THE CITY GENT

Bradford City

Ah, the invitation to contribute to *SOTF5* wings its way to me from our esteemed editorial team. Once again they ask for anecdotes, gossip and key features from the season - and not a match by match report. Once again we would have had to do this anyway, as the amount of ale drunk before and after (and even during) the games renders it difficult even to recall some games, let alone report on them.

We can start off with gossip, or rather the lack of it. No club officials photographed exposing Sophie Rees-Mogg's breasts. No players outed by the *News of the Screws* (and who cares, if they play well for your club). No drug hells to be overcome. Not even a love rat to be exposed (even figuratively).

THE
CITY GENT
The Voice of Bantam Progressivism
The Fifteenth Season

ISSUE 82   SPRING 1999

ONE THING THAT'S
DEFINITELY GOING UP AT   **£1**
VALLEY PARADE THIS SEASON !

All we got to hear about was the usual transfer guff (and we never believed we were going to sign the entire Albanian national side at the time) and non-gossip. You know, this sort of thing:

"Hey, I've got something for *City Gent*, I saw player X and player Y down club A on Saturday night."

"It's an absolute bloody disgrace."

"Hey, it isn't that bad. They deserve a drink after a win like that."

"No, club A is an absolute bloody disgrace - the prices they charge for drinks."

Key features is a different matter and it's so difficult to choose. Off the field was a mixed bag. The club staff have worked marvellously hard all season (can I have my photo pass now?), especially the delightful Sarah. Sarah runs the reception, answers the phone at Valley Parade, and has some weird and wonderful people with whom to deal (posh prose, eh?), and that's just the *City Gent* team. Just one example of an overheard telephone call should illustrate this:

"Good morning, Bradford City; how may I help?" "You want the club's address to post something to us? Certainly. It's Bradford City AFC, Valley Parade, Bradford..."

"No, that's Bradford."

"No, Bradford, as in the name of the club. B-R-A-D-F-O-R-D, West Yorkshire..."

"No, West Yorkshire..."

Obviously the ground redevelopment, now that the Labour Party have reneged on their election promises to retain terracing in football grounds, has gone ahead. The new stand is going to be really imposing (especially if you live on Rock Terrace behind it), and even those who wanted to retain the terrace are by and large impressed. Even in its partly-built state, you can see the ground from distant parts of the city, where it was never visible/noticeable from before. (Especially galling to a L**ds fan I know, who bought his house because he couldn't see Valley Parade from there. No doubt he will be investing in some of those fast-growing conifers during the summer months.)

The financial side has looked good throughout the season, particularly comforting when you remember the crises of years gone by and see what can happen at other clubs. However, all these plus points are overturned by two heinous crimes against the City faithful. Crime number one - a mind-sapping blow to both male and female fans. No repeat of the club shop catalogue. The last issue was so popular, I don't think you could buy a copy nowadays. Yet no repeat for this season. Total, total, abject disappointment. Crime number two - there were matches when the bar didn't open at half-time! In days gone by you could sneak out to the Belle Vue for a quick pint if this absolutely horrendous event occurred. Now this famous hostelry is closed, not even that avenue was open and we were left staring for quarter of an hour at the grass growing. At least it was Bradford grass on these occasions, but unforgivable nevertheless. Off the pitch, and in the stands, Huddersfield Town fans (TBs) won the 'filth of the year' award. Having no Chris Kamara to sing racists songs about, they returned to Bradford fire jibes this year.

In particular during the announcement for the minute's silence for Hillsborough victims, there were shouts of "burn you fuckers, burn". The second the whistle sounded after the minute silence, the same pathetic vitriol was repeated.

However, loathsome as you are, we hope it doesn't happen to you.

Anyway, on to the playing side.

The season, or rather pre-season dawned, with City fans' opinion divided as to the managerial appointment. Some believed a 'big name' or more experienced manager should have been appointed. Others, myself included, felt a big name would bugger off at the first sign of a bigger salary, and someone who had pledged themselves to the club would do better for us.

The usual pre-season friendlies gave no real indication as to how we would fair come league kick-off time. For example, my local non-league side, Thackley, looked better than City for periods of our game at Dennyfield, and it was 'only' a penalty that saw us to victory.

So the season proper kicked off with a good-looking (football-wise anyway) City team. Our most expensive forward line ever, and a good mixture of experience and youth, steel and flair, pace and power, Dolland and Aitchison - sorry, got a bit carried away there - in the side. Optimists thought we'd do it, pessimists knew we wouldn't, and those in between just hoped and prayed.

And what a hectic, frantic, breathless season it turned out to be. The side was so erratic: brilliant one game, disinterested the next, then bloody dreadful; then solid, then brilliant, then solid, and so on. Neither could the usual suspects, who haunted the stand or clubhouse bar during these performances, make out any pattern to our form. Valley Parade, Throstle Nest, Former Tory Party Treasure Stadium or Bramall Lane - you never knew what to expect.

Clubs we expected to take three easy points from gave us a hard time. The 'better' (in their view anyway) sides were often overcome with ease. The runaway league leaders from the north-east were given a hell of a game. (We were talking for ages to their Peruvian star in the bar at half-time, before one of their other players came over to tell us he didn't speak a word of English.) Even John McGinlay tried in this one.

Our rivals' results appeared somewhat similar, with many discussions about how one team could beat another, yet lose to a third. Sometimes other results went our way, sometimes not. Many fans' views changed from doom and gloom to hope and glory (I really must stop this) on a regular basis, whilst the optimists (few) remained optimistic and the pessimists (many more) remained pessimistic.

However, the run-in to the end of the season all proved at bit too much and Bradford City reserves remained in Pontin's League Division Two. However, the first team got promoted to the Premiership, so that was a bit of a consolation. But when the usual suspects found out that this meant the reserves getting automatic promotion to the new Premiership Reserve League, we went wild. I don't think the town has seen a night of celebrating like that since VL (Victory over L**ds) night back in the Eighties. A bloody big thank you to everyone at the club for all their efforts this season. Well done.

And finally an anecdote to sum up our season. On our visit to Newcastle for the FA Cup, the first person our crew saw on the station when they arrived was a well-known and loyal supporter last heard of on his holidays in Australia. Apparently, despite his Antipodean absence (sorry), he had managed to obtain a ticket and flown back. Arriving at Heathrow the evening before, he had travelled up to Newcastle on the train overnight. The reason he was staggering, he claimed, was not the strong drink he had consumed but was caused by jet and train lag. Hmm, I think that, metaphorically, just about sums up our season.

John Watmough

THE FOX

Leicester City

Back in August 1996, wide-eyed Premiership new boys Leicester City were overwhelmingly backed to go straight back from where they had come. It was a return trip... behave yourselves, don't create a scene, wipe your feet on the way out and best not sew those Premiership patches too securely on your sleeves, eh?

Three seasons later, after early May's Sunday shakedown, City yet again find themselves settled on page one of the Ceefax Premier League table... i.e. the top half... i.e. how the hell did we do that?

City have occupied the mid-table for nearly all that time.

We have occasionally drifted upwards as far as second, and downwards to the edge of the panic zone, but not too convincingly in either direction.

We have a manager with an eye for a bargain that makes the settlers who exchanged a handful of brightly coloured beads for Manhattan Island look as if they had been badly ripped off.

Martin O'Neill has created the club's best side for over 30 years, with funds as close to bugger-all as makes no odds. Despite lazy media comparisons with Wimbledon and unfounded accusations of spoiling tactics, City have done it with a certain amount of style, too. If we are such a physical side, then how (Spurs fans may want to ask themselves) did we finish second in the Fair Play League?

But despite finishing tenth and competing in (another) cup final, I don't think the season will go down as many City followers' favourite year. In a way, the highlight of the campaign came when the new season was only 75 minutes old. That was the moment when Tony Cottee put us 2-0 up against eventual Treble winners Manchester United, and just for the briefest moment I thought, "Bloody hell! We're going to win the league." Unfortunately due to too many City players having to withdraw with lumps kicked out of them and the ref applying the Old Trafford bye-law of playing on until United equalise, we had to be content with a point. But until that disappointing climax we had been absolutely superb against a team who turned out to be the European Champions.

After that (almost) glorious start we seemed to have alternate good and bad months. There was a disappointing run in September, but then things on the field picked up in October, whilst off the field a worrying advance from Leeds smarmy chairman Peter Ridsdale was eventually beaten off. O'Neill would almost certainly have left for Elland Road had he been given permission to speak to Leeds, but that permission was never forthcoming, as chairman John Elsom did a passable impression of a brick wall. He may no longer be on O'Neill's Christmas card list, but at least he held on to the biggest asset the club has. November bad, December good. January and February rotten... but patchy league form, especially at Filbert Street, was threaded through with another march on Wembley as a succession of Premier League sides were hurdled in the League Cup.

The last-minute defeat at Wembley as ten-man Spurs snatched the trophy from under our noses, actually signalled a big upturn in league fortunes. A marvellous April saw City enjoy instant revenge, with a 2-0 victory at Spurs, gain the usual win at Anfield, dent Chelsea's hopes of the title beyond repair with a late equaliser at Stamford Bridge, and beat local rivals Coventry at home - dispelling any lingering fear of relegation in the process. May saw City stumble to three defeats in a disappointing end to matters, but tenth place was secured despite an awful defeat at Forest on the final Sunday.

So we find ourselves in an odd position. For a set of supporters who endured the Plymouth, Bournemouth, Hull, Portsmouth, Swindon... circuit for far too long, we are still appreciative of our top-flight place. But do we want to finish tenth from now until the end of time? Like Coventry, only better?

Martin O'Neill and his side now seem to be banging their heads on a glass ceiling. The board still regard 1988 prices for players as impressive and it is becoming increasingly difficult to buy players who are an improvement on what we already have. The latest crop of arrivals: Gerry Taggart, Andrew Impey, Frank Sinclair and Arnar Gunnlaugsson have yet to replace the first wave of O'Neill signings in our affections or in the starting XI.

The only way through, onto higher and better things, would be a new stadium to replace the 22,000 capacity Filbert Street, two sides of which would be laughed at by opposing supporters, even if we played in the Nationwide Conference. O'Neill has made no attempt to hide his contempt for the "humble surroundings" he is forced to ply his trade in and is only half-joking when he claims that he tries to keep the 'bike shed' East Stand out of sight when bringing potential new signings to the club.

You can't tread water forever, and what we now desperately need is one of those shiny new grounds that everyone else seems to be getting. So the key to further progress now rests firmly on the shoulders of those charged with getting Leicester City FC moved lock, stock and no smoking areas the short hop over the canal to the proposed new site on Bede Island.

At times progress has been encouraging. We have a little model of the ground to look at (very nice). We have architects drawings, with the bluest of blue skies and the waters of the canal gently lapping against its banks, onto grassy areas where the artist must seriously have considered adding picnicking, kite-flying families (lovely). But as for any activity involving big yellow diggers and blokes in construction helmets... nothing doing. At the time of writing, City have had a green light from the local Council... which arrived on the same night that City won their League Cup Semi-final against Sunderland and was announced after the game, producing a bigger roar than the final whistle. But there is the usual resident opposition to the plans and our particular buff-coloured folder has currently entered the warren of corridors in Whitehall, whilst the government decides whether it is worthy of a hearing.

Until then, we are still waiting, suspended in time and space, for the great leap forward.

If we can oversimplify things just a little, two scenarios present themselves:

Firstly, and this is my preferred option, the ground is okayed in time for work to start this summer and Leicester City have a stadium worthy of their players and manager in time for the start of the 2000/01 campaign. The crowds who stayed away when it became too difficult to get tickets at Filbert Street come flocking back, O'Neill manages to keep his side together, adds to it significantly, and goes on to do what his old boss Brian Clough did at East Midlands rivals Derby and Forest in the Seventies. Hurrah!

The alternative, is that the ground plans get caught up in red tape, the new ground might be ready, who knows when, O'Neill gets fed up waiting and starts looking for a club with facilities and funds to match his ambitions, and every player worthy of the name follows him out of the door. We probably wouldn't need a 40,000 stadium then.

Oh bugger.

This club has stood at the gateway of the big boys playground before, and those within the oak-panelled boardroom have opted for the quiet life... this time, they really do have to get it right.

Gary Silke

THE GOONER

Arsenal

There's one player I'd love to be able to ignore in this review of Arsenal's '98-99 season, but unfortunately he provided the beginning and the ending to a memorable, yet somehow forgettable campaign, thus making it impossible. Who am I referring to? One Edward Sheringham.

Our benevolent act of inviting Manchester United to join our Double Double party, also known as the Charity Shield, at Wembley in August was surely centred round this sad individual who has in the past expressed a deep lying hatred of all things Goonerish. Even so, he had managed to endear himself to the red and white half of North London when, on leaving White Hart Lane to join United in the summer of 1997, he declared he was moving to "win medals", the insinuation obviously being that Spurs would never be able to help him achieve that particular goal.

How funny was it, therefore, that in his first season at Old Trafford, not only did he end up with none (we had a rather less polite way of phrasing it, but apparently I shouldn't use such language in a family publication such as this), but that we were the team to deprive him on two fronts.

Consequently, his appearance on the United substitute bench for this annual curtain-raiser was met with much amusement from the triumphant Arsenal fans. The tabloid hacks had hyped themselves into a frenzy over the anticipated jeering which David Beckham would endure after his World Cup *faux pas* and yet, whilst not ignoring Posh's bloke, we were clearly more interested in baiting his loud-mouthed team-mate. By the time we were 3-0 up and cruising to victory, we were even proclaiming "We want Teddy"; and, once Ferguson had duly obliged, requesting that his team-mates "Give the ball to Teddy". How we laughed when he placed the easiest of chances into the side netting. Everything was well with the world.

Nine months later and the same Mr Sheringham was standing on the same turf being interviewed by some Sky commentator having just won the Man of the Match award in the FA Cup Final. "It's been some week for you, Teddy," we were breathlessly told. "Seven days ago you had no medals and now you've got two!"

"Yeah," said Teddy. "I've certainly proved some people wrong. Here's to all you Gooners!"

At first I couldn't believe my ears and then it was all my family could do to prevent me putting my foot through the telly. Little did I know then that just four days later he was going to play an equally large part in spoiling our celebrations to commemorate the tenth anniversary of that moment at Anfield in 1989 when Mickey Thomas went "charging through the midfield" (© Brian Moore 1989) to score the goal which won the Championship and inspired *Fever Pitch* - the best football-related film ever. However, if you think you've heard the last of the "Ooooh Teddy, Teddy" song, don't bet on it. With the number of talented intellectuals among our following, the new lyrics took all of 30 seconds to dream up: "You might have won the treble, but you're still a c..."

So am I jealous of United's treble success? Of course I bloody well am. You've got to be, haven't you? They outshone our Double, nicked our ownership of the most famous last-minute goal in history, and even managed to pinch our most revered date. Bastards! However, I'm not one to try to argue that they were lucky, because I've always felt that the team who wins the league are the best side in the country; and anyway, any argument raised would be devaluing our own achievements of twelve months ago. Nevertheless, my motto for the close season has been: "Great sides know how to finish second." And my reasoning is that you've got to accept that you can't win everything every year. The important thing is that if you are not winning, you've got to be in the next best place, and that's second. Look back at the Liverpool sides of the Seventies and Eighties, from 1972 until 1991, they only failed to finish in the top two once (1980-81). And during the Nineties, Manchester United have had eight consecutive years of finishing no lower than second. This is a habit which Arsenal have never really mastered, having only come second in English football's top division three times and, before last season, the most recent occasion as long ago as 1972-73; and before that not since the early Thirties. If we are to be regarded as a genuine force in European football, this is the kind of consistency we must demonstrate.

Don't get me wrong, though, there's no way anyone should regard this season as a flop and it has disappointed me to hear so many disparaging remarks from fellow supporters. It doesn't matter whether you support Manchester United or Scarborough, there will have been moments throughout the season which you can look back on and think about what might have been 'if' those incidents had seen the ball bounce a different way. For me, there were four such moments that contrived to rob us of not one, not two, but in fact all three trophies which are now residing at Old Trafford.

Firstly, had we not conceded soft, late equalisers in our Champions League games against Lens and Dynamo Kiev, not only would we have been progressing to the quarter-finals as group winners, but it could also have meant Manchester United's elimination from the competition, since they only just squeezed through as one of the best runners-up.

By the time we visited The Dell at Easter, the Premiership title race was moving into its final furlong and the difference between a win and a draw was looking increasingly likely to be a critical factor in the eventual reckoning. So when Kanu was presented with an opportunity to turn one point into three from close-range and only managed to steer the ball into Francis Benali's stomach rather than the back of the net, many suspected that the writing was on the wall.

And then there was Dennis Bergkamp's penalty miss in the last minute of normal time in what was rightly billed as the Match of the Season - the FA Cup Semi-final replay. It's not stretching the point too far to say that moment may well have decided not only the FA Cup, but also the league, such was the impetus handed to United. Of course, I appreciate that Alex Ferguson (you can't tell me who I have to call 'Sir') would be whining as only he can if these had all fallen our way, but do you really think I'd care?

OK, so those were the low points, but it would be unforgivable not to mention at least some of the events which made up the rest of Arsenal's season. After the highs of the previous campaign, it was always going be difficult, if not impossible, to emulate those achievements. Some pundits questioned whether the appetite would still be there and, indeed, at the start of the season, one of our regular columnists expressed some concern that French World Cup winner Emmanuel Petit, in particular, would struggle to "get really stoked up about Charlton's visit" to Highbury at the end of August. Perhaps Manu read this and, determined to show his hunger was anything but lacking, promptly got himself sent off in said game; probably the one red card of the three he was to collect that you couldn't argue with.

Indiscipline was to be a stick with which the press beat us throughout the campaign, as referees waved their cards at our players with an infuriating regularity. Suspensions to key players at key times caused Arsene Wenger selection problems, most of which he circumnavigated with extraordinary ease. But it remains an area where there is plenty of room for improvement.

If the media were quick to criticise when things weren't going our way, it was pleasing, if a little unusual, to be the recipients of their praise for an unprecedented act of sportsmanship which shook the football world. Our FA Cup Fifth Round tie against First Division Sheffield United was locked at one goal apiece when one of the visiting players suffered an injury which left him prostrate on the Highbury turf. Play carried on for a short while before the Sheffield United goalkeeper cleared the ball into touch, although whether this was done deliberately is perhaps debatable. However, it was clear that at least 20 players on the pitch were prepared to accept this to be the case and, once treatment had been administered to the injured player, took up their positions in expectation of the ball being thrown back to the goalkeeper, as football protocol dictates. Indeed that was what Ray Parlour appeared to attempt, but our Nigerian international, Kanu, who having appeared as a substitute a few minutes earlier was making his Arsenal debut, ran on to the ball and seeing Marc Overmars also making ground in the middle, crossed for the Dutch winger to tap into what was practically an unguarded net. No official rules had been broken, so the goal had to stand, but our cheers were muted and for a while it seemed unlikely that the match would reach its conclusion as Sheffield United manager Steve Bruce stormed on to the pitch to remonstrate with the referee, and he even attempted to call his team off the pitch in disgust. Fortunately, some sense of order was restored and the game was allowed to continue, although in the most surreal of atmospheres. The 'goal' did prove decisive and, not surprisingly, was the main talking point as Gooners left the ground and made their way to the nearby pubs. The debate was quickly silenced, however, by the sight of Arsene Wenger appearing on television screens and offering to replay the game. To many people's surprise, the FA quickly agreed and we met again at Highbury ten days later when, with supreme irony, we again ran out 2-1 winners, thanks to goals from the villain of the first game, Marc Overmars, and an exquisite chip from Dennis Bergkamp.

Arsenal fans were quick to point out that there were no conciliatory gestures two years previously when we were the victims of a similar incident involving Chris Sutton, which deprived us of a Champions League spot. It will be interesting to see whether a precedent has now been set, but I think the most important thing was that the integrity of Arsenal Football Club remained unblemished and the credit for this must rest with Arsene Wenger, who has made such an impact in his two and a half years with us that it's embarrassing to remember our indifferent reaction to his appointment. I'd be hard pushed to name another manager in the English game who would have been able to handle the situation with such dignity.

George Graham, perhaps? Hmmm... couldn't see it somehow, but then perhaps I'm a touch biased now that he is in residence down the road at White Hart Lane. Unthinkable as it may have been five years ago, the man whose study is (was) a shrine to Arsenal and their history, has now been charged with attempting to recreate the glory days for our biggest rivals. It would be something of an understatement to say that his decision to take up the post was not well received at Highbury. Those who were prepared to forgive and forget his involvement in the bung allegations, saw this as a crime far more heinous and were not slow to let Mr Graham know their feelings when he visited Highbury in November with his new friends. The ensuing goalless draw will undoubtedly have brought a smile to his face, since it not only proved that his current crop of defenders were already picking up the art of keeping clean sheets, but the home side's defence, which incidentally was on its way to a new Premiership record of conceding only 18 goals in 38 matches, still had a remarkably familiar look to it!

Of course, George did lead Spurs to their first silverware in eight years, even if it was only the Worthless Cup which we, like the other big sides, regard as little more than practice sessions for our reserves. Needless to say their fans didn't see it in quite the same light and were "giving it plenty" when we went to White Hart Lane for a critical league fixture in early May. Thankfully, our 3-1 victory put them firmly in their place and was capped by a high class goal from Kanu, chipping the ball over the head of the defender and then running round to hit it powerfully past Ian Walker. The Nigerian international had certainly made his mark since his arrival from Internazionale in January, because apart from his involvement in the Sheffield United debacle and this goal against the ol' enemy, he had enchanted fans with his incredibly laid back approach and delightful touch. You had to see a slow motion replay of his second goal in the 6-1 drubbing of Middlesbrough to appreciate the sublime piece of skill he had executed to back-heel a Lee Dixon cross into the corner of the goal from fully 15 yards out. More than anything, it is his form that allows us to look forward with such optimism to the challenge that lies ahead.

However, at the time of writing, it looks certain that Nicolas Anelka has played his last game for the club and although we will be collecting a record fee from his transfer, his departure will leave a gaping hole which will not be easy to fill. The new format of the Champions League is going to put an enormous strain on our playing resources and I don't doubt that we'll be a major player in the transfer market during the close season as a consequence. Nevertheless, I'm sure Monsieur Wenger has a few names up his sleeve and he'll pluck us another gem or two from somewhere... just so long as it ain't Teddy bloody Sheringham.

Mike Francis

Source: Moulin Rouge

THE HANGING SHEEP

Leeds United

Having attained a place in the UEFA Cup in George Graham's first full season, the emphasis was on consolidating that position in the hope that a bit of success might tempt top names to set down roots here at Elland Road. Well, that was my theory at least.

All through the summer of 1998 we had to endure chairman Peter Ridsdale stating that Leeds would back the manager financially, whilst Graham countered that funds didn't seem to be available. Given that Leeds United have been consistently tight (tight in top-flight terms) with transfer payouts, then Graham's words sounded neither unreasonable or, perhaps more worryingly, untrue.

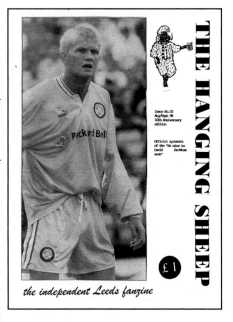

the independent Leeds fanzine

Early matches were blighted by a never-ending cluster of drawn matches when victories should have been assured. These results were further interspersed by the never-ending claim and counter-claim from manager and chairman respectively. Although it all seemed within context, underlying differences were there to be seen if you cared to read between the lines.

All this led to Spurs sticking their noses into the argument when yet another of their managers had to leave. Surely Graham wouldn't undo all the hard work that he, O'Leary and the often-understated Eddie Gray had put in over the past two years?

Graham's reluctance to state his intentions and continued appearances on *Match Of The Day*, when questions about his future were met with the trademark smile (that is about as sincere as a crocodile's just before it lunches on your bollocks), further fuelled the fire.

During the trip to Maritimo (a small Portugese colony in the middle of nowhere), Peter Ridsdale attempted to calm the travelling Leeds fans by climbing into our section of the ground and relaying the situation first hand. His words will echo in my head forever. Surrounded by the masses, our esteemed chairman simply stated: "Fuck George Graham, he's off. Let's get behind the team."

Although the supporters rallied for the lads, Graham still got the abuse he deserved - and more. Ironically, as he sat impassively on the bench all game, we perhaps had a glimpse of things to come when his number two, David O'Leary,

---

was banished to the dressing-room for constantly leaving his seat and arguing the toss with the officials, rival team coaches and anyone else who wanted it. He was eventually sent off but not before two-fingering the jeering home supporters in the main stand. A bloke who gets right into the situation, I'm sure you'll agree.

Lunching the following day, we came across the Maritimo manager enjoying the fruits of his labour. He was delighted to go out on penalties after a 1-1 aggregate draw, when anything less than a complete rout would have been considered a success. He revealed that his players hadn't been paid for three months prior to the first-leg and that they'd returned to the dressing-room, after warming up at Leeds, shit-scared of the capacity crowd!

He'd simply instructed them to play for their pride - and play they did over those two legs. He even agreed to sign as Leeds manager for the princely sum of two English pints. What a contrast then to our overpaid, pampered players who won't consider getting into their flash cars for less than £10,000 per week. Days later and Graham was gone.

Just how anyone could be surprised by his lack of loyalty is beyond me. After all, he's always been one to put himself first and just because Leeds had been the only club to touch him with a very long stick after the bung scandal, it didn't necessarily follow that he would swallow his self-interest this time. He hadn't, he wouldn't - and I don't believe he ever will.

O'Leary immediately said he didn't want the job, as it was too big a task. This translated that he was to join Graham back home in London. Leeds then went on the prowl and ended up with Martin O'Neill as top candidate. O'Neill said he'd be interested in talking to Leeds as long as the board let him. They wouldn't. Leeds wouldn't approach him illegally but made it known that if he walked out they would talk to him. O'Neill said he wouldn't walk out but wanted to talk to Leeds. O'Leary (still at Leeds) said he would be interested in the job after all. Leicester said that Leeds couldn't talk to O'Neill. The PFA got involved, as did the Managers Association and the United Nations, NATO, The Salvation Army and Jerry Springer. But nothing changed - and after weeks of basically arsing around, we were back to square one.

So, we still didn't have a manager, Spurs had a new one and Leicester had their old one. Following all that? Ridsdale then went after O'Leary who, after days of intense talks, agreed to take over "for the time being".

Immediately youngsters and fringe players were plunged into the first team. A bold, attacking plan almost worked against Roma in the Olympic Stadium in the UEFA Cup. A 1-0 defeat didn't tell the story, as a ten-man Leeds ran the Italians ragged, the men in White rattling the woodwork twice in Rome. A similar scoreline in the second-leg meant the European tour was over but the new look Leeds team had done their new manager and, more importantly, themselves proud. There *was* life after Graham then.

Five weeks in and O'Leary's first signing was a familiar name. One David Batty returning home after five years away. Another great piece of Leeds transfer business meant that he left us for £2.7m and returned costing some £4.5m. In typical Batty fashion, he was booked, and therefore suspended again, and also cracked ribs, keeping him out for a couple of months. What a way to make a second debut.

The team continued to play ever more free-flowing attack-minded football, the likes of which have been sadly lacking at Leeds for years. Let's face it, O'Leary's predecessors, Graham and Wilkinson, haven't exactly got a great reputation for putting together teams who play exhilarating stuff. My fears were that, after so many years having Graham as a mentor, O'Leary would be cast in the same mould. I hold my hands up to the fact that I was way off the mark.

A potential cup upset at Portsmouth was to prove a test for O'Leary and his team, with Leeds' record in cup competitions not brilliant to say the least. A 5-1 demolition of Pompey masked the true dominance of the Leeds youngsters - we could and should have reached double figures that day.

The Leeds bandwagon rumbled on and despite Graham returning to knock us out of the cup after a replay, O'Leary's policy of keeping faith with the youngsters was paying dividends. Even our traditional enemy, the press, were beginning to wake up to the fact that we had a team to be proud of. The praise heaped upon Leeds United was quite unprecedented and even a tad disturbing, given that they have lunched on Leeds for three decades or more, with a frenzied enthusiasm bordering on the obsessive.

Alan Smith has made the U-21 England squad after only a handful of appearances and promises much for the future, as does Jonathan Woodgate, who went from reserve team player to full England international in an amazing 33 matches. Not only that, he was about the only English player to come away from the Euro 2000 flop in Bulgaria with any credit. The only downside was the excellent Lee Bowyer being completely overlooked for all England squads, despite having a superb season. This stemmed from a set-to with Peter Taylor in the summer of 1997. With Wilko now in charge of the U-21s, Bowyer's chance should come.

Even whilst partaking in an incredibly booze-fuelled stag week in Benidorm did we encounter more praise for our team. None other than a pissed up David Fairclough (yes, super sub himself) was announcing his admiration for the Leeds team. Oh, and by the way readers, he reckons he's got strawberry blond hair!

So, where do we go from here? Everything in the garden is rosy and O'Leary has got the team playing some superb football, with more yet to come. Europe will again prove a test for us, but given our performances against Roma, when the club was in turmoil, I feel reasonably confident that progress can be made on that front domestically, in terms of spending, we are still light years behind the top three, who are surely going to be scrapping once more for the top spots. Leeds have been widely tipped to have an influence on the title - and who would bet against us causing an upset?

Personally speaking, I think we're more likely to grab the odd win against the top three rather than challenging outright, but it'd be nice to get in amongst them.

From the fanzine point of view, this season saw our 50th edition roll off the press, and after ten years we decided to retire. Countless letters asked us to reconsider, but retire we have. So, once again may we thank our loyal readership for a decade of support and encouragement, and also outlets such as *SOTF* for allowing us the opportunity to bring our views to a wider audience. Cheers.

Chris Stringer

THE HATCHET

Bury

In '97-98, Bury had just about managed to hang onto their newly-found status in Division One, once again confounding critics and pundits alike. By the start of '98-99, however, things were already looking ominous. Stan Ternent and Sam Ellis, our most successful (if least photogenic) management team ever, chose to enhance their CV's by moving down a division to nearby Burnley.

Some fans hoped that this would be the perfect opportunity to get Sammy McIlroy in as manager. McIlroy, famed as the last of the Busby Babes, ended his playing career with something of a flourish at Gigg Lane some ten years ago, and is still seen by some Shakers fans as a potential messiah. That McIlroy stayed at

Macclesfield Town may say even more about Bury's lack of pulling power then Ternent's defection to the Purples. After some apparent hesitation, Bury finally secured the services of Neil Warnock who, it has been alleged, delayed joining us in the hope of being offered the job at his beloved Bramall Lane.

Our sense of gloom deepened when star defender Paul Butler joined Sunderland for the standard maximum fee of £1m - like Dr Evil, the villain in the Austin Powers films, our directors seem incapable of imagining a sum any higher than this. Worst of all, we still had 'Robbie the Bobby' as our mascot. This polystyrene monstrosity is supposed to be the club's tribute to Robert Peel, but (like most mascots, I suppose) merely succeeds in reminding any of us who are old enough of the nightmare that was *It's a Knockout*. Having any sort of mascot is bad enough; but what sort of street cred does it give you to have one who is named after the founder of the Dibble?

Despite these worrying portents, The Shakers got off to a surprisingly good start, climbing briefly to third place in the table, and then securing a money-spinning cup-tie at Old Trafford. Even at this stage, though, Neil Warnock's sober realism/complete lack of ambition (delete as preferred) was evident, as he pointed out that he would be delighted if we finished fourth from bottom. Some fans were beginning to doubt Warnock's judgement of players too, when it seemed that most of his signings turned out to be a) right-sided defenders; b) players he had signed before at previous clubs; and, of course, c) free transfers. And, although he revealed himself to be a reasonably witty speaker at various club functions, Warnock got the prize for Gigg Lane's PR gaffe of the season when he turned up for our match against Sheffield United wearing a Blades tie!

In a season of disappointments, the undoubted low point came at the end of November, when three thousand Bury fans travelled, more in hope than expectation, to Bolton's new Breezeblock Stadium, only to see the Scum give us a thoroughly deserved 4-0 tonking. After this gutless display, Warnock and his players were treated to a holiday in St Lucia, which is in contrast to the Bury fans, a fair proportion of whom were treated for chronic depression. We eventually got our revenge at the end of April, with our customary victory over Bolton at Gigg Lane, but by now we were in the bottom three and looking odds-on for relegation. The death knell finally sounded on Sunday 9 May when, despite a 1-0 win over Port Vale, we were relegated instead of Vale (with whom we were on equal points) on the basis of goals scored. The club, incidentally, chose this fixture as a 'family fun day' - free admission for kids, face-painting, disco and fun quiz, tour of the ground and dressing-rooms... all this *and* relegation. When it comes to putting on a show, we can't half show those Premiership boys a thing or two.

During the course of the season, the football was often dire, sometimes inspired, but however well or badly we played, the enduring problem was hitting the back of the net. It was our inability to score goals that ultimately cost us our hard-won place on football's mezzanine floor. Meanwhile, directors and commercial types at the club seemed to spend too much time repeating their old mantra - "We've got no money, we've got no fans, so what do you expect?" - whilst berating fans (and fanzines) for daring to comment on "things you know nothing about" (always a good standby, that one). We all know that Bury have never had money to burn - but are they trying to tell us that all those £1m transfers, the fees from Sky for live matches, *and* our Old Trafford bonanza really made no difference at all?

As the new season approaches, even more star players have left the sunken ship - for example, goalkeeper Dean Kiely and defender Chris Lucketti - leaving us with a major rebuilding job on our hands. Only time will tell if Warnock is up to it, but there has already been some talk in the local papers about Bury 'bouncing straight back' - I hope they mean Division One, not Division Three.

On a more positive note, last season saw the formation of the new Bury FC Supporters Association, which has the potential to be a force for real change and progress for the club. Work has also commenced on the new Cemetery End Stand, which will replace Gigg Lane's last remaining terrace and complete the process of transforming the ground into an all-seater stadium. All we need now is a decent team to watch and a few thousand more fans.

One thing last season showed me was that if Bury really want to make progress, build the supporter base and compete with the best, then the club needs to take a long, hard look at the way it promotes and markets itself. The club still relies far too heavily on the blind loyalty of a small but dedicated hard-core of fans. We need radical changes, plenty of imagination, and new vision, and the courage to go for it - after all, what have we got to lose? If relegation has done anything positive, it has surely proved - hopefully, once and for all - that you can't survive just by trying to stand still.

Chris Bainbridge

THE HOLY TRINITY

Aston Villa

Of all the clubs in all the world, only Aston Villa can put their supporters through the frustrations and disappointments that we had to suffer eventually during the season. Top of the pile on New Year's Day - having held the position for four months - Villa ended the season 24 points adrift from the eventual Champions; and, in sixth position, we didn't even manage to qualify for any kind of European competition for the coming campaign.

The warning signs were there from the outset. Despite John Gregory's amazing start at the Villa helm at the beginning of 1998, the summer transfer activity was more about departures than arrivals.

The Holy Trinity

Issue 19   February / March 1999   £1.00

COLLY

MAKES

SMALL

HEATH

DEBUT

AN ASTON VILLA FANZINE

Alan Thompson came from Bolton to give us balance on the left side of midfield, but out of the door went Milosevic, Nelson and Staunton (on a Bosman). The summer was spent holding negotiations with five players who had just twelve months left on their current contract - in order to avoid another Bosman-style departure. Then there was the little matter of Dwight Yorke.

Dwight Yorke was a hero down at Villa Park, idolised by grown men in the same vein as ex-players Brian Little and Paul McGrath. He had been the main reason for Villa's achievements over the past few years. The guy was (and still is) an absolute gem. The problem is, when you have players of such calibre, the bigger clubs start sniffing around - in this case, the hunter was Manchester United. All summer long, you couldn't open the newspapers without reading the latest developments in the 'Yorke to United' saga. Villa resisted all the initial approaches, but it was clear that Dwight's heart was set on the move. He appeared in the Villa team photo with the number 19 on his back (his squad number at Man United), and when he played his last-ever game for us, at Everton on the opening day of the season, he gave one of the most anonymous performances of his career. Villa finally surrendered for a bargain £12m at noon on European transfer deadline day. Within five hours, Yorke had driven to Manchester, passed a medical, agreed personal terms, and had registered as a United player. Hmmm.

The problem now for Villa was that it was too late for us to sign anyone for our own UEFA Cup campaign, and our squad was considerably weaker through the loss of our best player. We had the absurd situation of Riccardo Scimeca - a reserve central defender - playing in attack alongside Julian Joachim. In fact, our European adventure was almost over before it had started, as Stromsgodset (Norwegian for relegation-fodder) had taken a 2-0 lead at Villa Park in the first-round, first-leg. Luckily, Dariusz Vassell made a name for himself with injury-time goals - and Collymore wrapped it up with a hat-trick in the return leg. However, we met sterner opposition in the next round, in the form of Celta Vigo. Despite a fine performance in Spain, where Villa came away with a rare European away win, the Spaniards taught us a lesson in the European game in the return leg. Villa had been eliminated from the competition without even worrying the trophy-engravers.

The League Cup offered a similar disappointment. Having been handed a bye in round two because of our European commitments, Villa started their challenge with a tough trip to Chelsea in round three. In his infinite wisdom, Gregory decided to 'do a Manchester United', and fielded a severely weakened side. Unfortunately, the Villa squad doesn't compare to the Manc outfit and we were hammered 1-4, despite taking the lead. The supporters weren't happy: the League Cup still offers a European place and a Wembley final, which is something that you don't experience every year. Those who had made the journey down to Stamford Bridge were even more pissed off, having paid £35+ for ticket and travel, and having taken time off work just to see a team made up of reserves and fringe players wave the white flag.

If we thought that was bad, then much, much worse was to follow in the FA Cup, known on the Holte as Villa's holy grail (we haven't won the damn thing for 42 years). Collymore decided to play for us in the third round, first v 92nd clash as we eased past Hull City 3-0. However, Gregory left him out of the squad for the game against Fulham. Stan went AWOL for a month and Villa crashed out to Keegan's side in another humiliating surrender. The worst part about this day was that Villa didn't even look like scoring past the Second Division outfit - and the 30,000 or so Villa fans who had turned up knew that it wasn't going to get any better.

Anyway, the cups didn't really matter (Mickey Mouse competitions the lot of them...) because Villa were going to win the big one - the FA Carling Premiership. If your side has ever been top of its respective league, then you will know that it is a bloody marvellous feeling. While your team is in pole position, then no-one can take away the fact that your team is the best at that particular moment in time. Before the big clubs start to dominate and spoil the fun, a couple of the other runners usually get the chance to be top of the shop for a couple of weeks, and the fans get to experience briefly the unconfined joy that comes with being top of the league. Villa supporters didn't just get a couple of weeks - we got four months.

It all started after only the third game of the season, Villa went top for 24 hours with a good 1-0 away win at Sheffield Wednesday; yet even the most optimistic of Villa fans knew that it was way too early to start getting excited. But then we remained unbeaten in September and October, and started to pull away from the chasing pack. Everything that Gregory touched was turning to gold. We needed creativity after the loss of Yorke, so we bought Paul Merson. Gary Charles was struggling as a right wing-back, so the versatile Steve Watson arrived from

Newcastle. And when Collymore failed to stick the ball in the back of the net, Dion Dublin arrived on the scene and scored seven goals in his first three games. Everything in the garden was coming up claret and blue roses, but still no-one would take us seriously. The media continued to focus on the big three - Manchester United, Arsenal and Chelsea. Villa played all three in the space of a week in December. Despite outplaying Manchester United, we only came away with a point; we came from 2-0 down to beat Arsenal; and we only lost to Chelsea thanks to an injury-time goal scored in the early hours of Thursday morning. The toughest test of the season had been endured, and we were still on top.

This may have been the moment when Villa lost their bottle; when it suddenly dawned on the team that they were actually serious contenders and could actually do it. Certainly, after the amazing comeback against Arsenal (three goals in the second-half; the Gunners only conceded 17 league goals all season), the standard of Villa's performances dropped considerably. We were lucky to get three points against Charlton and Sheffield Wednesday; we were beaten by lowly Blackburn Rovers on Boxing Day; and after a terrible Everton provided us with what was to be our only league win during the first three months of 1999, came the Fulham debacle.

We thought that things couldn't possibly get any worse, but they did. Villa lost seven of their next eight league games, only a point against Wimbledon at Selhurst Park saving the team from an unwanted club record. Off the pitch, Collymore had officially become a part-timer, spending more time at the clinic than he did on the training pitch. Things weren't going our way in the transfer market either. Despite the player arriving by private jet at Birmingham airport, and holding a meeting at Villa Park itself, Juninho did not join the ranks, as the club refused to splash the cash.

The season was now beginning to drag and there were still a couple of months to go. As each Saturday went by without a Villa victory, Manchester United and Arsenal pulled further away and our title challenge seemed a distant memory. Soon, Chelsea had overtaken us and we were waving goodbye to our place in the exclusive UEFA Champions League. Next it was the turn of Leeds to bypass us, nabbing the one position available for UEFA Cup entry in the process. The final ignominy came on the last weekend of the season. Defeat at Arsenal and victory for West Ham meant that we hadn't even managed to qualify for the Inter-Toto Cup (although the damage had been done with a home defeat against Charlton the week before). After promising so much at the start of 1999, Villa finished the season with the same reward as the likes of Coventry City, Southampton and Wimbledon (no disrespect to the Saints or the Dons).

At the end, our squad was immediately weakened by Bosnich's decision to take advantage of the Bosman ruling to join Manchester United. To make matters worse, speculation continues about the future of our best remaining player - Ugo Ehiogu. As long as Villa continue to sell top players, rather than buy them; and as long as they turn down players of the calibre of Juninho, and settle instead for players such as Steve Stone - then they are never going to worry the Manchester Uniteds and Arsenals of this world.

Steve Whitehouse

THE LATIC FANATIC

Wigan Athletic

We've been left wondering how the '98-99 season could be labelled as a failure. Ray Mathias must be wondering as well. For, despite winning the Auto Windscreens Shield at Wembley and making the play-off semi-finals after coming through a punishing seven games in 15 days, Mathias was sacked in the most ruthless axeing by a chairman you're ever likely to see. In truth, if Mr Whelan is looking for a scapegoat for Latics' failure to make the First Division, then he need only look as far as the mirror. His refusal to invest any money into an adequate drainage system on the Springfield Park pitch during the pre-season surprised no-one. What was the point of throwing money into an outdated ground, when we were moving to a new stadium in twelve months time? But, in retrospect, this school of thought was extremely short-sighted and cost the club a lot more money than it saved them. Game after game was postponed as Latics fans were starved of any action on their own doorstep for the first month and a half of 1999, and in no small way helped clog up the fixture backlog at the end of the season.

The chairman's inability to appoint a new manager after Deehan's expected departure to Sheffield United in June, was also a cause of great concern. Whilst other clubs in our division were improving and fine-tuning their squads, Wigan were left with three players signed under the Bosman ruling by Deehan, none of whom were to play any significant role during the forthcoming season, and no new manager to access the first team squad and add any new signings of his own. The list of supposed candidates was endless: Molby, Macari, Kendall, Spackman, Rush, Stapleton, Pearson, Walsh, Heath, to name but a few. But as the weeks elapsed and the new season crept ever slowly nearer, the silence from Springfield Park became increasingly more deafening. With just one week to go, Whelan finally appointed Ray Mathias, one of the few names no-one had mentioned. Reserve team manager at Tranmere and previously manager at Latics in the Eighties, when he was unlucky to have been given the boot then, his appointment brought a mixed reaction from the fans. Everyone had expected a big name, and even though his arrival smacked of last minute desperation (the chairman was unwilling to offer a contract in no uncertain terms), there was a sense of relief that at least we were able to start the new season with a successor to Deehan, even if most of the summer had been wasted.

Therefore it was no real surprise that, after the first eight games of the season, Latics found themselves up to the knees in the relegation mire, with just two wins under their belt. Former captain Colin Greenall had supposedly retired at the end of the previous season, but now found himself thrust into first team action to cover for injuries. The thought suddenly occurred to the chairman that ambitious words need to be backed up with ambitious actions and his cheque book, currently enjoying a six-month vacation, had to be reunited with his pen - and quickly - otherwise the new stadium would be on the verge of becoming the largest white elephant in Western Europe and could soon be playing host to Third Division football. His great enthusiasm for the Bosman Ruling had eventually begun to wear thin. Within the space of a month, Liddell, Haworth, O'Neill and Balmer had arrived. A million plus had been spent, the transfer record had almost been doubled and, as a result, by the time we reached December, Latics had climbed up into the top half of the table. Pity Whelan wasn't quite as aware two months previous at how the squad needed strengthening. The playing staff was now of a sufficient standard to launch a serious challenge on the promotion places. The chairman had eventually got to grips with the situation, and Mathias' tactics of employing five at the back and using the speed of Barlow, Liddell and Haworth up front to catch teams on the counter-attack had seen us beat Fulham and do the double over Walsall. Lady Luck abandoned us in the FA Cup when we were denied a chance of a reunion with John Deehan in the third round at Sheffield United, Notts County beating us on penalties after 120 minutes of dreadful football. Unfortunately, just as things were improving on the pitch, the pitch itself was about to play a significant role in thwarting promotion chances. Latics played four consecutive away games in the new year, thanks to continual postponements at Springfield Park, including one game called off, against Notts County, just 40 minutes before the kick-off.

Coupled with progression in the Auto Windscreens Shield, Latics games for the remainder of the season were already beginning to mount up. To make matters worse we were due to face a Rochdale team (whose own pitch was more suited to Sellafield) in the AWS Northern Semi-final. After several postponements, the game eventually went ahead in mid-March, and yet more league games had to be rescheduled in the process. But at least Latics progressed 2-0 in an ill-tempered affair to reach the Northern Area Final with Wrexham. A 2-0 home first-leg advantage against the Welshmen always made Wigan the favourites, and a trip to the Twin Towers was never in much doubt as goals from Haworth and O'Neill ensured a second-leg 3-2 triumph - and a Wembley showdown with Millwall.

Little did we know at this stage how Wrexham were to play such a significant role in deciding how the season would finish. Three weeks later and

Wembley threatened to resemble Rourkes Drift as Latics fans were outnumbered 5-1 by their Millwall counterparts. The omens weren't good. Widespread media bias (we all know Danny Baker's a cockney twat, but Chris Evans is supposed to hail from the north-west, would you believe?) towards the Lions made it hard to believe the match was being contested by two teams. Millwall had done the double over us in the league fixtures; in fact Wigan had never managed to beat Millwall. And so a scrappy game ensued. Both teams came close to scoring, penalty appeals were turned down, but chances were few and far between, as a tense match headed for extra-time. Suddenly, out of nothing, Paul Rogers silenced his Latics critics and sent 8,000 or so Wiganers into ecstasy by stroking the ball home with just seconds remaining before the final whistle. We certainly had a longer trip home than they did, but I bet it was a damn sight more pleasurable.

Back in the league, Latics began to close the gap on the top six clubs. Promotion rivals Bournemouth and Gillingham were both beaten convincingly at Springfield Park during a run of eight consecutive wins that equalled the club record, and it looked as though the record was going to be beaten when we went 2-0 up at home to Stoke. Unfortunately we became complacent, Stoke pulled two goals back and the worst fears of the fans were realised as ex-Latics player Greg Strong grabbed a late winner for the Potters. Fortunately our home form for the remainder of the season remained consistently good, even if the fixture backlog was taking its toll on the players, and performances became more dogged than the stylish way we'd been sweeping teams to one side as witnessed earlier in the season. Despite defeats at Man City, Fulham and Wycombe in the closing weeks of the season, we still had an outside chance of making the play-offs on the final day of the season if Wrexham could snatch a point at Bournemouth and we could beat Chesterfield for the last-ever league game at Springfield Park. If the truth be known, most Latics fans entered the ground that day expecting it to be the last time we would venture foot onto the terracing of Springfield Park, our tired players would do well to beat Chesterfield and no-one expected Wrexham to bring anything back from the south coast.

But, to use a well known quote, "football's a funny old game" - and so it proved on May 8. Latics recovered from being a goal down to beat Chesterfield 3-1, whilst news filtered through on the many radios that were clamped to ears around Springfield Park that Wrexham had held Bournemouth at Dean Court. Scenes of jubilation took over the ground and requests for fans to keep off the pitch at the end of the game were completely ignored as thousands ran on to celebrate. And so to the inflated egos from Moss Side and Man City, in the play-offs. Both league games had been close run things. The game at Wigan should never have been given the go-ahead and only added to pitch problems we encountered later in the season. As a result, City scraped a 1-0 win with their only serious threat on goal, whilst Latics splashed round and did everything but find the net. At Maine Road, a rare mistake by Roy Carroll gifted City's winner in another close encounter. The play-off games followed in similar vein. Stuart Barlow put Latics ahead with one of the quickest goals ever scored at Springfield Park, following a mix-up between the 'keeper and a defender, before City equalised in the second period. The second-leg at Maine Road saw Wigan narrowly beaten by Shaun Goater's goal, a Graeme Jones header coming back off the crossbar later in the game. However, what was disturbing over the course of the two games were some of the refereeing decisions we witnessed. The first-leg saw the referee ignore appeals for a blatant handball, whilst the game in Manchester had Kevin Sharp hacked down in the penalty-area and the referee remarkably award a goal-kick. TV replays confirmed that the penalty wasn't even debatable, the ball had long since gone as Sharp was flattened, and City fans sat in the background could be seen putting their heads in their hands. Joe Royle later admitted it was the most blatant penalty he'd ever seen. The referee was perfectly placed - but then again this was the same official who apparently ran up to Goater after the winning goal to ask him if the ball had struck his chest or his arm, after it looked suspiciously like Goater used his forearm to bundle the ball in. As if he's going to admit he used his arm! All of which begs the question of what exactly Wigan's chances were of beating City. There certainly seems to have been a hidden agenda amongst match officials when smaller clubs like Wigan face the likes of Man City in end-of-season deciders. And this isn't sour grapes - look at what happened to Gillingham in the final: five minutes of injury-time conjured up from nowhere. These refereeing 'oversights' cost Ray Mathias his job.

John Benson has since been appointed successor to Mathias. Benson was offered the job twelve months ago but declined on health grounds, and it now looks increasingly likely that Mathias was simply 'used' for twelve months, while Benson recovered from illness. Should Wigan make a poor start to the forthcoming season Benson could suffer a relapse as fans are still angered over the dismissal of Mathias. He's supposedly been given £3m to spend by Whelan on boosting the squad, though whether £3m gets spent remains to be seen.

Andrew Werrill

THE LION ROARS

Millwall

THE LI N ROARS

THE ALTERNATIVE MILLWALL SUPPORTER'S MAGAZINE   WEMBLEY SPECIAL

TLR 109   £1.50

I BELIEVE IN MIRACLES

As Newcastle have spent the last two FA Cup Finals proving, a trip to Wembley can often hide a multitude of sins. But, for Millwall, a first visit to the national stadium in over 50 years showed that the club was finally moving in the right direction.

The Auto Windscreens Shield is seen by many as the ultimate 'Mickey Mouse' cup. But for 48,000 Millwall supporters watching their side contest the final of that much-maligned competition with Wigan on a sunny Sunday in April, the tournament was proof that the club's future is brighter than at any time for many years.

Supporting Millwall in the second half of the Nineties has been an utterly miserable experience. Relegation to the Second Division in 1996 was quickly followed by a spell in administration and the complete disintegration of the playing staff. The '97-98 season ended with manager Billy Bonds' sacking, as chairman Theo Paphitis handed the reigns to Millwall legends Keith Stevens and Alan Mcleary, which was seen as a huge gamble given their lack of any significant managerial experience.

So despite the disappointment of losing at Wembley to an injury-time Wigan winner, the management duo were rightly pleased with the efforts of their players. The fact that half of the team who played at Wembley had started the season in the youth side made the achievement even more remarkable. Another after-effect of the Bonds regime was a lack of money for the new bosses to spend in the transfer market. Bonds had emptied the coffers with a string of unsuccessful high-profile signings and Stevens and McLeary were left rooting around amongst other clubs' cast-offs.

As a result, the only new faces in the starting line-up for the first game of the season were Jamie Stuart, returning to football after a drugs ban whilst at Charlton, and former Millwall favourite Jimmy Carter, back at the Den from Portsmouth on a free transfer. QPR goalkeeper Tony Roberts also joined on a free but his stay was short-lived and he retired with a finger-injury after just a few weeks.

That first game ended in a 1-0 win at eventual Wembley opponents, Wigan, and the goal-scorer that day was a man who spent the rest of the season frustrating and delighting Millwall fans in equal measures.

Paul Shaw had cost £500,000 from Arsenal the previous season and had looked like one of Billy Bonds' few decent signings. His goal at Wigan, a 25-yard lob with the outside of his foot, looked like signalling the beginning of another good season for the striker. However, by the time the Lions walked out at Wembley, Shaw had been dropped and had developed a reputation for scoring the occasional brilliant goal in between periods of complete anonymity. Shaw's role as main striker had been taken by 21-year-old Neil Harris and it was his arrival in the first team that provided Millwall with their first prolific striker since the days of Teddy Sheringham.

Harris, signed from non-league Cambridge City for £30,000 the previous season, started this season on the bench but claimed his first goal for Millwall during a 2-1 home win against Northampton in September. His eye for goal, determination and no little skill quickly made him the first choice forward. The new management team had instilled a work ethic and commitment to direct football that meant the Irish youngster Richard Sadlier, a tall target man whose skills complemented Harris, often played ahead of Shaw. Although Shaw continued to be a favourite among the fans, a series of poor performances meant their loyalty seemed more misplaced as the season progressed.

The Lions new-found will to win was in stark contrast to the anaemic performances that had characterised the previous season. That passion led Trevor Francis to accuse Millwall of playing "like Wimbledon" after his Birmingham side had completed a closely-fought 3-1 aggregate win over the Lions in the Worthington Cup First Round.

His comments overlooked the presence of a posse of enthusiastic youngsters in the Millwall side. Stevens and Mcleary had made it clear that several of the older players were on their way out and once the youngsters had been given a chance, their commitment showed how much they wanted to repay the managers' faith in them.

A trip to league leaders Stoke in September gave the mid-table Lions the chance to measure themselves against the Second Division's form side. In the event, Millwall dominated from start to finish, missed a hatful of chances and proceeded to lose to a last-minute goal, a trend that haunted the team throughout the season. Not surprisingly for a team containing so many youngsters, results varied wildly from one match to the next. During the course of the season, eight members of the youth team made their debuts for the first team and the likes of Tim Cahill, Joe Dolan and Steven Reid all looked at ease in their new surroundings.

A tumultuous 1-1 home draw with Manchester City saw Paul Shaw sent off and the Lions throw away the points again in the last minute. Shaw showed why he could be so frustrating, with a virtuoso performance a couple of weeks later at Blackpool. Two superb finishes secured a 3-2 win but the striker failed to match that display for the rest of the season.

Throughout the campaign, the chequebook remained under lock and key as chairman Paphitis struggled to cut the club's huge running costs, and the visit of money-bags Fulham couldn't have presented a greater contrast in spending power.

Over 11,000 turned up at the Den to see Kevin Keegan and his travelling all-stars take on the Lions but another bad-tempered match was spoilt by some awful refereeing. It ended in heated scenes, with the home side reduced to ten men and eventually losing 1-0 to a Kit Symons header in – yes, you guessed it – the last minute.

A 3-0 hammering at Walsall in early November was the least the Lions deserved for an abysmal performance and little was expected from the visit a few days later to a Preston side defending an unbeaten home record. However, a header from Shaw capped an excellent display by the Lions and an unlikely 1-0 victory was secured. The roller-coaster week finished on a wet Friday night in South Wales. Taken apart by Third Division Swansea, the Lions were dumped out of the FA Cup almost before it began and had gone yet again from the sublime to the ridiculous.

Success against Cardiff in the Auto Windscreens Shield started a winning run that took the team to the fringes of the play-off race. A trip to Luton is usually a guarantee of three points for Millwall. This year was no exception and a late Lucas Neill goal snatched a 2-1 win.

Emerging with a 1-1 draw from promotion-chasing Gillingham was the highlight of the Christmas period, despite red cards for Gerard Lavin and Scott Fitzgerald. Australian youngster Lucas Neill scored the equaliser and, after a poor start to the season, the was recapturing the form that he had shown when first bursting into the team two years ago. Together with Harris, he helped rout Brighton 5-1 away in the second round of the Auto Windscreens Shield; and on the league front, three wins in the next four games kept the play-off chase alive. The return fixture with Gillingham at the Den produced the most exciting game by some way. After falling behind early on, Millwall twice took the lead and twice the Kent side came back to force a 3-3 draw. Tim Cahill's late dismissal took the red card count to nine for the season.

Bournemouth had already beaten Millwall twice by the time the sides met in the third round of the Auto Windscreens Shield. Mark Stein's early strike looked likely to complete the hat-trick but a Paul Shaw goal levelled the match and only poor finishing prevented the tie from being won in normal time. In the end a penalty-shoot was all that separated the sides. This time Stein was the villain as he blasted his kick against the bar, to set up another clash with Gillingham in the next round.

At just £5 per ticket, this nail-biting encounter was played out before a crowd of nearly 12,000. Seemingly destined to get to Wembley the hard way, this time it took a goalden goal to earn Millwall the win. Richard Sadlier's two-yard tap-in was enough to spark wild celebrations on and off the pitch. That result finally made clear the importance of the competition to the success-starved Millwall public. As if that wasn't enough, the following Saturday, we played over an hour with nine men and still completely outfought Stoke to claim a 2-0 win that prompted City manager Brian Little to describe the defeat as the worst of his career.

By now the side contained seven players of 21 or under and the feat of Stevens and Mcleary in continuing to get results from this incredibly inexperienced team was becoming clear. Off the field, the club's reputation proved as hard to shake-off as ever when a factless article in the *Independent* tried to suggest that Millwall was a breeding ground for the type accused of murdering Stephen Lawrence.

Promotion-chasing Walsall were the last obstacle between Millwall and their first visit to Wembley since 1945. The first-leg of the Auto Windscreens Shield Semi-final at the Den was tight throughout, with Walsall dominating possession but wasting their opportunities. Tim Cahill's third-minute goal had put the Lions in front but Walsall should have drawn level in the second-half when the outstanding Darren Wrack was tripped in the area. Neil Pointon took the penalty but Ben Roberts' outstretched legs preserved the lead and Millwall held on for a 1-0 win.

Over 2,000 fans made the trip to Walsall for the second-leg and they were rewarded with a magnificent performance. Previously mediocre players were suddenly playing like World Cup winners. Richard Sadlier gave Millwall the lead and, despite a late equaliser and some 'heart in the mouth' defending in stoppage-time, the job had been done - and on the final whistle the party started.

The build-up to Wembley featured all the usual fun and games. The players recorded a reggae version of club song *Let 'em Come*, all manner of merchandise flew out of the club shop faster than they could stock it and, most amazing of all, the club suddenly discovered 35,000 new supporters. The sight of queues forming outside the ticket office has been fairly rare in recent years but the demand was so high that additional tickets were requested from Wembley to cater for what seemed like the whole of South London.

Sensibly using the big day to promote Millwall in the right light, hundreds of local school children were given free tickets and the players wore anti-racism slogans on their tracksuits. The whole day was a complete carnival from start to finish and despite some predictions of Millwall fans ransacking and pillaging the national stadium, the Twin Towers were still standing at the final whistle and the eleven arrests (six from Wigan out of their 8,000 fans) was the lowest total for any Wembley final for over a decade, a fact that didn't make the papers.

The game itself could never have lived up to the anticipation. Both sides struggled to get going in a nervous first-half and both should have had penalties in the second. In the end Paul Rogers handball went unnoticed by the referee as he capitalised on some poor defending to score the winner in - when else? - the last minute.

Although the Wembley defeat precipitated a dramatic slump in form, which saw just one point taken from the last five matches, the tenth place finish and impressive cup run are solid foundations for next season. Whether the club will capitalise on the potential of their best group of players for many years remains to be seen. But the opportunity is there, and if we are to achieve any sort of success it must not be wasted.

Steve Griffiths

THE MIGHTY SHREW

Shrewsbury Town

After finishing the '97-98 season on a high note with a string of excellent performances, as usual Town fans thought that this was going to be our year. Jake King had changed the team around and in his second season in charge would surely give us something to shout about. How wrong could we be?

The new season kicked off, ironically, as the old one had ended, with a home fixture against Scunthorpe United. An own-goal and a Paul Evans thunderbolt set up a great opening day 2-1 victory over ex-Town 'keeper Tim Clarke's side, who as usual endured a large percentage of the taunts. However, all our dreams of a great season seemed to fade in the first two months. After trailing 4-0 from the away-leg of the Worthington Cup First Round at Bristol City, Town produced a cup classic with one of their best displays, as they fought back at the Meadow in the second-leg to win 4-3. But, sadly, even a Paul Evans hat-trick couldn't save them, as Town went out 7-4 on aggregate.

Things got worse as a run of five straight defeats rooted the team to the bottom of the pile, and without a goal in over 450 hours of league football. Defeats against Cardiff, Halifax, Barnet, Rochdale and Scarborough led to Town ultimately being judged, as Jake King admitted, "The worst team in the league."

King brought in two trialists to try to stop the rot, and also brought in old favourite Mark Rutherford from Ireland. You could feel the relief all around the Meadow as the goal-drought was finally broken by Kevin Seabury in the home mid-September 1-1 draw with Peterborough United. Neither trialist was ever to been seen again, and Rutherford only managed three substitute appearances before crossing the Irish Sea again because his girlfriend didn't want to move to England.

Mark Winstanley arrived on-loan from Burnley and produced some wonderful displays alongside Gayle and Wilding to tie up the leaky defence. During his stay, Town only lost once (unluckily at Darlington), had four draws and managed to notch-up two victories. Everyone wanted Mark to stay but unfortunately the small aspect of money reared its ugly head again and Winstanley disappointedly returned to Burnley.

Still stuck at the bottom of the league and going nowhere fast, Shrewsbury needed a kick-start - and truly got it in the form of an eight-match unbeaten run throughout October and the start of November. Town scored draws against Hartlepool United, with a rare Brian Gayle strike, Cambridge, and a lucky 1-1 at Chester. Victories over Rotherham, Plymouth Argyle, Swansea, and a fantastic 2-0 win over Brentford lifted Town into 18th position. This revival gained Jake King the Manager of the Month award for October, a fantastic achievement by the Scot, proving the few doubters that he is definitely up to the managerial task.

Town managed to find the money to sign Spencer Whelan from border rivals Chester City, which left many Town fans confused. Whelan plays in the same position as Winstanley and the small matter of him being better than Whelan probably didn't even come into it. Yet another great mistake by the Gay Meadow board.

High spirits following Shrewsbury's recent improvement were soon dampened and the Town players brought back down to earth in the FA Cup First Round tie at non-league Rushden & Diamonds. Over four thousand packed into the host's neat stadium to watch Town slump to a 1-0 defeat. It was especially disappointing, as Town were backed by a large and noisy following who did themselves proud, even if the team didn't.

This defeat certainly had an effect on the boys, as they slumped to six straight defeats, including in the Auto Windscreens Shield at home to Wycombe. Scott Cooksey played his debut senior game in that match and was soon called into action again against Cardiff and Hull, deputising for the injured Paul Edwards. 'Eagle' was injured at home to Torquay, which lead to central defender Peter Wilding having to take over the 'keeper's jersey and playing well opposite goalkeeping legend Neville Southall.

The lack of goals was again proving to be a problem for manager King, and with star man Lee Steele and strike-partner Steve Kerrigan failing to hit the net with any consistency, Paul Beavers was brought in on a month's loan from Sunderland to add some firepower to the attack. Sadly, Paul spent most of his time scoring off the pitch, constantly waving to his girlfriend sitting in the stand, rather than on it as his manager had anticipated. Mind you, looking the way she did, maybe he had a point - very tidy indeed!

Edwards returned to the side for the New Year's Day visit of Halifax, but it was up-front where Town shone. With Beavers back at Sunderland, Town's strike-force of Jagielka, Kerrigan and Steele were on fire. Youngster Jagielka, tireless as ever, ran his heart out but simply failed to find the target. As for the other two, Kerrigan and Steele were scoring for fun.

Following the 2-2 versus Halifax, Steele grabbed a brace against Barnet, two more against Rochdale, a fine solo effort against Scarborough, before grabbing two against Darlington and two more at home to Chester. His goals kept Town unbeaten during the month of February and the side only lost once in March, away at ex-favourite Nigel Pearson's Carlisle United. On his day, Steele is as good as anybody there is in the lower divisions but can be so frustrating. The ability he possesses is frightening and Steele's form was attracting scouts from all over the country to the Meadow. Not since Carl Griffiths' departure to Manchester City had the scouts been out in such force.

The match against Darlington proved to be the last in the blue of Shrewsbury for captain Paul Evans. The inspirational midfield player, with the knack of scoring spectacular goals, moved to Brentford and was immediately installed as their captain. Evo's departure left a massive gap at the club, but he wanted to give something back to the club he loved so much. By leaving when he did, Evo earned Town some desperately-needed income. Evo was adored by the supporters and it was the fans who had the last laugh. His second game for Brentford was against us and when he screwed a shot wide, the away end rose, singing, "What a waste of money..." Evo laughed, and clapped the Shrewsbury fans at the end of the game - before being showered with a bucket of water from his old team-mates.

A Friday night epic (that Sky refused to show) at home to Cambridge showed the fighting spirit that was now in the squad. Roared on by a noisy crowd, the two sides produced a cracking display of football, easily the best seen at the Meadow all season, with Kevin Seabury grabbing a late equaliser and snatching victory from under the nose of title-chasing Cambridge. The match was a credit to the Third Division. It's just a shame that more than the 3,247 at the Meadow could not have seen it. Due to Scarborough falling from league football, Shrewsbury Town are now the only team in any of the four divisions not to be shown live on television. Sky have promised to stage a game next season, but many Town fans will believe that when they see it.

Following the Cambridge game, Town were in 15th place in the table, and a good April could have seen them claim a play-off spot. However, April proved an absolute disaster. Town lost five of their seven games, most notably at Leyton Orient (6-1) and couldn't manage a victory. Town secured their Division Three status with victory over Mansfield on the penultimate game of the season.

With safety assured, Town made the long trip to Torquay with two things on their mind: a victory and a stag night. The scouts were out in force at Plainmoor, as Town gave a debut to teenage goalkeeper Glyn Thompson. Thompson, who has been tracked long-term by Manchester City, had a fantastic season in youth and reserve football and deserved his chance in the first team. Arsenal, Sheffield United and Manchester City were among the onlookers, as Thompson made an assured and confident debut in front of the large Town following. Town strolled with ease to a 3-0 victory. Lee Steele, later to become the first visiting player ever to be given the Torquay sponsors' Man of the Match award scored twice, with Steve Kerrigan netting the other. The victory was made even sweeter by the fact that the trip also hosted Kerrigan's stag night. The players, management and fans had a few headaches the next morning after a massive night out.

As for the future? Town desperately need at least three additions to the squad to have any chance of promotion next year. A successor to midfield player Paul Evans is a definite, with an attacker and possibly a defender needed to add strength in depth. As for the Gay Meadow, the club has announced plans to move into a 10,000 capacity all-seater stadium by the start of the 2001/2002 season. The move to the 'New Meadow' has received the backing of the majority of the club's supporters. Let's just hope that we can hold on to the quality players that we have, to play in our smart new home.

Mark Fielden

THE OATCAKE

Stoke City

One of the most common mistakes made by Stoke City supporters when talking about the declining fortunes of our club in recent years is to say, "Oh well, at least it can't get any worse." Always a fatal mistake, as things can, and invariably do, get worse - usually much worse. Not many thought things could get any worse than the '97-98 season (the year of FOUR managers) but the folly of such thinking would soon be cruelly exposed.

In the wake of a calamitous relegation in our inaugural season at the Britannia Stadium, our loathed board of directors acted with unusual speed and vision to appoint Brian Little as the man to

THE OATCAKE
Issue 195
Saturday August 15th 1998
v Macclesfield Town   Price £1
Stoke City Fanzine

Warning: Managing Stoke City can turn your hair grey...

...Well, greyer!

lead our club out of the mire. To say that the Stoke City faithful were stunned by the arrival of Brian Little would be an understatement of the highest order. Few could understand what had possessed a man with his undoubted managerial credentials to accept a job as difficult and potentially damaging as the Britannia Stadium hot-seat. When we say there is no money available to spend at Stoke, we mean NO money; and yet Brian Little professed himself happy and indeed eager to work under such restrictions.

There was a general wave of euphoria and optimism at the appointment of Brian Little but as always there were the merchants of doom; or as they prefer to be called, the realists. Some pointed out Little's track record of having walked out on every club - Darlington, Leicester and Aston Villa - he had previously managed, called him a quitter and predicted that he would do likewise at Stoke once he realised what he'd let himself in for. Sadly, as always at Stoke, it would be the pessimists who would be proved right.

All such negative thoughts were blown away during Little's whirlwind start to his time at Stoke. He turned around the routines at the club, won the respect of the players and took the plaudits that came his way as we made a flying start to the season. Only Fulham took any points off us in the opening nine games, and they danced around the pitch as though they'd won a cup final when they beat us 1-0 in a tense match at Craven Cottage. Other than that, it was wins all the way for the Potters, including an incredible game at Deepdale, where Preston battered us for nigh on 70 minutes, only for Stoke to come back from 1-3 down and snatch a sensational 4-3 win.

In hindsight we can see though that our 27-points-from-30 start to the season wasn't really as convincing as we'd believed at the time. We seldom looked as good as we should have done for a team with such a record, and at times we enjoyed some considerable amount of good fortune. However, the general consensus of opinion at the time was that if we were winning like this while playing so moderately, then what the hell would we be like once we really did start playing so well?

In truth, we never did start playing well and many began to have nagging doubts about our long-term ability to sustain a genuine push for promotion, even though we were still managing to hang on to top spot as we approached Christmas and the halfway stage of the season. At this point, I can well remember saying something rather foolish. Given the amount of points already amassed, I noted that even if we weren't good enough for a top-two place, we would have to produce relegation form to miss out on the play-offs. How prophetic!

The Christmas programme proved to be the catalyst which unmasked our phoney promotion credentials. Faced with four straight games against promotion-chasing Gillingham, Walsall, Preston and Man City, we were found somewhat wanting - managing just one goal and one point from the four matches. As well as realising that we weren't anywhere near as good as we'd wanted to believe, we also got the first real insight into the weakness of our big name manager. Prior to this crunch run of matches, he stated that he would be happy to get four draws from the four games. If you aim low, then you're not likely to score high - and the first serious doubts about the ability of our manager begin to be openly discussed by supporters and some media pundits alike.

The second half of the season turned out to be a nightmare. You kept pinching yourself to see if you could wake up but this was a living nightmare from which there was no escape. While most of us had known that we weren't as good as early form suggested, few of us could believe we were really as bad as we looked from December to May.

The team simply fell apart, especially in home matches, and it was really quite frightening to watch. The forward line disappeared from sight and the defence started to play in such a generous manner that they should have been afforded charity status. Teams lost the fear and respect they'd had for us earlier in the season and instead came looking for blood when they visited the Potteries. We embarked upon a shocking sequence of home results, which saw us lose six on the trot at the Brit, including a 2-1 defeat to mighty (any sarcasm is purely intentional) Rochdale in the Auto Windscreens Shield, where we were two down with less than four minutes on the clock.

Away from home, we fared slightly better, but even then there were some truly forgettable moments. A 4-0 thrashing at Bournemouth was bad but nothing could compare with a 2-0 defeat at Millwall, where we had numerical superiority for practically the whole match. The Lions had a man sent off after three minutes, and another after 65, but still managed almost completely to out-play Stoke. It was incredible to see Millwall's nine men looking the side more likely to score in the closing stages; and there was also the unbelievable sight of Millwall with just six players standing at one point, as three went down with cramp. Nearly all the Stokies present agreed it was the worst Stoke performance of all-time. Even Brian Little agreed he had never seen anything so poor but added that he wasn't the kind of man who went around shouting at the players. A good shouting at is the very least of things the players need, along with a kick up the backside, a boot in the bollocks, their wages being docked, and their heads held in a lavatory bowl whilst it was being flushed!

Led by a manager who could do nothing to address our considerable problems, Stoke suffered further embarrassment and were thrashed in home games by quality opposition such as Wrexham, Notts County, Reading, Bristol Rovers and Burnley (most of whom were battling against relegation). Not surprisingly this appalling sequence of results had an effect of the long-suffering Stoke support. Many stayed away from games, but those who did turn up staged protest after protest - and two home matches finished with fans spilling onto the pitch to vent their fury. Displaying all of their legendary tact, the board blamed the trouble on a "handful of agitators" and tried to make some correlation between the protests and the poor results (though there is simply no 'chicken and egg' mystery about which came first) and pointed to our very respectable away form, although refusing to acknowledge that two of the most visible and vocal protests against them had actually come in away games at Blackpool and Luton.

Our ridiculously poor form had the effect of bringing about the previously unthinkable as we slipped out of the play-offs and thus the promotion picture altogether. And yet the board clung to their fantasies and harped on about everybody pulling together and making one last push at the top six. They sounded every bit as convincing and ludicrous as the German High Command in 1945, which was mustering mythical divisions to repel the Russian swarms outside Berlin.

For his part, Brian Little assured supporters that he was doing everything in his power to turn things around, which from the outside looked suspiciously like doing nothing all, and our season began to draw towards a merciful conclusion. In the final weeks the Stoke support accepted their fate - and those who still turned up, adopted the gallows humour approach and put a brave face on it. Not an easy thing to do when you're watching the Chaplin-esque comic routines of Stoke City, for whom the arrival of a cross into our penalty-area is every bit a portent of disaster as the fall-guy walking towards a banana skin in a black and white movie of yesteryear.

After a 4-0 defeat at Gillingham on the penultimate Saturday of the season, where the home side appeared to declare at half-time, Brian Little's patience with his failing players finally snapped. The midweek visit to struggling Oldham saw him put out nearly all of our young reserve players (which went down a treat among Oldham's relegation rivals, I can tell you!). And although we went on to lose against ten men, the youngsters gave a good enough account of themselves, persuading Little Brian (no mistake) to repeat the experiment on the final day of the season when celebrating Walsall rolled into town.

No-one could really believe that Walsall had managed to stay the pace and clinch promotion behind Fulham; but done it they had and their success was an acute reminder to Stoke supporters of just how much we'd managed to balls-up our own season. It's probable that Walsall would have been afforded a generous ovation by Stoke supporters had a sizeable section of their travelling support not kept up a constant barrage of noise during a minute silence to mourn the death of a former manager's youngest son. After that the Stoke fans were incensed and wanted to see Walsall get their arses kicked. The young players responded to the wishes of the fans and played superbly to win 2-0. With nothing to play for, Walsall probably weren't at their best but they didn't roll over and die, and the young Stoke lads emerged from the game with great credit for their efforts.

And so ended another campaign of misery for Stokies, though the bad news extended beyond our own fortunes and also beyond the season's conclusion. Our two nearest local rivals, Port Vale and Crewe, both avoided relegation at the death (having both looked doomed a few weeks earlier), which was another kick in the teeth for Stokies, who would have to spend the summer listening to unabated gloating from two sets of supporters whose only ambition in this world is to see their clubs finish higher than Stoke City.

On top of that there was also the question of Brian Little. Despite persistent rumours about his imminent departure, he vowed in the final week of the season that he would see out the second year of his contract and was already looking at how to improve things during the summer. He then packed off on his summer holiday (not even pausing to give after-match interviews following the Walsall game) and nobody heard anything off him for five weeks. When he did finally resurface, it was to announce his resignation for "personal reasons", thus fulfilling the quitter predictions that had accompanied his arrival one year earlier. The saddest thing, though, was that nobody really cared that he left, except that it took him five weeks to make his decision, which had the effect of dropping us right in it with regards to looking for a new manager.

Looking back at the joy and optimism that followed his appointment, it's difficult to come to terms with the legacy left by Brian Little. We may have finished eighth in the Second Division but most fans accept that, without our lightning start to the season, we would have been struggling against relegation and Little's season at the club will be remembered as one of the worst in living memory. Where we go from here under Gary Megson is anybody's guess, but in the wake of this latest calamity many Stoke fans have vowed not to return.

Martin Smith

THE PIE

Notts County

The secret Chronicles of a Fanzine Editor's Wife

New Readers Start Here: Electric Sue is married to a member of *The Pie* editorial team. She is a long-suffering beer and football widow, or rather she is a Notts County, *Pie* fanzine and real ale widow, as her old man doesn't actually like football; which is why he is a Notts fan, he reckons. In a special feature, she opens up her personal diary to give an insight into living with a man sometimes described as the most boring in Britain, but more often as "that short, fat, obnoxious little git". **Now Read On.**

No.56
ONE POUND
May 1999

The Original Notts County Fanzine

NOTTS' FIND SUMMER INCOME

"Well we've certainly got the sand. Now where's the sun, sex and sangria we were promised?"

Yes it's me again, I thought I'd write about fat men again in this year's book in an attempt to contact my husband. 'Electric Steve' he calls himself. What a bloody stupid name. Well, anyway, he is one of the boring farts who puts this *Pie* flanzine thingy together; or rather, the other bloke does it and he just gets in the way. I haven't actually lost my old man, you understand. I don't get that lucky. He still lives at our house. Or at least, I think he does, as his bit of the bed appears to get slept in and I still get all his smelly underwear to wash. It's just that I never actually get to speak to him. He's either at work, down the pub or locked away in the spare room, or "the Pie office" as he calls it.

I have been trying to get him to do some work around the house and garden for months, but he doesn't listen. Not that I actually get to talk directly to him, mind you. I have to push notes under his office door or pass messages via the barmaid at the Royal Oak.

But the last 12 months didn't start off quite so bad. I'll tell you what happened. Well, he always claims not to like football, so I say: "Right, you can take me away for two weeks on an exotic holiday and I want no word of football breathed the whole time. And definitely none of this boring World Cup rubbish." To my amazement, he actually agreed and booked us a tour of the Far East, even though this meant missing two England games. He assured me that where we were going they weren't interested in football and, as a bonus, he didn't think there were any interesting beers or brew-pubs either. Having lived with him all these years, I suppose I ought to have known better.

Before we set off on our travels, he bought himself a new shaver. Nothing odd about that you might think. But it is a battery shaver. His old one plugged into the wall and he had bought it for a purpose. He worked out that he could sit on the toilet, read his paper, listen to the radio and shave all at the same time. Multi-tasking he calls it.

Anyway, on to our exotic holiday (no, I didn't say romantic, not with my husband). Our first stop was Bangkok and, if you listen to him, when we went through immigration the officer couldn't believe he had brought his wife with him. Apparently you just don't go to Bangkok with your own woman. The officer pointed out this strange Brit to his incredulous colleagues and at first they weren't going to let me in, but eventually they agreed on condition he paid corkage. Of course it isn't true - the little fat git nicked the story from Jasper Carrot.

Later that day we were walking along one of the main shopping streets (don't panic he was looking for a bar, not taking me shopping). This guy approached us and said he was a boy scout, even though he didn't look a day under 30. He claimed he was collecting signatures from tourists to try to win a trip to Birmingham - a likely story for a start. Who the hell would want to go there?

My old man entered his name and when he wrote 'Nottingham' at the side of it, quick as a flash the smartarse guy said: "Ah, Nottingham Forest." Well that did it. His lordship crossed his name out, threw the book to the ground, swore and stormed off - leaving the bewildered boy scout shouting after him to spare a few quid for his trip. Some bloody hope now, sunshine.

That night we were wandering through the notorious Patpong area of the city and Himself was searching intensely for something. Well, whatever it is he's looking for, there's no way he's having it, I thought. Then suddenly he looks at his watch, decides it's time to eat and drags me into this candlelit restaurant. He orders the works - champagne, the lot. The old bugger's gone romantic at last, I think (although I discovered afterwards that the bill only came to eight quid).

As we are tucking into this Thai feast, unbeknown to me, a screen is being put in place on the wall behind my back. The first I know of it is when I hear a football commentary start up in English. In fact it is that boring John Motson bloke. I have been done again. He has taken me for a meal, so he can watch the chuffing England game. I realised too late that he had not been walking around Patpong to view the more carnal facilities on offer, but to look for a place showing the footie game.

The next night he took me for a meal at this large American-style place. There was a rather good band on stage. Odd, I thought, his lordship can't stand music, let alone a live band. The place was in pitch darkness and we were shown to our table by a waiter carrying a torch, just like the old usherettes at Lenton Abbey Essoldo. This was great. The food was excellent, as were the band.

After a bit it became possible to see what was around us and I then twigged that the little sod had brought me to a brew-pub, which explains why he was ordering beers three at a time. Then things went rapidly downhill. A screen appeared behind the band and they started to show a football match - Scotland this time. The band played on through the whole match, but were drowned out by the cheers and boos of the audience. And he said they weren't interested in football in the Far East!

Two days later we left for Hong Kong, with Himself wearing the brand new Rolex watch he had bought off a guy in the street. He had believed this guy when he had told him it was genuine - after all, he did pay four quid for it!

For our first night in Hong Kong, he takes me to an Irish bar. Bloody odd, I think, as he always says the only place for Irish bars is Ireland, and he refuses to set foot in them at home. Stranger still, sat in this bar, he suddenly pulls out a pile of his *Pie* flanzines that he had secreted about his person and tries to flog them!

More amazingly, this guy rushes across to us and wants to buy the lot! But I smell a rat. He's set me up again. It turns out that he has arranged to deliver back copies of the *Pie* to a Notts fan who is working in Hong Kong. So instead of exploring the delights of the Orient, he is discussing Neil Warnock's flat back-four system and Stan Marshall's strike-rate (whatever they are). Chuffing fine exotic night out that turned out to be.

The next day he is moaning that the strap on his new Rolex watch has broken. Poor workmanship from such a prestige company, he reckons. So he buys a replacement for six quid, two more than the watch cost him. That night we ate in another brew-pub, and once again the World Cup is being shown on every blank wall in the place. No, they aren't interested in football in the Far East - they can't be, because my dear husband said so.

Next stop Bali, where our tour guide turns out to be obsessed with football. On our journey from the airport he asks us where we come from and when we say Nottingham, he replies: "Ah yes, Tottingham Hotspur and Tottingham Forest!" That did it - Himself went into an instant sulk and refused to speak to the guy again.

Our first morning in Bali was prompted by a burst of bad language as his lordship discovered he had left all his clean underwear back in Hong Kong. Brand new they were as well. He spent the next two hours trying to phone the hotel in Hong Kong about them, only to find he couldn't make anyone understand.

England had another game that night, only it kicked off at three in the morning local time. They were showing it in the hotel bar and the little git apparently decided he was going to watch it. The first I know of it is when he slams his way into the room at 5.00am, waking me up with his cursing and swearing because they had lost. It turns out he didn't wake up till four, so he missed half of the game anyway. Serves him right.

THE PIE

The final stage of our 'football-free' holiday was in Singapore. I knew things were amiss when the phone rang as soon as we checked into our hotel room. The call was from the only Notts fan in Singapore, offering to take him out for a beer so they could bore each other to death remembering past glories at Meadow Lane. The fact I couldn't join them was some compensation for the 'Delhi Belly' I had picked up on my travels that meant I could not go further than ten yards from the bathroom.

So that was our holiday this year. No football? No brew-pubs? I had been done again but I had the last laugh. It cost him £25 to have his underpants mailed from Hong Kong and then when he got his phone bill, discovered that the calls to the hotel to retrieve them had cost another £25. So, at £50, the tight sod has got the dearest Marks & Sparks knickers in Nottinghamshire!

Well of course the football season started again soon after we returned and he was quickly back to his usual moaning self. He was hoping his team, "Super Notts", were going to storm the division like they had the year before. But apparently not.

By Christmas he was wandering round in an alcoholic daze, and just like Private Fraser in *Dads Army*, kept whining "doomed, doomed, we're all doomed". Apparently they were in the deep brown stuff (not quite his words) and his messiah of last season, "Big Sam", was now "a clueless *&%£$".

But then they brought these three strikers - Rapley, Stallard and Beadle - who are according to his lordship "shit hot" and by the end of the season he was a relieved man. So now he reckons Big Sam is the messiah again and they are going to storm the division next season. Well according to the barmaid in the Royal Oak that is, as he hasn't spoken to me for ages.

Well that's about it. If you do see my old fella please tell him that he either decorates the downstairs toilet and puts the knob back on the kitchen door, or the signed photograph of his hero and role model, Jack Duckworth, goes in the dustbin along with his collection of Shipstone's beer mats.

Electric Sue

THE SECOND OF MAY

Bristol Rovers

There were times during the season when it looked as if we were deeply in the excrement normally associated with the south side of Bristol. The 'play-off curse' well and truly struck us, and for a while the 'R' word was on the tip of everyone's tongues, with the pessimists genuinely believing we'd hit the Third Division for the first time in our history. Thankfully they were proved wrong - and surely the motto for the season has to be: "It all came up smelling of Rovers in the end."

We'd hoped that the tenth anniversary season of *The Second of May* would be witness to events reminiscent of those of '89-90, which saw the fanzine renamed in

honour of Rovers' achievements in beating BCFC '82 to the Third Division Championship. It didn't, though many of the foundations laid in the past 12 months could help to achieve more success than we've ever had before. It's very easy to be short-termist in football - witness Bristol City, who showered the best part of £5m on new players in a bid for Premiership football, and instead returned to the Second with a hapless Swede in charge, whose managerial skills were more akin to his twin brother, Krusty the Clown. Meanwhile, a Turnip found the route to the Premiership for a paltry outlay of £500k and a great deal of team spirit.

In terms of the longer outlook, Rovers have much more in common with Watford than our neighbours; and looking at the whole picture, there are more than a few reasons to be cheerful about '98-99. The Memorial Ground became solely owned by Rovers (quite an achievement after over half a century of renting), and it's even likely to have four sides and a roof by the Millennium. The purchase of the Mem was the most visible sign of Rovers' increasingly stable finances. The club is certainly not 'wealthy' - as Tony Pulis claimed - but finances are on a much more even footing than only a decade ago, when the thought of relegation would almost certainly have carried with it the threat of bankruptcy. The Rovers board showed their faith in Ian Holloway's long-term plans by giving him a five-year contract and allowing some serious team rebuilding to go on which, whilst not bringing instant success, is likely to have future, lasting rewards. The youth system produced yet more gems, and despite losing both top goal-scorers from the previous season, Rovers ended up with the hottest strike-force in the division. The gloom of the league was punctuated by the best cup run Rovers have had for 20 years, Sky came to the Mem and, in the end, relegation was comfortably avoided.

The season had not even begun when our one-time tenants, Bristol Rugby Club, finally went into receivership and the Memorial Ground - which Rovers had bought a half-share in six months previously - became the sole property of Bristol Rovers. The local press, aided by the odd City fan, were quick to paint the Rovers board as the modern-day incarnation of the club's nickname 'The Pirates'. Accused of looting from the less fortunate, those desperate to discredit Rovers conveniently forgot about the £2.6m that had already been paid to the ailing rugby club, which was in itself a quarter of a million higher than another bid which had fallen through. Meanwhile, over in south Bristol, City chairman Scott Davidson, desperate to deflect attention from the appalling results his team were getting, began talking about hosting the 2006 World Cup at a new stadium. Odd that this proposed ground was at a site on which Rovers had previously been refused planning permission. Davidson refused to entertain the thought of groundsharing, and despite a previously impressive record at fooling half the population of Bristol, got made to look like a spoilt child. Not too many people were surprised when, having got the unbuilt and unfunded stadium onto the World Cup 'B' list (luckily there was a City fan sorting things out at the FA), talk of the super-stadium disappeared before the idea was publicly put on the back of what would appear to be a burner a long, long way away from Bristol.

Unfortunately, our joy at acquiring one asset was soon tempered by the loss of another. Barry Hayles, Golden Boot winner of the previous season, had long been linked with transfers to any club with money to spend. Rumours had him heading for the Stadium of Light, Upton Park and White Hart Lane amongst others, but time and time again they were proven unfounded. Nobody was kidding themselves, though, and we all knew that we had to resign ourselves to losing Bazza at some point. What we hadn't prepared ourselves for, though, was the possibility of losing Hayles to a club in the same division as Rovers. So when the news broke that he was leaving for Fulham, Gasheads were stunned. OK, they had loads of cash to tempt him with but the thought of having to play against him later in the season was awful - and how on earth could we want him to have the success he deserved when he was prostituting himself to a club which was the antithesis of everything football fans believed in, run by the loathsome Al Fayed. It got worse. Once they had Hayles, the Fulham fans, including a good proportion of the nouveau variety, failed to appreciate his talent. Rumours of Bazza being booed hit the Mem and Gasheads felt even more aggrieved that he'd left for a club whose supporters clearly didn't deserve him. As time wore on, it did get better - the newer Fulham fans worked out that the ball was supposed to be round and on the floor, not oval and in players' hands, and Hayles' confidence grew. He did the decent thing at the Mem and had a mediocre game, the Fulham freak show was easily promoted as Champions, and Barry ended up slightly nearer the level he should have gone to in the first place. In the cold light of the close season, we can also reflect on the thoughts of one Gashead at a pre-season game, when he said that he'd sacrifice Hayles if it meant Rovers finally owning a ground and having the security that the nomads of English football had been seeking for the past 50 years.

Apart from the ground, the best thing to come out of the Hayles transfer had nothing to do with the cash it raised. His departure allowed the partnership of Jason Roberts and Jamie Cureton to take shape, and become the most potent in the division. For a pair who only led Rovers attack for two-thirds of a season, the 52 goals they netted between them was pretty impressive. Cureton's 29-goal haul earned him the title of 'lazy bastard' from certain myopic members of the crowd, although he'll probably appreciate the Golden Boot that he got from the league more. Roberts had to settle for the equivalent award in the cup, though many of us thought he'd have rivalled Jamie's league total if he hadn't spent a whopping nine games in the stand on enforced breaks.

Jase wasn't the only offender - it's fair to say that Rovers' disciplinary record didn't improve on '97-98. Mind you, with six red cards by mid-October the end result could have been much greater than the nine we ended up with and the most we ever managed to get sent off in a game this season was a paltry two (three times). Rovers certainly weren't angels but reputation didn't help on the discipline front, and neither did the appalling refereeing that the whole of the Nationwide League was forced to endure. While incidents involving Di Canio, Petit and co may have made the headlines, those of us in the less glamorous reaches of the lower divisions were forced to endure the refs deemed too poor for the Prem. The likes of Hall, Singh and Lynch made fans and players' lives a misery week in and week out, seemingly without the authorities noticing a thing. You get the feeling that if Paulo and Emmanuel had played a few games in the Nationwide, refs would be suffering far greater injuries than the odd poke in the chest.

Suspensions certainly didn't help Rovers' league position and, despite our prolific goal-scorers, the Third Division had become perilously close by April. Together with enforced absences, Rovers were plagued by injuries, and ended the season having used 32 players - about twice as many as we had in the squad a week before the start. It was clear that on our day, and with something resembling a first team, Rovers were a match for anyone - doubles against Reading (10-1 on aggregate) and Stoke (5-1 on aggregate) showed that. And on the whole, performances against the top teams were better than those against the lowlier clubs. Consistency was definitely lacking, though, and it wasn't until the final month of the campaign that we got to see back-to-back league wins, which coincidentally guaranteed our safety. At least the cup run had provided some relief from the league. It certainly wasn't glamorous, as Rovers dispatched Welling, Exeter, Rotherham and Leyton Orient before losing to Barnsley in the fifth round, but just getting that far was an achievement - we were only a couple of games from Europe after all.

It was also the season that saw the Sky cameras roll into the Mem for the very first time. In the past Rovers have been shunned, partly because the 60-watt bulbs in our floodlights aren't good enough for the cameras, which rules us out for half the televised Nationwide games. When they did finally arrive on May 1, it would be fair to say that they weren't really there for our benefit. The visitors were Man City, accompanied by the now familiar-through-Division-Two whine that they didn't have enough tickets, which prompted Mr Murdoch to spot a chance to make some cash of his own by including the game in the Pay-Per-View experiment. No-one who supports a lower division club and has any semblance of sanity can advocate Pay-Per-View - doing so would be like signing your own death warrant. But such was the excitement of being on TV that half the Rovers fans in the ground had paid for the game twice and were videoing it at home. So much for solidarity against Murdoch but at least they'll all have a record of the catering-for-the-Mancs commentary team becoming ever more upset, as Rovers fought back from 2-0 down to get a draw.

Finally, it may be petty and it may be immature, but Gasheads treasured the moment last season when we could at last let rip at our neighbours. A year beforehand some of the more arrogant of their number had talked of the "Last-ever Bristol derby" (The quote from *SOTF4* goes something like: "It was patently obvious that in the future we would never again slump to their level..."), shortly before getting out their slightly inaccurate 'Second Division Champions' banner. Now, it was only right that we should enjoy the sight of them with egg on their faces as 'The Benny Hill Show' drew to a close with relegation. A word of advice for next year guys - it's probably better to wait until you've won the Championship until you get that banner out...

Hazel Potter & Ian Marriott

Separated at Birth

Krusty the clown   Benny Lennartsson

THE SHEEPING GIANT

Wrexham

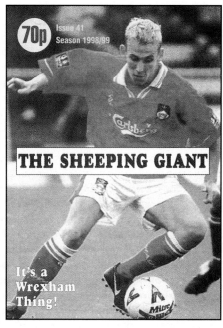

That it should come to this! After five outstanding years, it has fallen to me, Dai Shovett, runner-up in the 'North-East Wales Regional Newspaper Wrexham FC Reporter named Dai of the Year Award' (also placed in the 'Longest Sentence with Least Punctuation' Category), to reveal a shocking scandal at the heart of the *SOTF* series. Have you noticed the number of chapters that contain a mention of a Duran Duran song? *Grorty Dick* compares West Brom's season to *Hungry Like The Wolf*; *The Tea Party's* piece is entitled *Girls On Film*; and you can't move for Brighton publications asking *Is There Something I Should Know?*. Rumours abound of huge cash sums being offered by shady go-betweens to contributors who are willing to sell their creative souls in order to facilitate a spread-betting scam, based on the number of times Duran Duran songs are mentioned in this once-proud publication. I smell a Malaysian gambling syndicate - a line from my strangely unsuccessful footie panto *Jack and the Ormondroyd*.

But enough of that. It's not often that a journalist is able to be present at the making of history. It is even less often when that journalist happens to be Dai Shovett. And yet that was the case this season, as I was privileged to be in the right place at the right time, able to chronicle the historic sporting event which, as the Millennium drew to a close, gripped the whole nation, and perhaps the world. I'm sure you're all miles ahead of me now; I know this gladiatorial duel between two greats of the game needs no introduction. As the year drew on, rickshaw drivers in Bangkok refused to pick up fares as they plodded around the city, gripped by their radios. Sports lovers in Australia and New Zealand sat glued to the Internet all night, hoping for news. And cable shopping channels trashed their schedules to devote hour upon hour of programming to analysing this contest, while Andy Gray modelled diamante chokers on Sky Sports. It was a clash of the titans: Gog versus Magog, Ali versus Foreman, George versus Mildred, Godzilla versus Mothra, Goliath versus a large David. It was the question which gripped the world: who would score the most goals this season, Ian Rush or Mark Hughes?

So how did Rush come to sign for Wrexham? Well, it's a long story, and I'm going to use as many unnecessary words as possible in telling it because I've got to string this out to 2,000 words, and I'm used to writing a quick 300 on a Wrexham match on the back of an old envelope for a living.

When the World Cup ended, I immediately set about the most important part of any sports journalist's work - making up stories which would raise artificially high expectations for the coming season. I wrote an article about Wrexham swooping to sign some top international players. The headline is self-explanatory: 'FLYNN DEMANDS: "I REALLY REALLY REALLY WANT ZIEGE, ZIDANE".' How prophetic these words would be!

The season started quietly for me, as I forgot when it began and had already booked a holiday in Rhyl. I returned to find that Wrexham had already been knocked out of the Worthington Cup, and my house had been burned down by my Dad in a misguided protest against Members of the Welsh Assembly buying holiday homes in Wales. Imagine my surprise when I found Wrexham had indeed signed a top international player in the shape of Ian Rush. With Hughes signing simultaneously for something called Southampton, battle was well and truly joined.

Actually, people said Wrexham had signed a pale imitation of Rush, but he was tanned and the real thing, as I ascertained by stealing a glimpse of the unique birthmark in the shape of Flint Municipal Baths on his left buttock while he took a sauna in Wrexham's Swedish quarter.

He started in devastating style, blowing Colchester out of the water as we pulled off a memorable 4-2 home loss and nearly lasting an hour against Millwall. Soon the nation was buzzing as it followed the battle between the two fiery Welshmen. Who would be the first to hit the net? Hughes went close against Middlesbrough, while Rush was only 20 yards away as Karl Connolly scored a penalty past Blackpool.

While Rush flourished, Wrexham's season stank like a sandal in the wind. The team distracted fans from their poor away form by consistently losing at home, but still the supporters called for their heads - or failing that, a header. At least an impressive new stand was being built with a combination of Lottery money and a con which involved switching road signs, adopting southern accents, and convincing a group of builders that they were working on Oxford's new ground.

December came and went with the thrilling battle between Rush and Hughes locked at 0-0, and Wrexham's season began to look up as Carl Griffiths was brought in on loan from Orient Are. However, we couldn't quite afford to buy him, and although the club added a pound onto ticket prices for the rest of the season, they still couldn't rustle up the extra £150. I did my bit by arranging a fund-raising hot air balloon journey from Wrexham to Buenos Aires, where snooker loopy Orient boss Barry Hearn was said to be residing. I got sponsorship for the journey from the Meat Marketing Board, who put their slogan 'Bacon Your Mind Up' on the side of the balloon, but sadly the plan was hampered by technical problems. Our gas canister, commissioned by the sponsors in the shape of a calf's liver, contained plenty of gas, but its narrow aperture meant it couldn't release it quickly enough to enable us to gain altitude. As a result we were to try to travel across the Atlantic three feet in the air, but had to give up due to bumping into children and Sammy 'Fats and Small' Lee on our test flight. However, I did manage to fit in a bit of moonlighting, making personal appearances on behalf of the BBC's logo at bar mitzvahs and plastics' conventions.

Little Brian Flynn dropped a bombshell as the end of the season came near, when he gave a free transfer to Peter Ward, our resident old pro (although not in the Karren Brady sense). This led to a proud moment in my professional career, though, as I managed my longest-ever headline for the story: '"WARD, HUH! WHAT ON EARTH'S HE GOOD FOR? ABSOLUTELY NOTHING, SAY IT AGAIN!" SLAMS FLYNN.' Most sports journalists are paid by the word, so this was a particularly good moment for me.

As Wrexham's season faded away, the editor made a decision, ruling that we should place more emphasis on the interests of football fans in the Wrexham area, namely Manchester United and Liverpool. Thus the seeds of my downfall were planted in the allotment of fate by the seed-hurler of destiny. Naturally our coverage was slanted more towards Liverpool's heroic pursuit of an Inter-Toto Cup place than the confusing quests of Ferguson's team; and after a particularly awful performance by Monsieur Houllier's defence, I advocated the sale of their back-four under the headline 'BABB ALL OVER'. In the article, I made the innocent assertion that David James is paying for his sins in a past life - like the disabled and Chester fans. This didn't go down well, and neither did the immediate press release I issued to clear it all up:

"Obviously I never meant to cause offence with them things I said, although it wouldn't matter if I offended the disabled because they're all vegetables aren't they?"

I must admit that the media reaction to my comments scared me. I hadn't been in so much trouble since November, when I breached the National Union of Journalists' guidelines by writing a piece about Wales without referring to Cerys of Catatonia.

The worst came to the worst and I was summoned to Lancaster Gate to explain myself to the all-powerful supremo of football: Howard Wilkinson. Just before I went in to see him, I discovered that my daughter had faxed a touching letter to Ceefax pleading for me to maintain my post as football correspondent. I was astonished, not least because I don't have a daughter. Then I got a call from Honest Bill Cashpayment, my agent. He said he had written the letter on her behalf as he didn't want to cause her unnecessary distress, which was nice.

Dear Mr Ceefax,

I am Agnetha Shovett and I would like to say that I am very supportive of disabled people, so is my dad (except for the really disfigured ones, obviously!) but I think that this situation is the most pathetic reason for someone to have maybe lost their job and to have so much hassle over. If you'd just take the time to listen to what my client's explanation is then maybe you'd understand it a bit more. So please consider this from my dad's point of view and hopefully everything will be back to normal soon.

Thank you,

Anna-Frid Shovett

I thought that would get me out of the hole, but it was not to be. I entered Wilkinson's office to be confronted by the little big man himself, stroking a white fluffy cat in front of a large map of the world with the title 'WORLD DOMINATION AND STUFF'.

"Come in Mr Shovett, we were expecting you," he said. "I see you're admiring my map. Let me explain. The red dots are areas I wish to conquer by 2003. The blue dots are the sites of my network of laser guns, which will link to offer a high-tech umbrella protecting my territory from nuclear attack. The green dots are towns with shops that sell decent ties."

I was beginning to get edgy, so I decided to get down to business. I was willing to knuckle down, hang tough and stand my ground, to refuse to leave until I'd put my case, even if it meant staying overnight and eating Chinese takeaways on my expense account. Then he said I was never allowed to work in football again and I thanked him and left. It was only as I stood in the corridor that it hit me: didn't he used to have a big spot on his face?

Then it hit me that my life in football was over. I was left to reflect on the good times. It's amazing how quickly things have changed in the game. Was it really just 20 years ago that only James Bond had an autowindscreen? That chapter of my life was over, and I had to resign myself to spending mornings sitting around watching Richard and Judy (they sunbathe naked in next door's garden).

I still went to Wrexham's games, but it wasn't the same. Do you realise fans have to pay to get in these days? Still, I was hooked - I had to see how the battle of the century would turn out. You can't imagine the communal grief at the Racecourse when the news came through that Hughes had scored in April. It would have made our home match against Oldham seem pointless if it hadn't already been.

Rush's season ended with an heroic final push against Barry Town in the final of the Welsh Premier Cup, but he was not able to achieve that holy grail, that impossible dream of scoring a goal in just 2,000 minutes on the pitch. Defences as stern as Macclesfield, Caernarfon and Newtown had proved unyielding, and the great man was forced to walk away with his head held high and his weekly wage of five shillings in luncheon vouchers tucked away in his pocket as the campaign ended. And me? Well, now I'm out of a job and desperate for paid work. But, don't say a prayer for me now. Save it for the morning after.

***DAI SHOVETT HAS enjoyed a distinguished career as a local newspaper reporter, covering a series of diverse issues from Wrexham home games to Wrexham away games. In 1996, his work for the football magazine *Smells Like Kharine Spirit* was described by Gary Bushell as "...prose purpler than that weedy bloke from the *Carry On* films' face after a fight with Mike Tyson."

He has no wife or children, but harbours an unhealthy regard for Carol Vorderman.***

Richard Sympson

THE SILENCE OF THE LAMB

Preston North End

"It's full-time at the Priestfield Stadium - Gillingham 0 Preston North End 1. Preston are going to Wembley!" screams the commentator on Radio Lancashire... I get brought back to reality by the sound of my alarm clock and realise it was just a dream, as my head is banging with the most terrible hangover ever - from a night of drowning my sorrows. It's the day after our exit from the play-offs, losing to a no-hope team called Gillingham, and I thought it's as good a time as any to write my review.

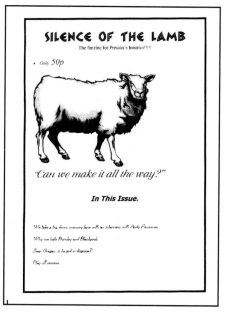

SILENCE OF THE LAMB

The fanzine for Preston's lunatics!!!!!

Only *50p*

"Can we make it all the way?"

In This Issue.

We take a trip down memory lane with an interview with Andy Parsons.

Why we hate Burnley and Blackpool.

Sean Gregan - is he god in disguise?

Play off reviews.

Well, Preston have had one hell of a season - certainly one to be remembered for the good and the bad. I'll start at the beginning. A good start came with a home win against York City, the first season's opener we had won for donkeys years. Fairly lowish crowds for the North End saw Nogan finally getting his act together and scoring goals, and Mark Rankine actually making an effort in midfield. It took us up to second in the league. I didn't really bother about league status until October, when Preston shot from seventh to the top. In the Worthington Cup, Preston got beaten by a group of fisherman from the beautiful town of Grimsby - 7-6 on penalties - as if anybody was bothered. In the league, we had a lucky win at Maine Road, in front of a 28,000 crowd, thanks to the ever-reliable Gazza Parkinson coming up with a cracking shot. That boosted the fans' confidence. Four weeks later, we beat the Turf Moan mob at Deepdale, 4-1, with two of their ex-players scoring for us.

But it wasn't all laughs and cruel jibes when it came to rival clubs. This was the season when we failed to beat B*******l (how degrading). This was also the season where we entertained Arsenal in the Sweet FA Cup. Earlier, we beat the likes of Ford United (next season we'll be playing Vauxhall Rovers) and Walsall but never thought we would have Arsehole Wenger at Deepdale. I still remember that Sunday night as the numbers were being pulled out: when I heard "Preston North End to play Arsenal", you could have cut the atmosphere in our house with a knife. As ever with the wonderful club I support, they decided to make a complete balls up of the ticket allocation, which meant long-suffering fans (like me) being left to watch the game in the pub and some glory-supporting time-waster being allowed to see the game. That pissed me off for weeks... and we haven't had another crowd of 21,000 since.

Going in front at an early stage, we knew damn well we'd get slaughtered. But 4-2 is better than losing 8-0. After all that excitement, it was back to league reality. For the next month we stayed fourth in the league and remained hopeful of automatic promotion. We were playing well as a side, results were going in our favour, but somehow we got beaten to the post by Walsall. No offence, but they'll be back down by the end of next season. During this time we had a few loan players, including Steve Basham. What can I say? What a guy - nine goals in 15 appearances. I was impressed too by Graham Alexander, who was bought from Luton Town and performed well in the right-back position, working brilliantly with the rest of the defence. From mid-January to the beginning of April, Preston were up and down between second and first like a big dipper. Losing to Macclesfield saw us go from second to fifth, where we finished. From the final whistle at Deepdale, after losing to the Scum, we knew it would be an uphill struggle getting back into automatic promotion. Even though we battled, we didn't get the points and had to settle for the dreaded play-offs. First it was Gillingham at home. A slow start, a first-half goal, a good crowd, but Dave Lucas made a stupid mistake 15 minutes from time and there was all to play for in the second-leg.

Three days later, at the Priestfield, Lucas let the ball in to the back of the net with only a minute played. It was bad luck for the lad. As we only had 1,300 tickets for the game, we had the dubious privilege of watching the game on a large TV screen at Deepdale, where 8,000 fans turned up (more than B*******I get at a home).

I'm not going into the game, because I'll get depressed again. The funny thing was that when the stadium announcer said he was sorry we lost and thanked us for being great supporters, I had to keep my mouth shut because the mood I was in, the bloke would have been wearing the bloody microphone. As I returned home that night and sat in the pub drowning my sorrows, I remembered the season we lost to Bury in the play-offs. The following season we went up as Champions.

Lucky omen, or what?
Sheridan Monks

THE TEA PARTY

Stockport County

So the remit was to deliver 2,000 words on the '98-99 season. It's hardly a case of where to start, more a debate on whether it started at all. At a time when the rest of the local clubs were involved right to the end, our season effectively finished with an Easter Monday victory at the Reebok. To those of us who believe that Bolton have ideas far beyond their station, this at least gave consolation that their self-proclaimed rightful return to the Premiership more than likely could now only be through the play-offs. We watched on as City and Wigan battled to join us, and as Oldham, Bury, Rochdale and Macclesfield fought the spectre of relegation with varying degrees of

the tea party

stockport county fanzine

HODDLE OUTLINES HIS FUTURE PLANS

I've had a great offer. You remember that bloke used to play in goal for Coventry? Went to work for the BBC? Well...

issue 80   price £1

failure. The less said about events in Stretford the better. For virtually the first time in 30 years this was a non-season - for County followers used to fighting re-election battles for the greater part of that time, and more recently moving upwards, the 50 games (only one more than the bare minimum) are long forgotten, even though the season is but a month gone.

And yet, as August dawned, there was a fair degree of optimism around Edgeley. After all, the previous campaign had seen County reach the highest position in their history. Megson seemed to have taken on where Dave Jones had left off, despite the crucial loss of Paul Jones and Todd. The selling frenzy continued in his first year, with Marsden and Armstrong disappearing to fellow Division One outfits, and with them any seeming ambition. And yet we still finished eighth. On reflection it was pretty galling that the side Jones brought up would, if kept together, have more than likely been in the play-offs. But there were no real complaints, other than from some of the Johnny Come Lately's who hadn't experienced the really dark days; and there had been plenty of them. The summer passed quietly, with Megson bringing in Carlo Nash from Palace, seemingly more famous for male modelling than any expertise between the sticks. Nothing else happened until a week before the season, when chairman Elwood finally released the Edgeley purse strings - which had seemed more secure than the Bank of England - and lashed out £800,000 on Ian Moore. This was spending totally unheard of, and was further bolstered by the Bosman acquisition of Graham Branch (undoubtedly one of the most spineless players ever to don the blue and white) from Tranmere, more than likely as a result of the short-lived McNally connection.

That initial optimism continued apace, as an opening-day victory at Valley Parade, in a game of three penalties, saw the faithful return over the hills in good heart. And that's about where it stopped, as three days later a truly dismal display against Hull in the League Cup set the scene for months to come. Briefly, highlights were few: A fighting display at a snowbound Stadium of Light, which saw the locals fairly muted; a truly satisfying beating of Birmingham, which evinced the normal moans, groans and pitiful excuses from Francis, and which came in the middle of a three-game winning spell that effectively banished the spectre of relegation; and that display at the Reebok. And that's about it. Lowlights were far too many to mention - suffice it to say that it was a common perception that the team seemed to have got their swimming trunks and sun tan oil out by early April, as a veritably abject run-in culminated in a five-goal pasting at relegated Oxford on the last day. The last month was about no pride and no heart. Frankly, in that time, the support they got at Ipswich, Pompey and the Manor Ground (none of them a five-minute jaunt) was undeserved - because those who did travel were more than short-changed.

So, how to review a season? You've got to look at the management first of all - and plenty did over that last month. There was a distinct impression that Megson's judgement of a player is open to question. After all Phillips, Alsaker, eventually Cook, and maybe Nixon were all found wanting. But that was about operating in the bargain sales - Elwood provided precious little cash, and certainly nowhere near enough to compete in the division. Megson unearthed a gem in McIntosh, but Moore proved a sore disappointment. Those who called for Megson's head seemed to have an incredibly short memory, and certainly not one that stretched back to February, when investment was sorely needed, and he was provided with a king's ransom of £10,000 (yes, *ten thousand*). Clubs in the Unibond League were spending more than that. To his credit, for the equivalent of three days' pay for the likes of Beckham, he went out and got Dave Smith from Oxford (a true bargain) and old-stager Tony Ellis, whose six goals from 16 starts, proved that he hadn't lost the knack of finding the back of the net, which he'd shown at a myriad of clubs over the years. But, I ask you, ten grand when two-bit players from all over Europe command £5m fees! And Megson was hardly helped with the long-term absence of the truly class Tom Bennett (whose return at Huddersfield some 13 months after a horrific leg break brought probably the biggest cheer of the season). Equally, scally Chris Byrne, another big plus in Megson's favour, lasted just 12 games before a serious injury put him out for the duration. The 'Ginger Whinger' ([©] mailing list moaners) had to turn to loanees, and uncovered a cracker in Derek McInnes, who subsequently returned to a cup winner's medal at Ibrox, and Paul Hughes from Chelsea.

In summary, Megson was expected to run a First Division club with Second Division (or maybe even lower) resources. That's sadly the nub of the problem and an appropriate time to turn to the board. Two years ago County exceeded all expectations. A run to the Coke semi, FA Cup progress and then promotion - all filled the Edgeley Park coffers as never before. Add to that a whole shedload of incoming transfer cash as the promotion team was broken up, and fans had the right to expect some serious investment, if not for a push to the eldorado of the Premiership, then at least to be able to compete in the top 44 clubs in English football. Well, that certainly never happened, and questions began to be asked about the whereabouts of this cash. In its own inimitable style, and true to form, the board were less than forthcoming about this until eventually, and mysteriously, two years' accounts were produced at one go. And they had an interesting tale to tell, to say the least. A net profit of over £2m had accrued over the two years.

Fans were well aware that there had been precious little put back into team affairs. There was a new stand to marvel at and the pitch had needed relaying. But the true tale was that well over £1m had disappeared back into directors' pockets, by them (and most of it presumably relates to Elwood) having their loans repaid. There was a bit of indignation about this, but on reflection what galled most people was the cloak of secrecy which had surrounded the issue. The board had a perfect right to take the money - after all, it was they who had put it in the club in the first place - but the resolute indifference to letting people know what was going on (much of it at the margins of company law in terms of the publication of accounts) led to a lot of exasperation from those who began to see themselves purely as turnstile fodder, who were expected to pay well over odds any time a big match loomed up at Edgeley Park.

The board hardly did themselves any favours as fans' favourite Mike Flynn was courted by our old chum Jasper (aka Trevor Francis), who was keen to spend more of the porn millions. Flynny, rightly recognising his value to the team, but wrongly not feeling bound to a contract he had signed, held out for a better deal, after having heard that Spurs were purportedly interested as well. The board apparently made offers, then promptly withdrew them, leaving the fans angry and bemused as they saw the prospect of Flynn disappearing. After two or three weeks of pretty unsavoury goings-on, and much to the relief of all, the cash was stumped up and Flynny is due to be with us for another four years.

Despite the calls for Megson to go, it really is about investing for the future - and make no bones about it, that's just for First Division survival. So the grand news, announced in April, of substantial resources being ploughed into the club was greeted with a huge sigh of complete indifference, once the plans came to light. A new stand (admittedly long-awaited), which will bring much-needed succour to the long-suffering away fans, who currently have to brave the elements, together with hotel and conference facilities, was hardly what was demanded or needed.

Failing desperately to gain the headlines on the back page, there seemed to be some kind of death wish to appear in the news pages. Firstly, Aaron Wilbraham, finding it difficult to live up to the promise that he showed in a few games at the back end of the previous season, found himself up before the beak after an incident with a baseball bat in leafy Knutsford. Not long after that came the summary dismissal of 'Mad Harry' McNally, Megson's chief scout. Sent to Scotland to eye some talent, by all accounts a three-day long trip ended with no players but a hefty bar bill, which led to a swift and unceremonious departure. Then there was long-term injury victim Chris Byrne, obviously with too much time on his hands, who came to the attention of the constabulary as he left a chemist's shop, which unfortunately for him was closed to customers at the time. Finding himself in the dock some months later, he must have been relieved not to be given a room at the Strangeways Hotel, but instead gave us a new angle on the 'County in the Community' programme, with a sentence of 240 hours community service.

But the most bizarre episode came with Dessie Byrne - a 17-year-old just breaking into the first team. An incident in a local club, involving what might allegedly and euphemistically be called a 'glassing', left Ian Moore sporting a black eye amongst other things. Dessie had apparently displeased some of the (ahem) tougher elements of the Salford area. Retribution was sought as a vanload of hooded and tooled-up characters descended on a training session. Showing much of the spirit they did throughout the season, the players fled to the sanctuary of the dressing-room leaving Megson to face the foe. Showing the same oratorical skills he displayed in his on-pitch addresses to the fans, but with perhaps more success, he managed to calm the situation. It led to Byrne's quick trip to the airport, more for his own safety, but with employment at County terminated. The whole affair was cloaked in secrecy, with all the players under orders not to comment. There was lots of talk about Byrne being a fall-guy for a more senior player in the episode, but the fundamental question as to why senior professionals were encouraging under-age drinking still remains unanswered - and, given the Tribunal's verdict that the dismissal was not unfair, will presumably remain a mystery.

So, if next year is about making headlines for the right reasons, what are the prospects? The return of Bennett and Chris Byrne will bring much-needed guile to the middle of the park - it'll be like two quality signings. With that, the problem will remain up front. A four-goal return from 42 games leaves many a question around Moore. A strike-force of 60-odd years and no pace between them, in Angell and Ellis, will hardly leave Division One defences quaking, good players that they both are. Overall, Division One football demands Division One commitment, both on and off the field. We didn't see too much of the former for much of last year and I'm afraid that however attractive to the corporate customer hotels, restaurants and leisure facilities might be, if the product isn't good on the field, then there'll be plenty of vacant sponsorship spots. The board at County seemingly have a lot of ambition, but it's perceived as being directed towards business plans which concentrate on corporate hospitality rather than football. All in all, it's time for them to give the manager the resources to do the job properly - only then can he be properly judged. Last season was a pretty wearying nine months - and sadly the only conclusion can be that, without a redirection of ambition at board level, the Millennium campaign could well be a long and sorry winter.

The above was written on June 10. It's now June 25 - and the news has just been confirmed, after a week of speculation, that Megson has been fired. Opinions will undoubtedly be mixed, but I stand by all that is written above. Whatever the reasons underlying the sacking, there can still be no escaping the fact that no-one can do a First Division job without the tools. So, six weeks from opening day, we find ourselves rudderless, with Andy Kilner, the club's 'football in the community' supremo elevated, but only on a temporary basis. What a way to prepare for a season - the phrase 'a long and sorry winter' may well be something of an understatement.

Martin Frost

THE THIN BLUE LINE

Cardiff City

How to get promoted - the Cardiff City way.

Is your club stuck in a rut? Not going anywhere? Tired of playing the same old clubs every season? Then why not get yourselves promoted? OK, it's not easy, but you can do it - why not? And what's more, you can do it without any costly signings, and without a sugar-daddy chairman. Don't believe me? Well, it's true - it can be done. I know, because Cardiff City have just done it. And we want to share our secrets with you. So, if your side is stuck in the basement of the Football League, and you want to get promoted, just follow this easy ten-step guide, and get promoted - the Cardiff City way.

THE

THIN BLUE LINE

UP, UP, AND AWAY - WITH CARDIFF CITY

JUST ONE POINT

Hey, there's my granny up in the stand

Did she bring her boots with her?

ARE THE BLUES GOING UP AT LAST?

ISSUE THIRTY   FIFTY PENCE

AND INSIDE THIS END-OF-SEASON ISSUE....... Promoted at last?, Cambridge, Thoughts on the Delaney sale, Six page players special, including Player of the Year and Marks out of ten, plus a day in the life of Kenny Hibbitt.......

1. Don't bother trying to find a mega-rich chairman. You won't - but never mind, because you don't need one anyway. Samesh Kumar has been chairman of Cardiff City since the end of the '94-95 season. He didn't have any money then, and if he's honest, still doesn't now. He borrowed the cash to buy the club, with the very optimistic idea that if the team succeeded on the pitch, the resulting crowds would fund any future spending. Needless to say, it didn't work. By time last season came around, things had come to a head. We had finished the '97-98 season in 20th place. Desperately short of cash, the future was looking well dodgy, and the club was fighting off the creditors. With no money for players, and performances dipping, the dreaded spectre of relegation to the Conference could not be ignored. Does any of this sound familiar to you? It does? So what do you do?

2. Get the supporters involved. OK, we're not talking about your average supporter here, but local men, fans of the club, who might have a bit of spare money. Every club has them. They're not millionaires, but they've done well for themselves, and they want to help the club. Don't ignore them, they can help, and they'll know more people who will want to help as well. But the best thing of all is that they have the best interests of the club at heart, and they're not just coming on board to make a quick buck. Steve Borley was brought up literally a stone's throw from Ninian Park, and has supported the club man and boy since then. A life of hard graft has left him in a position to help, and he bought into the club during the '97-98 season at a time when we needed him most. It wasn't long before his friends and relations were joining him, all of them bringing their own brand of experience, and their own little bit of cash. Following their example, more local men came aboard, perhaps glad to see the club going in the right direction at last, and maybe a bit more keen to deal with someone they knew. Maybe one of them by himself couldn't raise half a million quid, but ten of them together could - and that's exactly what they did. Samesh Kumar sold them parcels of shares, slowly reducing his holding in the club until he became a figurehead with no real power. With just 37 per cent of the shares, he no longer had a majority. The real supporters were in control. So what did they do next?

3. Bring in a manager with a proven record at this level. OK, this may not be as easy as it sounds, but they are out there. Decide who you want, track him down, and tempt him back. The board of Cardiff City decided towards the end of the '97-98 season that they wanted Frank Burrows back at Cardiff. He'd got us promoted back in '87-88, and he'd done it on a shoestring. Burrows was by now head coach at West Ham, following spells at Portsmouth and Swansea. A nice cushy job with a Premiership side, and he packed it all in to come back to Cardiff? It's true. We'll be honest and say that we didn't think it was a very good idea at the time; and we even went on television (cringe) to tell the world that we thought it was a step backwards. We're quite happy to admit here and now that we were wrong. Frankie is a top guy, and perhaps the best manager in the lower divisions. His achievements at Cardiff this season say it all.

4. Let him choose his own staff. Frankie's first appointment was not a new goalkeeper (we already had the best, in the shape of Jon Hallworth), or a new striker (although perhaps we could have done with one of those), but a coach - Billy Ayre, to be precise. Now, Frankie has years of experience of man-management, but Billy knows the lower divisions like the back of his hand, and knew just who could fill the gaping holes in the Bluebirds first team line-up. When Burrows started to rebuild his side, between the two of them, they knew just who to go for.

5. Sign your players on free transfers. OK, it helps if you have a manager with the acumen of Burrows, and a coach with the eyes of Ayre, but the players you need are all out there, if you look hard enough. Frankie brought in a lot, and some of his 'purchases' really opened our eyes. But only one of them cost us money, when Burrows paid £60,000 to bring Dai Thomas from Watford. Strangely, that was perhaps the least successful of his signings. The others were all free transfers, or 'Bosman signings' as Frankie likes to call them. To shore up the defence - Graham Mitchell and Mike Ford. To beef up the midfield - Richard Carpenter (no, not that one) and Mark Bonner. To add pace to the front line - John Williams. And to spice up the wings - Andrew Legg and Mark Delaney. Never heard of that last one? Well, you may not now, but this time next year you will, because we've just sold him to Aston Villa. We got him for nothing from League of Wales side Carmarthen Town, he played 20-odd games, and we sold him for a cool half-million quid. Good business, or the same old story of a club selling its players to survive? Needless to say, the fans were split over this decision, and now that we are promoted, you can't help but think that perhaps we should have held on to him. But how can you tell a young player he can't go to a Premiership side? And how do you turn down £500,000 for a player who cost nothing? At this level, if we're honest, you can't, can you? But to go back to the players who were brought in, they may have been free, but they still cost us a lot in terms of their wages, with the rumour being that Hallworth was the highest paid player in the Third, and so perhaps Delaney had to go just to keep the wage bill under control. Burrows also wanted every position covered in case of injury, and although it meant the club had to pay the salaries of a massive squad, for the best part of the season, it worked. We were nearly caught out when two of Orient's forwards conspired to mug Hallworth, breaking two of his ribs. It was past the transfer deadline, so rookie Seamus Kelly was roped into service, and didn't do too badly; but it could have ended in tears.

6. Play good football. The one good thing about Cardiff City - although it can sometimes be a millstone around the club's neck - is that it has huge potential. With no other club within 40 miles and a population of close on a million people within that distance, if City do well, they pull in massive crowds. And it's not all about winning, although that obviously helps. Good football is what people like to see, and for one three-month purple patch, that's what City delivered. From November to February, City swept aside all in their path, and camped in at the top of the table. It looked like we were to repeat Notts County's performance of the previous season, and run away with the title; but, sadly, it wasn't to be. As the season took its toll, the form began to slip... but that comes under another section.

7. Keep the defence tight. OK, we'll admit that this one is easier said than done, but if you get the right players, it is possible. We had a head start by having the brilliant Jon Hallworth in goal, and in front of him, we tended to play three at the back (usually Ford, Mitchell, Eckhardt), five in midfield, and two up front. The theory is that this formation can convert quickly from 3-5-2 to 5-3-2, turning a strong midfield into a packed defence at a moment's notice; and for us, it worked very well. Only eight teams conceded fewer goals than Cardiff's 39 last season, and four of those were at the top end of the Premiership. At the other end of the pitch, the goals were a bit harder to come by, but if the opposition doesn't score, then they can't win. Nineteen clean sheets tell their own story.

8. Get forward and score goals. This wasn't quite the success it should have been, but with Kevin Nugent and John Williams up front, we had strength and pace, and for the most part, a refusal to give up. They got 20 goals each this season, but perhaps the biggest boost to our promotion challenge was the fact that just about every player in the side scored at least once. Jason Fowler, Jeff Eckhardt, Dai Thomas, and Craig Middleton all got respectable totals, but of the 25 players used over the season, only five failed to score, and three of those were Hallworth, Mitchell and Ford - our rock-solid defence.

9. Don't panic. We can't claim that it was all plain sailing. It wasn't. We had our bad days as well as our good ones. The sale of Delaney prompted a lot anti-Kumar protest, with graffiti spayed on the walls of Ninian Park, and a group of moaning fans invading the boardroom. Strange really - there we were, top of the table, unbeaten at home for months, we'd just netted half a million quid for a player most fans laughed at when he was signed, and they're complaining? But the sale did have an effect. Delaney was a better attacker than defender, while his replacement, Wayne O'Sullivan, was a better defender than attacker. When Delaney went, the goals started to dry up. Instead of the two-pronged attack - Legg on the left, Delaney on the right - we suddenly had a one-sided team, and it didn't take long for the other sides to catch on. OK, so the defence stayed pretty watertight, but the string of wins became a string of draws, and the pack started to close in. It wasn't long before we were down to third, and although we were to return to the top briefly before the end of the season, all the other clubs had games in hand, and at the death, it was a close thing. With two months to go before the end of the season, we'd identified four games that looked vital to our promotion hopes. Cambridge and Leyton Orient away, plus Swansea and Scunthorpe at home. They were all draws - every one of them, and pretty dull ones too, but the one point against Scunthorpe meant that they couldn't catch us for the last automatic spot. We were up. So what did we do to celebrate? We went to Mansfield, and got thrashed 3-0, that's what.

10. Celebrate, and build for the future. But we were up, and that was all that mattered. Ninian Park saw another pitch invasion, the first since we went up at the end of the '92-93 season. Then, we were back down within two seasons, but this time things look a lot healthier. Despite a massive 75% increase in season ticket prices (last season they were so cheap the club may as well have given them away), we've already broken all pre-season sales records, all our players are under contract, and manager Frankie Burrows has agreed a new deal to keep him at the club. Samesh Kumar has resigned as chairman, but remains as a director, and is apparently keen to sell his remaining shares. A share issue is to be launched in July, which is hoped will raise over a million pounds to spend on players, and the redevelopment of the ground has commenced, with plans for new seating areas, and at long last, some executive boxes. Blimey.

And that's how it's done - at least, that's the way we did it. Sure, I've left loads out, and have probably made it sound really simple, when it wasn't. But at the end of the day, if you boil it down to the basics, it's this: In Frank Burrows we had a good manager, with a board who would back him. They signed players who would run themselves into the ground for the club, and at last the club started to pay some attention to the fans. Do that, and you're laughing. That's what they're doing at Cardiff, and I'm just so glad I'm here to see it happen after so long.

This summer the club celebrates its centenary - one hundred years since Riverside FC, later to become Cardiff City, were formed at a house in a Cardiff suburb. Happy birthday, Bluebirds.

Andrew Turton

THE VALE PARK BEANO

Port Vale

Events during the season at Burslem were responsible for many ex-smokers taking to the wonderful weed again, in desperation. As the comings and goings, both on and off the pitch continued, so sales of Park Drive soared, as we could hardly believe what was going on around us.

Two main stories dominated the pages of our little organ. One you probably already know about, concerning our beloved ex-leader, Rudgie (more about that later). The other, not as newsworthy nationally, but very important to us, and some might say even more important, as it concerns free speech (or rather the lack of it) and censorship on a certain local BBC radio station.

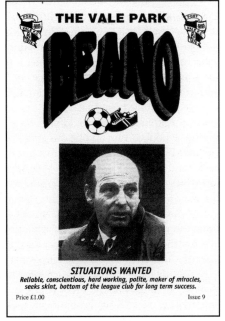

THE VALE PARK

SITUATIONS WANTED
Reliable, conscientious, hard working, polite, maker of miracles, seeks skint, bottom of the league club for long term success.
Price £1.00   Issue 9

Our local talk-based radio station is the unfortunately-named BBC Radio Stoke, a station that appears to do everything in its power to live up to its unfortunate moniker. Although the station claims not to be biased towards one team or another (Port Vale and Stoke City both being within its broadcasting area), the vast majority of its broadcasting staff, all except for one to be precise, make no secret of the fact that their support is not with Port Vale. It's not necessarily because they say "Port Vale are crap", or "We love Stoke". It's the little throwaway remarks that presenters use: "A good result last week for City"; or, "We'll be at the Brit, as usual." Just everyday, throwaway remarks that aren't offensive, but do emphasise which team they follow. But when the team you support is continually ignored, whilst it is impossible to escape references to another, *then* it becomes more than an irritation. Fortunately up until October, we did have one Vale fan on the payroll at the station. His name was George Andrews. He was the station commentator on all Vale matches, and he was a complete and absolute Port Vale nut. He was also good at his job; bloody good. He brought a game to life, even if it was dead: he was overtly exciting, humorous, and sometimes completely over the top. But we loved him because he was better than all the other Stokie-loving lot put together; and they knew it and were as jealous as hell.

One day in October, he disappeared from the airwaves, never to be heard again. He was gone, just like that, with no explanation or reason. Calls to the station were answered with: "We cannot comment. You'll have to ring the BBC press office at Pebble Mill for information." Calls to the press office were answered with "no comment". This is the BBC press office remember, the place to ring if you want information. And all we wanted to know was what had happened to George. After a few days, the local paper got hold of the story, which went along the lines of "he had been 'relieved of his duties' and would not be heard on the station again". Eventually, we discovered that George had indeed been sacked for a misdemeanour for which a verbal, or at worst, a written warning would have been sufficient punishment. But no, they threw the book at him and he was gone. Telephone calls to the station, and to Pebble Mill, were still answered by "no comment". The mighty BBC closed ranks and clammed up. Many Vale supporters tried on phone-in shows to raise the subject of what had happened to him, but as soon as they mentioned the words "George Andrews", they were cut off in mid-sentence. Some were even shouted off the air: "Shut up, I'm not going to talk about George Andrews," came the reply from one particularly obnoxious presenter. We were later to find out that presenters were in fear for their jobs. If they mentioned the words "George Andrews", they'd be in deep water - even drowned by the management.

What made it even more galling was the fact that the station was running some gooey jingles at the time, telling us "We're your friendly local station", and inviting us to "Ring our phone-in show and talk about anything you like - go on, get it off your chest and talk about it". Yeah, sure, ring in by all means - but what they didn't tell us was, that if they didn't like what you wanted to speak about, you'd not get on, old chum.

A sympathetic insider was later to tell us that George was disliked by the high-ups, as he didn't conform. He wasn't kosher BBC, old chap, and he had his own way of doing things, including not keeping to a script. But it was this that made him so damned good, so brilliant and so popular. Then, when he stepped ever so slightly over their dogmatic line... bingo, he's gone. Sod the listeners - even though other presenters break the rules, they can stay 'cos they're not Vale supporters.

On BBC TV at about this time, viewers were being asked to send for the 'Statement of Promises' because, we were told, "The BBC is unique in the way it is funded. It is funded by the viewers and listeners who all have a right to know what is going on." So we sent for it, and we read that the BBC was an open organisation that would respond to viewers' and listeners' queries, and so on and so on. But when we tried, without success, to obtain information about George, we discovered that their promises are just a load of words that don't mean a thing - like a worthless guarantee. So much then for the 'Statement of Promises' - or should it be 'Statement of Broken Promises'?

Eventually we were given a new Vale commentator - an ex-player in fact. The only problem was that he came from the wrong side of town, and although he gave his all for the club when they were paying his wages, it was no secret that his sympathies and passion belonged elsewhere - a couple of miles down the A50, in fact. This was borne out when on his first Radio Stoke interview, he was welcomed to the station as the "new Vale commentator", and asked: "But weren't you a Stoke season ticket holder, and aren't all your family true red and white?" "Oh yes," he replied - and the rest of the programme was devoted to talking about the good old days at the Victoria Stadium, their favourite players, and practically bugger all about Vale. Doesn't it just make you weep that they're so thick they can't see how they are throwing one insult after another at us. It really is an incredible situation that has resulted in Vale fans tuning to Talk Radio, where George now plies his trade. He is also working for Planet TV, and also employed by Port Vale for presentations, etc.

So just beware - when you next hear a BBC station inviting you to phone in and talk about anything you want - you can, as long as they agree with your subject, which cannot be controversial or critical. The only way around it is to say you want to talk about horse shit, or something equally riveting - then, when you get on, quickly ignore the horse shit bit and talk about whatever you want. The problem is, if you live in this area, they'll cut you off immediately. They're nothing more than a Government-lackey propaganda machine, making umpteen false claims and talking absolute bollocks, whilst trying to brainwash their listeners who are maybe under the impression that radio, free of censorship, did not die with the demise of Radio Caroline all those years ago.

The BBC's motto is 'Nation shall speak unto nation'. But our experiences over the last few months have revealed that you'll only hear what they want you to hear and that free speech is as restricted as it ever was. Frightening, isn't it?

But of course, all this pales into insignificance when compared to the events of January 18 and the dismissal of Our Main Man, John Rudge.

The season, up until then, had been poor, very poor - although not entirely Rudgie's fault. Top-scorer Lee Mills had suddenly upped and gone at the beginning of the season, after being offered bucketfuls of cash by Bradford. Fans' favourite, Gareth Ainsworth, had been sold to Wimbledon behind Rudgie's back, whilst he was abroad scouting. Team regulars Tony Naylor, Neil Aspen, Matt Carragher and Michael Walsh were out, long-term injured. Loan players came in, got injured and left. On January 16 we were second from the bottom, having just lost in a dismal fashion at home to Swindon. It was our twelfth defeat in 14 games and, to top it all, the heavens opened one hour before kick-off to give us one of the worst blizzards of the season. To rub salt into the wound, the snow stopped at 3.00pm prompt, so the match could go on, but hardly any spectators had turned up - only 5,405 in fact. But chairman Bill Bell had had enough - and on the following Monday, he announced that, after 15 years, John Rudge had been dismissed. It came as a bombshell to the supporters - even though we had been watching one defeat after another and the team were firmly ensconced at the wrong end of the league table. We fully expected the old magician to pull another rabbit out of his flat cap, turn him into another Robbie Earle, and start us climbing up the table. He'd done it before, and we fully expected him to do it again. Distraught fans held peaceful demonstrations, a 'flat cap' march was held, in which 843 black balloons were released, one for each of the games he presided over whilst manager. But Bill Bell had made up his mind, and threatened to sell the club if the unrest and discontent continued. It wasn't helped by the fact that some morons damaged some cars on his garage forecourt. A few days later, it was announced that ex-Vale player Brian Horton would be taking over. Sure enough, at the next home match, against Huddersfield, the same set of players who had performed so abysmally against Swindon and got Rudgie sacked, took all the points and ended the losing run. Gradually, Brian Horton brought his own players in, and come the end of the season we finished in 21st place, equal in points with the two teams immediately above us. First Division football was assured for another season, and a few voices were being heard saying that perhaps Bill Bell had done the right thing. Whether Rudgie would have pulled things around is impossible to say, but one thing's for certain, the great man will never be forgotten.

At the end of the season, a star-studded testimonial match was held for ex-Vale captain Ned Aspin. When Robbie Williams, Steve Guppy, Robbie Earle, Mark Bright and even Steve Bull turned up, they all received cheers and applause from the Vale faithful. But the biggest cheer went up when Rudgie appeared, to bid his final farewells to his long-time supporters, who could still hardly believe the tumultuous events of the previous few weeks.

Visitors to Vale Park next season shouldn't be surprised when they hear the chant "Brian Horton's black and white army...", followed by "John Rudge, there's only one John Rudge...". Rudgie was a one-off - a true gentleman and admired by everyone. He brought us four promotions, three Wembley visits and several giant-killing matches. It should be pointed out that even in our darkest days, even after losing at home to Swindon in front of 5,405 spectators, in the snow, there wasn't a "Rudgie out" to be heard. He and George Andrews were both one of us; they were our mates. They didn't just say they supported Port Vale because they were paid to say it - they really meant it, and that's what makes it so hard to come to terms with the fact that they've been sacked.

Brian Horton has certainly got a hard act to follow - a bloody hard act. He's done OK so far, but watch this space next year. And why not give a listen to George Andrews? He's on Talk Radio most Saturdays. You never know, our loss could be your gain.

We're not a big club, neither are we rich, but loyalty in this business is a rarity and last season we lost two of the most loyal people that you could wish to meet. It's no wonder that one of them was nicknamed 'The Voice of Vale' and the other 'Mr Port Vale'. It's also no wonder that many of us now suspect that the initials 'BBC' stand for 'Bringing Back Censorship'!

Dick Dale

THE WEARSIDE ROAR

Sunderland

When we started *The Wearside Roar* in the spring of 1998, we chose our title in homage to the 'Roker Roar' which, in reality, had only been heard in full effect on limited occasions in the couple of decades prior to Roker Park giving way to a housing estate in 1997.

However, *The Wearside Roar* has proven to be an inspired title choice for our unashamedly glossy A4 mag, as the atmosphere at the Stadium of Light is more often than not absolutely superb. Any misconceptions that moving to a new state-of-the-art 40,000-plus all-seater stadium was not the best thing for Sunderland have been shattered in the first two seasons at our beloved new home. A lot of

supporters of so-called Premiership big guns will be awe-struck at Wearside's new citadel, the focal point of Britain's newest city, when they visit our shrine of worship in the '99-2000 season. This season ended in gloriously spectacular fashion with promotion from the First Division, and although it can be argued that a club of Sunderland's size should never have had any problems in gaining Premier League status, the manner in which season '97-98 ended could have had catastrophic consequences for many sides of lesser character, for years to come.

The 4-4 Wembley play-off spectacular against Charlton was indeed a memorable affair and one of Wembley's genuinely all-time great matches. But for Sunderland, a season's graft was ended by Mickey Gray's now almost mythical penalty-miss, and 1998 was the longest close season in history for the loyal red and white army foot soldiers of SAFC. It was almost typical of Sunderland that, after having failed to scare at Wembley in every visit since the 1973 FA Cup Final (0-1 v Norwich, 1985 Milk Cup Final; 0-1 v Swindon, 1990 Play-off Final; 0-2 v Liverpool, 1992 FA Cup Final), they scored ten times, including their six penalties against the Valiants, and still went home defeated!

The 1-0 victory, courtesy of a Kevin Phillips penalty, against QPR at the beginning of the season, was of huge psychological importance and set the tone for a memorable campaign that saw the lads only lose three times throughout. There had been no long-yearned-for big-name signings by the single-minded Peter Reid during the summer. However, the main names who came in ultimately made massive contributions to our Wearside war effort, and emphasised that there are still bargains around if you know where to look. Not one to suffer fools, and even less so egocentric and eccentric French goalkeepers, Reidy let the peroxide blond Lionel Perez depart for Newcastle Disunited. Many fans were outraged that such a terrace hero was allowed to leave for the forces of darkness up the road on Tyneside. Enter the hitherto unheard-of Danish 'keeper Thomas Sorensen, currently on the verge of replacing the veteran legend Peter Schmeichel in the Denmark team. At only 22 years of age, this 6'4" goalkeeping colossus cost only £500,000 and is a truly brilliant prospect, as Premiership fans will see. Perez ended his first season at Newcastle on the transfer list and as third choice. His season's highlight was winning the Northumberland Senior Club, in front of one man and his dog, against Blyth Spartans. Oh dear! As defensive lapses cost Sunderland dearly towards the end of '97-98, Reid also caused raised eyebrows and groans of "Who is he" after paying Bury £1m for Paul Butler, a centre-half of the old school, circa Ron Yeats, Jack Charlton 'brick shithouse' stylee. Sorensen and Butler were exactly what Doctor Football ordered for Sunderland's shaky defence, and allied to the goals of Kevin Phillips and Niall Quinn, the silky skills of Nicky Summerbee and Allan Johnston, the Championship was destined for Wearside from the opening day.

Key players such as Lee Clark, Niall Quinn and Kevin Phillips missed large chunks of the season but the squad system advocated by Reid paid dividends. It was quite a feat for Sunderland to see players like Darren Williams, Darren Holloway and the outrageously-talented Michael Bridges, for example, regularly represent England U-21s whilst not regulars at what was, after all, still a First Division club. After their lacklustre showing in the Premiership in '96-97, Reid has totally remoulded his team, which is based on defensive strength but which scored goals from all over the place in Division One. As our season developed, it was also amusing for a large percentage of Sunderland supporters to see Newcastle continue to prove that money cannot guarantee success. They have too many soccer nomads from all over the world. Common sense tells you they cannot have any genuine team spirit or camaraderie in a dressing-room with around ten different nationalities in their set-up. Half of them will do well to speak and understand basic English, never mind enjoy the banter which successful football dressing-rooms always have. Under Keegan, the Mags thrived, and it was hard being a Sunderland fan three or four years ago, as they played football that even the most ardent Mackem secretly admired. Now, post-Keegan, post-flotation, post-Ginola, Ferdinand, etc, and post-arrogant directors, they are in a mess that even Mr Suave Gullit may struggle to cope with. What a shame for north-east football. Not.

Disunited even had the decency to make fools of themselves in the FA Cup Final for the second year in succession as Man United ambled to victory. The ease with which Sunderland took their divisional title, however, does not of course guarantee Premiership success. Bolton's runaway triumph a couple of years ago and subsequent placings illustrate this. However, there is genuine optimism amongst our supporters that a new era really is on the horizon. The current side needs strengthening, but the basis is there. Denmark's next international 'keeper in goal, a defence that includes England new boy Mickey Gray, Scotland's influential winger Allan 'Magic' Johnston in midfield, and the 'little and large' England-Ireland strike-partnership up front in Phillips and Quinn. There are no excuses available to Sunderland's hierarchy for failure any longer. Crowds are averaging over 40,000, bringing in revenue in the region of £1m a game, plus income from sponsorship, merchandising, corporate hospitality, and the riches that go with simply being in the Premiership via Sky revenue, etc. To the neutral, Sunderland are perceived as a yo-yo club, who have flattered to deceive for too long in spite of being well supported. But if Peter Reid goes for the jugular and fine tunes a promising side with genuine class in key central areas of his side, then a club which has not finished in the top half of the top-flight since the mid-1950s will flourish. Scouser Reid has been compared to his boyhood idol, Bill Shankly, on many occasions; and the similarities in character make-up to the Anfield idol are many. Indeed, Shanks once referred to the then Bolton schemer Reid as a "yard dog scrapper" - which was clearly a comment showing mutual respect. For Peter Reid now, however, read Sir Alex Ferguson. Reidy's management philosophy shows many striking reflections. Like Ferguson, he places great importance in a good youth set-up; he tends not to always look at the obvious big names with regard to signings; he generally prefers to sign British, Irish, Scandanavian or Northern European players; and remains seemingly sceptical of the more temperamental footballers of Latin origins.

Like Fergie, Reid is fiercely protective of his players in the public arena, although privately he tells them in no uncertain terms if he is unhappy. But now Reid knows that he has to do the business in the top flight amongst the big boys and really prove himself as worthy of being on the opposing bench as Ferguson, Wenger, Vialli and Graham. Sunderland fans were often complacent going to games last season, even though you can only beat what is in front of you. It was all very nice beating Oxford 7-0 or Tranmere 5-0, but the underlying fact was that most fans were bored with second-rate opposition and went to games almost expecting to win and thinking, "We shouldn't even be in this division." The fact was that we were. Wimbledon, Southampton, Coventry and co have survived in the top flight over the years, despite having lesser histories, traditions and support than the likes of Sunderland. The cliché that success has to be earned rings only too loudly for the Wearsiders. Kevin Ball, the club skipper, ran around the pitch after the final match of the season wearing a *TWR* 'Sunderland Till We Die' sweatshirt. And a player who has been crucial to our rise from Division One, also personifies the close relationship that has grown up between the club and the supporters, particularly after what everyone went through after the play-off final with Charlton. The key thing now is for everyone to stick together; to be resilient and we'll succeed. Sunderland need to indulge in 'controlled arrogance'. They should not talk about consolidation but have the confidence to set their goals higher than in the past - European qualification for starters - invest in class, whilst still retaining the work ethic and team sprit that has brought them relative success in the form of promotion.

After a record Stadium of Light crowd of 41,634 witnessed the final game of last season against Birmingham, the PA played Van Morrison's *Days Like This* and there was hardly a dry eye in the house. Sunderland fans are looking forward to crying more tears of emotion in the future but not ones concerned with relegation fights. Roll on the Premiership and to all away fans coming to our ground next season, be warned for the 2.50pm onslaught when Republica's *Ready To Go* precedes Prokofiev's *Dance of the Knights* as the teams get ready to enter the country's greatest football arena. The Wearside Roar awaits you all.

Tom Lynn

THE WHIFF

Reading

Ah, the optimism. Every fan of every team in the country goes into a new season knowing that this one could be theirs. Some have good reasons, others just the blind faith of the true believer. Reading fans had more reasons than most. A new stadium, good enough to rival any in the division, and most in the country, albeit a ground built on a swamp (alright, land-fill site), with access roads at least a year off completion. A host of new players we were assured were good enough to win the title. A division full of mediocrity and no-hopers in equal measure. And last but by no means least, a new(ish) manager, who had come from Celtic via Newcastle - Tommy Burns, the saviour of the Royals.

The Whiff

Alternative Reading   Issue 8 Feb 99   1.43 Euros

New Robin Friday T-shirt - Page 14   £1

CLUB ROCKED BY HUGE JOCK COCK SHOCK!

A large erection yesterday   The Shocking Story - In Full! - Page 3

The warning signs were there all along. At the end of the '97-98 season, Burns had brought in seven players on deadline day in a desperate attempt to avoid the spectre of relegation from Division One. It was a hopeless cause. The team were demoralised, tired, lacking in confidence - or to put it another way, just plain crap. We won two of the last 17 games, and the teams we beat (Man City and Stoke) joined us in Division Two.

Change is not necessarily for the better, however. Certainly in the short-term, wholesale changes to a team are unlikely to improve results, and *The Whiff* cautioned against high hopes, at least for a few months. We were totally, horribly, right to do so. Early away thrashings by Wrexham and Bristol Rovers were briefly forgotten with a 3-0 inaugural victory at the Madejski Stadium (hereafter referred to as the Mad Stad or the Ego-Dome) against Luton Town, but the end of September saw us languishing at the foot of the table, having taken a meagre five points from nine games.

However, the changes kept coming thick and fast. Early on, Carl Asaba was flogged to Gillingham at a loss, and went on to be one of the top scorers in the division, making it to the play-off final with the Gills, and even scoring at Wembley (alas for him, to no avail). Michael Meaker was sold to Bristol Rovers, and in time-honoured fashion scored against us in the second match of the season. A host of other players were told they were no longer required by the club, and went on to skulk about for the next few months as no other bugger wanted them either. Jason Bowen, Gareth Davies, James Lambert, Andy Legg and Steve Swales became known as 'The Death Row Five', and there were rumours of hangman nooses being left around should they feel the need to do everyone a favour.

Neville Roach also left the club after it appeared that he had got back into the side. Nev grew up almost next door to Elm Park, was Reading through and through, scored on his debut a couple of years ago, but was now deemed surplus to requirements. Southend have got themselves a good buy.

On the bright side, one player did redeem himself. Phil Parkinson, known to the local press as 'Captain Courageous' for his somewhat robust style of play, was told he could leave in August, but refused an offer from Wycombe, and by the end of October had regained his place in the centre of the pitch, as well as the captain's armband. For the second year in a row, he was voted Player of the Season by a considerable margin, and Tommy Burns had the decency to swallow his pride and admit that he'd made a mistake. Parky's contribution to Reading on and off the pitch is an example to every other player at the club, and he even managed to score some goals, which is better than one of our so-called strikers managed all season. Stand up and take a bow, Paul Brayson.

Another glimmer of hope amongst the torrent of despondency was an almost miraculous run of away form. Before September 30, Reading had gone eight months without an away win. Thank you, Walsall. We went on to gain points from every away fixture until the end of February, including a run of four wins. Christmas saw us in contention for the play-offs and all seemed right with the world.

Despite a peculiar result in January, and Bristol Rovers fans know what we're talking about, so there's no need to elaborate, by the end of March, we were still in contention; but this being Reading, it all slipped from our grasp. The closing stages of the season were epitomised by two results.

Firstly, Blackpool 2 Reading 0. The editorial team went to Blackpool for the weekend, along with about 800 others, and had a great time. The weather held out, the funfair was fantastic, silly hats and beer were abundant, and one of us even won something on the Grand National, but the match was utter, utter dross. It was the worst performance all season, against some stiff competition. We'll be going again next year, and would urge any occasional away-tripper to do the same, but our attendance at the game itself is under some doubt.

Secondly, Reading 2 Millwall 0. The last fixture at the Mad Stad until next season. Mathematically impossible to reach the play-offs, as it had been for two weeks. A nothing game. Reading dominated, with Parky scoring probably the best goal of his career, but that's what we needed to do in February. And April. Oh, and August, September and November.

Those twin excuses of injuries and the pitch were paraded all too frequently by management and media alike. Injuries have been a theme for a couple of years. Erstwhile captain, Barry Hunter, often described as a giraffe on roller-skates, finally played in April after a break of over two years (and then had the gall to ask for a pay rise). Star-signing Graeme Murty made his first appearance in February after a transfer from York in the summer. It turns out that he had one leg shorter than the other, a fact not picked up in the no doubt extensive medical. Numerous players picked up hamstring injuries on the training pitch. Most importantly, Martin Williams was sidelined in February when on target for 20-plus goals in the season, and there was no replacement. Richmond Rugby Club, who have now been swallowed up and spat out by some other bunch of egg-chasers, shared the Ego-Dome, and completely buggered the playing surface. So the pitch was a factor, but both teams have to cope with that.

It may seem from this that we had little to enjoy this season, but that's not strictly true. *The Whiff* scraped together enough money to sponsor a match ball in November, and had a fine day out being wined and dined in the sumptuous surroundings of the Thames Room in the West Stand. In fact, we were so well wined that we don't remember much about it, but Reading won 2-1 against a feeble Lincoln side. The stadium is fantastic, although it will be better with capacity crowds, and that's unlikely to happen if we continue to potter around in Division Two. Oxford's fall from Division One has been greeted with some glee. Not gloating, you understand, just the fact that we'll have a local derby other than Wycombe next year. Honest. The departure of long-serving Keith McPherson to Brighton was marked with a testimonial dinner in the even more sumptuous Princess Suite on Cup Final day, and *The Whiff* splashed out again for a table of ten and more wining and dining. Macca turned up at our end of season party a few weeks earlier, and this was *after* he'd left, so it was the least we could do.

And next season? Optimism is at a premium, and the word 'if' is on everyone's lips. If we can keep a stable team, if we can get a good start, if we can turn those far too frequent home draws into home wins, if Martin Williams is fit, if we can stop injuring our players on the training pitch, if our goal-scorers (Williams apart) can score some goals, we have a chance. A prediction? Champions. Or second. A realistic prediction? Fifth, but that's the worst of all options. Just ask Gillingham how they feel after their trip to the home of football. We've been there before, against Bolton for a place in the Premiership (well done, and thank you to Watford, by the way), and it's bloody hard to take. It's surely better to finish seventh than risk that heartache again. Or is it?
    Peter Cook

THE YELLOW BELLY

Lincoln City

Impudence

After a surging late run and the failings of others, the Imps had the audacity to win promotion last season. Having rubbed up their Third Division opponents the wrong way, as decreed by previous manager John Beck, City now had the cheek to inflict the same style on more illustrious adversaries. Although Beck had been sent on his way, the direct tactics remained under new manager Shane Westley, with one subtle difference from last year - they didn't work.

Full of optimism, around 600 Lincoln supporters went to the first game, at Bournemouth. And witnessed a horror story - in the first-half at least. The home side tore City to shreds and every time the ball was launched into their half, they controlled it and attacked Lincoln's defence at will. At half-time the home fans chanted "Going down, going down..." to us. Perhaps they knew something that took us another 45 games to work out.

Despite this grim start, City won their first home league game, got a couple of away draws, and should have beaten Preston when they were 3-1 up, only to concede three in the last 20 minutes. Then the rot set in and they lost six in a row, and the struggle to survive began.

Impecunious

Meaning skint. On the eve of the first home game of the season, chairman John Reames announced that Lincoln City were up for sale. He said that he couldn't put any more money into the club and a new backer was urgently needed to inject in large funds to meet the financial demands of playing at a higher level. This set the tone for the rest of the season, with the dire financial situation being a constant problem

Supporters heard what some of the players were getting and it was clear that the income from attendances would never match the outgoings in wages. Rumour had it that player X, who shall remain nameless (Leo Fortune-West), was on £1,700 a week and he wasn't even in the team.

In October the media reported that City were going bust. John Reames quickly denied these reports and a public meeting, previously arranged to talk about routine football matters, suddenly became a crisis meeting, with hundreds of supporters cramming in. Most fans were more than cheesed off that all this monetary gloom was casting a depressing shadow over what should have been the most exciting season for the Imps for years, after so long in the basement division. Despite this, most people were sympathetic rather than angry, and the idea of a fighting fund was agreed.

Impetus

After the public meeting, a small group of fans spoke to the board and a Bournemouth-type rescue scheme was agreed. Called the Impetus Campaign (or 'Impotence Campaign' by some of the more cynical around us), it had the dual aim of raising much-needed funds for the club in the way of donations from fans and businesses, and the elevation of an elected supporter onto the board. That way, fans could help City survive and could have a say in the running of the club. In addition, the organisation had other ideas, including getting reduced admission prices for youngsters, and lobbying the football club to bring on younger players instead of spending a fortune on has-beens. Much work was put into the scheme and, from October to January, it raised £1,000 per week.

Sadly, the optimism generated by Impetus was not matched by the results on the pitch - and by mid-November, City had won only three league games. One of them was a marvellous 2-1 defeat of Manchester City - the third time in a row that we had beaten them, including in cup games the season before last. Although the Imps were not getting hammered regularly (see later), they kept losing games they could have won or drawn, and relegation was already being talked about, albeit in hushed tones.

Impatience

Two defeats in three days in November at Chesterfield and Walsall were the final straw for the chairman, and Westley and his assistant, Wally Downes, were shown the door. At Saltergate, the Imps fell behind when the referee adjudged that Perry's well-timed tackle was a foul and he gave the home side a penalty. Lincoln never looked like getting back into the game, though, and ended up losing 3-0. At Walsall, City scored first, through Tony Battersby, but yet again lost a game they had been winning. At this game, too, the refereeing was appalling. Gavin Gordon was harshly sent off, and late on Walsall took a free-kick for offside well into Lincoln's half of the pitch!

Just like Beck, Shane Westley worked to a rigidly inflexible system, and there was no imagination behind Lincoln's tactics. Opponents preparing to play us didn't need to be Oxbridge graduates to know that they would he bombarded with long balls and long throw-ins, and teams were generally too good to fall for it. Exit Westley.

Imposter

I suppose most City fans reacted the same way when they heard a) Westley was sacked, and b) who was taking over. That would be a) thank God and b) are you taking the piss? Yes, as you probably know, the chairman took over as manager. He argued that the club couldn't afford anything other than an untried man in charge, and as he'd been at the club for 16 years, he thought he knew enough to do the job just as well as anyone.

Thankfully he decided not to do it all on his own and employed senior player Phil Stant as assistant. Stant did all the day-to-day training and coaching, and Reames picked the team on matchdays. Although this was considered a more-than-dodgy arrangement by the supporters, it was instantly noticeable that they had responded to popular opinion and changed the style of play. At last - football!

Improvement

As the new management team took over, the FA Cup was upon us, starting with a difficult away game at Cheltenham. They were top of the Conference and must have fancied their chances. As it was, City played well and won, and then hammered cocky Stevenage in the next round.

These confidence-boosting wins, allied with the players having the freedom to express themselves a bit, brought about an improvement in the team's performances in the league. From the end of November onwards, City were unbeaten in nine consecutive home league games, winning six and drawing three. Away games didn't yield much, but a win at Blackpool in February saw City out of the bottom four for the first time in months. Teams who had hammered us at their grounds - Chesterfield, Bristol Rovers, Bournemouth and Millwall - went away from Sincil Bank bemused and pointless, wondering why they didn't get an easy three-point haul like they did in the first game. At last City looked like a Second Division team.

Impoverished

And then came the turning point. Home form was giving City real hope and York came to Sincil Bank without a win since early January. Even better, they'd just sold leading scorer Richard Cresswell to Sheffield Wednesday. And when Paul Miller put us one up after four minutes, it was deep joy all round. City then eased up and, as the game wore on, changed from a confident, well-oiled machine to a bumbling, dismal shower devoid of ideas.

York striker Williams, making his debut after being bought from Halifax for £970,000 less than they got for Cresswell, scored two - and we left the ground stunned at Lincoln's transformation from winners to sinners. After this disaster we got stuffed at Stoke, mauled at Maine Road, and walloped at Wigan. Again we found ourselves thinking uneasy thoughts of Underhill, Gay Meadow, and other unpleasant places.

Improbable

As the season drew to a close, our attention was divided between Lincoln's games and results elsewhere. Just when things looked better, we found out that another relegation candidate had pulled off a shock win somewhere or other. City won at Colchester and beat Wrexham before the last game, at home to Wycombe. The biggest home crowd of the season willed the Imps to win, whilst at the same time hoping for an unlikely combination of results elsewhere. To complicate the formula, Wycombe needed to win to stay up - which they did, with a goal late on. It made no difference to us because

Oldham were quickly 2-0 up against useless Reading and we were down. We'd had our season in the sun and it was time to crawl back under the stone that is the Third Division.

Important

Several crucial matters need to be resolved by the Imps before next season. The Second Division seemed to us to be freakishly strong and we nearly did enough to stay in it - so surely we should do well back in the Third. To do this the best players must be persuaded to stay, and this is down to chairman Reames.

Another issue for him to sort out is the position of manager. He says he wants to carry on doing the job, but most supporters want Phil Stant to do it on his own. We have been told that he is not experienced enough to be appointed, but Graham Taylor had no experience when he started at Lincoln, and you can still read in *Rothmans* the unbeaten records set by City with him in charge.

Recently, Impetus and the existing membership scheme were combined to form a substantial supporters organisation. It will raise money for the Imps and fans will have a much bigger part to play in the running of the club. Already the club have responded to the grass-root support, and season ticket prices for under-16s have been made much cheaper. New youth policies are being set up to bring in new talent and to save paying out loads on players with limited ability and unlimited wage demands. Clubs who do not attract large crowds, and who do not have the benefit of a rich backer, will surely have to follow this route. It is important that the people who run Lincoln City do so in a way that does not jeopardise the future of the club. Involving the supporters much more, instead of just expecting to take their money off them, will he one way of doing that.

Finally, and most importantly, football has to look at the way it is going. The vast TV and corporate sums being greedily grasped by clubs in the Premiership is rapidly spoiling the competitive pyramid system that keeps the leagues alive. The influx of so many foreign players is forcing good players down the league, and small clubs are trying to meet their large salaries in the effort to succeed. Some players we saw last season - Asaba, Stein, Caskey, and so on - should be in the First Division at least, and clubs like Lincoln struggle to compete on and off the pitch, having gone up only one division, let alone anything more ambitious. All small teams dream of doing a Wimbledon and climbing to the top. These days if you haven't got any dosh, forget it.

Rob Bradley

THE ZULU

Birmingham City

Behind The Scenes

At long last, and for the first time in our history, the Blues are being run efficiently and in a business-like fashion, and showing a profit, which is another first. And pulling the strings we have Karren Brady, the first bird to control a football club. Karren has got things done, got results and, further more, got a lot of people's backs up. Oh dear! Jolly Jack Wiseman came with the furniture and fittings - he's been at the club since the year dot. We all love him. Everybody at the club mucks in; even the kit-man doubles up as a sign writer. Then we have the moneymen - multi-millionaires,

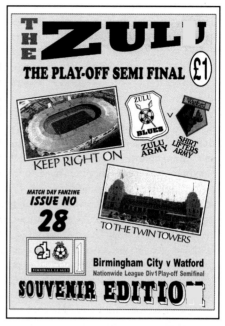

whose personal fortunes increase annually. David Sullivan and the Gold brothers will tell you proudly that they made their empires out of sex; who would have believed there was that much money in dirty postcards? They say you can't take it with you when you go. Well, don't you believe it. I'm positive the three of them have found a way to do it - otherwise they'd give Trevor a measly £50m to start getting his Premiership side together. At St Andrews, the ground improvements are looking good. Mind you, I was rather fond of those old asbestos sheets. The new stand at the Railway End will be open for business in the new year. That will just leave the old main stand to replace. Old? My God, it's the third one I can remember; whilst Jack Wiseman can remember the gypsies camping there in 1906.

The Playing Side

At the helm we have Trevor Francis, who also moonlights for Sky. Trevor's a living legend at St Andrews, and can do no wrong. 'Charisma' as the players affectionately refer to him, has completely changed the playing staff; we're looking good, and Trevor is about to deliver us to the promised land. Mick Mills (assistant-manager and part-time model for Kays catalogue): He is a bit of a flash harry, and if this former England international defender knows how to defend a dead-ball situation, he's certainly not letting on. Ian Bennett (goalkeeper): A great shot-stopper, but prone to suffering from a touch of the Draculas. Does he not like crosses. Jonathan Bass: It's common knowledge that all great players are ugly, so Jon's too pretty to be a footballer. Never mind Jon, all the lady Bluenoses love you. Tony Hey: Yet to deliver the goods, but with a raving beauty like his missus, the last thing I'd be thinking about is football. Simon Charlton: Not so simple is our Simon, and we've missed him. Get well soon Simon. Jerry Gill: Did everything asked of him when thrown in the deep end, and was unlucky to lose his place in the team. Time's on Jerry's side. Chris Holland: Lost the sight of one eye in an accident, but played out of his skin for us on loan. As soon as he signed on the dotted line, it appeared his other eye failed to focus, but seeing things a lot clearer now. Martin Grainger: He has a knack for finding space, then putting a telling ball through, right to the feet of the opposition. Jon McCarthy: Some fans are now getting on his back. But to his credit, Jon never hides, and is always looking for the ball. Give him a chance. Bryan Hughes: Destroyed us when playing against us for Wrexham in the FA Cup, but failed to live up to that at St Andrews. He was just getting there when he got injured. Going to be missed. Gary Ablett: This old Scouser is doing a great job by taking the place of that obese Geordie, Bruce. Michael Johnson: 'Magic' Johnson to the Tilton. Never gives less than one hundred per cent. A great favourite with the fans. Nicky Forster: Still to repay the great confidence Trevor has in his ability, but just lately showing signs. Keep taking the tablets, Nicky. Kevin Poole (reserve goalkeeper): He's spent that long on the bench, the others refer to him as "your honour". Peter Ndlovu: How can you go wrong with a good old-fashioned Brummie name like that? No messing with Peter. He goes straight for the jugular. A very shrewd bit of business for Trevor. Paul Furlong: Or 'sick note' as he's fast becoming known. Thank goodness he's got private medical insurance, otherwise he'd bankrupt the National Health Service. Dele Adebola: Strange how these old Brummie names keep cropping up. This man is built like the proverbial outside brick toilet. Defenders just bounce off him. He's fast becoming a cult figure with Bluenoses.

To Sum Up

Well to put it in a nutshell, this time next year we'll be playing in the Premiership. All we have to do for now, is to keep turning up and taking the points - forget the play-offs. An automatic place awaits us. OK so we came unstuck at Bradford and Bolton, mere hiccups on the road to glory. The way I see it, promoted by Christmas. And by the end of January crowned Champions. Then we can concentrate on the FA Cup and the League Cup. A treble is a distinct possibility. And if the men in the white coats leave me alone, and I continue with the medication, I'll be there at the end of the road!

Postscript

You learn what it's all about very early when you become a Bluenose. That is never be too optimistic. That way you will never be too disappointed. Because at the end of the day, they always let you down. Forget all that crap about a gypsy curse. We've never won a major prize because we've always been crap. We Bluenoses take all this in our stride - that is why we are so fanatical. I'll give you a good example of a Bluenose. In the seventies, we were once playing the great Leeds United side of that time in the FA Cup Semi-final at Hillsborough. We were losing 3-0 with about ten minutes to go - and, believe me, we were lucky to get nil. The Leeds fans, spoilt by success, were leaving the ground early in their hundreds. But not the Bluenoses - they stayed to the end, giving the team a support worthy of Champions. This is a fact, and is backed up by that great former Leeds United player Johnny Giles, who told me so recently, adding how impressed he was with our fans. And that's what it's all about, following the Blues - the fans, who without a doubt are the best in the country, and I love them all. So back in September when I was invited by Norwich Football Club to write the profile on the Blues, it's why I wrote it with a sense of humour. This went down like a lead balloon with the Blues. Trevor Francis went apeshit before the kick-off, inviting Tom Ross our local radio commentator into the dressing-room, telling him how upset the players were with the match programme. This resulted in Tom Ross slagging me off non-stop on the radio all day Saturday. We lost 2-0 and Trevor put this down to me, not the fact that we were crap.

The item made the front page of our Saturday sports paper, and the *Sunday Mercury*. Martin Grainger stated that I don't know anything about football and, if he had his way, he'd ban me from the ground. Now, being a Bluenose, I couldn't argue about knowing anything about football. But wanting me banned from the ground was another matter - so I wrote to Grainger telling him that just because he had been playing like one, didn't give him the excuse to start talking like one. It reached the Danny Baker show, where it went down well, whilst Karren Brady wrote to Norwich FC demanding an apology. The following Monday evening, I received a phone call from a Blues player who told me how much he and most of the players had enjoyed the programme, but asked me not to reveal his identity. Later in the season, I met and spoke to two more players who confirmed this. The fans, though, were the ones who really mattered - and they liked it. Several asked me to autograph the programme.

Later in the season, I upset the club again, when I went on the telly to denounce a company trying to sell the Blues fans a watch through dodgy means. Then, on *The Vanessa Show*, Karren Brady described me as a bitter old man. Coming from an old slapper, I found this amusing. I don't take myself seriously, and I don't take offence when I get criticised. Following the Blues has given me a very thick skin indeed.

Dave Small

THERE'S ONLY ONE F IN FULHAM

Fulham

How Fulhamish! We grab our first Championship for 50 years, doing so with a record points haul, only to have our last day of the season celebrations tainted.

There can surely never have been so many flags and banners at the Cottage. Yet before the game - against Preston - most were being dragged along, or even held as if at half-mast, rather than thrust skywards and waved in jubilation. Why? Well, with immaculate timing, King Kev, who had steered the club to the Division Two title and tremendous performances against several Premiership sides, had in the previous 48 hours decided he was off.

To be precise, it wasn't his

leaving that left a nasty taste in the mouth - he was off to the England hot-seat after all, not another domestic post - but that he had pledged time and again he would not be leaving Fulham. That's what grated. Massive media coverage of the Keegan-for-England campaign had consisted of rumour, speculation, supposition, jingoistic tub-thumping and incredibly patronising garbage, with an occasional well-balanced, reasoned piece of reporting thrown in for good measure. What remained constant, however, were Kevin Keegan's quotes that he was remaining loyal to Fulham.

To be honest, it was no real surprise that he went. And, by and large, he did so with the good wishes of the Fulham faithful. It was the broken promises that hurt, and the timing that stank. And the acute awareness that, not for the first time, a resurgent Fulham FC could possibly come off the rails. The main difference this time, we hope, is that the real key player - Mohammed Al Fayed - is as ebulliently enthusiastic as ever.

To put everything in context, and to counter the relentlessly-sung "Where were you when you were shit?" by opposing supporters, you must remember that it's only three years since we sat one off the bottom of the entire league, went to visit the bottom club - and lost. Those Fulham die-hards at Torquay in February 1996 and the devoted stalwarts who did so much to keep the club afloat during the dire decade when FFC plunged from crisis to crisis (a 'shoestring' was considered a veritable luxury in those dark days!) are now getting their pay-back. Big time.

But let's be honest, if anybody then had suggested that, three years on, we'd be bemoaning the loss of Kevin Keegan, but that at least we'd won the Division Two title in barnstorming fashion and had played the Premiership leaders off the (Villa) Park - not to mention having immense financial clout - then they'd have been deemed madder than a fusion of Collymore and Gascoigne.

Now would be an appropriate juncture to recognise and thank the assistance of non-Fulham fans. Our fundraising campaign, Fulham 2000, which wound up just recently with the balance of some £360,000 going towards ground improvements, received marvellous support from all over the country and abroad. Then we were perceived as many people's 'second-favourite club' or 'dear old Fulham'. Odd then that once we were fortunate enough to receive an unexpected and massive cash injection, we became the club that many loved to hate, with the dreadful consequence of one supporter, Matthew Fox, losing his life.

If a club is to get stronger, it's vital that gates go up, and yet in some ways we're as cheesed off at the bandwagon jumpers as anyone else. It's human nature for crowds to drift away when the team struggles and for attendances to rise as soon as things improve. But during those awful times when we begged for even the slightest financial assistance, the vast majority of the new Fulham faithful were nowhere to be seen. 'Nuff said.

If Micky Adams set the ball rolling in quite remarkable fashion, then history will record that Keegan's influence, especially once he was in a hands-on role, was phenomenal (Ray Wilkins, you'll recall, was jettisoned as we scraped into the '97-98 play-offs). His enthusiasm is boundless and incredibly infectious, and he helped to make Fulham newsworthy once again. Keegan's talismanic qualities meant we were linked, often realistically, with a host of big name players possibly prepared to drop a division or two because KK was at the helm. So, all in all, and allied to an ever-increasingly professional approach behind the scenes, it was clear to everyone that the club was going places.

On the field, the team amassed a record 101 points in winning the division, overcame Premiership side Southampton in the Worthington Cup before bowing out to Liverpool - where Paul Peschisolido netted our goal of the season. We enjoyed an even better run in the FA Cup, during which the Saints were again marched out. Aston Villa were outplayed 2-0 and it took all-conquering Manchester United narrowly to halt matters, 1-0, at Old Trafford. We were very nicely poised for a jump back into the big time.

For all the relevant pomp and majesty in the cup, however, it was very much bread and butter stuff in the league. Forget anything you may have read about 'Keegan's cavalier Fulham' - it was much more formulaic than that. Some league encounters were truly awful (not helped by team after team simply shutting up shop) - but we ground out the all-important points. Forget, too, any thoughts of big money 'fancy dans'. It was great to see our team consistently turn in performances of terrific character. And it was all too apparent that there was a wonderful squad spirit. Yes, it's boring to prattle on about work-rate and application. But they're priceless commodities, even to a team with supposedly millions in the kitty.

One or two sparkling league showings stood out, including the early-season drubbing of Man City, when two-goal Dirk 'German Porn Star' Lehmann thrust himself into the limelight. We enjoyed exciting encounters with Reading, 3-1, and Millwall, 4-1; won 4-0 at Kenilworth Road; defeated rivals and good friends Walsall 4-1; and had a cracking evening at home to Gillingham. The 3-0 scoreline flattered us that night, but who cared - promotion had been secured. Enter, stage right, our chairman for a prolonged jig of delight.

Non-Fulhamites may be surprised to learn that the key contributors on the park were not 'Super Geoffrey' Horsfield, the expensive Berry Berries, or even Mail Terror, whose goalkeeping performances from the turn of the year were hugely impressive. In fact John Gregory got it right (for once!) after our wonderful win at Villa Park. "Fulham's success was based on the form of their back three." And so it was for the whole season. Stand up and be counted Chris Coleman, Simon Morgan and Kit Symons.

Apparently, Kevin Keegan was keen to play with a flat back-four but had his hand forced by these three - two of them Welsh internationals and the other, Morgan, an Englishman with the most Welsh-sounding name of all. Stoic, brave and utterly committed, the trio blended so well that they took it in turns to pop upfield to score. Symons, in fact, threatened the goal-scoring feat of centre-half and war-horse Roger Brown, who scored an incredible 12 in 81/82. Kit finished one short of the record but treated us to some unexpected dribbling skills, which dear old Roger could only have dreamt about! 'Cookie' Coleman helped himself to five goals and earned the label "Best player outside the Premiership" from our ex-leader. Slightly biased, maybe, but more than slightly true all the same.

Then there is Simon Morgan. Where do you start? Successful author (his book *On Song for Promotion*, which recorded all the insider wheelings and dealings of our previous promotion year, 96/97, was lapped up by the fans); a great favourite for giving his absolute all for season upon season (and with a wholly deserved testimonial in the offing); labelled the 'Moaning Minnie' by the fanzine for championing the cause of whinging, whether at training or in the thick of a game ... but supposedly finished according to some as we kicked off the season.

Finished? Ha-bloody-ha! He scored eight times. But sod the goals. Even Keegan had to concede that "Simon Morgan has surprised me time and again", as he named him his Man of the Match for the umpteenth time. If ever there was a player who deserved this season's success it was our Simon. And if ever there was a moment to capture what he's all about, then it came in the first-half of the final match. Determined to play in our 'party day' game with Preston, despite five stitches in his leg, courtesy of a really dreadful tackle by a rather rugged Burnley chappie, Morgs was our last hope as Preston breached our defence in the first-half and homed in on goal. Morgan tracked his man and made his move. We all winced - and with reason. It was a bone-shuddering (stitch-splitting?) tackle, but one timed to absolute perfection and all carried out in his usual matter-of-fact fashion. The danger was cleared and, with spirits raised, forgotten man Paul Moody grabbed a second-half hat-trick to ensure we all went home smiling. Even Kevin Keegan.

Champions. Following a decade or more of despair, I could get used to this. More please...

David Lloyd

THORNE IN THE SIDE

Brentford

Brentford fans are never satisfied! A few years ago the last games of the season were simply to determine whether our beloved Bees would finish in thirteenth position or the dizzy heights of twelfth. We always ended up in mid-table - and then the Gods answered our prayers. "You want excitement? You'll get excitement!" From then on, it seems Brentford have always have something major to play for come that final curtain-call in May.

Little did we know that those final-day tears would be ones of heartache more often than joy, as apart from our flirt with the big time in 1992, two relegations, a defeat at Wembley

THORNE IN THE SIDE

OUTLOOK - North: Dull and gloomy South: Much brighter

ISSUE 28
£1

Brentford FC

BRENTFORD DRUGS SHOCK...
BATES CAUGHT WITH PERFORMANCE ENHANCHING DRUGS

and two play-off disappointments all within six years, were enough to send the sensible insane.

Fortunately, just over a regular 5,000 of us, insane or not, stuck by the club and reaped the rewards of our Championship season that unfolded just as dramatically as the previous campaign had ended. At the end of '97-98, we'd been kicked as hard as you can imagine and fell as low as we had experienced for as long as I can remember. David Webb sneaked out the back door after milking the club dry and dismembering a side that, 12 months earlier, had come within 90 minutes of being a Division One outfit again. Now we found ourselves in the basement league and allegedly up to £2m in debt.

Up stepped Ron Noades - 'The Ego had landed'. Like him or loathe him (and up until the Goldberg fiasco most Palace fans apparently loathed him), Ron Noades had come along as a knight in red and white armour. A few of us tried to fight his arrogance all season, but with the predicament our club was in, for the first time in ages, Ron Noades' hidden agenda, if he had one at all, was brushed under the carpet by supporters who were dreaming of any salvation.

Uncle Ron called us "morons", stuck up for David Webb, swigged beer from a bottle whilst wearing snowboots during press conferences, ditched favourite players, and argued rather than talked to fans in eventful fans forum evenings. But he did what he said he was going to do and made a good few eat humble pie come the end of the campaign. Noades himself laughed off media suggestions that he was a "God-like character with the supporters at Griffin Park". "They would have had anyone after David Webb!" he replied, and he was right.

Ron Noades was now the owner, chairman and manager; and *Thorne In The Side* teamed up with William Hill bookmakers to lay odds on him becoming 'player' with a tongue-in-cheek wager at 100-1.

It was to be popular feature in our fanzine. One punter took 1,000-1 on Uncle Ron becoming the next England manager, and Hills' Graeme Sharp quoted a 5,000-1 price on Noades actually scoring a hat-trick for the Bees! Brentford were in no doubt Ron was going to rule the world (or TW18 at least) as Noades euphoria took over. But before a ball was kicked, maybe the more serious punter would have done well to take the 7-1 on offer about us actually winning the Championship.

After a somewhat interesting start to the season, Brentford looked world-beaters in the opening game, where we stuffed Mansfield 3-0, but looked decidedly poor in the next match, losing to new recruits Halifax at the Shay, where we barely competed.

It was the way the early weeks of the season mapped out - brilliant one Saturday and bloody awful the next, sandwiched in between with outstanding midweek performances against West Brom in the cup, and a creditable slim defeat at the hands of Tottenham in the following round.

Noades told fans and press alike that he had the best coaching staff in the business at Griffin Park, and with the help of the chequebook to secure the services of three or four low-priced steals from non-league, Brentford began to build for the future.

Try telling that to impatient supporters - we wanted success right away. With respect to our new opponents, Brentford felt that we didn't belong in the Third Division. For once, we were the big boys, for once we had some money, and rather patronisingly at away grounds, the familiar song "We're only here for a year..." echoed at the likes of Hartlepool and Barnet. But I still needed convincing.

Despite never falling lower than seventh all season, it wasn't the stroll in the park that most had hoped for.

The rest of the division made sure Brentford weren't going to have it all their own way, as Scunthorpe, Plymouth and Rotherham joined us as early pace-setters - and because of all the attention Noades had brought with him, games against Brentford suddenly became the smaller clubs' cup finals.

If only we could have read the last page in the book instead of having to follow the mystery through the chapters, then Bees fans could have relaxed and actually enjoyed Division Three. As it was, at least it meant a few new grounds along the way.

On the whole, our away support was good both in attendance and vocal backing, the map books dusted off to find delights such as Scunthorpe,

Darlington and Rochdale. Maine Road and the Britannia Stadium may have been only one division higher, but they seemed light years away. Trips away from home, although enjoyable for the experience, didn't harvest many fruits for the first half of the season. Brentford's indifferent form was worrying, and although on the surface our promotion campaign was spluttering rather than gathering momentum, at least no-one in the basement seemed capable of putting a string of results together either.

A fortnight spell in December proved vital for the Bees. A TV-covered top of the table clash with Cambridge saw Brentford outplayed, but a 40-yard chip from Tony Folan in the fifth minute was enough to put us into second spot and gain valuable points against a strong Cambridge outfit. An equally important victory over Cardiff a week later, in an incident-packed game both on and off the field, witnessed by 9,500, cemented our promotion credentials.

The club then faced another first - international call-ups! This usually meant it was the Tenerife end of season tour, but this was the Ron Noades era and Hreidarsson, Folan, Boxall and Quinn were all called up to represent variously Iceland at full level and Republic of Ireland U-21s.

Brentford's young side, though, were feeling the strain, as the club then hit a barren spell, picking up one point from a possible 15 after the new year. Bees fans panicked, and Uncle Ron's answer was to rest key players, adopting a squad system normally reserved for the Premiership. Some fans moaned, some scoffed, and there were reports of frustrations amongst the camp after being dropped, or as the manager put it "rested". But drastic measures proved positive as Brentford were on the slide, and were barely holding onto the final play-off position.

As results improved and confidence grew, Brentford composed themselves, got back on course and never slipped below third place after a 4-2 win at fellow contenders Rotherham. In fact, a 16-match unbeaten run took us to the end of the season. The first milestone was reached with six games to spare - we were guaranteed a play-off place at least, which although didn't spark off too many celebrations amongst the faithful (judging by our play-off record of past), it was a cushion to fall onto should someone cut our strings to promotion.

Two thousand travellers packed into Roots Hall, sensing a win over lowly Southend would pave the way to the 'bigger' time; the Second Division, bar a major catastrophe, was within touching distance, and the players didn't disappoint. Even the Southend fans gave Bees leading-scorer Lloyd Owusu a standing ovation as he hit his second hat-trick over the Shrimpers, as Brentford demolished United 4-1. A 2-2 draw at Darlington, on a night where our rivals slipped up, set up promotion fever for the following weekend, a home game with Exeter. It was almost an anti-climax as the West Country side fell apart, the Bees winning 3-0. At last we were back where we had come from - promotion was ours.

All of a sudden the last home game of the campaign had added significance - a win would set up a Championship decider with Cambridge on the following Saturday. For once, Brentford read the script and gave Swansea City a lesson in football. The Bees, confident and playing their best football of the season, swept aside City and the crunch game was on...

The scene was set: both Cambridge and Brentford were already promoted, but whoever won claimed the title.

Bees fans were in good voice. After all, the last time we won the league, it was in Cambridgeshire and Evans was our captain: Peterborough and Terry were fond memories of the past - now it was the turn of Cambridge and Paul.

In a cracker of a game, that man Owusu did it again - a fine 1-0 victory and the Bees were crowned Champions. Brentford were smiling again. What a difference a year makes. The players celebrated to the end but few of them knew what this result meant to us. We'd been put through hell and back over the past two seasons and today was the first time it seemed to hurt a little less.

Even Uncle Ron managed a grin. With rumours around about a return to Crystal Palace, no-one knows how long he is to orchestrate his fine-tuned ensemble. But this is the new Brentford - farewell to the old, with the nightmare of the predecessor finally being put to rest. Ron Noades and his coaching team delivered the goods and proved many people wrong, and with a young squad, hungry for more, the future looks bright.

And as for David Webb? He can kiss my arse...
Nick Hester

THOSE WERE THE DAYS

Ipswich Town

The Price of Failure

This piece was written a few days after our third consecutive failure to win promotion to the Premiership through the play-offs. Increasingly the rest of the season seems irrelevant as whatever happens (a bad start, good start, goal famine, goal-glut), we always seem to finish third, fourth, fifth or sixth. And I, for one, am getting fed up with it. I'm also starting to find the annual look back at our season for *SOTF* an increasingly depressing exploit. Oh well, there's always next year, I suppose...

"The unluckiest team in the world." That's what the Guardian's *Fiver* football news

service called us this week, and I'm not one to argue with that assessment. What more could we have done on Wednesday? We got the performance we wanted from the team, but unfortunately the need for us to push forward left us exposed at the back and gave Bolton the opportunities to grab three goals.

A terrible way to end the season once more; particularly depressing this year as we came so close to an automatic place.

Where did it all go wrong? I think to an extent we can point to far too many home defeats. If just one had been turned into a victory it would have been us looking forward to the likes of Man United and Liverpool next season, and not Bradford City in our stead. We dominated most of those games - matches against Barnsley, Bolton, Grimsby and Crewe - but couldn't turn our superiority into goals. Our stuttering end to the season and goalless start also robbed us of valuable points which, when it came to the crunch, would have been vital.

Some also point to the transfers of Alex Mathie, Mauricio Taricco and, to a lesser extent, Danny Sonner. Would we have fared better with any of these players still at the club? Alex Mathie has had a nightmare season at Dundee United, with injuries, lack of fitness and an inability to settle seemingly to blame. Would things have worked out any differently for him at Portman Road if he had stayed? Very difficult to say. However, we certainly needed greater strength in depth up front, especially around Christmas when we lost both David Johnson and James Scowcroft to injury.

The transfer of Mauricio Taricco was probably the most controversial point in Town's season and it seems unlikely that we would have sold Mathie had the Taricco transfer come through a few weeks earlier. As things panned out, we replaced Mauricio fairly rapidly, and more than adequately, with Fabian Wilnis, a player who has already become a bit of a fans' favourite.

It is an unfortunate fact of football that clubs the size of Town need to sell to survive. We will always (unless we acquire a sugar daddy from somewhere) have situations where popular players will be sold. Whether the timing and fee were right for Mauricio can be questioned, but someone would have to have gone at some point to avoid the club getting into the kind of debt that has so crippled clubs like Crystal Palace.

Once again it seems we will be facing the loss of players in order to balance the books. Once again we will have a summer of wondering whether each day will bring a new sale. Mind you it's been like that all season. We've had rumours that Kieron Dyer is off to virtually every Premiership club, Richard Wright to Liverpool and Manchester United, David Johnson and James Scowcroft have both been linked with Charlton, and Bobby Petta with Barnsley.

With our season only over for five days, I have already heard or read speculation surrounding half the team. Apparently Kieron is off to Leeds or Arsenal, Richard Wright to Liverpool or Manchester United, David Johnson is off come what may, and Matt Holland and Bobby Petta are going to Fulham, or Petta to Celtic. We have also had Kieron Dyer and Richard Wright pledging to stay at the club, and David Sheepshanks admitting that someone will be sold over the summer. Oh and John Gorman hasn't committed himself to Town either. All this uncertainty means that it is going to be a very difficult summer for George Burley. What will the squad look like in August? What money will he have to play with to replace any players who are sold?

It is going to be very difficult for Town to repeat the performance of this season next year, given all this uncertainty. The ideal situation would be for all transfers to be done and dusted before pre-season training starts so that any new players have time to bed in. However, we all know that situations never end up being ideal for Town.

Another season ultimately ending in disappointment then, but once again Town have more than matched most of the richer clubs in the division. Look at the table: Sunderland, Bradford, Birmingham, Watford, Bolton, Wolves and others all have far greater financial resources than Town, and yet there we were in amongst them, and hugely unlucky not to be the ones promoted. The team have, by and large, performed superbly and given us fine entertainment. The good attitude and commitment to the cause of most of the players (and, sadly, we must say 'most' as certain players haven't always appeared to be totally committed to the club - Town fans all know who they are) has been evident throughout and were epitomised by Kieron's tears at the end of the final game, against Sheffield United. It'll be a shame to see this side broken up, as we've played some excellent and attractive football, but sadly this seems likely. All rather depressing.

On the upside, George Burley's purchasing of players in his four years at the club has been very astute. With the exceptions perhaps of Chris Swailes, Danny Sonner and Marco Holster, every player he has bought has done well. To be fair to Holster, he still has time to prove himself, in the same way that Bobby Petta did in his second season.

Once it becomes clear where we need to fill gaps in the team, and once it becomes evident what (if any) money there is available to spend, I think we can expect more signings of the class of Manuel Thetis, Jim Magilton and Fabian Wilnis. I just hope that everything is set in place soon enough for us to start a really serious assault on the division once more. One thing is for certain: with the likes of Fulham, Blackburn, Nottingham Forest, Wolves, Birmingham, Charlton and others, the First Division is going to be an incredibly difficult challenge next year. But it seems almost inevitable that we will finish in the top six, although the top two positions seem worryingly out of reach...

Philip Ham

Source: *One More Point*

THREE LIONS

Shrewsbury Town

The '97-98 season finished with Shrewsbury occupying their lowest league position for over 40 years, having lost in the opening round of every cup competition. Surely things couldn't get much worse? I was naive in thinking so. I'll spoil the ending of this season's tale by telling you that we finished even lower down the league snake (it's not been a ladder for some time now) than previously, and repeated our cup non-success, with the added bonus of being knocked out of the FA Cup by a non-league side.

Hopes began high enough after finishing the previous campaign with a flourish; and despite losing 3-0 to Northwich Victoria, pre-season had gone well, with victories over

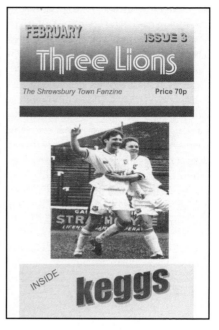

Sheffield Wednesday and Northampton. We had unearthed a gem of a striker, Lee Steele, from the aforementioned Conference club and had the two best full-backs in the division. Fate would give us an early chance to avenge last season's last-game defeat by Scunthorpe, as the opening fixture was a repeat - although the result was encouragingly different. We went to Trashton in the Worthington Cup and saw First Division Bristol City put four past us with the help of an assistant referee with the sun in his eyes. The 803 optimistic home fans who turned up at the Meadow thinking we still had a chance in the second-leg were soon scouring their mental record books as City soon put another couple past us to lead 6-0 on aggregate. Then the unthinkable almost happened. Town quickly pulled four goals back and, with 40 minutes still to go, the City defence were poo-ing their collective pants. It wasn't to be - but our victory on the night was an ill-omen for Bristol City.

Suitably spurred on, league defeat followed league defeat. Despite Rotherham's perennial generosity at Millmoor, we were soon cast adrift at the foot of the table. We lost at home to struggling teams like Barnet and were roundly thumped both home and away by Cardiff. At 3-0 down, just after the break at Ninian Park, Town fans were taunted with "It's just like watching Brazil". Self-deprecating as always, the Town faithful, watching the now familiar struggle in the new red away kit, responded with "It's just like watching Wales!" Terrace humour at its best. In fact of all the teams who were bottom at some point in the season, we lost to them all, except ourselves. Then, inexplicably, we started winning everything. We beat top teams like Plymouth and Brentford, before embarking on yet another slide down the table. Our two full-backs begun to perform as if the previous season had been erased from their memory and our star striker was dropped and seemingly uninterested. In fact we had four strikers all going through a 'lean spell' at the same time. It was 12 games before any of them found the net - and after 27 matches our top quartet had notched just three goals between them. It was just as well our midfield knew where the net was. Steve Kerrigan, complete with dodgy knee, still looked the most likely to form a partnership with Lee Steele, and slowly but surely things started to click. Another good run accompanied Lee's return to form and we headed off up the table once again.

Transfer deadline day has long since been anything except one of trepidation and this season's casualty was captain Paul Evans, who left to join upwardly-mobile Brentford. After eight years at the club, Paul could have gone for free at the end of the season but had obviously foreseen that he would be lifting the Championship trophy well before then, and that it wouldn't be with us. Town banked the cheque and reluctantly bade him farewell. With a bigger than ever hole in our midfield, another losing sequence wasn't entirely surprising or slow in coming. In an inconsistent division, we were more erratic than most; although over 45 games we did just enough to survive. At the last home game of the season, a match we actually won to dash Mansfield's play-off hopes, the usual messages and announcements were made not to invade the pitch at the end of the game. (It's five years now since anybody did.) Paul 'Eddie the Eagle' Edwards was deservedly named Player of the Year and at the final whistle, ran over to the Riverside terrace to throw his goalkeeping gloves into the crowd. Typically, he missed. The only incursion onto the playing area was the one bloke who had to be helped over the low wall by a steward to retrieve his own personal momento of our custodian's finest year. Somehow this incident encapsulated the whole season.

You may have noticed that I said 45 games earlier on. That was no error, as our visit to Torquay to complete our fixtures bore no relation to the events we had witnessed all year long. At 40, Neville Southall was presented with their Player of the Season award before the game, whilst we gave a goalkeeping debut to a 17-year-old, Glyn Thompson. One was commanding in keeping a clean sheet, bossing the defence admirably, whilst the other relied on his woodwork to reduce the number of occasions that he picked up the ball from the back of the net in the first-half alone, to five. You guessed it, Big Nev was having a tawdry time of it. Despite the referee cruelly chalking off two of them, this only served to confuse the poor Radio Devon reporter, who faithfully reported Torquay's 4-0 defeat. After witnessing just 12 away goals all season long, the 500 or so who'd made the five-hour journey were amply rewarded for their loyalty and the evening's celebrations merged into those for Stevie Kerrigan's stag night. Shrewsbury were just unbelievably rampant. Now hold that thought until August will you lads?

Chris Jarvis

TO ELL AND BACK

Leeds United

The summer of 1998... and there remained lingering doubts in the minds of Leeds United fans. George Graham had hardly been what you could call a productive or imaginative operator in the transfer market, bringing in two virtually unknowns, in Chelsea's third-choice left-back Danny Granville and a striker from Holland, Clyde Wijnhard. Alan Thompson, highly coveted by Leeds, had opted to go to Aston Villa instead because he wanted to win things - the mug! The ultimate snub, though, had to be Port Vale's Gareth Ainsworth, who admitted he was uncertain about leaving the splendour of deepest, darkest Burslem for the bright

AN UNOFFICIAL VIEW OF LEEDS UNITED #10 AUG 99

64 56 pages crammed FULL of LEEDS-PRICE £1.00
Warning! May contain language unsuitable for children

THE LATEST BOOK FROM THOSE LITERACY GENIUS AT SCUM:

"Leeds fans are identikit skinheads" - G & P Neville

Ralf Barker enjoys his first big day out at Elland Road during Leeds 4-1 thrashing of Derby last season. Mum Saffron is on hand to ensure be be saved!

lights of the Premiership. Graham, too, had doubts - whether or not to pay £2m for Ainsworth, and eventually the player ended up in Wimbledon's star-studded reserve team.

Leeds, however, did top the table after thrashing Southampton 3-0 at Elland Road. "There's only one George Graham!" the fans boomed. Up until then we had received Graham in somewhat lukewarm fashion. Those of us with reservations were proved ultimately correct - as Graham waved back that night, really he was waving goodbye.

London beckoned and poor homesick George wanted to be back in the capital rather than trudging up and down the M1 to Leeds and back every day. No doubt if Barnet had been on the lookout for a new boss, he would have taken a drastic pay-cut to join the Underhill outfit. Instead he chose to join lowly Tottenham. As a result, he managed to simultaneously piss off three sets of fans in one swoop! His one-time Arsenal fans were mortified that he'd joined the old enemy; Spurs die-hards at the time raged that they didn't want him due to his Arsenal connections (but shut up whining when he won a few matches); and left somewhere in the middle of the media circus were us Leeds fans, rightfully disgusted that he should break a four-year contract just six months down the line, when we'd rescued him off the scrapheap and made him the best-paid manager in the country.

The saga rumbled on. There followed a botched attempt to capture Leicester's Martin O'Neill. Suddenly Leeds were resembling the sad old bag at the ball who nobody wants to tango with. However, waiting quietly and patiently in the wings was David O'Leary.

No-one - I repeat, no-one - could have predicted the impact O'Leary made on the Leeds team. It was as if we turned full circle overnight without really making that many changes. The prodigal son, David Batty, returned and Leeds were not just beating opponents for fun, they were steamrollering them. The crowds flocked back to Elland Road. It was at times breathtaking stuff and hugely satisfying because the names on the team-sheet were home-grown ones, such as Harte, Kewell, Smith, Woodgate, Jones and McPhail. Faced with a defensive injury crisis, O'Leary gambled on the kids - and it paid off.

When we did slip up, we emerged from those matches with great credit. The negativity of Graham and the humdrum ending to the Wilkinson era was forgotten. Even the press men were forced to swallow the anti-Leeds bile, concocted since the days of the late, great Don Revie, and pencil in new superlatives about this Leeds team.

Inevitably, envious eyes were being cast upon our team. In particular it was rumoured from London N17 that Graham, armed with Alan Sugar's money, would take his pick of up to eight Leeds stars. The board moved quickly to secure Nigel Martyn and Lucas Radebe on improved, long-term deals and have no option but to do the same with half a dozen others this summer.

Cup success, as it always has been for Leeds was somewhat bleak. We bowed out of the UEFA Cup in the second round, somewhat tamely it has to be said against a below-par AS Roma side. The Worthless Cup campaign ended at eventual-finalists Leicester. And the gloomiest night of the season came when Tottenham put us out of the FA Cup, with two amazing goals from Anderton and Ginola.

After that Spurs defeat, great heart was taken by the fans in the way that Leeds picked themselves up and again began mercilessly to crush their opponents. Only a negative Liverpool denied us a club record for the most consecutive league wins. There was talk of the Champions League, with third spot in sight and Chelsea rapidly dropping points, but really that was optimistic; and most fans were more than happy when we confirmed another UEFA Cup campaign, routing eight-man West Ham 5-1 on their own turf.

O'Leary has since been tied down to a whopping five-year deal, with no 'get out' clauses (so we are told), and if our exciting young team can be kept together with similar long-term contracts then maybe, just maybe, we could be on to a winner. Whatever may be, but for the first time in years, Leeds United fans are eagerly renewing their season tickets out of anticipation rather than duty.

Mark Monk

TORA, TORA, TORA

Chesterfield

Swine Before Pearl's Harbour

The most exciting events at Chesterfield this season have all happened off the pitch - yes, it's been another one of those years. In February 1998, the local Borough Council rejected plans for Town's proposed move to Brimington - since which time, there has been much speculation about where the club would relocate after our board, in their infinite wisdom (don't make me laugh), decided that it was financially unfeasible to do anything with the splendid Saltergate, one of the last bastions of real footie grounds, with the possibility for home fans to walk round at half-time (or whenever they feel like it, in truth). Saltergate is also the oldest continually used league ground in the world - but, hey, don't let this nugget of historical truth stand in the way of 'progress'.

With, at the time of writing, the deadline day looming for new ground plans to be, at least, lodged with the necessary authorities, things have finally started to happen. Rumours had been flying about for ages that Mike McDonald, the ex-chairman of Sheffield United ('Deedahs' to those of us in north-east Derbyshire), was going to take over from the incumbent - some would say incompetent - J Norton Lee, and also build us a ground on a site behind the railway station. Following an article in the local press, in which McDonald accused Norton of not signing the contract to confirm that funding for the ground was in place, you could feel the hackles rising on the back of the chairman's neck. He's none too good at taking advice offered - and certainly not if that advice comes through the local press, whom he appears to hate. A week after the offending article, and (no coincidence, this) the day after both the *Derbyshire Times* and *Deedah Star Green 'Un* had gone to press, he called a meeting, limited to the first 100 members of the official supporters club who had a ticket, and from which all press were banned, to give his side of the new ground story. Only just over half of these supposed 'real fans' bothered to show up, which made it even more of a joke. Basically it appears we will have a 10,000 all-seater affair, built as cheaply as he can fund through grants, plus a million quid from his own company. Estimated cost of the entire ground will be less than Birmingham City paid for their new stand this season. Bescot Stadium 2 - can't wait... Oh, and McDonald is not going to be involved with the development, and presumably will not therefore be the new chairman of Town, so at least something good has come of this entire debacle. There was a statement in the programme for the home game following this meeting, but that was even more of a joke. It basically said, "Yes we will have a new ground and it will be behind the railway station." Nothing else. Is that keeping the fans informed? I think not. Meanwhile, Saltergate has been threatened with having the three terraced sides closed unless money is spent to bring them up to scratch, but late meetings with the Licensing Authorities have given us a year extension on our gaff. If this fails, Derby have supposedly offered us the Baseball Ground for next season - which would be a hoot, having to get coaches to attend home games.

September saw us smash our transfer record and pay a quarter of a million (wow!) for Jason Lee from Watford. We had first been linked with the possibility of signing Jason on transfer deadline day two seasons back, just days before the FA Cup semi-final game with Middlesburger at Old Trafford (aaaargh, I mentioned it - I'm sorry). Sadly the deal didn't go through due to... er, vehicular problems. We were linked with him again in the close season, but he chose to go back to Watford, where he failed to make it as a regular in the first team. The strange thing about the deal bringing him to Saltergate at last was that our cuddly chairman allegedly signed him behind the manager's back. Duncan claims he was kept *au fait* with the deal, but a body of evidence points to the fact that he only found out about it when it was sealed and delivered. You probably won't be too surprised to find then that big Jason's appearances in the first team have been few and far between, largely due to injury and also the burgeoning relationship between our front two of David Reeves and Jonathan Howard. However, even with Jason on the bench and the front pairing struggling, John Duncan has used him but sparingly. Rumours continue to circulate about discontent in the camp due to the fact that Jason is earning way more than anybody else. There was one brilliant tale of a training ground bust-up between Jason and Mark 'Bomber' Williams, in which Bomber is supposed to have smacked Jason. He's a brave boy.

Yes, let's mention Bomber. He almost certainly won't be here next season, as his contract is up and he's hoping to use his call-up to the Northern Ireland squad as a shop window for other clubs. He played at Wrexham against Wales in a B-team international and by all accounts had a cracking game. With his appearance against Germany and Moldova, he becomes the first Town man to play a full international, whilst still with the club, since Gerry Armstrong in 1986, who also turned out for Northern Ireland. In fact he is likely to equal the club record of appearances as an international (four!).

More on players: we were lucky enough to secure the services of the (hopefully) reformed Shane Nicholson, sacked by West Brom last season for failing, or not taking a drugs test - their loss has definitely been our gain. Shinner has the ultimate in cultured left feet and has been responsible for putting over many corners and crosses this season that even a blind player could have scored from. He's way too good for this division and is another one of our players who seems unlikely to kick-off with Town next season. Sadly, we lost the services of Andy 'Bruno' Morris, who was offered a contract by Rochdale (he was on week-to-week terms here) and has since been doing the business in Lancashire. I'm sure all the fans at the club wish him the best, until he plays us. He will long be remembered for that mazy dribble (so un-Brunolike) at York last season and for his magnificent 20-incher at Old Trafford (fnarr fnarr).

When the season kicked off, I wouldn't have given you money on Town appearing above tenth all season. Some people were openly talking about relegation even. Yet somehow we spent a couple of months on the fringes of the play-offs. We finished ninth but our away form scuppered any realistic push for promotion. Our victory at Reading on January 2 was our first Saturday away win in the league for 616 days (88 weeks if that sounds better). The last time was at Crewe shortly after we were dispatched by a bunch of child molesters from the north-east (or, I suppose, by a balding schoolteacher from Harrow) from a certain cup competition I've vowed not to mention again. Coincidentally, this was the same day as Exeter won their first away game in 14 months: good old New Year resolutions. Strangely, we repeated the feat for the next away match, but soon reverted to form. Our season expired with eight weeks and 12 games to go after a dull, dull, dull 0-0 draw at Rectum (one of those games when Jason Lee just about made it on, far too late to have any effect, though) and a dismal 2-0 defeat at a resurgent (yawn) Lincoln, where Duncan's tactical nous reached new heights, playing a formation of a Bomber-less five at the back (Jason Lee often making it six), two in midfield (they might as well have stayed at home) and three up front, allegedly. Reeves was so wide and Howard so fluffy, Lee was left to try to hold it together all on his own. He was rewarded for his efforts by being substituted with ten minutes to go - smart move, John. If this is the sign of things to come next season, then we are in big trouble.

We've had to stand or sit through some incredible crap this season. *Tora Tora Tora* was born out of the pathetic display at Colchester on the first day of the season. Who can forget the inept and dismal twin performances at Wycombe, firstly in the cup, supposedly after having had them watched many times, then weeks later in the league? Or what about Northampton? Hadn't won at home in months but... yes, here come Chesterfield, easy meat. This was so poor that one of our number even wrote to our chairman demanding his money back. I've never seen so many angry Town fans as after this shambles. Similarly at home, it hasn't been pretty much of the time. In the good old days, they used to open the gates at half-time and you could get in free. If they had been doing that this season, then, with few exceptions, you could have seen some good matches by entering just before four o'clock. Sadly, first halves for the most part pass far too slowly; thank goodness there's enough happening off the pitch and enough great rumours circulating to keep us amused. But then again, with fans beginning to call for the manager's head (again), Duncan rallies the troops and we score three goals in three consecutive home games for the first time in... ooh, bloody ages. Notts County and Lincoln were smit by the wrath of the gods before Town turned in their best performance in many a year by defeating the Dorset Cherries 3-1.

This season has also seen the emergence of SIFA (the Spireites Independent Fans Association), largely as a result of the frustration felt by a group of supporters at the lack of progress over the new ground. Membership has exceeded all expectations, with over 500 fans parting with their hard-earned dosh. All is not rosy, though. SIFA have upset the club big style by running their own, cheaper travel to away games and, so claim the club, taking money from them. The chairman met with a SIFA delegation early in the season but has since refused to have anything else to do with them. Grow up. (Although after the team and board shared a hotel in Bournemouth, things have improved and further meetings have taken place. Well, one anyway.) SIFA have managed to get up the noses of the club once or twice, whilst maintaining a cordial and useful arrangement with the local press, so they must be doing something right.

This season has also been Jamie Hewitt's testimonial. His committee have tended to go for the big events rather than something that the average fan can feel he can afford. But good luck, they seem to have raised a very reasonable amount of cash for this good cause. SIFA raised £750 at a race night - a victory for the common man.

In closing for this season, can I just say well done to Cambridge for a splendid double over our nearests and dearests - firstly for putting Deedah Stupidname out of the Worthington (headline in the *Star* as both Deedah clubs exited on the same night: 'Misery as Blades and Owls crash out' - I don't think so!) and then for an inspired rollicking of the Scabs 7-2. What a way to notch up your record league tally.

Fred Tomsett

TOSS!

Hull City

Tiger Tales: Tennis Balls, Tantrums and Take-overs

A tart's tights have had less ups and downs than the supporters of Hull City over the last 12 months. Even as I write, a court battle looms, threatening our hopes of a stable future. Meanwhile, in the background, the omnipresent evil that is David Lloyd still rants and raves like the lunatic we know and loathe - and still attempts to destroy the club he once owned. A tart's tights? The width and length of the ladders in such whore's hosiery can be nothing compared to far-reaching ramifications of a season, which saw Hull City Football Club

Issue 5
£1.00
April '99

THE PUCKISHLY INDEPENDENT
HULL CITY FANZINE

MISSING

- Have You Seen Neil? -

He was either last spotted hanging around the centre of Hull City's defence one Saturday afternoon or on the floor of a well known nightclub. Both sightings occurred approximately three months ago. Neil was a member of the so-called 'wing back formation' Hateley gang. Police wish to question the leader of this group, a tall straggly haired man also known as 'Atilla'. This man apparently befriended Neil but has also not been seen recently having absconded from former employers with over £75,000. Anyone with information about either man should contact TOSS! immediately.

INSIDE: ALLISON AND PALIN / THE CARTER STORY (PART II)
OUR LOCAL MEDIA CONSIDERED / DAVID D'AURIA ON THE COUCH
ANDY DAYKIN / VILLA EXAMINED / CITY 7 - CREWE 1
MORE PSYCHOS TO COMPLAIN ABOUT / PHIL PINDER.

ready to be closed down in October; virtually relegated out of the Football League by December, and then begin a revival of Lazarus-like proportions at the beginning of January.

Possibly our season is best exemplified by the events surrounding the traumatised Tigers' two highest attended games of the season under review. The first, against Cardiff on a Friday night in October, was publicised to Max Clifford extremes as the last chance to see Hull City play at Boothferry Park, and attracted a gate of 8,594. The second was an April Saturday against Scarborough, which was touted for months beforehand as a relegation decider, and drew a crowd of 13,958.

Ah, but back to those hazy, lazy, crazy days of last summer. The season started on an unexpected high. At 3:06pm on Saturday 8 August 1998, we were top of the league... I said, we were top of the league! At that precise moment, David D'Auria had put us 1-0 up at Rotherham. The first Third Division goal of the '98-99 season. This was a bonus. Having lost our top-scorer and then not invested in another striker during the close season, we didn't really travel to Millmoor thinking we'd find the net. Rotherham were promotion favourites and a 0-0 would have done us fine. But, for a moment, on that sunny first Saturday, we celebrated wildly and imagined all was well in our world.

The lead lasted ten minutes. We went in 2-1 down at half-time and by the end were lucky to lose only 3-1. From six minutes into the first game of the new season, it was all downward motion for the next five months. The Cardiff match came right in the middle of that run, and was the first game of the '98-99 campaign which featured us as the 92nd-placed club in the English football. We had, of course, flirted with that position briefly the previous season, but that didn't count; everyone knew Doncaster were going down. However, a 0-3 home defeat to Cambridge had dumped us back at the plug-end of the lowest league and this time it was serious. The whirlpool of neglect, incompetence and mismanagement that swirled through the club threatened to suck us down to the Conference and perhaps further.

The build-up to the Cardiff game, coming six days after the Cambridge defeat, was not encouraging. The media circus, featuring vultures as the main act, billed the game as maybe the last chance to see Hull City at Boothferry Park - or perhaps anywhere, ever again. David Lloyd - City owner, former tennis-playing also-ran and Essex entrepreneur - had been on radio's *Five Live* and in a voice rising in octaves ever higher, said of Hull: "They're living in the dark ages. They don't want to move to the future. They want to have their showers that don't work; they want to have their courts that have holes in their nets. That's what they want, and that's what they'll get. I'm out! I'm going! I'm not going to stay!" When asked if he had any advice for anyone willing to invest in the football club he simply screeched, "Don't!" He claimed he was subsidising losses of between £8,000 to £10,000 a week. With such recommendations, who in their right mind was going to buy, let alone invest in the shabby Tigers? Surprisingly, offers did come in. Most notably from two sources - former chairman, and much-loved saviour from the past, Don Robinson and a new consortium headed by former Scunthorpe chairman Tom Belton. Lloyd turned down both offers.

We had witnessed the Lloyd temper tantrums many times since he took over the club in the summer of 1997. But putting the club up for sale and then refusing to sell to anybody interested in football seemed much too an unsubtle backhand stroke, even for the centre court never-was.

The 'Lloyd out' taunts had become the matchday norm since the announcement that he would move Hull City to Hull Sharks' rugby league Shed of Shite stadium. Relations between fans and chairman reached the point of no return when we visited the Reebok Stadium in the League Cup. We knew this could be our biggest match of the season and that the press would be there in numbers. In the bar of a local sports centre one Wednesday evening, a form of peaceful protest was decided upon. The idea was simple: buy hundreds of tennis balls, write 'NO' on them, and throw them on the pitch just prior to kick-off. Unfortunately none of the instigators of this idea realised how far away from the pitch most of the City fans would be standing. The majority of bright yellow tennis balls only reached into a small corner and were quickly cleared by a battalion of ball-boys booting them off. The match was delayed by a couple of minutes at the most but Lloyd himself increased the incident's publicity value immeasurably by claiming that we'd been throwing tennis balls *at* him. The next day he put Boothferry Park, separate from the football club, up for sale.

Lloyd's aim was to build a Council-sponsored super stadium for the football club and rugby club. He owned both teams and the sale of their grounds, together with the franchises available around a super stadium, would net David Lloyd plc loadsamoney. It didn't seem to matter to him whether Hull City were a league club or not.

Meanwhile, Boothferry Park was left to rot. A deserted relic to better times. The players trained at the University. The club staff were in situ at the rugby ground and our once-prized and publicly-praised playing surface was left uncared for and deteriorated rapidly.

This was the scenario as 8,594 packed into Boothferry Park on that cold, wet Friday night, with Europe's largest travelling fair offering a bigger, brighter, warmer attraction just half a mile down the road. These hardy spectators did not go to see City beat Cardiff, especially given City's recent run of results. They went to show that, if the right people invested in the club, there was support out there to back them. Predictably, a typically inept 2-1 defeat followed. Mark Hateley's team, despite the healthy show of support, gave the same lacklustre performance they had managed all season. Hateley had promised, a year earlier, that once he got his own players in, performances and league position would improve. Neither did. In his defence he did have to rely on the Bosman Bargain Bin for recruitment. But the team's performances in general just mirrored the manager's off-field body language. Hateley stood stoic and mainly silent, arms folded, as we suffered defeat after defeat. It was obvious he couldn't instil passion into his charges. The ideas were good - plenty of passing and neat moves played into feet. The execution was not. Games were simply gifted to opponents. The toothless Tigers didn't have the bite to win back possession, which they lost trying to pass their way out of defence in eight moves when most of them couldn't string three passes together.

Following the defeat by Cardiff, on-field events went from bad to worse. But, off the pitch, help was at hand. New owners eventually prised Hull City's name and its players from Lloyd. Unfortunately, they did not succeed in obtaining the ground. Lloyd's grabbing claws were keeping a tight grip on the short hairs of the club's major asset. One casualty of this take-over was certain. The club, even if they wanted to, couldn't afford Hateley. Temporary control was given to Warren Joyce, who immediately brought in John McGovern to assist him.

The first game with Joyce in charge ended in a dreadful 2-0 home defeat against a red-carded, nine-man Brighton. We did beat Salisbury 2-0 in a drab cup game we probably expected to lose, and then battled well in the 3-2 defeat at near top of the table Scunthorpe.

We signed a 6' 3" goalkeeper, Paul Gibson, on loan from Manchester United. He was excellent in the next game, against Carlisle, and it was in that match that another loanee, Craig Dudley, scored the 89th-minute winner, his second goal in successive games. Unfortunately Notts County would not agree on any longer-term deal for Dudley and he only started one more game for us before heading back to Meadow Lane. Then Gibson broke a finger apparently saving a shot in training from recently-replaced 'keeper Steve Wilson. He returned to Old Trafford.

More new signings promised much in the way of ambition but delivered little on the field, and 1998 ended with us looking a lot less like pushovers but still ominously beatable. On December 28 our tenure as a Football League club seemed to have all but ended. The 3-2 defeat at Shrewsbury appeared to book our place in the Conference. We were then adrift at the bottom, nine points behind Scarborough, and well up shit creek.

The new year started with another defeat. This time it was at Villa Park, which at least increased our coffers. Fresh funds now enabled Joyce to further strengthen his squad for a last-ditch dash for survival. It was a near impossible task. But as results started to go our way, everyone began to anticipate the meeting with the boys from the Chip Pan Stadium at Scarborough as a possible lifeline.

One of Joyce's signings was Colin Alcide from Lincoln, who scored on his debut in our memorable away victory at Brentford. Big Col is not what you might call a total footballer, but he was an ever-present in the side for the four games in February. Unfortunately, we had had only one home fixture that month, and that was a not-too-enticing game against Barnet. Under 7,000 turned up. City, now with 39 professionals on their books, required crowds over 8,000 each fortnight to break even and the bank, not surprisingly due to our precarious position, refused us an overdraft facility. We were unable to pay the next monthly instalment on Alcide's £60,000 fee, so John Reames called the player back to Sincil Bank. Forget loan deals, Alcide became the first time-share footballer. After playing for us at Halifax one week Alcide turned out for Lincoln the following Saturday and, after we collected gate receipts for a home game against Mansfield and paid the Imps, he was back to play for us three days later at Cambridge.

Initially the new signings hadn't gelled but Warren, with board backing, had bought wisely and gradually it began to come right. Defeat at the beginning of January at home to Rotherham could have put us 12 points behind Scarborough. Luckily the Millers travelled with injury problems and a turning point of sorts occurred. It wasn't pretty and it wasn't clever, but we outfought our visitors and for once won the majority of 50-50 balls in a deserved 1-0 victory. Not many fans dared to raise their hopes at this point. Most saw it as a stay of execution, rather than the start of a revival.

Typically our next game, at Darlington, was called off. But with one win and one postponement, we set off to Peterborough carrying our best run of results for a long while and on a relative roll. Fantastic - we scored the winner with only a couple of minutes to go. Bollocks - it wasn't the winner... Posh equalised with the very last touch of the game. Disappointment, yes, but we would have settled for a draw before the game, and at least it showed that the players had acquired the will and belief to win.

We then incredibly went four games unbeaten - until a couple of thousand travelled to Spotland, and many more watched on Sky as Rochdale humiliated us 3-0.

Luckily this embarrassing trial by television was just a blip and a further unbeaten sequence dragged Scarborough, Carlisle, Hartlepool and even Southend into the relegation gutter with us. Hull City v Scarborough was for weeks clearly seen as a do-or-die decider, although with our run of form by the time the encounter took place, only Scarborough, of the two, realistically looked likely to go down. The official attendance for this bottom of the league local derby was 13,459. This is 500 more than our legal capacity, but probably 2,000 less than a lot of people's impartial estimate. A mainly uneventful 1-1 draw was probably a better result for Scarborough than us but the point was another step closer to mathematical safety.

The weeks surrounding the Scarborough match witnessed the first murmurings that all was not well in the Boothferry Park battle bunker. Word was that the generals and majors who supervised our survival strategy with great success were now fighting among themselves. Lawsuits at ten paces ensued. Major shareholder David Bennett was banned from the ground and rumours spread that there were plans to unseat chairman Tom Belton, who had in a short time become a press and fans' favourite. He was always available for a chat and a quote but, apparently, was not seen by other directors as a team player.

The season had ended but a summer of discontent had begun. The rumours circulating on that sunny Saturday against Scarborough soon became truth. Bennett took the City board to court, saying the club was being run illegally. Belton was sacked, and Steven Hinchcliffe, major shareholder, vice-president and friend of new chairman Nick Buchanan was asked by the FA to explain his involvement in a football club while being barred from any directorship for seven years.

As I write, these events are mainly unresolved. Also on-going are David Lloyd's ubiquitous pique practices. His latest cunning stunt was to try to prohibit necessary ground improvements on his land and also to suggest that there was asbestos in the popular East Stand roof. These measures would have forced our capacity down to 3,000, well below the Nationwide League's 6,000 minimum, and could have meant we could not continue as a league club. He has also suggested that had he remained in control at Boothferry Park, he would now himself be manager. A frightening thought.

Hopefully the new regime will overcome their problems and see off Lloyd once and for all. Yes, I know I'm being optimistic and any optimism in Hull City is as flimsy, and just as likely to be pulled out of shape as those previously-mentioned, ever-symbolic tart's tights. But it is a new season... and I've got a gusset feeling.

Ian Farrow

TRIPE 'N' TROTTERS

Bolton Wanderers

Cash no problem?

One of the most misquoted sayings in the English language is the one about money being the root of all evil. The actual quote refers to *the love* of money being the root of all evil, not money itself. This couldn't be truer for Bolton Wanderers in the past season.

The Bolton board had tempered the loss of the Premiership money, after midfield maestro Alan Thompson had utilised the 'relegation' release-clause in his contract and departed to Aston Villa for £4.5m during the summer. You can't blame the lad: after all, he was being tipped for an England call-up, and when duty calls, it tends to shout quite loudly. Unfortunately the money gained from the sale was not to be put into replacing the talented Geordie. But surely the most expensively-assembled squad in the division could cope.

From the early conflicts, it was apparent that the midfield lacked a certain something that only opening the coffers could provide. Bolton coughed and spluttered their way through the first month, with unconvincing draws teaming up with the inevitable disappointing draws, only brightened by the performances of a bald-headed Icelander going by the name of Arnar Gunnlaugsson.

Following a Premiership season of appearances lasting no longer than two minutes at a time, the shiny one was thrusted into the team as Colin Todd spoke the words, "Come, oh creator spirit, come." Come he did. Bright was the vision that delighted the division during the month of September, when he enthralled not just the slumbering masses at the Reebok, but the whole football-watching population.

Not that follicly-challenged forwards were the only ones capable of capturing the eyes of the so-called bigger fish. Oh no. Fair waved the golden corn in front of (cliché alert) Welsh dragon Nathan Blake, and the board weren't about to let another golden carrot pass them by. Hark! A hundred notes are swelling. In fact, they swelled to about £4m as Nat made his way along the devil's highway (the A666) to Blackburn.

Two days later, the 'title decider' was played at the Reebok, as Sunderland were the visitors. The powers-that-be witnessed the share value plummet as Bolton silently surrendered.

Twelfth position in the first week of November was not where most fans expected us to be. Surely now we'd see some fireworks on the transfer front? Be serious - this is Bolton. Burnden Park hadn't been sold, so money was scarce, apparently. Why wouldn't, or couldn't we strengthen our squad, when it was blatant that our depleted playing staff were not equipped for the task? The answers were not forthcoming. It seems as though the board cannot even tell the truth about simple matters - as though honest speech was biologically impossible for them.

Then - lo and behold! - the Bolton bedclothes became whiter than white for just a short time, following the arrival (on loan, obviously, thanks to our financial status) of bold Jon Newsome. The Whites managed to avoid soiling sheets for the first time in two months. All we wanted was to buy him. All the players wanted was to play alongside him. All the directors wanted to do was protect their dividends. Speculate to accumulate anyone? Not in Bolton, matey.

Newsome returned from whence he came, but the men in suits had noticed a cheaper alternative, with longer hair. Enter Paul Warhurst. Half a million well spent. Thanks a lot. I'll remember you in my will. You're not getting anything, but I'll certainly not forget you, you tight-arses.

The defence failed to be watertight for much longer, but the Wanderers went through the festive month unbeaten, albeit in the same unconvincing fashion of the opening month or so. The Reebok advent calendar revealed an unbeaten run of five games before the ultimately disappointing final window as Santa failed to bring a sackful of goals.

Hark, the herald angels sing. The much-hated Wolverhampton Wanderers would surely perish in the FA Cup game that was eagerly anticipated in the press. Unfortunately, the crowd failed to anticipate it with the same vigour. The Trotters, both on and off the pitch did just that, as we ignored all past rivalries and gifted a place in the next round to our former rivals. A couldn't-care-less attitude prevailed at the Reebok in our last FA Cup tie of the Twentieth Century. Millennium fever, anyone?

Only the soldier who has fought his way back from defeat truly understands the joy of victory, and it was following this setback that the Trotters decided to set upon what is commonly known in the trade (of cliché writers) as a hotspot. Fifteen points were taken, with no sign of a clanger, as former bosses and players were seen off by a team who seemed to have rediscovered some of their hunger and passion.

As hearts and flowers were being bandied about by romantics the world over, Bolton were right back on the promotion trail. Just eight points separated the Whites from league leaders (still) Sunderland and, with a game in hand, people believed in the power of good over evil - even after the departure of the Bald One to Leicester City, as the hype and adoration appeared to get too much for him. No-one could blame the directors for cashing in on someone who was obviously unsettled, and unsettling in the dressing-room. Well, not if the money was going to be spent on replacing an obviously talented player, that is.

Since relegation last season, £11m has disappeared into the coffers, with £4m outgoing on players to win us promotion. Good work, fellas. On the upside of all this is the fact that there is going to be a hotel built in the Reebok. Its cost is only a mere £9m or thereabouts. Coincidence or bullshit?

The signing of the hotel seemed to unsettle the Whites again, and the defence was soon back to its old tricks. The promotion-hungry Trotters conceded nine goals in three games, and Todd's remarks about catching Sunderland were thrown back in his face. Very hard. Inconsistency took over then, with the odd decent performance lit up slightly by the form of another Icelandic striker. Not an expensive one, you won't be surprised to hear, but a free transfer during the summer. Eidur Gudjohnsen - a former team-mate of Ronaldo (so we keep being told by the local rag). Eidur's scoring exploits rescued, and kept alive, fading hopes of promotion, whilst most others under-achieved. At least Colin Todd had promised us that they'd do their best to avoid the play-offs. That's alright, then.

Transfer deadline day arrived, and the club bigwigs delved into the cash pot, and splashed out a massive £50,000 on a much-needed acquisition. Steve Banks travelled from Blackpool and put in some towering performances behind a defence that sometimes appeared to be wearing bells and giving rides on the beach. Are you sure you can really afford that much money? After all, hotels aren't cheap. Perhaps a B&B would be more appropriate?

April arrived and was only marginally wetter than some of the performances. Todd's promotion aspirations were doused by several piss-poor performances against relegation-haunted local rivals. Beaten by Bury, for Christ's sake. And bloody Stockport. At home. But at least the chairman's building company had got the contract to build the hotel. Everything's OK, then.

Colin's pledge to avoid the play-offs looked like coming true after a draw against former rivals Wolverhampton took destiny out of our own hands, with a week of the season remaining. Who would dare bet on Grimsby coming to our rescue? Especially with a 12-year-old in goal (or something). However, the Mariners did us (and themselves, of course) proud against Wolves, meaning we only needed to beat Portsmouth to book our place in the play-offs. No problem.

Ipswich were our opponents - a team we had already beaten home and away this season. Come now all, keep high mirth, for the play-offs aren't all that bad. Bolton were 1-0 up from the first-leg at home, and the scene was set. The second-leg was not a place for faint hearts, literally. Heart attacks, angina attacks and other nervous ailments were in abundance as the Trotters took us on a roller-coaster ride of emotions as pride, passion and commitment reared its collective head and stared towards the Twin Towers. Perhaps it would have been easier if Ipswich had won, but they didn't: Wembley beckoned Bolton.

Watford had done the double over us during the season, with Taylor's long-ball hoofers having the advantage over our clueless defence. Now it was time for the most expensively-assembled and most talented yet under-achieving squad in the Nationwide to put them in their place... wasn't it?

We should have known better. Graham Taylor did. 'Ne'er cast a cloud 'til May is out' goes the saying. Bolton had no idea when it came to handling the direct style of football favoured by Watford. To be fair to them, the first goal was a cracker - but if football was fair, Ipswich would have been there, not us. All's fair in love and war. Watford were rubbish, but they were better at being rubbish that we were. It's as simple as that.

So a season that had promised so much before it began, gave us nothing in return for vast amounts of suffering - financially, emotionally and physically. I'd like to wish Watford all the best in the Premiership, but I won't. I hope they get no more than a dozen points next season. They might be in the top echelon of English football, but at least we'll have a hotel.

In short, the Bolton board has become a flabby self-indulgent giant, whilst the team itself floundered and starved. This is Bolton. Sponsor this space.

Dave Conliffe

Source: *A Load of Bull*

TWO TOGETHER

Barnet

A frequent refrain on performance is: "Two minutes and it's all over." In Barnet's case, the season had come and gone after just two matches. An impressive 2-0 away win at Darlington started the campaign, due mainly to heroics from goalkeeper and Player of the Year Lee Harrison, followed by a 2-1 win at home to Wolves in the Worthington Cup, which featured the goal of the season from new signing Darren Currie (nephew of the famous Tony). Then it was downhill all the way.

The next four matches were all goalless losses. After a brief resurgence away to Shrewsbury, confidence, aspirations and pride hit an all-time low with the 9-1 home

TWO TOGETHER

A **Barnet** FC
Supporters
Magazine

Keep Barnet Alive!

defeat by Peterborough - and Barry Fry of all people! Barnet started the game missing three key defenders and the inspiring figure of Harrison. So when the referee sent off two Barnet defenders and chose to let off the villain of the piece, Jimmy Quinn, our defence was as makeshift as a wooden computer. By this time goals were arriving like missiles over Kosovo. It would be unfair to name the young stand-in goalkeeper making his debut, but by the end of the game, traumatised by the experience, he was as mobile as a Serbian tank factory. Even our one goal was gifted to us by an ex-player, Mickey Bodley, with a freak own-goal.

To be fair to manager John Still, an awful string of injuries, including an horrific double fracture to the excellent youngster Warren Goodhind, and some pathetic refereeing displays, accounted for major inconsistency and many poor results. But who wants to be fair? Still's neanderthal tactics and curious team selections perplexed the players almost as much as the crowd. His ranting from the sidelines and total abandonment of any pretence to having a midfield on occasions caused dismay. Briefly the club flirted with the ultimate disaster, but in the second half of the season recovered a little, to establish mid-table mediocrity. Team performances were often worse than mediocre. Particularly at home, unimaginative and uncommitted displays tested the patience of supporters to the limit. In between, the sparkle was occasionally rekindled and three of the four promoted sides were beaten at Underhill. In the return game at Peterborough, any thoughts of revenge were dashed before the game started when Lee Harrison was ruled out through injury. He only missed three games all season but two of them were against Peterborough. Has Barry Fry taken up witchcraft? The inevitable result from our seemingly spellbound defence was another goal-feast and a 5-2 defeat.

Still does not appear to be the ultimate tactician or man-manager. In a time when football is a 14-man game, Still - a self-confessed fan of John Beck - rarely gets around to using any substitute before the 82nd minute; another source of frustration. The current team, apart from the stoical Paul Wilson and one or two survivors from the best-forgotten days of Mullery, are all Still signings. A few of those have been disastrous and some of the worst have moved on. Supporters did not see the funny side of resident joker Billy Manuel, and will be relieved that he was one of them. Sean Devine, widely regarded as the best striker in the Third Division over the last few seasons, had managed one goal under the delicate guidance of Still. His departure was inevitable but his relief at finding a more sympathetic environment to display his skills was underlined by scoring almost a goal a game after joining Wycombe, and being instrumental in keeping them up. But Still has also brought in some excellent players, and if he knew how to exploit their ability there would be a danger of Barnet becoming a decent side. Credit must go to the chairman, Tony Kleanthous for continuing to find money for these signings, in difficult times for the club, and his commitment to developing a good young team.

The season fizzled out to a predictably aimless conclusion, off-field disputes and countless long balls hoofed up and down the famous slope. But one bad result, far worse than the 9-1 defeat remained. John Prescott, the portly piranha, cunningly waiting for the close season, when football supporters might not notice such things, announced the shock news that Barnet's application to develop Copthall Stadium, approved by the local Council, had been thrown out. And for good measure, Underhill wasn't deemed capable of redevelopment to Taylor Report standards either.

Suddenly the club was plunged into crisis, with all doors to a suitable stadium being slammed in Barnet's face. Refusal was really unexpected, since Copthall is an existing sports stadium, in its own isolated grounds, highly accessible in the centre of the borough and a burden to the Council because of its advance state of dilapidation. Almost every potential site in the area is green belt and if the government were not prepared to approve Copthall, then what would they approve?

And so the KBA - Keep Barnet Alive - campaign has been born to fight vigorously for the survival of the club. Without the campaign Barnet would probably be playing their last season in the league, irrespective of their performance on the pitch. The stakes are high, the politicians and bureaucrats doggedly disinterested in Barnet's fate. But we are getting considerable interest from the media and great support from fans of other clubs, for which we are very grateful.

Football is all about dreams. Barnet supporters are currently dreaming about a midfield who can hold and pass the ball, a manager who doesn't need continually to scream at the players and, most of all, the security of a new ground, where we will be safe from the menace of rules, regulations and hidden agendas from those who seek to manipulate and hijack the people's game.

Tony Thornton

UGLY INSIDE

Southampton

The Premier League table shows Southampton survived by five points. Just how that was achieved defies logic. If you landed on Planet Southampton on the last Sunday of the season, you would have thought we'd won the league. The joy and ecstasy experienced that lovely sunny day hid nine months of hurt and embarrassment.

We took a gamble in *SOTF4* by predicting the proposed new stadium at Stoneham would collapse because the club wanted to put a huge retail development on the site. We warned about the dealings of the then FA chairman and club director

Keith Wiseman, and sounded the possibility of our Council offering Saints an inner-city site as an alternative to Stoneham. It was a one hundred per cent success rate that Uri Geller and Mystic Meg would be proud of.

Club chairman Rupert Lowe has tried every dirty trick in his political book to minimise the effect of the fanzine and indeed the sterling efforts of Southampton Independent Supporters Association (SISA). We have encountered some farcical situations in the last year. He even went to the extremes of planting his own people at supposed fans meetings to try to disrupt the questions we wanted answering. He has embarked on a vicious campaign to intimidate all forms of local media to such an extent that they are now frightened to say anything detrimental regarding Saints. Thankfully the fanzine copy remains as strong as ever and, in a land where free speech is a right, we sincerely thank *SOTF*, Channel 4 Teletext, and the excellent *Sport First* newspaper for giving us that unedited platform.

Fans around the country now associate Saints with relegation escapes, and whilst that is true in the Nineties, it certainly wasn't in the Eighties. People pat us on the back and say: "Well done, Saints. You've done it again. Marvellous achievement with gates of 15,000." "Bollocks," I say, "we should be at least halfway up the Premiership and attracting gates of 30,000 plus." We shouldn't have to keep selling our best young players. We should be signing two or three class players and looking to improve our standards all the time. I didn't always see eye to eye with Lawrie McMenemy, but he set the club up for the big time, only to see it eroded by gross mis-management at boardroom level.

The saga of the new stadium rolls on and on like a pantomime. "We want to build at Stoneham," say Saints. "Oh no you can't," say Hampshire County Council. "Oh yes you can," say Southampton County Council. Then, 18 months later, "Oh yes you can," say Hampshire. "Oh no you can't," say Eastleigh Borough Council. Finally all councils agree: "Oh yes you can." "Great - get on with it," say the fans. "Just a minute, we need a retail site to fund it," say the club. "Fuck off," say Eastleigh (what a rude pantomime!), "it's only a mile from our shopping centre." Some fans, keen to blame Eastleigh for the project's failure, are totally wrong. In the original memorandum of agreement signed by all three councils and the club, there was no mention of a large-scale retail operation. So, after seven wasted years, God knows how much cash gone in surveys, meetings and the like, we are back to square one.

We were led to believe that when Saints became a plc, Rupert Lowe and his chums were bringing the necessary expertise and finance to deliver us the stadium. The Stoneham dream had died and had it not been for the desire and effort of the ruling Labour group at Southampton City Council liasing closely with SISA, we would be condemned to a life sentence at the Dell. As predicted in *SOTF4*, Saints have another chance to move home, this time to an inner-city site, half a mile from St Mary's church, where the club was founded (hence the nickname). The surrounding area is made up of many ethnic minorities and is predominantly working class. Despite the sensitive nature of plonking a football ground in the middle of a working community very little effort, if any, was made by the club to reassure residents of their fears of potential racial abuse and disruption. In fact it was left to the individual representation from SISA at community meetings to be the only football voice crying in the wilderness. Eventually Mohamed (although it's very hard to imagine Rupert Lowe as Mohamed; more like a cross between Adolf Hitler and Margaret Thatcher) came to the mountain. The residents by no means appeased by this public relations stunt continued their argument at a very lively civic planning meeting. Fans and residents openly talked together, and despite being on opposing sides, there was much common ground. A genuine feeling developed that, should the stadium materialise, both sides would work closely together to help minimise the effect on residents.

At last the green light was given to the plans and all that remains now is for Saints to fund the project and build it. You might have expected us to be popping champagne corks and cart-wheeling down the high street at this point. Had Lowe guaranteed funding, we would have. Recent history has taught all Saints fans to be cynical, so this day was just another hurdle in a never-ending saga which threatens to outrun *Coronation Street*.

Then relegation was 50/50, so Lowe started making noises about its effect making the stadium difficult to fund. This put the idea into many fans' heads that survival would ensure its development. The emotional blackmail heightened the end of season escape push to such an extent that over 12,000 travelled to our last away match at Wimbledon. A marvellous day out brought flooding back memories of semi-finals and Wembley visits. The equation facing us was simple: beat Everton at home and we stay up. It doesn't matter how many last-day escape acts you experience, that horrible fear of failure lays in the pit of your stomach like a ton weight. Fans try to console each other that everything is going to be alright, but inside you are shitting it. The relief felt when Latvian Marians Pahars hammered home our opening goal was enormous. The second, quickly followed by news that Charlton were losing, brought pandemonium - the Dell was rocking! I have not seen the kind of celebration that ensued that night since we won the cup in '76. The city was alive in the belief that this, our greatest escape act ever, had guaranteed the new stadium.

The huge tidal wave of emotion over, it was back to reality and another summer of gross incompetence at the Dell (business as usual, you might say). The funding has to be in place by the end of September if Saints are to begin the 2001/2 season there. The monetary position of the plc wobbles like our away form. The number of scandals which have disgraced the club's name in the last three years must have disturbed financial institutions looking to invest.

Firstly, a local BBC documentary, *Southern Eye*, questioning the motives of the original take-over, backed up by a national appearance on *Panorama*. Then this season's upheaval when plc director Keith Wiseman was voted out as chairman of the Football Association in the much-publicised 'cash for votes' allegations. Yet again Southampton's name was dragged through the mud. Things on the pitch didn't get much better. Mark Hughes amassed a record number of bookings. Stuart Ripley arrested at Christmas for an alleged attack on a fan, then proceeded to punch the lights out of a Swindon youth in a reserve match. Even our own Dennis Rofe described it as the worst violence he had seen by a pro-footballer on the pitch.

The summer of discontent started when one of our most loyal servants, Ken Monkou, was refused an extension to his contract. Ken wanted to see out his playing days here but Rupert Lowe decided otherwise. A bitter blow to the fans who voted Ken runner-up to James Beattie as Player of the Season. Then came the real sledgehammer: season ticket prices up 15% for renewals and nearly 30% for new takers. This the reward for unstinting loyalty and, as yet, no major signings. In June a new kit arrived and – surprise, surprise - it is horrendous. There has been no consultation with the fans concerning its design, which is as far away as you could imagine from the traditional red and white stripes previously campaigned for. It looks like something you'd buy at Kwik Save but at least Kwik Save carrier bags have red and white stripes. Now, if rumours are to be believed, we are to have a blue away kit. Horror upon horror - would you see Newcastle fans in red and white or Liverpool fans in blue? No! So why should we be inflicted with wearing the colours of our biggest enemy? It's like the Pope marrying the Queen. Unfortunately we, as Saints fans, have become immune to all this crap. Nothing surprises us any more, not even our manager being arrested, linked to a child abuse scandal in

Liverpool. Season after season of neglect has made us tired and weary, but we must fight on and stick to the main issue. Has the plc the money to fund the new stadium? The planning is in place; there are no more excuses.

Some of you may be wondering why we put ourselves through all this. Well, from our point of view, it is my comradeship with my fellow fans. Everything hit home to me in a five-minute spell on exiting the Dell after our triumphal survival. In Archers Road, I met Kevin and David Roberts, two neighbours from a childhood spent playing football on an adapted allotment at every available opportunity. We used to build our own goalposts, turf the goalmouth, and even put sand slits in the pitch to copy Saints. As we danced with exuberance in Archers Road, we were kids again, with the love and enthusiasm of a simple working man's game hijacked by the City and greed.

Walking on now to Milton Road, I spotted Timmy Vokes with his two kids, Sam and Matthew. Tim was my companion on many an away jaunt in the Eighties, including an epic rail journey to Sporting Lisbon. This season he had been a major help with transport to away games, and for once Sam and Matt weren't fighting, just beaming with delight. Finally, as I made my way up Milton Road towards the Fitzhugh pub, I saw Grace Bennett sitting by a wall. I don't know how old Grace is, and she probably doesn't want me to tell you. But her husband, Sid, used to take her on motorcycle sidecar to away games when we played in Division Three South. Unfortunately she has missed a few games of late due to problems with her legs, but it was great to see her present on this very happy day.

All these people described and thousands like them are real genuine football people - the game is in their blood. Every time ticket prices rise, we lose a few of them replaced by Johnny Come Lately walking cash machines. I love football people... I love football... please don't let it die.

On the dawn of a new season, it seems that nationally there is at last a new fans' organisation that will present a single unified voice for campaigning supporters. Supported by the FSA, the National Federation of Supporters Clubs, and many leading ISA's, COFS, the Coalition of Football Supporters held its inaugural conference in Leicester on June 27, and over the coming season will be launching a national campaign calling for an independent regulator for football. We at Southampton have learnt that a regulator is probably the only answer to many of football's financial problems, not least in being given the power to monitor the type of people suitable to own football clubs. Our club truly is in the hands of a bunch of greedy, manipulative ex-public schoolboys with no previous affinity for either football or Southampton itself. As one long-term fan put it in a conversation with the chairman: "I'm sick of watching you lot use this club as a gravy train." And so said millions of traditional fans across the country. With an election to win, Tony Blair would do well to wake up to a populist issue, which would at least go a little way towards proving that this Labour government still cares about its traditional support base. We shall see, won't we?

Clive Foley

UNITED WE STAND

Manchester United

Wow. This is the one we've waited for. Barcelona 1999 - and a date with destiny. The Stone Roses had unwittingly written about this game a decade before. A decade that had started with an incompetent United side managed by a manager who looked a little out of his (English) league. How wrong we all were.

When Mark Robins notched against Forest at the City Ground, most said it saved the Wizard's job. By May, we'd won the FA Cup. And it was a big deal. City, then a big club, may have beaten us 5-1, but we'd won the silverware. Now it seems it's not such a big deal. We may not even regard it enough of a

deal to even defend the trophy. How times have changed. How football has changed. And how Manchester United has changed.

This last ten years have seen us steadily climb to the pinnacle of European football. We can thank Eric Cantona for giving us the belief, and Alex Ferguson for giving us the ability. But on May 26 we had the players to thank. Between the awesome squad assembled over the last few years, they managed to do the impossible. They won everything they seriously entered. To write this piece without it sounding the most anal dirge of gloating is impossible. But then why should I try? Manchester United, my Manchester United, had won the fucking lot. And knowing just how much we're hated makes the pleasure of that the most incredible footballing orgasm of all time.

Eleven games have probably shaped our season. The two 3-3 draws against Barcelona confirmed the long-held belief that, as an attacking force, we could more than hold our own. But defensively? Yips Jaap Stam and Schmeichs seemed to want to even up each game with a little help from their friends. Sandwiched between these results was a performance at Highbury that was a joy to watch. Unfortunately it came from Arsenal - and we were left with the feeling that the Gunners, with their World Cup winning players, were still the best in the land.

By the new year we'd settled down defensively, and once again Schmeichel was back at his best. He'd also announced his retirement from English football. Up front we were still as devastating, and when the FA Cup tie with Liverpool was played, billed as the battle of the strikers, we knew we were in for the promise of a 90-minute fiesta. Ninety minutes and a Michael Owen/Liverpool 1-0 victory. We were gutted. Defeat by our bitterest rivals? Fortunately, Fergie's watch was on the wrist of the referee - Dwight Yorke and Ole Gunnar Solskjaer, refusing to accept defeat, or even a replay, killing off the Anfield challenge.

The little gunner, Ole G Superstar, then featured heavily in the next definitive game, despite only being on the field for 15 minutes. Scoring four times at Forest, taking our total to eight, he seemed to be questioning his inclusion only as a substitute. He had been offered the chance of a first team place at Tottenham, but said he preferred to take his chances at Old Trafford. Later, when his last kick of the season made me, like thousands of others, the happiest man on Planet Earth, how thankful we would be that he did.

Inter Milan in the quarter-finals were our next big test. In a hard-fought 2-0 win, we'd had to rely on an outstanding defensive display by Henning Berg. It was enough to see us through, as the away-leg petered out into a draw, thanks to a late Scholes' equaliser. By now the games were coming thick and fast, and every one was as massive as Roy Keane. His resurgence in midfield on the back of his career-threatening injury was the reason for our still being touted as possible Treble winners. We scoffed as the press piled on the pressure. We'd be happy with just one trophy after last season. In the FA Cup semi replay against Arsenal, however, even we began to believe. After dominating for a game and a half, we found ourselves down to ten men, thanks to the usual woeful refereeing dominating the Premiership these days. To make matters worse, Arsenal had rightly been awarded a penalty in the final minute of the game, and with the scores deadlocked, and Bergkamp 12 yards away from guiding Arsenal towards another domestic double, all seemed lost. Then Schmeichel, who had been written-off earlier in the year, saved, diving low to his left; but fate has always had its own inimitable way of saying, "Sod's law, mate? I wrote it, and I'll use it at every opportunity to make you look stupid." The rest is history, or a part of our history that'll never be forgotten, thanks to Giggs revealing his Gary Glitter chest rug, after the maziest of dribbles over 70 yards saw us through to an incredible victory.

However, Turin again, for a second-leg match in the European Champions League, would see us finally and irrevocably broken-hearted. The first-leg last-minute equaliser, now becoming a habit, had given us slight hope, but the two early Juve goals had finished us off. Keane decided he wanted to play in a European final, and dragged us back into the game with a solo display of perfection. Blomqvist then made sure Keane wouldn't play in the final by giving him a pass of such ineptitude a booking was inevitable, and as we all sighed in desperation, Keane merely shrugged his shoulders, and made sure that even if he wouldn't be playing, his team-mates would. Three goals later, and we were in our second cup final of the season.

With three games left, we'd still won nothing. But three wins would see us finally surpass any of the feats achieved by our Merseyside foes. Tottenham were the first hurdle we had to jump. Despite going a goal behind, we once again fought our way back, and at the end of the final Sunday of the season, we'd won our fifth Championship in seven years. Six days later, Newcastle succumbed to the irresistible force we'd become, and a third Treble and fourth FA Cup of the decade were secured. Now only Bayern Munich came between us and immortality.

In the Nou Camp, we failed to entertain, and with time up had lost 1-0 to the German Champions-elect. But once again fate decided otherwise. A Mr Edward Sheringham, scapegoat turned hero, offered us a lifeline. We took it. Less than two minutes later we were Champions of Europe. Simply the best. And the tears that filled in our eyes as the final whistle blew were as much of sadness as of joy. We'd climbed a mountain - and however long we may live, however many more miles we would travel, however many more times we would watch our beloved United play, it would never ever get any better than this. For us now football is finished.

When Beckham kicked his first football after the nightmare of the World Cup, he couldn't have hoped, never mind dreamt of this ending. So it is to him we dedicate this season. The guy has been awesome. In effort, he was never questioned; in performance, never matched; in attitude, never touched. Schmeichel, the best goalkeeper ever to grace the global game of football, left with chants of "We are the Champions - Champions of Europe" ringing in his ears. It was Sir Matt's birthday, and somewhere up there in heaven, he'd seen that his club had been blessed. For his part, Fergie got a knighthood. As for us? We got the biggest hangover of all time, something only matched by our overdrafts. To support United is divine. It is to be blessed - touched by the hand of God. To be loved and loathed with the same passion. There is no in-between. It must never be any other way.

Steve Black

101 Bad Buys

No. 43 A Bayern Munich Scarf.
Hope he gets many hours of fun out of it.

WAR OF THE MONSTER TRUCKS

Sheffield Wednesday

Issue 20 of *War of the Monster Trucks,* the first of the season, was entitled *The New Deal* and had a front cover with Danny Wilson and Sergeant Wilson from *Dad's Army.* Danny is saying, "The board have promised me all the money I need to rebuild the squad, and I believe them." Sgt Wilson is saying, "Do you think that's wise, sir?"

Inside the mag we reproduced the Premier League table from *The Green 'Un*, our local sports paper in which we do a weekly column. The table had been produced before any games were played and therefore had Wednesday, alphabetically, in 16th place, two places above the relegation drop zone. "Okay we'll settle for that!" read our caption.

And those two pages just about sum up our season. We expected to struggle and had little or no money to buy our way out. So the same squad of about 14 players featured in pretty much every game and most of those brought mediocre performances from our blue and white heroes.

The summer started with the surprise departure of Big Fat Ron. We swilled our pints of Old Dog's Bollocks down at the New Barrack Tavern, smug in the belief that our chairman, Dave Richards, must have some big name lined up. It appeared we were going French, with first Gerard Houllier, then Philippe Trousier. But it was not to be, and Uncle Dave turned out to be all mouth and no Trousier. We became nervous, as names such as Howard Kendall, Graham Souness, and then Walter Smith, started to circulate around the taprooms of north Sheffield. For a while, it really looked like it would be the ex-Rangers boss, but on the way down from Glasgow his points were changed at Carlisle Junction, and he ended up in Liverpool saying, "The fact I chose Everton speaks volumes." The fact Everton came a lot closer to getting relegated than Wednesday spoke a few volumes more.

At the start of all the manager malarkey, we at *WOTMT* had said in the local press and on our Radio Sheffield spot that our choice would be Danny

Wilson. (If only because we all thought *Second Summer of Love* was such a great record.) But we didn't think he would leave Barnsley - not even for a Golden Pig. However, it *was* Danny and as the news broke we got on to the jungle phones of Sheffield 6, sounding like we all had arthritis - "Daneee, Daneee, Daneee" was the shout.

The season crawled into life with two home defeats, but a 3-0 away win over Tottingham away gave us some cheer. It also signalled the first bit of awkwardness from Paolo Di Canio, who said something along the lines of, "For us to beat them by that much must make them a pretty crap side." The mutton-chopped marauder had started to get himself revved up well before THAT incident. Danny had a right old go after Cambridge beat us at home in the League Cup. Paolo pouted, took off and then came back again best of mates with Sheffield Wednesday FC and gave us the "best fans in the world" routine.

Paolo was our hero - so much so that when he pushed over pirouetting Paul Alcock (who we think made a meal of it), we backed him through the FA hearing and his suspension and his self-enforced rest back home in Italy. Then it started to go wrong. We have a phrase in Sheffield which is "reyt mardy". It doesn't really translate, but this is exactly what Paolo was. The nearest you could probably get is petulant. Here was a man who we had stuck with, whilst he continued to draw his weekly wage that was more than many Sheffielders earn in a year, now saying he couldn't come back because he was feeling depressed.

Later it transpired that he had "misplaced" the London Owls' Player of the Year trophy from last season. He poured petrol on this particular fire by saying something along the lines of, "I don't even remember receiving it - why should I when I'm used to receiving things like the UEFA Cup." That finished it off for us, and he can expect a rough ride when he visits Hillsborough next season with twitching Hairy Redbat's 'Ammers.

Unlike his disgraced countryman, tiny Italian Beni Carbone became our new joint-hero. The gap left by Di Canio gave Beni the opportunity to become one of the two key players of the season. He is a top striker, who can dribble, shoot and hit a dead ball. At the time of writing, he's negotiating a new contract and we at *Truck Towers* have everything crossed hoping for a new deal.

The other hero for the season has been Emerson Thome, nicknamed 'the Wall'. This giant Brazilian centre-half played his heart out for the Wednesday. Signed on a free from Benfica, Emerson has demonstrated the sort of passion that we should see from all professional footballers, rather than the overpaid *prima donnas* who fill up much of the Premiership. Emerson makes at least one crucial tackle each game, usually where he throws his most sensitive part of his anatomy in front of a power shot from the likes of Shearer or Keane. Emerson also loves the crowd at Hillsborough, so much that when a chant starts up for him he stops and acknowledges the Kop - in the middle of the game.

Disappointments for the season have included Wim Jonk, who has ability but doesn't look bothered; Andy Booth, who looks a bit out of his depth in the Premiership; and Richie Humpreys, who despite a promising start a couple of seasons ago, now looks as portly as Kevin Pressman. Big Kev has given us a lot of copy and, like every chip shop in South Yorkshire, we'll be sorry to see him go - which is looking inevitable now Pavel the surly Czech has taken the goalkeeping spot. Kev has the sort of pork products' predilection that would balance out on one end of a see-saw with Jan Molby, and the *WOTMT* editorial board on the other.

In the end we finished 12th in the league, so our prediction wasn't that far off. Next season will be an important one for the Wednesday. We have, in Danny Wilson, one of the best young managers around, but he needs money to buy (at least) a quality striker, a dominant midfielder and a right-back. There's a feeling in Sheffield that if this is not forthcoming from the chairman in the close season, it might be time for a change - both in the way the club is run and also by whom. The Wednesday have been a nearly club for far too long and it seems like the board's ambition has extended no further than to stop in the Premiership. That's not enough for Wednesdayites, and whilst we are sensible enough to realise we cannot at the moment compete with Fergie's Follies over the Pennines, we do expect a good cup run and to challenge for a European place.

As a final torment, the season dangled a Fair Play UEFA spot tantalisingly in front of our eyes, only for this to be snatched away by Captain Biffa Atherton's sending-off in the last game against already doomed Charlton. Next season we need to be more consistent and win that place on merit by finishing in the top six.

There is a beer in Sheffield called Wards. It acts as a big-time laxative the morning after a proper session the night before. Our bet is that, before the start of next season, we are due the sort of clear-out that six pints of Wards brings - with the first team squad looking very different from the one at the end of the last season. And at Truck Towers we continue to be the only fanzine (to our knowledge) to be edited by a big black labrador, formulating his editorials whilst gently lapping half a Barnsley Bitter from an ashtray in front of the coal fire in the taproom.

God bless you, Young Mr Wilson - and may the summer bring you all that you (and we) wish for.

Sir Stanley Headfire and the WOTMT Editorial Board (Nick Riley, Paul Taylor and Andy Selman).

WE ARE CREWE

Crewe Alexandra

Despite the fact that *The Great Escape* has been over-used in football circles in recent years, it really is the only way to sum up '98-99 at the Alex. Dead and buried by November, safe before the last game of the season, this must surely be one of the best escapes. It was almost unbelievable. If you'd said in mid-December that the Alex would finish 18th, you would have been laughed at by most people.

The season didn't actually start badly. That is if you ignore being 3-0 down to Oldham at half-time in the League Cup. Bring on Rodney Jack to put that right in the second-leg. Dubbed somewhere as the 'Ronaldo of South Cheshire', his debut promised much. League victories over Barnsley and Bradford in August were the only wins we had until December, though. The Bradford one was particularly sweet. Their big-spending team contained two ex-Alex players stolen from us pre-season. City chairman Geoffrey Richmond had even threatened legal action because the tribunal system, which was seeing Ashley Westwood transferred, was illegal! The season's prize pillock found, even before it had started.

September, October and November were full of grim results. Four goals down at home to Tranmere after 15 minutes wasn't particularly clever, but at times we were playing some good stuff. After finally getting a win, at QPR in December, we started to pick up even more, a bit of confidence working wonders. This was shown well when we lost 2-0 at Sunderland, as the local radio phone-ins were full of the home fans moaning about how they deserved to have lost. The match reports asking who was the team at the top and who was at the bottom were to become a regular feature of the next few months.

January and February showed how quickly hope can turn into despair. Losing 2-0 to Norwich with eight minutes left, a 3-2 win put us right back in the hunt. Two weeks later, as the ideas for the fanzine began to take shape, we were losing hope as we outplayed Sheffield United only to lose to an injury-time goal-line scramble. Quite how Sheffield United can claim to play football is a mystery to many Alex fans, though. On the two occasions we have seen them this year,

'I BET THE THROW-IN GOES TO THIS BLOKE!'
THE NEW ALEX FANZINE
ISSUE ONE: ONLY £1

they have been - shall we say - 'physical'. We had the misfortune to face them live on Sky earlier in the season and Dave Walton found a boot in his face as he went for a header. This prompted a memorable response to a TV interview question, from Dario. Sky: "Is Dave Walton all right?" Dario: "Yes, he's fine. We always send them to hospital when they are." It's not often Dario is wound up so much by the performance of a referee, but he has been with good reason regularly this year. Step forward Mr Wolstenholme, the joker of the Battle of Bramall Lane, and the man who gave two of the three red cards to Alex players this year.

At this point there were those of us who were beginning to give up hope. The next week saw Rodney Jack's season catch fire, two exceptional goals giving us a 2-0 lead over Barnsley - which of course we went and surrendered. Talking of Barnsley, what kind of joke for an away end is that? Seats on open terracing - marvellous, especially in the middle of a Yorkshire winter. Fifteen quid, horizontal rain - and they actually have the balls to bring round plastic macs and charge £1 for them.

This was forgotten by the end of the month, as we destroyed Bolton's 15-match unbeaten run, with a superb 3-1 win at the Reebok. The few Bolton fans left at the end applauded off the Alex team, although not Rodney Jack, who had been clattered before the end after ripping their defence to shreds. With wins over Swindon and Oxford, we were really giving ourselves hope. We were playing well - and there was a team below us in the table for the first time since November. The way we were playing we looked certainties to stay up.

Ha! Two 3-0 defeats on the trot put us back bottom and sapped confidence once more. But, with a twisty-turny end to the season taking another turn, we won 5-1 at West Brom. That game included a first senior goal from David Wright, an 18-year-old right-back, who for the second half of the season has kept Marcus Bignot, Player of the Year and trailed by Arsenal twelve months previously, out of the team. One of the real high spots of the season, his goal was a cracker from all of 35 yards. Remember the name - it'll be on the back of an England shirt in a few years.

And of course then we had to look like we'd blown it again, taking only one point from two home games, one against local and relegation rivals Port Vale. So, naturally enough, we follow that up with a 2-1 win at Ipswich. Some day I will work out this game of ours, but it'll take me a helluva long time. We then went into a real do-or-die clash with Bristol City on a Tuesday night. With the best atmosphere I can ever remember at Gresty Road, we grabbed a 1-0 win. All three sides of home support were up and singing, the ground was buzzing, helped by the Bristol City fans who had made the trek up. The goal that day was scored by Seth Johnson. Seth is now a Premiership player, and rightfully so. But Seth should be applauded because he is one of that rare commodity in the modern game who actually know the meaning of the word loyalty. Offered a big money move to Derby before the deadline, he declined, saying he would rather stay and help the Alex stay up. That's another name for England in a few years. An absolute class act. Seeing him in tandem with the on-loan Danny Murphy has to be one of the best midfields ever seen at

Gresty Road. The majority of the Alex fans are relieved that Seth didn't follow Murph to Anfield, though.

The penultimate day saw the Alex safe. Three-up by half-time, despite Pompey grabbing a goal back, Bury losing meant we were safe. We were something like eight points adrift at one point, yet going into the last game we didn't have to have radios clasped to our ears because we knew that we would be staying up. Steve Rider on *Grandstand* suggested that Dario Gradi MBE should be renamed Dario Houdini. If Alex Ferguson was knighted, I think Dario should be up for a sainthood and anything else that's going. The bloke is an absolute genius, no question about it.

The unthinkable a few months earlier, of going to Huddersfield without dire need for points, was reality. The usual committed performance that we have seen in the past few months was again turned out by the Alex. Some players have bounced back from perhaps justified, if overly vocal criticism to turn in some cracking performances. Step forward, Mark Rivers - superb, 110 per cent effort towards the end of the year; Shaun Smith - unquestionably inspirational captain, who can still ping a few crossfield balls to perfection; Jason Kearton - worked out what those glove things on the end of his arms were for again, in time to pull off some world-class saves. There are others who have been outstanding throughout. Every player deserves credit for rescuing a seemingly lost cause. The club can now move on with our new stand. Much as we liked it, the Paddock and Main Stand were not up to First Division standard. The club shop has gone up market as well - mini-kits and mouse mats... whatever next!

It's just a shame that the club has felt the need to mess around with tradition for the last year or so. We started this season with a new badge, about which no fans were consulted. Then we are told that for next season we will not be playing at Gresty Road, but at The Alexandra Stadium. No, not some out of town MFI contraption - the present ground apparently needs renaming. Again the fans were not consulted. Add to that the fact that the home shirt for next season is apparently red and blue, and not the traditional red and white, then there is an undercurrent of disappointment with the board. Despite this, the board *have* listened to the fans on various points, and seemingly forged a better relationship. But there always seems to be something there to let them down.

It's just a shame that for next season we will have lost Seth Johnson and Murphy. But with our continuing supply of youth team players, we're all confident at the moment. We'll carry on producing cracking young players and defying the prophets of doom. Like I said at the beginning, we've got a better claim than most on *The Great Escape* theme (just why is it played at England games?). Fair enough, it's been a memorable season, and the relegation fight has got just about the whole of an Alex crowd behind the team. Some of the SCAF's, as they have been christened (So-Called Alex Fans), have even been heard to give positive support! But I'll sleep a lot happier if we don't need to be singing some film theme-tune next May.

Michael Lazenby

WE ARE LEEDS

Leeds United

Its Thursday ten June - and about time I sat down and wrote this year's contribution to SOTF.

Yesterday, Jonathon Woodgate made his full international debut at 19 years of age. That is still very, very young for a centre-half. But in his usual calm, confident way he coped exceptionally well. The national press afforded him their begrudging praise in the usual manner they reserve for anyone who does well but doesn't actually play for Manchester United. Still, to play for your country in that position at that age is praise enough.

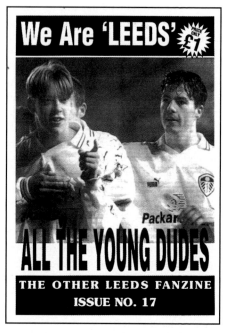

And that's really how '98-99 was for Leeds United. Nobody, least of all journalists and football commentators, gave us a cat in hell's chance of doing anything. They all laughed at our pre-season signings. They all laughed when George Graham found a new sugar daddy. They laughed at our squad, and how - but ho, ho, ho, who's got the last laugh now?

Yes, everyone from Match of the Day to the Hotten Courier said the same old thing: "Leeds United don't have the strength in depth." When David O'Leary started his tenure of the Elland Road office, even rival managers rang him to tell him we were going nowhere. They obviously told that to Alan Thompson, Dion Dublin, Ashley Ward and Martin O'Neill, whilst they were about it. They all turned down Leeds - but, as I said, ho, ho, ho, who's got the last laugh now?

Don't get me wrong. I am a Leeds fan of thirty-odd years on the terraces. I don't mistake mere qualification for the UEFA Cup as the height of success. But I know how close we came to more, and what we had to go through to get there.

Had any other team - even the three above us - had our injury problems, a complete back-four out long-term, Kelly and Robertson all season, Molenaar and Hiden out since just before Christmas, Lee Sharpe hardly kicking a ball, the international commitments of Lucas Radebe and the young players, plus injuries to Batty, Martyn and Riberio - then even those great squads above us would have wilted. Did you hear all the fuss the Chelsea fans caused on 6.06 because they thought Ken Bates should panic-buy an Italian striker because they had two players injured?

How many other clubs could have carried on regardless when the early season was all but written off, when the manager took a month over leaving, then the second choice took another month to turn us down. We did - and we came out better and stronger for it. David O'Leary was third choice and, if I'm honest, he wasn't even that for me. But I'm so glad he took the post. He proved everyone wrong.

For the first time in years, football at Elland Road is fun again; and what's more we are winning again, and how.

As the season passed, the average age of the Leeds United team got younger and younger and our critics, still bitter and jealous over things that happened 25 to 30 years ago, crowed louder and louder over the strength of our squad. It wasn't until nearly the end that they realised we were keeping the pace rather well. In fact when you compared O'Leary's lions to those wonderful squads at Liverpool, Newcastle, Middlesbrough and... wait for it, Blackburn, they didn't really have much of a leg to stand on.

We had a quick romance with European football, a respectable cup run and finished fourth. What would we have done with a fully-fit squad, or if Jimmy had put that penalty away against Chelsea, or if we never dropped so many silly points early on because George Graham daren't go for 2-0 away from home.

I don't care if they did the Treble, I don't care if Ginola won Footballer of the Year. We've got Kewell, Hasselbaink and Lucas Radebe, as well as our most promising youngsters since Major Buckley said: "That Charles lad, he must be worth a try." For the first time in years, we look forward to the new season with optimism and confidence. And if the plc do the right thing, who knows where we will be this time next year.

The future's white, the future's Leeds United.

From a supporting point of view, does anyone out there know the whereabouts of Sheffield Wednesday? Early on they were supposed to visit Elland Road, making the 30-mile trip in less than an hour. Strangely this big club had less support than any other at Elland Road all season. Shown up by Wimbledon, Southampton, Roma, Maritimo (one plane a day) and Rushden & Diamonds. If their silly band had been allowed in, it would have doubled their turnout. Probably the best turnout was Arsenal, who thought we were going to lay down and die for them (ho, ho, ho, who's got the last laugh now?). Then there's all those other teams coming and singing "Stand up if you hate Man U", then they applaud us for it. Where were you 30 years ago, boys? I thought Newcastle hated Sunderland, I thought Arsenal hated Tottenham, I thought Villa hated the Blues, and I thought Liverpool's rivals were Everton. Thirty years ago they all hated Leeds and Leeds and Leeds, Leeds and Leeds and Leeds and Leeds, Leeds and Leeds and Leeds, they all fucking hated Leeds. There's more than one bandwagon in football, lads. When it all started there was us and City. Manchester United were everyone else's second team. Now we all seem like jealous, bitter, lost sheep, allowing the self-professed biggest club in the world to put years of bitterness down to seven years of success. Never mind, soon you will all be jealous of Leeds and Leeds and Leeds again.

Steve Abbot

WHAT A LOAD OF COBBLERS

Northampton Town

I sometimes wonder just why I follow the Cobblers. Why can't I follow a team who you know will just plod along quite nicely, with the occasional cup run, the occasional flirtation with success, but never really forcing anyone to get over-excited (or drop into deep depression)?

No, fate demanded that my team was to be Northampton - and for years we were like I described - a nondescript Fourth Division side, with the occasional cup run (playing European Champions Aston Villa in the third round of the FA Cup springs to mind). But in the last decade or so there has rarely been a season where we, as Northampton Town fans, haven't had to face either deep joy or deep depression.

WALOC Reveals The Rejected Strips ....
"Too Sensible" said a Spokesperson

We had Graham Carr's marvellous Fourth Division Champions, then almost made the play-offs, then flirted with relegation, then relegation. Then Theo Foley's side who led the table until January, only to blow it big style and, in a three-horse race, finish tenth. Then the deep depression, where the club so nearly folded, a last-day win at Shrewsbury keeping us in the league. Then the following season finishing bottom, only to be reprieved because Kidderminster's ground was not good enough. Struggling at the foot of the table again - until the sacking of Barnwell and the arrival of Ian Atkins. A 'successful' 17th led to rising mediocrity - we actually had a mid-table finish the following season. Then Wembley and promotion, followed by Wembley again but no fairytale ending this time.

So what did the season bring us? Well, there was no consolation. Once again the extremes that are Northampton Town FC surfaced, and depression returned.

In the close season Atkins had made a few changes - discarding 'Super' Johnny Gayle and bringing in ageing target man Paul Wilkinson. I heard on the grapevine that Millwall fans had been pissing themselves with laughter when they heard we'd signed him. It soon became pretty apparent why.

An opening-day defeat didn't really faze us. We were down to ten men after only six minutes against one of the sides predicted to do well, Stoke City. We played pretty well, but in the heat, against 11, that numerical supremacy did for us. Little did we know at that stage that Corazzin's screaming free-kick into the top corner was probably going to be as good as it got.

A less than inspiring Worthington Cup second-leg victory over Brighton was followed by what proved to be the enduring pattern over the season - away defeats by the odd goal, and home draws. Our only home wins in August and September came in the Worthington Cup against the aforementioned Brighton, and another Sixfields' magical night, when we played West Ham off the park, live on Sky, and won 2-0. It was to be the only high point in the entire season. By this time, we were 20th in the Division - but, following that performance, realised what a false position we were in. If we could produce that sort of football against a side so high in the Premiership, then it was only a matter of time before we headed back towards the upper reaches of the division. Four days later we returned to Planet Earth, as Millwall - still laughing about Paul Wilkinson - reminded us what Division Two was about.

The return leg against West Ham was also on Sky (just as well because I couldn't travel to London). It was real backs to the wall stuff, and Andy Woodman was magnificent in goal. That game also showed up the nasty side of Ian Wright, a great goal-scorer but a lousy sportsman. I believe though that one moment of that game set our demise in motion. Chris Freestone had scored both our goals at Sixfields. He had been so instrumental in getting us to Wembley the previous season, and was just getting back to form after his obvious distraught state at Wembley. He was near the halfway line, the ball was cleared yet again by our hard-working defence, their defender mistimed his header and skidded to Freestone. He had half the length of the pitch to run, but no-one near him and only Shaka Hislop to beat. He looked so tentative, and although he got it around Hislop, the time he had taken had allowed a West Ham player to get back and clear off the line. He was never the same again, and only scored two more goals for us before being transferred on deadline day to Hartlepool, where he managed to help keep them in the League.

The draw for the next round gave us Tottenham at home, and when the draw was made we all fancied our chances - they still had Christian Gross in charge, and the media were picking the bones of the carcass that was the once mighty Spurs. But before then we had to start winning some league games. Man City came (apparently this and the away game at Maine Road, according to the City whingers, were "our cup finals"). Another game we should have won - but let slip. This was becoming the story of our season. Get in front but fail to capitalise. Our first league home win of the season came on October 10, against Bristol Rovers. Their fans were hoping to avenge last season's play-off defeat and our form going into the game suggested they might. But the Sixfields crowd in full voice ("3-1 and you fucked it up" being the favoured chant of the day), saw a thoroughly deserved victory and we climbed to the giddy heights of 19th. A draw at Bournemouth followed - perhaps we were getting it together. Wrong! A stupifyingly boring 1-0 defeat at Luton saw rumblings of discontent against manager Atkins' tactics. You don't mind winning and playing crap football, but to endure crap and lose makes people question just why they spend vast amounts of money travelling all over the country. Another home draw followed against Preston - in the league we had now played seven home games, won one, lost one and drawn five.

But all this was forgotten for a night after the Preston game. The visitors were Tottenham, but by now they had a new man at the helm - a certain George Graham. We went 1-0 up and had we been able to hang on to that until half-time, who knows? But Spurs pulled it back, and in the end were comfortable 3-1 winners - but at least we did go out to the eventual Worthington Cup winners (well, you have to have some reflected glory!)

An away win followed at Macclesfield - incidentally, Kidderminster's ground must have been *really* bad five years ago, because Moss Rose was a tip. But the pubs were good. It was in one of these that we watched the draw for the first round of the FA Cup. It was to be Lancaster or Leek at Sixfields. But before the glory of the FA Cup, two more league games - home draw number six and another 1-0 away defeat. Lancaster won through and came to Sixfields. In the first minute we were down to ten men - David Seal sent off for kicking at the goalkeeper, and then the non-league side taking the lead. We managed to get back on terms and then get a second, but it was no cakewalk. The draw for the next round gave us Yeovil away. It came as no shock to most of us that we lost. What was more surprising was that the media saw it as a shock. They obviously never watched any of our away performances.

By this time there were strong rumours that all was not well behind the scenes. We had sold our inspirational captain Ray Warburton and the mercurial Carl Heggs to local rich boys Rushden & Direones, and 'keeper Andy Woodman had been despatched into the stiffs to be replaced by Billy Turley. Word had it that Woody was not amused by this turn of events.

Amazingly, on the back of all this unrest, we recorded back-to-back wins - one at a home, the other at struggling Burnley. This took us into Christmas in our highest league position of the season, 18th. We would achieve nothing higher. Boxing Day defeat at Notts County made it a depressing Christmas, but then our usual tormenting of Fulham saw us get a deserved point. It was to be the last highlight for some time. As we went all of January without a point, including an uncharacteristic surrender at Craven Cottage (if there was one game in recent seasons the players seemed 'up for it' it was Fulham away). We just rolled over and played dead. Atkins came under further stick from the crowd and was seen laughing at and taking the piss out of the fans. But for some reason we remained cautiously optimistic. Out of the next six games, five were at home, and we had to start converting these home draws into wins.

Out of those six games we won just one of them - and that was away. But two of those games were beyond belief. We battered Walsall... and lost 1-0; then played Millwall off the park... and lost 2-1. The writing was on the wall. And I was resigned to relegation after we capitulated totally to a Macclesfield side who clearly wanted it far more than we did. We again had the experience of playing at home with five defenders, only two midfield and three up front. It didn't work - Macclesfield had done their homework, won the high ball easily, played it through the midfield, and took us to the cleaners. A further humiliation at Preston and we were down to 23rd.

But on Good Friday, enter Kevin Wilson. We did not lose another match all season. His influence was immediately obvious. He was what we had been missing all season: a bit of guile, and the ability to put a foot on the ball and create. Why couldn't he have been brought in sooner? With his introduction, we looked more dangerous going forward - unfortunately without a goalie the defence could trust, Woodman having long since gone to Brentford, Turley dropping more balls than the England cricket team and his temporary stand-in, Steve Francis, the role model for the joke about a 'keeper nicknamed Dracula. So we still couldn't win. And it was this ultimate failure to win home games (just four all season) that cost us our place in the division. But both Notts County and Brentford have trod similar promotion and relegation paths in recent seasons, before returning as Champions, so there's hope yet. Straw-clutching, you'll note, remains alive and well in Northampton.

Rob Marshall

Source: Clap Your Hands, Stamp Your Feet!

WHAT'S THE STORY, SOUTHEND GLORY

Southend United

Surely there's a common denominator. There must have been *something*. One single fathomable reason for our recent plunge into near-oblivion, one palpable cause for Southend United's downfall, one explanation why we now say Cheltenham instead of Charlton.

Managerial incompetence? Directorial impotence? Sun-spots? Black magic? Sheer bad luck?

I've sussed it out. There's a solid tangible reason, a three-dimensional manifestation of our recent past, a rationale. I have the answer. My car mini-kit. It seems so obvious now.

Late 1996 and the Fat Hamsters opened their scummy little boutique in our high street. Forgetting the sheer bad manners of the decision, it was a legitimate business venture, which was to create animosity where none previously existed. My personal defiance knowing no bounds, off to the SUFC Hyperstore I stomped, with anger in my heart and a fiver in my pocket. "One Action Man footie kit for my motor vehicle, please!" I roared.

A fancy mini-kit in purest bri-nylon? No. A miniature masterpiece of sweat-shop sewing correct in every detail? Heaven forbid. Cut with garden shears from the finest polypropylene, lovingly detailed in splodgy screen-print one-sided because, after all, you can only see one side at once, can't you? And topped with the weediest, crappiest rubber sucker, which wouldn't hold a flea onto a bulldog's bollocks. And only £2.99! Bargain-on-sea! It managed to hang onto my window for one game. We lost. I stuck it back up. We lost again. It fell onto the floor. I didn't notice. We won. The sucker broke, I jammed it into the windowsill. We lost. Three times. The kids pulled it down and bent it. We drew and won. So I put it up again, jammed next to the seatbelt, loud and proud. You know the rest.

And so it went on, and as the wheels came off Whelan's wagon, and we stared relegation in the face, I cleaned my little plastic flat-man, straightened him out, restored him to semi-glory and drove to Grimsby for our last game in

Division One. We lost 4-0. The car-kit yo-yoed during season '97-98, Alvin's doomed efforts to avoid successive relegations were useless against the voodoo power of painted PVC. The kit was in pole position now in my back window, especially prominent for weekend trips to Carlisle (0-5), Northampton (1-3), Blackpool (0-3), and final confirmation of our fate at York. Where I chucked it in a bin. July 1998, and I shook Alvin's hand and said "Champions by Easter!" The look of sheer horror and consternation on his face should really have given me a clue.

Holidays meant I missed the first four games of the season. We won them all. And what should catch my eye in the window of the SUFC Megastore? Yes, a brand new car-kit, new sponsors, new chunky industrial strength sucker and made from a substance, which, in a certain light, if you were pissed, that could almost be mistaken for *cloth!* Yes, I bought it. Yes, it was all downhill from then on. The kids mangled it beyond repair around the time Alvin went. I threw it in a Southend gutter before the Orient away game. We won 3-0. And stayed unbeaten away from home. But when we played at the Hall, suspiciously near the kit's resting place, we lost. I'm going to find the little bugger. And burn it.

Tony Hall

Source: *Shayven Haven*

WHEN SKIES ARE GREY

Everton

Three cheers for racism

Before you turn purple and start ranting about "typical Everton", let me expand on my opening statement. Just as chaos theory purports that a butterfly fluttering its wings in China causes an earthquake in Brazil, it is undeniable that the president of Trabzonspor's outrageous assertion that Kevin Campbell is a "discoloured cannibal" ultimately led to Everton FC surviving in the top flight of English football. And although we deplore bigotry and intolerance of any kind - except maybe against Kopites from Devon - we have to concede in this case that one man's meat is another man's poison - boom-boom.

WHEN SKIES ARE GREY
ISSUE 69   FEBRUARY 1999   £1

At the beginning of the season we never would have dreamt that the big, awkward, sulky bloke who used to play for Arsenal and Forest would be our saviour. In fact, we never thought we'd need saving at all. It had all looked so promising, you see. After pushing poor old Howard Kendall out of the club again, our somewhat unpopular chairman, Peter Johnson, sought to win the fans (and more importantly their season ticket money) back round in the most tried and trusted manner - buying players. Now, if you're going to spend big money in the transfer market, you need someone with a proven track record, and they don't come much better at splashing out someone else's wedge than Walter Smith. Some doubts were raised about his pedigree at the time, given that he had unlimited funds at Rangers and yet they conceded the Championship as soon as Celtic got their act together. Their less than impressive showings in Europe were also considered a moot point. However, these doubts were shelved temporarily as the likes of John Collins, Olivier Dacourt and Marco Materazzi arrived at the club. Fair enough, we'd never even heard of the last one but he sounded fantastic. And so, despite the numerous false dawns we've experienced at Everton over the years, we allowed ourselves once again to get sucked in – and the odd over-zealous punter was even heard to mutter the words "European place" - until, of course, we actually saw them play.

Straight from the off they were rubbish. The opening game, against Aston Villa, summed up much of what was to come. Everton packed their defence and humped the ball down the pitch towards the head of an isolated Duncan Ferguson. When we did get a clear chance - a penalty - John Collins went and put it in the same spot that most of the world and, more importantly, Mark Bosnich had seen him put one in the World Cup against Brazil. It had even been on *Football Focus* that morning. Scoring was proving to be something of a problem, particularly at home. Indeed, until we beat Middlesbrough 5-0 in February, Manchester United had scored more league goals at Goodison than us. This was despite the purchase of Ibrahima Bakayoko from Montpellier- a highly sought-after Ivory Coast international, apparently. We were told that he was a cross between George Weah and Ian Wright. After about half an hour of his debut, against Liverpool (which included missing a free header in front of goal), it was obvious that he was a little - how can I put it? - unconventional. For those of you unaccustomed to the finer points of soccerspeak, that's really just a polite way of saying that he's shit. It was once said of an American president that he couldn't walk and chew gum at the same time; in Bakayoko, we had a player who couldn't control a ball and stand up simultaneously. Think headless, think chicken... think somewhere in the region of five million quid. And people wonder how such a big club as Everton is in financial difficulties. The financial difficulties I'm referring to only really came to light following our first home league win of the season, when Michael Ball's penalty sent Ruud Gullit home with no points, but with Duncan Ferguson bound and gagged in the boot of the coach.

Remember a programme called *The Gaffer* starring Bill Maynard? During the title sequence, he would rip a parking ticket off the windscreen of his car and sling it over his shoulder onto the back seat, where there was a massive pile of them. It transpired that a similar scenario had been taking place in the office of Peter Johnson, although his pile contained demands for millions of pounds by the club's creditors. When he and his colleague, Cliff Finch, could no longer avoid the banks by ducking behind their desks and shouting "There's nobody here - you might as well just go away", it appeared that they were threatened with GBH unless they paid off some of their debt. They searched down the back of the couch and even tried to flog some of Cliff's old Bowie albums at a car boot sale, but to no avail. Sod it, they decided in the end - and sold Duncan Ferguson without bothering to tell the manager. To say that the fans were upset would be like saying Bill Gates is quite well off. They were livid. "We've never been so disillusioned since Suez" was the cry from the terraces, along with "It's worse than Dylan going electric". Hang on, now that I think about it, it might just have been "Fuck off Johnson". It felt like the club would collapse around our ears with the departure of Ferguson, much like the situation with the ravens at the Tower of London, but in hindsight things didn't turn out that badly.

Firstly, the ensuing furore made even the rhino-skinned Johnson's position untenable, and he stepped aside as chairman, although as I write this he still owns the club. Secondly, it would appear that big Fergie's groin fell off as soon as he arrived in the north-east, where he has hardly played a game. He made a brief appearance in the FA Cup Final, where he was patently unfit, and rumours abound that he is deeply unhappy playing for the biggest bunch of jumped up phoneys in English football. Something tells us that Everton may never get to see the extra million they are due once he plays 30 games for Newcastle. With the benefit of hindsight, a strange clause to have in the deal, don't you think?

One of the highlights of this season has been watching our loveable neighbours across Stanley Park trying to convince themselves that the good times are just around the corner. Their pathetic joint-managership scheme was hilarious. It was meant to be a blend of continental flair and boot-room basics - instead it just showed that two clueless buffoons do not equal one good manager. It was even funnier when they got rid of the lesser of the two evils and retained the permanently bemused-looking Gerard Houllier. His bumbling Inspector Clouseau impersonation reached its zenith when he tried to convince the watching public that Robbie Fowler's celebration in the derby was meant to be something to do with eating grass and nothing at all to do with snorting cocaine or anything like that. Apparently they are planning to spend all their money on various foreign mercenaries this summer - will they never learn from Everton's mistakes?

Our season changed on transfer deadline day, although we didn't know it at the time. To much consternation from fans, including yours truly, Walter Smith drafted in Scott Gemmill and Kevin Campbell and we lost our first derby game for years. Apparently the celebrations are still going on in parts of Norway. Then we lost at home to Sheffield Wednesday in the most bizarre manner. After teen striking sensation Francis Jeffers lobbed us into the lead, two outrageous back passes from David Unsworth and Marco Materazzi gifted Wednesday a game they hadn't even been trying to win. The drop looked likely at this point. But in the next game, against Coventry (a team we hadn't beaten for years), everything seemed to click, especially the two new signings, and we beat them 2-0.

That was the beginning of a run of form that even saw us win 3-1 at St James' Park - one of our many traditional bogey grounds - with the aid of Shay Given's Hans Segers impression for Kevin Campbell's second goal. After the goal-drought of the first half of the season, it was satisfying to see the net bulging with alarming regularity during our two final home games, when we put four past Charlton and six past the desperate West Ham United. Heaven only knows what the future holds for the Toffees. Some of our supposedly better players will be on the move to appease the bank manager - hopefully they'll take Slaven Bilic with them (we've got fans who've spent longer on the pitch than this big-mouthed tart). But, whatever happens, at least we live to fight another day, thanks mainly, as I've said, to the words of a Turkish Nazi. Who knows, we may get even luckier next season, and Inter Milan's president might call Ronaldo a goofy twat.

Mark O'Brien

WHEN YOU'RE SMILING

Leicester City

If you walk into a pub and order a pint of cheap, strong and unsophisticated ale, then you could - with good cause - believe you were on for a good bowel-bashing and a wicked pukey hangover. But this is nearly the Millennium - and things should be changing...

Three and a half years ago, Leicester City fans found themselves going through the turnstiles into the Fox and Donkey - an interactive football theme pub and brewery, with an excessively large kiddies' play-area. Until new management had arrived, the beer had been over-priced, and was a mixture of 'not properly fermented' and just plain 'out of date'. The new landlord was called Martin and we soon found out that what he didn't know about spicing up the banal, below average and frankly bog standard, wasn't worth knowing at all.

He was very much his own man, and soon had regulars, locals, barmen and brewery executives scuttling for cover. Arguments over opening times, wages and the price of a pint were never far from the surface.

The Fox and Donkey's own-brewed concoctions were soon getting rave reviews the length and breadth of the country. But just like all real ales (such as the Dog's Bollocks Knee Wobbler), they have their detractors as well. Whilst a surprising consistency and strength won its 1997 brews a national competition, it also brought unjust criticism. "Boring", "predictable" and "too hard". But hang on, this is beer you're talking about and not a McDonalds hamburger.

There were several brews which continued to draw much of the praise and slating from the Fox and Donkey's selection.

Not least was the ginger (top) beer - 18% proof and reaches the parts others don't! It gets your balls with both feet and leaves you completely legless. It's so potent as to only be sold in half-pint sized glasses. And it looks like it's here to stay.

Matty's Hairless Hoofer Stout is a popular brew throughout the UK - except for, oddly, in Scotland, where Mulder and Scully have been called in to investigate this normally dependable stout for pouring itself back into its original barrel. "You're going the wrong way," can be heard exclaimed throughout bars and pubs all over the land of the tartan. Its head is said to be its most potent part - however, even this has been claimed to be 'missing the spot' recently.

Old Walshy's Peculiar was a firm favourite amongst the real ale bores. Very rough, with a history of unpredictability - it has mellowed slightly with a better head on it. Unfortunately it isn't largely available, due to its age and fragile condition.

Kellweiser beer is the cool lager brewed on temporary licence from the old US of A. Tastes OK, but kicks you in the bollocks when you're least expecting it. Soon to be replaced by a continental lager called Peggy's Revenge. "Finely brewed over time on the bench" is what it says in the advertising.

Rob's Legbreaker is another brew on the way out; and Savo's Silencer hit an unexplainable run of popularity during the spring, but has largely reduced again to cult popularity for its blonde appearance and extra fizz.

TC's Surprise was the Fox and Donkey's top brew. It nearly doubled the amount of pints sunk next to the others. However, this probably has something to do with the fact that it can be traced back to when Stella Artois was first brewed, in 1366.

Gerry's Benchwarmer goes well on those cold winter nights - and brings a smile to everyone's lips in the Fox and Donkey, knowing it's still on the bench!

Muzzy's Mystifying Merriment has been one of the Fox's most keenly sought-after exports recently, but apart from occasional flashes (drinking it from long-range is said to reap most pleasure) it has been more subdued of late. Heskenbrau has had a similarly poor time recently - particularly in view of the enormous price of a pint. Very strong, but often too quick and misses the mark every time.

Gupps' Fisherater is always there when you fancy putting a pint in a box - it doesn't pour very fast but it is consistent. Not a word to describe the Scruffy Scouser Snakebite - but God, don't we at the Fox and Donkey love this one? It's likely that in any other boozer, this wouldn't ever have seen the light of day. But the F and D regulars have taken this brew to their hearts and regularly toast in honour of it - even though it's that dodgy a pint, it's rarely on sale.

Just once in a while, the Fox and Donkey is host to a guest ale or two, which manage to make an impression. David's Shampoo and Set was one of the most over-rated beers to appear all last year. With its scent of patchouli oils and a tendency to be very flat, this was one which cut no ice with the F and D regulars at all. And whilst this beer was heaped with national accolades, the remaining stocks were being used to kill an infestation in the toilets!

This is not to say that Fox and Donkey brews had their own way - no, not at all. In fact when some were exported to the land of the Woolybacks, F and D beers were soon slung onto the street due to their poor performance. And to our total shame, they waltzed all over our own brews when THEY visited us. Oh the shame of it all. Being humiliated by both Mancunian and North London ales was pretty much as to form.

The highlight of the year should have been winning back the crown of achievement from the alternative national Beer Festival held in Wembley. Things had been going smoothly - if not exactly to plan - and it was heading for a lock-in. When all of a sudden the Kellweiser went flat and all was lost on the stroke of 'time'. Shite - still there's always next time. Cheers.

Geoff Davison

WHERE'S THE MONEY GONE?

Darlington

You Crazy Son of a Pitch!

Darlington 3 Scunthorpe United 1; Scunthorpe United 3 Swansea City 1; Swansea City 1 West Ham United 0; West Ham United 4 Middlesbrough 0; Manchester United 2 Middlesbrough 3.

These results clearly show that Darlington are better than Manchester United. Yet whilst United won the Championship, the FA Cup and the European Champions League, The Quakers had to settle for finishing 11th in Division Three. United's players earn up to £40,000 per week, and they're the richest club in Europe. The average wage for a Darlo

We Defy (Alleged) Asset Strippers

☐ Issue 18 ☐ Official sponsors of David Preece's gloves ☐ Only 30p

Oliver appeals for more first team chances:

Please sir, can I have a game?

Only 30p!

player is £500, and we're lucky to still have a club. In fact, the only thing the two clubs have got in common is that Darlington's super utility-man, Glen Naylor, dyed his hair the same colour as David Beckham's earlier in the season. And they both looked ridiculous.

But let us go back, back... way back to August 1998 (screen goes all wobbly). The signings of ex-Sunderland and Derby County hero Marco Gabbiadini, Middlesbrough's Craig Liddle, the experienced Gary Bennett, and former Feethams' favourite Adam Reed from Blackburn, encouraging results in the pre-season friendlies and a fantastic new 8,500 all-seater stand, on top of the high expectations that always accompany a new season, meant that hopes were high. Darlo would surely storm to the league title, amassing 153 points and 211 goals along the way. Some optimistic souls thought we could even reach the second round of the Creamy Worthington Cup, something almost unthinkable in recent years.

A superb exhibition of free-flowing football against Barnet in the first game of the season saw betting shops stop taking bets on Darlo winning the Third Division. Or perhaps I'm lying. We missed numerous scoring opportunities in that game, and slumped to a 2-0 defeat after Barnet scored two late contenders for goal of the season, despite only having seven per cent of the possession.

Advancing beyond the first round of the Wortho Cup proved beyond us, as Sheffield United won 3-1 at Bramall Lane. Despite a valiant fightback at Feethams, where we took the First Division side to extra-time, we eventually bowed out 5-3 on aggregate. But by the end of August, Quakers had climbed up to eighth in the Division, with average crowds of about 4,000. Eighteen-year-old defender Carl Pepper had been superb in the opening games, but was dropped after making a couple of mistakes, and only started one more game in the season.

We only lost once in September, to eventual champions Brentford, and we hit the summit of the table for two weeks. Hartlepooh United had been comfortably dispatched at Feethams, earning Darlo the first silverware of the season in the form of the Comcast Challenge Cup, awarded to the victors between ourselves and the Funky Monkeys. October saw us head the league table again, but our Canadian international defender Jason DeVos was sold to Dundee United for £500,000, a move that probably cost us promotion. Darlo allegedly pocketed only £125,000 once our previous owner Reg Brealey had got his grubby hands on some of the money, and DeVos' former side had picked up their share. That's how they do business at Feethams.

A variety of foreign trialists arrived in November, but Salif Bagayoko, Juan Fernandez and Raphael Andrade were all released - in the latter's case probably because he was a Teenage Mutant Hero Turtle. It soon became apparent that it wasn't new players we needed, but a new pitch, as our current one had less grass than Hartlefool's assistant manager, Brian Honour, has hair - even though it had only been laid in the close season. Nobody knew why it was in such a state, although the club blamed everything from the wrong kind of pipes, to the turf being poor. It wasn't affecting the players' performances at Feethams yet, but it was clear that something needed to be done, especially as our away form was deteriorating just as quickly as the pitch.

The solution was to buy some special water-soaking worms on the advice of Manchester United. The Reds had used them when they encountered problems with their Field of Dreams™, but had to relay their pitch all the same. It didn't do us any good either, and within a couple of weeks, our turf had been dug up. At least we had another tenuous link with Man United.

It was these pitch problems that led to Darlo's home FA Cup tie with Burnley being switched to Middlesbrough's Riverside Stadium. With nine minutes to go, the Clarets were 2-0 up and, although down to ten men after the dismissal of Boro reject Andy Payton, looked to be progressing through to the second round. However, Darlo were then awarded our first penalty of the season, which the rejuvenated Brian Atkinson slotted away. With two minutes remaining, substitute Mario Dorner scrambled home an equaliser. Deep into injury-time, boo-boy target Mark Barnard smacked home a dramatic winner. Hooray!

Our reward was a plum tie at home to Manchester City, which was also shown on Sky. Gary Bennett headed in a rehearsed corner routine, but Paul Dickov earned himself a nickname amongst Darlo fans not too dissimilar to his surname by scoring a spectacular equaliser. The replay also finished level, but former Hartlepool player Michael Brown scored in extra-time to knock us out. Now our only chance of cup glory was in the prestigious Auto Wind-Breaking Shield, where we pushed aside Second Division Oldham Athletic, but Chesterfield deposited us in the second round.

By now, tales of the club's financial troubles were being exposed by the three fanzines, and majority shareholder Mike Peden responded to an article in *WTMG* by setting up an interview. However, he then decided not to talk to us, therefore missing out on a chance to deny everything, which is what he undoubtedly would have done. Defender Richard Hope was sold for a nominal fee, which probably means a fiver (which is about all he's worth). Not exactly going to clear up the debts, but the club's spin-doctors maintained that everything was rosy in the Garden of Peden.

In the league, our defence was being exposed even more than the accounts, and although Marco Gabbiadini was starting to score freely, we had slipped down to 14th by the end of January, albeit with a few games in hand. The club announced plans to relay the pitch, but it was obvious that we simply couldn't afford to, so we made do with stabbing it with a garden fork in an attempt to stem the flooding. Needless to say, it didn't work.

However, we opened a can of whoop-ass on promotion chasing Mansfield Town, coming back from 1-0 down at half-time to beat the Stags 5-1, no doubt leaving them feeling even more bitter than their beer. Then we travelled to Sicktoria Park to play Fartlepool, who by now had signed Peter Beardsley and his famous chin. He was totally anonymous as Darlo stormed into a 3-0 lead, and remained just as quiet as the Poolies pulled two goals back. After chatting to a few of our mates from other fanzines, it transpired that Beardsley had been equally poor against their teams, and that he was clearly a spent force; although it can't help when you're playing with players of the quality that Hartlepool have. Therefore, it was worrying when we were linked with him this summer, but thankfully nothing came of it.

Four consecutive defeats in February and March seemed to have ended our hopes of the play-offs, but this was overshadowed by the club's financial plight. That was exposed even further as the local newspapers latched onto the fanzines' hatchet job on the club's accounts and begun to expose even more debts. It was soon revealed that we owed money to the tune of almost £5m, and that the players and staff hadn't been paid on three occasions.

Despite all this, the players avoided being dragged down, and managed to keep their play-off hopes alive until the last game of April, where a 2-2 draw with Brentford all but mathematically killed us off. However, *WTMG* revealed that local businessman George Reynolds was at the game. Reynolds is worth £250m, and is the 84th richest person in the country. Unfortunately, the club's response that Reynolds would not be buying the club brought us back down to earth. However, George was at the next game too, and it was announced that he might be buying the club after all. This was confirmed three days later, when Reynolds was introduced on the pitch before our last home game against Exeter City. The players were obviously pleased, as they stormed to a 4-0 win.

George Reynolds has pledged to put Darlington in the Premiership, and move us to a new 25,000 all-seater stadium. Sure, nearly every new chairman promises the same thing when they take over. Just look at Carlisle United, where Michael Knighton promised something similar; yet they should technically be playing in the Nationwide Conference next season. However, all his business partners can vouch that he is a man of his word, and he's already delivered on one of his promises - to cut ticket prices by nearly 50 per cent. Besides, he's the richest football chairman in the north-east, and if he's prepared to put his money where his mouth is, we really can achieve what he has vowed. The bookmakers certainly seem to think so - the odds of us reaching the Premiership in six years are only 25-1. Words like 'frightening' are being bandied around by the local press and disbelieving fans, and to a certain extent, it is. But it's not as frightening as seeing your football team come as close to extinction as ours did.

Daniel King, 'Peter Graham's Bandy Legs', Robbie Bear, Phillip 'Feethams' Bear.

Source: Monkey Business

WHITE LOVE

Bolton Wanderers

The unbearable lightness of Bolton

When Bolton play their opening game at Selhurst Park, the omens are never good for the rest of the season. Looking back with hindsight, whilst we thought there would be some 'easy' games and a few 'harder' ones, we never thought that the Wanderers would be their own worst enemies in their quest to return once again for a bite of the very lucrative Premiership cherry.

We couldn't have got a more difficult opening fixture if a Bury fan had drawn them up. From a 1-0 lead courtesy of Deano,

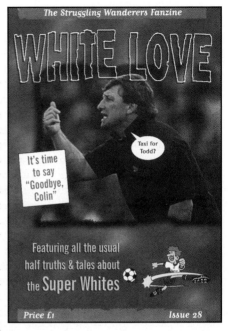

The Struggling Wanderers Fanzine

WHITE LOVE

Taxi for Todd?

It's time to say "Goodbye, Colin"

Featuring all the usual half truths & tales about the **Super Whites**

Price £1   *Issue 28*

we found ourselves 2-1 down, and just as the fat lady was clearing her throat, up stepped Arnie 'The Iceman' Gunnlaugsson to save the bacon. The match was a taste of the season to come from Bolton.

The Grimsby match was regarded as one of these 'easy' games for the Whites, but Grimsby, like many teams to come, had other plans, and exposed our shoddy and naive defence for what they were. Thank God we were playing an 'average' team, we thought. We needed a solid performance to calm our nerves after that less than promising start, but what we got was another defensive shambles - this time away at Bradford City. With the Whites leading 2-1 and only minutes remaining, our kamikaze defence produced another cock-up special to fritter away two more points. We hoped, and some of us even prayed, that our defensive lapses were just a case of early season jitters. However, the home match against Sheffield United confirmed our worst fears as the Wanderers let in a last-gasp equaliser to give the Blades a 2-2 draw. You would have thought we had Helen Keller and Stevie Wonder, or Shaun Ryder and Bez for that matter, manning our defence - not a brace of experienced international players.

When we went 2-0 up against West Brom at the Hawthorns, we all thought that surely this time we couldn't blow the lead. But we did! It took a last-minute wonder goal from our Jamaican international Ricardo 'Yardie' Gardener to produce a turn-up for the books. By the time we went 2-0 at home against Birmingham, the script for the rest of the match could easily have been written as we conceded a sloppy goal from a corner ball, but 'Super Bob' Taylor, scourge of the West Midlands, had other ideas and headed home to give us a 3-1 win. We repeated the performance at home to Hull City in the Worthington Cup, against a surreal backdrop of hundreds of tennis balls being thrown on the pitch in protest against Hull City owner David Lloyd.

Then came the trip to Gresty Road. With the Wanderers now operating a 4-4-2 system, we reckoned that our days of defensive errors and squandering two-goal leads were well and truly behind us. We couldn't have been more wrong - 2-1 down, 4-2 up, 4-4 draw at the end. What an utter shambles. It saw the pro- and anti- Todd factions in the crowd at each other's throats once more. It took a 3-0 tanking of league leaders Huddersfield to produce a huge sigh of relief that could be heard throughout the whole of Lancashire. A scabby home win against Swindon put us back on track to the promised land. After two draws against Barnsley and Oxford, came our home encounter with our soon-to-be nemesis, Watford, as the pigeons finally came home to roost for a team that couldn't tackle its way out of a paper bag. Graham Taylor's post-match comments on our 2-1 defeat turned out to be somewhat prophetic, with the turnip declaring that, "We were put to the sword by a side full of gifted players, but we defended well and rode our luck." Hmmm.

Once again the kamikaze tendencies of the Wanderers took control, this time at Ashton Gate, as the team crashed to a 2-1 defeat by Bristol City. It was obvious that we needed something more than Dyno-Rod to sort out our leaky defence. Worse was to come as the tabloid press informed us, and the rest of the world, that the Wanderers had serious cash-flow problems. The club reckoned it was down to the fact that we had not sold the Burnden Park site. With a third of the seats empty for every match due to ever-spiralling ticket prices, and no sign of our much-promised railway station, we could think of other reasons. We might have a spanking state-of-the-art stadium, with flushing toilets and hand-dryers, but our new home had high running costs, and the present gates wouldn't sustain some of the champagne lifestyles that players and backroom staff had become accustomed to.

The club saw the sale of Nathan Blake as a short-term solution to their problems, and he duly trudged northwards up the A666 to play for T'Rovers to the tune of £4.25m. Had we off-loaded a duffer or sold our star player? The fans' opinions were divided on this back at T'Reebok.

The Whites were going through a dicky patch that every Bolton fan could foresee, with Sunderland, QPR and Tranmere taking advantage of a suspect defence and weak midfield. Toddy finally realised that the team he had fashioned were not going to coast it in the First Division. It seemed our prayers were answered in the forms of Jon Newsome and Paul Warhurst, both brought in on loan to shore up a shaky back-four. Conceding goals became a thing of the past as Big Jon took a firm grip of things and we dished out punishments to the likes of Ipswich and Stockport. Oops, we nearly missed out a certain local derby... er, 4-0 against Bury, wasn't it? Bury were laughed out of the Reebok and the borough itself, as Michael 'Smurf' Johansen and Arnie went through their defence like shit through a goose.

After drawing with Wolves came a trip to Trashmere and another case of dubious refereeing that saw the Whites concede a 94th minute equaliser. Big Jon's last game was against Portsmouth and we all reckoned that pen would be put to paper as a matter of priority. It wasn't. The results over the Christmas period thankfully went right for us, with a draw against an ever-improving Bradford side, and a fine 2-0 win at Port Vale. The FA Cup made its debut at the Reebok and it brought our favourite whipping boys, Wolves, with it. This time we were on the receiving end, courtesy of two goals from Robbie Keane. Two weeks later, with wins over Palace and Sheffield United, this little blip in our progress was forgotten about. Palace were a pushover, with Warhurst now on board full-time, the only downside of the 3-0 win was the absence of 'Judas' Curcic. However his presence was felt as Arnie the Iceman came down with a case of 'Sasa-itis', when he declared he was to good for the team. Since the departure of Blakey, Arnie had become a bloody good little goal machine for the Whites. Yet once again a talented player chose to diss the Super-Whites. Toddy had learned by his mistakes and the half-season wonder was efficiently offloaded to Leicester City and replaced with another Scandinavian - this time Bo Hansen from Brondby. The Whites could now field four Danes, a Finn and two Icelandic players in their starting line-up. Wins over Norwich, Grimsby and West Brom lifted the Wanderers into third place, and the quest for promotion was back on track. The West Brom match in particular was memorable thanks to the myopic ref and his linesmen failing to see Lee Hughes put the ball across the goal-line, twice!

Then the wheels fell off the trolley again as we lost to bottom place Crewe, courtesy of Rodney Jack, and we hit the self-destruct button at Huddersfield, Swindon and Barnsley. It was clear that any chance of automatic promotion had gone out of the window. The phrase 'play-offs' rang out loud and clear for the Wanderers. A pitiful home defeat to Stockport rammed home the message. For many fans, Colin Todd's head was well and truly on the chopping block after this defeat. Toddy and the club took a huge gamble when they didn't cough up the cash for Jon Newsome, and it was a gamble that had sadly gone wrong. The truth had dawned for many Wanderers fans - the team were a bunch of lightweights and any return to the big time would be the footballing equivalent of hari-kari. There was only one person in the whole of Bolton who thought differently by this stage, and - yes, you guessed it - it was good old Toddy.

The 2-0 defeat to Watford at Vicarage Road saw perhaps the most lacklustre display of the season from the Wanderers, with the only credit going to our newly-signed 'keeper Steve 'Gordon' Banks for his penalty save. The away end rose in unison to let Todd know that the taxi was waiting outside for him. We had gone from being potential champions to scrambling for a play-off place in six sorry weeks.

As for the rest of the season... well, you know the story. By this stage there were few people in Bolton who wanted the Wanderers to get promoted, and especially with Colin Todd still at the helm. After wins over Ipswich and Portsmouth (and after giving Bury a little relegation sweetener!), we entered the play-offs. Things went from bad to worse as we defeated Ipswich on aggregate (by away goals after extra-time) to reach the Twin Towers once again.

Two Bolton supporters, a father and young son, had their lives abruptly ended on the way back from Ipswich, killed in the early hours in a motorway smash. Suddenly football, and winning promotion, seemed unimportant.

We made our way to Wembley like a condemned man on his way to the electric chair, to face a team who had already done the double on us. The Wanderers performance on the day summed up the season. It lacked any clout whatsoever, and by the time the second Watford goal went in many of us were already back on the North Circular and the M1. There were few tears shed by the Bolton fans, only the numb realisation that the team shouldn't have been there at all on the day. The consolation came in the fact that Watford, not us, would be next season's sacrificial offering to the Premier League. The masochists here at the Reebok would be planning our trips to Nottingham, Walsall, Fulham, Charlton and, more sweetly, a couple of local derbies involving our neighbours to the south, Manchester City, and our neighbours to the north, T'Rovers. We looked forward to Blakey keeping up his tradition of not being able to score at either ground!

Dick Smiley, Ray Burke, Paul Hanley and the Unknown Wanderer

> Three Wolves fans walk into a pub, order a round of drinks, raise their glasses and toast to "51 days." After the third round and toast, the barman is curious, and asks "What does "to 51 days" mean?" One of the Wolves fans tells him "We're celebrating the completion of a jigsaw puzzle in 51 days — 'cos on the box it says 2 to 4 years!"

YELLOW FEVER

Oxford United

Readers of last year's *SOTF* would have found both of the Oxford fanzines in fine fettle, and with every justification. We'd survived a nasty dose of *Financius Crisisus* (it's spreading - be careful), fan power had seen the appointment of the moustachioed messiah Malcolm Shotton as manager, and after a flirt with relegation, we'd finished nicely in the upper half of the table. It was one of the most enjoyable seasons I had experienced as an Oxford fan, and I was overflowing with optimism for this season.

What a fool.

You may know what happened. But the chances are you won't, as the average football lover

Yellow Fever is the official sponsor of Malcolm Shotton's moustache

Yellow Fever Issue 5   August 1998   Moustache Special   Only £1

OXFORD ANNOUNCE NEW MINCHERY OWNER...

THE VIAGRA STADIUM

VIAGRA - THE ONLY THING THAT CAN FINISH THIS ERECTION

Inside: Whitehurst, Geoff Coppock's World Cup Scrapbook, Deano, Robinson's Cordial

these days appears to struggle with the concept of football existing outside the Theatre of Dreams. Those of you who do care about all things Nationwide won't know much either, simply because none of the papers or TV channels seem interested either. So, let me give you a recap.

Let's start with what you will know. Sky and *Match of the Day* viewers will recall that we were robbed of a famous FA Cup victory over Chelsea on that fateful Monday night by Mike Reed and his love of big teams. Think back to what was said by those patronising commentators that night. "Plucky Oxford, the famous slope at the quirky Manor Ground with so much giant-killing tradition... how ironic that, if everything had gone to plan, Oxford would be playing not at the Manor, but at their new stadium, which has stood two-thirds unfinished for the past two years."

Yes, that's us. We're the ones who made a sow's ear of trying to move to a new ground and have paid the price ever since. This year it resulted in relegation to the Second Division. Our relegation wasn't a heartbreaker (like Scarborough's), nor a real sickener (like York's), nor was it hilarious (like Blackburn's)... it was just dreadfully inevitable. After just a few games, it became clear that there was too much wrong with the club, and that the heroics of the management and the team in the previous campaign weren't going to happen again. We started the season badly and got gradually worse, ending with a woeful run-in which sent us down.

You could argue that any team conceding seven twice in a season (once away, once at home) deserved to go down. If you'd seen our display for the second of those games (Oxford 1 Birmingham 7), you'd be justified in thinking the team deserved to be put down. But then, any team which had to sell its star 'keeper and its only left-back for next to nothing to keep the club afloat was always going to struggle. Playing two-thirds of a season without a genuine left-back was a problem, but we had no choice. Our left-back was sold to Birmingham (where he is now doing well, as their third choice) three days before the seven-goal calamity, and only a few weeks after we'd beaten said Brummie outfit at St Andrews. All season we kept selling our best players. The price we paid was relegation; the price we received was peanuts.

What else might you recall about Oxford? Go on, think hard. Who scored our goal against Chelsea? You must remember him. An odd looking bloke with big ears and a name that sounds like a fart... that's right, Dean Windass.

Deano joined us at the start of the season from Aberdeen. I knew all about Windass, because he played for Hull, when I lived there for three years, and I remembered what a great player he was. When I actually saw him play in an Oxford shirt, it was a dream come true - except, of course, it went wrong. After just a few months, he started moaning about wanting to move. After a while, he started demanding a move. Come February (18 goals and a few dazzling displays later), he'd become so unbearable in training that Malcolm Shotton (whose close friendship with Deano had secured his signature) made him train with the kids.

Eventually the spoilt, dim-witted, lug-eared, but oh so brilliant goal-machine got his way, and we sold him to Bradford for just under a million. We immediately tried to buy Steve Flack from Exeter for £250,000 to bolster our forward line but, ill-advisedly, the Grecians turned us down, expecting us to come along with a bigger offer. Oxford never improve their offers, mainly because they never can. The £250,000 offer was made on a Friday. By the following Monday, we had no money left. You see, despite reports suggesting that we'd paid £450,000 to Aberdeen for Windass, in truth we paid nothing; but promised them we would when we could. As Deano packed his bags for sunny Valley Parade, £450,000 flew off to Aberdeen, and the bank swallowed the rest, and would not let us have any of it to replace him. Lloyds Bank effectively relegated us, and ultimately cost us £600,000 in TV money. With that sort of financial judgement, I can see why they had that bit of bother a while back.

The last few months of the season, post-Deano, were horrendous. We were unlucky, it has to be said, but we were desperately poor, too. Our forwards would take it in turns to miss chance after chance, our defence would make one mistake, and we'd lose 1-0. It was as bad as it gets. Take the Bury game at the Manor, for instance. In the first half-hour, we had a hatful of open goals, and missed the lot. In the last 13 minutes of the first-half, we hit the bar three times. In the last minute of the half, we conceded a soft goal from a duff back-pass. We lost 1-0, as for the entire second-half, we simply chose to whack the ball up to Big Kev Francis.

Ah, yes. Big Kev. You'll remember him. As every matchday programme in the country will tell you when Oxford come to town, "At 6' 7", Kevin Francis is the tallest player in the Football League." (If someone had the foresight to put a copyright on that quote, they'd have made millions by now. Maybe I should do it quickly.) Big Kev was one of the stars in the previous season's great escape, signing towards the end of the season, banging in seven goals in no time at all, and giving the place a lift with his personality.

Big Kev is easily mocked because he is tall and ungainly, and yet he's got a strike-rate to compare with anyone and was recently voted Stockport's Player of All-time. The man is a genuine superstar... except this year. Throughout his career, as the opposition fans have taunted him, he's answered by scoring. This year, having missed the first half of the season through an appalling injury (almost life-threatening, if rumours are to be believed), he made his comeback against Chelsea when only 50 per cent fit, missed an open goal - and then conceded the penalty that never was. The big fella never recovered from this, lost his confidence, and for the first time in his career, he played like the donkey people expect him to be. If you play with two wingers who can cross the ball, Kev will score shed-loads for you. If you aimlessly whack the ball in his direction, he'll look crap. Guess what we did?

The annoying thing is, despite our appalling form during the run-in, the teams around us were crap, too, and we could have stayed up. Despite defeats by QPR, Crewe and Bury, and even after producing one of the worst displays in living memory at Port Vale (despite a huge support of over 2,000 travelling U's fans), a win in our penultimate home game against a care-free Norwich side would have kept us up. But we capitulated, and now we're down.

So, who do we blame for this whole fiasco? Certainly Malcolm Shotton (remember him? - big jaw, porno 'tache) has lost his God-like status, and in some quarters, is now quite unpopular. Some inhabitants of the Beech Road stand lost patience with him because of the torrent of foul language that poured from his mouth each game, usually aimed at the referee or the opposition, but occasionally at our own players (this in the year that he fronted a campaign to cut out swearing at the Manor). Others were put off by a stream of rumours emanating from Oxford night clubs regarding his lager-based antics. Many were just pissed off because, for the first time in recent memory, we became an ugly, long ball team - and still got relegated.

Blaming Shotton would be unfair. Some of his decisions were duff, his treatment of various players was poor, and tactically we were naive at times. But, in truth, I doubt many managers in the world would have kept us up with the squad that finished the season. In fact, most managers would have quit long before the season ended, faced with the problems he was. Despite not being paid for two months, despite having to sell three of our best players, despite not even being able to afford to take (on trial!) a goal-scoring sensation playing at Oxford City, Malcolm stayed because he genuinely loves Oxford United Football Club. I know a lot of people tore their hair out at some of his decisions, but deep down, we love him.

If you are going to apportion blame, you need to look back to the previous owners of our club, who have ruined us. I imagine that *Rage On* will cover this in more detail, but if one good thing happened this year, it is that we have finally bid farewell to ex-chairman Robin Herd (a nice man, loved the club, couldn't run a business) and managing director Keith Cox (nasty man, loved money, couldn't run a business). Herd finally found a buyer for his shares and sold up (we'll reserve judgement on the new owner), and Cox resigned after a Sunday paper revealed that in his previous employment, he allegedly profited from a company which lost millions in a dubious land development deal. Hmmm, sounds familiar. Apparently, we still owe them both money, so although now absent, their legacies still haunts us.

So, there we are. Another bizarre season at Oxford. A relegation, a striking striker, continuing problems with the new ground, the resignation of our £67 per hour managing director, a new owner, two seven-goal drubbings, the failed take-over by a consortium led by TV's Jim Rosenthal, rumours galore, and - crikey - we even saw Nicky Banger score twice in a game. Strangest of all though is, at the time of writing, Oxford have a squad of 12 players for next season. I don't know about you, but I see a problem arising.

A huge mess, certainly, but we're not alone. There's a lot of shit happening at just about every Nationwide League club, and it is all pretty worrying. Chester, Portsmouth, Crystal Palace, Luton, Scarborough... we're all going through the same problems. Our teams are in danger of dying, and no-one knows or cares about it because our teams are not considered interesting or trendy by the wanky media-types who cover our game. If you do follow a bigger team and you are reading this, take note of what is going on. The football bubble will burst soon, and then we will all be fucked. Fans need to reclaim their clubs before this happens and - as Bournemouth proved - it *is* possible.

Weird but true, I felt angrier when bloody Manchester United scored twice in the last minute of *that* final than I did after the final whistle blew on our last Sunday of the season. Relegation is bad news - especially to a team in our position - but so was the world's worst plc doing the Treble, and having it heralded by their floppy-haired friends in the media as the greatest ever thing to ever happen ever in the world ever. If you tell kids that Manchester United are the greatest team in the world and that we should support them because they're English and the best, then kids are going to support them. A generation will grow up as true Red Devils, drinking Carling, eating football (whatever that means), wearing replicas, and spending £400 on a dish and a subscription to MUTV, rather than a £200 season ticket for the local team which is struggling to survive.

Future generations may never get the chance to know what football is really about, and that's their loss.
Daniel Curtis

YIDAHO!

Wimbledon

The biggest story in the season of Wimbledon Football Club happened a month after the season had finished, when our popular manager, Joe Kinnear, was replaced by former Norway boss Egil Olsen. This may have come as a shock to football fans around the country, who saw Joe as a successful manager - but it shouldn't have to the average Wimbledon fan. Two weeks earlier, our Norwegian owners had threatened to pull out of the club and look for some other suckers... sorry, investment. When they had first taken over the club they had wanted Olsen, so it was no surprise that they should stoop to blackmail to get their man.

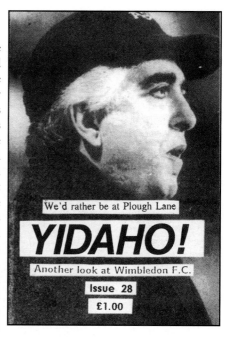

We'd rather be at Plough Lane

YIDAHO!

Another look at Wimbledon F.C.

Issue 28

£1.00

The announcement of Joe's departure was relayed in typically melodramatic fashion by Sam Hamman. Apparently Hamman and Kinnear would continue to "live in each other's underpants" - which had the *News of the World* back at the press conference slavering with lust. It was simple really: Joe wanted to manage a bigger club; no, he wasn't leaving because of his heart attack a few months earlier; and, yes, of course he would stay on to help the new man settle into the job. Everything was just so amicable.

The departure of Joe had put a crimp in to what had become a dull and uninspired season. The season had begun so promisingly, with no new signings to fire the interest of Dons supporters. However, our pessimism was banished on the opening day of the season as we swept past the dreaded Spurs with a convincing 3-1 victory. We followed up with two draws, before fashioning the most unlikely victory of the season, away at West Ham. Looking at the Wimbledon team sheet before kick-off, it was difficult to see where a goal was coming from with such a defensive line-up. However, goals did come. Four of them. All the more remarkable - as West Ham were three up at the time. As Ekoku fired home the late winner, I was dreaming of seeing us play in more exotic locations than Upton Park. Would I have to renew that passport I got ten years ago on the off-chance that English clubs would be readmitted into

Europe? Well, probably not - but you can't help getting emotional after a couple of bottles of Merrydown and a four-match unbeaten start to the season.

Eastbourne seemed to a more likely holiday destination a month later, as reality began to sink in. After defeats at Villa and Old Trafford, we continued to lose at home to Everton - of all teams - and this was at the time that Everton were *really* bad, as opposed to the normal times, when they're just awful.

As a backdrop to the season, we had the continuing saga of where the club would be playing home games in the future. The long-standing Dublin option seemed to be kicked into touch - for now, and we feverishly celebrated the idea that we might get to play football in our own country. Various proposals were flying around, none of which seemed to involve building our own stadium back in Wimbledon. The proposals ranged from the viable (a groundshare with QPR), to the insulting - a merger with Palace, and the club renamed as Selhurst Sharks... I ask you! Most puzzling proposal was a merger with West Brom, and the most suicidal, a deal with Man City, where we sold them all our best players and gave them our place in the Premiership. I'm not quite sure what Wimbledon were to gain from this arrangement. I don't know who the Man City agent was during all this but I'd like him to represent me. There still hasn't been any decision made as to where we're going to end up but I do know we have £40m tucked away in the bank just waiting to be spent on the construction of a new stadium, hopefully back in the London Borough of Merton. So next time you hear a story about "poor old penniless Wimbledon", remember, it's complete bullshit.

November Spawned a Monster, so the song goes - but for us it brought our first signing and a run to the fifth round of the League Cup. I think Morrissey's lyrics fit better. With the likes of Michael Hughes, Neal Ardley and Mark Kennedy in the squad, what we really needed was another winger, so we bought one - Gareth Ainsworth from Port Vale, for a cool £2m. Gareth said he is occasionally mistaken for Ryan Giggs, but that is just ridiculous. I mean, Gareth is available for international duty. The Worthington Cup seemed to bring our best chance of some well-earned silverware for the season, with impressive victories over a trio of Division One clubs - Portsmouth, Birmingham and Bolton. In the fifth round of the Copa Worthington, we were drawn at home to Chelsea. Bryan Butler once described Tottenham as an "international sweet trolley of a team". This lot was enough to make you want to reach for the sick-bag. Still, it was always Wimbledon's ambition to play foreign opposition in a competitive competition, so we were going to make the most of it. Despite a gloriously one-eyed performance from referee Graham Poll, we managed a 2-1 win. Chelsea may have had most of the skill on show but we beat them with the good old British qualities of determination, passion, doggedness and will to win. They don't like it up 'em, Mr Vialli! As we left the stadium that night, lifted by the euphoria of the evening, we sensed something special was awaiting us. It was a sense that glorious failure was not far around the corner.

While the cups were our best chance of success, we were still going along nicely in the league. Although performances weren't always impressive, we managed to secure victories over the likes of Arsenal and Liverpool and stayed within the top eight, giving ourselves a slight chance of UEFA Cup football. Everything was going along too well, as we looked at the remainder of the season with a highly inflated sense of optimism.

That inflated sense of optimism seemed to be justified when Wimbledon did something that shook the football world. Not only did we sign someone, but we paid £7.5m for the privilege. The arrival of John Hartson from West Ham could have been the catalyst for a memorable season. The last time we made such a shock of a signing was 12 years previously when we signed John Fashanu and the man got us promotion. However, the signing of Hartson coincided with a dismal run to the end of the season.

I've never been a fan of Tottenham Hotspur. In fact it would probably be fair to say that I despise them to the very core of my being. They are the southern equivalent of Man United - only without any of the success to back it up. From the arrogance of the management, to their fans' insistence that they are a massive club with a divine right to success, they look down on other clubs through sheer snobbery – and that gets on my tits. It's a bit much to take from a club who have only been League Champions twice. Taking my views into consideration, you can understand why it was a bit galling for me to see our season ruined by those bastards. The fourth round FA Cup defeat I could deal with, but to lose the Worthington Semi-final by a single goal was too much to take. Even worse was the arrogance of the Spurs fans afterwards, saying they hoped we were relegated as we didn't play their 'beautiful football'. A bit of success and Spurs fans revert to type.

If this wasn't bad enough, the disappointment of the loss killed our season and we went from bad to worse. We were never seriously in danger of relegation, but it was still a worry. Maybe if Joe Kinnear hadn't had his heart attack up at Hillsborough, we would have turned things around. But really it was not excuse for the dire performances we had to endure for the rest of the season, including a spell where we went six games without a goal. I'd love to be able to tell you of an ending to the season that gave us hope for the future, but sadly that wasn't to be.

The highlight of the season was undoubtedly the first half - not that there was much to compare it to. A long cup run is the most we can ever really hope for – but, for a while, the league kept us interested. The Player of the Season was deservedly our 'keeper Neil Sullivan. His frequent match-winning performance earned him rave reviews, envious glances from other clubs and an established international spot with Scotland. I just hope that we can keep hold of him. Our defence, whilst conceding too many goals were often outstanding individually. In the forward positions, there were two shining lights. Winger Michael Hughes and young Jason Euell. We look so much more dangerous when Hughes is playing and we missed him badly when he was out injured for the last couple of months of the season. Jason Euell is our star in the making, if not already. Able to play as comfortably in midfield as attack, he is already spoken of as a future England player.

Wimbledon's fight to remain in the Premiership will be harder than ever next season and a lot depends on how new manager Olsen can wheel and deal in the transfer market. Whatever happens though, the effort and spirit will still be there.

Colin Leonard

Source: Everywhere We Go